C# 9 and .NET 5 – Mode
Cross-Platform Development

Fifth Edition

Build intelligent apps, websites, and services with
Blazor, ASP.NET Core, and Entity Framework Core
using Visual Studio Code

Mark J. Price

BIRMINGHAM - MUMBAI

C# 9 and .NET 5 – Modern Cross-Platform Development
Fifth Edition

Producer: Ben Renow-Clarke
Acquisition Editor – Peer Reviews: Divya Mudaliar
Content Development Editors: Joanne Lovell, Bhavesh Amin
Technical Editor: Aniket Shetty
Project Editor: Radhika Atitkar
Copy Editor: Safis Editing
Proofreader: Safis Editing
Indexer: Rekha Nair
Presentation Designer: Sandip Tadge

First published: March 2016
Second edition: March 2017
Third edition: November 2017
Fourth edition: October 2019
Fifth edition: November 2020

Production reference: 1051120

Published by Packt Publishing Ltd.
Livery Place
35 Livery Street
Birmingham B3 2PB, UK.

ISBN 978-1-80056-810-5

www.packt.com

packt.com

Subscribe to our online digital library for full access to over 7,000 books and videos, as well as industry leading tools to help you plan your personal development and advance your career. For more information, please visit our website.

Why subscribe?

- Spend less time learning and more time coding with practical eBooks and Videos from over 4,000 industry professionals

- Learn better with Skill Plans built especially for you

- Get a free eBook or video every month

- Fully searchable for easy access to vital information

- Copy and paste, print, and bookmark content

Did you know that Packt offers eBook versions of every book published, with PDF and ePub files available? You can upgrade to the eBook version at www.Packt.com and as a print book customer, you are entitled to a discount on the eBook copy. Get in touch with us at customercare@packtpub.com for more details.

At www.Packt.com, you can also read a collection of free technical articles, sign up for a range of free newsletters, and receive exclusive discounts and offers on Packt books and eBooks.

Contributors

About the author

Mark J. Price is a Microsoft Specialist: Programming in C# and architecting Microsoft Azure Solutions, with more than 20 years of educational and programming experience.

Microsoft
C E R T I F I E D
Solutions Developer

App Builder

Microsoft
Specialist

Programming in C#

epi

Episerver CMS
Certified Developer

Since 1993, Mark has passed more than 80 Microsoft programming exams and specializes in preparing others to pass them too. His students range from professionals with decades of experience to 16-year-old apprentices with none. He successfully guides all of them by combining educational skills with real-world experience in consulting and developing systems for enterprises worldwide.

Between 2001 and 2003, Mark was employed full time to write official courseware for Microsoft in Redmond, USA. His team wrote the first training courses for C# while it was still an early alpha version. While with Microsoft, he taught "train-the-trainer" classes to get other MCTs up to speed on C# and .NET.

Currently, Mark creates and delivers training courses for Episerver's Digital Experience Platform, including Content Cloud, Commerce Cloud, and Intelligence Cloud.

In 2010, Mark studied for a Postgraduate Certificate in Education (PGCE). He taught GCSE and A-Level mathematics in two London secondary schools. He holds a Computer Science BSc. Hons. degree from the University of Bristol, UK.

Thank you to my parents, Pamela and Ian, for raising me to be polite, hardworking, and curious about the world. Thank you to my sisters, Emily and Juliet, for loving me despite being their awkward older brother. Thank you to my friends and colleagues who inspire me technically and creatively. Lastly, thanks to all the students I have taught over the years for motivating me to be the best teacher that I can be.

About the reviewer

Damir Arh has many years of experience with software development and maintenance; from complex enterprise software projects to modern consumer-oriented mobile applications. Although he has worked with a wide spectrum of different languages, his favorite language remains C#. In his drive toward better development processes he is a proponent of test-driven development, continuous integration, and continuous deployment. He shares his knowledge by speaking at local user groups and conferences, blogging, and writing articles. He has received the prestigious Microsoft MVP award for developer technologies 9 times in a row. In his spare time, he's always on the move: hiking, geocaching, running, and rock climbing.

I'd like to thank my family and friends for their patience and understanding during the weekends and evenings I spent on my computer to help make this book better for everyone.

Table of Contents

Preface

There are programming books that are thousands of pages long that aim to be comprehensive references to the C# language and the .NET platform.

This book is different. It is concise and aims to be a brisk, fun read that is packed with practical hands-on walkthroughs of each subject. The breadth of the overarching narrative comes at the cost of some depth, but you will find many signposts to explore further if you wish.

This book is simultaneously a step-by-step guide to learning modern C# proven practices using cross-platform .NET and a brief introduction to the main types of applications that can be built with them. This book is best for beginners to C# and .NET, or programmers who have worked with C# in the past but feel left behind by the changes in the past few years.

If you already have experience with older versions of C#, then in the first topic of *Chapter 2, Speaking C#*, you can review tables of the new language features and jump straight to them. If you already have experience with older versions of .NET, then in the first topic of *Chapter 7, Understanding and Packaging .NET Types*, you can review tables of the new platform features and jump straight to them.

I will point out the cool corners and gotchas of C# and .NET, so you can impress colleagues and get productive fast. Rather than slowing down and boring some readers by explaining every little thing, I will assume that you are smart enough to Google an explanation for topics that are related but not necessary to include in a beginner-to-intermediate guide.

You can clone solutions for the step-by-step guided tasks and exercises from the GitHub repository at the following link: https://github.com/markjprice/cs9dotnet5.

If you don't know how, then I provide instructions on how to do this using Visual Studio Code at the end of *Chapter 1, Hello, C#! Welcome, .NET!*.

What this book covers

Chapter 1, Hello, C#! Welcome, .NET!, is about setting up your development environment and using Visual Studio Code to create the simplest application possible with C# and .NET. You will learn how to write and compile code on any of the supported operating systems: Windows, macOS, and Linux variants. For simplified console apps, you will see the use of the top-level program feature introduced in C# 9. You will also learn the best places to look for help.

Chapter 2, Speaking C#, introduces the versions of C# and has tables showing which version introduced new features, and then explains the grammar and vocabulary that you will use every day to write the source code for your applications. In particular, you will learn how to declare and work with variables of different types, and about the big change in C# 8 with the introduction of nullable reference types.

Chapter 3, Controlling Flow and Converting Types, covers using operators to perform simple actions on variables including comparisons, writing code that makes decisions, pattern matching in C# 7 to C# 9, repeating a block of statements, and converting between types. It also covers writing code defensively to handle errors when they inevitably occur.

Chapter 4, Writing, Debugging, and Testing Functions, is about following the **Don't Repeat Yourself (DRY)** principle by writing reusable functions using both imperative and functional implementation styles. You will also learn how to use debugging tools to track down and remove bugs, monitoring your code while it executes to diagnose problems, and rigorously testing your code to remove bugs and ensure stability and reliability before it gets deployed into production.

Chapter 5, Building Your Own Types with Object-Oriented Programming, discusses all the different categories of members that a type can have, including fields to store data and methods to perform actions. You will use **object-oriented programming (OOP)** concepts, such as aggregation and encapsulation. You will learn language features such as tuple syntax support and out variables, and default literals and inferred tuple names, as well as how to define and work with immutable types using the new record keyword, init-only properties, and with expressions introduced in C# 9.

Chapter 6, Implementing Interfaces and Inheriting Classes, explains deriving new types from existing ones using OOP. You will learn how to define operators and local functions, delegates and events, how to implement interfaces about base and derived classes, how to override a type member, how to use polymorphism, how to create extension methods, and how to cast between classes in an inheritance hierarchy.

Chapter 7, Understanding and Packaging .NET Types, introduces the versions of .NET and has tables showing which version introduced new features, and then presents .NET types that are compliant with .NET Standard, and how they relate to C#. You will learn how to deploy and package your own apps and libraries.

Chapter 8, Working with Common .NET Types, discusses the types that allow your code to perform common practical tasks, such as manipulating numbers and text, storing items in collections, and implementing internationalization.

Chapter 9, Working with Files, Streams, and Serialization, talks about interacting with the filesystem, reading and writing to files and streams, text encoding, and serialization formats like JSON and XML, including the improved functionality and performance of the `System.Text.Json` classes in .NET 5.

Chapter 10, Protecting Your Data and Applications, is about protecting your data from being viewed by malicious users using encryption, and from being manipulated or corrupted using hashing and signing. You will also learn about authentication and authorization to protect applications from unauthorized users.

Chapter 11, Working with Databases Using Entity Framework Core, explains reading and writing to databases, such as Microsoft SQL Server and SQLite, using the **object-relational mapping (ORM)** technology named Entity Framework Core.

Chapter 12, Querying and Manipulating Data Using LINQ, teaches you **Language INtegrated Queries (LINQ)** — language extensions that add the ability to work with sequences of items and filter, sort, and project them into different outputs.

Chapter 13, Improving Performance and Scalability Using Multitasking, discusses allowing multiple actions to occur at the same time to improve performance, scalability, and user productivity. You will learn about the `async Main` feature and how to use types in the `System.Diagnostics` namespace to monitor your code to measure performance and efficiency.

Chapter 14, Introducing Practical Applications of C# and .NET, introduces you to the types of cross-platform applications that can be built using C# and .NET. You will also build an entity model to represent the Northwind database that will be used throughout Chapters 15 to 21.

Chapter 15, Building Websites Using ASP.NET Core Razor Pages, is about learning the basics of building websites with a modern HTTP architecture on the server side using ASP.NET Core. You will learn how to implement the ASP.NET Core feature known as Razor Pages, which simplifies creating dynamic web pages for small websites, and about building the HTTP request and response pipeline.

Chapter 16, Building Websites Using the Model-View-Controller Pattern, is about learning how to build large, complex websites in a way that is easy to unit test and manage with teams of programmers using ASP.NET Core MVC. You will learn about startup configuration, authentication, routes, models, views, and controllers.

Chapter 17, Building Websites Using a Content Management System, explains how a web **Content Management System (CMS)** can enable developers to rapidly build websites with a customizable administration user interface that non-technical users can use to create and manage their own content. As an example, you will learn about a simple open source .NET-based one named Piranha CMS.

Chapter 18, Building and Consuming Web Services, explains building backend REST architecture web services using the ASP.NET Core Web API and how to properly consume them using factory-instantiated HTTP clients.

Chapter 19, Building Intelligent Apps Using Machine Learning, introduces you to Microsoft's open source ML.NET package of machine learning algorithms, which can be used to embed adaptive intelligence into any cross-platform .NET app, such as a digital commerce website that provides product recommendations for visitors to add to their shopping cart.

Chapter 20, Building Web User Interfaces Using Blazor, introduces how to build web user interface components using Blazor that can be executed either on the server side or inside the client-side web browser. You will see the differences between Blazor Server and Blazor WebAssembly and how to build components that are easier to switch between the two hosting models.

Chapter 21, Building Cross-Platform Mobile Apps, introduces you to taking C# mobile by building a cross-platform app for iOS and Android. The app for this chapter will be built using Visual Studio 2019 for Mac on macOS.

Appendix A, Answers to the Test Your Knowledge Questions, has the answers to the test questions at the end of each chapter.

Appendix B, Building Windows Desktop Apps, introduces you to how .NET 5 and its Windows Desktop Pack enable Windows Forms and WPF apps to benefit from running on .NET 5. You will then learn the basics of XAML, which can be used to define the user interface for a graphical app for **Windows Presentation Foundation (WPF)** or the **Universal Windows Platform (UWP)**. You will apply the principles and features of Fluent Design to light up a UWP app. The apps for this chapter must be built using Visual Studio 2019 on Windows 10.

You can read both appendices at the following link: `https://static.packt-cdn.com/downloads/9781800568105_Appendices.pdf`.

What you need for this book

You can develop and deploy C# and .NET apps using Visual Studio Code on many platforms, including Windows, macOS, and many varieties of Linux. An operating system that supports Visual Studio Code and an internet connection is all you need to complete Chapters 1 to 20.

You will need macOS to build the apps in *Chapter 21, Building Cross-Platform Mobile Apps,* because you must have macOS and Xcode to compile iOS apps.

You will need Windows 10 to build the apps in *Appendix B, Building Windows Desktop Apps.*

Downloading the color images of this book

We also provide you with a PDF file that has color images of the screenshots/diagrams used in this book. The color images will help you better understand the changes in the output.

You can download this file from `https://static.packt-cdn.com/downloads/9781800568105_ColorImages.pdf`.

Conventions

In this book, you will find a number of text styles that distinguish between different kinds of information. Here are some examples of these styles and an explanation of their meaning.

CodeInText: Indicates code words in text, database table names, folder names, filenames, file extensions, pathnames, dummy URLs, user input, and Twitter handles. For example; "The Controllers, Models, and Views folders contain ASP.NET Core classes and the .cshtml files for execution on the server."

A block of code is set as follows:

```
// storing items at index positions
names[0] = "Kate";
names[1] = "Jack";
names[2] = "Rebecca";
names[3] = "Tom";
```

When we wish to draw your attention to a particular part of a code block, the relevant lines or items are highlighted:

```
// storing items at index positions
names[0] = "Kate";
names[1] = "Jack";
names[2] = "Rebecca";
names[3] = "Tom";
```

Any command-line input or output is written as follows:

```
dotnet new console
```

Bold: Indicates a new term, an important word, or words that you see on the screen, for example, in menus or dialog boxes, also appear in the text like this. For example: "Clicking on the **Next** button moves you to the next screen."

More Information: Links to external sources of further reading appear in a box like this.

Good Practice: Recommendations for how to program like an expert appear like this.

Get in touch

Feedback from our readers is always welcome.

General feedback: If you have questions about any aspect of this book, mention the book title in the subject of your message and email us at customercare@packtpub.com.

Errata: Although we have taken every care to ensure the accuracy of our content, mistakes do happen. If you have found a mistake in this book we would be grateful if you would report this to us. Please visit, www.packtpub.com/support/errata, selecting your book, clicking on the Errata Submission Form link, and entering the details.

Piracy: If you come across any illegal copies of our works in any form on the Internet, we would be grateful if you would provide us with the location address or website name. Please contact us at copyright@packt.com with a link to the material.

If you are interested in becoming an author: If there is a topic that you have expertise in and you are interested in either writing or contributing to a book, please visit authors.packtpub.com.

Reviews

Please leave a review. Once you have read and used this book, why not leave a review on the site that you purchased it from? Potential readers can then see and use your unbiased opinion to make purchase decisions, we at Packt can understand what you think about our products, and our authors can see your feedback on their book. Thank you!

For more information about Packt, please visit packt.com.

01

Hello, C#! Welcome, .NET!

In this first chapter, the goals are setting up your development environment, understanding the similarities and differences between .NET 5, .NET Core, .NET Framework, and .NET Standard, and then creating the simplest application possible with C# 9 and .NET 5 using Microsoft's Visual Studio Code.

After this first chapter, this book can be divided into three parts: first, the grammar and vocabulary of the C# language; second, the types available in .NET for building app features; and third, examples of common cross-platform apps you can build using C# and .NET.

Most people learn complex topics best by imitation and repetition rather than reading a detailed explanation of the theory; therefore, I will not overload you with detailed explanations of every step throughout this book. The idea is to get you to write some code, build an application from that code, and then for you to see it run.

You don't need to know all the nitty-gritty details immediately. That will be something that comes with time as you build your own apps and go beyond what any book can teach you.

In the words of Samuel Johnson, author of the English dictionary in 1755, I have committed "a few wild blunders, and risible absurdities, from which no work of such multiplicity is free." I take sole responsibility for these and hope you appreciate the challenge of my attempt to *lash the wind* by writing this book about rapidly evolving technologies like C# and .NET, and the apps that you can build with them.

This first chapter covers the following topics:

- Setting up your development environment
- Understanding .NET
- Building console apps using Visual Studio Code
- Downloading solution code from a GitHub repository
- Looking for help

Setting up your development environment

Before you start programming, you'll need a code editor for C#. Microsoft has a family of code editors and **Integrated Development Environments (IDEs)**, which include:

- Visual Studio Code
- GitHub Codespaces
- Visual Studio 2019
- Visual Studio 2019 for Mac

Using Visual Studio Code for cross-platform development

The most modern and lightweight code editor to choose, and the only one from Microsoft that is cross-platform, is Microsoft Visual Studio Code. It is able to run on all common operating systems, including Windows, macOS, and many varieties of Linux, including **Red Hat Enterprise Linux (RHEL)** and Ubuntu.

Visual Studio Code is a good choice for modern cross-platform development because it has an extensive and growing set of extensions to support many languages beyond C#, and being cross-platform and lightweight it can be installed on all platforms that your apps will be deployed to for quick bug fixes and so on.

Visual Studio Code is by far the most popular development environment with over half of developers selecting it in the Stack Overflow 2019 survey (the question was not asked in the 2020 survey), as shown in the following chart:

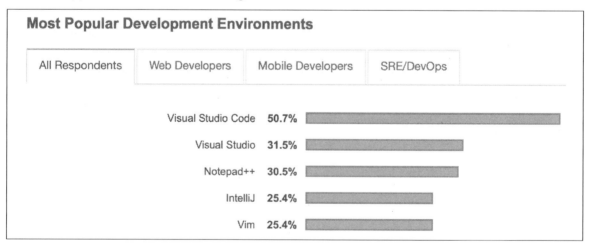

Figure 1.1: The most popular development environments

More Information: You can read the survey at the following link: `https://insights.stackoverflow.com/survey/2019#development-environments-and-tools`

Using Visual Studio Code means a developer can use a cross-platform code editor to develop cross-platform apps. Therefore, I have chosen to use Visual Studio Code for all but the last chapter of this book, because it needs special features not available in Visual Studio Code for building mobile apps.

 More Information: You can read about Microsoft's plans for Visual Studio Code at the following link: `https://github.com/Microsoft/vscode/wiki/Roadmap`

If you prefer to use Visual Studio 2019 or Visual Studio for Mac instead of Visual Studio Code, then of course you can, but I will assume that you are already familiar with how to use them and so I will not give step-by-step instructions for using them in this book. This book does not teach how to use code editors, it teaches how to write code, and that is the same regardless of the tool.

 More Information: You can read a comparison of Visual Studio Code and Visual Studio 2019 at the following link: `https://www.itworld.com/article/3403683/visual-studio-code-stepping-on-visual-studios-toes.html`

Using GitHub Codespaces for development in the cloud

GitHub Codespaces is a fully configured development environment based on Visual Studio Code that can be spun up in an environment hosted in the cloud and accessed through any web browser. It supports Git repos, extensions, and a built-in command-line interface so you can edit, run, and test from any device.

 More Information: Read more about GitHub Codespaces at the following link: `https://docs.github.com/en/github/developing-online-with-codespaces/about-codespaces`

Using Visual Studio 2019 for Windows app development

Microsoft Visual Studio 2019 only runs on Windows, version 7 SP1 or later. You must run it on Windows 10 to create **Universal Windows Platform (UWP)** apps that are installed from the Windows Store and run in a sandbox to protect your computer. It is the only Microsoft developer tool that can create Windows apps, so we will use it in *Appendix B, Building Windows Desktop Apps,* which is available as a PDF document at the following link:
`https://static.packt-cdn.com/downloads/9781800568105_Appendices.pdf`.

Using Visual Studio for Mac for mobile development

To compile apps for Apple operating systems like iOS to run on devices like the iPhone and iPad, you must have Xcode, but that tool only runs on macOS. Although you can use Visual Studio 2019 on Windows with its Xamarin extensions to write a cross-platform mobile app, you still need macOS and Xcode to compile it.

So, we will use Visual Studio 2019 for Mac on macOS in *Chapter 21, Building Cross-Platform Mobile Apps.*

Recommended tools for chapters

To help you to set up the best environment to use in this book, the following table summarizes which tools and operating systems I recommend be used for each of the chapters in this book:

Chapters	Tool	Operating systems
Chapters 1 to 20	Visual Studio Code	Windows, macOS, Linux
Chapter 21	Visual Studio 2019 for Mac	macOS
Appendix B	Visual Studio 2019	Windows 10

To write this book, I used my MacBook Pro and the following listed software:

- Visual Studio Code on macOS as my primary code editor.
- Visual Studio Code on Windows 10 in a virtual machine to test OS-specific behavior like working with the filesystem.
- Visual Studio 2019 on Windows 10 in a virtual machine to build Windows apps.
- Visual Studio 2019 for Mac on macOS to build mobile apps.

 More Information: Google and Amazon are supporters of Visual Studio Code, as you can read at the following link: `https://www.cnbc.com/2018/12/20/microsoft-cmo-capossela-says-google-employees-use-visual-studio-code.html`

Deploying cross-platform

Your choice of code editor and operating system for development does not limit where your code gets deployed.

.NET 5 supports the following platforms for deployment:

- **Windows**: Windows 7 SP1, or later. Windows 10 version 1607, or later. Windows Server 2012 R2 SP1, or later. Nano Server version 1809, or later.
- **Mac**: macOS High Sierra (version 10.13), or later.
- **Linux**: Alpine Linux 3.11, or later. CentOS 7, or later. Debian 9, or later. Fedora 30, or later. Linux Mint 18, or later. openSUSE 15, or later. Red Hat Enterprise Linux (RHEL) 7, or later. SUSE Enterprise Linux 12 SP2, or later. Ubuntu 18.04, 19.10, 20.04, or later.

> **More Information**: You can read the official list of supported operating systems at the following link: `https://github.com/dotnet/core/blob/master/release-notes/5.0/5.0-supported-os.md`

Windows ARM64 support in .NET 5 and later means you can now develop on and deploy to Windows ARM devices like Microsoft Surface Pro X.

> **More Information**: You can read more about Windows ARM64 support at the following link: `https://github.com/dotnet/runtime/issues/36699`

Understanding Microsoft Visual Studio Code versions

Microsoft releases a new feature version of Visual Studio Code (almost) every month and bug fix versions more frequently. For example:

- Version 1.49, August 2020 feature release
- Version 1.49.1, August 2020 bug fix release

> **More Information**: You can read about the latest versions at the following link: `https://code.visualstudio.com/updates`

The version used in this book is 1.49 released on September 10, 2020, but the version of Microsoft Visual Studio Code is less important than the version of the **C# for Visual Studio Code** extension that you will install later.

While the C# extension is not required, it provides IntelliSense as you type, code navigation, and debugging features, so it's something that's very handy to install. To support C# 9, you should install the C# extension version 1.23 or later.

In this book, I will show keyboard shortcuts and screenshots of Visual Studio Code using the macOS version. Visual Studio Code on Windows and variants of Linux are practically identical, although keyboard shortcuts are likely different.

Some common keyboard shortcuts that we will use are shown in the following table:

Action	macOS	Windows
Show Command Palette	*Cmd + Shift + P*	*Ctrl + Shift + P*
Show Command Palette	*F1*	*F1*
Go To Definition	*F12*	*F12*
Go Back	*Ctrl + -*	*Alt + ←*
Go Forward	*Ctrl + Shift + -*	*Alt + →*
Show Terminal	*Ctrl + ` (backtick)*	*Ctrl + ' (quote)*
New Terminal	*Ctrl + Shift + ` (backtick)*	*Ctrl + Shift + ' (quote)*
Toggle Line Comment	*Ctrl + /*	*Ctrl + /*
Toggle Block Comment	*Shift + Option + A*	*Shift + Alt + A*

I recommend that you download a PDF of keyboard shortcuts for your operating system from the following list:

- **Windows**: https://code.visualstudio.com/shortcuts/keyboard-shortcuts-windows.pdf
- **macOS**: https://code.visualstudio.com/shortcuts/keyboard-shortcuts-macos.pdf
- **Linux**: https://code.visualstudio.com/shortcuts/keyboard-shortcuts-linux.pdf

 More Information: You can learn about the default key bindings for Visual Studio Code and how to customize them at the following link: https://code.visualstudio.com/docs/getstarted/keybindings

Visual Studio Code has rapidly improved over the past couple of years and has pleasantly surprised Microsoft with its popularity. If you are brave and like to live on the bleeding edge, then there is an Insiders edition, which is a daily build of the next version.

Downloading and installing Visual Studio Code

Now you are ready to download and install Visual Studio Code, its C# extension, and the .NET 5 SDK:

1. Download and install either the Stable build or the Insiders edition of Visual Studio Code from the following link: `https://code.visualstudio.com/`.

2. Download and install the .NET 5 SDK from the following link: `https://www.microsoft.com/net/download`.

3. To install the C# extension, you must first launch the Visual Studio Code application.

4. In Visual Studio Code, click the **Extensions** icon or navigate to **View | Extensions**.

5. C# is one of the most popular extensions available, so you should see it at the top of the list, or you can enter `C#` in the search box, as shown in the following screenshot:

Figure 1.2: The C# extension

6. Click **Install** and wait for supporting packages to download and install.

 More Information: You can read more about Visual Studio Code support for C# at the following link: `https://code.visualstudio.com/docs/languages/csharp`

0

Installing other extensions

In later chapters of this book, you will use more extensions. If you want to install them now, all the extensions that we will use are shown in the following table:

Extension	Description
C# for Visual Studio Code (powered by OmniSharp) `ms-vscode.csharp`	C# editing support, including syntax highlighting, IntelliSense, Go to Definition, Find All References, debugging support for .NET, and support for `csproj` projects on Windows, macOS, and Linux.
MSBuild project tools `tinytoy.msbuild-project-tools`	Provides IntelliSense for MSBuild project files, including auto-complete for `<PackageReference>` elements.
C# XML Documentation Comments `k--kato.docomment`	Generate XML documentation comments.
REST Client `humao.rest-client`	Send an HTTP request and view the response directly in Visual Studio Code.
ILSpy .NET Decompiler `icsharpcode.ilspy-vscode`	Decompile MSIL assemblies – support for .NET Framework, .NET Core, and .NET Standard.

Understanding .NET

.NET 5, .NET Framework, .NET Core, and Xamarin are related and overlapping platforms for developers used to build applications and services. In this section, I'm going to introduce you to each of these .NET concepts.

Understanding .NET Framework

.NET Framework is a development platform that includes a **Common Language Runtime (CLR)**, which manages the execution of code, and a **Base Class Library (BCL)**, which provides a rich library of classes to build applications from. Microsoft originally designed .NET Framework to have the possibility of being cross-platform, but Microsoft put their implementation effort into making it work best with Windows.

Since .NET Framework 4.5.2 it has been an official component of the Windows operating system. .NET Framework is installed on over one billion computers so it must change as little as possible. Even bug fixes can cause problems, so it is updated infrequently.

All of the apps on a computer written for .NET Framework share the same version of the CLR and libraries stored in the **Global Assembly Cache (GAC)**, which can lead to issues if some of them need a specific version for compatibility.

Good Practice: Practically speaking, .NET Framework is Windows-only and a legacy platform. Do not create new apps using it.

Understanding the Mono and Xamarin projects

Third parties developed a .NET Framework implementation named the **Mono** project. Mono is cross-platform, but it fell well behind the official implementation of .NET Framework.

More Information: You can read more about the Mono project at the following link: http://www.mono-project.com/

Mono has found a niche as the foundation of the **Xamarin** mobile platform as well as cross-platform game development platforms like **Unity**.

More Information: You can read more about Unity at the following link: https://docs.unity3d.com/

Microsoft purchased Xamarin in 2016 and now gives away what used to be an expensive Xamarin extension for free with Visual Studio 2019. Microsoft renamed the **Xamarin Studio** development tool, which could only create mobile apps, to **Visual Studio for Mac** and gave it the ability to create other types of projects like console apps and web services. With Visual Studio 2019 for Mac, Microsoft has replaced parts of the Xamarin Studio editor with parts from Visual Studio for Windows to provide closer parity of experience and performance.

Understanding .NET Core

Today, we live in a truly cross-platform world where modern mobile and cloud development have made Windows, as an operating system, much less important. Because of that, Microsoft has been working on an effort to decouple .NET from its close ties with Windows. While rewriting .NET Framework to be truly cross-platform, they've taken the opportunity to refactor and remove major parts that are no longer considered core.

This new product was branded .NET Core and includes a cross-platform implementation of the CLR known as **CoreCLR** and a streamlined library of classes known as **CoreFX**.

Scott Hunter, Microsoft Partner Director Program Manager for .NET, has said that "Forty percent of our .NET Core customers are brand-new developers to the platform, which is what we want with .NET Core. We want to bring new people in."

.NET Core is fast-moving and because it can be deployed side by side with an app, it can change frequently, knowing those changes will not affect other .NET Core apps on the same machine. Improvements that Microsoft makes to .NET Core cannot be added to .NET Framework.

More Information: You can read more about Microsoft's positioning of .NET Core and .NET Framework at the following link: `https://devblogs.microsoft.com/dotnet/update-on-net-core-3-0-and-net-framework-4-8/`

Understanding .NET 5 and the journey to one .NET

At the Microsoft Build developer conference in May 2020, the .NET team announced that their plans for the unification of .NET had been delayed. They said .NET 5 would be released on November 10, 2020 and it would unify all the various .NET platforms except mobile. It will not be until .NET 6 in November 2021 that mobile will also be supported by the unified .NET platform.

.NET Core has been renamed .NET and the major version number has skipped the number four to avoid confusion with .NET Framework 4.x. Microsoft plans on annual major version releases every November, rather like Apple does major version number releases of iOS every September.

More Information: You can read more about Microsoft's plans for the journey to one .NET at the following link: `https://devblogs.microsoft.com/dotnet/announcing-net-5-preview-4-and-our-journey-to-one-net/`

The following table shows when the key versions of modern .NET were released, when future releases are planned, and which version is used by the various editions of this book:

Version	Released	Edition	Published
.NET Core RC1	November 2015	First	March 2016
.NET Core 1.0	June 2016		
.NET Core 1.1	November 2016		
.NET Core 1.0.4 and .NET Core 1.1.1	March 2017	Second	March 2017
.NET Core 2.0	August 2017		
.NET Core for UWP in Windows 10 Fall Creators Update	October 2017	Third	November 2017
.NET Core 2.1 (LTS)	May 2018		
.NET Core 2.2 (Current)	December 2018		
.NET Core 3.0 (Current)	September 2019	Fourth	October 2019
.NET Core 3.1 (LTS)	December 2019		
.NET 5.0 (Current)	November 2020	Fifth	November 2020
.NET 6.0 (LTS)	November 2021	Sixth	November 2021

Understanding .NET support

.NET versions are either **Long-Term Support (LTS)** or Current, as described in the following list:

- **LTS** releases are stable and require fewer updates over their lifetime. These are a good choice for applications that you do not intend to update frequently. LTS releases will be supported for 3 years after general availability.

- **Current** releases include features that may change based on feedback. These are a good choice for applications that you are actively developing because they provide access to the latest improvements. After a 3-month maintenance period, the previous minor version will no longer be supported.

Both receive critical fixes throughout their lifetime for security and reliability. You must stay up to date with the latest patches to get support. For example, if a system is running 1.0 and 1.0.1 has been released, 1.0.1 will need to be installed to get support.

To better understand your choices of Current and LTS releases, it is helpful to see it visually with three-year-long blue bars that do not fade for LTS; and for Current, variable-length green bars that fade to pale green to show the three months after a new release before a Current release reaches end of life, as shown in the following diagram:

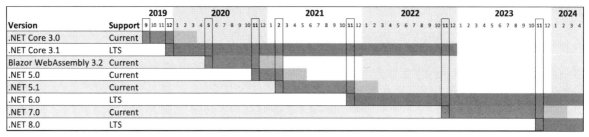

Figure 1.3: Support for various versions

For example, if you create a project using .NET 5.0 and Microsoft releases .NET 5.1 in February 2021, then you will need to upgrade your project to .NET 5.1 by the end of May 2021.

If you need longer-term support from Microsoft, then choose .NET Core 3.1 today, not .NET 5.0. Once .NET 6.0 releases in November 2021, you will still have more than another year of support before you will have to upgrade your project to .NET 6.0.

All versions of .NET Core have reached end of life except the LTS versions that will reach end of life as shown in the following list:

- .NET Core 2.1 will reach end of life on August 21, 2021.

- .NET Core 3.1 will reach end of life on December 3, 2022.

- .NET 6.0 will reach end of life in November 2024 if it releases as planned in November 2021.

 More Information: You can read more about .NET Support Policy at the following link: https://dotnet.microsoft.com/platform/support/policy/dotnet-core

Understanding .NET Runtime and .NET SDK versions

.NET Runtime versioning follows semantic versioning, that is, a major increment indicates breaking changes, minor increments indicate new features, and patch increments indicate bug fixes.

.NET SDK versioning does not follow semantic versioning. The major and minor version numbers are tied to the runtime version it is matched with. The patch number follows a convention that indicates the major and minor version of the SDK. You can see an example of this in the following table:

Change	Runtime	SDK
Initial release	5.0.0	5.0.100
SDK bug fix	5.0.0	5.0.101
Runtime and SDK bug fix	5.0.1	5.0.102
SDK new feature	5.0.1	5.0.200

 More Information: You can learn more about how versions work at the following link: https://docs.microsoft.com/en-us/dotnet/core/versions/

Removing old versions of .NET

.NET Runtime updates are compatible with a major version such as 5.x and updated releases of the .NET SDK maintain the ability to build applications that target previous versions of the runtime, which enables the safe removal of older versions.

You can see which SDKs and runtimes are currently installed using the following commands:

- `dotnet --list-sdks`
- `dotnet --list-runtimes`

On Windows, use the **App & features** section to remove .NET SDKs.

On macOS or Windows, use the `dotnet-core-uninstall` tool.

 More Information: You can read about the .NET Uninstall Tool at the following link: https://docs.microsoft.com/en-us/dotnet/core/additional-tools/uninstall-tool

For example, while writing the fourth edition I used the following command every month:

```
dotnet-core-uninstall --all-previews-but-latest --sdk
```

 More Information: You can read about removing .NET SDKs and runtimes at the following link: https://docs.microsoft.com/en-us/dotnet/core/install/remove-runtime-sdk-versions

What is different about .NET Core and .NET 5?

Modern .NET is smaller than the current version of .NET Framework due to the fact that legacy and non-cross-platform technologies have been removed. For example, **Windows Forms** and **Windows Presentation Foundation (WPF)** can be used to build **graphical user interface (GUI)** applications, but they are tightly bound to the Windows ecosystem, so they have been removed from .NET on macOS and Linux.

One of the features of .NET 5 is support for running old Windows Forms and WPF applications using the **Windows Desktop Pack** that is included with the Windows version of .NET 5, which is why it is bigger than the SDKs for macOS and Linux. You can make some small changes to your legacy Windows app if necessary, and then rebuild it for .NET 5 to take advantage of new features and performance improvements. You'll learn about support for building these types of Windows apps in *Appendix B, Building Windows Desktop Apps*.

ASP.NET Web Forms and **Windows Communication Foundation (WCF)** are old web application and service technologies that fewer developers are choosing to use for new development projects today, so they have also been removed from .NET 5. Instead, developers prefer to use ASP.NET MVC and ASP.NET Web API. These two technologies have been refactored and combined into a platform that runs on .NET 5, named **ASP.NET Core**. You'll learn about the technologies in *Chapter 15, Building Websites Using ASP.NET Core Razor Pages*, *Chapter 16, Building Websites Using the Model-View-Controller Pattern*, and *Chapter 18, Building and Consuming Web Services*.

More Information: Some .NET Framework developers are upset that ASP.NET Web Forms, WCF, and Windows Workflow (WF) are missing from .NET 5 and would like Microsoft to change their minds. There are open source projects to enable WCF and WF to migrate to .NET 5. You can read more at the following link: `https://devblogs.microsoft.com/dotnet/supporting-the-community-with-wf-and-wcf-oss-projects/`. There is an open source project for Blazor Web Forms components at the following link: `https://github.com/FritzAndFriends/BlazorWebFormsComponents`

Entity Framework (EF) 6 is an object-relational mapping technology that is designed to work with data that is stored in relational databases such as Oracle and Microsoft SQL Server. It has gained baggage over the years, so the cross-platform API has been slimmed down, has been given support for non-relational databases like Microsoft Azure Cosmos DB, and has been renamed **Entity Framework Core**. You will learn about it in *Chapter 11, Working with Databases Using Entity Framework Core*.

If you have existing apps that use the old EF, then version 6.3 is supported on .NET Core 3.0 or later.

More Information: Although .NET 5 has dropped the word Core in its branding, ASP.NET Core and Entity Framework Core will retain the word Core to help differentiate from older legacy versions of those technologies, as explained at the following link: `https://docs.microsoft.com/en-us/dotnet/core/dotnet-five`

In addition to removing large pieces from .NET Framework in order to make .NET Core, Microsoft has componentized .NET into NuGet packages, those being small chunks of functionality that can be deployed independently.

Microsoft's primary goal is not to make .NET smaller than .NET Framework. The goal is to componentize .NET to support modern technologies and to have fewer dependencies, so that deployment requires only those packages that your application needs.

Understanding .NET Standard

The situation with .NET in 2019 was that there were three forked .NET platforms controlled by Microsoft, as shown in the following list:

- **.NET Core**: for cross-platform and new apps
- **.NET Framework**: for legacy apps
- **Xamarin**: for mobile apps

Each had strengths and weaknesses because they were all designed for different scenarios. This led to the problem that a developer had to learn three platforms, each with annoying quirks and limitations. Because of that, Microsoft defined **.NET Standard**: a specification for a set of APIs that all .NET platforms could implement to indicate what level of compatibility they have. For example, basic support is indicated by a platform being compliant with .NET Standard 1.4.

With .NET Standard 2.0 and later, Microsoft made all three platforms converge on a modern minimum standard, which made it much easier for developers to share code between any flavor of .NET.

For .NET Core 2.0 and later, this added a number of the missing APIs that developers need to port old code written for .NET Framework to the cross-platform .NET Core. However, some APIs are implemented but throw an exception to indicate to a developer that they should not actually be used! This is usually due to differences in the operating system on which you run .NET. You'll learn how to handle these exceptions in *Chapter 2, Speaking C#*.

It is important to understand that .NET Standard is just a standard. You are not able to install .NET Standard in the same way that you cannot install HTML5. To use HTML5, you must install a web browser that implements the HTML5 standard.

To use .NET Standard, you must install a .NET platform that implements the .NET Standard specification. .NET Standard 2.0 is implemented by the latest versions of .NET Framework, .NET Core, and Xamarin.

The latest .NET Standard, 2.1, is only implemented by .NET Core 3.0, Mono, and Xamarin. Some features of C# 8.0 require .NET Standard 2.1. .NET Standard 2.1 is not implemented by .NET Framework 4.8 so we should treat .NET Framework as legacy.

Once .NET 6 is released in November 2021, the need for .NET Standard will significantly reduce, because there will be a single .NET for all platforms, including mobile. Even then, apps and websites created for .NET Framework will need to be supported so understanding that you can create .NET Standard 2.0 class libraries that are backward compatible with legacy .NET platforms is important to know.

 More Information: .NET Standard versions and which .NET platforms support them are listed at the following link: https://github.com/dotnet/standard/blob/master/docs/versions.md

By the end of 2021, Microsoft promises that there will be a single .NET platform. .NET 6 is planned to have a single BCL and two runtimes: one optimized for server or desktop scenarios like websites and Windows desktop apps based on the .NET Core runtime, and one optimized for mobile apps based on the Xamarin runtime.

.NET platforms and tools used by the book editions

For the first edition of this book, which was written in March 2016, I focused on .NET Core functionality but used .NET Framework when important or useful features had not yet been implemented in .NET Core, because that was before the final release of .NET Core 1.0. Visual Studio 2015 was used for most examples, with Visual Studio Code shown only briefly.

The second edition was (almost) completely purged of all .NET Framework code examples so that readers were able to focus on .NET Core examples that truly run cross-platform.

The third edition completed the switch. It was rewritten so that all of the code was pure .NET Core. But giving step-by-step instructions for both Visual Studio Code and Visual Studio 2019 for all tasks added unnecessary complexity.

The fourth edition continued the trend by only showing coding examples using Visual Studio Code for all but the last two chapters of this book. In *Chapter 20, Building Windows Desktop Apps*, it used Visual Studio 2019 running on Windows 10, and in *Chapter 21, Building Cross-Platform Mobile Apps*, it used Visual Studio 2019 for Mac.

In this fifth edition, *Chapter 20, Building Windows Desktop Apps*, was moved to *Appendix B* to make space for a new *Chapter 20, Building Web User Interfaces Using Blazor*. Blazor projects can be created using Visual Studio Code.

In the planned sixth edition, *Chapter 21, Building Cross-Platform Mobile and Desktop Apps*, will be completely rewritten to show how mobile and desktop cross-platform apps can be created using Visual Studio Code and an extension to support .NET MAUI (Multi-platform App UI). This has to wait until the sixth edition because Microsoft will release .NET MAUI with .NET 6 in November 2021. At that point, the whole book will use Visual Studio Code for all examples.

Understanding intermediate language

The C# compiler (named **Roslyn**) used by the dotnet CLI tool converts your C# source code into **intermediate language** (**IL**) code and stores the IL in an assembly (a DLL or EXE file). IL code statements are like assembly language instructions, which are executed by .NET's virtual machine, known as CoreCLR.

At runtime, CoreCLR loads the IL code from the assembly, the **just-in-time** (**JIT**) compiler compiles it into native CPU instructions, and then it is executed by the CPU on your machine. The benefit of this three-step compilation process is that Microsoft is able to create CLRs for Linux and macOS, as well as for Windows. The same IL code runs everywhere because of the second compilation process, which generates code for the native operating system and CPU instruction set.

Regardless of which language the source code is written in, for example, C#, Visual Basic, or F#, all .NET applications use IL code for their instructions stored in an assembly. Microsoft and others provide disassembler tools that can open an assembly and reveal this IL code, such as the ILSpy .NET Decompiler extension.

Comparing .NET technologies

We can summarize and compare .NET technologies in 2020, as shown in the following table:

Technology	Description	Host OSes
.NET 5	Modern feature set, full C# 9 support, port existing and create new Windows and Web apps and services.	Windows, macOS, Linux
.NET Framework	Legacy feature set, limited C# 8 support, no C# 9 support, maintain existing applications.	Windows only
Xamarin	Mobile and desktop apps only.	Android, iOS, macOS

Building console apps using Visual Studio Code

The goal of this section is to showcase how to build a console app using Visual Studio Code. Both the instructions and screenshots in this section are for macOS, but the same actions will work with Visual Studio Code on Windows and Linux variants.

The main differences will be native command-line actions such as deleting a file: both the command and the path are likely to be different on Windows or macOS and Linux. Luckily, the dotnet command-line tool will be identical on all platforms.

Writing code using Visual Studio Code

Let's get started writing code!

1. Start Visual Studio Code.

2. On macOS, navigate to **File** | **Open…**. On Windows, navigate to **File** | **Open Folder…**. On both OSes, you can click the **Open Folder** button in the **EXPLORER** pane or click the **Open folder…** link on the **Welcome** tab, as shown in the following screenshot:

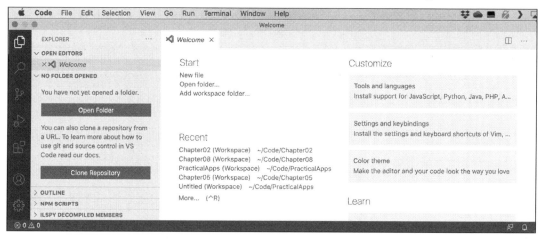

Figure 1.4: The Visual Studio Code Welcome tab

3. In the dialog box, navigate to your user folder on macOS (mine is named markjprice), your Documents folder on Windows, or any directory or drive in which you want to save your projects.

4. Click the **New Folder** button and name the folder Code.

5. In the Code folder, create a new folder named Chapter01.

6. In the Chapter01 folder, create a new folder named HelloCS.

7. Select the HelloCS folder and on macOS click **Open** or on Windows click **Select Folder**.

8. Navigate to **View** | **Terminal**, or on macOS press *Ctrl* + ` (backtick) and on Windows press *Ctrl* + ' (single quote). Confusingly, on Windows, the key combination *Ctrl* + ` (backtick) splits the current window!

9. In **TERMINAL**, enter the following command:

```
dotnet new console
```

10. You will see that the dotnet command-line tool creates a new **Console Application** project for you in the current folder, and the **EXPLORER** window shows the two files created, HelloCS.proj and Program.cs, as shown in the following screenshot:

Figure 1.5: Your EXPLORER window should show both files have been created

11. In **EXPLORER**, click on the file named `Program.cs` to open it in the editor window. The first time that you do this, Visual Studio Code may have to download and install C# dependencies like OmniSharp, the Razor Language Server, and the .NET Core debugger, if it did not do this when you installed the C# extension.

12. If you see a warning saying that required assets are missing, click **Yes**, as shown in the following screenshot:

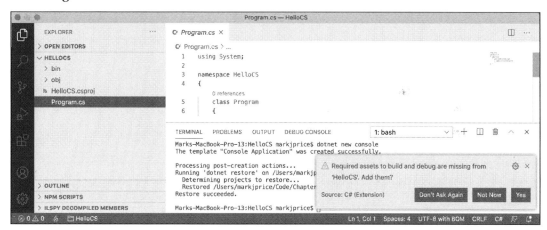

Figure 1.6: Warning message to add required build and debug assets

13. After a few seconds, a folder named `.vscode` will appear in the **EXPLORER** pane with some files that are used during debugging, as you will learn in *Chapter 4, Writing, Debugging, and Testing Functions*.

14. In `Program.cs`, modify line 9 so that the text that is being written to the console says, **Hello, C#!**

15. Navigate to **File | Auto Save**. This toggle will save the annoyance of remembering to save before rebuilding your application each time.

Compiling and running code using the dotnet CLI

The next task is to compile and run the code.

1. Navigate to **View | Terminal** and enter the following command:

```
dotnet run
```

2. The output in the **TERMINAL** window will show the result of running your application, as shown in the following screenshot:

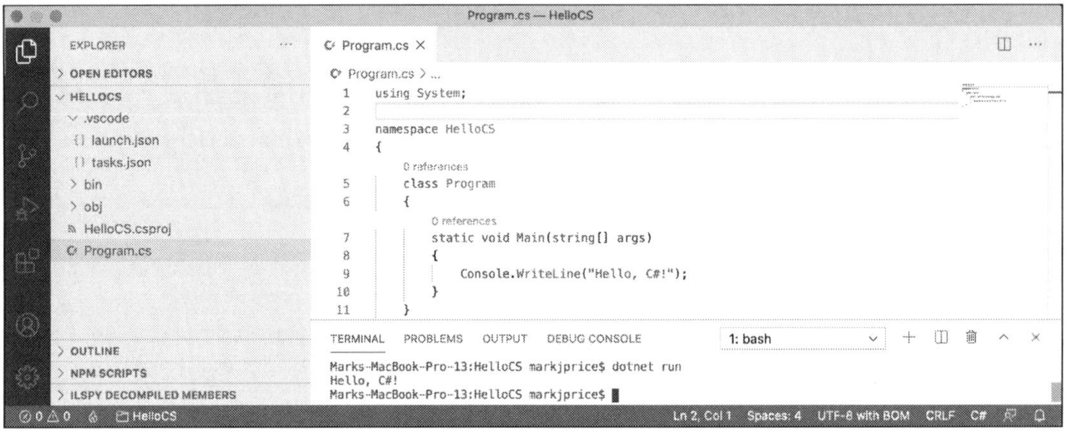

Figure 1.7: The output of running your application

Writing top-level programs

You might be thinking that was a lot of code just to output Hello, C#! Although the boilerplate code is written for you by the project template, is there a simpler way?

Well, in C# 9 there is, and it is known as **top-level programs**.

Let's compare the traditional minimum console app, as shown in the following code:

```
using System;

class Program
{
  static void Main(string[] args)
  {
    Console.WriteLine("Hello World!");
  }
}
```

To the new top-level program minimum console app, as shown in the following code:

```
using System;

Console.WriteLine("Hello World!");
```

That is a lot simpler, right? If you had to start with a blank fiie and write all the statements yourself, this is better.

During compilation, all the boilerplate code to define the `Program` class and its `Main` method is generated and wrapped around the statements you write. Any `using` statements still have to go at the top of the file. There can be only one file like this in a project.

Personally, especially when teaching C#, I plan to continue to use the traditional project template since it is true to reality. I am not keen on magic hidden code for the same reason I do not like graphical user interfaces that hide elements in an attempt to simplify the experience but frustrate users because they cannot discover features that they need.

For example, arguments can be passed into a console app. With a top-level program, you would need to know that the `args` parameter exists even though you cannot see it.

Downloading solution code from the GitHub repository

Git is a commonly used source code management system. GitHub is a company, website, and desktop application that makes it easier to manage Git. Microsoft purchased GitHub in 2018, so it will continue to get closer integration with Microsoft tools.

I used GitHub to store solutions to all the practical exercises that are featured at the end of each chapter. You will find the repository for this chapter at the following link: `https://github.com/markjprice/cs9dotnet5`.

I recommend that you add the preceding link to your favorite bookmarks because I use the GitHub repository for this book for publishing errata and other useful links.

Using Git with Visual Studio Code

Visual Studio Code has support for Git, but it will use your OS's Git installation, so you must install Git 2.0 or later first before you get these features.

You can install Git from the following link: `https://git-scm.com/download`.

If you like to use a GUI, you can download GitHub Desktop from the following link:

`https://desktop.github.com`

Cloning the book solution code repository

Let's clone the book solution code repository.

1. Create a folder named `Repos` in your user or `Documents` folder, or wherever you want to store your Git repositories.

2. In Visual Studio Code, open the `Repos` folder.

3. Navigate to **View | Terminal**, and enter the following command:

```
git clone https://github.com/markjprice/cs9dotnet5.git
```

4. Note that cloning all of the solutions for all of the chapters will take a minute or so, as shown in the following screenshot:

Figure 1.8: Cloning the book solution code

 More Information: For more information about source code version control with Visual Studio Code, visit the following link: `https://code.visualstudio.com/Docs/editor/versioncontrol`

Looking for help

This section is all about how to find quality information about programming on the web.

Reading Microsoft documentation

The definitive resource for getting help with Microsoft developer tools and platforms is **Microsoft Docs**, and you can find it at the following link: `https://docs.microsoft.com/`.

Getting help for the dotnet tool

At the command line, you can ask the `dotnet` tool for help with its commands.

1. To open the official documentation in a browser window for the dotnet new command, enter the following at the command line or in Visual Studio Code Terminal:

```
dotnet help new
```

2. To get help output at the command line, use the -h or --help flag, as shown in the following command:

```
dotnet new console -h
```

3. You will see the following partial output:

```
Console Application (C#)
Author: Microsoft
Description: A project for creating a command-line application that can
run on .NET Core on Windows, Linux and macOS
Options:
  -f|--framework  The target framework for the project.
                      net5.0           - Target net5.0
                      netcoreapp3.1    - Target netcoreapp3.1
                      netcoreapp3.0    - Target netcoreapp3.0
                  Default: net5.0


  --langVersion   Sets langVersion in the created project file
                  text - Optional


  --no-restore    If specified, skips the automatic restore of the project
on create.

                  bool - Optional
                  Default: false / (*) true


* Indicates the value used if the switch is provided without a value.
```

Getting definitions of types and their members

One of the most useful keyboard shortcuts in Visual Studio Code is F12 to **Go To Definition**. This will show what the public definition of the type or member looks like by reading the metadata in the compiled assembly. Some tools, such as ILSpy .NET Decompiler, will even reverse-engineer from the metadata and IL code back into C# for you.

Let's see how to use the Go To Definition feature.

1. In Visual Studio Code, open the HelloCS folder.

2. In Program.cs, inside the Main method, enter the following statement to declare an integer variable named z:

```
int z;
```

3. Click inside `int` and then press *F12*, or right-click and choose **Go To Definition**. In the new code window that appears, you can see how the `int` data type is defined, as shown in the following screenshot:

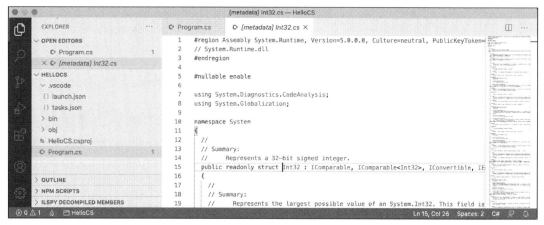

Figure 1.9: The int data type

You can see that `int`:

- Is defined using the `struct` keyword.
- Is in the `System.Runtime` assembly.
- Is in the `System` namespace.
- Is named `Int32`.
- Is therefore an alias for the `System.Int32` type.
- Implements interfaces such as `IComparable`.
- Has constant values for its maximum and minimum values.
- Has methods like `Parse`.

 Good Practice: When you try to use **Go To Definition**, you will sometimes see an error saying **No definition found**. This is because the C# extension does not know about the current project. Navigate to **View | Command Palette**, enter and select **OmniSharp: Select Project**, and then select the correct project that you want to work with.

Right now, the **Go To Definition** feature is not that useful to you because you do not yet know what these terms mean.

By the end of the first part of this book, which teaches you about C#, you will know enough for this feature to become very handy.

4. In the code editor window, scroll down to find the `Parse` method with a single `string` parameter and the comments that document it, starting on line 87, as shown in the following screenshot:

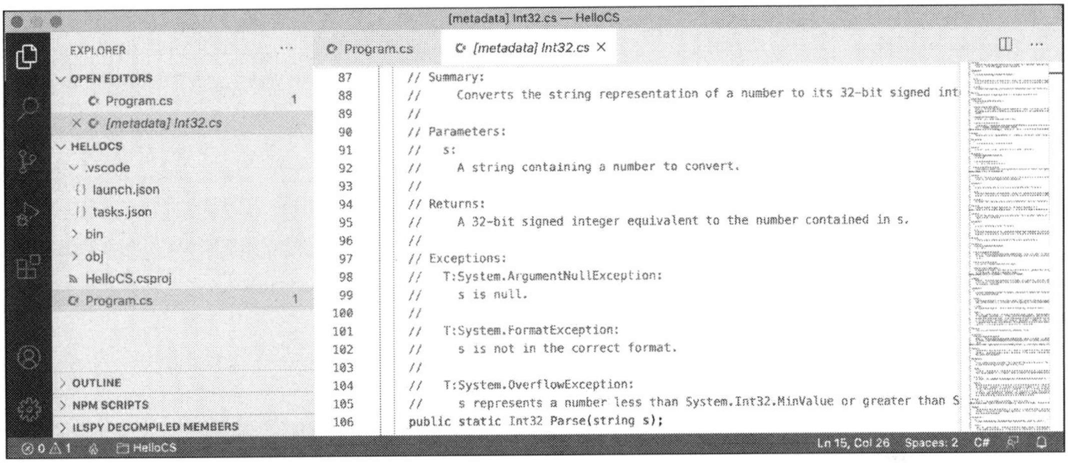

Figure 1.10: The comments for the Parse method

In the comments, you will see that Microsoft has documented what exceptions might occur if you call this method, including `ArgumentNullException`, `FormatException`, and `OverflowException`. Now, we know that we need to wrap a call to this method in a `try` statement and which exceptions to catch.

Hopefully, you are getting impatient to learn what all this means!

Be patient for a little longer. You are almost at the end of this chapter, and in the next chapter, you will dive into the details of the C# language. But first, let's see where else you can look for help.

Looking for answers on Stack Overflow

Stack Overflow is the most popular third-party website for getting answers to difficult programming questions. It's so popular that search engines such as **DuckDuckGo** have a special way to write a query to search the site.

1. Start your favorite web browser.
2. Navigate to `DuckDuckGo.com`, enter the following query, and note the search results, which are also shown in the following screenshot:

```
!so securestring
```

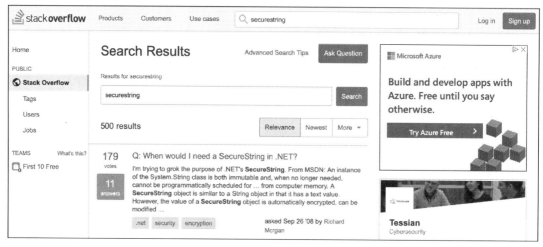

Figure 1.11: Stack Overflow search results for securestring

Searching for answers using Google

You can search **Google** with advanced search options to increase the likelihood of finding what you need.

1. Navigate to Google.

2. Search for information about `garbage collection` using a simple Google query, and note that you will probably see a lot of ads for garbage collection services in your local area before you see the Wikipedia definition of garbage collection in computer science.

3. Improve the search by restricting it to a useful site such as Stack Overflow, and by removing languages that we might not care about such as C++, Rust, and Python, or by adding C# and .NET explicitly, as shown in the following search query:

```
garbage collection site:stackoverflow.com +C# -Java
```

Subscribing to the official .NET blog

To keep up to date with .NET, an excellent blog to subscribe to is the official **.NET Blog** written by the .NET engineering teams, and you can find it at the following link: `https://devblogs.microsoft.com/dotnet/`.

Scott Hanselman's videos

Scott Hanselman from Microsoft has an excellent YouTube channel about computer stuff they didn't teach you. I recommend it to everyone working with computers.

 More Information: You can watch Scott's video series at the following link: `http://computerstufftheydidnteachyou.com/`

Practicing and exploring

Let's now test your knowledge and understanding by trying to answer some questions, getting some hands-on practice, and exploring with deeper research into the topics covered throughout this chapter.

Exercise 1.1 – Test your knowledge

Try to answer the following questions, remembering that although most answers can be found in this chapter, some online research or code writing will be needed to answer others:

1. Why can a programmer use different languages, for example, C# and F#, to write applications that run on .NET?
2. What do you type at the prompt to create a console app?
3. What do you type at the prompt to build and execute C# source code?
4. What is the Visual Studio Code keyboard shortcut to view Terminal?
5. Is Visual Studio 2019 better than Visual Studio Code?
6. Is .NET Core better than .NET Framework?
7. What is .NET Standard and why is it still important?
8. What is the name of the entry point method of a .NET console application and how should it be declared?
9. Where would you look for help about a C# keyword?
10. Where would you look for solutions to common programming problems?

Exercise 1.2 – Practice C# anywhere

You don't need Visual Studio Code or even Visual Studio 2019 or Visual Studio 2019 for Mac to write C#. You can go to .NET Fiddle – `https://dotnetfiddle.net/` – and start coding online.

Exercise 1.3 – Explore topics

You can use the following links to read more details about the topics we've covered in this chapter:

- **Visual Studio Code documentation**: `https://code.visualstudio.com/docs`
- **.NET**: `https://dotnet.microsoft.com`
- **.NET Core Command-Line Interface (CLI) tool**: `https://aka.ms/dotnet-cli-docs`
- **.NET Core runtime, CoreCLR**: `https://github.com/dotnet/runtime`
- **.NET Core Roadmap**: `https://github.com/dotnet/core/blob/master/roadmap.md`

- **.NET Standard FAQ**: `https://github.com/dotnet/standard/blob/master/docs/faq.md`
- **Stack Overflow**: `https://stackoverflow.com/`
- **Google Advanced Search**: `https://www.google.com/advanced_search`
- **Microsoft Learn**: `https://docs.microsoft.com/en-us/learn/`
- **.NET Videos**: `https://dotnet.microsoft.com/learn/videos`
- **Microsoft Channel 9** – .NET Videos: `https://channel9.msdn.com/Search?term=.net&lang-en=true`

Summary

In this chapter, we:

- Set up your development environment.
- Discussed the differences between .NET 5, .NET Core, .NET Framework, Xamarin, and .NET Standard.
- Used Visual Studio Code and .NET SDK to create a simple console application.
- Learned how to download the solution code for this book from a GitHub repository.
- And most importantly, we learned how to find help.

In the next chapter, you will learn to speak C#.

02

Speaking C#

This chapter is all about the basics of the C# programming language. Over the course of this chapter, you'll learn how to write statements using the grammar of C#, as well as being introduced to some of the common vocabulary that you will use every day. In addition to this, by the end of the chapter, you'll feel confident in knowing how to temporarily store and work with information in your computer's memory.

This chapter covers the following topics:

- Introducing C#
- Understanding the basics of C#
- Working with variables
- Working with null values
- Further exploring console applications

Introducing C#

This part of the book is about the C# language—the grammar and vocabulary that you will use every day to write the source code for your applications.

Programming languages have many similarities to human languages, except that in programming languages, you can make up your own words, just like Dr. Seuss!

In a book written by Dr. Seuss in 1950, *If I Ran the Zoo*, he states this:

> "*And then, just to show them, I'll sail to Ka-Troo And Bring Back an It-Kutch, a Preep, and a Proo, A Nerkle, a Nerd, and a Seersucker, too!*"

Understanding language versions and features

This part of the book covers the C# programming language and is written primarily for beginners, so it covers the fundamental topics that all developers need to know, from declaring variables to storing data to how to define your own custom data types.

Advanced and obscure topics like ref local variable reassignment and reference semantics with value types are not covered.

This book covers features of the C# language from version 1.0 up to the latest version, 9.0. If you already have some familiarity with older versions of C# and are excited to find out about the new features in the most recent versions of C#, I have made it easier for you to jump around by listing language versions and their important new features below, along with the chapter number and topic title where you can learn about them.

More Information: You can learn more about the current status of the C# language at this link: `https://github.com/dotnet/roslyn/blob/master/docs/Language%20Feature%20Status.md`

C# 1.0

C# 1.0 was released in 2002 and included all the important features of a statically typed object-oriented modern language, as you will see throughout chapters 2 to 6.

C# 2.0

C# 2.0 was released in 2005 and focused on enabling strong data typing using generics, to improve code performance and reduce type errors, including the topics listed in the following table:

Feature	Chapter	Topic
Nullable value types	2	Making a value type nullable
Generics	6	Making types more reusable with generics

C# 3.0

C# 3.0 was released in 2007 and focused on enabling declarative coding with **Language INtegrated Queries (LINQ)** and related features like anonymous types and lambda expressions, including the topics listed in the following table:

Feature	Chapter	Topic
Implicitly typed local variables	2	Inferring the type of a local variable
LINQ	12	All topics in *Chapter 12, Querying and Manipulating Data Using LINQ*

C# 4.0

C# 4.0 was released in 2010 and focused on improving interoperability with dynamic languages like F# and Python, including the topics listed in the following table:

Feature	Chapter	Topic
Dynamic types	2	The `dynamic` type
Named/optional arguments	5	Optional parameters and named arguments

C# 5.0

C# 5.0 was released in 2012 and focused on simplifying asynchronous operation support by automatically implementing complex state machines while writing what looks like synchronous statements, including the topics listed in the following table:

Feature	Chapter	Topic
Simplified asynchronous tasks	13	Understanding `async` and `await`

 More Information: You can download the **C# Language Specification 5.0** from the following link: `https://www.microsoft.com/en-us/download/details.aspx?id=7029`

C# 6.0

C# 6.0 was released in 2015 and focused on minor refinements to the language, including the topics listed in the following table:

Feature	Chapter	Topic
`Static` imports	2	Simplifying the usage of the console
Interpolated strings	2	Displaying output to the user
Expression bodied members	5	Defining read-only properties

 More Information: You can read draft proposals for C# Language Specifications for 6.0 and later at the following link: `https://docs.microsoft.com/en-us/dotnet/csharp/language-reference/`

C# 7.0

C# 7.0 was released in March 2017 and focused on adding functional language features like tuples and pattern matching, as well as minor refinements to the language, including the topics listed in the following table:

Feature	Chapter	Topic
Binary literals and digit separators	2	Storing whole numbers
Pattern matching	3	Pattern matching with the `if` statement
`out` variables	5	Controlling how parameters are passed
Tuples	5	Combining multiple values with tuples
Local functions	6	Defining local functions

C# 7.1

C# 7.1 was released in August 2017 and focused on minor refinements to the language, including the topics listed in the following table:

Feature	Chapter	Topic
Default literal expressions	5	Setting fields with default literal
Inferred tuple element names	5	Inferring tuple names
`async Main`	13	Improving responsiveness for console apps

C# 7.2

C# 7.2 was released in November 2017 and focused on minor refinements to the language, including the topics listed in the following table:

Feature	Chapter	Topic
Leading underscores in numeric literals	2	Storing whole numbers
Non-trailing named arguments	5	Optional parameters and named arguments
`private protected` access modifier	5	Understanding access modifiers
You can test `==` and `!=` with tuple types	5	Comparing tuples

C# 7.3

C# 7.3 was released in May 2018 and focused on performance-oriented safe code that improves ref variables, pointers, and stackalloc. These are advanced and rarely needed for most developers, so they are not covered in this book.

 More Information: If you're interested, you can read the details at the following link: https://docs.microsoft.com/en-us/dotnet/csharp/whats-new/csharp-7-3

C# 8.0

C# 8.0 was released in September 2019 and focused on a major change to the language related to null handling, including the topics listed in the following table:

Feature	Chapter	Topic
Nullable reference types	2	Making a reference type nullable
Switch expressions	3	Simplifying `switch` statements with switch expressions
Default interface methods	6	Understanding default interface methods

C# 9.0

C# 9.0 was released in November 2020 and focused on record types, refinements to pattern matching, and minimal-code console apps, including the topics listed in the following table:

Feature	Chapter	Topic
Minimal-code console apps	1	Top-level programs
Enhanced pattern matching	5	Pattern matching with objects
Records	5	Working with records

 More Information: You can read more about new C# 9.0 features at the following link: https://docs.microsoft.com/en-us/dotnet/csharp/ whats-new/csharp-9

Discovering your C# compiler versions

With the C# 7.x generation, Microsoft decided to increase the cadence of language releases, releasing minor version numbers, also known as point releases, for the first time since C# 1.1.

.NET language compilers for C# and Visual Basic, also known as Roslyn, along with a separate compiler for F#, are distributed as part of .NET SDK. To use a specific version of C#, you must have at least that version of .NET SDK installed, as shown in the following table:

.NET SDK	Roslyn	C#
1.0.4	2.0 - 2.2	7.0
1.1.4	2.3 - 2.4	7.1
2.1.2	2.6 - 2.7	7.2
2.1.200	2.8 - 2.10	7.3
3.0	3.0 - 3.4	8.0
5.0	5.0	9.0

 More Information: You can see a list of versions at the following link: https://github.com/dotnet/roslyn/blob/master/docs/wiki/NuGet-packages.md

Let's see what .NET SDK and C# language compiler versions you have available:

1. Start Visual Studio Code.
2. Navigate to **View | Terminal**.
3. To determine which version of the .NET SDK you have available, enter the following command:

```
dotnet --version
```

4. Note the version at the time of writing is 5.0.100, indicating that it is the initial version of the SDK without any bug fixes or new features yet, as shown in the following output:

```
5.0.100
```

5. To determine which versions of the C# compiler you have available, enter the following command:

```
csc -langversion:?
```

6. Note all the versions available at the time of writing, as shown in the following output:

```
Supported language versions:
default
1
2
3
4
5
6
7.0
7.1
7.2
7.3
8.0
9.0 (default)
latestmajor
preview
latest
```

More Information: On Windows, the preceding command returns the error, `The name "csc" is not recognized as the name of a command, function, script file, or executable program. Check the spelling of the name, as well as the presence and correctness of the path.` To fix this issue, follow the instructions at the following link: https://docs.microsoft.com/en-us/dotnet/csharp/language-reference/compiler-options/command-line-building-with-csc-exe

Enabling a specific language version compiler

Developer tools like Visual Studio Code and the `dotnet` command-line interface assume that you want to use the latest major version of a C# language compiler by default. Before C# 8.0 was released, C# 7.0 was the latest major version and was used by default. To use the improvements in a C# point release like 7.1, 7.2, or 7.3, you had to add a configuration element to the project file, as shown in the following markup:

```
<LangVersion>7.3</LangVersion>
```

After the release of C# 9.0 with .NET 5.0, if Microsoft releases a C# 9.1 compiler and you want to use its new language features then you will have to add a configuration element to your project file, as shown in the following markup:

```
<LangVersion>9.1</LangVersion>
```

Potential values for the `<LangVersion>` are shown in the following table:

LangVersion	Description
7, 7.1, 7.2, 7.3, 8, 9	Entering a specific version number will use that compiler if it has been installed.
`latestmajor`	Uses the highest major number, for example, 7.0 in August 2019, 8.0 in October 2019, 9.0 in November 2020.
`latest`	Uses the highest major and highest minor number, for example, 7.2 in 2017, 7.3 in 2018, 8 in 2019, 9 in 2020, perhaps 9.1 in early 2021.
`preview`	Uses the highest available preview version, for example, 9.0 in May 2020 with .NET 5.0 Preview 4 installed.

After creating a new project with the `dotnet` command-line tool, you can edit the `.csproj` file and add the `<LangVersion>` element, as shown highlighted in the following markup:

```
<Project Sdk="Microsoft.NET.Sdk">
  <PropertyGroup>
    <OutputType>Exe</OutputType>
    <TargetFramework>net5.0</TargetFramework>
    <LangVersion>preview</LangVersion>
  </PropertyGroup>
</Project>
```

Your projects must target `net5.0` to use the full features of C# 9.

If you have not done so already, install the extension **MSBuild project tools**. This will give you IntelliSense while editing `.csproj` files, including making it easy to add the `<LangVersion>` element with appropriate values.

> **More Information**: You can read about C# language versioning at the following link: https://docs.microsoft.com/en-us/dotnet/csharp/language-reference/configure-language-version

Understanding C# basics

To learn C#, you will need to create some simple applications. To avoid overloading you with too much information too soon, the chapters in the first part of this book will use the simplest type of application: a console application.

Let's start by looking at the basics of the grammar and vocabulary of C#. Throughout this chapter, you will create multiple console applications, with each one showing a feature of the C# language. We will start by creating a console app that shows the compiler version.

1. If you've completed *Chapter 1, Hello, C#! Welcome, .NET!*, then you will already have a Code folder in your user folder. If not, then you'll need to create it.

2. Create a subfolder named Chapter02, with a sub-folder named Basics.

3. Start Visual Studio Code and open the Chapter02/Basics folder.

4. In Visual Studio Code, navigate to **View | Terminal**, and enter the following command:

```
dotnet new console
```

5. In **EXPLORER**, click the Program.cs file, and then click on **Yes** to add the missing required assets.

6. Open the Program.cs file, and at the top of the file, under the using statement, add a statement to show the current C# version as an error, as shown in the following code:

```
#error version
```

7. Navigate to **View | Problems**, and note the compiler version and language version appear as a compiler error message number CS8304, as shown in the following screenshot:

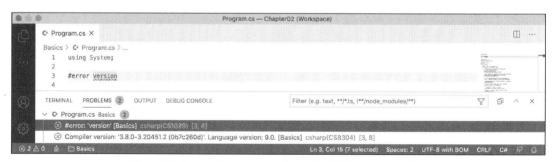

Figure 2.1: A compiler error that shows the C# language version

8. Comment out the statement that causes the error, as shown in the following code:

```
// #error version
```

Understanding C# grammar

The grammar of C# includes statements and blocks. To document your code, you can use comments.

 Good Practice: Comments should never be the only way that you document your code. Choosing sensible names for variables and functions, writing unit tests, and creating literal documents are other ways to document your code.

Statements

In English, we indicate the end of a sentence with a full stop. A sentence can be composed of multiple words and phrases, with the order of words being part of the grammar. For example, in English, we say "the black cat."

The adjective, *black*, comes before the noun, *cat*. Whereas French grammar has a different order; the adjective comes after the noun: "le chat noir." What's important to take away from this is that the order matters.

C# indicates the end of a **statement** with a semicolon. A statement can be composed of multiple **variables** and **expressions**. For example, in the following statement, `totalPrice` is a variable and `subtotal + salesTax` is an expression:

```
var totalPrice = subtotal + salesTax;
```

The expression is made up of an operand named `subtotal`, an operator +, and another operand named `salesTax`. The order of operands and operators matters.

Comments

When writing your code, you're able to add comments to explain your code using a double slash, `//`. By inserting `//` the compiler will ignore everything after the `//` until the end of the line, as shown in the following code:

```
// sales tax must be added to the subtotal
var totalPrice = subtotal + salesTax;
```

Visual Studio Code will add or remove the comment double slashes at the start of the currently selected line(s) if you press *Ctrl + K + C* to add them or *Ctrl + K + U* to remove them. In macOS, press *Cmd* instead of *Ctrl*.

To write a multiline comment, use `/*` at the beginning and `*/` at the end of the comment, as shown in the following code:

```
/*
This is a multi-line
comment.
*/
```

Blocks

In English, we indicate a new paragraph by starting a new line. C# indicates a **block** of code with the use of curly brackets, { }. Blocks start with a declaration to indicate what is being defined. For example, a block can define a **namespace**, **class**, **method**, or a **statement**, something we will learn more about later.

In your current project, note that the grammar of C# is written for you by the dotnet CLI tool. I've added some comments to the statements written by the project template, as shown in the following code:

```
using System; // a semicolon indicates the end of a statement

namespace Basics
{ // an open brace indicates the start of a block
  class Program
  {
    static void Main(string[] args)
    {
      Console.WriteLine("Hello World!"); // a statement
    }
  }
} // a close brace indicates the end of a block
```

Understanding C# vocabulary

The C# vocabulary is made up of **keywords**, **symbol characters**, and **types**.

Some of the predefined, reserved keywords that you will see in this book include using, namespace, class, static, int, string, double, bool, if, switch, break, while, do, for, and foreach.

Some of the symbol characters that you will see include ", ', +, -, *, /, %, @, and $.

Changing the color scheme for syntax

By default, Visual Studio Code shows C# keywords in blue in order to make them easier to differentiate from other code. Visual Studio Code allows you to customize the color scheme:

1. In Visual Studio Code, navigate to **Code | Preferences | Color Theme** (it is on the **File** menu on Windows), or press *Ctrl* or *Cmd + K, Ctrl* or *Cmd + T*.

2. Select a color theme. For reference, I'll use the **Light+ (default light)** color theme so that the screenshots look good in a printed book.

There are other contextual keywords that only have a special meaning in a specific context. However, that still means that there are only about 100 actual C# keywords in the language.

Comparing programming languages to human languages

The English language has more than 250,000 distinct words, so how does C# get away with only having about 100 keywords? Moreover, why is C# so difficult to learn if it has only 0.0416% of the number of words in the English language?

One of the key differences between a human language and a programming language is that developers need to be able to define the new "words" with new meanings. Apart from the 104 keywords in the C# language, this book will teach you about some of the hundreds of thousands of "words" that other developers have defined, but you will also learn how to define your own "words."

> **More Information**: Programmers all over the world must learn English because most programming languages use English words such as namespace and class. There are programming languages that use other human languages, such as Arabic, but they are rare. If you are interested in learning, this YouTube video shows a demonstration of an Arabic programming language:
> `https://youtu.be/dkO8cdwf6v8`

Help for writing correct code

Plain text editors such as Notepad don't help you write correct English. Likewise, Notepad won't help you write correct C# either.

Microsoft Word can help you write English by highlighting spelling mistakes with red squiggles, with Word saying that "icecream" should be ice-cream or ice cream, and grammatical errors with blue squiggles, such as a sentence should have an uppercase first letter.

Similarly, Visual Studio Code's C# extension helps you write C# code by highlighting spelling mistakes, such as the method name should be `WriteLine` with an uppercase `L`, and grammatical errors, such as statements that must end with a semicolon.

The C# extension constantly watches what you type and gives you feedback by highlighting problems with colored squiggly lines, similar to that of Microsoft Word.

Let's see it in action:

1. In `Program.cs`, change the `L` in the `WriteLine` method to lowercase.
2. Delete the semicolon at the end of the statement.
3. Navigate to **View** | **Problems**, or press *Ctrl* or *Cmd* + *Shift* + *M*, and note that a red squiggle appears under the code mistakes and details are shown in the **PROBLEMS** window, as you can see in the following screenshot:

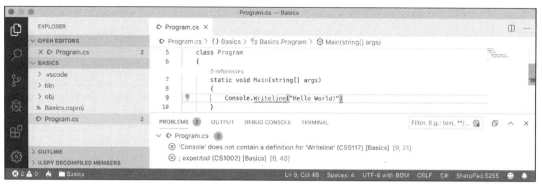

Figure 2.2: The PROBLEMS window showing two compile errors

4. Fix the two coding mistakes.

Verbs are methods

In English, verbs are doing or action words, like run and jump. In C#, doing or action words are called **methods**. There are hundreds of thousands of methods available to C#. In English, verbs change how they are written based on when in time the action happens. For example, Amir *was jumping* in the past, Beth *jumps* in the present, they *jumped* in the past, and Charlie *will jump* in the future.

In C#, methods such as WriteLine change how they are called or executed based on the specifics of the action. This is called **overloading**, which is something we will cover in more detail in *Chapter 5, Building Your Own Types with Object-Oriented Programming*. But for now, consider the following example:

```
// outputs a carriage-return
Console.WriteLine();

// outputs the greeting and a carriage-return
Console.WriteLine("Hello Ahmed");

// outputs a formatted number and date and a carriage-return
Console.WriteLine(
  "Temperature on {0:D} is {1}°C.", DateTime.Today, 23.4);
```

A different analogy is that some words are spelled the same, but have different meanings depending on the context.

Nouns are types, fields, and variables

In English, nouns are names that refer to things. For example, Fido is the name of a dog. The word "dog" tells us the type of thing that Fido is, and so in order for Fido to fetch a ball, we would use his name.

In C#, their equivalents are **types**, **fields**, and **variables**. For example, Animal and Car are **types**; that is, they are nouns for categorizing things. Head and Engine are fields, that is, nouns that belong to Animal and Car. While Fido and Bob are variables, that is, nouns for referring to a specific thing.

There are tens of thousands of types available to C#, though have you noticed how I didn't say, "There are tens of thousands of types in C#?" The difference is subtle but important. The language of C# only has a few keywords for types, such as string and int, and strictly speaking, C# doesn't define any types. Keywords such as string that look like types are **aliases**, which represent types provided by the platform on which C# runs.

It's important to know that C# cannot exist alone; after all, it's a language that runs on variants of .NET. In theory, someone could write a compiler for C# that uses a different platform, with different underlying types. In practice, the platform for C# is .NET, which provides tens of thousands of types to C#, including System.Int32, which is the C# keyword alias int maps to, as well as many more complex types, such as System.Xml.Linq.XDocument.

It's worth taking note that the term **type** is often confused with **class**. Have you ever played the parlor game *Twenty Questions*, also known as *Animal, Vegetable, or Mineral?* In the game, everything can be categorized as an animal, vegetable, or mineral. In C#, every **type** can be categorized as a class, struct, enum, interface, or delegate. The C# keyword string is a class, but int is a struct. So, it is best to use the term **type** to refer to both.

Revealing the extent of the C# vocabulary

We know that there are more than 100 keywords in C#, but how many types are there? Let's now write some code to find out how many types (and their methods) are available to C# in our simple console application.

Don't worry about how this code works for now; it uses a technique called reflection:

1. We'll start by adding the following statements at the top of the Program.cs file:

```
using System.Linq;
using System.Reflection;
```

2. Inside the Main method, delete the statement that writes Hello World! and replace it with the following code:

```
// loop through the assemblies that this app references
foreach (var r in Assembly.GetEntryAssembly()
  .GetReferencedAssemblies())
{
  // load the assembly so we can read its details
  var a = Assembly.Load(new AssemblyName(r.FullName));

  // declare a variable to count the number of methods
  int methodCount = 0;
```

```
    // loop through all the types in the assembly
    foreach (var t in a.DefinedTypes)
    {
        // add up the counts of methods
        methodCount += t.GetMethods().Count();
    }

    // output the count of types and their methods
    Console.WriteLine(
        "{0:N0} types with {1:N0} methods in {2} assembly.",
        arg0: a.DefinedTypes.Count(),
        arg1: methodCount,
        arg2: r.Name);
}
```

3. Navigate to **View | Terminal**.

4. In **TERMINAL**, enter the following command:

```
dotnet run
```

5. After running that command, you will see the actual number of types and methods that are available to you in the simplest application when running on your OS. The numbers of types and methods displayed will be different depending on the operating system that you are using, as shown in the following outputs:

```
// Output on Windows
0 types with 0 methods in System.Runtime assembly.
103 types with 1,094 methods in System.Linq assembly.
46 types with 662 methods in System.Console assembly.

// Output on macOS
0 types with 0 methods in System.Runtime assembly.
103 types with 1,094 methods in System.Linq assembly.
57 types with 701 methods in System.Console assembly.
```

6. Add statements to the top of the Main method to declare some variables, as shown highlighted in the following code:

```
static void Main(string[] args)
{
    // declare some unused variables using types
    // in additional assemblies
    System.Data.DataSet ds;
    System.Net.Http.HttpClient client;
```

By declaring variables that use types in other assemblies, those assemblies are loaded with our application, which allows our code to see all the types and methods in them. The compiler will warn you that you have unused variables but that won't stop your code from running.

7. Run the console application again and view the results, which should look similar to the following outputs:

```
// Output on Windows
0 types with 0 methods in System.Runtime assembly.
376 types with 6,763 methods in System.Data.Common assembly.
533 types with 5,193 methods in System.Net.Http assembly.
103 types with 1,094 methods in System.Linq assembly.
46 types with 662 methods in System.Console assembly.

// Output on macOS
0 types with 0 methods in System.Runtime assembly.
376 types with 6,763 methods in System.Data.Common assembly.
522 types with 5,141 methods in System.Net.Http assembly.
103 types with 1,094 methods in System.Linq assembly.
57 types with 701 methods in System.Console assembly.
```

Now, you have a better sense of why learning C# is a challenge, because there are so many types and methods to learn. Methods are only one category of a member that a type can have, and other programmers are constantly defining new members!

Working with variables

All applications process data. Data comes in, data is processed, and then data goes out. Data usually comes into our program from files, databases, or user input, and it can be put temporarily into variables that will be stored in the memory of the running program. When the program ends, the data in memory is lost. Data is usually output to files and databases, or to the screen or a printer. When using variables, you should think about, firstly, how much space the variable takes in the memory, and, secondly, how fast it can be processed.

We control this by picking an appropriate type. You can think of simple common types such as int and double as being different-sized storage boxes, where a smaller box would take less memory but may not be as fast at being processed; for example, adding 16-bit numbers might not be processed as fast as adding 64-bit numbers on a 64-bit operating system. Some of these boxes may be stacked close by, and some may be thrown into a big heap further away.

Naming things and assigning values

There are naming conventions for things, and it is good practice to follow them, as shown in the following table:

Naming convention	Examples	Used for
Camel case	`cost`, `orderDetail`, `dateOfBirth`	Local variables, private fields.
Title case	`String`, `Int32`, `Cost`, `DateOfBirth`, `Run`	Types, non-private fields, and other members like methods.

> **Good Practice**: Following a consistent set of naming conventions will enable your code to be easily understood by other developers (and yourself in the future!). You can read more about naming guidelines at the following link: https://docs.microsoft.com/en-us/dotnet/standard/design-guidelines/naming-guidelines

The following code block shows an example of declaring a named local variable and assigning a value to it with the = symbol. You should note that you can output the name of a variable using a keyword introduced in C# 6.0, `nameof`:

```
// let the heightInMetres variable become equal to the value 1.88
double heightInMetres = 1.88;
Console.WriteLine($"The variable {nameof(heightInMetres)} has the value
{heightInMetres}.");
```

The message in double quotes in the preceding code wraps onto a second line because the width of a printed page is too narrow. When entering a statement like this in your code editor, type it all in a single line.

Literal values

When you assign to a variable, you often, but not always, assign a **literal** value. But what is a literal value? A literal is a notation that represents a fixed value. Data types have different notations for their literal values, and over the next few sections, you will see examples of using literal notation to assign values to variables.

Storing text

For text, a single letter, such as an A, is stored as a char type and is assigned using single quotes around the literal value, or assigning the return value of a function call, as shown in the following code:

```
char letter = 'A'; // assigning literal characters
char digit = '1';
char symbol = '$';

char userChoice = GetKeystroke(); // assigning from a function
```

For text, multiple letters, such as Bob, are stored as a `string` type and are assigned using double quotes around the literal value, or assigning the return value of a function call, as shown in the following code:

```
string firstName = "Bob"; // assigning literal strings
string lastName = "Smith";
string phoneNumber = "(215) 555-4256";

// assigning a string returned from a function call
string address = GetAddressFromDatabase(id: 563);
```

Understanding verbatim strings

When storing text in a `string` variable, you can include escape sequences, which represent special characters like tabs and new lines using a backslash, as shown in the following code:

```
string fullNameWithTabSeparator = "Bob\tSmith";
```

 More Information: You can read more about escape sequences at the following link: https://devblogs.microsoft.com/csharpfaq/what-character-escape-sequences-are-available/

But what if you are storing the path to a file, and one of the folder names starts with a T, as shown in the following code:

```
string filePath = "C:\televisions\sony\bravia.txt";
```

The compiler will convert the \t into a tab character and you will get errors!

You must prefix with the @ symbol to use a **verbatim** literal string, as shown in the following code:

```
string filePath = @"C:\televisions\sony\bravia.txt";
```

 More Information: You can read more about verbatim strings at the following link: https://docs.microsoft.com/en-us/dotnet/csharp/language-reference/tokens/verbatim

To summarize:

- **Literal string**: Characters enclosed in double-quote characters. They can use escape characters like \t for tab.
- **Verbatim string**: A literal string prefixed with @ to disable escape characters so that a backslash is a backslash.

- **Interpolated string**: A literal string prefixed with $ to enable embedded formatted variables. You will learn more about this later in this chapter.

Storing numbers

Numbers are data that we want to perform an arithmetic calculation on, for example, multiplying. A telephone number is not a number. To decide whether a variable should be stored as a number or not, ask yourself whether you need to perform arithmetic operations on the number or whether the number includes non-digit characters such as parentheses or hyphens to format the number as (414) 555-1234. In this case, the number is a sequence of characters, so it should be stored as a string.

Numbers can be **natural numbers**, such as 42, used for counting (also called **whole numbers**); they can also be negative numbers, such as -42 (called **integers**); or, they can be **real numbers**, such as 3.9 (with a fractional part), which are called **single-** or **double-precision floating point numbers** in computing.

Let's explore numbers.

1. Create a new folder inside the Chapter02 folder named Numbers.
2. In Visual Studio Code, open the Numbers folder.
3. In **TERMINAL**, create a new console application using the dotnet new console command.
4. Inside the Main method, type statements to declare some number variables using various data types, as shown in the following code:

```
// unsigned integer means positive whole number
// including 0
uint naturalNumber = 23;

// integer means negative or positive whole number
// including 0
int integerNumber = -23;

// float means single-precision floating point
// F suffix makes it a float literal
float realNumber = 2.3F;

// double means double-precision floating point
double anotherRealNumber = 2.3; // double literal
```

Storing whole numbers

You might know that computers store everything as bits. The value of a bit is either 0 or 1. This is called a **binary number system**. Humans use a **decimal number system**.

The decimal number system, also known as Base 10, has 10 as its **base**, meaning there are ten digits, from 0 to 9. Although it is the number base most commonly used by human civilizations, other number-base systems are popular in science, engineering, and computing. The binary number system also known as Base 2 has two as its base, meaning there are two digits, 0 and 1.

The following table shows how computers store the decimal number 10. Take note of the bits with the value 1 in the 8 and the 2 columns; 8 + 2 = 10:

128	64	32	16	8	4	2	1
0	0	0	0	1	0	1	0

So, 10 in decimal is 00001010 in binary.

Two of the improvements seen in C# 7.0 and later are the use of the underscore character, _, as a digit separator, and support for binary literals. You can insert underscores anywhere into the digits of a number literal, including decimal, binary, or hexadecimal notation, to improve legibility. For example, you could write the value for 1 million in decimal notation, that is, Base 10, as 1_000_000.

To use binary notation, that is, Base 2, using only 1s and 0s, start the number literal with 0b. To use hexadecimal notation, that is, Base 16, using 0 to 9 and A to F, start the number literal with 0x. Let's enter some code to see some examples.

1. At the bottom of the Main method, type statements to declare some number variables using underscore separators, as shown in the following code:

```
// three variables that store the number 2 million
int decimalNotation = 2_000_000;
int binaryNotation = 0b_0001_1110_1000_0100_1000_0000;
int hexadecimalNotation = 0x_001E_8480;

// check the three variables have the same value
// both statements output true
Console.WriteLine($"{decimalNotation == binaryNotation}");
Console.WriteLine(
    $"{decimalNotation == hexadecimalNotation}");
```

2. Run the console app and note the result is that all three numbers are the same, as shown in the following output:

```
True
True
```

Computers can always exactly represent integers using the int type or one of its sibling types such as long and short.

Storing real numbers

Computers cannot always exactly represent floating point numbers. The `float` and `double` types store real numbers using single- and double-precision floating points.

Most programming languages implement the IEEE Standard for Floating-Point Arithmetic. IEEE 754 is a technical standard for floating-point arithmetic established in 1985 by the **Institute of Electrical and Electronics Engineers (IEEE)**.

 More Information: If you want to dive deep into understanding floating point numbers, then you can read an excellent primer at the following link: `https://ciechanow.ski/exposing-floating-point/`

The following table shows a simplification of how a computer represents the number 12.75 in binary notation. Note the bits with the value 1 in the 8, 4, ½, and ¼ columns.

$8 + 4 + \frac{1}{2} + \frac{1}{4} = 12\frac{3}{4} = 12.75$.

128	64	32	16	8	4	2	1	.	½	¼	1/8	1/16
0	0	0	0	1	1	0	0	.	1	1	0	0

So, 12.75 in decimal is `00001100.1100` in binary. As you can see, the number 12.75 can be exactly represented using bits. However, some numbers can't, something that we'll be exploring shortly.

Writing code to explore number sizes

C# has an **operator** named `sizeof()` that returns the number of bytes that a type uses in memory. Some types have members named `MinValue` and `MaxValue`, which return the minimum and maximum values that can be stored in a variable of that type. We are now going to use these features to create a console application to explore number types.

1. Inside the `Main` method, type statements to show the size of three number data types, as shown in the following code:

```
Console.WriteLine($"int uses {sizeof(int)} bytes and can store numbers in
the range {int.MinValue:N0} to {int.MaxValue:N0}.");
Console.WriteLine($"double uses {sizeof(double)} bytes and can store
numbers in the range {double.MinValue:N0} to {double.MaxValue:N0}.");
Console.WriteLine($"decimal uses {sizeof(decimal)} bytes and can store
numbers in the range {decimal.MinValue:N0} to {decimal.MaxValue:N0}.");
```

The width of the printed pages in this book make the `string` values (in double-quotes) wrap over multiple lines. You must type them on a single line, or you will get compile errors.

2. Run the console application by entering `dotnet run`, and view the output, as shown in the following screenshot:

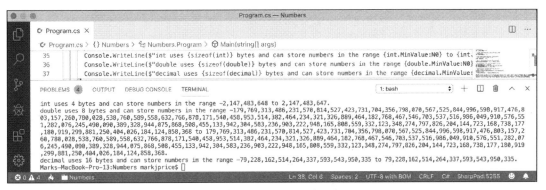

Figure 2.3: Information on number data types

An `int` variable uses four bytes of memory and can store positive or negative numbers up to about 2 billion. A `double` variable uses eight bytes of memory and can store much bigger values! A `decimal` variable uses 16 bytes of memory and can store big numbers, but not as big as a `double` type.

But you may be asking yourself, why might a `double` variable be able to store bigger numbers than a `decimal` variable, yet it's only using half the space in memory? Well, let's now find out!

Comparing double and decimal types

You will now write some code to compare double and decimal values. Although it isn't hard to follow, don't worry about understanding the syntax right now:

1. Under the previous statements, enter statements to declare two `double` variables, add them together and compare them to the expected result, and write the result to the console, as shown in the following code:

```
Console.WriteLine("Using doubles:");
double a = 0.1;
double b = 0.2;

if (a + b == 0.3)
{
  Console.WriteLine($"{a} + {b} equals 0.3");
}
else
{
  Console.WriteLine($"{a} + {b} does NOT equal 0.3");
}
```

2. Run the console application and view the result, as shown in the following output:

```
Using doubles:
0.1 + 0.2 does NOT equal 0.3
```

The `double` type is not guaranteed to be accurate because some numbers literally cannot be represented as floating-point values.

> **More Information**: You can read more about why 0.1 does not exist in floating-point numbers at the following link: `https://www.exploringbinary.com/why-0-point-1-does-not-exist-in-floating-point/`

As a rule of thumb, you should only use `double` when accuracy, especially when comparing the equality of two numbers, is not important. An example of this may be when you're measuring a person's height.

The problem with the preceding code is illustrated by how the computer stores the number `0.1`, or multiples of `0.1`. To represent `0.1` in binary, the computer stores 1 in the 1/16 column, 1 in the 1/32 column, 1 in the 1/256 column, 1 in the 1/512 column, and so on.

The number `0.1` in decimal is `0.00011001100110011…` repeating forever:

4	2	1	.	½	¼	1/8	1/16	1/32	1/64	1/128	1/256	1/512	1/1024	1/2048
0	0	0	.	0	0	0	1	1	0	0	1	1	0	0

> **Good Practice**: Never compare `double` values using `==`. During the First Gulf War, an American Patriot missile battery used `double` values in its calculations. The inaccuracy caused it to fail to track and intercept an incoming Iraqi Scud missile, and 28 soldiers were killed; you can read about this at `https://www.ima.umn.edu/~arnold/disasters/patriot.html`.

3. Copy and paste the statements that you wrote before (that used the `double` variables).

4. Modify the statements to use `decimal` and rename the variables to c and d, as shown in the following code:

```csharp
Console.WriteLine("Using decimals:");
decimal c = 0.1M; // M suffix means a decimal literal value
decimal d = 0.2M;

if (c + d == 0.3M)
{
  Console.WriteLine($"{c} + {d} equals 0.3");
}
else
{
  Console.WriteLine($"{c} + {d} does NOT equal 0.3");
}
```

5. Run the console application and view the result, as shown in the following output:

```
Using decimals:
0.1 + 0.2 equals 0.3
```

The decimal type is accurate because it stores the number as a large integer and shifts the decimal point. For example, 0.1 is stored as 1, with a note to shift the decimal point one place to the left. 12.75 is stored as 1275, with a note to shift the decimal point two places to the left.

> **Good Practice**: Use int for whole numbers and double for real numbers that will not be compared to other values. Use decimal for money, CAD drawings, general engineering, and wherever the accuracy of a real number is important.

The double type has some useful special values: double.NaN means not-a-number, double.Epsilon is the smallest positive number that can be stored in a double, and double.Infinity means an infinitely large value.

Storing Booleans

Booleans can only contain one of the two literal values true or false, as shown in the following code:

```
bool happy = true;
bool sad = false;
```

They are most commonly used to branch and loop. You don't need to fully understand them yet, as they are covered more in *Chapter 3, Controlling Flow and Converting Types*.

Using Visual Studio Code workspaces

Before we create any more projects, let's talk about workspaces.

Although we could continue to create and open separate folders for each project, it can be useful to have multiple folders open at the same time. Visual Studio has a feature called workspaces that enables this.

Let's create a workspace for the two projects we have created so far in this chapter:

1. In Visual Studio Code, navigate to **File | Save Workspace As...**.
2. Enter Chapter02 for the workspace name, change to the Chapter02 folder, and click **Save**, as shown in the following screenshot:

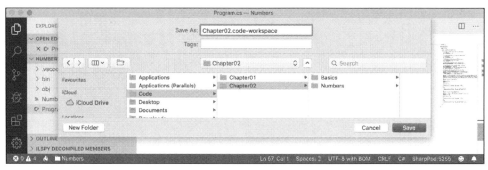

Figure 2.4: Saving a workspace

3. Navigate to **File | Add Folder to Workspace...**

4. Select the `Basics` folder, click **Add**, and note that both `Basics` and `Numbers` are now part of the `Chapter02` workspace.

 Good Practice: When using workspaces, be careful when entering commands in Terminal. Be sure that you are in the correct folder before entering potentially destructive commands! You will see how in the next task.

Storing any type of object

There is a special type named `object` that can store any type of data, but its flexibility comes at the cost of messier code and possibly poor performance. Because of those two reasons, you should avoid it whenever possible. The following steps show how to use `object` types if you need to use them:

1. Create a new folder named `Variables` and add it to the `Chapter02` workspace.

2. Navigate to **Terminal | New Terminal**.

3. Select the **Variables** project, as shown in the following screenshot:

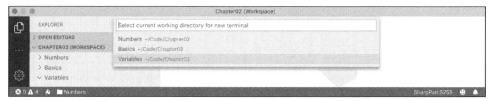

Figure 2.5: Selecting the Variables project

4. Enter the command to create a new console application: `dotnet new console`.

5. Navigate to **View | Command Palette**.

6. Enter and select **OmniSharp: Select Project**.

7. Select the **Variables** project, and if prompted, click **Yes** to add required assets to debug.

8. In **EXPLORER**, in the **Variables** project, open `Program.cs`.

9. In the `Main` method, add statements to declare and use some variables using the `object` type, as shown in the following code:

```
object height = 1.88; // storing a double in an object
object name = "Amir"; // storing a string in an object
Console.WriteLine($"{name} is {height} metres tall.");

int length1 = name.Length; // gives compile error!
int length2 = ((string)name).Length; // tell compiler it is a string
Console.WriteLine($"{name} has {length2} characters.");
```

10. In **TERMINAL**, execute the code by entering dotnet run, and note that the fourth statement cannot compile because the data type of the name variable is not known by the compiler.

11. Add comment double slashes to the beginning of the statement that cannot compile to "comment it out."

12. In **TERMINAL**, execute the code by entering dotnet run, and note that the compiler can access the length of a string if the programmer explicitly tells the compiler that the object variable contains a string, as shown in the following output:

```
Amir is 1.88 metres tall.
Amir has 4 characters.
```

The object type has been available since the first version of C#, but C# 2.0 and later have a better alternative called **generics**, which we will cover in *Chapter 6, Implementing Interfaces and Inheriting Classes*, which will provide us with the flexibility we want, but without the performance overhead.

Storing dynamic types

There is another special type named dynamic that can also store any type of data, but even more than object, its flexibility comes at the cost of performance. The dynamic keyword was introduced in C# 4.0. However, unlike object, the value stored in the variable can have its members invoked without an explicit cast. Let's make use of a dynamic type:

1. In the Main method, add statements to declare a dynamic variable and assign a string value, as shown in the following code:

```
// storing a string in a dynamic object
dynamic anotherName = "Ahmed";
```

2. Add a statement to get the length of the string value, as shown in the following code:

```
// this compiles but would throw an exception at run-time
// if you later store a data type that does not have a
// property named Length
int length = anotherName.Length;
```

One limitation of dynamic is that Visual Studio Code cannot show IntelliSense to help you write the code. This is because the compiler cannot check what the type is during build time. Instead, the CLR checks for the member at runtime and throws an exception if it is missing.

Exceptions are a way to indicate that something has gone wrong. You will learn more about them and how to handle them in *Chapter 3, Controlling Flow and Converting Types.*

Declaring local variables

Local variables are declared inside methods, and they only exist during the execution of that method, and once the method returns, the memory allocated to any local variables is released.

Strictly speaking, value types are released while reference types must wait for a garbage collection. You will learn about the difference between value types and reference types in *Chapter 6, Implementing Interfaces and Inheriting Classes.*

Specifying and inferring the type of a local variable

Let's explore local variables declared with specific types and using type inference.

1. Inside the `Main` method, enter statements to declare and assign values to some local variables using specific types, as shown in the following code:

```
int population = 66_000_000; // 66 million in UK
double weight = 1.88; // in kilograms
decimal price = 4.99M; // in pounds sterling
string fruit = "Apples"; // strings use double-quotes
char letter = 'Z'; // chars use single-quotes
bool happy = true; // Booleans have value of true or false
```

Visual Studio Code will show green squiggles under each of the variable names to warn you that the variable is assigned but its value is never used.

You can use the var keyword to declare local variables. The compiler will infer the type from the value that you assign after the assignment operator, =.

A literal number without a decimal point is inferred as an int variable, that is, unless you add the L suffix, in which case, it infers a long variable.

A literal number with a decimal point is inferred as double unless you add the M suffix, in which case, it infers a decimal variable, or the F suffix, in which case, it infers a float variable. Double quotes indicate a string variable, single quotes indicate a char variable, and the true and false values infer a bool type.

2. Modify the previous statements to use var, as shown in the following code:

```
var population = 66_000_000; // 66 million in UK
var weight = 1.88; // in kilograms
var price = 4.99M; // in pounds sterling
var fruit = "Apples"; // strings use double-quotes
var letter = 'Z'; // chars use single-quotes
var happy = true; // Booleans have value of true or false
```

Good Practice: Although using var is convenient, some developers avoid using it, to make it easier for a code reader to understand the types in use. Personally, I use it only when the type is obvious. For example, in the following code statements, the first statement is just as clear as the second in stating what the type of the xml variable is, but it is shorter. However, the third statement isn't clear, so the fourth is better. If in doubt, spell it out!

3. At the top of the class file, import some namespaces, as shown in the following code:

```
using System.IO;
using System.Xml;
```

4. Under the precious statements, add statements to create some new objects, as shown in the following code:

```
// good use of var because it avoids the repeated type
// as shown in the more verbose second statement
var xml1 = new XmlDocument();
XmlDocument xml2 = new XmlDocument();

// bad use of var because we cannot tell the type, so we
// should use a specific type declaration as shown in
// the second statement
var file1 = File.CreateText(@"C:\something.txt");
StreamWriter file2 = File.CreateText(@"C:\something.txt");
```

Using target-typed new to instantiate objects

With C# 9, Microsoft introduced another syntax for instantiating objects known as **target-typed new**. When instantiating an object, you can specify the type first and then use new without repeating the type, as shown in the following code:

```
XmlDocument xml3 = new(); // target-typed new in C# 9
```

Getting default values for types

Most of the primitive types except string are **value types**, which means that they must have a value. You can determine the default value of a type using the default() operator.

The string type is a **reference type**. This means that string variables contain the memory address of a value, not the value itself. A reference type variable can have a null value, which is a literal that indicates that the variable does not reference anything (yet). null is the default for all reference types.

You'll learn more about value types and reference types in *Chapter 6, Implementing Interfaces and Inheriting Classes*.

Let's explore default values.

1. In the `Main` method, add statements to show the default values of an `int`, `bool`, `DateTime`, and `string`, as shown in the following code:

```
Console.WriteLine($"default(int) = {default(int)}");
Console.WriteLine($"default(bool) = {default(bool)}");
Console.WriteLine(
    $"default(DateTime) = {default(DateTime)}");
Console.WriteLine(
    $"default(string) = {default(string)}");
```

2. Run the console app and view the result, noting that your output for the date and time might be formatted differently if you are not running it in the UK, as shown in the following output:

```
default(int) = 0
default(bool) = False
default(DateTime) = 01/01/0001 00:00:00
default(string) =
```

Storing multiple values

When you need to store multiple values of the same type, you can declare an **array**. For example, you may do this when you need to store four names in a `string` array.

The code that you will write next will allocate memory for an array for storing four `string` values. It will then store `string` values at index positions 0 to 3 (arrays count from zero, so the last item is one less than the length of the array). Finally, it will loop through each item in the array using a `for` statement, something that we will cover in more detail in *Chapter 3, Controlling Flow and Converting Types*.

Let's look at how to use an array in detail:

1. In the `Chapter02` folder, create a new folder named `Arrays`.
2. Add the `Arrays` folder to the `Chapter02` workspace.
3. Create a new Terminal window for the `Arrays` project.
4. Create a new console application project in the `Arrays` folder.
5. Select `Arrays` as the current project for OmniSharp.
6. In the `Arrays` project, in `Program.cs`, in the `Main` method, add statements to declare and use an array of string values, as shown in the following code:

```
string[] names; // can reference any array of strings

// allocating memory for four strings in an array
names = new string[4];
```

```
// storing items at index positions
names[0] = "Kate";
names[1] = "Jack";
names[2] = "Rebecca";
names[3] = "Tom";

// looping through the names
for (int i = 0; i < names.Length; i++)
{
  // output the item at index position i
  Console.WriteLine(names[i]);
}
```

7. Run the console app and note the result, as shown in the following output:

```
Kate
Jack
Rebecca
Tom
```

Arrays are always of a fixed size at the time of memory allocation, so you need to decide how many items you want to store before instantiating them.

Arrays are useful for temporarily storing multiple items, but **collections** are a more flexible option when adding and removing items dynamically. You don't need to worry about collections right now, as we will cover them in *Chapter 8, Working with Common .NET Types*.

Working with null values

You have now seen how to store primitive values like numbers in variables. But what if a variable does not yet have a value? How can we indicate that? C# has the concept of a null value, which can be used to indicate that a variable has not been set.

Making a value type nullable

By default, value types like int and DateTime must always have a value, hence their name. Sometimes, for example, when reading values stored in a database that allows empty, missing, or null values, it is convenient to allow a value type to be null. We call this a **nullable value type**.

You can enable this by adding a question mark as a suffix to the type when declaring a variable. Let's see an example:

1. In the Chapter02 folder, create a new folder named NullHandling.

2. Add the NullHandling folder to the Chapter02 workspace.

3. Create a new Terminal window for the NullHandling project.

4. Create a new console application project in the `NullHandling` folder.

5. Select `NullHandling` as the current project for OmniSharp.

6. In the `NullHandling` project, in `Program.cs`, in the `Main` method, add statements to declare and assign values, including `null`, to `int` variables, as shown in the following code:

```
int thisCannotBeNull = 4;
thisCannotBeNull = null; // compile error!

int? thisCouldBeNull = null;
Console.WriteLine(thisCouldBeNull);
Console.WriteLine(thisCouldBeNull.GetValueOrDefault());

thisCouldBeNull = 7;
Console.WriteLine(thisCouldBeNull);
Console.WriteLine(thisCouldBeNull.GetValueOrDefault());
```

7. Comment out the statement that gives a compile error.

8. Run the application and view the result, as shown in the following output:

```
0
7
7
```

The first line is blank because it is outputting the `null` value!

Understanding nullable reference types

The use of the `null` value is so common, in so many languages, that many experienced programmers never question the need for its existence. But there are many scenarios where we could write better, simpler code if a variable is not allowed to have a `null` value.

 More Information: You can find out more through the following link, where the inventor of `null`, Sir Charles Antony Richard Hoare, admits his mistake in a recorded hour-long talk: `https://www.infoq.com/presentations/Null-References-The-Billion-Dollar-Mistake-Tony-Hoare`

The most significant change to the language in C# 8.0 was the introduction of nullable and non-nullable reference types. "But wait!", you are probably thinking, "Reference types are already nullable!"

And you would be right, but in C# 8.0 and later, reference types can be configured to no longer allow the `null` value by setting a file- or project-level option to enable this useful new feature. Since this is a big change for C#, Microsoft decided to make the feature opt-in.

It will take multiple years for this new C# language feature to make an impact since there are thousands of existing library packages and apps that will expect the old behavior. Even Microsoft has not had time to fully implement this new feature in all the main .NET 5 packages.

 More Information: You can read the tweet about achieving 80% annotations in .NET 5 at the following link: `https://twitter.com/terrajobst/ status/1296566363880742917`

During the transition, you can choose between several approaches for your own projects:

- **Default**: No changes are needed. Non-nullable reference types are not supported.
- **Opt-in project, opt-out files**: Enable the feature at the project level and, for any files that need to remain compatible with old behavior, opt out. This is the approach Microsoft is using internally while it updates its own packages to use this new feature.
- **Opt-in files**: Only enable the feature for individual files.

Enabling nullable and non-nullable reference types

To enable the feature at the project level, add the following to your project file:

```
<PropertyGroup>
    <Nullable>enable</Nullable>
</PropertyGroup>
```

To disable the feature at the file level, add the following to the top of a code file:

```
#nullable disable
```

To enable the feature at the file level, add the following to the top of a code file:

```
#nullable enable
```

Declaring non-nullable variables and parameters

If you enable nullable reference types and you want a reference type to be assigned the `null` value, then you will have to use the same syntax as making a value type nullable, that is, adding a ? symbol after the type declaration.

So, how do nullable reference types work? Let's look at an example. When storing information about an address, you might want to force a value for the street, city, and region, but the building can be left blank, that is, null:

1. In `NullHandling.csproj`, add an element to enable nullable reference types, as shown highlighted in the following markup:

```
<Project Sdk="Microsoft.NET.Sdk">
```

```
    <PropertyGroup>
      <OutputType>Exe</OutputType>
      <TargetFramework>net5.0</TargetFramework>
      <Nullable>enable</Nullable>
    </PropertyGroup>
</Project>
```

2. In `Program.cs`, at the top of the file add a statement to enable nullable reference types, as shown in the following code:

```
#nullable enable
```

3. In `Program.cs`, in the `NullHandling` namespace, above the `Program` class, add statements to declare an `Address` class with four fields, as shown in the following code:

```
class Address
{
    public string? Building;
    public string Street;
    public string City;
    public string Region;
}
```

4. After a few seconds, note that the C# extension warns of problems with non-nullable fields like `Street`, as shown in the following screenshot:

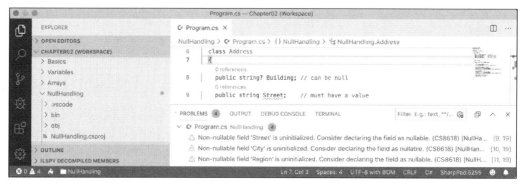

Figure 2.6: Warning messages about non-nullable fields in the PROBLEMS window

5. Assign the empty string value to each of the three fields that are non-nullable, as shown in the following code:

```
public string Street = string.Empty;
public string City = string.Empty;
public string Region = string.Empty;
```

6. In `Main`, add statements to instantiate an `Address` and set its properties, as shown in the following code:

```
var address = new Address();
address.Building = null;
address.Street = null;
address.City = "London";
address.Region = null;
```

7. Note the warnings, as shown in the following screenshot:

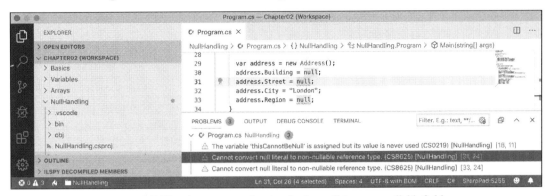

Figure 2.7: Warning message about assigning null to a non-nullable field

So, this is why the new language feature is named nullable reference types. Starting with C# 8.0, unadorned reference types can become non-nullable, and the same syntax is used to make a reference type nullable as is used for value types.

> **More Information**: You can watch a video to learn how to get rid of null reference exceptions forever at the following link: `https://channel9.msdn.com/Shows/On-NET/This-is-how-you-get-rid-of-null-reference-exceptions-forever`

Checking for null

Checking whether a nullable reference type or nullable value type variable currently contains null is important because if you do not, a `NullReferenceException` can be thrown, which results in an error. You should check for a null value before using a nullable variable, as shown in the following code:

```
// check that the variable is not null before using it
if (thisCouldBeNull != null)
{
  // access a member of thisCouldBeNull
  int length = thisCouldBeNull.Length; // could throw exception
  ...
}
```

If you are trying to use a member of a variable that might be null, use the null-conditional operator `?.`, as shown in the following code:

```
string authorName = null;

// the following throws a NullReferenceException
int x = authorName.Length;

// instead of throwing an exception, null is assigned to y
int? y = authorName?.Length;
```

More Information: You can read more about the null-conditional operator at the following link: https://docs.microsoft.com/en-us/dotnet/csharp/language-reference/operators/null-conditional-operators

Sometimes you want to either assign a variable to a result or use an alternative value, such as 3, if the variable is null. You do this using the null-coalescing operator, ??, as shown in the following code:

```
// result will be 3 if authorName?.Length is null
var result = authorName?.Length ?? 3;
Console.WriteLine(result);
```

 More Information: You can read about the null-coalescing operator at the following link: https://docs.microsoft.com/en-us/dotnet/csharp/language-reference/operators/null-coalescing-operator

Exploring console applications further

We have already created and used basic console applications, but we're now at a stage where we should delve into them more deeply.

Console applications are text-based and are run at the command line. They typically perform simple tasks that need to be scripted, such as compiling a file or encrypting a section of a configuration file.

Equally, they can also have arguments passed to them to control their behavior. An example of this would be to create a new console app using the F# language with a specified name instead of using the name of the current folder, as shown in the following command line:

```
dotnet new console -lang "F#" --name "ExploringConsole"
```

Displaying output to the user

The two most common tasks that a console application performs are writing and reading data. We have already been using the WriteLine method to output, but if we didn't want a carriage return at the end of the lines, we could have used the Write method.

Formatting using numbered positional arguments

One way of generating formatted strings is to use numbered positional arguments.

This feature is supported by methods like Write and WriteLine, and for methods that do not support the feature, the string parameter can be formatted using the Format method of string.

Let's begin formatting:

1. Add a new console application project named `Formatting` to the `Chapter02` folder and workspace.

2. In the `Main` method, add statements to declare some number variables and write them to the console, as shown in the following code:

```
int numberOfApples = 12;
decimal pricePerApple = 0.35M;

Console.WriteLine(
  format: "{0} apples costs {1:C}",
  arg0: numberOfApples,
  arg1: pricePerApple * numberOfApples);

string formatted = string.Format(
  format: "{0} apples costs {1:C}",
  arg0: numberOfApples,
  arg1: pricePerApple * numberOfApples);

//WriteToFile(formatted); // writes the string into a file
```

The `WriteToFile` method is a nonexistent method used to illustrate the idea.

Formatting using interpolated strings

C# 6.0 and later has a handy feature named **interpolated strings**. A string prefixed with $ can use curly braces around the name of a variable or expression to output the current value of that variable or expression at that position in the string as the following shows:

1. In the `Main` method, enter a statement at the bottom of the `Main` method, as shown in the following code:

```
Console.WriteLine($"{numberOfApples} apples costs {pricePerApple *
numberOfApples:C}");
```

2. Run the console app, and view the result, as shown in the following partial output:

```
12 apples costs £4.20
```

For short formatted strings, an interpolated string can be easier for people to read. But for code examples in a book, where lines need to wrap over multiple lines, this can be tricky. For many of the code examples in this book, I will use numbered positional arguments.

Understanding format strings

A variable or expression can be formatted using a format string after a comma or colon.

An `N0` format string means a number with thousand separators and no decimal places, while a `C` format string means currency. The currency format will be determined by the current thread. For instance, if you run this code on a PC in the UK, you'll get pounds sterling with commas as the thousand separators, but if you run this code on a PC in Germany, you will get Euros with dots as the thousand separators.

The full syntax of a format item is:

```
{ index [, alignment ] [ : formatString ] }
```

Each format item can have an alignment, which is useful when outputting tables of values, some of which might need to be left- or right-aligned within a width of characters. Alignment values are integers. Positive integers are right-aligned and negative integers are left-aligned.

For example, to output a table of fruit and how many of each there are, we might want to left-align the names within a column of 8 characters and right-align the counts formatted as numbers with zero decimal places within a column of six characters:

1. In the `Main` method, enter the following statements at the bottom:

    ```csharp
    string applesText = "Apples";
    int applesCount = 1234;

    string bananasText = "Bananas";
    int bananasCount = 56789;

    Console.WriteLine(
      format: "{0,-8} {1,6:N0}",
      arg0: "Name",
      arg1: "Count");

    Console.WriteLine(
      format: "{0,-8} {1,6:N0}",
      arg0: applesText,
      arg1: applesCount);

    Console.WriteLine(
      format: "{0,-8} {1,6:N0}",
      arg0: bananasText,
      arg1: bananasCount);
    ```

2. Run the console app and note the effect of the alignment and number format, as shown in the following output:

    ```
    Name      Count
    Apples    1,234
    Bananas  56,789
    ```

More Information: You can read more details about formatting types in .NET at the following link: https://docs.microsoft.com/en-us/dotnet/standard/base-types/formatting-types

Getting text input from the user

We can get text input from the user using the ReadLine method. This method waits for the user to type some text, then as soon as the user presses *Enter*, whatever the user has typed is returned as a string value:

1. In the Main method, type statements to ask the user for their name and age and then output what they entered, as shown in the following code:

```
Console.Write("Type your first name and press ENTER: ");
string firstName = Console.ReadLine();

Console.Write("Type your age and press ENTER: ");
string age = Console.ReadLine();

Console.WriteLine(
    $"Hello {firstName}, you look good for {age}.");
```

2. Run the console application.
3. Enter a name and age, as shown in the following output:

```
Type your name and press ENTER: Gary
Type your age and press ENTER: 34
Hello Gary, you look good for 34.
```

Importing a namespace

You might have noticed that unlike our very first application in *Chapter 1, Hello, C#! Welcome, .NET!*, we have not been typing System before Console. This is because System is a namespace, which is like an address for a type. To refer to someone exactly, you might use Oxford.HighStreet.BobSmith, which tells us to look for a person named *Bob Smith on the High Street in the city of Oxford*.

The System.Console.WriteLine line tells the compiler to look for a method named WriteLine in a type named Console in a namespace named System. To simplify our code, the dotnet new console command added a statement at the top of the code file to tell the compiler to always look in the System namespace for types that haven't been prefixed with their namespace, as shown in the following code:

```
using System;
```

We call this *importing the namespace*. The effect of importing a namespace is that all available types in that namespace will be available to your program without needing to enter the namespace prefix and will be seen in IntelliSense while you write code.

Simplifying the usage of the console

In C# 6.0 and later, the using statement can be used to further simplify our code. Then, we won't need to enter the Console type throughout our code. We can use Visual Studio Code's Replace feature to remove the times we have previously written Console.:

1. Add a statement to statically import the System.Console class to the top of the Program. cs file, as shown in the following code:

   ```
   using static System.Console;
   ```

2. Select the first Console. in your code, ensuring that you select the dot after the word Console too.

3. Navigate to **Edit | Replace** and note that an overlay dialog appears ready for you to enter what you would like to replace Console. with, as shown in the following screenshot:

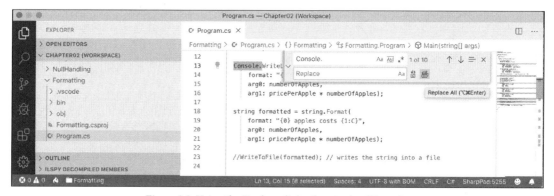

Figure 2.8: Using the Replace dialog box to simplify code

4. Click on the **Replace All** button (the second of the two buttons to the right of the replace box) or press *Alt + A* or *Alt + Cmd + Enter* to replace all, and then close the replace box by clicking on the cross in its top-right corner.

Getting key input from the user

We can get key input from the user using the ReadKey method. This method waits for the user to press a key or key combination that is then returned as a ConsoleKeyInfo value:

1. In the Main method, type statements to ask the user to press any key combination and then output information about it, as shown in the following code:

   ```
   Write("Press any key combination: ");
   ConsoleKeyInfo key = ReadKey();
   WriteLine();
   WriteLine("Key: {0}, Char: {1}, Modifiers: {2}",
   ```

```
        arg0: key.Key,
        arg1: key.KeyChar,
        arg2: key.Modifiers);
```

2. Run the console application, press the K key, and note the result, as shown in the following output:

```
Press any key combination: k
Key: K, Char: k, Modifiers: 0
```

3. Run the console application, hold down Shift and press the K key, and note the result, as shown in the following output:

```
Press any key combination: K
Key: K, Char: K, Modifiers: Shift
```

4. Run the console application, press the F12 key, and note the result, as shown in the following output:

```
Press any key combination:
Key: F12, Char: , Modifiers: 0
```

When running a console application in Terminal within Visual Studio Code, some keyboard combinations will be captured by the code editor or operating system before they can be processed by your app.

Getting arguments

You might have been wondering what the string[] args arguments are in the Main method. They're an array used to pass arguments into a console application; let's take a look to see how it works.

Command-line arguments are separated by spaces. Other characters like hyphens and colons are treated as part of an argument value. To include spaces in an argument value, enclose the argument value in single or double quotes.

Imagine that we want to be able to enter the names of some colors for the foreground and background, and the dimensions of the Terminal window at the command line. We would be able to read the colors and numbers by reading them from the args array, which is always passed into the Main method of a console application.

1. Create a new folder for a console application project named Arguments and add it to the Chapter02 workspace.

2. Add a statement to statically import the System.Console type and a statement to output the number of arguments passed to the application, as shown highlighted in the following code:

```
using System;
using static System.Console;
```

```
namespace Arguments
{
  class Program
  {
    static void Main(string[] args)
    {
      WriteLine($"There are {args.Length} arguments.");
    }
  }
}
```

 Good Practice: Remember to statically import the System.Console type in all future projects to simplify your code, as these instructions will not be repeated every time.

3. Run the console application and view the result, as shown in the following output:

```
There are 0 arguments.
```

4. In **TERMINAL**, enter some arguments after the dotnet run command, as shown in the following command line:

```
dotnet run firstarg second-arg third:arg "fourth arg"
```

5. Note the result indicates four arguments, as shown in the following output:

```
There are 4 arguments.
```

6. To enumerate or iterate (that is, loop through) the values of those four arguments, add the following statements after outputting the length of the array:

```
foreach (string arg in args)
{
  WriteLine(arg);
}
```

7. In **TERMINAL**, repeat the same arguments after the dotnet run command, as shown in the following command line:

```
dotnet run firstarg second-arg third:arg "fourth arg"
```

8. Note the result shows the details of the four arguments, as shown in the following output:

```
There are 4 arguments.
firstarg
second-arg
third:arg
fourth arg
```

Setting options with arguments

We will now use these arguments to allow the user to pick a color for the background, foreground, and cursor size of the output window. The cursor size can be an integer value from 1, meaning a line at the bottom of the cursor cell, up to 100, meaning a percentage of the height of the cursor cell.

The System namespace is already imported so that the compiler knows about the ConsoleColor and Enum types. If you cannot see either of these types in the IntelliSense list, it is because you are missing the using System; statement at the top of the file.

1. Add statements to warn the user if they do not enter three arguments and then parse those arguments and use them to set the color and dimensions of the console window, as shown in the following code:

```
if (args.Length < 3)
{
  WriteLine("You must specify two colors and cursor size, e.g.");
  WriteLine("dotnet run red yellow 50");
  return; // stop running
}

ForegroundColor = (ConsoleColor)Enum.Parse(
  enumType: typeof(ConsoleColor),
  value: args[0],
  ignoreCase: true);

BackgroundColor = (ConsoleColor)Enum.Parse(
  enumType: typeof(ConsoleColor),
  value: args[1],
  ignoreCase: true);

CursorSize = int.Parse(args[2]);
```

2. Enter the following command in **TERMINAL**:

```
dotnet run red yellow 50
```

On Linux, this will work correctly. On Windows, this will run, but the cursor will not change size. On macOS, you'll see an unhandled exception, as shown in the following screenshot:

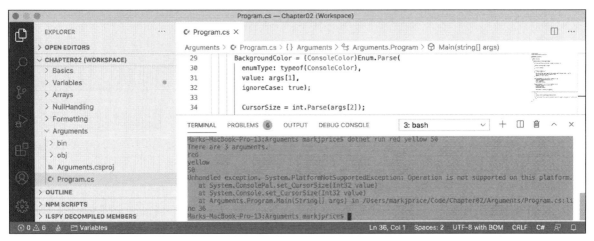

Figure 2.9: An unhandled exception on unsupported macOS

Although the compiler did not give an error or warning, at runtime some API calls may fail on some platforms. Although a console application running on Linux can change its cursor size, on macOS, it cannot, and complains if you try.

Handling platforms that do not support an API

So how do we solve this problem? We can solve this by using an exception handler. You will learn more details about the `try-catch` statement in *Chapter 3, Controlling Flow and Converting Types*, so for now, just enter the code.

1. Modify the code to wrap the lines that change the cursor size in a `try` statement, as shown in the following code:

```
try
{
  CursorSize = int.Parse(args[2]);
}
catch (PlatformNotSupportedException)
{
  WriteLine("The current platform does not support changing the size of
the cursor.");
}
```

2. Rerun the console application; note the exception is caught, and a friendlier message is shown to the user.

Another way to handle differences in operating systems is to use the `OperatingSystem` class, as shown in the following code:

```
if (OperatingSystem.IsWindows())
{
  // execute code that only works on Windows
}
```

The OperatingSystem class has equivalent methods for other common OSes like Android, iOS, Linux, macOS, and even the browser, which is useful for Blazor web components.

Practicing and exploring

Test your knowledge and understanding by answering some questions, get some hands-on practice, and explore the topics covered in this chapter with deeper research.

Exercise 2.1 – Test your knowledge

To get the best answer to some of these questions, you will need to do your own research. I want you to "think outside the book" so I have deliberately not provided all the answers in the book.

I want to encourage you to get in the good habit of looking for help elsewhere, following the principle of "teach a person to fish."

What type would you choose for the following "numbers"?

1. A person's telephone number
2. A person's height
3. A person's age
4. A person's salary
5. A book's ISBN
6. A book's price
7. A book's shipping weight
8. A country's population
9. The number of stars in the universe
10. The number of employees in each of the small or medium businesses in the United Kingdom (up to about 50,000 employees per business)

Exercise 2.2 – Practice number sizes and ranges

Create a console application project named Exercise02 that outputs the number of bytes in memory that each of the following number types uses, and the minimum and maximum values they can have: sbyte, byte, short, ushort, int, uint, long, ulong, float, double, and decimal.

 More Information: You can always read the documentation, available at https://docs.microsoft.com/en-us/dotnet/standard/base-types/composite-formatting for Composite Formatting to learn how to align text in a console application

The result of running your console application should look something like the following screenshot:

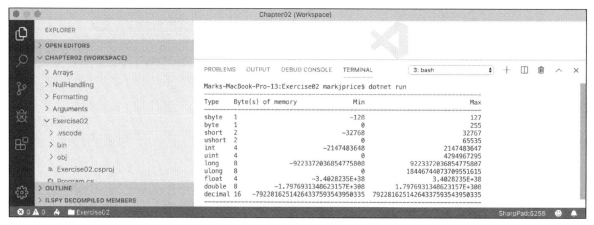

Figure 2.10: The result of the console application

Exercise 2.3 – Explore topics

Use the following links to read more about the topics covered in this chapter:

- **C# Keywords**: https://docs.microsoft.com/en-us/dotnet/csharp/language-reference/keywords/index
- **Main() and command-line arguments (C# Programming Guide)**: https://docs.microsoft.com/en-us/dotnet/csharp/programming-guide/main-and-command-args/
- **Types (C# Programming Guide)**: https://docs.microsoft.com/en-us/dotnet/csharp/programming-guide/types/
- **Statements, Expressions, and Operators (C# Programming Guide)**: https://docs.microsoft.com/en-us/dotnet/csharp/programming-guide/statements-expressions-operators/
- **Strings (C# Programming Guide)**: https://docs.microsoft.com/en-us/dotnet/csharp/programming-guide/strings/
- **Nullable Types (C# Programming Guide)**: https://docs.microsoft.com/en-us/dotnet/csharp/programming-guide/nullable-types/
- **Nullable reference types**: https://docs.microsoft.com/en-us/dotnet/csharp/nullable-references
- **Console Class**: https://docs.microsoft.com/en-us/dotnet/api/system.console

Summary

In this chapter, you learned how to declare variables with a specified or an inferred type; we discussed some of the built-in types for numbers, text, and Booleans; we covered how to choose between number types; we covered the nullability of types; we learned how to control output formatting in console apps.

In the next chapter, you will learn about operators, branching, looping, and converting between types.

03

Controlling Flow and Converting Types

This chapter is all about writing code that performs simple operations on variables, makes decisions, performs pattern matching, repeats blocks of statements, converts variable or expression values from one type to another, handles exceptions, and checks for overflows in number variables.

This chapter covers the following topics:

- Operating on variables
- Understanding selection statements
- Understanding iteration statements
- Casting and converting between types
- Handling exceptions
- Checking for overflow

Operating on variables

Operators apply simple operations such as addition and multiplication to **operands** such as variables and literal values. They usually return a new value that is the result of the operation that can be assigned to a variable.

Most operators are binary, meaning that they work on two operands, as shown in the following pseudocode:

```
var resultOfOperation = firstOperand operator secondOperand;
```

Some operators are unary, meaning they work on a single operand, and can apply before or after the operand, as shown in the following pseudocode:

```
var resultOfOperation = onlyOperand operator;
var resultOfOperation2 = operator onlyOperand;
```

Examples of unary operators include incrementors and retrieving a type or its size in bytes, as shown in the following code:

```
int x = 5;
int incrementedByOne = x++;
int incrementedByOneAgain = ++x;
Type theTypeOfAnInteger = typeof(int);
int howManyBytesInAnInteger = sizeof(int);
```

A ternary operator works on three operands, as shown in the following pseudocode:

```
var resultOfOperation = firstOperand firstOperator
secondOperand secondOperator thirdOperand;
```

Unary operators

Two common unary operators are used to increment, ++, and decrement, --, a number. Let us write some example code to show how they work:

1. If you have completed the previous chapters, then you will already have a Code folder in your user folder. If not, create it.
2. In the Code folder, create a folder named Chapter03.
3. Start Visual Studio Code and close any open workspace or folder.
4. Save the current workspace in the Chapter03 folder as Chapter03.code-workspace.
5. Create a new folder named Operators and add it to the Chapter03 workspace.
6. Navigate to **Terminal | New Terminal**.
7. In **TERMINAL**, enter a command to create a new console application in the Operators folder.
8. Open Program.cs.
9. Statically import System.Console.
10. In the Main method, declare two integer variables named a and b, set a to three, increment a while assigning the result to b, and then output their values, as shown in the following code:
    ```
    int a = 3;
    int b = a++;
    WriteLine($"a is {a}, b is {b}");
    ```

11. Before running the console application, ask yourself a question: what do you think the value of b will be when output? Once you've thought about that, run the console application, and compare your prediction against the actual result, as shown in the following output:

```
a is 4, b is 3
```

The variable b has the value 3 because the ++ operator executes after the assignment; this is known as a postfix operator. If you need to increment before the assignment, then use the prefix operator.

12. Copy and paste the statements, and then modify them to rename the variables and use the prefix operator, as shown in the following code:

```
int c = 3;
int d = ++c; // increment c before assigning it
WriteLine($"c is {c}, d is {d}");
```

13. Rerun the console application and note the result, as shown in the following output:

```
a is 4, b is 3
c is 4, d is 4
```

Good Practice: Due to the confusion between prefix and postfix for the increment and decrement operators when combined with assignment, the Swift programming language designers decided to drop support for this operator in version 3. My recommendation for usage in C# is to never combine the use of ++ and -- operators with an assignment operator, =. Perform the operations as separate statements.

Binary arithmetic operators

Increment and decrement are unary arithmetic operators. Other arithmetic operators are usually binary and allow you to perform arithmetic operations on two numbers as the following shows:

1. Add the statements to the bottom of the Main method to declare and assign values to two integer variables named e and f, and then apply the five common binary arithmetic operators to the two numbers, as shown in the following code:

```
int e = 11;
int f = 3;
WriteLine($"e is {e}, f is {f}");
WriteLine($"e + f = {e + f}");
WriteLine($"e - f = {e - f}");
WriteLine($"e * f = {e * f}");
WriteLine($"e / f = {e / f}");
WriteLine($"e % f = {e % f}");
```

2. Rerun the console application and note the result, as shown in the following output:

```
e is 11, f is 3
e + f = 14
e - f = 8
e * f = 33
e / f = 3
e % f = 2
```

To understand the divide / and modulo % operators when applied to integers, you need to think back to primary school. Imagine you have eleven sweets and three friends. How can you divide the sweets between your friends? You can give three sweets to each of your friends, and there will be two left over. Those two sweets are the **modulus**, also known as the **remainder** after dividing. If you have twelve sweets, then each friend gets four of them, and there are none left over, so the remainder would be 0.

3. Add statements to declare and assign a value to a double variable named g to show the difference between whole number and real number divisions, as shown in the following code:

```
double g = 11.0;
WriteLine($"g is {g:N1}, f is {f}");
WriteLine($"g / f = {g / f}");
```

4. Rerun the console application and note the result, as shown in the following output:

```
g is 11.0, f is 3
g / f = 3.6666666666666665
```

If the first operand is a floating-point number, such as g with the value 11.0, then the divide operator returns a floating-point value, such as 3.6666666666665, rather than a whole number.

Assignment operators

You have already been using the most common assignment operator, =.

To make your code more concise, you can combine the assignment operator with other operators like arithmetic operators, as shown in the following code:

```
int p = 6;
p += 3; // equivalent to p = p + 3;
p -= 3; // equivalent to p = p - 3;
p *= 3; // equivalent to p = p * 3;
p /= 3; // equivalent to p = p / 3;
```

Logical operators

Logical operators operate on Boolean values, so they return either true or false.

Let's explore binary logical operators that operate on two Boolean values:

1. Create a new folder and console application named `BooleanOperators` and add
    it to the `Chapter03` workspace. Remember to use the Command Palette to select
    `BooleanOperators` as the active project.

> **Good Practice**: Remember to statically import the `System.Console`
> type to simplify statements in a console app.

2. In `Program.cs`, in the `Main` method, add statements to declare two Boolean variables with
    values `true` and `false`, and then output truth tables showing the results of applying
    AND, OR, and XOR (exclusive OR) logical operators, as shown in the following code:

```
bool a = true;
bool b = false;
WriteLine($"AND | a       | b ");
WriteLine($"a   | {a & a,-5} | {a & b,-5} ");
WriteLine($"b   | {b & a,-5} | {b & b,-5} ");
WriteLine();
WriteLine($"OR  | a       | b ");
WriteLine($"a   | {a | a,-5} | {a | b,-5} ");
WriteLine($"b   | {b | a,-5} | {b | b,-5} ");
WriteLine();
WriteLine($"XOR | a       | b ");
WriteLine($"a   | {a ^ a,-5} | {a ^ b,-5} ");
WriteLine($"b   | {b ^ a,-5} | {b ^ b,-5} ");
```

3. Run the console application and note the results, as shown in the following output:

```
AND | a     | b
a   | True  | False
b   | False | False
OR  | a     | b
a   | True  | True
b   | True  | False
XOR | a     | b
a   | False | True
b   | True  | False
```

For the AND `&` logical operator, both operands must be `true` for the result to be `true`. For the
OR `|` logical operator, either operand can be `true` for the result to be `true`. For the XOR `^` logical
operator, either operand can be `true` (but not both!) for the result to be `true`.

> **More Information**: Read about truth tables at the following link:
> https://en.wikipedia.org/wiki/Truth_table

Conditional logical operators

Conditional logical operators are similar to logical operators, but you use two symbols instead of one, for example, && instead of &, or || instead of |.

In *Chapter 4, Writing, Debugging, and Testing Functions*, you will learn about functions in more detail, but I need to introduce functions now to explain conditional logical operators, also known as short-circuiting Boolean operators.

A function executes statements and then returns a value. That value could be a Boolean value like true that is used in a Boolean operation. Let's make use of conditional logical operators:

1. After and outside the Main method, write statements to declare a function that writes a message to the console and returns true, as shown highlighted in the following code:

```
class Program
{
  static void Main(string[] args)
  {
    ...
  }

  private static bool DoStuff()
  {
    WriteLine("I am doing some stuff.");
    return true;
  }
}
```

2. Inside and at the bottom of the Main method, perform an AND & operation on the a and b variables and the result of calling the function, as shown in the following code:

```
WriteLine($"a & DoStuff() = {a & DoStuff()}");
WriteLine($"b & DoStuff() = {b & DoStuff()}");
```

3. Run the console app, view the result, and note that the function was called twice, once for a and once for b, as shown in the following output:

```
I am doing some stuff.
a & DoStuff() = True
I am doing some stuff.
b & DoStuff() = False
```

4. Change the & operators into && operators, as shown in the following code:

```
WriteLine($"a && DoStuff() = {a && DoStuff()}");
WriteLine($"b && DoStuff() = {b && DoStuff()}");
```

5. Run the console app, view the result, and note that the function does run when combined with the a variable. It does not run when combined with the b variable because the b variable is `false` so the result will be `false` anyway, so it does not need to execute the function, as shown in the following output:

```
I am doing some stuff.
a && DoStuff() = True
b && DoStuff() = False // DoStuff function was not executed!
```

 Good Practice: Now you can see why the conditional logical operators are described as being short-circuiting. They can make your apps more efficient, but they can also introduce subtle bugs in cases where you assume that the function would always be called. It is safest to avoid them when used in combination with functions that cause side effects.

 More Information: You can read about side effects at the following link: https://en.wikipedia.org/wiki/Side_effect_(computer_science)

Bitwise and binary shift operators

Bitwise operators affect the bits in a number. Binary shift operators can perform some common arithmetic calculations much faster than traditional operators.

Let's explore bitwise and binary shift operators:

1. Create a new folder and console application named `BitwiseAndShiftOperators` and add it to the workspace.

2. Add statements to the `Main` method to declare two integer variables with values `10` and `6`, and then output the results of applying AND, OR, and XOR bitwise operators, as shown in the following code:

```
int a = 10; // 0000 1010
int b = 6;  // 0000 0110
WriteLine($"a = {a}");
WriteLine($"b = {b}");
WriteLine($"a & b = {a & b}"); // 2-bit column only
WriteLine($"a | b = {a | b}"); // 8, 4, and 2-bit columns
WriteLine($"a ^ b = {a ^ b}"); // 8 and 4-bit columns
```

3. Run the console application and note the results, as shown in the following output:

```
a = 10
b = 6
a & b = 2
a | b = 14
```

```
a ^ b = 12
```

4. Add statements to the Main method to output the results of applying the left-shift operator to move the bits of the variable a by three columns, multiplying a by 8, and right-shifting the bits of the variable b by one column, as shown in the following code:

```
// 0101 0000 left-shift a by three bit columns
WriteLine($"a << 3 = {a << 3}");


// multiply a by 8
WriteLine($"a * 8 = {a * 8}");


// 0000 0011 right-shift b by one bit column
WriteLine($"b >> 1 = {b >> 1}");
```

5. Run the console application and note the results, as shown in the following output:

```
a << 3 = 80
a * 8 = 80
b >> 1 = 3
```

The 80 result is because the bits in it were shifted three columns to the left, so the 1-bits moved into the 64- and 16-bit columns and 64 + 16 = 80. This is the equivalent of multiplying by 8 but CPUs can perform a bit-shift faster. The 3 result is because the 1-bits in b were shifted one column into the 2- and 1-bit columns.

Miscellaneous operators

nameof and sizeof are convenient operators when working with types:

- nameof returns the short name (without the namespace) of a variable, type, or member as a string value, which is useful when outputting exception messages.
- sizeof returns the size in bytes of simple types, which is useful for determining the efficiency of data storage.

There are many other operators; for example, the dot between a variable and its members is called the **member access operator** and the round brackets at the end of a function or method name is called the **invocation operator**, as shown in the following code:

```
int age = 47;


// How many operators in the following statement?
char firstDigit = age.ToString()[0];


// There are four operators:
// = is the assignment operator
// . is the member access operator
// () is the invocation operator
```

```
// [] is the indexer access operator
```

More Information: You can read more about some of these miscellaneous operators at the following link: https://docs.microsoft.com/en-us/dotnet/csharp/language-reference/operators/member-access-operators

Understanding selection statements

Every application needs to be able to select from choices and branch along different code paths. The two selection statements in C# are if and switch. You can use if for all your code, but switch can simplify your code in some common scenarios such as when there is a single variable that can have multiple values that each require different processing.

Branching with the if statement

The if statement determines which branch to follow by evaluating a Boolean expression. If the expression is true, then the block executes. The else block is optional, and it executes if the if expression is false. The if statement can be nested.

The if statement can be combined with other if statements as else if branches, as shown in the following code:

```
if (expression1)
{
  // runs if expression1 is true
}
else if (expression2)
{
  // runs if expression1 is false and expression2 if true
}
else if (expression3)
{
  // runs if expression1 and expression2 are false
  // and expression3 is true
}
else
{
  // runs if all expressions are false
}
```

Each if statement's Boolean expression is independent of the others and, unlike switch statements, does not need to reference a single value.

Let's create a console application to explore selection statements like `if`:

1. Create a folder and console application named `SelectionStatements` and add it to the workspace.

2. Add the following statements inside the `Main` method to check whether this console application has any arguments passed to it:

```
if (args.Length == 0)
{
  WriteLine("There are no arguments.");
}
else
{
  WriteLine("There is at least one argument.");
}
```

3. Run the console application by entering the following command into the **TERMINAL**:

```
dotnet run
```

Why you should always use braces with if statements

As there is only a single statement inside each block, the preceding code *could* be written without the curly braces, as shown in the following code:

```
if (args.Length == 0)
  WriteLine("There are no arguments.");
else
  WriteLine("There is at least one argument.");
```

This style of `if` statement should be avoided because it can introduce serious bugs, for example, the infamous #gotofail bug in Apple's iPhone iOS operating system. For 18 months after Apple's iOS 6 was released, in September 2012, it had a bug in its **Secure Sockets Layer (SSL)** encryption code, which meant that any user running Safari, the device's web browser, who tried to connect to secure websites, such as their bank, was not properly secure because an important check was being accidentally skipped.

 More Information: You can read about this infamous bug at the following link: https://gotofail.com/

Just because you can leave out the curly braces doesn't mean you should. Your code is not "more efficient" without them; instead, it is less maintainable and potentially more dangerous.

Pattern matching with the if statement

A feature introduced with C# 7.0 and later is **pattern matching**. The if statement can use the is keyword in combination with declaring a local variable to make your code safer:

1. Add statements to the end of the Main method so that if the value stored in the variable named o is an int, then the value is assigned to the local variable named i, which can then be used inside the if statement. This is safer than using the variable named o because we know for sure that i is an int variable and not something else, as shown in the following code:

```
// add and remove the "" to change the behavior
object o = "3";
int j = 4;

if (o is int i)
{
  WriteLine($"{i} x {j} = {i * j}");
}
else
{
  WriteLine("o is not an int so it cannot multiply!");
}
```

2. Run the console application and view the results, as shown in the following output:

```
o is not an int so it cannot multiply!
```

3. Delete the double-quote characters around the "3" value so that the value stored in the variable named o is an int type instead of a string type.

4. Rerun the console application to view the results, as shown in the following output:

```
3 x 4 = 12
```

Branching with the switch statement

The switch statement is different from the if statement because it compares a single expression against a list of multiple possible case statements. Every case statement is related to the single expression. Every case section must end with:

- The break keyword (like case 1 in the following code),
- Or the goto case keywords (like case 2 in the following code),
- Or they should have no statements (like case 3 in the following code),
- Or the return keyword to leave the current function (not shown in the code).

Let's write some code to explore the `switch` statements:

1. Enter some statements for a `switch` statement after the `if` statements that you wrote previously. You should note that the first line is a label that can be jumped to, and the second line generates a random number. The `switch` statement branches are based on the value of this random number, as shown in the following code:

```
A_label:
var number = (new Random()).Next(1, 7);
WriteLine($"My random number is {number}");

switch (number)
{
  case 1:
    WriteLine("One");
    break; // jumps to end of switch statement
  case 2:
    WriteLine("Two");
    goto case 1;
  case 3:
  case 4:
    WriteLine("Three or four");
    goto case 1;
  case 5:
    // go to sleep for half a second
    System.Threading.Thread.Sleep(500);
    goto A_label;
  default:
    WriteLine("Default");
    break;
} // end of switch statement
```

Good Practice: You can use the `goto` keyword to jump to another case or a label. The `goto` keyword is frowned upon by most programmers but can be a good solution to code logic in some scenarios. However, you should use it sparingly.

More Information: You can read about the `goto` keyword and examples of when it can be used at the following link: `https://docs.microsoft.com/en-us/dotnet/csharp/language-reference/keywords/goto`

2. Run the console application multiple times in order to see what happens in various cases of random numbers, as shown in the following example output:

```
bash-3.2$ dotnet run
My random number is 4
Three or four
One
bash-3.2$ dotnet run
My random number is 2
Two
One
bash-3.2$ dotnet run
My random number is 1
One
```

Pattern matching with the switch statement

Like the if statement, the switch statement supports pattern matching in C# 7.0 and later. The case values no longer need to be literal values; they can be patterns.

Let's see an example of pattern matching with the switch statement using a folder path. If you are using macOS, then swap the commented statement that sets the path variable and replace my username with your user folder name:

1. Add the following statement to the top of the file to import types for working with input/output:

```
using System.IO;
```

2. Add statements to the end of the Main method to declare a string path to a file, open it as either a readonly or writeable stream, and then show a message based on what type and capabilities the stream has, as shown in the following code:

```
// string path = "/Users/markjprice/Code/Chapter03";
string path = @"C:\Code\Chapter03";

Write("Press R for readonly or W for write: ");
ConsoleKeyInfo key = ReadKey();
WriteLine();

Stream s = null;

if (key.Key == ConsoleKey.R)
{
  s = File.Open(
    Path.Combine(path, "file.txt"),
    FileMode.OpenOrCreate,
    FileAccess.Read);
```

```
    }
    else
    {
      s = File.Open(
        Path.Combine(path, "file.txt"),
        FileMode.OpenOrCreate,
        FileAccess.Write);
    }

    string message = string.Empty;

    switch (s)
    {
      case FileStream writeableFile when s.CanWrite:
        message = "The stream is a file that I can write to.";
        break;
      case FileStream readOnlyFile:
        message = "The stream is a read-only file.";
        break;
      case MemoryStream ms:
        message = "The stream is a memory address.";
        break;
      default: // always evaluated last despite its current position
        message = "The stream is some other type.";
        break;
      case null:
        message = "The stream is null.";
        break;
    }
    WriteLine(message);
```

3. Run the console app and note that the variable named s is declared as a `Stream` type so it could be any subtype of stream, like a memory stream or file stream. In this code, the stream is created using the `File.Open` method, which returns a file stream and, depending on your keypress, it will be writeable or readonly, so the result will be a message that describes the situation, as shown in the following output:

```
The stream is a file that I can write to.
```

In .NET, there are multiple subtypes of `Stream`, including `FileStream` and `MemoryStream`. In C# 7.0 and later, your code can more concisely branch, based on the subtype of stream, and declare and assign a local variable to safely use it. You will learn more about the `System.IO` namespace and the `Stream` type in *Chapter 9, Working with Files, Streams, and Serialization*.

Additionally, case statements can include a `when` keyword to perform more specific pattern matching. In the first `case` statement in the preceding code, s will only be a match if the stream is a `FileStream` and its `CanWrite` property is `true`.

More Information: You can read more about pattern matching at the following link: https://docs.microsoft.com/en-us/dotnet/csharp/pattern-matching

Simplifying switch statements with switch expressions

In C# 8.0 or later, you can simplify switch statements using **switch expressions**.

Most switch statements are very simple, yet they require a lot of typing. Switch expressions are designed to simplify the code you need to type while still expressing the same intent in scenarios where all cases return a value to set a single variable. Switch expressions use a lambda => to indicate a return value.

Let's implement the previous code that uses a switch statement using a switch expression so that you can compare the two styles:

1. Add statements to the end of the Main method to set the message based on what type and capabilities the stream has using a switch expression, as shown in the following code:

```
message = s switch
{
  FileStream writeableFile when s.CanWrite
    => "The stream is a file that I can write to.",
  FileStream readOnlyFile
    => "The stream is a read-only file.",
  MemoryStream ms
    => "The stream is a memory address.",
  null
    => "The stream is null.",

  _
    => "The stream is some other type."
};
WriteLine(message);
```

The main differences are the removal of the case and break keywords. The underscore character is used to represent the default return value.

2. Run the console app, and note the result is the same as before.

More Information: You can read more about patterns and switch expressions at the following link: https://devblogs.microsoft.com/dotnet/do-more-with-patterns-in-c-8-0/

Understanding iteration statements

Iteration statements repeat a block of statements either while a condition is true or for each item in a collection. The choice of which statement to use is based on a combination of ease of understanding to solve the logic problem and personal preference.

Looping with the while statement

The while statement evaluates a Boolean expression and continues to loop while it is true. Let's explore iteration statements:

1. Create a new folder and console application project named IterationStatements and add it to the workspace.
2. Type the following code inside the Main method:

```
int x = 0;

while (x < 10)
{
  WriteLine(x);
  x++;
}
```

3. Run the console application and view the results, which should be the numbers 0 to 9, as shown in the following output:

```
0
1
2
3
4
5
6
7
8
9
```

Looping with the do statement

The do statement is like while, except the Boolean expression is checked at the bottom of the block instead of the top, which means that the block always executes at least once, as the following shows:

1. Type the following code at the end of the `Main` method:

```
string password = string.Empty;

do
{
  Write("Enter your password: ");
  password = ReadLine();
}
while (password != "Pa$$w0rd");

WriteLine("Correct!");
```

2. Run the console application, and note that you are prompted to enter your password repeatedly until you enter it correctly, as shown in the following output:

```
Enter your password: password
Enter your password: 12345678
Enter your password: ninja
Enter your password: correct horse battery staple
Enter your password: Pa$$w0rd
Correct!
```

3. As an optional challenge, add statements so that the user can only make ten attempts before an error message is displayed.

Looping with the for statement

The `for` statement is like `while`, except that it is more succinct. It combines:

- An **initializer expression**, which executes once at the start of the loop.
- A **conditional expression**, which executes on every iteration at the start of the loop to check whether the looping should continue.
- An **iterator expression**, which executes on every loop at the bottom of the statement.

The `for` statement is commonly used with an integer counter. Let's explore some code.

1. Enter a for statement to output the numbers 1 to 10, as shown in the following code:

```
for (int y = 1; y <= 10; y++)
{
  WriteLine(y);
}
```

2. Run the console application to view the result, which should be the numbers 1 to 10.

Looping with the foreach statement

The foreach statement is a bit different from the previous three iteration statements.

It is used to perform a block of statements on each item in a sequence, for example, an array or collection. Each item is usually read-only, and if the sequence structure is modified during iteration, for example, by adding or removing an item, then an exception will be thrown. Try the following example:

1. Type statements to create an array of string variables and then output the length of each one, as shown in the following code:

```
string[] names = { "Adam", "Barry", "Charlie" };

foreach (string name in names)
{
  WriteLine($"{name} has {name.Length} characters.");
}
```

2. Run the console application and view the results, as shown in the following output:

```
Adam has 4 characters.
Barry has 5 characters.
Charlie has 7 characters.
```

Understanding how foreach works internally

Technically, the foreach statement will work on any type that follows these rules:

1. The type must have a method named GetEnumerator that returns an object.
2. The returned object must have a property named Current and a method named MoveNext.
3. The MoveNext method must return true if there are more items to enumerate through or false if there are no more items.

There are interfaces named IEnumerable and IEnumerable<T> that formally define these rules, but technically the compiler does not require the type to implement these interfaces.

The compiler turns the foreach statement in the preceding example into something similar to the following pseudocode:

```
IEnumerator e = names.GetEnumerator();

while (e.MoveNext())
{
  string name = (string)e.Current; // Current is read-only!
  WriteLine($"{name} has {name.Length} characters.");
}
```

Due to the use of an iterator, the variable declared in a `foreach` statement cannot be used to modify the value of the current item.

Casting and converting between types

You will often need to convert values of variables between different types. For example, data input is often entered as text at the console, so it is initially stored in a variable of the `string` type, but it then needs to be converted into a date/time, or number, or some other data type, depending on how it should be stored and processed.

Sometimes you will need to convert between number types, like between an integer and a floating-point, before performing calculations.

Converting is also known as **casting**, and it has two varieties: **implicit** and **explicit**. Implicit casting happens automatically, and it is safe, meaning that you will not lose any information.

Explicit casting must be performed manually because it may lose information, for example, the precision of a number. By explicitly casting, you are telling the C# compiler that you understand and accept the risk.

Casting numbers implicitly and explicitly

Implicitly casting an `int` variable into a `double` variable is safe because no information can be lost as the following shows:

1. Create a new folder and console application project named `CastingConverting` and add it to the workspace.

2. In the `Main` method, enter statements to declare and assign an `int` variable and a `double` variable, and then implicitly cast the integer's value when assigning it to the `double` variable, as shown in the following code:

```
int a = 10;
double b = a; // an int can be safely cast into a double
WriteLine(b);
```

3. In the `Main` method, enter the following statements:

```
double c = 9.8;
int d = c; // compiler gives an error for this line
WriteLine(d);
```

4. View the **PROBLEMS** window by navigating to **View | Problems**, and note the error message, as shown in the following screenshot:

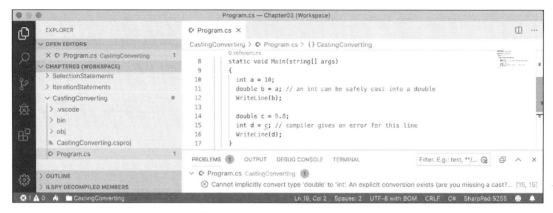

Figure 3.1: Note the error message

If you need to create the required assets to show **PROBLEMS**, then try closing and reopening the workspace, select the correct project for OmniSharp, and then click **Yes** when prompted to create missing assets, for example, the .vscode folder. The status bar should show the currently active project, like **CastingConverting** in the preceding screenshot.

You cannot implicitly cast a double variable into an int variable because it is potentially unsafe and could lose data.

5. View the **TERMINAL** window, and enter the dotnet run command, and note the error message, as shown in the following output:

```
Program.cs(19,15): error CS0266: Cannot implicitly convert type 'double'
to 'int'. An explicit conversion exists (are you missing a cast?) [/Users/
markjprice/Code/Chapter03/CastingConverting/CastingConverting.csproj]
The build failed. Fix the build errors and run again.
```

You must explicitly cast a double variable into an int variable using a pair of round brackets around the type you want to cast the double type into. The pair of round brackets is the **cast operator**. Even then, you must beware that the part after the decimal point will be trimmed off without warning because you have chosen to perform an explicit cast and therefore understand the consequences.

6. Modify the assignment statement for the d variable, as shown in the following code:

```
int d = (int)c;
WriteLine(d); // d is 9 losing the .8 part
```

7. Run the console application to view the results, as shown in the following output:

```
10
9
```

We must perform a similar operation when converting values between larger integers and smaller integers. Again, beware that you might lose information because any value too big will have its bits copied and then be interpreted in ways that you might not expect!

8. Enter statements to declare and assign a `long` 64-bit variable to an `int` 32-bit variable, both using a small value that will work and a too-large value that will not, as shown in the following code:

```
long e = 10;
int f = (int)e;
WriteLine($"e is {e:N0} and f is {f:N0}");
e = long.MaxValue;
f = (int)e;
WriteLine($"e is {e:N0} and f is {f:N0}");
```

9. Run the console application to view the results, as shown in the following output:

```
e is 10 and f is 10
e is 9,223,372,036,854,775,807 and f is -1
```

10. Modify the value of e to 5 billion, as shown in the following code:

```
e = 5_000_000_000;
```

11. Run the console application to view the results, as shown in the following output:

```
e is 5,000,000,000 and f is 705,032,704
```

Converting with the System.Convert type

An alternative to using the cast operator is to use the `System.Convert` type. The `System.Convert` type can convert to and from all the C# number types as well as Booleans, strings, and date and time values.

Let's write some code to see this in action:

1. At the top of the `Program.cs` file, statically import the `System.Convert` class, as shown in the following code:

```
using static System.Convert;
```

2. Add statements to the bottom of the `Main` method to declare and assign a value to a `double` variable, convert it to an integer, and then write both values to the console, as shown in the following code:

```
double g = 9.8;
int h = ToInt32(g);
WriteLine($"g is {g} and h is {h}");
```

3. Run the console application and view the result, as shown in the following output:

```
g is 9.8 and h is 10
```

One difference between casting and converting is that converting rounds the `double` value `9.8` up to `10` instead of trimming the part after the decimal point.

Rounding numbers

You have now seen that the cast operator trims the decimal part of a real number and that the `System.Convert` methods round up or down. However, what is the rule for rounding?

Understanding the default rounding rules

In British primary schools for children aged 5 to 11, pupils are taught to round *up* if the decimal part is .5 or higher and round *down* if the decimal part is less.

Let's explore if C# follows the same primary school rule:

1. At the bottom of the `Main` method, add statements to declare and assign an array of `double` values, convert each of them to an integer, and then write the result to the console, as shown in the following code:

```
double[] doubles = new[]
   { 9.49, 9.5, 9.51, 10.49, 10.5, 10.51 };

foreach (double n in doubles)
{
   WriteLine($"ToInt({n}) is {ToInt32(n)}");
}
```

2. Run the console application and view the result, as shown in the following output:

```
ToInt(9.49) is 9
ToInt(9.5) is 10
ToInt(9.51) is 10
ToInt(10.49) is 10
ToInt(10.5) is 10
ToInt(10.51) is 11
```

We have shown that the rule for rounding in C# is subtly different from the primary school rule:

- It always rounds *down* if the decimal part is less than the midpoint .5.
- It always rounds *up* if the decimal part is more than the midpoint .5.
- It will round *up* if the decimal part is the midpoint .5 and the non-decimal part is odd, but it will round *down* if the non-decimal part is even.

This rule is known as **Banker's Rounding**, and it is preferred because it reduces bias by alternating when it rounds up or down. Sadly, other languages such as JavaScript use the primary school rule.

Taking control of rounding rules

You can take control of the rounding rules by using the Round method of the Math class:

1. At the bottom of the Main method, add statements to round each of the double values using the "away from zero" rounding rule also known as rounding "up," and then write the result to the console, as shown in the following code:

```
foreach (double n in doubles)
{
  WriteLine(format:
    "Math.Round({0}, 0, MidpointRounding.AwayFromZero) is {1}",
    arg0: n,
    arg1: Math.Round(value: n, digits: 0,
          mode: MidpointRounding.AwayFromZero));
}
```

2. Run the console application and view the result, as shown in the following output:

```
Math.Round(9.49, 0, MidpointRounding.AwayFromZero) is 9
Math.Round(9.5, 0, MidpointRounding.AwayFromZero) is 10
Math.Round(9.51, 0, MidpointRounding.AwayFromZero) is 10
Math.Round(10.49, 0, MidpointRounding.AwayFromZero) is 10
Math.Round(10.5, 0, MidpointRounding.AwayFromZero) is 11
Math.Round(10.51, 0, MidpointRounding.AwayFromZero) is 11
```

> **More Information**: MidpointRounding.AwayFromZero is the primary school rule. You can read more about taking control of rounding at the following link: https://docs.microsoft.com/en-us/dotnet/api/system.math.round

> **Good Practice**: For every programming language that you use, check its rounding rules. They may not work the way you expect!

Converting from any type to a string

The most common conversion is from any type into a string variable for outputting as human-readable text, so all types have a method named ToString that they inherit from the System.Object class.

The ToString method converts the current value of any variable into a textual representation. Some types can't be sensibly represented as text, so they return their namespace and type name.

Let's convert some types into a string:

1. At the bottom of the Main method, type statements to declare some variables, convert them to their string representation, and write them to the console, as shown in the following code:

    ```
    int number = 12;
    WriteLine(number.ToString());

    bool boolean = true;
    WriteLine(boolean.ToString());

    DateTime now = DateTime.Now;
    WriteLine(now.ToString());

    object me = new object();
    WriteLine(me.ToString());
    ```

2. Run the console application and view the result, as shown in the following output:

    ```
    12
    True
    27/01/2019 13:48:54
    System.Object
    ```

Converting from a binary object to a string

When you have a binary object like an image or video that you want to either store or transmit, you sometimes do not want to send the raw bits, because you do not know how those bits could be misinterpreted, for example, by the network protocol transmitting them or another operating system that is reading the store binary object.

The safest thing to do is to convert the binary object into a string of safe characters. Programmers call this **Base64** encoding.

The Convert type has a pair of methods, ToBase64String and FromBase64String, that perform this conversion for you. Let's see them in action:

1. Add statements to the end of the Main method to create an array of bytes randomly populated with byte values, write each byte nicely formatted to the console, and then write the same bytes converted to Base64 to the console, as shown in the following code:

    ```
    // allocate array of 128 bytes
    byte[] binaryObject = new byte[128];

    // populate array with random bytes
    ```

```
(new Random()).NextBytes(binaryObject);

WriteLine("Binary Object as bytes:");

for(int index = 0; index < binaryObject.Length; index++)
{
  Write($"{binaryObject[index]:X} ");
}
WriteLine();

// convert to Base64 string and output as text
string encoded = Convert.ToBase64String(binaryObject);

WriteLine($"Binary Object as Base64: {encoded}");
```

By default, an int value would output assuming decimal notation, that is, base10. You can use format codes such as :X to format the value using hexadecimal notation.

2. Run the console application and view the result:

```
Binary Object as bytes:
B3 4D 55 DE 2D E BB CF BE 4D E6 53 C3 C2 9B 67 3 45 F9 E5 20 61 7E 4F 7A
81 EC 49 F0 49 1D 8E D4 F7 DB 54 AF A0 81 5 B8 BE CE F8 36 90 7A D4 36 42
4 75 81 1B AB 51 CE 5 63 AC 22 72 DE 74 2F 57 7F CB E7 47 B7 62 C3 F4 2D
61 93 85 18 EA 6 17 12 AE 44 A8 D B8 4C 89 85 A9 3C D5 E2 46 E0 59 C9 DF
10 AF ED EF 8AA1 B1 8D EE 4A BE 48 EC 79 A5 A 5F 2F 30 87 4A C7 7F 5D C1 D
26 EE
Binary Object as Base64: s01V3i0Ou8++TeZTw8KbZwNF +eUgYX5PeoHsSfBJHY7U99tU
r6CBBbi+zvg2kHrUNkIEdYEbq1HOBWOsInLedC9Xf8vnR7diw/QtYZOFGOoGFxKuRKgNuEyJha
k81eJG4FnJ3xCv7e+KobGN7kq+SO x5pQpfLzCHSsd/XcENJu4=
```

Parsing from strings to numbers or dates and times

The second most common conversion is from strings to numbers or date and time values.

The opposite of ToString is Parse. Only a few types have a Parse method, including all the number types and DateTime.

Let's see Parse in action:

1. Add statements to the Main method to parse an integer and a date and time value from strings and then write the result to the console, as shown in the following code:

```
int age = int.Parse("27");
DateTime birthday = DateTime.Parse("4 July 1980");

WriteLine($"I was born {age} years ago.");
WriteLine($"My birthday is {birthday}.");
WriteLine($"My birthday is {birthday:D}.");
```

2. Run the console application and view the result, as shown in the following output:

```
I was born 27 years ago.
My birthday is 04/07/1980 00:00:00.
My birthday is 04 July 1980.
```

By default, a date and time value outputs with the short date and time format. You can use format codes such as D to output only the date part using long date format.

 More Information: There are many other format codes for common scenarios that you can read about at the following link: `https://docs.microsoft.com/en-us/dotnet/standard/base-types/standard-date-and-time-format-strings`

One problem with the Parse method is that it gives errors if the string cannot be converted.

3. Add a statement to the bottom of the Main method to attempt to parse a string containing letters into an integer variable, as shown in the following code:

```
int count = int.Parse("abc");
```

4. Run the console application and view the result, as shown in the following output:

```
Unhandled Exception: System.FormatException: Input string was not in a
correct format.
```

As well as the preceding exception message, you will see a stack trace. I have not included stack traces in this book because they take up too much space.

Avoiding exceptions using the TryParse method

To avoid errors, you can use the TryParse method instead. TryParse attempts to convert the input string and returns true if it can convert it and false if it cannot.

The out keyword is required to allow the TryParse method to set the count variable when the conversion works.

Let's see TryParse in action:

1. Replace the int count declaration with statements to use the TryParse method and ask the user to input a count for a number of eggs, as shown in the following code:

```
Write("How many eggs are there? ");
int count;
string input = ReadLine();

if (int.TryParse(input, out count))
{
    WriteLine($"There are {count} eggs.");
```

```
    }
    else
    {
        WriteLine("I could not parse the input.");
    }
```

2. Run the console application.

3. Enter 12 and view the result, as shown in the following output:

```
How many eggs are there? 12
There are 12 eggs.
```

4. Run the console application again.

5. Enter twelve and view the result, as shown in the following output:

```
How many eggs are there? twelve
I could not parse the input.
```

You can also use methods of the System.Convert type to convert string values into other types; however, like the Parse method, it gives an error if it cannot convert.

Handling exceptions when converting types

You've seen several scenarios where errors have occurred when converting types. When this happens, we say *a runtime exception has been thrown*.

As you have seen, the default behavior of a console application is to write a message about the exception, including a stack trace in the output, and then stop running the application.

 Good Practice: Avoid writing code that will throw an exception whenever possible, perhaps by performing if statement checks, but sometimes you can't. In those scenarios, you could catch the exception and handle it in a better way than the default behavior.

Wrapping error-prone code in a try block

When you know that a statement can cause an error, you should wrap that statement in a try block. For example, parsing from text to a number can cause an error. Any statements in the catch block will be executed only if an exception is thrown by a statement in the try block. We don't have to do anything inside the catch block. Let's see this in action:

1. Create a folder and console application named HandlingExceptions and add it to the workspace.

2. In the Main method, add statements to prompt the user to enter their age and then write their age to the console, as shown in the following code:

```
WriteLine("Before parsing");
Write("What is your age? ");
string input = ReadLine();
try
{
  int age = int.Parse(input);
  WriteLine($"You are {age} years old.");
}
catch
{
}
WriteLine("After parsing");
```

This code includes two messages to indicate *before* parsing and *after* parsing to make clearer the flow through the code. These will be especially useful as the example code grows more complex.

3. Run the console application.

4. Enter a valid age, for example, 47, and view the result, as shown in the following output:

```
Before parsing
What is your age? 47
You are 47 years old.
After parsing
```

5. Run the console application again.

6. Enter an invalid age, for example, kermit, and view the result, as shown in the following output:

```
Before parsing
What is your age? Kermit
After parsing
```

When the code executed, the error exception was caught and the default message and stack trace were not output, and the console application continued running. This is better than the default behavior, but it might be useful to see the type of error that occurred.

Catching all exceptions

To get information about any type of exception that might occur, you can declare a variable of type System.Exception to the catch block:

1. Add an exception variable declaration to the catch block and use it to write information about the exception to the console, as shown in the following code:

```
catch(Exception ex)
{
    WriteLine($"{ex.GetType()} says {ex.Message}");
}
```

2. Run the console application.

3. Enter an invalid age, for example, kermit, and view the result, as shown in the following output:

```
Before parsing
What is your age? kermit
System.FormatException says Input string was not in a correct format.
After parsing
```

Catching specific exceptions

Now that we know which specific type of exception occurred, we can improve our code by catching just that type of exception and customizing the message that we display to the user:

1. Leave the existing catch block, and above it, add a new catch block for the format exception type, as shown in the following highlighted code:

```
catch (FormatException)
{
    WriteLine("The age you entered is not a valid number format.");
}
catch (Exception ex)
{
    WriteLine($"{ex.GetType()} says {ex.Message}");
}
```

2. Run the console application.

3. Enter an invalid age, for example, kermit, and view the result, as shown in the following output:

```
Before parsing
What is your age? kermit
The age you entered is not a valid number format.
After parsing
```

The reason we want to leave the more general catch below is because there might be other types of exceptions that can occur.

4. Run the console application.

5. Enter a number that is too big for an integer, for example, 9876543210, and view the result, as shown in the following output:

```
Before parsing
What is your age? 9876543210
System.OverflowException says Value was either too large or too small for
an Int32.
After parsing
```

Let's add another `catch` block for this type of exception.

6. Leave the existing `catch` blocks, and add a new `catch` block for the overflow exception type, as shown in the following highlighted code:

```
catch (OverflowException)
{
   WriteLine("Your age is a valid number format but it is either too big or
small.");
}
catch (FormatException)
{
   WriteLine("The age you entered is not a valid number format.");
}
```

7. Run the console application.

8. Enter a number that is too big, and view the result, as shown in the following output:

```
Before parsing
What is your age? 9876543210
Your age is a valid number format but it is either too big or small.
After parsing
```

The order in which you catch exceptions is important. The correct order is related to the inheritance hierarchy of the exception types. You will learn about inheritance in *Chapter 5, Building Your Own Types with Object-Oriented Programming*. However, don't worry too much about this—the compiler will give you build errors if you get exceptions in the wrong order anyway.

Checking for overflow

Earlier, we saw that when casting between number types, it was possible to lose information, for example, when casting from a `long` variable to an `int` variable. If the value stored in a type is too big, it will overflow.

Throwing overflow exceptions with the checked statement

The checked statement tells .NET to throw an exception when an overflow happens instead of allowing it to happen silently, which is done by default for performance reasons.

We will set the initial value of an int variable to its maximum value minus one. Then, we will increment it several times, outputting its value each time. Once it gets above its maximum value, it overflows to its minimum value and continues incrementing from there. Let's see this in action:

1. Create a folder and console application named CheckingForOverflow and add it to the workspace.

2. In the Main method, type statements to declare and assign an integer to one less than its maximum possible value, and then increment it and write its value to the console three times, as shown in the following code:

    ```
    int x = int.MaxValue - 1;
    WriteLine($"Initial value: {x}");
    x++;
    WriteLine($"After incrementing: {x}");
    x++;
    WriteLine($"After incrementing: {x}");
    x++;
    WriteLine($"After incrementing: {x}");
    ```

3. Run the console application and view the result, as shown in the following output:

    ```
    Initial value: 2147483646
    After incrementing: 2147483647
    After incrementing: -2147483648
    After incrementing: -2147483647
    ```

4. Now, let's get the compiler to warn us about the overflow by wrapping the statements using a checked statement block, as shown highlighted in the following code:

    ```
    checked
    {
      int x = int.MaxValue - 1;
      WriteLine($"Initial value: {x}");
      x++;
      WriteLine($"After incrementing: {x}");
      x++;
      WriteLine($"After incrementing: {x}");
      x++;
      WriteLine($"After incrementing: {x}");
    }
    ```

5. Run the console application and view the result, as shown in the following output:

```
Initial value: 2147483646
After incrementing: 2147483647
Unhandled Exception: System.OverflowException: Arithmetic operation
resulted in an overflow.
```

6. Just like any other exception, we should wrap these statements in a try statement block and display a nicer error message for the user, as shown in the following code:

```
try
{
    // previous code goes here
}
catch (OverflowException)
{
    WriteLine("The code overflowed but I caught the exception.");
}
```

7. Run the console application and view the result, as shown in the following output:

```
Initial value: 2147483646
After incrementing: 2147483647
The code overflowed but I caught the exception.
```

Disabling compiler overflow checks with the unchecked statement

A related keyword is unchecked. This keyword switches off overflow checks performed by the compiler within a block of code. Let's see how to do this:

1. Type the following statement at the end of the previous statements. The compiler will not compile this statement because it knows it would overflow:

```
int y = int.MaxValue + 1;
```

2. View the **PROBLEMS** window by navigating to **View | Problems**, and note a **compile-time** check is shown as an error message, as shown in the following screenshot:

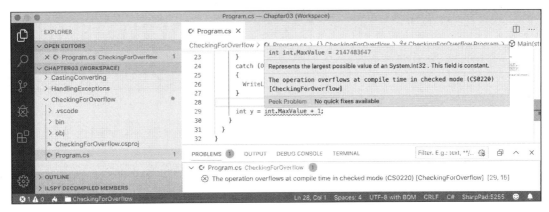

Figure 3.2: A compile-time check in the PROBLEMS window

3. To disable compile-time checks, wrap the statement in an unchecked block, write the value of y to the console, decrement it, and repeat, as shown in the following code:

```
unchecked
{
  int y = int.MaxValue + 1;
  WriteLine($"Initial value: {y}");
  y--;
  WriteLine($"After decrementing: {y}");
  y--;
  WriteLine($"After decrementing: {y}");
}
```

4. Run the console application and view the results, as shown in the following output:

```
Initial value: -2147483648
After decrementing: 2147483647
After decrementing: 2147483646
```

Of course, it would be rare that you would want to explicitly switch off a check like this because it allows an overflow to occur. But, perhaps, you can think of a scenario where you might want that behavior.

Practicing and exploring

Test your knowledge and understanding by answering some questions, get some hands-on practice, and explore with deeper research into this chapter's topics.

Exercise 3.1 – Test your knowledge

Answer the following questions:

1. What happens when you divide an `int` variable by 0?
2. What happens when you divide a `double` variable by 0?
3. What happens when you overflow an `int` variable, that is, set it to a value beyond its range?
4. What is the difference between x = y++; and x = ++y;?
5. What is the difference between `break`, `continue`, and `return` when used inside a loop statement?
6. What are the three parts of a `for` statement and which of them are required?
7. What is the difference between the = and == operators?
8. Does the following statement compile? for (; true;) ;
9. What does the underscore _ represent in a switch expression?
10. What interface must an object implement to be enumerated over by using the `foreach` statement?

Exercise 3.2 – Explore loops and overflow

What will happen if this code executes?

```
int max = 500;
for (byte i = 0; i < max; i++)
{
  WriteLine(i);
}
```

Create a console application in `Chapter03` named `Exercise02` and enter the preceding code. Run the console application and view the output. What happens?

What code could you add (don't change any of the preceding code) to warn us about the problem?

Exercise 3.3 – Practice loops and operators

FizzBuzz is a group word game for children to teach them about division. Players take turns to count incrementally, replacing any number divisible by three with the word *fizz*, any number divisible by five with the word *buzz*, and any number divisible by both with *fizzbuzz*.

Some interviewers give applicants simple FizzBuzz-style problems to solve during interviews. Most good programmers should be able to write out on paper or a whiteboard a program to output a simulated FizzBuzz game in under a couple of minutes.

Want to know something worrisome? Many computer science graduates can't. You can even find senior programmers who take more than 10-15 minutes to write a solution.

> *"199 out of 200 applicants for every programming job can't write code at all. I repeat: they can't write any code whatsoever."*

> *– Reginald Braithwaite*

This quote is taken from the following website: `http://blog.codinghorror.com/why-cant-programmers-program/`.

 More Information: Refer to the following link for more information: `http://imranontech.com/2007/01/24/using-fizzbuzz-to-find-developers-who-grok-coding/`

Create a console application in `Chapter03` named `Exercise03` that outputs a simulated FizzBuzz game counting up to 100. The output should look something like the following screenshot:

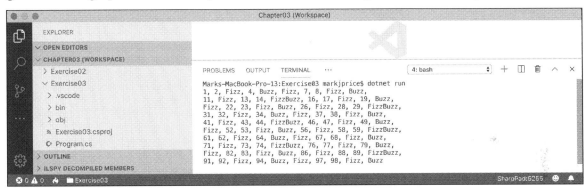

Figure 3.3: A simulated FizzBuzz game output

Exercise 3.4 – Practice exception handling

Create a console application in `Chapter03` named `Exercise04` that asks the user for two numbers in the range 0-255 and then divides the first number by the second:

```
Enter a number between 0 and 255: 100
Enter another number between 0 and 255: 8
100 divided by 8 is 12
```

Write exception handlers to catch any thrown errors, as shown in the following output:

```
Enter a number between 0 and 255: apples
Enter another number between 0 and 255: bananas
FormatException: Input string was not in a correct format.
```

Exercise 3.5 – Test your knowledge of operators

What are the values of x and y after the following statements execute?

1. ```
   x = 3;
   y = 2 + ++x;
   ```
2. ```
   x = 3 << 2;
   y = 10 >> 1;
   ```
3. ```
   x = 10 & 8;
   y = 10 | 7;
   ```

Exercise 3.6 – Explore topics

Use the following links to read in more detail about the topics covered in this chapter:

- **C# operators**: https://docs.microsoft.com/en-us/dotnet/csharp/programming-guide/statements-expressions-operators/operators

- **Bitwise and shift operators**: https://docs.microsoft.com/en-us/dotnet/csharp/language-reference/operators/bitwise-and-shift-operators

- **Statement keywords (C# Reference)**: https://docs.microsoft.com/en-us/dotnet/csharp/language-reference/keywords/statement-keywords

- **Casting and type conversions (C# Programming Guide)**: https://docs.microsoft.com/en-us/dotnet/articles/csharp/programming-guide/types/casting-and-type-conversions

Summary

In this chapter, you experimented with some operators, learned how to branch and loop, how to convert between types, and how to catch exceptions.

You are now ready to learn how to reuse blocks of code by defining functions, how to pass values into them and get values back, and how to track down bugs in your code and squash them!
   ```

04

Writing, Debugging, and Testing Functions

This chapter is about writing functions to reuse code, debugging logic errors during development, logging exceptions during runtime, and unit testing your code to remove bugs and ensure stability and reliability.

This chapter covers the following topics:

- Writing functions
- Debugging during development
- Logging during runtime
- Unit testing

Writing functions

A fundamental principle of programming is **Don't Repeat Yourself** (**DRY**).

While programming, if you find yourself writing the same statements over and over again, then turn those statements into a function. Functions are like tiny programs that complete one small task. For example, you might write a function to calculate sales tax and then reuse that function in many places in a financial application.

Like programs, functions usually have inputs and outputs. They are sometimes described as black boxes, where you feed some raw materials in one end and a manufactured item emerges at the other. Once created, you don't need to think about how they work.

Let's say that you want to help your child learn their times tables, so you want to make it easy to generate a times table for a number, such as the 12 times table:

```
1 x 12 = 12
2 x 12 = 24
...
12 x 12 = 144
```

You previously learned about the for statement earlier in this book, so you know that for can be used to generate repeated lines of output when there is a regular pattern, like the 12 times table, as shown in the following code:

```
for (int row = 1; row <= 12; row++)
{
  Console.WriteLine($"{row} x 12 = {row * 12}");
}
```

However, instead of outputting the 12 times table, we want to make this more flexible, so it could output the times table for any number. We can do this by creating a function.

Writing a times table function

Let's explore functions by creating a function to draw a times table:

1. In your Code folder, create a folder named Chapter04.

2. Start Visual Studio Code. Close any open folder or workspace and save the current workspace in the Chapter04 folder as Chapter04.code-workspace.

3. In the Chapter04 folder, create a folder named WritingFunctions, add it to the Chapter04 workspace, and create a new console application project in WritingFunctions.

4. Modify Program.cs, as shown in the following code:

```
using static System.Console;

namespace WritingFunctions
{
  class Program
  {
    static void TimesTable(byte number)
    {
      WriteLine($"This is the {number} times table:");

      for (int row = 1; row <= 12; row++)
      {
```

```
      WriteLine(
        $"{row} x {number} = {row * number}");
    }
    WriteLine();
  }

  static void RunTimesTable()
  {
    bool isNumber;
    do
    {
      Write("Enter a number between 0 and 255: ");

      isNumber = byte.TryParse(
        ReadLine(), out byte number);

      if (isNumber)
      {
        TimesTable(number);
      }
      else
      {
        WriteLine("You did not enter a valid number!");
      }
    }
    while (isNumber);
  }

  static void Main(string[] args)
  {
    RunTimesTable();
  }
 }
}
```

In the preceding code, note the following:

- We have statically imported the Console type so that we can simplify calls to its methods such as WriteLine.

- We have written a function named TimesTable that must have a byte value passed to it named number.

- TimesTable does not return a value to the caller, so it is declared with the void keyword before its name.

- TimesTable uses a for statement to output the times table for the number passed to it.

- We have written a function named `RunTimesTable` that prompts the user to enter a number, and then calls `TimesTable`, passing it the entered number. It loops while the user enters valid numbers.

- We call `RunTimesTable` in the `Main` method.

5. Run the console application.

6. Enter a number, for example, 6, and then view the result, as shown in the following output:

```
Enter a number between 0 and 255: 6
This is the 6 times table:
1 x 6 = 6
2 x 6 = 12
3 x 6 = 18
4 x 6 = 24
5 x 6 = 30
6 x 6 = 36
7 x 6 = 42
8 x 6 = 48
9 x 6 = 54
10 x 6 = 60
11 x 6 = 66
12 x 6 = 72
```

Writing a function that returns a value

The previous function performed actions (looping and writing to the console), but it did not return a value. Let's say that you need to calculate sales or **valued-added tax (VAT)**. In Europe, VAT rates can range from 8% in Switzerland to 27% in Hungary. In the United States, state sales taxes can range from 0% in Oregon to 8.25% in California:

1. Add a function to the `Program` class named `CalculateTax`, with a second function to run it, as shown in the following code. Before you run the code, note the following:

    - The `CalculateTax` function has two inputs: a parameter named `amount` that will be the amount of money spent, and a parameter named `twoLetterRegionCode` that will be the region the amount is spent in.

    - The `CalculateTax` function will perform a calculation using a `switch` statement, and then return the sales tax or VAT owed on the amount as a `decimal` value; so, before the name of the function, we have declared the data type of the return value.

    - The `RunCalculateTax` function prompts the user to enter an amount and a region code, and then calls `CalculateTax` and outputs the result:

```
static decimal CalculateTax(
  decimal amount, string twoLetterRegionCode)
```

```
{
  decimal rate = 0.0M;

  switch (twoLetterRegionCode)
  {
    case "CH": // Switzerland
      rate = 0.08M;
      break;
    case "DK": // Denmark
    case "NO": // Norway
      rate = 0.25M;
      break;
    case "GB": // United Kingdom
    case "FR": // France
      rate = 0.2M;
      break;
    case "HU": // Hungary
      rate = 0.27M;
      break;
    case "OR": // Oregon
    case "AK": // Alaska
    case "MT": // Montana
      rate = 0.0M;
      break;
    case "ND": // North Dakota
    case "WI": // Wisconsin
    case "ME": // Maryland
    case "VA": // Virginia
      rate = 0.05M;
      break;
    case "CA": // California
      rate = 0.0825M;
      break;
    default: // most US states
      rate = 0.06M;
      break;
  }

  return amount * rate;
}

static void RunCalculateTax()
{
  Write("Enter an amount: ");
  string amountInText = ReadLine();
```

```
    Write("Enter a two-letter region code: ");
    string region = ReadLine();

    if (decimal.TryParse(amountInText, out decimal amount))
    {
      decimal taxToPay = CalculateTax(amount, region);
      WriteLine($"You must pay {taxToPay} in sales tax.");
    }
    else
    {
      WriteLine("You did not enter a valid amount!");
    }
  }
```

2. In the `Main` method, comment the `RunTimesTable` method call, and call the `RunCalculateTax` method, as shown in the following code:

    ```
    // RunTimesTable();
    RunCalculateTax();
    ```

3. Run the console application.

4. Enter an amount like 149 and a valid region code like FR to view the result, as shown in the following output:

    ```
    Enter an amount: 149
    Enter a two-letter region code: FR
    You must pay 29.8 in sales tax.
    ```

Can you think of any problems with the `CalculateTax` function as written? What would happen if the user enters a code like `fr` or `UK`? How could you rewrite the function to improve it? Would using a **switch expression** instead of a **switch statement** be clearer?

Writing mathematical functions

Although you might never create an application that needs to have mathematical functionality, everyone studies mathematics at school, so using mathematics is a common way to learn about functions.

Converting numbers from cardinal to ordinal

Numbers that are used to count are called **cardinal** numbers, for example, 1, 2, and 3, whereas numbers used to order are **ordinal** numbers, for example, 1st, 2nd, and 3rd. Let's create a function to convert cardinals to ordinals:

1. Write a function named `CardinalToOrdinal` that converts a cardinal `int` value into an ordinal `string` value; for example, it converts 1 into 1st, 2 into 2nd, and so on, as shown in the following code:

```
static string CardinalToOrdinal(int number)
{
  switch (number)
  {
    case 11: // special cases for 11th to 13th
    case 12:
    case 13:
      return $"{number}th";
    default:
      int lastDigit = number % 10;

      string suffix = lastDigit switch
      {
        1 => "st",
        2 => "nd",
        3 => "rd",
        _ => "th"
      };
      return $"{number}{suffix}";
  }
}

static void RunCardinalToOrdinal()
{
  for (int number = 1; number <= 40; number++)
  {
    Write($"{CardinalToOrdinal(number)} ");
  }
  WriteLine();
}
```

From the preceding code, note the following:

- The CardinalToOrdinal function has one input: a parameter of the int type named number, and one output: a return value of the string type.

- A switch statement is used to handle the special cases of 11, 12, and 13.

- A switch expression then handles all other cases: if the last digit is 1, then use st as the suffix, if the last digit is 2, then use nd as the suffix, if the last digit is 3, then use rd as the suffix, and if the last digit is anything else, then use th as the suffix.

- The RunCardinalToOrdinal function uses a for statement to loop from 1 to 40, calling the CardinalToOrdinal function for each number and writing the returned string to the console, separated by a space character.

2. In the `Main` method, comment the `RunCalculateTax` method call, and call the `RunCardinalToOrdinal` method, as shown in the following code:

```
// RunTimesTable();
// RunCalculateTax();
RunCardinalToOrdinal();
```

3. Run the console application and view the results, as shown in the following output:

```
1st 2nd 3rd 4th 5th 6th 7th 8th 9th 10th 11th 12th 13th 14th 15th 16th
17th 18th 19th 20th 21st 22nd 23rd 24th 25th 26th 27th 28th 29th 30th 31st
32nd 33rd 34th 35th 36th 37th 38th 39th 40th
```

Calculating factorials with recursion

The factorial of 5 is 120, because factorials are calculated by multiplying the starting number by one less than itself, and then by one less again, and so on, until the number is reduced to 1. An example can be seen in: 5 x 4 x 3 x 2 x 1 = 120.

Factorials are written like this: 5!, where the exclamation mark is read as *bang*, so 5! = 120, that is, *five bang equals one hundred and twenty*. Bang is a good name for factorials because they increase in size very rapidly, just like an explosion.

We will write a function named `Factorial`; this will calculate the factorial for an int passed to it as a parameter. We will use a clever technique called **recursion**, which means a function that calls itself within its implementation, either directly or indirectly:

 More Information: Recursion is clever, but it can lead to problems, such as a stack overflow due to too many function calls because memory is used to store data on every function call and it eventually uses too much. Iteration is a more practical, if less succinct, solution in languages like C#. You can read more about this at the following link: https://en.wikipedia.org/wiki/Recursion_(computer_science)#Recursion_versus_iteration

1. Add a function named `Factorial`, and a function to call it, as shown in the following code:

```
static int Factorial(int number)
{
  if (number < 1)
  {
    return 0;
  }
  else if (number == 1)
  {
    return 1;
  }
  else
```

```
    {
        return number * Factorial(number - 1);
    }
}

static void RunFactorial()
{
    for (int i = 1; i < 15; i++)
    {
        WriteLine($"{i}! = {Factorial(i):N0}");
    }
}
```

As before, there are several noteworthy elements of the preceding code, including the following:

- If the input number is zero or negative, Factorial returns 0.

- If the input number is 1, Factorial returns 1, and therefore stops calling itself. If the input number is larger than one, Factorial multiplies the number by the result of calling itself and passing 1 less than the number. This makes the function recursive.

- RunFactorial uses a for statement to output the factorials of numbers from 1 to 14, calls the Factorial function inside its loop, and then outputs the result, formatted using the code N0, which means number format uses thousands separators with zero decimal places.

2. In the Main method, comment the RunCardinalToOrdinal method call, and call the RunFactorial method.

3. Run the console application, and view the results, as shown in the following output:

```
1! = 1
2! = 2
3! = 6
4! = 24
5! = 120
6! = 720
7! = 5,040
8! = 40,320
9! = 362,880
10! = 3,628,800
11! = 39,916,800
12! = 479,001,600
13! = 1,932,053,504
14! = 1,278,945,280
```

It is not immediately obvious in the previous output, but factorials of 13 and higher will overflow the int type because they are so big. 12! is 479,001,600, which is about half a billion. The maximum positive value that can be stored in an int variable is about two billion. 13! is 6,227,020,800, which is about six billion and when stored in a 32-bit integer it overflows without showing any problem.

What should you do to get notified when an overflow happens? Of course, we could solve the problem for 13! and 14! by using a long 64-bit integer instead of an int 32-bit integer, but we will quickly hit the overflow limit again. The point of this section is to understand that numbers can overflow and how to handle that, not how to calculate factorials!

4. Modify the Factorial function to check for overflows, as shown in the following code:

```
checked // for overflow
{
    return number * Factorial(number - 1);
}
```

5. Modify the RunFactorial function to handle overflow exceptions when calling the Factorial function, as shown in the following code:

```
try
{
    WriteLine($"{i}! = {Factorial(i):N0}");
}
catch (System.OverflowException)
{
    WriteLine($"{i}! is too big for a 32-bit integer.");
}
```

6. Run the console application, and view the results, as shown in the following output:

```
1! = 1
2! = 2
3! = 6
4! = 24
5! = 120
6! = 720
7! = 5,040
8! = 40,320
9! = 362,880
10! = 3,628,800
11! = 39,916,800
12! = 479,001,600
13! is too big for a 32-bit integer.
14! is too big for a 32-bit integer.
```

Documenting functions with XML comments

By default, when calling a function like `CardinalToOrdinal`, Visual Studio Code will show a tooltip with basic information, as shown in the following screenshot:

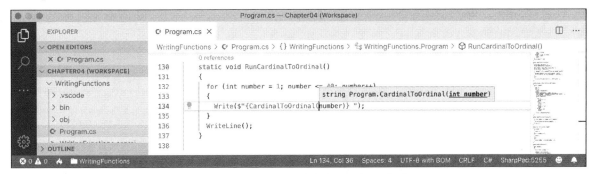

Figure 4.1: A tooltip showing the default simple method signature

Let's improve the tooltip by adding extra information:

1. If you haven't already installed the **C# XML Documentation Comments** extension, do so now. Instructions for installing extensions for Visual Studio Code were covered in *Chapter 1, Hello, C#! Welcome, .NET!*.

2. On the line above the `CardinalToOrdinal` function, type three forward slashes, and note the extension expands this into an XML comment and recognizes that it has a single parameter named `number`.

3. Enter suitable information for the XML documentation comment, as shown in the following code and screenshot:

```
/// <summary>
/// Pass a 32-bit integer and it will be converted into its ordinal
equivalent.
/// </summary>
/// <param name="number">Number is a cardinal value e.g. 1, 2, 3, and so
on.</param>
/// <returns>Number as an ordinal value e.g. 1st, 2nd, 3rd, and so on.</
returns>
```

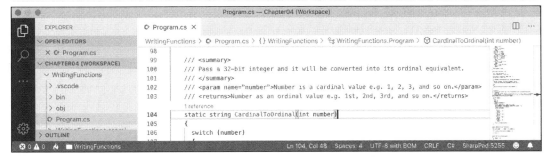

Figure 4.2: XML documentation comment

4. Now, when calling the function, you will see more details, as shown in the following screenshot:

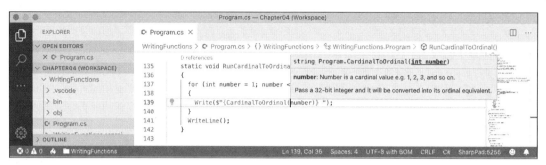

Figure 4.3: A tooltip showing the more detailed method signature

 Good Practice: Add XML documentation comments to all your functions.

Using lambdas in function implementations

F# is Microsoft's strongly typed functional-first programming language that, like C#, compiles to IL to be executed by .NET. Functional languages evolved from lambda calculus; a computational system based only on functions. The code looks more like mathematical functions instead of steps in a recipe.

Some of the important attributes of functional languages are defined in the following list:

- **Modularity**. The same benefit of defining functions in C# applies to functional languages. Break up a large complex code base into smaller pieces.

- **Immutability**. Variables in the C# sense do not exist. Any data value inside a function cannot change. Instead, a new data value can be created from an existing one. This reduces bugs.

- **Maintainability**. Code is cleaner and clearer (for mathematically inclined programmers!)

Since C# 6, Microsoft has worked to add features to the language to support a more functional approach. For example, adding tuples and pattern matching in C# 7, non-null reference types in C# 8, improving pattern matching, and adding records, that is, immutable class objects in C# 9.

In C# 6, Microsoft added support for expression-bodied function members.

The Fibonacci sequence of numbers always starts with 0 and 1. Then the rest of the sequence is generated using the rule of adding together the previous two numbers, as shown in the following sequence of numbers:

```
0 1 1 2 3 5 8 13 21 34 65 ...
```

The next term in the sequence would be 34 + 65, which is 89.

We will use the Fibonacci sequence to illustrate the difference between an imperative and declarative function implementation:

1. Add an imperative function named `FibImperative`, and a function to call it inside a `for` statement that loops from 1 to 30, as shown in the following code:

```
static int FibImperative(int term)
{
  if (term == 1)
  {
    return 0;
  }
  else if (term == 2)
  {
    return 1;
  }
  else
  {
    return FibImperative(term - 1) + FibImperative(term - 2);
  }
}

static void RunFibImperative()
{
  for (int i = 1; i <= 30; i++)
  {
    WriteLine("The {0} term of the Fibonacci sequence is {1:N0}.",
      arg0: CardinalToOrdinal(i),
      arg1: FibImperative(term: i));
  }
}
```

2. In the `Main` method, comment the other method calls, and call the `RunFibImperative` method.

3. Run the console application, and view the results, as shown in the following output:

```
The 1st term of the Fibonacci sequence is 0.
The 2nd term of the Fibonacci sequence is 1.
The 3rd term of the Fibonacci sequence is 1.
The 4th term of the Fibonacci sequence is 2.
The 5th term of the Fibonacci sequence is 3.
The 6th term of the Fibonacci sequence is 5.
The 7th term of the Fibonacci sequence is 8.
The 8th term of the Fibonacci sequence is 13.
The 9th term of the Fibonacci sequence is 21.
The 10th term of the Fibonacci sequence is 34.
```

```
The 11th term of the Fibonacci sequence is 55.
The 12th term of the Fibonacci sequence is 89.
The 13th term of the Fibonacci sequence is 144.
The 14th term of the Fibonacci sequence is 233.
The 15th term of the Fibonacci sequence is 377.
The 16th term of the Fibonacci sequence is 610.
The 17th term of the Fibonacci sequence is 987.
The 18th term of the Fibonacci sequence is 1,597.
The 19th term of the Fibonacci sequence is 2,584.
The 20th term of the Fibonacci sequence is 4,181.
The 21st term of the Fibonacci sequence is 6,765.
The 22nd term of the Fibonacci sequence is 10,946.
The 23rd term of the Fibonacci sequence is 17,711.
The 24th term of the Fibonacci sequence is 28,657.
The 25th term of the Fibonacci sequence is 46,368.
The 26th term of the Fibonacci sequence is 75,025.
The 27th term of the Fibonacci sequence is 121,393.
The 28th term of the Fibonacci sequence is 196,418.
The 29th term of the Fibonacci sequence is 317,811.
The 30th term of the Fibonacci sequence is 514,229.
```

4. Add a declarative function named `FibFunctional`, and a function to call it inside a `for` statement that loops from 1 to 30, as shown in the following code:

```
static int FibFunctional(int term) =>
  term switch
  {
    1 => 0,
    2 => 1,
    _ => FibFunctional(term - 1) + FibFunctional(term - 2)
  };

static void RunFibFunctional()
{
  for (int i = 1; i <= 30; i++)
  {
    WriteLine("The {0} term of the Fibonacci sequence is {1:N0}.",
      arg0: CardinalToOrdinal(i),
      arg1: FibFunctional(term: i));
  }
}
```

5. In the `Main` method, comment the `RunFibImperative` method call, and call the `RunFibFunctional` method.

6. Run the console application and view the results (which will be the same as before).

Debugging during development

In this section, you will learn how to debug problems at development time.

 More Information: It can be tricky setting up the OmniSharp debugger for Visual Studio Code. If you have trouble, try reading the information at the following link: `https://github.com/OmniSharp/omnisharp-vscode/blob/master/debugger.md`

Creating code with a deliberate bug

Let's explore debugging by creating a console app with a deliberate bug that we will then use the OmniSharp debugger tools to track down and fix:

1. In `Chapter04`, create a folder named `Debugging`, add it to the workspace, and create a console application in the folder.

2. Navigate to **View | Command Palette**, enter and select **OmniSharp: Select Project**, and then select the **Debugging** project.

3. When you see the pop-up warning message saying that required assets are missing, click **Yes** to add them.

4. In the `Debugging` folder, open and modify `Program.cs` to define a function with a deliberate bug and call it in the `Main` method, as shown in the following code:

```
using static System.Console;

namespace Debugging
{
  class Program
  {
    static double Add(double a, double b)
    {
      return a * b; // deliberate bug!
    }

    static void Main(string[] args)
    {
      double a = 4.5; // or use var
      double b = 2.5;
      double answer = Add(a, b);
      WriteLine($"{a} + {b} = {answer}");
      ReadLine(); // wait for user to press ENTER
    }
  }
}
```

5. Run the console application and view the result, as shown in the following output:

```
4.5 + 2.5 = 11.25
```

6. Press *Enter* to end the console application.

But wait, there's a bug! 4.5 added to 2.5 should be 7, not 11.25!

We will use the debugging tools to hunt for and squash the bug.

Setting a breakpoint

Breakpoints allow us to mark a line of code that we want to pause at to inspect the program state and find bugs, as the following shows:

1. Click the open curly brace at the beginning of the Main method.

2. Navigate to **Debug | Toggle Breakpoint** or press *F9*. A red circle will then appear in the margin bar on the left-hand side to indicate that a breakpoint has been set, as shown in the following screenshot:

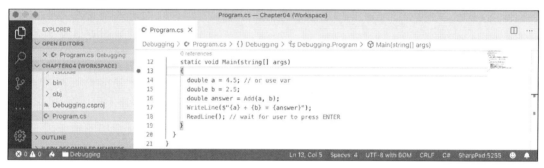

Figure 4.4: Toggling breakpoints

Breakpoints can be toggled with *F9*. You can also left-click in the margin to toggle the breakpoint on and off, or right-click to see more options, such as remove, disable, or edit an existing breakpoint, or adding a breakpoint, conditional breakpoint, or logpoint when a breakpoint does not yet exist.

3. In Visual Studio Code, go to **View | Run**, or press *Ctrl* or *Cmd + Shift + D*. Or you can click **Run** (the triangle "play" and "bug" icon) in the left navigation bar.

4. At the top of the **DEBUG** window, click on the dropdown to the right of the **Start Debugging** button (green triangular "play" button), and select **.NET Core Launch (console) (Debugging)**, as shown in the following screenshot:

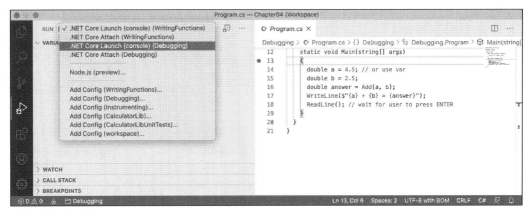

Figure 4.5: Debugging

5. At the top of the **DEBUG** window, click the **Start Debugging** button (green triangular "play" button), or press *F5*. Visual Studio Code starts the console application execution and then pauses when it hits the breakpoint. This is known as **break mode**. The line that will be executed next is highlighted in yellow, and a yellow block points at the line from the margin bar, as shown in the following screenshot:

Figure 4.6: Break mode

Navigating with the debugging toolbar

Visual Studio Code shows a floating toolbar with six buttons to make it easy to access debugging features, as described in the following list:

- **Continue**/*F5* (blue bar and triangle): This button will continue running the program from the current position until it ends or hits another breakpoint.

- **Step Over**/*F10*, **Step Into**/*F11*, and **Step Out**/*Shift + F11* (blue arrows over blue dots): These buttons step through the code statements in various ways, as you will see in a moment.

- **Restart**/*Ctrl* or *Cmd + Shift + F5* (green circular arrow): This button will stop and then immediately restart the program.

- **Stop**/*Shift + F5* (red square): This button will stop the program.

Debugging windows

RUN view on the left-hand side allows you to monitor useful information, such as variables, while you step through your code. It has four sections:

- **VARIABLES,** including **Locals**, which shows the name, value, and type for any local variables automatically. Keep an eye on this window while you step through your code.
- **WATCH,** which shows the value of variables and expressions that you manually enter.
- **CALL STACK,** which shows the stack of function calls.
- **BREAKPOINTS,** which shows all your breakpoints and allows finer control over them.

When in break mode, there is also a useful window at the bottom of the edit area:

- **DEBUG CONSOLE** enables live interaction with your code. You can interrogate the program state, for example, by entering the name of a variable. For example, you can ask a question such as, "What is 1+2?" by typing 1+2 and pressing *Enter*, as shown in the following screenshot:

Figure 4.7: Interrogating the program state

Stepping through code

Let's explore some ways to step through the code:

1. Navigate to **Run | Step Into** or click on the **Step Into** button in the toolbar or press *F11*. The yellow highlight steps forward one line.
2. Navigate to **Run | Step Over** or click on the **Step Over** button in the toolbar or press *F10*. The yellow highlight steps forward one line. At the moment, you can see that there is no difference between using **Step Into** or **Step Over**.
3. Press *F10* again so that the yellow highlight is on the line that calls the Add method, as shown in the following screenshot:

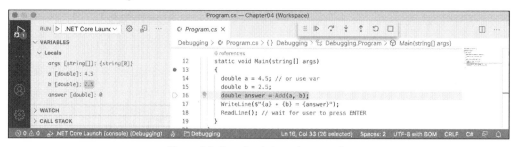

Figure 4.8: Stepping into and over code

The difference between **Step Into** and **Step Over** can be seen when you are about to execute a method call:

- If you were to click on **Step Into**, the debugger steps into the method so that you can step through every line in that method.

- If you were to click on **Step Over**, the whole method is executed in one go; it does not skip over the method without executing it.

4. Click on **Step Into** to step inside the method.

5. Select the expression a * b, right-click the expression, and select **Add to Watch…**.

   The expression is added to the **WATCH** window, showing that this operator is multiplying a by b to give the result 11.25. We can see that this is the bug, as shown in the following screenshot:

Figure 4.9: Adding elements to the WATCH window

If you hover your mouse pointer over the a or b parameters in the code editing window, then a tooltip appears showing the current value.

6. Fix the bug by changing * to + in both the watch expression and in the function.

7. Stop, recompile, and restart by clicking the green circular arrow **Restart** button or press *Ctrl* or *Cmd + Shift + F5*.

8. Step into the function, take a minute to note how it now calculates correctly, click the **Continue** button or press *F5*, and note that when writing to the console during debugging, the output appears in the **DEBUG CONSOLE** window instead of the **TERMINAL** window.

Customizing breakpoints

It is easy to make more complex breakpoints:

1. If you are still debugging, click the **Stop** button in the floating toolbar, or navigate to **Run | Stop Debugging**, or press *Shift + F5*.

2. In the **BREAKPOINTS** window, click the last button in its mini toolbar to **Remove All Breakpoints**, or navigate to **Run | Remove All Breakpoints**.

3. Click on the WriteLine statement.

4. Set a breakpoint by pressing *F9* or navigating to **Run | Toggle Breakpoint**.

5. Right-click the breakpoint and choose **Edit Breakpoint…**.

6. Enter an expression, like the answer variable must be greater than 9, and note the expression must evaluate to true for the breakpoint to activate, as shown in the following screenshot:

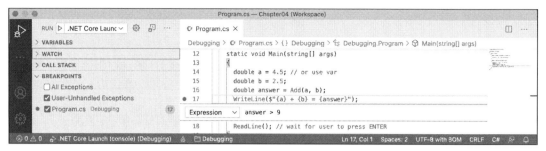

Figure 4.10: Customizing a breakpoint

7. Start debugging and note the breakpoint is not hit.

8. Stop debugging.

9. Edit the breakpoint and change its expression to less than 9.

10. Start debugging and note the breakpoint is hit.

11. Stop debugging.

12. Edit the breakpoint and select **Hit Count**, then enter a number like 3, meaning that you would have to hit the breakpoint three times before it activates.

13. Hover your mouse over the breakpoint's red circle to see a summary, as shown in the following screenshot:

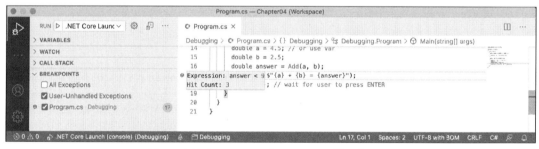

Figure 4.11: A summary of a customized breakpoint

You have now fixed a bug using some debugging tools and seen some advanced possibilities for setting breakpoints.

> **More Information**: You can read more about using the Visual Studio Code debugger at the following link: https://code.visualstudio.com/docs/editor/debugging

Logging during development and runtime

Once you believe that all the bugs have been removed from your code, you would then compile a release version and deploy the application, so that people can use it. But no code is ever bug free, and during runtime unexpected errors can occur.

End users are notoriously bad at remembering, admitting to, and then accurately describing what they were doing when an error occurred, so you should not rely on them accurately providing useful information to reproduce the problem in order to understand what caused the problem and then fix it.

> **Good Practice**: Add code throughout your application to log what is happening, and especially when exceptions occur, so that you can review the logs and use them to trace the issue and fix the problem.

There are two types that can be used to add simple logging to your code: Debug and Trace.

Before we delve into them in more detail, let's look at a quick overview of each one:

- Debug is used to add logging that gets written during development.
- Trace is used to add logging that gets written during both development and runtime.

Instrumenting with Debug and Trace

You have seen the use of the Console type and its WriteLine method to provide output to the console or **TERMINAL** or **DEBUG CONSOLE** windows in Visual Studio Code.

We also have a pair of types named Debug and Trace that have more flexibility in where they write out to.

> **More Information**: You can read more about the Debug class at the following link: https://docs.microsoft.com/en-us/dotnet/api/system.diagnostics.debug

The Debug and Trace classes can write to any **trace listener**. A trace listener is a type that can be configured to write output anywhere you like when the Trace.WriteLine method is called. There are several trace listeners provided by .NET, and you can even make your own by inheriting from the TraceListener type.

> **More Information**: You can see the list of trace listeners that derive from TraceListener at the following link: https://docs.microsoft.com/en-us/dotnet/api/system.diagnostics.tracelistener

Writing to the default trace listener

One trace listener, the DefaultTraceListener class, is configured automatically and writes to Visual Studio Code's **DEBUG CONSOLE** window. You can configure others manually using code:

1. In Chapter04, create a folder named Instrumenting, add it to the workspace, and create a console application project in the folder.

2. Modify Program.cs, as shown in the following code:

```csharp
using System.Diagnostics;

namespace Instrumenting
{
  class Program
  {
    static void Main(string[] args)
    {
      Debug.WriteLine("Debug says, I am watching!");
      Trace.WriteLine("Trace says, I am watching!");
    }
  }
}
```

3. Navigate to the **RUN** view.

4. Start debugging by launching the Instrumenting console application, and note that **DEBUG CONSOLE** shows the two messages in blue, mixed with other debugging information like loaded assembly DLLs in orange, as shown in the following screenshot:

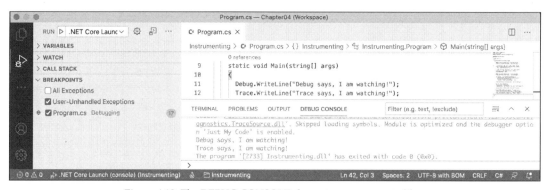

Figure 4.12: The DEBUG CONSOLE shows two messages in blue

Configuring trace listeners

Now, we will configure another trace listener that will write to a text file:

1. Modify the code to add a statement to import the System.IO namespace, create a
    new text file for logging to, and enable automatic flushing of the buffer, as shown
    highlighted in the following code:

```
using System.Diagnostics;
using System.IO;

namespace Instrumenting
{
  class Program
  {
    static void Main(string[] args)
    {
      // write to a text file in the project folder
      Trace.Listeners.Add(new TextWriterTraceListener(
        File.CreateText("log.txt")));

      // text writer is buffered, so this option calls
      // Flush() on all listeners after writing
      Trace.AutoFlush = true;

      Debug.WriteLine("Debug says, I am watching!");
      Trace.WriteLine("Trace says, I am watching!");
    }
  }
}
```

Any type that represents a file usually implements a buffer to improve performance.
Instead of writing immediately to the file, data is written to an in-memory buffer and
only once the buffer is full will it be written in one chunk to the file. This behavior can
be confusing while debugging because we do not immediately see the results! Enabling
AutoFlush means it calls the Flush method automatically after every write.

2. Run the console application by entering the following command in the **TERMINAL**
    window for the Instrumenting project and note that nothing will appear to have
    happened:

```
dotnet run --configuration Release
```

3. In **EXPLORER**, open the file named log.txt and note that it contains the message,
    "Trace says, I am watching!".

4. Run the console application by entering the following command in the **TERMINAL**
    window for the Instrumenting project:

```
dotnet run --configuration Debug
```

5. In **EXPLORER**, open the file named `log.txt` and note that it contains both the message, "Debug says, I am watching!" and "Trace says, I am watching!".

 Good Practice: When running with the `Debug` configuration, both `Debug` and `Trace` are active and will show their output in **DEBUG CONSOLE**. When running with the `Release` configuration, only the `Trace` output is shown. You can therefore use `Debug.WriteLine` calls liberally throughout your code, knowing they will be stripped out automatically when you build the release version of your application.

Switching trace levels

The `Trace.WriteLine` calls are left in your code even after release. So, it would be great to have fine control over when they are output. This is something we can do with a **trace switch**.

The value of a trace switch can be set using a number or a word. For example, the number 3 can be replaced with the word **Info**, as shown in the following table:

Number	Word	Description
0	Off	This will output nothing.
1	Error	This will output only errors.
2	Warning	This will output errors and warnings.
3	Info	This will output errors, warnings, and information.
4	Verbose	This will output all levels.

Let's explore using trace switches. We will need to add some packages to enable loading configuration settings from a JSON `appsettings` file:

1. Navigate to the **TERMINAL** window.
2. Enter the following command:
    ```
    dotnet add package Microsoft.Extensions.Configuration
    ```
3. Enter the following command:
    ```
    dotnet add package Microsoft.Extensions.Configuration.Binder
    ```
4. Enter the following command:
    ```
    dotnet add package Microsoft.Extensions.Configuration.Json
    ```
5. Enter the following command:
    ```
    dotnet add package Microsoft.Extensions.Configuration.FileExtensions
    ```
6. Open `Instrumenting.csproj` and note the extra `<ItemGroup>` section with the extra packages, as shown highlighted in the following markup:
    ```
    <Project Sdk="Microsoft.NET.Sdk">
      <PropertyGroup>
    ```

```
      <OutputType>Exe</OutputType>
      <TargetFramework>net5.0</TargetFramework>
    </PropertyGroup>
  <ItemGroup>
    <PackageReference
      Include="Microsoft.Extensions.Configuration"
      Version="5.0.0" />
    <PackageReference
      Include="Microsoft.Extensions.Configuration.Binder"
      Version="5.0.0" />
    <PackageReference
      Include="Microsoft.Extensions.Configuration.FileExtensions"
      Version="5.0.0" />
    <PackageReference
      Include="Microsoft.Extensions.Configuration.Json"
      Version="5.0.0" />
  </ItemGroup>
</Project>
```

7. Add a file named appsettings.json to the Instrumenting folder.

8. Modify appsettings.json, as shown in the following code:

```
{
  "PacktSwitch": {
    "Level": "Info"
  }
}
```

9. In Program.cs, import the Microsoft.Extensions.Configuration namespace.

10. Add some statements to the end of the Main method to create a configuration builder that looks in the current folder for a file named appsettings.json, build the configuration, create a trace switch, set its level by binding to the configuration, and then output the four trace switch levels, as shown in the following code:

```
var builder = new ConfigurationBuilder()
  .SetBasePath(Directory.GetCurrentDirectory())
  .AddJsonFile("appsettings.json",
  optional: true, reloadOnChange: true);

IConfigurationRoot configuration = builder.Build();

var ts = new TraceSwitch(
  displayName: "PacktSwitch",
  description: "This switch is set via a JSON config.");

configuration.GetSection("PacktSwitch").Bind(ts);
```

```
Trace.WriteLineIf(ts.TraceError, "Trace error");
Trace.WriteLineIf(ts.TraceWarning, "Trace warning");
Trace.WriteLineIf(ts.TraceInfo, "Trace information");
Trace.WriteLineIf(ts.TraceVerbose, "Trace verbose");
```

11. Set a breakpoint on the `Bind` statement.

12. Start debugging the `Instrumenting` console application.

13. In the **VARIABLES** window, expand the `ts` variable watch, and note that its `Level` is `Off` and its `TraceError`, `TraceWarning`, and so on are all `false`.

14. Step into the call to the `Bind` method by clicking the **Step Into** or **Step Over** buttons or pressing *F11* or *F10* and note the `ts` variable watch updates to `Info` level.

15. Step into or over the four calls to `Trace.WriteLineIf` and note that all levels up to `Info` are written to the **DEBUG CONSOLE** but not `Verbose`, as shown in the following screenshot:

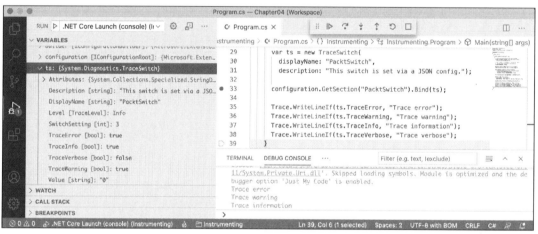

Figure 4.13: Different trace levels shown in the DEBUG CONSOLE

16. Stop debugging.

17. Modify `appsettings.json` to set a level of 2, which means warning, as shown in the following JSON file:

```json
{
  "PacktSwitch": {
    "Level": "2"
  }
}
```

18. Save the changes.

19. Run the console application by entering the following command in the **TERMINAL** window for the `Instrumenting` project:

```
dotnet run --configuration Release
```

20. Open the file named `log.txt` and note that this time, only trace error and warning levels are the output of the four potential trace levels, as shown in the following text file:

```
Trace says, I am watching!
Trace error
Trace warning
```

If no argument is passed, the default trace switch level is Off (0), so none of the switch levels are output.

Unit testing functions

Fixing bugs in code is expensive. The earlier that a bug is discovered in the development process, the less expensive it will be to fix.

Unit testing is a good way to find bugs early in the development process. Some developers even follow the principle that programmers should create unit tests before they write code, and this is called **Test-Driven Development** (TDD).

> **More Information**: You can learn more about TDD at the following link: https://en.wikipedia.org/wiki/Test-driven_development

Microsoft has a proprietary unit testing framework known as **MS Test**; however, we will use the free and open source third-party framework **xUnit.net**.

Creating a class library that needs testing

First, we will create a function that needs testing. We will create it in a class library project. A class library is a package of code that can be distributed and referenced by other .NET applications:

1. Inside the Chapter04 folder, create two subfolders named CalculatorLib and CalculatorLibUnitTests, and add them each to the workspace.

2. Navigate to **Terminal | New Terminal** and select CalculatorLib.

3. Enter the following command in **TERMINAL**:
   ```
   dotnet new classlib
   ```

4. Rename the file named Class1.cs to Calculator.cs.

5. Modify the file to define a `Calculator` class (with a deliberate bug!), as shown in the following code:

```
namespace Packt
{
  public class Calculator
  {
    public double Add(double a, double b)
    {
      return a * b;
    }
  }
}
```

6. Enter the following command in **TERMINAL**:

```
dotnet build
```

7. Navigate to **Terminal | New Terminal** and select `CalculatorLibUnitTests`.

8. Enter the following command in **TERMINAL**:

```
dotnet new xunit
```

9. Click on the file named `CalculatorLibUnitTests.csproj`, and modify the configuration to add an item group with a project reference to the `CalculatorLib` project, as shown highlighted in the following markup:

```
<Project Sdk="Microsoft.NET.Sdk">
  <PropertyGroup>
    <TargetFramework>net5.0</TargetFramework>
    <IsPackable>false</IsPackable>
  </PropertyGroup>
  <ItemGroup>
    <PackageReference Include="Microsoft.NET.Test.Sdk"
      Version="16.8.0" />
    <PackageReference Include="xunit"
      Version="2.4.1" />
    <PackageReference Include="xunit.runner.visualstudio"
      Version="2.4.3" />
    <PackageReference Include="coverlet.collector"
      Version="1.3.0" />
  </ItemGroup>
  <ItemGroup>
    <ProjectReference
      Include="..\CalculatorLib\CalculatorLib.csproj" />
  </ItemGroup>
</Project>
```

More Information: You can view Microsoft's NuGet feed for the latest `Microsoft.NET.Test.Sdk` and other packages at the following link: https://www.nuget.org/

10. Rename the file `UnitTest1.cs` to `CalculatorUnitTests.cs`.

11. Enter the following command in **TERMINAL**:

```
dotnet build
```

Writing unit tests

A well-written unit test will have three parts:

- **Arrange**: This part will declare and instantiate variables for input and output.
- **Act**: This part will execute the unit that you are testing. In our case, that means calling the method that we want to test.
- **Assert**: This part will make one or more assertions about the output. An assertion is a belief that, if not true, indicates a failed test. For example, when adding 2 and 2, we would expect the result to be 4.

Now, we will write the unit tests for the `Calculator` class:

1. Open `CalculatorUnitTests.cs`, rename the class to `CalculatorUnitTests`, import the `Packt` namespace, and modify it to have two test methods for adding 2 and 2, and adding 2 and 3, as shown in the following code:

```csharp
using Packt;
using Xunit;

namespace CalculatorLibUnitTests
{
  public class CalculatorUnitTests
  {
    [Fact]
    public void TestAdding2And2()
    {
      // arrange
      double a = 2;
      double b = 2;
      double expected = 4;
      var calc = new Calculator();

      // act
      double actual = calc.Add(a, b);
```

```
      // assert
      Assert.Equal(expected, actual);
   }

   [Fact]
   public void TestAdding2And3()
   {
      // arrange
      double a = 2;
      double b = 3;
      double expected = 5;
      var calc = new Calculator();

      // act
      double actual = calc.Add(a, b);

      // assert
      Assert.Equal(expected, actual);
   }
 }
}
```

Running unit tests

Now we are ready to run the unit tests and see the results:

1. In the `CalculatorLibUnitTest` **TERMINAL** window, enter the following command:

   ```
   dotnet test
   ```

2. Note that the results indicate that two tests ran, one test passed, and one test failed, as shown in the following screenshot:

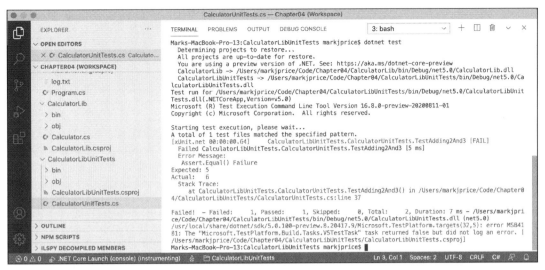

Figure 4.14: The unit test results

3. Fix the bug in the Add method.

4. Run the unit tests again to see that the bug has now been fixed.

5. Close the workspace.

Practicing and exploring

Test your knowledge and understanding by answering some questions, get some hands-on practice, and explore with deeper research into the topics covered in this chapter.

Exercise 4.1 – Test your knowledge

Answer the following questions. If you get stuck, try Googling the answers if necessary:

1. What does the C# keyword void mean?

2. What are some differences between imperative and functional programming styles?

3. In Visual Studio Code, what is the difference between pressing *F5*, *Ctrl* or *Cmd* + *F5*, *Shift* + *F5*, and *Ctrl* or *Cmd* + *Shift* + *F5*?

4. Where does the Trace.WriteLine method write its output to?

5. What are the five trace levels?

6. What is the difference between Debug and Trace?

7. When writing a unit test, what are the three As?

8. When writing a unit test using xUnit, what attribute must you decorate the test methods with?

9. What dotnet command executes xUnit tests?

10. What is TDD?

Exercise 4.2 – Practice writing functions with debugging and unit testing

Prime factors are the combination of the smallest prime numbers that, when multiplied together, will produce the original number. Consider the following example:

- Prime factors of 4 are: 2 x 2
- Prime factors of 7 are: 7
- Prime factors of 30 are: 5 x 3 x 2
- Prime factors of 40 are: 5 x 2 x 2 x 2
- Prime factors of 50 are: 5 x 5 x 2

Create a workspace named `PrimeFactors` to contain three projects; a class library with a method named `PrimeFactors` that, when passed an `int` variable as a parameter, returns a string showing its prime factors; a unit tests project; and a console application to use it.

To keep it simple, you can assume that the largest number entered will be 1000.

Use the debugging tools and write unit tests to ensure that your function works correctly with multiple inputs and returns the correct output.

Exercise 4.3 – Explore topics

Use the following links to read more about the topics covered in this chapter:

- **Debugging in Visual Studio Code**: https://code.visualstudio.com/docs/editor/debugging
- **Instructions for setting up the .NET debugger**: https://github.com/OmniSharp/omnisharp-vscode/blob/master/debugger.md
- **System.Diagnostics Namespace**: https://docs.microsoft.com/en-us/dotnet/core/api/system.diagnostics
- **Unit testing in .NET**: https://docs.microsoft.com/en-us/dotnet/core/testing/
- **xUnit.net**: http://xunit.github.io/

Summary

In this chapter, you learned how to write reusable functions, in both an imperative and functional style, and then how to use the Visual Studio Code debugging and diagnostic features to fix any bugs in them, and finally you learned how to unit test your code.

In the next chapter, you will learn how to build your own types using object-oriented programming techniques.

05

Building Your Own Types with Object-Oriented Programming

This chapter is about making your own types using **object-oriented programming** (OOP). You will learn about all the different categories of members that a type can have, including fields to store data and methods to perform actions. You will use OOP concepts such as aggregation and encapsulation. You will also learn about language features such as tuple syntax support, out variables, inferred tuple names, and default literals.

This chapter will cover the following topics:

- Talking about OOP
- Building class libraries
- Storing data with fields
- Writing and calling methods
- Controlling access with properties and indexers
- Pattern matching with objects
- Working with records

Talking about object-oriented programming

An object in the real world is a thing, such as a car or a person, whereas an object in programming often represents something in the real world, such as a product or bank account, but this can also be something more abstract.

In C#, we use the class (mostly) or struct (sometimes) C# keywords to define a type of object. You will learn about the difference between classes and structs in *Chapter 6, Implementing Interfaces and Inheriting Classes*. You can think of a type as being a blueprint or template for an object.

The concepts of object-oriented programming are briefly described here:

- **Encapsulation** is the combination of the data and actions that are related to an object. For example, a `BankAccount` type might have data, such as `Balance` and `AccountName`, as well as actions, such as `Deposit` and `Withdraw`. When encapsulating, you often want to control what can access those actions and the data, for example, restricting how the internal state of an object can be accessed or modified from the outside.

- **Composition** is about what an object is made of. For example, a car is composed of different parts, such as four wheels, several seats, and an engine.

- **Aggregation** is about what can be combined with an object. For example, a person is not part of a car object, but they could sit in the driver's seat and then becomes the car's driver — two separate objects that are aggregated together to form a new component.

- **Inheritance** is about reusing code by having a subclass derive from a base or superclass. All functionality in the base class is inherited by and becomes available in the derived class. For example, the **base** or **super** `Exception` class has some members that have the same implementation across all exceptions, and the sub or derived `SqlException` class inherits those members and has extra members only relevant to when a SQL database exception occurs, like a property for the database connection.

- **Abstraction** is about capturing the core idea of an object and ignoring the details or specifics. C# has an `abstract` keyword which formalizes the concept. If a class is not explicitly `abstract`, then it can be described as being concrete. Base or superclasses are often abstract, for example, the superclass `Stream` is `abstract` and its subclasses, like `FileStream` and `MemoryStream`, are concrete. Only concrete classes can be used to create objects; abstract classes can only be used as the base for other classes because they are missing some implementation. Abstraction is a tricky balance. If you make a class more abstract, more classes will be able to inherit from it, but at the same time, there will be less functionality to share.

- **Polymorphism** is about allowing a derived class to override an inherited action to provide custom behavior.

Building class libraries

Class library assemblies group types together into easily deployable units (DLL files). Apart from when you learned about unit testing, you have only created console applications to contain your code. To make the code that you write reusable across multiple projects, you should put it in class library assemblies, just like Microsoft does.

Creating a class library

The first task is to create a reusable .NET class library:

1. In your existing `Code` folder, create a folder named `Chapter05`, with a subfolder named `PacktLibrary`.

2. In Visual Studio Code, navigate to **File | Save Workspace As...**, enter the name Chapter05, select the Chapter05 folder, and click **Save**.

3. Navigate to **File | Add Folder to Workspace...**, select the **PacktLibrary** folder, and click **Add**.

4. In **TERMINAL**, enter the following command: dotnet new classlib.

5. Open the PacktLibrary.csproj file, and note that by default class libraries target .NET 5 and therefore can only work with other .NET 5-compatible assemblies, as shown in the following markup:

```
<Project Sdk="Microsoft.NET.Sdk">

  <PropertyGroup>
    <TargetFramework>net5.0</TargetFramework>
  </PropertyGroup>

</Project>
```

6. Modify the target framework to support .NET Standard 2.0, as shown in the following markup:

```
<Project Sdk="Microsoft.NET.Sdk">

  <PropertyGroup>
    <TargetFramework>netstandard2.0</TargetFramework>
  </PropertyGroup>

</Project>
```

7. Save and close the file.

8. In **TERMINAL**, compile the project, as shown in the following command: dotnet build.

 Good Practice: To use the latest C# language and .NET platform features, put types in a .NET 5 class library. To support legacy .NET platforms like .NET Core, .NET Framework, and Xamarin, put types that you might reuse in a .NET Standard 2.0 class library.

Defining a class

The next task is to define a class that will represent a person:

1. In **EXPLORER**, rename the file named Class1.cs to Person.cs.

2. Click Person.cs to open it and change the class name to Person.

3. Change the namespace to Packt.Shared.

Good Practice: We're doing this because it is important to put your classes in a logically named namespace. A better namespace name would be domain-specific, for example, `System.Numerics` for types related to advanced numbers, but in this case, the types we will create are `Person`, `BankAccount`, and `WondersOfTheWorld` and they do not have a normal domain.

Your class file should now look like the following code:

```
using System;

namespace Packt.Shared
{
  public class Person
  {
  }
}
```

Note that the C# keyword `public` is applied before `class`. This keyword is called an **access modifier**, and it allows for all the other code to access this class.

If you do not explicitly apply the `public` keyword, then it will only be accessible within the assembly that defined it. This is because the implicit access modifier for a class is `internal`. We need this class to be accessible outside the assembly, so we must make sure it is `public`.

Understanding members

This type does not yet have any members encapsulated within it. We will create some over the following pages. Members can be fields, methods, or specialized versions of both. You'll find a description of them here:

- **Fields** are used to store data. There are also three specialized categories of field, as shown in the following bullets:
    - **Constant**: The data never changes. The compiler literally copies the data into any code that reads it.
    - **Read-only**: The data cannot change after the class is instantiated, but the data can be calculated or loaded from an external source at the time of instantiation.
    - **Event**: The data references one or more methods that you want to execute when something happens, such as clicking on a button, or responding to a request from other code. Events will be covered in *Chapter 6, Implementing Interfaces and Inheriting Classes.*

- **Methods** are used to execute statements. You saw some examples when you learned about functions in *Chapter 4, Writing, Debugging, and Testing Functions*. There are also four specialized categories of method:

  - **Constructor**: The statements execute when you use the new keyword to allocate memory and instantiate a class.

  - **Property**: The statements execute when you get or set data. The data is commonly stored in a field but could be stored externally, or calculated at runtime. Properties are the preferred way to encapsulate fields unless the memory address of the field needs to be exposed.

  - **Indexer**: The statements execute when you get or set data using array syntax [ ].

  - **Operator**: The statements execute when you use an operator like + and / on operands of your type.

Instantiating a class

In this section, we will make an **instance** of the Person class, which is described as instantiating a class.

Referencing an assembly

Before we can instantiate a class, we need to reference the assembly that contains it:

1. Create a subfolder under Chapter05 named PeopleApp.

2. In **Visual Studio Code**, navigate to **File | Add Folder to Workspace…**, select the PeopleApp folder, and click **Add**.

3. Navigate to **Terminal | New Terminal** and select **PeopleApp**.

4. In **TERMINAL**, enter the following command: dotnet new console.

5. In **EXPLORER**, click on the file named PeopleApp.csproj.

6. Add a project reference to PacktLibrary, as shown highlighted in the following markup:

```
<Project Sdk="Microsoft.NET.Sdk">
  <PropertyGroup>
    <OutputType>Exe</OutputType>
    <TargetFramework>net5.0</TargetFramework>
  </PropertyGroup>
  <ItemGroup>
    <ProjectReference Include="../PacktLibrary/PacktLibrary.csproj" />
  </ItemGroup>
</Project>
```

7. In **TERMINAL**, enter a command to compile the PeopleApp project and its dependency PacktLibrary project, as shown in the following command: dotnet build.

8. Select PeopleApp as the active project for OmniSharp.

Importing a namespace to use a type

Now, we are ready to write statements to work with the Person class:

1. In **Visual Studio Code**, in the PeopleApp folder, open Program.cs.

2. At the top of the Program.cs file, enter statements to import the namespace for our People class and statically import the Console class, as shown in the following code:

```
using Packt.Shared;
using static System.Console;
```

3. In the Main method, enter statements to:

   • Create an instance of the Person type.

   • Output the instance using a textual description of itself.

   The new keyword allocates memory for the object and initializes any internal data. We could use Person in place of the var keyword, but the use of var involves less typing and is still just as clear, as shown in the following code:

```
var bob = new Person();
WriteLine(bob.ToString());
```

   You might be wondering, "Why does the bob variable have a method named ToString? The Person class is empty!" Don't worry, we're about to find out!

4. Run the application, by entering dotnet run in **TERMINAL**, and then view the result, as shown in the following output:

```
Packt.Shared.Person
```

Managing multiple files

If you have multiple files that you want to work with at the same time, then you can put them side by side as you edit them:

1. In **EXPLORER**, expand the two projects.

2. Open both Person.cs and Program.cs.

3. Click, hold, and drag the edit window tab for one of your open files to arrange them so that you can see both Person.cs and Program.cs at the same time.

You can click on the **Split Editor Right** button or press *Cmd + * so that you have two files open side by side vertically.

 More Information: You can read more about working with the Visual Studio Code user interface at the following link: https://code.visualstudio.com/docs/getstarted/userinterface

Understanding objects

Although our Person class did not explicitly choose to inherit from a type, all types ultimately inherit directly or indirectly from a special type named System.Object.

The implementation of the ToString method in the System.Object type simply outputs the full namespace and type name.

Back in the original Person class, we could have explicitly told the compiler that Person inherits from the System.Object type, as shown in the following code:

```
public class Person : System.Object
```

When class B **inherits** from class A, we say that A is the **base** or **superclass** and B is the **derived** or **subclass**. In this case, System.Object is the base or superclass and Person is the derived or subclass.

You can also use the C# alias keyword object:

```
public class Person : object
```

Inheriting from System.Object

Let's make our class explicitly inherit from object and then review what members all objects have:

1. Modify your Person class to explicitly inherit from object.
2. Click inside the object keyword and press *F12*, or right-click on the object keyword and choose **Go to Definition**.

You will see the Microsoft-defined `System.Object` type and its members. This is something you don't need to understand the details of yet, but notice that it has a method named `ToString`, as shown in the following screenshot:

```
●  ●  ●                              [metadata] Object.cs — Chapter05 (Workspace)
        ⚙ [metadata] Object.cs  ✕
    1      #region Assembly netstandard, Version=2.0.0.0, Culture=neutral, PublicKeyToken=cc7b13ffcd2ddd51
    2      // netstandard.dll
    3      #endregion
    4
    5      namespace System
    6      {
    7        public class Object
    8        {
    9          public Object();
   10
   11          ~Object();
   12
   13          public static bool Equals(Object objA, Object objB);
   14          public static bool ReferenceEquals(Object objA, Object objB);
   15          public virtual bool Equals(Object obj);
   16          public virtual int GetHashCode();
   17          public Type GetType();
   18          public virtual string ToString();
   19          protected Object MemberwiseClone();
   20        }
   21      }
⊗ 0 ⚠ 0   ♠   ■ PeopleApp                              Ln 7, Col 16   Spaces: 2   C#   SharpPad:5255   ☺  ▲
```

Figure 5.1: System.Object class definition

 Good Practice: Assume other programmers know that if inheritance is not specified, the class will inherit from `System.Object`.

Storing data within fields

In this section, we will be defining a selection of fields in the class in order to store information about a person.

Defining fields

Let's say that we have decided that a person is composed of a name and a date of birth. We will encapsulate these two values inside a person, and the values will be visible outside it.

Inside the `Person` class, write statements to declare two public fields for storing a person's name and date of birth, as shown in the following code:

```
public class Person : object
{
  // fields
  public string Name;
  public DateTime DateOfBirth;
}
```

You can use any type for a field, including arrays and collections such as lists and dictionaries. These would be used if you needed to store multiple values in one named field. In this example, a person only has one name and one date of birth.

Understanding access modifiers

Part of encapsulation is choosing how visible the members are.

Note that, as we did with the class, we explicitly applied the `public` keyword to these fields. If we hadn't, then they would be implicitly `private` to the class, which means they are accessible only inside the class.

There are four access modifier keywords, and two combinations of access modifier keywords that you can apply to a class member, such as a field or method, as shown in the following table:

Access Modifier	Description
private	Member is accessible inside the type only. This is the default.
internal	Member is accessible inside the type and any type in the same assembly.
protected	Member is accessible inside the type and any type that inherits from the type.
public	Member is accessible everywhere.
internal protected	Member is accessible inside the type, any type in the same assembly, and any type that inherits from the type. Equivalent to a fictional access modifier named `internal_or_protected`.
private protected	Member is accessible inside the type or any type that inherits from the type and is in the same assembly. Equivalent to a fictional access modifier named `internal_and_protected`. This combination is only available with C# 7.2 or later.

> **Good Practice**: Explicitly apply one of the access modifiers to all type members, even if you want to use the implicit access modifier for members, which is private. Additionally, fields should usually be `private` or `protected`, and you should then create `public` properties to get or set the field values. This is because it controls access. You will do this later in the chapter.

Setting and outputting field values

Now we will use those fields in the console app:

1. At the top of `Program.cs`, make sure the `System` namespace is imported.

2. Inside the `Main` method, change the statements to set the person's name and date of birth, and then output those fields nicely formatted, as shown in the following code:

```
var bob = new Person();
bob.Name = "Bob Smith";
bob.DateOfBirth = new DateTime(1965, 12, 22);
```

```
WriteLine(
    format: "{0} was born on {1:dddd, d MMMM yyyy}",
    arg0: bob.Name,
    arg1: bob.DateOfBirth);
```

We could have used string interpolation too, but for long strings it will wrap over multiple lines, which can be harder to read in a printed book. In the code examples in this book, remember that {0} is a placeholder for arg0, and so on.

3. Run the application and view the result, as shown in the following output:

```
Bob Smith was born on Wednesday, 22 December 1965
```

The format code for arg1 is made of several parts. dddd means the name of the day of the week. d means the number of the day of the month. MMMM means the name of the month. Lowercase m is used for minutes in time values. yyyy means the full number of the year. yy would mean the two-digit year.

You can also initialize fields using a shorthand object initializer syntax using curly braces. Let's see how.

4. Add the following code underneath the existing code to create another new person. Notice the different format code for the date of birth when writing to the console:

```
var alice = new Person
{
    Name = "Alice Jones",
    DateOfBirth = new DateTime(1998, 3, 7)
};

WriteLine(
    format: "{0} was born on {1:dd MMM yy}",
    arg0: alice.Name,
    arg1: alice.DateOfBirth);
```

5. Run the application and view the result, as shown in the following output:

```
Bob Smith was born on Wednesday, 22 December 1965
Alice Jones was born on 07 Mar 98
```

Remember that your output may look different based on your locale, that is, language and culture.

Storing a value using an enum type

Sometimes, a value needs to be one of a limited set of options. For example, there are seven ancient wonders of the world, and a person may have one favorite. At other times, a value needs to be a combination of a limited set of options. For example, a person may have a bucket list of ancient world wonders they want to visit.

We are able to store this data by defining an enum type.

An enum type is a very efficient way of storing one or more choices because, internally, it uses integer values in combination with a lookup table of string descriptions:

1. Add a new file to the class library by selecting PacktLibrary, clicking on the **New File** button in the mini toolbar, and entering the name WondersOfTheAncientWorld.cs.

2. Modify the WondersOfTheAncientWorld.cs file, as shown in the following code:

```
namespace Packt.Shared
{
  public enum WondersOfTheAncientWorld
  {
    GreatPyramidOfGiza,
    HangingGardensOfBabylon,
    StatueOfZeusAtOlympia,
    TempleOfArtemisAtEphesus,
    MausoleumAtHalicarnassus,
    ColossusOfRhodes,
    LighthouseOfAlexandria
  }
}
```

3. In the Person class, add the following statement to your list of fields:

```
public WondersOfTheAncientWorld FavoriteAncientWonder;
```

4. In the Main method of Program.cs, add the following statements:

```
bob.FavoriteAncientWonder =
  WondersOfTheAncientWorld.StatueOfZeusAtOlympia;

WriteLine(format:
  "{0}'s favorite wonder is {1}. Its integer is {2}.",
  arg0: bob.Name,
  arg1: bob.FavoriteAncientWonder,
  arg2: (int)bob.FavoriteAncientWonder);
```

5. Run the application and view the result, as shown in the following output:

```
Bob Smith's favorite wonder is StatueOfZeusAtOlympia. Its integer is 2.
```

The enum value is internally stored as an int for efficiency. The int values are automatically assigned starting at 0, so the third world wonder in our enum has a value of 2. You can assign int values that are not listed in the enum. They will output as the int value instead of a name since a match will not be found.

Storing multiple values using an enum type

For the bucket list, we could create a collection of instances of the enum, and collections will be explained later in this chapter, but there is a better way. We can combine multiple choices into a single value using **flags**:

1. Modify the enum by decorating it with the [System.Flags] attribute.

2. Explicitly set a byte value for each wonder that represents different bit columns, as shown in the following code:

```
namespace Packt.Shared
{
  [System.Flags]
  public enum WondersOfTheAncientWorld : byte
  {
    None                         = 0b_0000_0000, // i.e. 0
    GreatPyramidOfGiza           = 0b_0000_0001, // i.e. 1
    HangingGardensOfBabylon      = 0b_0000_0010, // i.e. 2
    StatueOfZeusAtOlympia        = 0b_0000_0100, // i.e. 4
    TempleOfArtemisAtEphesus     = 0b_0000_1000, // i.e. 8
    MausoleumAtHalicarnassus     = 0b_0001_0000, // i.e. 16
    ColossusOfRhodes             = 0b_0010_0000, // i.e. 32
    LighthouseOfAlexandria       = 0b_0100_0000  // i.e. 64
  }
}
```

We are assigning explicit values for each choice that would not overlap when looking at the bits stored in memory. We should also decorate the enum type with the System. Flags attribute so that when the value is returned it can automatically match with multiple values as a comma-separated string instead of returning an int value. Normally, an enum type uses an int variable internally, but since we don't need values that big, we can reduce memory requirements by 75%, that is, 1 byte per value instead of 4 bytes, by telling it to use a byte variable.

If we want to indicate that our bucket list includes the *Hanging Gardens and Mausoleum at Halicarnassus* ancient world wonders, then we would want the 16 and 2 bits set to 1. In other words, we would store the value 18:

64	32	16	8	4	2	1
0	0	1	0	0	1	0

In the Person class, add the following statement to your list of fields:

```
public WondersOfTheAncientWorld BucketList;
```

3. In the Main method of PeopleApp, add the following statements to set the bucket list using the | operator (bitwise logical OR) to combine the enum values. We could also set the value using the number 18 cast into the enum type, as shown in the comment, but we shouldn't because that would make the code harder to understand:

```
bob.BucketList =
  WondersOfTheAncientWorld.HangingGardensOfBabylon
  | WondersOfTheAncientWorld.MausoleumAtHalicarnassus;

// bob.BucketList = (WondersOfTheAncientWorld)18;

WriteLine($"{bob.Name}'s bucket list is {bob.BucketList}");
```

4. Run the application and view the result, as shown in the following output:

```
Bob Smith's bucket list is HangingGardensOfBabylon,
MausoleumAtHalicarnassus
```

 Good Practice: Use the enum values to store combinations of discrete options. Derive an enum type from byte if there are up to eight options, from ushort if there are up to 16 options, from uint if there are up to 32 options, and from ulong if there are up to 64 options.

Storing multiple values using collections

Let's now add a field to store a person's children. This is an example of aggregation because children are instances of a class that is related to the current person but are not part of the person itself. We will use a generic List<T> collection type:

1. Import the System.Collections.Generic namespace at the top of the Person.cs class file, as shown in the following code:

    ```
    using System.Collections.Generic;
    ```

    You will learn more about collections in *Chapter 8, Working with Common .NET Types*. For now, just follow along.

2. Declare a new field in the Person class, as shown in the following code:

    ```
    public List<Person> Children = new List<Person>();
    ```

List<Person> is read aloud as "list of Person," for example, "the type of the property named Children is a list of Person instances." We must ensure the collection is initialized to a new instance of a list of Person before we can add items to it, otherwise, the field will be null and it will throw runtime exceptions.

The angle brackets in the List<T> type is a feature of C# called **generics** that was introduced in 2005 with C# 2.0. It's just a fancy term for making a collection **strongly typed**, that is, the compiler knows more specifically what type of object can be stored in the collection. Generics improve the performance and correctness of your code.

Strongly typed is different from **statically typed**. The old `System.Collection` types are statically typed to contain weakly typed `System.Object` items. The newer `System.Collection.Generic` types are statically typed to contain strongly typed `<T>` instances. Ironically, the term generics means we can use a more specific static type!

1. In the `Main` method, add statements to add two children for Bob and then show how many children he has and what their names are, as shown in the following code:

    ```
    bob.Children.Add(new Person { Name = "Alfred" });
    bob.Children.Add(new Person { Name = "Zoe" });

    WriteLine(
      $"{bob.Name} has {bob.Children.Count} children:");

    for (int child = 0; child < bob.Children.Count; child++)
    {
      WriteLine($"  {bob.Children[child].Name}");
    }
    ```

    We could also use a `foreach` statement. As an extra challenge, change the `for` statement to output the same information using `foreach`.

2. Run the application and view the result, as shown in the following output:

    ```
    Bob Smith has 2 children:
      Alfred
      Zoe
    ```

Making a field static

The fields that we have created so far have all been **instance** members, meaning that a different value of each field exists for each instance of the class that is created. The bob variable has a different `Name` value to alice.

Sometimes, you want to define a field that only has one value that is shared across all instances. These are called **static** members because fields are not the only members that can be `static`.

Let's see what can be achieved using `static` fields:

1. In the `PacktLibrary` project, add a new class file named `BankAccount.cs`.

2. Modify the class to give it three fields, two instance fields and one static field, as shown in the following code:

    ```
    namespace Packt.Shared
    {
      public class BankAccount
      {
        public string AccountName; // instance member
    ```

```
    public decimal Balance; // instance member
    public static decimal InterestRate; // shared member
  }
}
```

Each instance of `BankAccount` will have its own `AccountName` and `Balance` values, but all instances will share a single `InterestRate` value.

3. In `Program.cs` and its `Main` method, add statements to set the shared interest rate and then create two instances of the `BankAccount` type, as shown in the following code:

```
BankAccount.InterestRate = 0.012M; // store a shared value

var jonesAccount = new BankAccount();
jonesAccount.AccountName = "Mrs. Jones";
jonesAccount.Balance = 2400;

WriteLine(format: "{0} earned {1:C} interest.",
  arg0: jonesAccount.AccountName,
  arg1: jonesAccount.Balance * BankAccount.InterestRate);

var gerrierAccount = new BankAccount();
gerrierAccount.AccountName = "Ms. Gerrier";
gerrierAccount.Balance = 98;

WriteLine(format: "{0} earned {1:C} interest.",
  arg0: gerrierAccount.AccountName,
  arg1: gerrierAccount.Balance * BankAccount.InterestRate);
```

`:C` is a format code that tells .NET to use the currency format for the numbers. In *Chapter 8, Working with Common .NET Types*, you will learn how to control the culture that determines the currency symbol. For now, it will use the default for your operating system installation. I live in London, UK, hence my output shows British Pounds (£).

4. Run the application and view the additional output:

```
Mrs. Jones earned £28.80 interest.
Ms. Gerrier earned £1.18 interest.
```

Making a field constant

If the value of a field will never **ever** change, you can use the `const` keyword and assign a literal value at compile time:

1. In the `Person` class, add the following code:

```
// constants
public const string Species = "Homo Sapien";
```

2. In the Main method, add a statement to write Bob's name and species to the console, as shown in the following code:

```
WriteLine($"{bob.Name} is a {Person.Species}");
```

To get the value of a constant field, you must write the name of the class, not the name of an instance of the class.

3. Run the application and view the result, as shown in the following output:

```
Bob Smith is a Homo Sapien
```

Examples of the const fields in Microsoft types include System.Int32.MaxValue and System.Math.PI because neither value will ever change, as you can see in the following screenshot:

```
[metadata] Math.cs — Chapter05 (Workspace)

C⁺ [metadata] Math.cs ×

1   #region Assembly System.Runtime, Version=5.0.0.0, Culture=neutral, PublicKeyToken=b03f5f7f11d50a3a
2   // System.Runtime.dll
3   #endregion
4
5
6   namespace System
7   {
8       //
9       // Summary:
10      //     Provides constants and static methods for trigonometric, logarithmic, and other
11      //     common mathematical functions.
12      public static class Math
13      {
14          //
15          // Summary:
16          //     Represents the natural logarithmic base, specified by the constant, e.
17          public const double E = 2.7182818284590451;
18          //
19          // Summary:
20          //     Represents the ratio of the circumference of a circle to its diameter, specified
21          //     by the constant, π.
22          public const double PI = 3.1415926535897931;
23          public const double Tau = 6.2831853071795862;
```

Figure 5.2: Examples of constants

Good Practice: Constants should be avoided for two important reasons: the value must be known at compile time, and it must be expressible as a literal string, Boolean, or number value. Every reference to the const field is replaced with the literal value at compile time, which will, therefore, not be reflected if the value changes in a future version and you do not recompile any assemblies that reference it to get the new value.

Making a field read-only

A better choice for fields that should not change is to mark them as read-only:

1. Inside the Person class, add a statement to declare an instance read-only field to store a person's home planet, as shown in the following code:

```
// read-only fields
public readonly string HomePlanet = "Earth";
```

You can also declare `static readonly` fields whose value will be shared across all instances of the type.

2. Inside the `Main` method, add a statement to write Bob's name and home planet to the console, as shown in the following code:

    ```
    WriteLine($"{bob.Name} was born on {bob.HomePlanet}");
    ```

3. Run the application and view the result, as shown in the following output:

    ```
    Bob Smith was born on Earth
    ```

> **Good Practice**: Use read-only fields over constant fields for two important reasons: the value can be calculated or loaded at runtime and can be expressed using any executable statement. So, a read-only field can be set using a constructor or a field assignment. Every reference to the field is a live reference, so any future changes will be correctly reflected by calling code.

Initializing fields with constructors

Fields often need to be initialized at runtime. You do this in a constructor that will be called when you make an instance of the class using the `new` keyword. Constructors execute before any fields are set by the code that is using the type.

1. Inside the `Person` class, add the following highlighted code after the existing read-only `HomePlanet` field:

    ```
    // read-only fields
    public readonly string HomePlanet = "Earth";
    public readonly DateTime Instantiated;

    // constructors
    public Person()
    {
        // set default values for fields
        // including read-only fields
        Name = "Unknown";
        Instantiated = DateTime.Now;
    }
    ```

2. Inside the `Main` method, add statements to instantiate a new person and then output its initial field values, as shown in the following code:

    ```
    var blankPerson = new Person();

    WriteLine(format:
        "{0} of {1} was created at {2:hh:mm:ss} on a {2:dddd}.",
        arg0: blankPerson.Name,
    ```

```
    arg1: blankPerson.HomePlanet,
    arg2: blankPerson.Instantiated);
```

3. Run the application and view the result, as shown in the following output:

```
Unknown of Earth was created at 11:58:12 on a Sunday
```

    You can have multiple constructors in a type. This is especially useful to encourage developers to set initial values for fields.

4. In the `Person` class, add statements to define a second constructor that allows a developer to set initial values for the person's name and home planet, as shown in the following code:

```
public Person(string initialName, string homePlanet)
{
  Name = initialName;
  HomePlanet = homePlanet;
  Instantiated = DateTime.Now;
}
```

5. Inside the `Main` method, add the following code:

```
var gunny = new Person("Gunny", "Mars");

WriteLine(format:
    "{0} of {1} was created at {2:hh:mm:ss} on a {2:dddd}.",
    arg0: gunny.Name,
    arg1: gunny.HomePlanet,
    arg2: gunny.Instantiated);
```

6. Run the application and view the result:

```
Gunny of Mars was created at 11:59:25 on a Sunday
```

Setting fields with default literals

A language feature introduced in C# 7.1 was **default literals**. Back in *Chapter 2*, *Speaking C#*, you learned about the `default(type)` keyword.

As a reminder, if you had some fields in a class that you wanted to initialize to their default type values in a constructor, you have been able to use `default(type)` since C# 2.0:

1. In the `PacktLibrary` folder, add a new file named `ThingOfDefaults.cs`.

2. In the `ThingOfDefaults.cs` file, add statements to declare a class with four fields of various types and set them to their default values in a constructor, as shown in the following code:

```
using System;
using System.Collections.Generic;

namespace Packt.Shared
{
  public class ThingOfDefaults
  {
    public int Population;
    public DateTime When;
    public string Name;
    public List<Person> People;

    public ThingOfDefaults()
    {
      Population = default(int); // C# 2.0 and later
      When = default(DateTime);
      Name = default(string);
      People = default(List<Person>);
    }
  }
}
```

You might think that the compiler ought to be able to work out what type we mean without being explicitly told, and you'd be right, but for the first 15 years of the C# compiler's life, it didn't. Finally, with the C# 7.1 and later compilers, it does.

3. Simplify the statements setting the defaults, as shown highlighted in the following code:

```
using System;
using System.Collections.Generic;

namespace Packt.Shared
{
  public class ThingOfDefaults
  {
    public int Population;
    public DateTime When;
    public string Name;
    public List<Person> People;

    public ThingOfDefaults()
    {
      Population = default; // C# 7.1 and later
```

```
        When = default;
        Name = default;
        People = default;
      }
    }
  }
```

Constructors are a special category of method. Let's look at methods in more detail.

Writing and calling methods

Methods are members of a type that execute a block of statements.

Returning values from methods

Methods can return a single value or return nothing.

- A method that performs some actions but does not return a value indicates this with the void type before the name of the method.
- A method that performs some actions and returns a value indicates this with the type of the return value before the name of the method.

For example, you will create two methods:

- WriteToConsole: This will perform an action (writing some text to the console), but it will return nothing from the method, indicated by the void keyword.
- GetOrigin: This will return a text value, indicated by the string keyword.

Let's write the code:

1. Inside the Person class, statically import System.Console.
2. Add statements to define the two methods, as shown in the following code:

```
// methods
public void WriteToConsole()
{
  WriteLine($"{Name} was born on a {DateOfBirth:dddd}.");
}

public string GetOrigin()
{
  return $"{Name} was born on {HomePlanet}.";
}
```

3. Inside the `Main` method, add statements to call the two methods, as shown in the following code:

```
bob.WriteToConsole();
WriteLine(bob.GetOrigin());
```

4. Run the application and view the result, as shown in the following output:

```
Bob Smith was born on a Wednesday.
Bob Smith was born on Earth.
```

Combining multiple returned values using tuples

Each method can only return a single value that has a single type. That type could be a simple type, such as `string` in the previous example, a complex type, such as `Person`, or a collection type, such as `List<Person>`.

Imagine that we want to define a method named `GetTheData` that returns both a `string` value and an `int` value. We could define a new class named `TextAndNumber` with a `string` field and an `int` field, and return an instance of that complex type, as shown in the following code:

```
public class TextAndNumber
{
  public string Text;
  public int Number;
}

public class Processor
{
  public TextAndNumber GetTheData()
  {
    return new TextAndNumber
    {
      Text = "What's the meaning of life?",
      Number = 42
    };
  }
}
```

But defining a class just to combine two values together is unnecessary, because in modern versions of C# we can use **tuples**. Tuples are an efficient way to combine two or more values into a single unit. I pronounce them as tuh-ples but I have heard other developers pronounce them as too-ples. To-may-toe, to-mah-toe, po-tay-toe, po-tah-toe, I guess.

Tuples have been a part of some languages such as F# since their first version, but .NET only added support for them in .NET 4.0 with the `System.Tuple` type.

It was only in C# 7.0 that C# added language syntax support for tuples using the parentheses characters () and at the same time, .NET added a new System.ValueTuple type that is more efficient in some common scenarios than the old .NET 4.0 System.Tuple type, and the C# tuple uses the more efficient one.

Let's explore tuples:

1. In the Person class, add statements to define a method that returns a string and int tuple, as shown in the following code:

```
public (string, int) GetFruit()
{
    return ("Apples", 5);
}
```

2. In the Main method, add statements to call the GetFruit method and then output the tuple's fields automatically named Item1 and Item2, as shown in the following code:

```
(string, int) fruit = bob.GetFruit();

WriteLine($"{fruit.Item1}, {fruit.Item2} there are.");
```

3. Run the application and view the result, as shown in the following output:

```
Apples, 5 there are.
```

Naming the fields of a tuple

To access the fields of a tuple, the default names are Item1, Item2, and so on.

You can explicitly specify the field names:

1. In the Person class, add statements to define a method that returns a tuple with named fields, as shown in the following code:

```
public (string Name, int Number) GetNamedFruit()
{
    return (Name: "Apples", Number: 5);
}
```

2. In the Main method, add statements to call the method and output the tuple's named fields, as shown in the following code:

```
var fruitNamed = bob.GetNamedFruit();

WriteLine($"There are {fruitNamed.Number} {fruitNamed.Name}.");
```

3. Run the application and view the result, as shown in the following output:

```
There are 5 Apples.
```

Inferring tuple names

If you are constructing a tuple from another object, you can use a feature introduced in C# 7.1 called **tuple name inference**.

In the Main method, create two tuples, made of a string and int value each, as shown in the following code:

```
var thing1 = ("Neville", 4);
WriteLine($"{thing1.Item1} has {thing1.Item2} children.");


var thing2 = (bob.Name, bob.Children.Count);
WriteLine($"{thing2.Name} has {thing2.Count} children.");
```

In C# 7.0, both things would use the Item1 and Item2 naming schemes. In C# 7.1 and later, the second thing can infer the names Name and Count.

Deconstructing tuples

You can also deconstruct tuples into separate variables. The deconstructing declaration has the same syntax as named field tuples, but without a named variable for the tuple, as shown in the following code:

```
// store return value in a tuple variable with two fields
(string name, int age) tupleWithNamedFields = GetPerson();
// tupleWithNamedFields.name
// tupleWithNamedFields.age

// deconstruct return value into two separate variables
(string name, int age) = GetPerson();
// name
// age
```

This has the effect of splitting the tuple into its parts and assigning those parts to new variables.

1. In the Main method, add the following code:

```
(string fruitName, int fruitNumber) = bob.GetFruit();

WriteLine($"Deconstructed: {fruitName}, {fruitNumber}");
```

2. Run the application and view the result, as shown in the following output:

```
Deconstructed: Apples, 5
```

 More Information: Deconstruction is not just for tuples. Any type can be deconstructed if it has a Deconstruct method. You can read about this at the following link: https://docs.microsoft.com/en-us/dotnet/csharp/deconstruct

Defining and passing parameters to methods

Methods can have parameters passed to them to change their behavior. Parameters are defined a bit like variable declarations but inside the parentheses of the method, as the following shows:

1. In the `Person` class, add statements to define two methods, the first without parameters and the second with one parameter, as shown in the following code:

    ```
    public string SayHello()
    {
      return $"{Name} says 'Hello!'";
    }

    public string SayHelloTo(string name)
    {
      return $"{Name} says 'Hello {name}!'";
    }
    ```

2. In the `Main` method, add statements to call the two methods and write the return value to the console, as shown in the following code:

    ```
    WriteLine(bob.SayHello());
    WriteLine(bob.SayHelloTo("Emily"));
    ```

3. Run the application and view the result:

    ```
    Bob Smith says 'Hello!'
    Bob Smith says 'Hello Emily!'
    ```

When typing a statement that calls a method, IntelliSense shows a tooltip with the name and type of any parameters, and the return type of the method, as shown in the following screenshot:

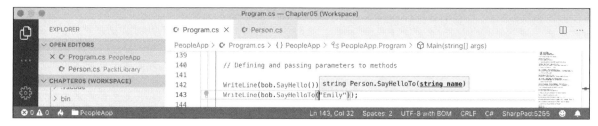

Figure 5.3: An IntelliSense tooltip for a method with no overloads

Overloading methods

Instead of having two different method names, we could give both methods the same name. This is allowed because the methods each have a different signature.

A **method signature** is a list of parameter types that can be passed when calling the method (as well as the type of the return value).

1. In the `Person` class, change the name of the `SayHelloTo` method to `SayHello`.

2. In `Main`, change the method call to use the `SayHello` method, and note that the quick info for the method tells you that it has one additional overload, **1/2**, as well as **2/2**, as shown in the following screenshot:

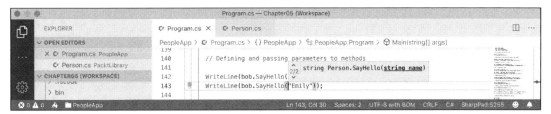

Figure 5.4: An IntelliSense tooltip for an overloaded method

 Good Practice: Use overloaded methods to simplify your class by making it appear to have fewer methods.

Passing optional parameters and naming arguments

Another way to simplify methods is to make parameters optional. You make a parameter optional by assigning a default value inside the method parameter list. Optional parameters must always come last in the list of parameters.

 More Information: There is one exception to optional parameters always coming last. C# has a `params` keyword that allows you to pass a comma-separated list of parameters of any length as an array. You can read about params at the following link: https://docs.microsoft.com/en-us/dotnet/csharp/language-reference/keywords/params

We will now create a method with three optional parameters.

1. In the `Person` class, add statements to define the method, as shown in the following code:

```csharp
public string OptionalParameters(
    string command = "Run!",
    double number = 0.0,
    bool active = true)
{
    return string.Format(
        format: "command is {0}, number is {1}, active is {2}",
        arg0: command, arg1: number, arg2: active);
}
```

2. In the `Main` method, add a statement to call the method and write its return value to the console, as shown in the following code:

```
WriteLine(bob.OptionalParameters());
```

3. Watch IntelliSense appear as you type the code. You will see a tooltip, showing the three optional parameters with their default values, as shown in the following screenshot:

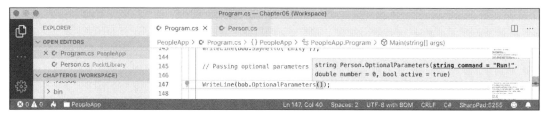

Figure 5.5: IntelliSense showing optional parameters as you type code

4. Run the application and view the result, as shown in the following output:

```
command is Run!, number is 0, active is True
```

5. In the `Main` method, add a statement to pass a `string` value for the `command` parameter and a `double` value for the `number` parameter, as shown in the following code:

```
WriteLine(bob.OptionalParameters("Jump!", 98.5));
```

6. Run the application and see the result, as shown in the following output:

```
command is Jump!, number is 98.5, active is True
```

The default values for `command` and `number` have been replaced, but the default for `active` is still `true`.

Optional parameters are often combined with naming parameters when you call the method, because naming a parameter allows the values to be passed in a different order than how they were declared.

7. In the `Main` method, add a statement to pass a `string` value for the `command` parameter and a `double` value for the `number` parameter but using named parameters, so that the order they are passed through can be swapped around, as shown in the following code:

```
WriteLine(bob.OptionalParameters(
    number: 52.7, command: "Hide!"));
```

8. Run the application and view the result, as shown in the following output:

```
command is Hide!, number is 52.7, active is True
```

You can even use named parameters to skip over optional parameters.

9. In the `Main` method, add a statement to pass a `string` value for the `command` parameter using positional order, skip the `number` parameter, and use the named `active` parameter, as shown in the following code:

```
WriteLine(bob.OptionalParameters("Poke!", active: false));
```

10. Run the application and view the result, as shown in the following output:

```
command is Poke!, number is 0, active is False
```

Controlling how parameters are passed

When a parameter is passed into a method, it can be passed in one of three ways:

- By **value** (this is the default): Think of these as being *in-only*.
- By **reference** as a `ref` parameter: Think of these as being *in-and-out*.
- As an out parameter: Think of these as being *out-only*.

Let's see some examples of passing parameters in and out.

1. In the `Person` class, add statements to define a method with three parameters, one in parameter, one `ref` parameter, and one out parameter, as shown in the following method:

```
public void PassingParameters(int x, ref int y, out int z)
{
  // out parameters cannot have a default
  // AND must be initialized inside the method
  z = 99;

  // increment each parameter
  x++;
  y++;
  z++;
}
```

2. In the `Main` method, add statements to declare some `int` variables and pass them into the method, as shown in the following code:

```
int a = 10;
int b = 20;
int c = 30;

WriteLine($"Before: a = {a}, b = {b}, c = {c}");
bob.PassingParameters(a, ref b, out c);
WriteLine($"After: a = {a}, b = {b}, c = {c}");
```

3. Run the application and view the result, as shown in the following output:

```
Before: a = 10, b = 20, c = 30
After: a = 10, b = 21, c = 100
```

When passing a variable as a parameter by default, its current *value* gets passed, *not* the variable itself. Therefore, x is a copy of the a variable. The a variable retains its original value of 10. When passing a variable as a ref parameter, a *reference* to the variable gets passed into the method.

Therefore, y is a reference to b. The b variable gets incremented when the y parameter gets incremented. When passing a variable as an out parameter, a *reference* to the variable gets passed into the method.

Therefore, z is a reference to c. The c variable gets replaced by whatever code executes inside the method. We could simplify the code in the Main method by not assigning the value 30 to the c variable since it will always be replaced anyway.

In C# 7.0 and later, we can simplify code that uses the out variables.

4. In the Main method, add statements to declare some more variables including an out parameter named f declared inline, as shown in the following code:

```
int d = 10;
int e = 20;

WriteLine(
    $"Before: d = {d}, e = {e}, f doesn't exist yet!");

// simplified C# 7.0 syntax for the out parameter
bob.PassingParameters(d, ref e, out int f);
WriteLine($"After: d = {d}, e = {e}, f = {f}");
```

Understanding ref returns

In C# 7.0 and later, the ref keyword is not just for passing parameters into a method; it can also be applied to the return value. This allows an external variable to reference an internal variable and modify its value after the method call. This might be useful in advanced scenarios, for example, passing around placeholders into big data structures, but it's beyond the scope of this book.

More Information: You can read more about using the ref keyword for return values at the following link: https://docs.microsoft.com/en-us/dotnet/csharp/programming-guide/classes-and-structs/ref-returns

Splitting classes using partial

When working on large projects with multiple team members, it is useful to be able to split the definition of a complex class across multiple files. You do this using the partial keyword.

Imagine we want to add statements to the Person class that are automatically generated by a tool like an object-relational mapper that reads schema information from a database. If the class is defined as partial, then we can split the class into an autogenerated code file and a manually edited code file.

1. In the Person class, add the partial keyword, as shown highlighted in the following code:

```
namespace Packt.Shared
{
    public partial class Person
    {
```

2. In **EXPLORER**, click on the **New File** button in the PacktLibrary folder, and enter a name of PersonAutoGen.cs.

3. Add statements to the new file, as shown in the following code:

```
namespace Packt.Shared
{
    public partial class Person
    {
    }
}
```

The rest of the code we write for this chapter will be written in the PersonAutoGen.cs file.

Controlling access with properties and indexers

Earlier, you created a method named GetOrigin that returned a string containing the name and origin of the person. Languages such as Java do this a lot. C# has a better way: **properties**.

A property is simply a method (or a pair of methods) that acts and looks like a field when you want to get or set a value, thereby simplifying the syntax.

Defining read-only properties

A readonly property only has a get implementation.

1. In the PersonAutoGen.cs file, in the Person class, add statements to define three properties:

   - The first property will perform the same role as the GetOrigin method using the property syntax that works with all versions of C# (although, it uses the C# 6 and later string interpolation syntax).

   - The second property will return a greeting message using the C# 6 and, later, the lambda expression (=>) syntax.

   - The third property will calculate the person's age.

Here's the code:

```
// a property defined using C# 1 - 5 syntax
public string Origin
{
  get
  {
    return $"{Name} was born on {HomePlanet}";
  }
}

// two properties defined using C# 6+ lambda expression syntax
public string Greeting => $"{Name} says 'Hello!'";

public int Age => System.DateTime.Today.Year - DateOfBirth.Year;
```

 More Information: Obviously, this isn't the best way to calculate someone's age, but we aren't learning how to calculate ages from dates of birth. If you need to do that properly, you can read a discussion at the following link: https://stackoverflow.com/questions/9/how-do-i-calculate-someones-age-in-c

2. In the `Main` method, add statements to get the properties, as shown in the following code:

```
var sam = new Person
{
  Name = "Sam",
  DateOfBirth = new DateTime(1972, 1, 27)
};

WriteLine(sam.Origin);
WriteLine(sam.Greeting);
WriteLine(sam.Age);
```

3. Run the application and view the result, as shown in the following output:

```
Sam was born on Earth
Sam says 'Hello!'
48
```

The output shows 48 because I ran the console application on August 15, 2020 when Sam was 48 years old.

Defining settable properties

To create a settable property, you must use the older syntax and provide a pair of methods —
not just a get part, but also a set part:

1. In the `PersonAutoGen.cs` file, add statements to define a `string` property that has both a
   get and set method (also known as a *getter* and *setter*), as shown in the following code:

   ```
   public string FavoriteIceCream { get; set; } // auto-syntax
   ```

   Although you have not manually created a field to store the person's favorite ice cream,
   it is there, automatically created by the compiler for you.

   Sometimes, you need more control over what happens when a property is set. In this
   scenario, you must use a more detailed syntax and manually create a `private` field to
   store the value for the property.

2. In the `PersonAutoGen.cs` file, add statements to define a `string` field and `string`
   property that has both a get and set, as shown in the following code:

   ```
   private string favoritePrimaryColor;

   public string FavoritePrimaryColor
   {
     get
     {
       return favoritePrimaryColor;
     }
     set
     {
       switch (value.ToLower())
       {
         case "red":
         case "green":
         case "blue":
           favoritePrimaryColor = value;
           break;
         default:
           throw new System.ArgumentException(
             $"{value} is not a primary color. " +
             "Choose from: red, green, blue.");
       }
     }
   }
   ```

3. In the `Main` method, add statements to set Sam's favorite ice cream and color, and then write them to the console, as shown in the following code:

```
sam.FavoriteIceCream = "Chocolate Fudge";

WriteLine($"Sam's favorite ice-cream flavor is {sam.FavoriteIceCream}.");

sam.FavoritePrimaryColor = "Red";

WriteLine($"Sam's favorite primary color is {sam.FavoritePrimaryColor}.");
```

4. Run the application and view the result, as shown in the following output:

```
Sam's favorite ice-cream flavor is Chocolate Fudge.
Sam's favorite primary color is Red.
```

If you try to set the color to any value other than red, green, or blue, then the code will throw an exception. The calling code could then use a `try` statement to display the error message.

> **Good Practice**: Use properties instead of fields when you want to validate what value can be stored when you want to data bind in XAML, which we will cover in *Chapter 21, Building Cross-Platform Mobile Apps*, and when you want to read and write to a field without using a method pair like `GetAge` and `SetAge`

> **More Information**: You can read more about the encapsulation of fields using properties at the following link: https://stackoverflow.com/questions/1568091/why-use-getters-and-setters-accessors

Defining indexers

Indexers allow the calling code to use the array syntax to access a property. For example, the `string` type defines an **indexer** so that the calling code can access individual characters in the string individually.

We will define an indexer to simplify access to the children of a person:

1. In the `PersonAutoGen.cs` file, add statements to define an indexer to get and set a child using the index of the child, as shown in the following code:

```
// indexers
public Person this[int index]
{
  get
  {
    return Children[index];
  }
}
```

```
  set
  {
    Children[index] = value;
  }
}
```

You can overload indexers so that different types can be used for their parameters. For example, as well as passing an int value, you could also pass a string value.

2. In the Main method, add the following code. After adding to the children, we will access the first and second child using the longer Children field and the shorter indexer syntax:

```
sam.Children.Add(new Person { Name = "Charlie" });
sam.Children.Add(new Person { Name = "Ella" });

WriteLine($"Sam's first child is {sam.Children[0].Name}");
WriteLine($"Sam's second child is {sam.Children[1].Name}");

WriteLine($"Sam's first child is {sam[0].Name}");
WriteLine($"Sam's second child is {sam[1].Name}");
```

3. Run the application and view the result, as shown in the following output:

```
Sam's first child is Charlie
Sam's second child is Ella
Sam's first child is Charlie
Sam's second child is Ella
```

Pattern matching with objects

In *Chapter 3*, *Controlling Flow and Converting Types*, you were introduced to basic pattern matching. In this section, we will explore pattern matching in more detail.

Creating and referencing a .NET 5 class library

The enhanced pattern matching features are only available in .NET 5 class libraries that support C# 9 or later. First, we will see what pattern matching features were available before the enhancements in C# 9.

1. Create a subfolder under Chapter05 named PacktLibrary9.
2. In Visual Studio Code, navigate to **File | Add Folder to Workspace…**, select the PacktLibrary9 folder, and click **Add**.
3. Navigate to **Terminal | New Terminal** and select **PacktLibrary9**.
4. In **TERMINAL**, enter the following command: dotnet new classlib.
5. In **EXPLORER**, in the PeopleApp folder, click on the file named PeopleApp.csproj.

6. Add a language version element to force the use of the C# 8 compiler, and add a project reference to PacktLibrary9, as shown highlighted in the following markup:

```xml
<Project Sdk="Microsoft.NET.Sdk">
  <PropertyGroup>
    <OutputType>Exe</OutputType>
    <TargetFramework>net5.0</TargetFramework>
    <LangVersion>8</LangVersion>
  </PropertyGroup>
  <ItemGroup>
    <ProjectReference Include="../PacktLibrary/PacktLibrary.csproj" />
    <ProjectReference Include="../PacktLibrary9/PacktLibrary9.csproj" />
  </ItemGroup>
</Project>
```

7. Navigate to **Terminal | New Terminal** and select **PeopleApp**.

8. In **TERMINAL**, enter a command to compile the PeopleApp project and its dependent projects, as shown in the following command: dotnet build.

Defining flight passengers

In this example, we will define some classes that represent various types of passengers on a flight and then we will use a switch expression with pattern matching to determine the cost of their flight.

1. In **EXPLORER**, in the PacktLibrary9 folder, delete the file named Class1.cs and add a new file named FlightPatterns.cs.

2. In the file FlightPatterns.cs, add statements to define three types of passengers with different properties, as shown in the following code:

```csharp
namespace Packt.Shared
{
  public class BusinessClassPassenger
  {
    public override string ToString()
    {
      return $"Business Class";
    }
  }

  public class FirstClassPassenger
  {
    public int AirMiles { get; set; }

    public override string ToString()
    {
```

```
      return $"First Class with {AirMiles:N0} air miles";
    }
  }

  public class CoachClassPassenger
  {
    public double CarryOnKG { get; set; }

    public override string ToString()
    {
      return $"Coach Class with {CarryOnKG:N2} KG carry on";
    }
  }
}
```

3. In the `PeopleApp` folder, open `Program.cs`, and add statements to the end of the `Main` method to define an object array containing five passengers of various types and property values, and then enumerate them, outputting the cost of their flight, as shown in the following code:

```
object[] passengers = {
  new FirstClassPassenger { AirMiles = 1_419 },
  new FirstClassPassenger { AirMiles = 16_562 },
  new BusinessClassPassenger(),
  new CoachClassPassenger { CarryOnKG = 25.7 },
  new CoachClassPassenger { CarryOnKG = 0 },
};

foreach (object passenger in passengers)
{
  decimal flightCost = passenger switch
  {
    FirstClassPassenger p when p.AirMiles > 35000 => 1500M,
    FirstClassPassenger p when p.AirMiles > 15000 => 1750M,
    FirstClassPassenger _                         => 2000M,
    BusinessClassPassenger _                      => 1000M,
    CoachClassPassenger p when p.CarryOnKG < 10.0 => 500M,
    CoachClassPassenger _                         => 650M,
    _                                             => 800M
  };

  WriteLine($"Flight costs {flightCost:C} for {passenger}");
}
```

While reviewing the preceding code, note the following:

- To pattern match on properties of an object, you must name a local variable that can then be used in an expression like p.
- To pattern match on a type only, you can use the _ to discard the local variable.
- The switch expression also uses the _ to represent its default branch.

4. Run the application and view the result, as shown in the following output:

```
Flight costs £2,000.00 for First Class with 1,419 air miles
Flight costs £1,750.00 for First Class with 16,562 air miles
Flight costs £1,000.00 for Business Class
Flight costs £650.00 for Coach Class with 25.70 KG carry on
Flight costs £500.00 for Coach Class with 0.00 KG carry on
```

Enhancements to pattern matching in C# 9

The previous examples worked with C# 8. Now we will look at some enhancements in C# 9 and later. First, you no longer need to use the underscore to discard when doing type matching:

1. In the PeopleApp folder, open Program.cs and remove the _ from one of the branches.
2. In **TERMINAL**, enter the dotnet build command to compile the console app, and note the compile error that explains this feature is not supported by C# 8.0.
3. Open PeopleApp.csproj and remove the language version element that forced the use of C# 8.0.
4. In the PeopleApp folder, open Program.cs and modify the branches for first-class passengers to use a nested switch expression and the new support for conditionals like >, as shown in the following code:

```
decimal flightCost = passenger switch
{
  /* C# 8 syntax
  FirstClassPassenger p when p.AirMiles > 35000 => 1500M,
  FirstClassPassenger p when p.AirMiles > 15000 => 1750M,
  FirstClassPassenger                           => 2000M, */

  // C# 9 syntax
  FirstClassPassenger p => p.AirMiles switch
  {
    > 35000 => 1500M,
    > 15000 => 1750M,
    _       => 2000M
  },

  BusinessClassPassenger                        => 1000M,
```

```
    CoachClassPassenger p when p.CarryOnKG < 10.0 => 500M,
    CoachClassPassenger                            => 650M,
    _                                              => 800M
  };
```

5. Run the application, view the results, and note they are the same as before.

 More Information: You can complete a detailed tutorial about pattern matching at the following link: https://docs.microsoft.com/en-us/dotnet/csharp/tutorials/pattern-matching

Working with records

Before we dive into the new records language feature of C# 9, let us see some other related new features.

Init-only properties

You have used object initialization syntax to instantiate objects and set initial properties throughout this chapter. Those properties can also be changed after instantiation.

Sometimes you want to treat properties like `readonly` fields so they can be set during instantiation but not after. The new `init` keyword enables this. It can be used in place of the `set` keyword:

1. In the `PacktLibrary9` folder, add a new file named `Records.cs`.

2. In the `Records.cs` file, define an immutable person class, as shown in the following code:

```
namespace Packt.Shared
{
  public class ImmutablePerson
  {
    public string FirstName { get; init; }
    public string LastName { get; init; }
  }
}
```

3. In `Program.cs`, at the bottom of the `Main` method, add statements to instantiate a new immutable person and then try to change one of its properties, as shown in the following code:

```
var jeff = new ImmutablePerson
{
  FirstName = "Jeff",
```

```
        LastName = "Winger"
    };


    jeff.FirstName = "Geoff";
```

4. Compile the console app and note the compile error, as shown in the following output:

```
Program.cs(254,7): error CS8852: Init-only property or indexer
'ImmutablePerson.FirstName' can only be assigned in an object initializer,
or on 'this' or 'base' in an instance constructor or an 'init' accessor.
[/Users/markjprice/Code/Chapter05/PeopleApp/PeopleApp.csproj]
```

5. Comment out the attempt to set the `LastName` property after instantiation.

Understanding records

Init-only properties provide some immutability to C#. You can take the concept further by using **Records**. These are defined by using the `record` keyword instead of the `class` keyword. That makes the whole object immutable, so it acts like a value.

Records should not have any state (properties and fields) that changes after instantiation. Instead, the idea is that you create new records from existing ones with any changed state. This is called **non-destructive mutation**. To do this, C# 9 introduces the `with` keyword:

1. Open `Records.cs`, and add a record named `ImmutableVehicle`, as shown highlighted in the following code:

```
public record ImmutableVehicle
{
    public int Wheels { get; init; }
    public string Color { get; init; }
    public string Brand { get; init; }
}
```

2. Open `Program.cs`, and at the bottom of the `Main` method, add statements to create a car and then a mutated copy of it, as shown in the following code:

```
var car = new ImmutableVehicle
{
    Brand = "Mazda MX-5 RF",
    Color = "Soul Red Crystal Metallic",
    Wheels = 4
};

var repaintedCar = car with { Color = "Polymetal Grey Metallic" };

WriteLine("Original color was {0}, new color is {1}.",
    arg0: car.Color, arg1: repaintedCar.Color);
```

3. Run the application, view the results, and note the change to the car color in the mutated copy, as shown in the following output:

```
Original color was Soul Red Crystal Metallic, new color is Polymetal Grey
Metallic.
```

Simplifying data members

In the following class, `Age` is a `private` field so it can only be accessed inside the class, as shown in the following code:

```
public class Person
{
  int Age; // private field by default
}
```

But with the `record` keyword, the field becomes an `init`-only `public` property, as shown in the following code:

```
public record Person
{
  int Age; // public property equivalent to:
  // public int Age { get; init; }
}
```

This is designed to make it clear and concise to define records.

Positional records

Instead of using object initialization syntax with curly braces, sometimes you might prefer to provide a constructor with positional parameters as you saw earlier in this chapter. You can also combine this with a deconstructor for splitting the object into individual parts, as shown in the following code:

```
public record ImmutableAnimal
{
  string Name; // i.e. public init-only properties
  string Species;

  public ImmutableAnimal(string name, string species)
  {
    Name = name;
    Species = species;
  }

  public void Deconstruct(out string name, out string species)
```

```
    {
        name = Name;
        species = Species;
    }
}
```

The properties, constructor, and deconstructor can be generated for you:

1. In the `Records.cs` file, add statements to define another record, as shown in the following code:

   ```
   // simpler way to define a record that does the equivalent
   public data class ImmutableAnimal(string Name, string Species);
   ```

2. In the `Program.cs` file, add statements to construct and deconstruct immutable animals, as shown in the following code:

   ```
   var oscar = new ImmutableAnimal("Oscar", "Labrador");
   var (who, what) = oscar; // calls Deconstruct method
   WriteLine($"{who} is a {what}.");
   ```

3. Run the application and view the results, as shown in the following output:

   ```
   Oscar is a Labrador.
   ```

Practicing and exploring

Test your knowledge and understanding by answering some questions, get some hands-on practice, and explore this chapter's topics with deeper research.

Exercise 5.1 – Test your knowledge

Answer the following questions:

1. What are the six combinations of access modifier keywords and what do they do?
2. What is the difference between the `static`, `const`, and `readonly` keywords when applied to a type member?
3. What does a constructor do?
4. Why should you apply the `[Flags]` attribute to an `enum` type when you want to store combined values?
5. Why is the `partial` keyword useful?
6. What is a tuple?
7. What does the C# `record` keyword do?
8. What does overloading mean?
9. What is the difference between a field and a property?
10. How do you make a method parameter optional?

Exercise 5.2 – Explore topics

Use the following links to read more about this chapter's topics:

- **Fields (C# programming guide)**: `https://docs.microsoft.com/en-us/dotnet/articles/csharp/programming-guide/classes-and-structs/fields`

- **Access modifiers (C# programming guide)**: `https://docs.microsoft.com/en-us/dotnet/articles/csharp/language-reference/keywords/access-modifiers`

- **Enumeration types (C# reference)**: `https://docs.microsoft.com/en-us/dotnet/csharp/language-reference/builtin-types/enum`

- **Constructors (C# programming guide)**: `https://docs.microsoft.com/en-us/dotnet/articles/csharp/programming-guide/classes-and-structs/constructors`

- **Methods (C# programming guide)**: `https://docs.microsoft.com/en-us/dotnet/articles/csharp/methods`

- **Properties (C# programming guide)**: `https://docs.microsoft.com/en-us/dotnet/articles/csharp/properties`

Summary

In this chapter, you learned about making your own types using OOP. You learned about some of the different categories of members that a type can have, including fields to store data and methods to perform actions, and you used OOP concepts, such as aggregation and encapsulation. You saw examples of how to use C# 9 features like object pattern matching enhancements, `init`-only properties, and records.

In the next chapter, you will take these concepts further by defining delegates and events, implementing interfaces, and inheriting from existing classes.

06

Implementing Interfaces and Inheriting Classes

This chapter is about deriving new types from existing ones using **object-oriented programming (OOP)**. You will learn about defining operators and local functions for performing simple actions and delegates and events for exchanging messages between types. You will learn how to implement interfaces for common functionality. You will learn about generics and the difference between reference and value types. You will learn how to inherit from a base class to create a derived class to reuse functionality, how to override an inherited type member, and how to use polymorphism. Finally, you will learn how to create extension methods, and how to cast between classes in an inheritance hierarchy.

This chapter covers the following topics:

- Setting up a class library and console application
- Simplifying methods
- Raising and handling events
- Implementing interfaces
- Making types more reusable with generics
- Managing memory with reference and value types
- Inheriting from classes
- Casting within inheritance hierarchies
- Inheriting and extending .NET types

Setting up a class library and console application

We will start by defining a workspace with two projects like the one created in *Chapter 5, Building Your Own Types with Object-Oriented Programming*. If you completed all the exercises in that chapter, then you can open the Chapter05 workspace and continue working with its projects.

Otherwise, follow the instructions given in this section:

1. In your existing Code folder, create a folder named Chapter06 with two subfolders named PacktLibrary and PeopleApp, as shown in the following hierarchy:

   - Chapter06

     - PacktLibrary
     - PeopleApp

2. Start Visual Studio Code.

3. Navigate to **File | Save As Workspace…**, enter the name Chapter06, and click **Save**.

4. Navigate to **File | Add Folder to Workspace…**, select the PacktLibrary folder, and click **Add**.

5. Navigate to **File | Add Folder to Workspace…**, select the PeopleApp folder, and click **Add**.

6. Navigate to **Terminal | New Terminal** and select PacktLibrary.

7. In **TERMINAL**, enter the following command:

```
dotnet new classlib
```

8. Navigate to **Terminal | New Terminal** and select **PeopleApp**.

9. In **TERMINAL**, enter the following command:

```
dotnet new console
```

10. In the **EXPLORER** pane, in the PacktLibrary project, rename the file named Class1.cs to Person.cs.

11. Modify the file contents, as shown in the following code:

```
using System;

namespace Packt.Shared
{
  public class Person
  {
  }
}
```

12. In the **EXPLORER** pane, expand the folder named `PeopleApp` and click on the file named `PeopleApp.csproj`.

13. Add a project reference to `PacktLibrary`, as shown in the following markup:

```
<Project Sdk="Microsoft.NET.Sdk">
  <PropertyGroup>
    <OutputType>Exe</OutputType>
    <TargetFramework>net5.0</TargetFramework>
  </PropertyGroup>

  <ItemGroup>
    <ProjectReference
      Include="..\PacktLibrary\PacktLibrary.csproj" />
  </ItemGroup>
</Project>
```

14. In the **TERMINAL** window for the `PeopleApp` folder, enter the `dotnet build` command, and note the output indicating that both projects have been built successfully.

15. Add statements to the `Person` class to define three fields and a method, as shown in the following code:

```
using System;
using System.Collections.Generic;
using static System.Console;

namespace Packt.Shared
{
  public class Person
  {
    // fields
    public string Name;
    public DateTime DateOfBirth;
    public List<Person> Children = new List<Person>();

    // methods
    public void WriteToConsole()
    {
      WriteLine($"{Name} was born on a {DateOfBirth:dddd}.");
    }
  }
}
```

Simplifying methods

We might want two instances of Person to be able to procreate. We can implement this by writing methods. Instance methods are actions that an object does to itself; static methods are actions the type does.

Which you choose depends on what makes the most sense for the action.

> **Good Practice**: Having both static and instance methods to perform similar actions often makes sense. For example, string has both a Compare static method and a CompareTo instance method. This puts the choice of how to use the functionality in the hands of the programmers using your type, giving them more flexibility.

Implementing functionality using methods

Let's start by implementing some functionality by using methods:

1. Add one instance method and one static method to the Person class that will allow two Person objects to procreate, as shown in the following code:

```
// static method to "multiply"
public static Person Procreate(Person p1, Person p2)
{
    var baby = new Person
    {
        Name = $"Baby of {p1.Name} and {p2.Name}"
    };

    p1.Children.Add(baby);
    p2.Children.Add(baby);

    return baby;
}

// instance method to "multiply"
public Person ProcreateWith(Person partner)
{
    return Procreate(this, partner);
}
```

Note the following:

- In the static method named Procreate, the Person objects to procreate are passed as parameters named p1 and p2.

- A new `Person` class named baby is created with a name made of a combination of the two people who have procreated. This could be changed later by setting the returned baby variable's `Name` property.

- The baby object is added to the `Children` collection of both parents and then returned. Classes are reference types, meaning a reference to the baby object stored in memory is added, not a clone of the baby. You will learn the difference between reference types and value types later in this chapter.

- In the instance method named `ProcreateWith`, the `Person` object to procreate with is passed as a parameter named `partner`, and it, along with `this`, is passed to the static `Procreate` method to reuse the method implementation. `this` is a keyword that references the current instance of the class.

 Good Practice: A method that creates a new object, or modifies an existing object, should return a reference to that object so that the caller can see the results.

2. In the `PeopleApp` project, at the top of the `Program.cs` file, import the namespace for our class and statically import the `Console` type, as shown highlighted in the following code:

```
using System;
using Packt.Shared;
using static System.Console;
```

3. In the `Main` method, create three people and have them procreate with each other, noting that to add a double-quote character into a `string`, you must prefix it with a backslash character like this: \", as shown in the following code:

```
var harry = new Person { Name = "Harry" };
var mary = new Person { Name = "Mary" };
var jill = new Person { Name = "Jill" };

// call instance method
var baby1 = mary.ProcreateWith(harry);
baby1.Name = "Gary";

// call static method
var baby2 = Person.Procreate(harry, jill);

WriteLine($"{harry.Name} has {harry.Children.Count} children.");
WriteLine($"{mary.Name} has {mary.Children.Count} children.");
WriteLine($"{jill.Name} has {jill.Children.Count} children.");
WriteLine(
    format: "{0}'s first child is named \"{1}\".",
    arg0: harry.Name,
    arg1: harry.Children[0].Name);
```

4. Run the application and view the result, as shown in the following output:

```
Harry has 2 children.
Mary has 1 children.
Jill has 1 children.
Harry's first child is named "Gary".
```

Implementing functionality using operators

The System.String class has a static method named Concat that concatenates two string values and returns the result, as shown in the following code:

```
string s1 = "Hello ";
string s2 = "World!";
string s3 = string.Concat(s1, s2);
WriteLine(s3); // Hello World!
```

Calling a method like Concat works, but it might be more natural for a programmer to use the + symbol operator to "add" two string values together, as shown in the following code:

```
string s1 = "Hello ";
string s2 = "World!";
string s3 = s1 + s2;
WriteLine(s3); // Hello World!
```

A well-known biblical phrase is *Go forth and multiply*, meaning to procreate. Let's write code so that the * (multiply) symbol will allow two Person objects to procreate.

We do this by defining a static operator for a symbol like *. The syntax is rather like a method, because in effect, an operator is a method, but uses a symbol instead of a method name, which makes the syntax more concise.

 More Information: The * symbol is just one of many that you can implement as an operator. The complete list of symbols is listed at this link: https://docs.microsoft.com/en-us/dotnet/csharp/programming-guide/statements-expressions-operators/overloadable-operators

1. In the PacktLibrary project, in the Person class, create a static operator for the * symbol, as shown in the following code:

```
// operator to "multiply"
public static Person operator *(Person p1, Person p2)
{
    return Person.Procreate(p1, p2);
}
```

Good Practice: Unlike methods, operators do not appear in IntelliSense lists for a type. For every operator you define, make a method as well, because it may not be obvious to a programmer that the operator is available. The implementation of the operator can then call the method, reusing the code you have written. A second reason for providing a method is that operators are not supported by every language compiler.

2. In the `Main` method, after calling the static `Procreate` method, use the `*` operator to make another baby, as shown in the following highlighted code:

```
// call static method
var baby2 = Person.Procreate(harry, jill);

// call an operator
var baby3 = harry * mary;
```

3. Run the application and view the result, as shown in the following output:

```
Harry has 3 children.
Mary has 2 children.
Jill has 1 children.
Harry's first child is named "Gary".
```

Implementing functionality using local functions

A language feature introduced in C# 7.0 is the ability to define a **local function**.

Local functions are the method equivalent of local variables. In other words, they are methods that are only accessible from within the containing method in which they have been defined. In other languages, they are sometimes called **nested** or **inner functions**.

Local functions can be defined anywhere inside a method: the top, the bottom, or even somewhere in the middle!

We will use a local function to implement a factorial calculation:

1. In the `Person` class, add statements to define a `Factorial` function that uses a local function inside itself to calculate the result, as shown in the following code:

```
// method with a local function
public static int Factorial(int number)
{
    if (number < 0)
    {
        throw new ArgumentException(
            $"{nameof(number)} cannot be less than zero.");
    }
```

```
        return localFactorial(number);

        int localFactorial(int localNumber) // Local function
        {
            if (localNumber < 1) return 1;
            return localNumber * localFactorial(localNumber - 1);
        }
    }
```

2. In `Program.cs`, in the `Main` method, add a statement to call the `Factorial` function and write the return value to the console, as shown in the following code:

```
WriteLine($"5! is {Person.Factorial(5)}");
```

3. Run the application and view the result, as shown in the following output:

```
5! is 120
```

Raising and handling events

Methods are often described as *actions that an object can perform, either on itself or to related objects.* For example, `List` can add an item to itself or clear itself, and `File` can create or delete a file in the filesystem.

Events are often described as *actions that happen to an object.* For example, in a user interface, `Button` has a `Click` event, a click being something that happens to a button. Another way of thinking of events is that they provide a way of exchanging messages between two objects.

Events are built on delegates, so let's start by having a look at how delegates work.

Calling methods using delegates

You have already seen the most common way to call or execute a method: use the `.` operator to access the method using its name. For example, `Console.WriteLine` tells the `Console` type to access its `WriteLine` method.

The other way to call or execute a method is to use a **delegate**. If you have used languages that support **function pointers**, then think of a delegate as being a **type-safe method pointer**.

In other words, a delegate contains the memory address of a method that matches the same signature as the delegate so that it can be called safely with the correct parameter types.

For example, imagine there is a method in the `Person` class that must have a `string` type passed as its only parameter, and it returns an `int` type, as shown in the following code:

```
public int MethodIWantToCall(string input)
{
    return input.Length; // it doesn't matter what this does
}
```

I can call this method on an instance of `Person` named p1 like this:

```
int answer = p1.MethodIWantToCall("Frog");
```

Alternatively, I can define a delegate with a matching signature to call the method indirectly. Note that the names of the parameters do not have to match. Only the types of parameters and return values must match, as shown in the following code:

```
delegate int DelegateWithMatchingSignature(string s);
```

Now, I can create an instance of the delegate, point it at the method, and finally, call the delegate (which calls the method!), as shown in the following code:

```
// create a delegate instance that points to the method
var d = new DelegateWithMatchingSignature(p1.MethodIWantToCall);

// call the delegate, which calls the method
int answer2 = d("Frog");
```

You are probably thinking, "What's the point of that?" Well, it provides flexibility.

For example, we could use delegates to create a queue of methods that need to be called in order. Queuing actions that need to be performed is common in services to provide improved scalability.

Another example is to allow multiple actions to perform in parallel. Delegates have built-in support for asynchronous operations that run on a different thread, and that can provide improved responsiveness. You will learn how to do this in *Chapter 13, Improving Performance and Scalability Using Multitasking*.

The most important example is that delegates allow us to implement **events** for sending messages between different objects that do not need to know about each other.

Delegates and events are two of the most confusing features of C# and can take a few attempts to understand, so don't worry if you feel lost!

Defining and handling delegates

Microsoft has two predefined delegates for use as events. Their signatures are simple, yet flexible, as shown in the following code:

```
public delegate void EventHandler(
  object sender, EventArgs e);

public delegate void EventHandler<TEventArgs>(
  object sender, TEventArgs e);
```

Good Practice: When you want to define an event in your own types, you should use one of these two predefined delegates.

1. Add statements to the Person class and note the following points, as shown in the following code:

   - It defines an EventHandler delegate field named Shout.
   - It defines an int field to store AngerLevel.
   - It defines a method named Poke.
   - Each time a person is poked, their AngerLevel increments. Once their AngerLevel reaches three, they raise the Shout event, but only if there is at least one event delegate pointing at a method defined somewhere else in the code; that is, it is not null.

```
// event delegate field
public EventHandler Shout;

// data field
public int AngerLevel;

// method
public void Poke()
{
  AngerLevel++;
  if (AngerLevel >= 3)
  {
    // if something is listening...
    if (Shout != null)
    {
      // ...then call the delegate
      Shout(this, EventArgs.Empty);
    }
  }
}
```

Checking whether an object is null before calling one of its methods is very common. C# 6.0 and later allows null checks to be simplified inline, as shown in the following code:

```
Shout?.Invoke(this, EventArgs.Empty);
```

2. In Program, add a method with a matching signature that gets a reference to the Person object from the sender parameter and outputs some information about them, as shown in the following code:

```
private static void Harry_Shout(object sender, EventArgs e)
{
  Person p = (Person)sender;
  WriteLine($"{p.Name} is this angry: {p.AngerLevel}.");
}
```

Microsoft's convention for method names that handle events is `ObjectName_EventName`.

3. In the `Main` method, add a statement to assign the method to the delegate field, as shown in the following code:

    ```
    harry.Shout = Harry_Shout;
    ```

4. Add statements to call the `Poke` method four times, after assigning the method to the `Shout` event, as shown highlighted in the following code:

    ```
    harry.Shout = Harry_Shout;
    harry.Poke();
    harry.Poke();
    harry.Poke();
    harry.Poke();
    ```

    Delegates are multicast, meaning that you can assign multiple delegates to a single delegate field. Instead of the = assignment, we could have used the += operator so we could add more methods to the same delegate field. When the delegate is called, all the assigned methods are called, although you have no control over the order that they are called in.

5. Run the application and view the result, as shown in the following output, and note that Harry says nothing the first two times he is poked, and only gets angry enough to shout once he's been poked at least three times:

    ```
    Harry is this angry: 3.
    Harry is this angry: 4.
    ```

Defining and handling events

You've now seen how delegates implement the most important functionality of events: the ability to define a signature for a method that can be implemented by a completely different piece of code, and then call that method and any others that are hooked up to the delegate field.

But what about events? There is less to them than you might think.

When assigning a method to a delegate field, you should not use the simple assignment operator as we did in the preceding example, and as shown in the following code:

```
harry.Shout = Harry_Shout;
```

If the Shout delegate field was already referencing one or more methods, by assigning a method, it would replace all the others. With delegates that are used for events, we usually want to make sure that a programmer only ever uses either the += operator or the -= operator to assign and remove methods:

1. To enforce this, add the event keyword to the delegate field declaration, as shown in the following code:

   ```
   public event EventHandler Shout;
   ```

2. In **TERMINAL**, enter the command dotnet build, and note the compiler error message, as shown in the following output:

   ```
   Program.cs(41,13): error CS0079: The event 'Person.Shout' can only appear
   on the left hand side of += or -=
   ```

   This is (almost) all that the event keyword does! If you will never have more than one method assigned to a delegate field, then you do not need "events."

3. Modify the method assignment to use +=, as shown in the following code:

   ```
   harry.Shout += Harry_Shout;
   ```

4. Run the application and note that it has the same behavior as before.

 More Information: You can define your own custom EventArgs-derived types so that you can pass additional information to an event handler method. You can read more at the following link: https://docs.microsoft.com/en-us/dotnet/standard/events/how-to-raise-and-consume-events

Implementing interfaces

Interfaces are a way of connecting different types together to make new things. Think of them like the studs on top of LEGO™ bricks, which allow them to "stick" together, or electrical standards for plugs and sockets.

If a type implements an interface, then it is making a promise to the rest of .NET that it supports a certain feature.

Common interfaces

Here are some common interfaces that your types might need to implement:

Interface	Method(s)	Description
IComparable	CompareTo(other)	This defines a comparison method that a type implements to order or sort its instances.
IComparer	Compare (first, second)	This defines a comparison method that a secondary type implements to order or sort instances of a primary type.

IDisposable	Dispose()	This defines a disposal method to release unmanaged resources more efficiently than waiting for a finalizer.
IFormattable	ToString (format, culture)	This defines a culture-aware method to format the value of an object into a string representation.
IFormatter	Serialize (stream, object) and Deserialize(stream)	This defines methods to convert an object to and from a stream of bytes for storage or transfer.
IFormat Provider	GetFormat(type)	This defines a method to format inputs based on a language and region.

Comparing objects when sorting

One of the most common interfaces that you will want to implement is IComparable. It allows arrays and collections of any type that implements it to be sorted.

1. In the Main method, add statements that create an array of Person instances and write the items to the console, and then attempt to sort the array and write the items to the console again, as shown in the following code:

```
Person[] people =
{
    new Person { Name = "Simon" },
    new Person { Name = "Jenny" },
    new Person { Name = "Adam" },
    new Person { Name = "Richard" }
};

WriteLine("Initial list of people:");
foreach (var person in people)
{
    WriteLine($"  {person.Name}");
}

WriteLine("Use Person's IComparable implementation to sort:");
Array.Sort(people);
foreach (var person in people)
{
    WriteLine($"  {person.Name}");
}
```

2. Run the application, and you will see the following runtime error:

```
Unhandled Exception: System.InvalidOperationException: Failed to compare
two elements in the array. ---> System.ArgumentException: At least one
object must implement IComparable.
```

As the error explains, to fix the problem, our type must implement IComparable.

3. In the `PacktLibrary` project, in the `Person` class, after the class name, add a colon and enter `IComparable<Person>`, as shown in the following code:

```
public class Person : IComparable<Person>
```

Visual Studio Code will draw a red squiggle under the new code to warn you that you have not yet implemented the method you have promised to. It can write the skeleton implementation for you if you click on the light bulb and choose the **Implement interface** option.

Interfaces can be implemented implicitly and explicitly. Implicit implementations are simpler. Explicit implementations are only necessary if a type must have multiple methods with the same name and signature. For example, both `IGamePlayer` and `IKeyHolder` might have a method called `Lose` with the same parameters. In a type that must implement both interfaces, only one implementation of `Lose` can be the implicit method. If both interfaces can share the same implementation, that works, but if not then the other `Lose` method will have to be implemented differently and called explicitly.

 More Information: You can read more about explicit interface implementations at the following link: `https://docs.microsoft.com/en-us/dotnet/csharp/programming-guide/interfaces/explicit-interface-implementation`

4. Scroll down to find the method that was written for you and delete the statement that throws the `NotImplementedException` error.

5. Add a statement to call the `CompareTo` method of the `Name` field, which uses the string type's implementation of `CompareTo`, as shown highlighted in the following code:

```
public int CompareTo(Person other)
{
    return Name.CompareTo(other.Name);
}
```

We have chosen to compare two `Person` instances by comparing their `Name` fields. `Person` instances will, therefore, be sorted alphabetically by their name.

For simplicity, I have not added `null` checks throughout these examples.

6. Run the application, and note that this time it works as expected, as shown in the following output:

```
Initial list of people:
  Simon
  Jenny
  Adam
  Richard
Use Person's IComparable implementation to sort:
  Adam
```

```
Jenny
Richard
Simon
```

 Good Practice: If anyone will want to sort an array or collection of instances of your type, then implement the IComparable interface.

Comparing objects using a separate class

Sometimes, you won't have access to the source code for a type, and it might not implement the IComparable interface. Luckily, there is another way to sort instances of a type. You can create a separate type that implements a slightly different interface, named IComparer:

1. In the PacktLibrary project, add a new class named PersonComparer that implements the IComparer interface that will compare two people, that is, two Person instances, by comparing the length of their Name field, or if the names are the same length, then by comparing the names alphabetically, as shown in the following code:

```csharp
using System.Collections.Generic;

namespace Packt.Shared
{
  public class PersonComparer : IComparer<Person>
  {
    public int Compare(Person x, Person y)
    {
      // Compare the Name Lengths...
      int result = x.Name.Length
        .CompareTo(y.Name.Length);

      // ...if they are equal...
      if (result == 0)
      {
        // ...then compare by the Names...
        return x.Name.CompareTo(y.Name);
      }
      else
      {
        // ...otherwise compare by the lengths.
        return result;
      }
    }
  }
}
```

2. In `PeopleApp`, in the `Program` class, in the `Main` method, add statements to sort the array using this alternative implementation, as shown in the following code:

```
WriteLine("Use PersonComparer's IComparer implementation to sort:");
Array.Sort(people, new PersonComparer());
foreach (var person in people)
{
  WriteLine($"  {person.Name}");
}
```

3. Run the application and view the result, as shown in the following output:

```
Initial list of people:
  Simon
  Jenny
  Adam
  Richard
Use Person's IComparable implementation to sort:
  Adam
  Jenny
  Richard
  Simon
Use PersonComparer's IComparer implementation to sort:
  Adam
  Jenny
  Simon
  Richard
```

This time, when we sort the `people` array, we explicitly ask the sorting algorithm to use the `PersonComparer` type instead, so that the people are sorted with the shortest names first, and when the lengths of two or more names are equal, to sort them alphabetically.

Defining interfaces with default implementations

A language feature introduced in C# 8.0 is **default implementations** for an interface. Let's see it in action:

1. In the `PacktLibrary` project, add a new file named `IPlayable.cs`.

2. Modify the statements to define a public `IPlayable` interface with two methods to `Play` and `Pause`, as shown in the following code:

```
using static System.Console;

namespace Packt.Shared
{
  public interface IPlayable
  {
    void Play();
```

```
    void Pause();
  }
}
```

3. In the `PacktLibrary` project, add a new file named `DvdPlayer.cs`.

4. Modify the statements in the file to implement the `IPlayable` interface, as shown in the following code:

```
using static System.Console;

namespace Packt.Shared
{
  public class DvdPlayer : IPlayable
  {
    public void Pause()
    {
      WriteLine("DVD player is pausing.");
    }

    public void Play()
    {
      WriteLine("DVD player is playing.");
    }
  }
}
```

This is useful, but what if we decide to add a third method, `Stop`? Before C# 8.0, this would be impossible once at least one type implements the original interface. One of the main points of an interface is that it is a fixed contract.

C# 8.0 allows an interface to add new members after release as long as they have a default implementation. C# purists do not like the idea, but for practical reasons it is useful, and other languages such as Java and Swift enable similar techniques.

 More Information: You can read about the design decisions around default interface implementations at the following link: https:// docs.microsoft.com/en-us/dotnet/csharp/language- reference/proposals/csharp-8.0/default-interface-methods

Support for default interface implementations requires some fundamental changes to the underlying platform, so they are only supported with C# if the target framework is .NET 5 or later, .NET Core 3.0 or later, or .NET Standard 2.1. They are therefore not supported by .NET Framework.

5. Modify the `IPlayable` interface to add a `Stop` method with a default implementation, as shown highlighted in the following code:

```
using static System.Console;

namespace Packt.Shared
{
  public interface IPlayable
  {
    void Play();
    void Pause();

    void Stop() // default interface implementation
    {
      WriteLine("Default implementation of Stop.");
    }
  }
}
```

6. In **TERMINAL**, compile the `PeopleApp` project by entering the command `dotnet build`, and note the projects compile successfully.

 More Information: You can read a tutorial about updating interfaces with default interface members at the following link: `https://docs.microsoft.com/en-us/dotnet/csharp/tutorials/default-interface-members-versions`

Making types safely reusable with generics

In 2005, with C# 2.0 and .NET Framework 2.0, Microsoft introduced a feature named **generics**, which enables your types to be more safely reusable and more efficient. It does this by allowing a programmer to pass types as parameters, similar to how you can pass objects as parameters.

First, let's look at an example of a non-generic type so that you can understand the problem that generics is designed to solve:

1. In the `PacktLibrary` project, add a new class named `Thing`, as shown in the following code, and note the following:

    *   `Thing` has an `object` field named `Data`.
    *   `Thing` has a method named `Process` that accepts an `object` input parameter and returns a `string` value.

    ```
    using System;

    namespace Packt.Shared
    ```

```
{
  public class Thing
  {
    public object Data = default(object);

    public string Process(object input)
    {
      if (Data == input)
      {
        return "Data and input are the same.";
      }
      else
      {
        return "Data and input are NOT the same.";
      }
    }
  }
}
```

2. In the `PeopleApp` project, add some statements to the end of `Main`, as shown in the following code:

```
var t1 = new Thing();
t1.Data = 42;
WriteLine($"Thing with an integer: {t1.Process(42)}");

var t2 = new Thing();
t2.Data = "apple";
WriteLine($"Thing with a string: {t2.Process("apple")}");
```

3. Run the application and view the result, as shown in the following output:

```
Thing with an integer: Data and input are NOT the same.
Thing with a string: Data and input are the same.
```

`Thing` is currently flexible, because any type can be set for the `Data` field and `input` parameter. But there is no type checking, so inside the `Process` method, we cannot safely do much and the results are sometimes not what you might expect; for example, when passing `int` values into an `object` parameter!

This is because the value 42 stored in the `Data` property is stored in a different memory address to the value 42 passed as a parameter and when comparing reference types like any value stored in `object`, they are only equal if they are stored at the same memory address, that is, the same object, even if their values are equal. We can solve this problem by using generics.

Working with generic types

Let's write some code to solve the problem by using generics:

1. In the `PacktLibrary` project, add a new class named `GenericThing`, as shown in the following code:

    ```csharp
    using System;

    namespace Packt.Shared
    {
      public class GenericThing<T> where T : IComparable
      {
        public T Data = default(T);

        public string Process(T input)
        {
          if (Data.CompareTo(input) == 0)
          {
            return "Data and input are the same.";
          }
          else
          {
            return "Data and input are NOT the same.";
          }
        }
      }
    }
    ```

    Note the following:

    - `GenericThing` has a generic type parameter named `T`, which can be any type that implements `IComparable`, so it must have a method named `CompareTo` that returns `0` if two objects are equal. By convention, name the type parameter `T` if there is only one type parameter.
    - `GenericThing` has a `T` field named `Data`.
    - `GenericThing` has a method named `Process` that accepts a `T` input parameter and returns a `string` value.

2. In the `PeopleApp` project, add some statements to the end of `Main`, as shown in the following code:

    ```csharp
    var gt1 = new GenericThing<int>();
    gt1.Data = 42;
    WriteLine($"GenericThing with an integer: {gt1.Process(42)}");

    var gt2 = new GenericThing<string>();
    gt2.Data = "apple";
    WriteLine($"GenericThing with a string: {gt2.Process("apple")}");
    ```

Note the following:

- When instantiating an instance of a generic type, the developer must pass a type parameter. In this example, we pass int as the type parameter for gt1 and string as the type parameter for gt2, so wherever T appears in the GenericThing class, it is replaced with int and string.

- When setting the Data field and passing the input parameter, the compiler enforces the use of an int value, such as 42, for the gt1 variable, and a string value, such as "apples", for the gt2 variable.

3. Run the application, view the result, and note the logic of the Process method correctly works for GenericThing for both int and string values, as shown in the following output:

```
Thing with an integer: Data and input are NOT the same.
Thing with a string: Data and input are the same.
GenericThing with an integer: Data and input are the same.
GenericThing with a string: Data and input are the same.
```

Working with generic methods

Generics can be used for methods as well as types, even inside a non-generic type:

1. In PacktLibrary, add a new class named Squarer, with a generic method named Square, as shown in the following code:

```
using System;
using System.Threading;

namespace Packt.Shared
{
  public static class Squarer
  {
    public static double Square<T>(T input)
      where T : IConvertible
    {
      // convert using the current culture
      double d = input.ToDouble(
        Thread.CurrentThread.CurrentCulture);

      return d * d;
    }
  }
}
```

Note the following:

- The `Squarer` class is non-generic.
- The `Square` method is generic, and its type parameter `T` must implement `IConvertible`, so the compiler will make sure that it has a `ToDouble` method.
- `T` is used as the type for the `input` parameter.
- `ToDouble` requires a parameter that implements `IFormatProvider` to understand the format of numbers for a language and region. We can pass the `CurrentCulture` property of the current thread to specify the language and region used by your computer. You will learn about cultures in *Chapter 8, Working with Common .NET Types*.
- The return value is the `input` parameter multiplied by itself, that is, squared.

2. In `PeopleApp`, in the `Program` class, at the bottom of the `Main` method, add the following code. Note that when calling a generic method, you can specify the type parameter to make it clearer, as shown in the first example, although the compiler can work it out on its own, as shown in the second example:

```
string number1 = "4";

WriteLine("{0} squared is {1}",
  arg0: number1,
  arg1: Squarer.Square<string>(number1));

byte number2 = 3;

WriteLine("{0} squared is {1}",
  arg0: number2,
  arg1: Squarer.Square(number2));
```

3. Run the application and view the result, as shown in the following output:

```
4 squared is 16
3 squared is 9
```

I have mentioned reference types a couple of times. Let's look at them in more detail.

Managing memory with reference and value types

There are two categories of memory: **stack** memory and **heap** memory. With modern operating systems, the stack and heap can be anywhere in physical or virtual memory.

Stack memory is faster to work with (because it is managed directly by the CPU and because it uses a last-in, first-out mechanism, it is more likely to have the data in its L1 or L2 cache) but limited in size, while heap memory is slower but much more plentiful.

For example, on my macOS, in **TERMINAL**, I can enter the command `ulimit -a` to discover that stack size is limited to 8,192 KB and other memory is "unlimited." This is why it is so easy to get a "stack overflow."

There are two C# keywords that you can use to create object types: `class` and `struct`. Both can have the same members, such as fields and methods. One difference between the two is how memory is allocated.

When you define a type using `class`, you are defining a **reference type**. This means that the memory for the object itself is allocated on the heap, and only the memory address of the object (and a little overhead) is stored on the stack.

 More Information: If you are interested in the technical details of the internal memory layout of types in .NET, you can read the article at the following link: `https://adamsitnik.com/Value-Types-vs-Reference-Types/`

When you define a type using `struct`, you are defining a **value type**. This means that the memory for the object itself is allocated on the stack.

If a `struct` uses field types that are not of the `struct` type, then those fields will be stored on the heap, meaning the data for that object is stored in both the stack and the heap!

These are the most common `struct` types:

- **Numbers**: `byte`, `sbyte`, `short`, `ushort`, `int`, `uint`, `long`, `ulong`, `float`, `double`, and `decimal`
- **Miscellaneous**: `char`, `DateTime`, and `bool`
- **System.Drawing**: `Color`, `Point`, and `Rectangle`

Almost all the other types are `class` types, including `string`.

Apart from the difference in where in memory the data for a type is stored, the other major difference is that you cannot inherit from a `struct`.

Working with struct types

Let's explore working with value types:

1. Add a file named `DisplacementVector.cs` to the `PacktLibrary` project.
2. Modify the file, as shown in the following code, and note the following:
   - The type is declared using `struct` instead of `class`.
   - It has two `int` fields, named `X` and `Y`.
   - It has a constructor for setting initial values for `X` and `Y`.

- It has an operator for adding two instances together that returns a new instance of the type with X added to X, and Y added to Y.

```
namespace Packt.Shared
{
  public struct DisplacementVector
  {
    public int X;
    public int Y;

    public DisplacementVector(int initialX, int initialY)
    {
      X = initialX;
      Y = initialY;
    }

    public static DisplacementVector operator +(
      DisplacementVector vector1,
      DisplacementVector vector2)
    {
      return new DisplacementVector(
        vector1.X + vector2.X,
        vector1.Y + vector2.Y);
    }
  }
}
```

3. In the `PeopleApp` project, in the `Program` class, in the `Main` method, add statements to create two new instances of `DisplacementVector`, add them together, and output the result, as shown in the following code:

```
var dv1 = new DisplacementVector(3, 5);
var dv2 = new DisplacementVector(-2, 7);
var dv3 = dv1 + dv2;

WriteLine($"({dv1.X}, {dv1.Y}) + ({dv2.X}, {dv2.Y}) = ({dv3.X}, {dv3.Y})");
```

4. Run the application and view the result, as shown in the following output:

```
(3, 5) + (-2, 7) = (1, 12)
```

Good Practice: If the total bytes used by all the fields in your type is 16 bytes or less, your type only uses struct types for its fields, and you will never want to derive from your type, then Microsoft recommends that you use struct. If your type uses more than 16 bytes of stack memory, if it uses class types for its fields, or if you might want to inherit from it, then use class.

Releasing unmanaged resources

In the previous chapter, we saw that constructors can be used to initialize fields and that a type may have multiple constructors. Imagine that a constructor allocates an unmanaged resource; that is, anything that is not controlled by .NET, such as a file or mutex under the control of the operating system. The unmanaged resource must be manually released because .NET cannot do it for us using its automatic garbage collection feature.

Garbage collection is an advanced topic, so for this topic, I will show some code examples, but you do not need to create them in your current project.

 More Information: You can read about garbage collection at the following link: https://docs.microsoft.com/en-us/dotnet/standard/garbage-collection/

Each type can have a single **finalizer** that will be called by the .NET runtime when the resources need to be released. A finalizer has the same name as a constructor; that is, the type name, but it is prefixed with a tilde, ~, as shown in the following code:

```
public class Animal
{
  public Animal()
  {
    // allocate any unmanaged resources
  }

  ~Animal() // Finalizer aka destructor
  {
    // deallocate any unmanaged resources
  }
}
```

Do not confuse a finalizer (also known as a **destructor**) with a **deconstruct** method. A destructor releases resources; that is, it destroys an object. A deconstruct method returns an object split up into its constituent parts and uses the C# deconstruction syntax, for example, when working with tuples.

The preceding code example is the minimum you should do when working with unmanaged resources. But the problem with only providing a finalizer is that the .NET garbage collector requires two garbage collections to completely release the allocated resources for this type.

Though optional, it is recommended to also provide a method to allow a developer who uses your type to explicitly release resources so that the garbage collector can release managed parts of an unmanaged resource, such as a file, immediately and deterministically, and then release the managed memory part of the object in a single garbage collection instead of two rounds of garbage collection.

There is a standard mechanism to do this by implementing the IDisposable interface, as shown in the following example:

```
public class Animal : IDisposable
{
  public Animal()
  {
    // allocate unmanaged resource
  }

  ~Animal() // Finalizer
  {
    if (disposed) return;
    Dispose(false);
  }

  bool disposed = false; // have resources been released?

  public void Dispose()
  {
    Dispose(true);
    GC.SuppressFinalize(this);
  }

  protected virtual void Dispose(bool disposing)
  {
    if (disposed) return;

    // deallocate the *unmanaged* resource
    // ...

    if (disposing)
    {
      // deallocate any other *managed* resources
      // ...
    }
    disposed = true;
  }
}
```

There are two Dispose methods, public and protected:

- The public void Dispose method will be called by a developer using your type. When called, both unmanaged and managed resources need to be deallocated.

- The `protected virtual void Dispose` method with a `bool` parameter is used internally to implement the deallocation of resources. It needs to check the `disposing` parameter and `disposed` flag because if the finalizer has already run and it called the `~Animal` method, then only unmanaged resources need to be deallocated.

The call to `GC.SuppressFinalize(this)` is what notifies the garbage collector that it no longer needs to run the finalizer, and removes the need for a second garbage collection.

More Information: You can read more about finalizers and disposing at the following link: `https://docs.microsoft.com/en-us/dotnet/standard/garbage-collection/unmanaged`

Ensuring that Dispose is called

When someone uses a type that implements `IDisposable`, they can ensure that the public `Dispose` method is called with the `using` statement, as shown in the following code:

```
using (Animal a = new Animal())
{
  // code that uses the Animal instance
}
```

The compiler converts your code into something like the following, which guarantees that even if an exception occurs, the `Dispose` method will still be called:

```
Animal a = new Animal();
try
{
  // code that uses the Animal instance
}
finally
{
  if (a != null) a.Dispose();
}
```

More Information: You can read more about the `IDisposable` interface at the following link: `https://docs.microsoft.com/en-us/dotnet/standard/garbage-collection/using-objects`

You will see practical examples of releasing unmanaged resources with `IDisposable`, `using` statements, and `try...finally` blocks in *Chapter 9, Working with Files, Streams, and Serialization.*

Inheriting from classes

The `Person` type we created earlier implicitly derived (inherited) from `System.Object`. Now, we will create a class that inherits from `Person`:

1. Add a new class named `Employee` to the `PacktLibrary` project.
2. Modify its statements, as shown in the following code:

```
using System;

namespace Packt.Shared
{
  public class Employee : Person
  {
  }
}
```

3. Add statements to the `Main` method to create an instance of the `Employee` class, as shown in the following code:

```
Employee john = new Employee
{
  Name = "John Jones",
  DateOfBirth = new DateTime(1990, 7, 28)
};
john.WriteToConsole();
```

4. Run the console application and view the result, as shown in the following output:

```
John Jones was born on a Saturday
```

Note that the `Employee` class has inherited all the members of `Person`.

Extending classes to add functionality

Now, we will add some employee-specific members to extend the class.

1. In the `Employee` class, add the following code to define two properties:

```
public string EmployeeCode { get; set; }
public DateTime HireDate { get; set; }
```

2. Back in the `Main` method, add statements to set John's employee code and hire date, as shown in the following code:

```
john.EmployeeCode = "JJ001";
john.HireDate = new DateTime(2014, 11, 23);
WriteLine($"{john.Name} was hired on {john.HireDate:dd/MM/yy}");
```

3. Run the console application and view the result, as shown in the following output:

```
John Jones was hired on 23/11/14
```

Hiding members

So far, the WriteToConsole method is inherited from Person, and it only outputs the employee's name and date of birth. We might want to change what this method does for an employee:

1. In the Employee class, add the following highlighted code to redefine the WriteToConsole method:

```
using System;
using static System.Console;

namespace Packt.Shared
{
  public class Employee : Person
  {
    public string EmployeeCode { get; set; }
    public DateTime HireDate { get; set; }

    public void WriteToConsole()
    {
      WriteLine(format:
        "{0} was born on {1:dd/MM/yy} and hired on {2:dd/MM/yy}",
        arg0: Name,
        arg1: DateOfBirth,
        arg2: HireDate);
    }
  }
}
```

2. Run the application and view the result, as shown in the following output:

```
John Jones was born on 28/07/90 and hired on 01/01/01
John Jones was hired on 23/11/14
```

The Visual Studio Code C# extension warns you that your method now hides the method by drawing a squiggle under the method name, the **PROBLEMS** window includes more details, and the compiler will output the warning when you build and run the console application, as shown in the following screenshot:

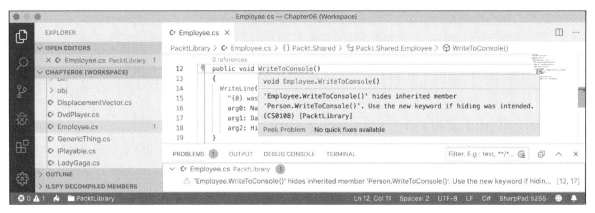

Figure 6.1: Hidden method warning

As the warning describes, you can remove this by applying the new keyword to the method, to indicate that you are deliberately replacing the old method, as shown highlighted in the following code:

```
public new void WriteToConsole()
```

Overriding members

Rather than hiding a method, it is usually better to **override** it. You can only override if the base class chooses to allow overriding, by applying the virtual keyword:

1. In the Main method, add a statement to write the value of the john variable to the console as a string, as shown in the following code:

    ```
    WriteLine(john.ToString());
    ```

2. Run the application and note that the ToString method is inherited from System.Object so the implementation returns the namespace and type name, as shown in the following output:

    ```
    Packt.Shared.Employee
    ```

3. Override this behavior for the Person class by adding a ToString method to output the name of the person as well as the type name, as shown in the following code:

    ```
    // overridden methods
    public override string ToString()
    {
        return $"{Name} is a {base.ToString()}";
    }
    ```

    The base keyword allows a subclass to access members of its superclass; that is, the base class that it inherits or derives from.

4. Run the application and view the result. Now, when the ToString method is called, it outputs the person's name, as well as the base class's implementation of ToString, as shown in the following output:

    ```
    John Jones is a Packt.Shared.Employee
    ```

Good Practice: Many real-world APIs, for example, Microsoft's Entity Framework Core, Castle's DynamicProxy, and Episerver's content models, require the properties that you define in your classes to be marked as `virtual` so that they can be overridden. Unless you have a good reason not to, mark your method and property members as `virtual`.

Preventing inheritance and overriding

You can prevent someone from inheriting from your class by applying the `sealed` keyword to its definition. No one can inherit from Scrooge McDuck, as shown in the following code:

```
public sealed class ScroogeMcDuck
{
}
```

An example of `sealed` in .NET is the `string` class. Microsoft has implemented some extreme optimizations inside the `string` class that could be negatively affected by your inheritance, so Microsoft prevents that.

You can prevent someone from further overriding a `virtual` method in your class by applying the `sealed` keyword to the method. No one can change the way Lady Gaga sings, as shown in the following code:

```
using static System.Console;

namespace Packt.Shared
{
  public class Singer
  {
    // virtual allows this method to be overridden
    public virtual void Sing()
    {
      WriteLine("Singing...");
    }
  }

  public class LadyGaga : Singer
  {
    // sealed prevents overriding the method in subclasses
    public sealed override void Sing()
    {
      WriteLine("Singing with style...");
    }
  }
}
```

You can only seal an overridden method.

Understanding polymorphism

You have now seen two ways to change the behavior of an inherited method. We can hide it using the new keyword (known as **non-polymorphic inheritance**), or we can override it (known as **polymorphic inheritance**).

Both ways can access members of the base class by using the base keyword, so what is the difference?

It all depends on the type of the variable holding a reference to the object. For example, a variable of the Person type can hold a reference to a Person class, or any type that derives from Person:

1. In the Employee class, add statements to override the ToString method so it writes the employee's name and code to the console, as shown in the following code:

```
public override string ToString()
{
  return $"{Name}'s code is {EmployeeCode}";
}
```

2. In the Main method, write statements to create a new employee named Alice, store it in a variable of type Person, and call both variables' WriteToConsole and ToString methods, as shown in the following code:

```
Employee aliceInEmployee = new Employee
  { Name = "Alice", EmployeeCode = "AA123" };

Person aliceInPerson = aliceInEmployee;
aliceInEmployee.WriteToConsole();
aliceInPerson.WriteToConsole();
WriteLine(aliceInEmployee.ToString());
WriteLine(aliceInPerson.ToString());
```

3. Run the application and view the result, as shown in the following output:

```
Alice was born on 01/01/01 and hired on 01/01/01
Alice was born on a Monday
Alice's code is AA123
Alice's code is AA123
```

When a method is hidden with new, the compiler is not smart enough to know that the object is an Employee, so it calls the WriteToConsole method in Person.

When a method is overridden with `virtual` and `override`, the compiler is smart enough to know that although the variable is declared as a `Person` class, the object itself is an `Employee` class and, therefore, the `Employee` implementation of `ToString` is called.

The member modifiers and the effect they have are summarized in the following table:

Variable type	Member modifier	Method executed	In class
Person		WriteToConsole	Person
Employee	new	WriteToConsole	Employee
Person	virtual	ToString	Employee
Employee	override	ToString	Employee

In my opinion, polymorphism is literally academic to most programmers. If you get the concept, that's cool; but, if not, I suggest that you don't worry about it. Some people like to make others feel inferior by saying understanding polymorphism is important for all C# programmers to learn, but IMHO it's not. You can have a successful career with C# and never need to be able to explain polymorphism, just as a racing car driver doesn't need to be able to explain the engineering behind fuel injection.

 Good Practice: You should use `virtual` and `override` rather than `new` to change the implementation of an inherited method whenever possible.

Casting within inheritance hierarchies

Casting between types is subtly different from converting between types. Casting is between similar types, like between a 16-bit integer and a 32-bit integer, or between a superclass and one of its subclasses. Converting is between dissimilar types, like between text and a number.

Implicit casting

In the previous example, you saw how an instance of a derived type can be stored in a variable of its base type (or its base's base type, and so on). When we do this, it is called **implicit casting**.

Explicit casting

Going the other way is an explicit cast, and you must use parentheses around the type you want to cast into as a prefix to do it:

1. In the `Main` method, add a statement to assign the `aliceInPerson` variable to a new `Employee` variable, as shown in the following code:

   ```
   Employee explicitAlice = aliceInPerson;
   ```

2. Visual Studio Code displays a red squiggle and a compile error, as shown in the following screenshot:

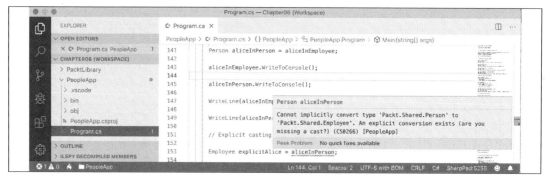

Figure 6.2: A missing explicit cast compile error

3. Change the statement to prefix the assigned variable named with a cast to the `Employee` type, as shown in the following code:

```
Employee explicitAlice = (Employee)aliceInPerson;
```

Avoiding casting exceptions

The compiler is now happy; but, because `aliceInPerson` might be a different derived type, like `Student` instead of `Employee`, we need to be careful. In a real application with more complex code, the current value of this variable could have been set to a `Student` instance and then this statement would throw an `InvalidCastException` error.

We can handle this by writing a `try` statement, but there is a better way. We can check the type of an object using the `is` keyword:

1. Wrap the explicit cast statement in an `if` statement, as shown in the following code:

```
if (aliceInPerson is Employee)
{
  WriteLine($"{nameof(aliceInPerson)} IS an Employee");
  Employee explicitAlice = (Employee)aliceInPerson;
  // safely do something with explicitAlice
}
```

2. Run the application and view the result, as shown in the following output:

```
aliceInPerson IS an Employee
```

Alternatively, you can use the `as` keyword to cast. Instead of throwing an exception, the `as` keyword returns `null` if the type cannot be cast.

3. Add the following statements to the end of the `Main` method:

```
Employee aliceAsEmployee = aliceInPerson as Employee;

if (aliceAsEmployee != null)
{
  WriteLine($"{nameof(aliceInPerson)} AS an Employee");
```

```
    // do something with aliceAsEmployee
  }
```

Since accessing a `null` variable can throw a `NullReferenceException` error, you should always check for `null` before using the result.

4. Run the application and view the result, as shown in the following output:

```
aliceInPerson AS an Employee
```

What if you want to execute a block of statements when Alice is not an employee?

In the past, you would have had to use the ! operator, as shown in the following code:

```
if (!(aliceInPerson is Employee))
```

With C# 9 and later, you can use the not keyword, as shown in the following code:

```
if (aliceInPerson is not Employee)
```

Good Practice: Use the `is` and `as` keywords to avoid throwing exceptions when casting between derived types. If you don't do this, you must write `try...catch` statements for `InvalidCastException`.

Inheriting and extending .NET types

.NET has prebuilt class libraries containing hundreds of thousands of types. Rather than creating your own completely new types, you can often get a head start by deriving from one of Microsoft's types to inherit some or all of its behavior and then overriding or extending it.

Inheriting exceptions

As an example of inheritance, we will derive a new type of exception:

1. In the `PacktLibrary` project, add a new class named `PersonException`, with three constructors, as shown in the following code:

```
using System;

namespace Packt.Shared
{
  public class PersonException : Exception
  {
    public PersonException() : base() { }

    public PersonException(string message) : base(message) { }
```

```
        public PersonException(
            string message, Exception innerException)
            : base(message, innerException) { }
    }
}
```

Unlike ordinary methods, constructors are not inherited, so we must explicitly declare and explicitly call the base constructor implementations in System.Exception to make them available to programmers who might want to use those constructors with our custom exception.

2. In the Person class, add statements to define a method that throws an exception if a date/time parameter is earlier than a person's date of birth, as shown in the following code:

```
public void TimeTravel(DateTime when)
{
    if (when <= DateOfBirth)
    {
        throw new PersonException("If you travel back in time to a date
earlier than your own birth, then the universe will explode!");
    }
    else
    {
        WriteLine($"Welcome to {when:yyyy}!");
    }
}
```

3. In the Main method, add statements to test what happens when employee John Jones tries to time travel too far back, as shown in the following code:

```
try
{
    john.TimeTravel(new DateTime(1999, 12, 31));
    john.TimeTravel(new DateTime(1950, 12, 25));
}
catch (PersonException ex)
{
    WriteLine(ex.Message);
}
```

4. Run the application and view the result, as shown in the following output:

```
Welcome to 1999!
If you travel back in time to a date earlier than your own birth, then the
universe will explode!
```

Good Practice: When defining your own exceptions, give them the same three constructors that explicitly call the built-in ones.

Extending types when you can't inherit

Earlier, we saw how the sealed modifier can be used to prevent inheritance.

Microsoft has applied the sealed keyword to the System.String class so that no one can inherit and potentially break the behavior of strings.

Can we still add new methods to strings? Yes, if we use a language feature named extension methods, which was introduced with C# 3.0.

Using static methods to reuse functionality

Since the first version of C#, we've been able to create static methods to reuse functionality, such as the ability to validate that a string contains an email address. This implementation will use a regular expression that you will learn more about in *Chapter 8, Working with Common .NET Types*:

1. In the PacktLibrary project, add a new class named StringExtensions, as shown in the following code, and note the following:

   - The class imports a namespace for handling regular expressions.

   - The IsValidEmail static method uses the Regex type to check for matches against a simple email pattern that looks for valid characters before and after the @ symbol.

```
using System.Text.RegularExpressions;

namespace Packt.Shared
{
  public class StringExtensions
  {
    public static bool IsValidEmail(string input)
    {
      // use simple regular expression to check
      // that the input string is a valid email
      return Regex.IsMatch(input,
        @"[a-zA-Z0-9\.-_]+@[a-zA-Z0-9\.-_]+");
    }
  }
}
```

2. Add statements to the bottom of the `Main` method to validate two examples of email addresses, as shown in the following code:

```
string email1 = "pamela@test.com";
string email2 = "ian&test.com";

WriteLine(
    "{0} is a valid e-mail address: {1}",
    arg0: email1,
    arg1: StringExtensions.IsValidEmail(email1));

WriteLine(
    "{0} is a valid e-mail address: {1}",
    arg0: email2,
    arg1: StringExtensions.IsValidEmail(email2));
```

3. Run the application and view the result, as shown in the following output:

```
pamela@test.com is a valid e-mail address: True
ian&test.com is a valid e-mail address: False
```

This works, but extension methods can reduce the amount of code we must type and simplify the usage of this function.

Using extension methods to reuse functionality

It is easy to make `static` methods into extension methods for their usage:

1. In the `StringExtensions` class, add the `static` modifier before the class, and add the `this` modifier before the `string` type, as highlighted in the following code:

```
public static class StringExtensions
{
    public static bool IsValidEmail(this string input)
    {
```

These two changes tell the compiler that it should treat the method as one that extends the `string` type.

2. Back in the `Program` class, add some new statements to use the extension method for string values:

```
WriteLine(
    "{0} is a valid e-mail address: {1}",
    arg0: email1,
    arg1: email1.IsValidEmail());

WriteLine(
    "{0} is a valid e-mail address: {1}",
```

```
    arg0: email2,
    arg1: email2.IsValidEmail());
```

Note the subtle simplification in the syntax for calling the `IsValidEmail` method. The older, longer syntax still works too.

3. The `IsValidEmail` extension method now appears to be a method just like all the actual instance methods of the `string` type, such as `IsNormalized` and `Insert`, as shown in the following screenshot:

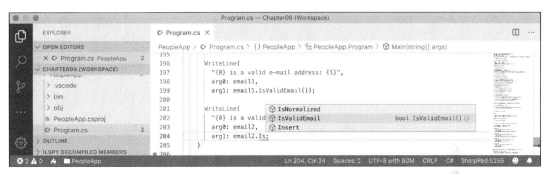

Figure 6.3: Using extension methods

Extension methods cannot replace or override existing instance methods, so you cannot, for example, redefine the `Insert` method. The extension method will appear as an overload in IntelliSense, but an instance method will be called in preference to an extension method with the same name and signature.

Although extension methods might not seem to give a big benefit, in *Chapter 12, Querying and Manipulating Data Using LINQ*, you will see some extremely powerful uses of extension methods.

Practicing and exploring

Test your knowledge and understanding by answering some questions. Get some hands-on practice and explore with deeper research into this chapter's topics.

Exercise 6.1 – Test your knowledge

Answer the following questions:

1. What is a delegate?
2. What is an event?
3. How are a base class and a derived class related and how can the derived class access the base class?
4. What is the difference between `is` and `as` operators?
5. Which keyword is used to prevent a class from being derived from or a method from being further overridden?

6. Which keyword is used to prevent a class from being instantiated with the new keyword?

7. Which keyword is used to allow a member to be overridden?

8. What's the difference between a destructor and a deconstruct method?

9. What are the signatures of the constructors that all exceptions should have?

10. What is an extension method and how do you define one?

Exercise 6.2 – Practice creating an inheritance hierarchy

Explore inheritance hierarchies by following these steps:

1. Add a new console application named Exercise02 to your workspace.

2. Create a class named Shape with properties named Height, Width, and Area.

3. Add three classes that derive from it—Rectangle, Square, and Circle—with any additional members you feel are appropriate and that override and implement the Area property correctly.

4. In Program.cs, in the Main method, add statements to create one instance of each shape, as shown in the following code:

```
var r = new Rectangle(3, 4.5);
WriteLine($"Rectangle H: {r.Height}, W: {r.Width}, Area: {r.Area}");
var s = new Square(5);
WriteLine($"Square H: {s.Height}, W: {s.Width}, Area: {s.Area}");
var c = new Circle(2.5);
WriteLine($"Circle H: {c.Height}, W: {c.Width}, Area: {c.Area}");
```

5. Run the console application and ensure that the result looks like the following output:

```
Rectangle H: 3, W: 4.5, Area: 13.5
Square H: 5, W: 5, Area: 25
Circle H: 5, W: 5, Area: 19.6349540849362
```

Exercise 6.3 – Explore topics

Use the following links to read more about the topics covered in this chapter:

- **Operator (C# reference)**: https://docs.microsoft.com/en-us/dotnet/csharp/language-reference/operators/operator-overloading

- **Delegates**: https://docs.microsoft.com/en-us/dotnet/csharp/tour-of-csharp/features-delegates-and-lambda-expressions

- **Events Change to: C# reference**: https://docs.microsoft.com/en-us/dotnet/csharp/language-reference/keywords/event

- **Interfaces**: https://docs.microsoft.com/en-us/dotnet/csharp/tour-of-csharp/types-interfaces

- **Generics (C# Programming Guide)**: https://docs.microsoft.com/en-us/dotnet/csharp/programming-guide/generics

- **Reference Types (C# Reference)**: https://docs.microsoft.com/en-us/dotnet/csharp/language-reference/keywords/reference-types

- **Value Types (C# reference)**: https://docs.microsoft.com/en-us/dotnet/csharp/language-reference/builtin-types/value-types

- **Inheritance (C# Programming Guide)**: https://docs.microsoft.com/en-us/dotnet/csharp/programming-guide/classes-and-structs/inheritance

- **Finalizers (C# Programming Guide)**: https://docs.microsoft.com/en-us/dotnet/csharp/programming-guide/classes-and-structs/destructors

Summary

In this chapter, you learned about local functions and operators, delegates and events, implementing interfaces, generics, and deriving types using inheritance and OOP. You also learned about base and derived classes, and how to override a type member, use polymorphism, and cast between types.

In the next chapter, you will learn how .NET 5 is packaged and deployed, and in the subsequent chapters the types that it provides you with to implement common functionality such as file handling, database access, encryption, and multitasking.

07

Understanding and Packaging .NET Types

This chapter is about how C# keywords are related to .NET types, and about the relationship between namespaces and assemblies. You'll also become familiar with how to package and publish your .NET apps and libraries for use cross-platform, how to use legacy .NET Framework libraries in .NET libraries, and the possibility of porting legacy .NET Framework code bases to .NET.

This chapter covers the following topics:

- Introducing .NET 5
- Understanding .NET components
- Publishing your applications for deployment
- Decompiling assemblies
- Packaging your libraries for NuGet distribution
- Porting from .NET Framework to .NET 5

Introducing .NET 5

This part of the book is about the functionality in the **Base Class Library** (BCL) APIs provided by .NET 5, and how to reuse functionality across all the different .NET platforms using .NET Standard.

.NET Core 2.0 and later's support for a minimum of .NET Standard 2.0 is important because it provides many of the APIs that were missing from the first version of .NET Core. The 15 years' worth of libraries and applications that .NET Framework developers had available to them that are relevant for modern development have now been migrated to .NET and can run cross-platform on macOS and Linux variants, as well as on Windows.

.NET Standard 2.1 added about 3,000 new APIs. Some of those APIs need runtime changes that would break backward compatibility, so .NET Framework 4.8 only implements .NET Standard 2.0. .NET Core 3.0, Xamarin, Mono, and Unity implement .NET Standard 2.1.

> **More Information**: The full list of .NET Standard 2.1 APIs and a comparison with .NET Standard 2.0 are documented at the following link: `https://github.com/dotnet/standard/blob/master/docs/versions/netstandard2.1.md`

.NET 5 removes the need for .NET Standard if all your projects can use .NET 5. Since you might still need to create class libraries for legacy .NET Framework projects, or for Xamarin mobile apps, then there is still a need to create .NET Standard 2.0 and 2.1 class libraries. Once .NET 6 is released in November 2021 with support for Xamarin mobile, then the need for .NET Standard will be further reduced.

> **More Information**: You can read more about the future of .NET Standard at the following link: `https://devblogs.microsoft.com/dotnet/the-future-of-net-standard/`

To summarize the progress that .NET has made over the past five years I have compared the major .NET Core and modern .NET versions with the equivalent .NET Framework versions in the following list:

- .NET Core 1.0: much smaller API compared to .NET Framework 4.6.1, which was the current version in March 2016.

- .NET Core 2.0: reached API parity with .NET Framework 4.7.1 for modern APIs because they both implement .NET Standard 2.0.

- .NET Core 3.0: larger API compared to .NET Framework for modern APIs because .NET Framework 4.8 does not implement .NET Standard 2.1.

- .NET 5: even larger API compared to .NET Framework 4.8 for modern APIs, with much-improved performance.

> **More Information**: You can search and browse all .NET APIs at the following link: `https://docs.microsoft.com/en-us/dotnet/api/`

.NET Core 1.0

.NET Core 1.0 was released in June 2016 and focused on implementing an API suitable for building modern cross-platform apps, including web and cloud applications and services for Linux using ASP.NET Core.

> **More Information**: You can read the .NET Core 1.0 announcement at the following link: `https://devblogs.microsoft.com/dotnet/announcing-net-core-1-0/`

.NET Core 1.1

.NET Core 1.1 was released in November 2016 and focused on fixing bugs, increasing the number of Linux distributions supported, supporting .NET Standard 1.6, and improving performance, especially with ASP.NET Core for web apps and services.

> **More Information**: You can read the .NET Core 1.1 announcement at the following link: `https://devblogs.microsoft.com/dotnet/announcing-net-core-1-1/`

.NET Core 2.0

.NET Core 2.0 was released in August 2017 and focused on implementing .NET Standard 2.0, the ability to reference .NET Framework libraries, and more performance improvements.

> **More Information**: You can read the .NET Core 2.0 announcement at the following link: `https://devblogs.microsoft.com/dotnet/announcing-net-core-2-0/`

The third edition of this book was published in November 2017, so it covered up to .NET Core 2.0 and .NET Core for UWP apps.

.NET Core 2.1

.NET Core 2.1 was released in May 2018 and focused on an extendable tooling system, adding new types like `Span<T>`, new APIs for cryptography and compression, a Windows Compatibility Pack with an additional 20,000 APIs to help port old Windows applications, Entity Framework Core value conversions, LINQ `GroupBy` conversions, data seeding, query types, and even more performance improvements, including the topics listed in the following table:

Feature	Chapter	Topic
Spans, indexes, ranges	8	Working with spans, indexes, and ranges
Brotli compression	9	Compressing with the Brotli algorithm
Cryptography	10	What's new in cryptography?
Lazy loading	11	Enabling lazy loading
Data seeding	11	Understanding data seeding

.NET Core 2.2

.NET Core 2.2 was released in December 2018 and focused on diagnostic improvements for the runtime, optional tiered compilation, and adding new features to ASP.NET Core and Entity Framework Core like spatial data support using types from the **NetTopologySuite** (**NTS**) library, query tags, and collections of owned entities.

 More Information: You can read the .NET Core 2.2 announcement at the following link: `https://devblogs.microsoft.com/dotnet/announcing-net-core-2-2/`

.NET Core 3.0

.NET Core 3.0 was released in September 2019 and focused on adding support for building Windows desktop applications using Windows Forms (2001), Windows Presentation Foundation (WPF; 2006), and Entity Framework 6.3, side-by-side and app-local deployments, a fast JSON reader, serial port access and other PIN access for **Internet of Things** (**IoT**) solutions, and tiered compilation by default, including the topics listed in the following table:

Feature	Chapter	Topic
Embedding .NET in-app	7	Publishing your applications for deployment
Index and Range	8	Working with spans, indexes, and ranges
System.Text.Json	9	High-performance JSON processing
Async streams	13	Working with async streams

The fourth edition of this book was published in October 2019, so it covered some of the new APIs added in later versions up to .NET Core 3.0.

 More Information: You can read the .NET Core 3.0 announcement at the following link: `https://devblogs.microsoft.com/dotnet/announcing-net-core-3-0/`

.NET 5.0

.NET 5.0 was released in November 2020 and focused on unifying the various .NET platforms, refining the platform, and improving performance, including the topics listed in the following table:

Feature	Chapter	Topic
Half type	8	Working with numbers
Regular expression performance improvements	8	Regular expression performance improvements

System.Text.Json improvements	9	High-performance JSON processing
A simple way to get generated SQL	11	Getting the generated SQL
Filtered Include	11	Filtering included entities
Scaffold-DbContext now singularizes using Humanizer	11	Scaffolding models using an existing database

 More Information: You can read the .NET 5 announcement at the following link: `https://devblogs.microsoft.com/dotnet/announcing-net-5-0`

Improving performance from .NET Core 2.0 to .NET 5

Microsoft has made significant improvements to performance in the past few years.

 More Information: You can read a detailed blog post at the following link: `https://devblogs.microsoft.com/dotnet/performance-improvements-in-net-5/`

Understanding .NET components

.NET is made up of several pieces, which are as follows:

- **Language compilers**: These turn your source code written with languages such as C#, F#, and Visual Basic into **intermediate language** (**IL**) code stored in assemblies. With C# 6.0 and later, Microsoft switched to an open source rewritten compiler known as Roslyn that is also used by Visual Basic.

 More Information: You can read more about Roslyn at the following link: `https://github.com/dotnet/roslyn`

- **Common Language Runtime** (**CoreCLR**): This runtime loads assemblies, compiles the IL code stored in them into native code instructions for your computer's CPU, and executes the code within an environment that manages resources such as threads and memory.

- **Base Class Libraries (BCLs) of assemblies in NuGet packages (CoreFX)**: These are prebuilt assemblies of types packaged and distributed using NuGet for performing common tasks when building applications. You can use them to quickly build anything you want, rather like combining LEGO™ pieces. .NET Core 2.0 implemented .NET Standard 2.0, which is a superset of all previous versions of .NET Standard, and lifted .NET Core up to parity with .NET Framework and Xamarin. .NET Core 3.0 implemented .NET Standard 2.1, which added new capabilities and enables performance improvements beyond those available in .NET Framework. .NET 5 implements a unified BCL across all types of apps (except mobile). .NET 6 will implement a unified BCL across all types of apps including mobile.

 More Information: You can read the announcement of .NET Standard 2.1 at the following link: `https://devblogs.microsoft.com/dotnet/announcing-net-standard-2-1/`

Understanding assemblies, packages, and namespaces

An **assembly** is where a type is stored in the filesystem. Assemblies are a mechanism for deploying code. For example, the `System.Data.dll` assembly contains types for managing data. To use types in other assemblies, they must be referenced.

Assemblies are often distributed as **NuGet packages**, which can contain multiple assemblies and other resources. You will also hear about **project SDKs** and **platforms**, which are combinations of NuGet packages.

A **namespace** is the address of a type. Namespaces are a mechanism to uniquely identify a type by requiring a full address rather than just a short name. In the real world, *Bob of 34 Sycamore Street* is different from *Bob of 12 Willow Drive*.

In .NET, the `IActionFilter` interface of the `System.Web.Mvc` namespace is different from the `IActionFilter` interface of the `System.Web.Http.Filters` namespace.

Understanding dependent assemblies

If an assembly is compiled as a class library and provides types for other assemblies to use, then it has the file extension `.dll` (dynamic link library), and it cannot be executed standalone.

Likewise, if an assembly is compiled as an application, then it has the file extension `.exe` (executable) and can be executed standalone. Before .NET Core 3.0, console apps were compiled to `.dll` files and had to be executed by the `dotnet run` command or a host executable.

Any assembly can reference one or more class library assemblies as dependencies, but you cannot have circular references. So, assembly *B* cannot reference assembly *A*, if assembly *A* already references assembly *B*. The compiler will warn you if you attempt to add a dependency reference that would cause a circular reference.

Good Practice: Circular references are often a warning sign of poor code design. If you are sure that you need a circular reference, then use an interface to solve it, as explained in the Stack Overflow answer at the following link: https://stackoverflow.com/questions/6928387/how-to-solve-circular-reference

Understanding the Microsoft .NET project SDKs

By default, console applications have a dependency reference on the Microsoft .NET SDK. This platform contains thousands of types in NuGet packages that almost all applications would need, such as the int and string types.

More Information: You can read more about .NET project SDKs at the following link: https://docs.microsoft.com/en-us/dotnet/core/project-sdk/overview

When using .NET, you reference the dependency assemblies, NuGet packages, and platforms that your application needs in a project file.

Let's explore the relationship between assemblies and namespaces:

1. In Visual Studio Code, create a folder named Chapter07 with a subfolder named AssembliesAndNamespaces, and enter dotnet new console to create a console application.

2. Save the current workspace as Chapter07 in the Chapter07 folder and add the AssembliesAndNamespaces folder to the workspace.

3. Open AssembliesAndNamespaces.csproj, and note that it is a typical project file for a .NET application, as shown in the following markup:

```
<Project Sdk="Microsoft.NET.Sdk">
  <PropertyGroup>
    <OutputType>Exe</OutputType>
    <TargetFramework>net5.0</TargetFramework>
  </PropertyGroup>
</Project>
```

Although it is possible to include the assemblies that your application uses with its deployment package, by default the project will probe for shared assemblies installed in well-known paths.

First, it will look for the specified version of .NET in the current user's .dotnet/store and .nuget folders, and then it looks in a fallback folder that depends on your OS, as shown in the following root paths:

- Windows: C:\Program Files\dotnet\sdk
- macOS: /usr/local/share/dotnet/sdk

Most common .NET types are in the `System.Runtime.dll` assembly. You can see the relationship between some assemblies and the namespaces that they supply types for, and note that there is not always a one-to-one mapping between assemblies and namespaces, as shown in the following table:

Assembly	Example namespaces	Example types
`System.Runtime.dll`	`System, System.Collections, System. Collections.Generic`	`Int32, String, IEnumerable<T>`
`System.Console.dll`	`System`	`Console`
`System.Threading.dll`	`System.Threading`	`Interlocked, Monitor, Mutex`
`System.Xml.XDocument.dll`	`System.Xml.Linq`	`XDocument, XElement, XNode`

Understanding NuGet packages

.NET is split into a set of packages, distributed using a Microsoft-supported package management technology named NuGet. Each of these packages represents a single assembly of the same name. For example, the `System.Collections` package contains the `System.Collections.dll` assembly.

The following are the benefits of packages:

- Packages can ship on their own schedule.
- Packages can be tested independently of other packages.
- Packages can support different OSes and CPUs by including multiple versions of the same assembly built for different OSes and CPUs.
- Packages can have dependencies specific to only one library.
- Apps are smaller because unreferenced packages aren't part of the distribution.

The following table lists some of the more important packages and their important types:

Package	Important types
`System.Runtime`	`Object, String, Int32, Array`
`System.Collections`	`List<T>, Dictionary<TKey, TValue>`
`System.Net.Http`	`HttpClient, HttpResponseMessage`
`System.IO.FileSystem`	`File, Directory`
`System.Reflection`	`Assembly, TypeInfo, MethodInfo`

Understanding frameworks

There is a two-way relationship between frameworks and packages. Packages define the APIs, while frameworks group packages. A framework without any packages would not define any APIs.

More Information: If you have a strong understanding of interfaces and types that implement them, you might find the following URL useful for grasping how packages, and their APIs, relate to frameworks such as the various .NET Standard versions: `https://gist.github.com/davidfowl/8939f305567e17` `55412d6dc0b8baf1b7`

.NET packages each support a set of frameworks. For example, the `System.IO.FileSystem` package version 4.3.0 supports the following frameworks:

- .NET Standard, version 1.3 or later.
- .NET Framework, version 4.6 or later.
- Six Mono and Xamarin platforms (for example, Xamarin.iOS 1.0).

More Information: You can read the details at the following link: `https://` `www.nuget.org/packages/System.IO.FileSystem/`

Importing a namespace to use a type

Let's explore how namespaces are related to assemblies and types:

1. In the `AssembliesAndNamespaces` project, in the `Main` method, enter the following code:

   ```
   var doc = new XDocument();
   ```

   The `XDocument` type is not recognized because we have not told the compiler what the namespace of the type is. Although this project already has a reference to the assembly that contains the type, we also need to either prefix the type name with its namespace or import the namespace.

2. Click inside the `XDocument` class name. Visual Studio Code displays a light bulb, showing that it recognizes the type and can automatically fix the problem for you.

3. Click the light bulb, or in Windows, press *Ctrl* + . (dot), or in macOS, press *Cmd* + . (dot).

4. Select `using System.Xml.Linq;` from the menu.

This will import the namespace by adding a `using` statement to the top of the file. Once a namespace is imported at the top of a code file, then all the types within the namespace are available for use in that code file by just typing their name without the type name needing to be fully qualified by prefixing it with its namespace.

Relating C# keywords to .NET types

One of the common questions I get from new C# programmers is, *What is the difference between* string *with a lowercase s and* String *with an uppercase S?*

The short answer is easy: none. The long answer is that all C# type keywords are aliases for a .NET type in a class library assembly.

When you use the string keyword, the compiler turns it into a System.String type. When you use the int type, the compiler turns it into a System.Int32 type:

1. In the Main method, declare two variables to hold string values, one using lowercase string and one using uppercase String, as shown in the following code:

```
string s1 = "Hello";
String s2 = "World";

WriteLine($"{s1} {s2}");
```

   At the moment, they both work equally well and literally mean the same thing.

2. At the top of the class file, comment out the using System; statement by prefixing the statement with //, and note the compiler error.

3. Remove the comment slashes to fix the error.

 Good Practice: When you have a choice, use the C# keyword instead of the actual type because the keywords do not need the namespace imported.

The following table shows the 16 C# type keywords along with their actual .NET types:

Keyword	.NET type	Keyword	.NET type
string	System.String	char	System.Char
sbyte	System.SByte	byte	System.Byte
short	System.Int16	ushort	System.UInt16
int	System.Int32	uint	System.UInt32
long	System.Int64	ulong	System.UInt64
float	System.Single	double	System.Double
decimal	System.Decimal	bool	System.Boolean
object	System.Object	dynamic	System.Dynamic.DynamicObject

Other .NET programming language compilers can do the same thing. For example, the Visual Basic .NET language has a type named Integer that is its alias for System.Int32.

4. Right-click inside XDocument and choose **Go to Definition** or press F12.

5. Navigate to the top of the code file and note the assembly filename is `System.Xml.XDocument.dll` but the class is in the `System.Xml.Linq` namespace, as shown in the following screenshot:

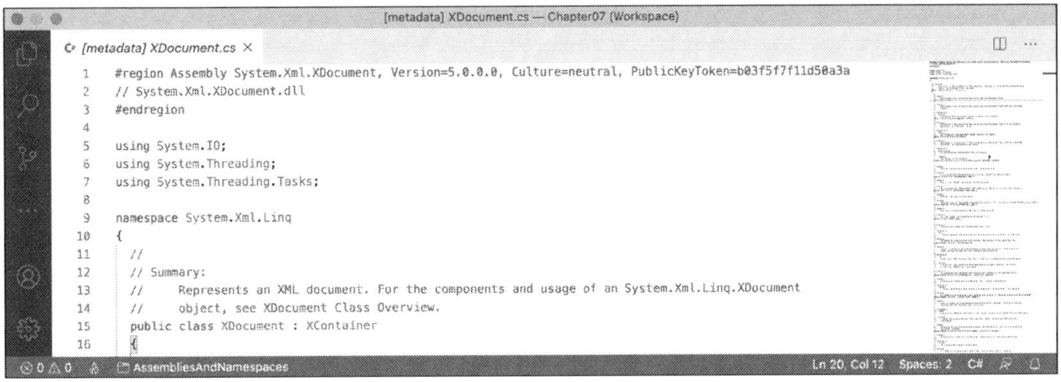

```
[metadata] XDocument.cs — Chapter07 (Workspace)

C* [metadata] XDocument.cs ×

1   #region Assembly System.Xml.XDocument, Version=5.0.0.0, Culture=neutral, PublicKeyToken=b03f5f7f11d50a3a
2   // System.Xml.XDocument.dll
3   #endregion
4
5   using System.IO;
6   using System.Threading;
7   using System.Threading.Tasks;
8
9   namespace System.Xml.Linq
10  {
11      //
12      // Summary:
13      //     Represents an XML document. For the components and usage of an System.Xml.Linq.XDocument
14      //     object, see XDocument Class Overview.
15      public class XDocument : XContainer
16      {

AssembliesAndNamespaces                                                    Ln 20, Col 12    Spaces: 2    C#
```

Figure 7.1: Information on the assembly file

6. Close the **[metadata] XDocument.cs** tab.

7. Right-click inside `string` or `String` and choose **Go to Definition** or press F12.

8. Navigate to the top of the code file and note the assembly filename is `System.Runtime.dll` but the class is in the `System` namespace.

Sharing code with legacy platforms using .NET Standard

Before .NET Standard, there were **Portable Class Libraries (PCLs)**. With PCLs, you could create a library of code and explicitly specify which platforms you want the library to support, such as Xamarin, Silverlight, and Windows 8. Your library could then use the intersection of APIs that are supported by the specified platforms.

Microsoft realized that this is unsustainable, so they created .NET Standard—a single API that all future .NET platforms would support. There are older versions of .NET Standard, but .NET Standard 2.0 was an attempt to unify all important recent .NET platforms. .NET Standard 2.1 was released in late 2019 but only .NET Core 3.0 and that year's version of Xamarin support its new features. For the rest of this book, I will use the term .NET Standard to mean .NET Standard 2.0.

.NET Standard is similar to HTML5 in that they are both standards that a platform should support. Just as Google's Chrome browser and Microsoft's Edge browser implement the HTML5 standard, .NET Core, .NET Framework, and Xamarin all implement .NET Standard. If you want to create a library of types that will work across variants of legacy .NET, you can do so most easily with .NET Standard.

Good Practice: Since many of the API additions in .NET Standard 2.1 required runtime changes, and .NET Framework is Microsoft's legacy platform that needs to remain as unchanging as possible, .NET Framework 4.8 remained on .NET Standard 2.0 rather than implementing .NET Standard 2.1. If you need to support .NET Framework customers, then you should create class libraries on .NET Standard 2.0 even though it is not the latest and does not support all the recent language and BCL new features.

Your choice of which .NET Standard version to target comes down to a balance between maximizing platform support and available functionality. A lower version supports more platforms but has a smaller set of APIs. A higher version supports fewer platforms but has a larger set of APIs. Generally, you should choose the lowest version that supports all the APIs that you need.

The versions of .NET Standard and which platforms they support are summarized in the following table:

Platform	1.1	1.2	1.3	1.4	1.5	1.6	2.0	2.1
.NET Core	→	→	→	→	→	1.0, 1.1	2.0	3.0
.NET Framework	4.5	4.5.1	4.6	→	→	→	4.6.1	n/a
Mono	→	→	→	→	→	4.6	5.4	6.2
Xamarin.iOS	→	→	→	→	→	10.0	10.14	12.12
UWP	→	→	→	10	→	→	10.0.16299	n/a

Creating a .NET Standard 2.0 class library

We will create a class library using .NET Standard 2.0 so that it can be used across all important .NET legacy platforms and cross-platform on Windows, macOS, and Linux operating systems while also having access to a wide set of .NET APIs:

1. In the Code/Chapter07 folder, create a subfolder named SharedLibrary.
2. In Visual Studio Code, add the SharedLibrary folder to the Chapter07 workspace.
3. Navigate to **Terminal | New Terminal** and select SharedLibrary.
4. In **TERMINAL**, enter the following command:

```
dotnet new classlib
```

5. Click on SharedLibrary.csproj and note that a class library generated by the dotnet CLI targets .NET 5.0 by default, as shown in the following markup:

```
<Project Sdk="Microsoft.NET.Sdk">
  <PropertyGroup>
    <TargetFramework>net5.0</TargetFramework>
  </PropertyGroup>
</Project>
```

6. Modify the target framework, as shown in the following markup:

```
<Project Sdk="Microsoft.NET.Sdk">
  <PropertyGroup>
    <TargetFramework>netstandard2.0</TargetFramework>
  </PropertyGroup>
</Project>
```

 Good Practice: If you need to create a type that uses new features in .NET 5, then create separate class libraries: one targeting .NET Standard 2.0 and one targeting .NET 5. You will see this in action in *Chapter 11, Working with Databases Using Entity Framework Core.*

Publishing your applications for deployment

There are three ways to publish and deploy a .NET application. They are:

1. **Framework-dependent deployment (FDD)**.
2. **Framework-dependent executables (FDEs)**.
3. Self-contained.

If you choose to deploy your application and its package dependencies, but not .NET itself, then you rely on .NET already being on the target computer. This works well for web applications deployed to a server because .NET and lots of other web applications are likely already on the server.

Sometimes, you want to be able to give someone a USB stick containing your application and know that it can execute on their computer. You want to perform a self-contained deployment. While the size of the deployment files will be larger, you'll know that it will work.

Creating a console application to publish

Let's explore how to publish a console application:

1. Create a new console application project named DotNetCoreEverywhere and add it to the Chapter07 workspace.

2. In Program.cs, add a statement to output a message saying the console app can run everywhere, as shown in the following code:

```
using static System.Console;

namespace DotNetCoreEverywhere
{
  class Program
  {
    static void Main(string[] args)
```

```
    {
        WriteLine("I can run everywhere!");
    }
  }
}
```

3. Open `DotNetCoreEverywhere.csproj` and add the runtime identifiers to target three operating systems inside the `<PropertyGroup>` element, as shown highlighted in the following markup:

```
<Project Sdk="Microsoft.NET.Sdk">
  <PropertyGroup>
    <OutputType>Exe</OutputType>
    <TargetFramework>net5.0</TargetFramework>
    <RuntimeIdentifiers>
      win10-x64;osx-x64;rhel.7.4-x64
    </RuntimeIdentifiers>
  </PropertyGroup>
</Project>
```

- The `win10-x64` RID value means Windows 10 or Windows Server 2016.
- The `osx-x64` RID value means macOS High Sierra 10.13 or later.
- The `rhel.7.4-x64` RID value means **Red Hat Enterprise Linux (RHEL)** 7.4 or later.

More Information: You can find the currently supported Runtime Identifier (RID) values at the following link: `https://docs.microsoft.com/en-us/dotnet/articles/core/rid-catalog`

Understanding dotnet commands

When you install .NET SDK, it includes the **command-line interface (CLI)** named dotnet.

Creating new projects

The dotnet CLI has commands that work on the current folder to create a new project using templates:

1. In Visual Studio Code, navigate to **TERMINAL**.
2. Enter the dotnet new -l command to list your currently installed templates, as shown in the following screenshot:

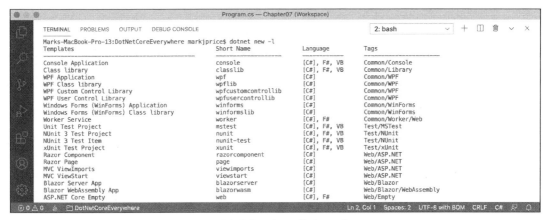

Figure 7.2: A list of installed templates

 More Information: You can install additional templates from the following link: https://dotnetnew.azurewebsites.net/

Managing projects

The `dotnet` CLI has the following commands that work on the project in the current folder, to manage the project:

- `dotnet restore`: This downloads dependencies for the project.
- `dotnet build`: This compiles the project.
- `dotnet test`: This runs unit tests on the project.
- `dotnet run`: This runs the project.
- `dotnet pack`: This creates a NuGet package for the project.
- `dotnet publish`: This compiles and then publishes the project, either with dependencies or as a self-contained application.
- `add`: This adds a reference to a package or class library to the project.
- `remove`: This removes a reference to a package or class library from the project.
- `list`: This lists the package or class library references for the project.

Publishing a self-contained app

Now that you have seen some example `dotnet` tool commands, we can publish our cross-platform console app:

1. In Visual Studio Code, navigate to **TERMINAL**, and enter the following command to build the release version of the console application for Windows 10:

```
dotnet publish -c Release -r win10-x64
```

Microsoft Build Engine will then compile and publish the console application.

2. In **TERMINAL**, enter the following commands to build release versions for macOS and RHEL:

```
dotnet publish -c Release -r osx-x64
dotnet publish -c Release -r rhel.7.4-x64
```

3. Open a macOS Finder window or Windows File Explorer, navigate to `DotNetCoreEverywhere\bin\Release\net5.0`, and note the output folders for the three operating systems.

4. In the `osx-x64` folder, select the `publish` folder, note all the supporting assemblies, and then select the `DotNetEverywhere` executable file, and note the executable is about 95 KB, as shown in the following screenshot:

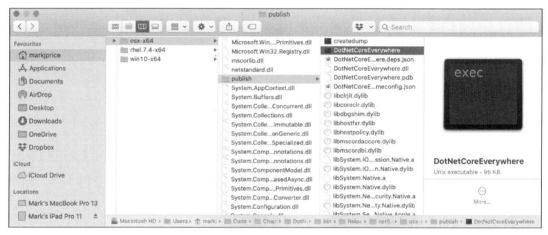

Figure 7.3: The DotNetEverywhere executable file for macOS

5. Double-click the executable and note the results, as shown in the following screenshot:

Figure 7.4: The results of executing DotNetEverywhere

If you copy any of those `publish` folders to the appropriate operating system, the console application will run; this is because it is a self-contained deployable .NET application.

Publishing a single-file app

To publish as a "single" file, you can specify flags when publishing. But in .NET 5.0, single-file apps are primarily focused on Linux because there are limitations in both Windows and macOS that mean true single-file publishing is not technically possible.

If you can assume that .NET 5 is already installed on a computer, then you can use the following flags:

```
dotnet publish -r win10-x64 -c Release --self-contained=false
/p:PublishSingleFile=true
```

This will generate two files: DotNetCoreEverywhere.exe and DotNetCoreEverywhere.pdb. The exe is the executable. The pdb is a program database file that stores debugging information.

 More Information: You can read about PDB files at the following link: https://www.wintellect.com/pdb-files-what-every-developer-must-know/

If you prefer the pdb file to be embedded in the exe file, then add an element to your csproj file, as shown in the following markup:

```
<PropertyGroup>
  <OutputType>Exe</OutputType>
  <TargetFramework>net5.0</TargetFramework>
  <DebugType>embed</DebugType>
</PropertyGroup>
```

If you cannot assume that .NET 5 is already installed on a computer, then although Linux also only generates the two files, expect the following additional files for Windows: coreclr.dll, clrjit.dll, clrcompression.dll, and mscordaccore.dll.

Let us see an example for macOS:

1. In Visual Studio Code, navigate to **TERMINAL**, and enter the following command to build the release version of the console application for Windows 10:

   ```
   dotnet publish -c Release -r osx-x64 /p:PublishSingleFile=true
   ```

2. Navigate to the DotNetCoreEverywhere\bin\Release\net5.0\osx-x64\publish folder, select the DotNetEverywhere executable file, and note the executable is now about 52 MB, and there is a pdb file and seven dylib files.

 More Information: You can read more about the single-file app issue at the following link: https://github.com/dotnet/runtime/issues/36590

Reducing the size of apps using app trimming

One of the problems with deploying a .NET app as a self-contained app is that the .NET 5 libraries take up a lot of space. One of the biggest needs for reduced size is Blazor WebAssembly components because all the .NET 5 libraries need to be downloaded to the browser.

Luckily, you can reduce this size by not packaging unused assemblies with your deployments. Introduced with .NET Core 3.0, the app trimming system can identify the assemblies needed by your code and remove those not needed.

With .NET 5, the trimming goes further by removing individual types and even members like methods from within an assembly if they are not used. For example, with a Hello World console app, the System.Console.dll assembly is trimmed from 61.5 KB to 31.5 KB. This is an experimental feature so use it with caution.

The catch is how well the trimming identifies unused assemblies, types, and members. If your code is dynamic, perhaps using reflection, then it might not work correctly, so Microsoft also allows manual control.

There are two ways to enable assembly-level trimming. First, add an element in the project file, as shown in the following markup:

```
<PublishTrimmed>true</PublishTrimmed>
```

Second, add a flag when publishing, as shown in the following command:

```
-p:PublishTrimmed=True
```

There are two ways to enable member-level trimming.

First, add an element in the project file, as shown in the following markup:

```
<PublishTrimmed>true</PublishTrimmed>
<TrimMode>Link</TrimMode>
```

Second, add a flag when publishing, as shown in the following command:

```
-p:PublishTrimmed=True -p:TrimMode=Link
```

 More Information: You can read more about app trimming at the following link: https://devblogs.microsoft.com/dotnet/app-trimming-in-net-5/

Decompiling assemblies

One of the best ways to learn how to code for .NET is to see how professionals do it.

For learning purposes, you can decompile any .NET assembly with a tool like **ILSpy**. If you have not already installed the **ILSpy .NET Decompiler** extension for Visual Studio Code, then search for it and install it now:

 Good Practice: You could decompile someone else's assemblies for non-learning purposes but remember that you are viewing their intellectual property so please respect that.

1. In Visual Studio Code, navigate to **View | Command Palette...** or press *Cmd + Shift + P*.

2. Type `ilspy` and then select **ILSpy: Decompile IL Assembly (pick file)**.

3. Navigate to the `Code/Chapter07/DotNetCodeEverywhere/bin/Release/net5.0/osx-x64` folder.

4. Select the **System.IO.FileSystem.dll** assembly and click **Select assembly**.

5. In the **EXPLORER** window, expand **ILSPY DECOMPILED MEMBERS**, select the assembly, and note the two edit windows that open showing assembly attributes using C# code and external DLL and assembly references using IL code, as shown in the following screenshot:

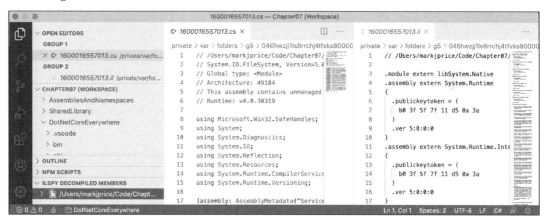

Figure 7.5: Expanding ILSPY DECOMPILED MEMBERS

6. In the IL code, note the reference to the `System.Runtime` assembly, including the version number, as shown in the following code:

```
.assembly extern System.Runtime
{
    .publickeytoken = (
      b0 3f 5f 7f 11 d5 0a 3a
    )
    .ver 5:0:0:0
}
```

`.module extern libSystem.Native` means this assembly makes function calls to macOS system APIs as you would expect from code that interacts with the filesystem. If we had decompiled the Windows equivalent of this assembly, it would use `.module extern kernel32.dll` instead, which is a Win32 API.

7. In the **EXPLORER** window, expand the namespaces, expand the **System.IO** namespace, select **Directory**, and note the two edit windows that open showing the decompiled `Directory` class using C# code and IL code, as shown in the following screenshot:

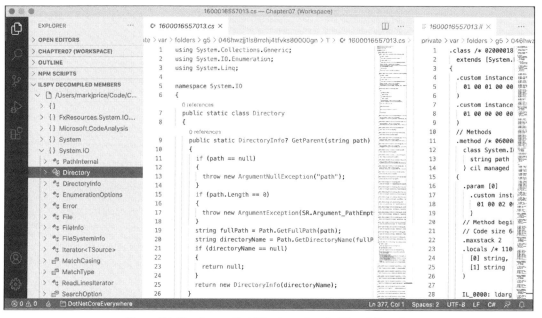

Figure 7.6: The decompiled Directory class in C# and IL code

8. Compare the C# source code for the `GetParent` method, shown in the following code:

```
public static DirectoryInfo GetParent(string path)
{
  if (path == null)
  {
    throw new ArgumentNullException("path");
  }
  if (path.Length == 0)
  {
    throw new ArgumentException(SR.Argument_PathEmpty, "path");
  }
  string fullPath = Path.GetFullPath(path);
  string directoryName = Path.GetDirectoryName(fullPath);
  if (directoryName == null)
  {
    return null;
  }
  return new DirectoryInfo(directoryName);
}
```

9. With the equivalent IL source code of the `GetParent` method, as shown in the following code:

```
.method /* 06000067 */ public hidebysig static
  class System.IO.DirectoryInfo GetParent (
    string path
  ) cil managed
{
  .param [0]
    .custom instance void System.Runtime.CompilerServices.
NullableAttribute::.ctor(uint8) = (
01 00 02 00 00
    )
  // Method begins at RVA 0x62d4
  // Code size 64 (0x40)
  .maxstack 2
  .locals /* 1100000E */ (
    [0] string,
    [1] string
  )

  IL_0000: ldarg.0
  IL_0001: brtrue.s IL_000e

  IL_0003: ldstr "path" /* 700005CB */
  IL_0008: newobj instance void
    [System.Runtime]System.ArgumentNullException::.ctor(string) /*
0A000035 */
  IL_000d: throw

IL_000e: ldarg.0
IL_000f: callvirt instance int32 [System.Runtime]System.String::get_
Length() /* 0A000022 */
IL_0014: brtrue.s IL_0026
IL_0016: call string System.SR::get_Argument_PathEmpty() /* 0600004C */
IL_001b: ldstr "path" /* 700005CB */
IL_0020: newobj instance void [System.Runtime]System.ArgumentException::.
ctor(string, string) /* 0A000036 */
IL_0025: throw
IL_0026: ldarg.0
IL_0027: call string [System.Runtime.Extensions]System.
IO.Path::GetFullPath(string) /* 0A000037 */
IL_002c: stloc.0
IL_002d: ldloc.0
IL_002e: call string [System.Runtime.Extensions]System.IO.Path::GetDirecto
ryName(string) /* 0A000038 */
IL_0033: stloc.1
```

```
IL_0034: ldloc.1
IL_0035: brtrue.s IL_0039
IL_0037: ldnull
IL_0038: ret
IL_0039: ldloc.1
IL_003a: newobj instance void System.IO.DirectoryInfo::.ctor(string) /*
06000097 */
IL_003f: ret
} // end of method Directory::GetParent
```

> **Good Practice:** The IL code edit windows are not especially useful unless you get very advanced with C# and .NET development where knowing how the C# compiler translates your source code into IL code can be important. The much more useful edit windows contain the equivalent C# source code written by Microsoft experts. You can learn a lot of good practices from seeing how professionals implement types.

10. Close the edit windows without saving changes.

11. In the **EXPLORER** window, in **ILSPY DECOMPILED MEMBERS**, right-click the assembly and choose **Unload Assembly**.

Packaging your libraries for NuGet distribution

Before we learn how to create and package our own libraries, we will review how a project can use an existing package.

Referencing a NuGet package

Let's say that you want to add a package created by a third-party developer, for example, Newtonsoft.Json, a popular package for working with the **JavaScript Object Notation (JSON)** serialization format:

1. In Visual Studio Code, open the AssembliesAndNamespaces project.

2. Enter the following command in **Terminal**:
   ```
   dotnet add package newtonsoft.json
   ```

3. Open AssembliesAndNamespaces.csproj, and you will see the package reference has been added, as shown in the following markup:
   ```
   <Project Sdk="Microsoft.NET.Sdk">
     <PropertyGroup>
       <OutputType>Exe</OutputType>
   ```

```
      <TargetFramework>net5.0</TargetFramework>
    </PropertyGroup>
    <ItemGroup>
      <PackageReference Include="newtonsoft.json"
        Version="12.0.3" />
    </ItemGroup>
  </Project>
```

If you have a more recent version of the newtonsoft.json package, then it has been updated since this book was published.

Fixing dependencies

To consistently restore packages and write reliable code, it's important that you **fix dependencies**. Fixing dependencies means you are using the same family of packages released for a specific version of .NET, for example, .NET 5.0.

To fix dependencies, every package should have a single version with no additional qualifiers. Additional qualifiers include betas (beta1), release candidates (rc4), and wildcards (*). Wildcards allow future versions to be automatically referenced and used because they always represent the most recent release. But wildcards are therefore dangerous because they could result in the use of future incompatible packages that break your code.

If you use the dotnet add package command, then it will always use the latest specific version of a package. But if you copy and paste configuration from a blog article or manually add a reference yourself, you might include wildcard qualifiers.

The following dependencies are NOT fixed and should be avoided:

```
<PackageReference Include="System.Net.Http"
  Version="4.1.0-*" />
<PackageReference Include="Newtonsoft.Json"
  Version="12.0.3-beta1" />
```

 Good Practice: Microsoft guarantees that if you fixed your dependencies to what ships with a specific version of .NET, for example, 5.0, those packages will all work together. Always fix your dependencies.

Packaging a library for NuGet

Now, let's package the SharedLibrary project that you created earlier:

1. In the SharedLibrary project, rename Class1.cs to StringExtensions.cs, and modify its contents to provide some useful extension methods for validating various text values using regular expressions, as shown in the following code:

```
using System.Text.RegularExpressions;

namespace Packt.Shared
{
  public static class StringExtensions
  {
    public static bool IsValidXmlTag(this string input)
    {
      return Regex.IsMatch(input,
        @"^<([a-z]+)([^<]+)*(?:>(.*)<\/\1>|\s+\/>)$");
    }

    public static bool IsValidPassword(this string input)
    {
      // minimum of eight valid characters
      return Regex.IsMatch(input, "^[a-zA-Z0-9_-]{8,}$");
    }

    public static bool IsValidHex(this string input)
    {
      // three or six valid hex number characters
      return Regex.IsMatch(input,
        "^#?([a-fA-F0-9]{3}|[a-fA-F0-9]{6})$");
    }
  }
}
```

You will learn how to write regular expressions in *Chapter 8, Working with Common .NET Types*.

2. Edit `SharedLibrary.csproj`, and modify its contents, as shown in the following markup, and note the following:

    - `PackageId` must be globally unique, so you must use a different value if you want to publish this NuGet package to the `https://www.nuget.org/` public feed for others to reference and download.

    - `PackageLicenseExpression` must be a value from the following link: `https://spdx.org/licenses/` or you could specify a custom license.

    - All the other elements are self-explanatory:

```
<Project Sdk="Microsoft.NET.Sdk">
  <PropertyGroup>
    <TargetFramework>netstandard2.0</TargetFramework>

    <GeneratePackageOnBuild>true</GeneratePackageOnBuild>
    <PackageId>Packt.CSdotnet.SharedLibrary</PackageId>
    <PackageVersion>5.0.0.0</PackageVersion>
```

```
        <Title>C# 9 and .NET 5 Shared Library</Title>
        <Authors>Mark J Price</Authors>
        <PackageLicenseExpression>
          MS-PL
        </PackageLicenseExpression>
        <PackageProjectUrl>
          http://github.com/markjprice/cs9dotnet5
        </PackageProjectUrl>
        <PackageIcon>packt-csdotnet-sharedlibrary.png</PackageIcon>
        <PackageRequireLicenseAcceptance>true
          </PackageRequireLicenseAcceptance>
        <PackageReleaseNotes>
          Example shared library packaged for NuGet.
        </PackageReleaseNotes>
        <Description>
          Three extension methods to validate a string value.
        </Description>
        <Copyright>
          Copyright © 2020 Packt Publishing Limited
        </Copyright>
        <PackageTags>string extensions packt csharp net5</PackageTags>
      </PropertyGroup>

      <ItemGroup>
        <None Include="packt-csdotnet-sharedlibrary.png">
          <Pack>True</Pack>
          <PackagePath></PackagePath>
        </None>
      </ItemGroup>
    </Project>
```

Configuration property values that are true or false values cannot have any whitespace so the `<PackageRequireLicenseAcceptance>` entry cannot have a carriage-return and indentation as shown in the preceding markup.

3. Download the icon file and save it in the SharedLibrary folder from the following link: https://github.com/markjprice/cs9dotnet5/tree/master/Chapter07/SharedLibrary/ packt-csdotnet-sharedlibrary.png.

4. Navigate to **Terminal** | **New Terminal** and select SharedLibrary.

5. In **TERMINAL**, enter commands to build the release assembly and then generate a NuGet package, as shown in the following commands:

```
dotnet build -c Release
dotnet pack -c Release
```

6. Start your favorite browser and navigate to the following link: https://www.nuget.org/ packages/manage/upload.

7. You will need to sign in with a Microsoft account at `https://www.nuget.org/` if you want to upload a NuGet package for other developers to reference as a dependency package.

8. Click on **Browse...** and select the `.nupkg` file that was created by the `pack` command. The folder path should be `Code\Chapter07\SharedLibrary\bin\Release` and the file is named `Packt.CSdotnet.SharedLibrary.5.0.0.nupkg`.

9. Verify that the information you entered in the `SharedLibrary.csproj` file has been correctly filled in, and then click on **Submit**.

10. Wait a few seconds, and you will see a success message showing that your package has been uploaded, as shown in the following screenshot:

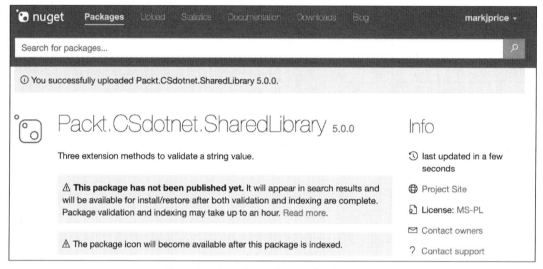

Figure 7.7: A NuGet package upload message

 More Information: If you get an error, then review the project file for mistakes, or read more information about the `PackageReference` format at the link: `https://docs.microsoft.com/en-us/nuget/reference/msbuild-targets`

Testing your package

You will now test your uploaded package by referencing it in the `AssembliesAndNamespaces` project:

1. Open `AssembliesAndNamespaces.csproj`.

2. Modify it to reference your package (or you could use the `dotnet add package` command), as shown highlighted in the following markup:

```
<Project Sdk="Microsoft.NET.Sdk">
  <PropertyGroup>
```

```
    <OutputType>Exe</OutputType>
    <TargetFramework>net5.0</TargetFramework>
  </PropertyGroup>
  <ItemGroup>
    <PackageReference Include="newtonsoft.json"
      Version="12.0.3" />
    <PackageReference Include="packt.csdotnet.sharedlibrary"
      Version="5.0.0" />
  </ItemGroup>
</Project>
```

In the preceding markup, I used my package reference. You should use your own if you successfully uploaded it.

3. Enter the command to restore packages and compile the console app: `dotnet build`.

4. Edit `Program.cs` to import the `Packt.Shared` namespace.

5. In the `Main` method, prompt the user to enter some `string` values, and then validate them using the extension methods in the package, as shown in the following code:

```
Write("Enter a color value in hex: ");
string hex = ReadLine();
WriteLine("Is {0} a valid color value? {1}",
  arg0: hex, arg1: hex.IsValidHex());

Write("Enter a XML element: ");
string xmlTag = ReadLine();
WriteLine("Is {0} a valid XML element? {1}",
  arg0: xmlTag, arg1: xmlTag.IsValidXmlTag());

Write("Enter a password: ");
string password = ReadLine();
WriteLine("Is {0} a valid password? {1}",
  arg0: password, arg1: password.IsValidPassword());
```

6. Run the application, enter some values as prompted, and view the results, as shown in the following output:

```
Enter a color value in hex: 00ffc8
Is 00ffc8 a valid color value? True
Enter an XML element: <h1 class="<" />
Is <h1 class="<" /> a valid XML element? False
Enter a password: secretsauce
Is secretsauce a valid password? True
```

Porting from .NET Framework to .NET 5

If you are an existing .NET Framework developer, then you may have existing applications that you are wondering if you should port to .NET 5. You should consider if porting is the right choice for your code, because sometimes, the best choice is not to port.

Could you port?

.NET 5 has great support for the following types of applications on Windows, macOS, and Linux:

- **ASP.NET Core MVC** web applications
- **ASP.NET Core Web API** web services (REST/HTTP)
- **Console applications**

.NET 5 has great support for the following types of applications on Windows:

- **Windows Forms applications**
- **Windows Presentation Foundation (WPF)** applications
- **Universal Windows Platform (UWP)** applications

 More Information: UWP apps can be created using C++, JavaScript, C#, and Visual Basic using a custom version of .NET Core. You can read more about this at the following link: https://docs.microsoft.com/en-us/windows/uwp/get-started/universal-application-platform-guide

.NET 5 does not support the following types of legacy Microsoft applications and many others:

- **ASP.NET Web Forms** web applications
- **Windows Communication Foundation** services
- **Silverlight** applications

Silverlight and ASP.NET Web Forms applications will never be able to be ported to modern .NET, but existing Windows Forms and WPF applications could be ported to .NET 5 on Windows in order to benefit from the new APIs and faster performance. Existing ASP.NET MVC web applications and ASP.NET Web API web services could be ported to .NET 5 on Windows, Linux, or macOS.

Should you port?

Even if you *could* port, *should* you? What benefits do you gain? Some common benefits include the following:

- **Deployment to Linux or Docker for web applications and web services**: These OSes are lightweight and cost-effective as web application and web service platforms, especially when compared to Windows Server.

- **Removal of dependency on IIS and System.Web.dll**: Even if you continue to deploy to Windows Server, ASP.NET Core can be hosted on lightweight, higher-performance Kestrel (or other) web servers.

- **Command-line tools**: Tools that developers and administrators use to automate their tasks are often built as console applications. The ability to run a single tool cross-platform is very useful.

Differences between .NET Framework and .NET 5

There are three key differences, as shown in the following table:

.NET 5	.NET Framework
Distributed as NuGet packages, so each application can be deployed with its own app-local copy of the version of .NET that it needs.	Distributed as a system-wide, shared set of assemblies (literally, in the **Global Assembly Cache** (**GAC**)).
Split into small, layered components, so a minimal deployment can be performed.	Single, monolithic deployment.
Removes older technologies, such as ASP.NET Web Forms, and non-cross-platform features, such as AppDomains, .NET Remoting, and binary serialization.	As well as some similar technologies to those in .NET 5, it retains some older technologies such as ASP.NET Web Forms.

Understanding the .NET Portability Analyzer

Microsoft has a useful tool that you can run against your existing applications to generate a report for porting. You can watch a demonstration of the tool at the following link: https://channel9.msdn.com/Blogs/Seth-Juarez/A-Brief-Look-at-the-NET-Portability-Analyzer

Using non-.NET Standard libraries

Most existing NuGet packages can be used with .NET 5, even if they are not compiled for .NET Standard. If you find a package that does not officially support .NET Standard, as shown on its nuget.org web page, you do not have to give up. You should try it and see if it works.

 More Information: You can search for useful NuGet packages at the following link: https://www.nuget.org/packages

For example, there is a package of custom collections for handling matrices created by Dialect Software LLC, documented at the following link:

https://www.nuget.org/packages/DialectSoftware.Collections.Matrix/

This package was last updated in 2013, which was long before .NET Core and .NET 5 existed, so this package was built for .NET Framework. As long as an assembly package like this only uses APIs available in .NET Standard, it can be used in a .NET 5 project.

Let's try using it and see if it works:

1. Open `AssembliesAndNamespaces.csproj`.

2. Add a `<PackageReference>` for Dialect Software's package, as shown in the following markup:

   ```
   <PackageReference
       Include="dialectsoftware.collections.matrix"
       Version="1.0.0" />
   ```

3. In **TERMINAL**, restore the dependent packages, as shown in the following command:

   ```
   dotnet restore
   ```

4. Open `Program.cs` and add statements to import the `DialectSoftware.Collections` and `DialectSoftware.Collections.Generics` namespaces.

5. Add statements to create instances of `Axis` and `Matrix<T>`, populate them with values, and output them, as shown in the following code:

   ```
   var x = new Axis("x", 0, 10, 1);
   var y = new Axis("y", 0, 4, 1);

   var matrix = new Matrix<long>(new[] { x, y });

   for (int i = 0; i < matrix.Axes[0].Points.Length; i++)
   {
     matrix.Axes[0].Points[i].Label = "x" + i.ToString();
   }

   for (int i = 0; i < matrix.Axes[1].Points.Length; i++)
   {
     matrix.Axes[1].Points[i].Label = "y" + i.ToString();
   }

   foreach (long[] c in matrix)
   {
     matrix[c] = c[0] + c[1];
   }

   foreach (long[] c in matrix)
   ```

```
{
  WriteLine("{0},{1} ({2},{3}) = {4}",
    matrix.Axes[0].Points[c[0]].Label,
    matrix.Axes[1].Points[c[1]].Label,
    c[0], c[1], matrix[c]);
}
```

6. Run the console application, noting the warning message and the results, as shown in the following output:

```
warning NU1701: Package 'DialectSoftware.Collections.Matrix
1.0.0' was restored using '.NETFramework,Version=v4.6.1,
.NETFramework,Version=v4.6.2, .NETFramework,Version=v4.7,
.NETFramework,Version=v4.7.1, .NETFramework,Version=v4.7.2,
.NETFramework,Version=v4.8' instead of the project target framework
'net5.0'. This package may not be fully compatible with your project.
x0,y0 (0,0) = 0
x0,y1 (0,1) = 1
x0,y2 (0,2) = 2
x0,y3 (0,3) = 3
...and so on.
```

Even though this package was created before .NET 5 existed, and the compiler and runtime have no way of knowing if it will work and therefore show warnings, because it happens to only call .NET Standard-compatible APIs, it works.

Practicing and exploring

Test your knowledge and understanding by answering some questions, get some hands-on practice, and explore with deeper research into topics of this chapter.

Exercise 7.1 – Test your knowledge

Answer the following questions:

1. What is the difference between a namespace and an assembly?
2. How do you reference another project in a `.csproj` file?
3. What is the benefit of a tool like ILSpy?
4. Which .NET type does the C# `float` alias represent?
5. What tool should you use before porting an application from .NET Framework to .NET 5?
6. What is the difference between framework-dependent and self-contained deployments of .NET applications?
7. What is a RID?

8. What is the difference between the dotnet pack and dotnet publish commands?

9. What types of applications written for the .NET Framework can be ported to .NET 5?

10. Can you use packages written for .NET Framework with .NET 5?

Exercise 7.2 – Explore topics

Use the following links to read in more detail the topics covered in this chapter:

- **Overview of porting from .NET Framework to .NET Core**: https://docs.microsoft.com/en-us/dotnet/core/porting/

- **.NET Core application publishing overview**: https://docs.microsoft.com/en-us/dotnet/core/deploying/

- **.NET Blog**: https://devblogs.microsoft.com/dotnet/

- **Tutorial: Create an item template**: https://docs.microsoft.com/en-us/dotnet/core/tutorials/cli-templates-create-item-template

- **What .NET Developers ought to know**: https://www.hanselman.com/blog/WhatNETDevelopersOughtToKnowToStartIn2017.aspx

- **CoreFX README.md**: https://github.com/dotnet/corefx/blob/master/Documentation/README.md

Summary

In this chapter, we explored the relationship between assemblies and namespaces, and we also discussed options for porting existing .NET Framework code bases, published your apps and libraries, and deployed your code cross-platform.

In the next chapter, you will learn about some common Base Class Library types that are included with .NET 5.

08

Working with Common .NET Types

This chapter is about some common types that are included with .NET. These include types for manipulating numbers, text, collections, network access, reflection, and attributes; improving working with spans, indexes, and ranges; and internationalization.

This chapter covers the following topics:

- Working with numbers
- Working with text
- Pattern matching with regular expressions
- Storing multiple objects in collections
- Working with spans, indexes, and ranges
- Working with network resources
- Working with types and attributes
- Working with images
- Internationalizing your code

Working with numbers

One of the most common types of data is numbers. The most common types in .NET for working with numbers are shown in the following table:

Namespace	Example type(s)	Description
System	SByte, Int16, Int32, Int64	Integers; that is, zero and positive and negative whole numbers
System	Byte, UInt16, UInt32, UInt64	Cardinals; that is, zero and positive whole numbers
System	Half, Single, Double	Reals; that is, floating point numbers
System	Decimal	Accurate reals; that is, for use in science, engineering, or financial scenarios
System .Numerics	BigInteger, Complex, Quaternion	Arbitrarily large integers, complex numbers, and quaternion numbers

 More Information: You can read more about this subject at the following link: https://docs.microsoft.com/en-us/dotnet/standard/numerics

.NET has had the 32-bit float and 64-bit double types since .NET Framework 1.0. The IEEE 754 specification also defines a 16-bit floating point standard. Machine learning and other algorithms would benefit from this smaller, lower-precision number type so Microsoft has added the System.Half type to .NET 5.

Currently, the C# language does not define a half alias so you must use the .NET type name Half. This might change in the future.

 More Information: You can read more about the Half type at the following link: https://devblogs.microsoft.com/dotnet/introducing-the-half-type/

Working with big integers

The largest whole number that can be stored in .NET types that have a C# alias is about eighteen and a half quintillion, stored in an unsigned long integer. But what if you need to store numbers larger than that? Let's explore numerics:

1. Create a new console application named WorkingWithNumbers in a folder named Chapter08.

2. Save the workspace as Chapter08 and add WorkingWithNumbers to it.

3. In Program.cs, add a statement to import System.Numerics, as shown in the following code:

```
using System.Numerics;
```

4. In `Main`, add statements to output the largest value of `ulong`, and a number with 30 digits using `BigInteger`, as shown in the following code:

```
var largest = ulong.MaxValue;
WriteLine($"{largest,40:N0}");

var atomsInTheUniverse =
    BigInteger.Parse("1234567890123456789012345678901234567890");
WriteLine($"{atomsInTheUniverse,40:N0}");
```

The `40` in the format code means right-align 40 characters, so both numbers are lined up to the right-hand edge. The `N0` means use thousand separators and zero decimal places.

5. Run the console application and view the result, as shown in the following output:

```
                 18,446,744,073,709,551,615
123,456,789,012,345,678,901,234,567,890
```

Working with complex numbers

A complex number can be expressed as $a + bi$, where a and b are real numbers, and i is an imaginary unit, where $i^2 = -1$. If the real part a is zero, it is a pure imaginary number. If the imaginary part b is zero, it is a real number.

Complex numbers have practical applications in many **STEM** (**science**, **technology**, **engineering**, and **mathematics**) fields of study. Additionally, they are added by separately adding the real and imaginary parts of the summands; consider this:

```
(a + bi) + (c + di) = (a + c) + (b + d)i
```

Let's explore complex numbers:

1. In `Main`, add statements to add two complex numbers, as shown in the following code:

```
var c1 = new Complex(4, 2);
var c2 = new Complex(3, 7);
var c3 = c1 + c2;
WriteLine($"{c1} added to {c2} is {c3}");
```

2. Run the console application and view the result, as shown in the following output:

```
(4, 2) added to (3, 7) is (7, 9)
```

Quaternions are a number system that extends complex numbers. They form a four-dimensional associative normed division algebra over the real numbers, and therefore also a domain.

Huh? Yes, I know. I don't understand that either. Don't worry; we're not going to write any code using them! Suffice to say, they are good at describing spatial rotations, so video game engines use them, as do many computer simulations and flight control systems.

Working with text

One of the other most common types of data for variables is text. The most common types in .NET for working with text are shown in the following table:

Namespace	Type	Description
System	Char	Storage for a single text character
System	String	Storage for multiple text characters
System.Text	StringBuilder	Efficiently manipulates strings
System.Text .RegularExpressions	Regex	Efficiently pattern-matches strings

Getting the length of a string

Let's explore some common tasks when working with text; for example, sometimes you need to find out the length of a piece of text stored in a string variable:

1. Create a new console application project named WorkingWithText in the Chapter08 folder and add it to the Chapter08 workspace.

2. Navigate to **View | Command Palette**, enter and select **OmniSharp: Select Project**, and select **WorkingWithText**.

3. In the WorkingWithText project, in Program.cs, in Main, add statements to define a variable to store the name of the city London, and then write its name and length to the console, as shown in the following code:

    ```
    string city = "London";
    WriteLine($"{city} is {city.Length} characters long.");
    ```

4. Run the console application and view the result, as shown in the following output:

    ```
    London is 6 characters long.
    ```

Getting the characters of a string

The string class uses an array of char internally to store the text. It also has an indexer, which means that we can use the array syntax to read its characters:

1. Add a statement to write the characters at the first and third position in the string variable, as shown in the following code:

    ```
    WriteLine($"First char is {city[0]} and third is {city[2]}.");
    ```

2. Run the console application and view the result, as shown in the following output:

    ```
    First char is L and third is n.
    ```

Array indexes start at zero, so the third character is at index 2.

Splitting a string

Sometimes, you need to split some text wherever there is a character, such as a comma:

1. Add statements to define a single `string` variable containing comma-separated city names, then use the `Split` method and specify that you want to treat commas as the separator, and then enumerate the returned array of `string` values, as shown in the following code:

```
string cities = "Paris,Berlin,Madrid,New York";

string[] citiesArray = cities.Split(',');

foreach (string item in citiesArray)
{
  WriteLine(item);
}
```

2. Run the console application and view the result, as shown in the following output:

```
Paris
Berlin
Madrid
New York
```

Later in this chapter, you will learn how to handle more complex scenarios; for example, what if a `string` variable contains film titles, as shown in the following example: `"Monsters, Inc."`,`"I, Tonya"`,`"Lock, Stock and Two Smoking Barrels"`.

Getting part of a string

Sometimes, you need to get part of some text. The `IndexOf` method has nine overloads that return the index position of a specified `char` or `string`. The `Substring` method has two overloads, as shown in the following list:

*   `Substring(startIndex, length)`: returns a substring starting at `startIndex` and containing the next length characters.
*   `Substring(startIndex)`: returns a substring starting at `startIndex` and containing all characters up to the end of the string.

Let's explore a simple example:

1. Add statements to store a person's full name in a `string` variable with a space character between the first and last name, find the position of the space, and then extract the first name and last name as two parts so that they can be recombined in a different order, as shown in the following code:

```
string fullName = "Alan Jones";
int indexOfTheSpace = fullName.IndexOf(' ');
```

```
string firstName = fullName.Substring(
    startIndex: 0, length: indexOfTheSpace);

string lastName = fullName.Substring(
    startIndex: indexOfTheSpace + 1);

WriteLine($"{lastName}, {firstName}");
```

2. Run the console application and view the result, as shown in the following output:

```
Jones, Alan
```

If the format of the initial full name was different, for example, `"LastName, FirstName"`, then the code would need to be different. As an optional exercise, try writing some statements that would change the input `"Jones, Alan"` into `"Alan Jones"`.

Checking a string for content

Sometimes, you need to check whether a piece of text starts or ends with some characters or contains some characters. You can achieve this with methods named `StartsWith`, `EndsWith`, and `Contains`:

1. Add statements to store a string value and then check if it starts with or contains a couple of different string values, as shown in the following code:

```
string company = "Microsoft";
bool startsWithM = company.StartsWith("M");
bool containsN = company.Contains("N");
WriteLine($"Starts with M: {startsWithM}, contains an N: {containsN}");
```

2. Run the console application and view the result, as shown in the following output:

```
Starts with M: True, contains an N: False
```

Joining, formatting, and other string members

There are many other `string` members, as shown in the following table:

Member	Description
`Trim`, `TrimStart`, and `TrimEnd`	These trim whitespace characters such as space, tab, and carriage return from the beginning and/or end of the string variable.
`ToUpper` and `ToLower`	These convert all the characters in the string variable into uppercase or lowercase.
`Insert` and `Remove`	These insert or remove some text in the string variable.
`Replace`	This replaces some text with other text.

`string.Concat`	This concatenates two string variables. The + operator calls this method when used between string variables.
`string.Join`	This concatenates one or more string variables with a character in between each one.
`string.IsNullOrEmpty`	This checks whether a string variable is null or empty ("").
`string.IsNullOrWhitespace`	This checks whether a string variable is null or whitespace; that is, a mix of any number of horizontal and vertical spacing characters, for example, tab, space, carriage return, line feed, and so on.
`string.Empty`	This can be used instead of allocating memory each time you use a literal string value using an empty pair of double-quotes ("").
`string.Format`	An older, alternative method of string interpolation to output formatted string variables, which uses positioned instead of named parameters.

Some of the preceding methods are `static` methods. This means that the method can only be called from the type, not from a variable instance. In the preceding table, I indicated the `static` methods by prefixing them with `string.`, like `string.Format`.

Let's explore some of these methods:

1. Add statements to take an array of `string` values and combine them back together into a single `string` variable with separators using the `Join` method, as shown in the following code:

    ```
    string recombined = string.Join(" => ", citiesArray);
    WriteLine(recombined);
    ```

2. Run the console application and view the result, as shown in the following output:

    ```
    Paris => Berlin => Madrid => New York
    ```

3. Add statements to use positioned parameters and interpolated `string` formatting syntax to output the same three variables twice, as shown in the following code:

    ```
    string fruit = "Apples";
    decimal price = 0.39M;
    DateTime when = DateTime.Today;

    WriteLine($"{fruit} cost {price:C} on {when:dddd}s.");
    WriteLine(string.Format("{0} cost {1:C} on {2:dddd}s.",
      fruit, price, when));
    ```

4. Run the console application and view the result, as shown in the following output:

    ```
    Apples cost £0.39 on Thursdays.
    Apples cost £0.39 on Thursdays.
    ```

Building strings efficiently

You can concatenate two strings to make a new `string` variable using the `String.Concat` method or simply by using the + operator. But both of these choices are bad practice because .NET must create a completely new `string` variable in memory.

This might not be noticeable if you are only adding two `string` values, but if you concatenate inside a loop with many iterations, it can have a significant negative impact on performance and memory use.

In *Chapter 13, Improving Performance and Scalability Using Multitasking,* you will learn how to concatenate `string` variables efficiently using the `StringBuilder` type.

Pattern matching with regular expressions

Regular expressions are useful for validating input from the user. They are very powerful and can get very complicated. Almost all programming languages have support for regular expressions and use a common set of special characters to define them:

1. Create a new console application project named `WorkingWithRegularExpressions`, add it to the workspace, and select it as the active project for OmniSharp.

2. At the top of the file, import the following namespace:

    ```
    using System.Text.RegularExpressions;
    ```

Checking for digits entered as text

Let's implement the common example of validating number input:

1. In the `Main` method, add statements to prompt the user to enter their age and then check that it is valid using a regular expression that looks for a digit character, as shown in the following code:

    ```
    Write("Enter your age: ");
    string input = ReadLine();

    var ageChecker = new Regex(@"\d");

    if (ageChecker.IsMatch(input))
    {
      WriteLine("Thank you!");
    }
    else
    {
      WriteLine($"This is not a valid age: {input}");
    }
    ```

The @ character switches off the ability to use escape characters in the string. Escape characters are prefixed with a backslash. For example, \t means a tab and \n means a new line.

When writing regular expressions, we need to disable this feature. To paraphrase the television show *The West Wing*, "Let backslash be backslash."

Once escape characters are disabled with @, then they can be interpreted by a regular expression. For example, \d means digit. You will learn more regular expressions that are prefixed with a backslash later in this topic.

2. Run the console application, enter a whole number such as 34 for the age, and view the result, as shown in the following output:

```
Enter your age: 34
Thank you!
```

3. Run the console application again, enter carrots, and view the result, as shown in the following output:

```
Enter your age: carrots
This is not a valid age: carrots
```

4. Run the console application again, enter bob30smith, and view the result, as shown in the following output:

```
Enter your age: bob30smith
Thank you!
```

The regular expression we used is \d, which means one digit. However, it does not specify what can be entered *before* and *after* that one digit. This regular expression could be described in English as "Enter any characters you want as long as you enter at least one digit character."

5. Change the regular expression to ^\d$, as shown in the following code:

```
var ageChecker = new Regex(@"^\d$");
```

6. Rerun the application. Now, it rejects anything except a single digit.

We want to allow one or more digits. To do this, we add a + after the \d expression to modify the meaning to *one or more*.

7. Change the regular expression, as shown in the following code:

```
var ageChecker = new Regex(@"^\d+$");
```

8. Run the application and see how the regular expression now only allows zero or positive whole numbers of any length.

Understanding the syntax of a regular expression

Here are some common regular expression **symbols** that you can use in regular expressions:

Symbol	Meaning	Symbol	Meaning
^	Start of input	$	End of input
\d	A single digit	\D	A single NON-digit
\s	Whitespace	\S	NON-whitespace
\w	Word characters	\W	NON-word characters
[A-Za-z0-9]	Range(s) of characters	\^	^ (caret) character
[aeiou]	Set of characters	[^aeiou]	NOT in a set of characters
.	Any single character	\.	. (dot) character

More Information: To specify a Unicode character, use \u followed by four characters specifying the number of the character. For example, \u00c0 is the À character. You can learn more at the following link: https://www.regular-expressions.info/unicode.html

In addition, here are some regular expression **quantifiers** that affect the previous symbols in a regular expression:

Symbol	Meaning	Symbol	Meaning
+	One or more	?	One or none
{3}	Exactly three	{3,5}	Three to five
{3,}	At least three	{,3}	Up to three

Examples of regular expressions

Here are some examples of regular expressions with a description of their meaning:

Expression	Meaning
\d	A single digit somewhere in the input
a	The character a somewhere in the input
Bob	The word Bob somewhere in the input
^Bob	The word Bob at the start of the input
Bob$	The word Bob at the end of the input
^\d{2}$	Exactly two digits
^[0-9]{2}$	Exactly two digits
^[A-Z]{4,}$	At least four uppercase English letters in the ASCII character set only
^[A-Za-z]{4,}$	At least four upper or lowercase English letters in the ASCII character set only

`^[A-Z]{2}\d{3}$`	Two uppercase English letters in the ASCII character set and three digits only
`^[A-Za-z \u00c0-\u017e]+$`	At least one uppercase or lowercase English letter in the ASCII character set or European letters in the Unicode character set, as shown in the following list: ÀÁÂÃÄ ÅÆÇÈÉÊËÌÍÎÏÐÑÒÓÔÕÖ×ØÙÚÛÜÝÞßàáâãäåæçèéêëìíîïðñòóôõö÷øùúûüýþÿıŒœŠšŸ Žž
`^d.g$`	The letter d, then any character, and then the letter g, so it would match both dig and dog or any single character between the d and g
`^d\.g$`	The letter d, then a dot (.), and then the letter g, so it would match d.g only

Good Practice: Use regular expressions to validate input from the user. The same regular expressions can be reused in other languages such as JavaScript and Python.

Splitting a complex comma-separated string

Earlier in this chapter, you learned how to split a simple comma-separated `string` variable. But what about the following example of film titles?

```
"Monsters, Inc.","I, Tonya","Lock, Stock and Two Smoking Barrels"
```

The `string` value uses double-quotes around each film title. We can use these to identify whether we need to split on a comma (or not). The `Split` method is not powerful enough, so we can use a regular expression instead.

More Information: You can read a fuller explanation in the Stack Overflow article that inspired this task at the following link: `https://stackoverflow.com/questions/18144431/regex-to-split-a-csv`

To include double-quotes inside a `string` value, we prefix them with a backslash:

1. Add statements to store a complex comma-separated `string` variable, and then split it in a dumb way using the `Split` method, as shown in the following code:

    ```
    string films = "\"Monsters, Inc.\",\"I, Tonya\",\"Lock, Stock and Two
    Smoking Barrels\"";

    string[] filmsDumb = films.Split(',');

    WriteLine("Dumb attempt at splitting:");
    foreach (string film in filmsDumb)
    {
      WriteLine(film);
    }
    ```

2. Add statements to define a regular expression to split and write the film titles in a smart way, as shown in the following code:

```
var csv = new Regex(
  "(?:^|,)(?=[^\"]|(\")?)\"?((?(1)[^\"]*|[^,\"]*))\"?(?=,|$)");

MatchCollection filmsSmart = csv.Matches(films);

WriteLine("Smart attempt at splitting:");
foreach (Match film in filmsSmart)
{
  WriteLine(film.Groups[2].Value);
}
```

3. Run the console application and view the result, as shown in the following output:

```
Dumb attempt at splitting:
"Monsters
 Inc."
"I
 Tonya"
"Lock
 Stock and Two Smoking Barrels"
Smart attempt at splitting:
Monsters, Inc.
I, Tonya
Lock, Stock and Two Smoking Barrels
```

 More Information: Regular expressions are a massive topic. Books more than an inch thick have been written about them. You can read more about them at the following link: https://www.regular-expressions.info

Regular expression performance improvements

The .NET types for working with regular expressions are used throughout the .NET platform and many of the apps built with it. As such, they have a significant impact on performance, but until now, they have not received much optimization attention from Microsoft.

With .NET 5, the `System.Text.RegularExpressions` namespace has rewritten internals to squeeze out maximum performance. Common regular expression benchmarks using methods like `IsMatch` are now five times faster. And the best thing is, you do not have to change your code to get the benefits!

 More Information: You can read details about the performance improvements at the following link: `https://devblogs.microsoft.com/dotnet/regex-performance-improvements-in-net-5/`

Storing multiple objects in collections

Another of the most common types of data is collections. If you need to store multiple values in a variable, then you can use a collection.

A **collection** is a data structure in memory that can manage multiple items in different ways, although all collections have some shared functionality.

The most common types in .NET for working with collections are shown in the following table:

Namespace	Example type(s)	Description
System .Collections	IEnumerable, IEnumerable<T>	Interfaces and base classes used by collections.
System .Collections .Generic	List<T>, Dictionary<T>, Queue<T>, Stack<T>	Introduced in C# 2.0 with .NET Framework 2.0. These collections allow you to specify the type you want to store using a generic type parameter (which is safer, faster, and more efficient).
System .Collections .Concurrent	BlockingCollection, ConcurrentDictionary, ConcurrentQueue	These collections are safe to use in multithreaded scenarios.
System .Collections .Immutable	ImmutableArray, ImmutableDictionary, ImmutableList, ImmutableQueue	Designed for scenarios where the contents of the original collection will never change, although they can create modified collections as a new instance.

 More Information: You can read more about collections at the following link: `https://docs.microsoft.com/en-us/dotnet/standard/collections`

Common features of all collections

All collections implement the ICollection interface; this means that they must have a Count property to tell you how many objects are in them.

For example, if we had a collection named passengers, we could do this:

```
int howMany = passengers.Count;
```

All collections implement the IEnumerable interface, which means that they must have a GetEnumerator method that returns an object that implements IEnumerator; this means that the returned object must have a MoveNext method and a Current property so that they can be iterated using the foreach statement.

For example, to perform an action on each object in the passengers collection, we could do this:

```
foreach (var passenger in passengers)
{
  // do something with each passenger
}
```

To understand collections, it can be useful to see the most common interfaces that collections implement, as shown in the following diagram:

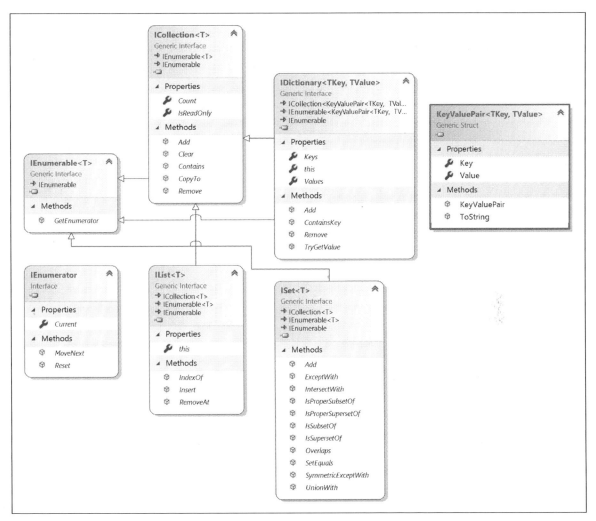

Figure 8.1: Common interfaces that collections implement

Lists, that is, a type that implements IList, are *ordered collections*. As you can see in the preceding diagram, IList<T> includes ICollection<T> so they must have a Count property, and an Add method to put an item at the end of the collection, as well as an Insert method to put an item in the list at a specified position, and RemoveAt to remove an item at a specified position.

Understanding collection choices

There are several different choices of collection that you can use for different purposes: lists, dictionaries, stacks, queues, sets, and many other more specialized collections.

Lists

Lists are a good choice when you want to manually control the order of items in a collection. Each item in a list has a unique index (or position) that is automatically assigned. Items can be any type defined by T and items can be duplicated. Indexes are int types and start from 0, so the first item in a list is at index 0, as shown in the following table:

Index	Item
0	London
1	Paris
2	London
3	Sydney

If a new item (for example, **Santiago**) is inserted between **London** and **Sydney**, then the index of **Sydney** is automatically incremented. Therefore, you must be aware that an item's index can change after inserting or removing items, as shown in the following table:

Index	Item
0	London
1	Paris
2	London
3	Santiago
4	Sydney

Dictionaries

Dictionaries are a good choice when each **value** (or object) has a unique sub value (or a made-up value) that can be used as a **key** to quickly find a value in the collection later. The key must be unique. For example, if you are storing a list of people, you could choose to use a government-issued identity number as the key.

Think of the key as being like an index entry in a real-world dictionary. It allows you to quickly find the definition of a word because the words (for example, keys) are kept sorted, and if we know we're looking for the definition of *manatee*, we would jump to the middle of the dictionary to start looking, because the letter *M* is in the middle of the alphabet.

Dictionaries in programming are similarly smart when looking something up. They must implement the interface IDictionary<TKey, TValue>.

The key and value can be any types defined by TKey and TValue. The example Dictionary<string, Person> uses a string as the key and a Person instance as the value. Dictionary<string, string> uses string values for both, as shown in the following table:

Key	Value
BSA	Bob Smith
MW	Max Williams

BSB	Bob Smith
AM	Amir Mohammed

Stacks

Stacks are a good choice when you want to implement **last-in, first-out** (LIFO) behavior. With a stack, you can only directly access or remove the one item at the top of the stack, although you can enumerate to read through the whole stack of items. You cannot, for example, directly access the second item in a stack.

For example, word processors use a stack to remember the sequence of actions you have recently performed, and then when you press *Ctrl + Z*, it will undo the last action in the stack, and then the next to last action, and so on.

Queues

Queues are a good choice when you want to implement the **first-in, first-out** (FIFO) behavior. With a queue, you can only directly access or remove the one item at the front of the queue, although you can enumerate to read through the whole queue of items. You cannot, for example, directly access the second item in a queue.

For example, background processes use a queue to process work items in the order that they arrive, just like people standing in line at the post office.

Sets

Sets are a good choice when you want to perform set operations between two collections. For example, you may have two collections of city names, and you want to know which names appear in both sets (known as the **intersect** between the sets). Items in a set must be unique.

Working with lists

Let's explore lists:

1. Create a new console application project named WorkingWithLists, add it to the workspace, and select it as the active project for OmniSharp.

2. At the top of the file, import the following namespace:

   ```
   using System.Collections.Generic;
   ```

3. In the Main method, type statements that illustrate some of the common ways of working with lists, as shown in the following code:

   ```
   var cities = new List<string>();
   cities.Add("London");
   cities.Add("Paris");
   cities.Add("Milan");
   ```

```
WriteLine("Initial list");
foreach (string city in cities)
{
  WriteLine($" {city}");
}

WriteLine($"The first city is {cities[0]}.");
WriteLine($"The last city is {cities[cities.Count - 1]}.");

cities.Insert(0, "Sydney");

WriteLine("After inserting Sydney at index 0");
foreach (string city in cities)
{
  WriteLine($" {city}");
}

cities.RemoveAt(1);
cities.Remove("Milan");

WriteLine("After removing two cities");
foreach (string city in cities)
{
  WriteLine($" {city}");
}
```

4.   Run the console application and view the result, as shown in the following output:

```
Initial list
 London
 Paris
 Milan
The first city is London.
The last city is Milan.
After inserting Sydney at index 0
 Sydney
 London
 Paris
 Milan
After removing two cities
 Sydney
 Paris
```

Working with dictionaries

Let's explore dictionaries:

1. Create a new console application project named WorkingWithDictionaries, add it to the workspace, and select it as the active project for OmniSharp.

2. Import the System.Collections.Generic namespace.

3. In the Main method, type statements that illustrate some of the common ways of working with dictionaries, as shown in the following code:

```
var keywords = new Dictionary<string, string>();
keywords.Add("int", "32-bit integer data type");
keywords.Add("long", "64-bit integer data type");
keywords.Add("float", "Single precision floating point number");

WriteLine("Keywords and their definitions");
foreach (KeyValuePair<string, string> item in keywords)
{
  WriteLine($" {item.Key}: {item.Value}");
}
WriteLine($"The definition of long is {keywords["long"]}");
```

4. Run the console application and view the result, as shown in the following output:

```
Keywords and their definitions
 int: 32-bit integer data type
 long: 64-bit integer data type
 float: Single precision floating point number
The definition of long is 64-bit integer data type
```

Sorting collections

A List<T> class can be sorted by manually calling its Sort method (but remember that the indexes of each item will change). Manually sorting a list of string values or other built-in types will work without extra effort on your part, but if you create a collection of your own type, then that type must implement an interface named IComparable. You learned how to do this in *Chapter 6, Implementing Interfaces and Inheriting Classes*.

A Dictionary<T>, Stack<T>, or Queue<T> collection cannot be sorted because you wouldn't usually want that functionality; for example, you would never sort a queue of guests checking into a hotel. But sometimes, you might want to sort a dictionary or a set.

Sometimes it would be useful to have an automatically sorted collection, that is, one that maintains the items in a sorted order as you add and remove them. There are multiple auto-sorting collections to choose from. The differences between these sorted collections are often subtle but can have an impact on the memory requirements and performance of your application, so it is worth putting effort into picking the most appropriate option for your requirements.

Some common auto-sorting collections are shown in the following table:

Collection	Description
SortedDictionary<TKey, TValue>	This represents a collection of key/value pairs that are sorted by key.
SortedList<TKey, TValue>	This represents a collection of key/value pairs that are sorted by key, based on the associated IComparer<TKey> implementation.
SortedSet<T>	This represents a collection of unique objects that are maintained in a sorted order.

Using specialized collections

There are a few other collections for special situations, as shown in the following table:

Collection	Description
System.Collections .BitArray	This manages a compact array of bit values, which are represented as Booleans, where true indicates that the bit is on (1) and false indicates the bit is off (0).
System.Collections .Generics.LinkedList<T>	This represents a doubly-linked list where every item has a reference to its previous and next items. They provide better performance compared to List<T> for scenarios where you will frequently insert and remove items from the middle of the list because in a LinkedList<T> the items do not have to be rearranged in memory.

Using immutable collections

Sometimes you need to make a collection **immutable**, meaning that its members cannot change; that is, you cannot add or remove them.

If you import the System.Collections.Immutable namespace, then any collection that implements IEnumerable<T> is given six extension methods to convert it into an immutable list, dictionary, hash set, and so on:

1. In the WorkingWithLists project, in Program.cs, import the System.Collections. Immutable namespace, and then add the following statements to the end of the Main method:

    ```
    var immutableCities = cities.ToImmutableList();

    var newList = immutableCities.Add("Rio");

    Write("Immutable list of cities:");
    foreach (string city in immutableCities)
    {
      Write($" {city}");
    }
    ```

```
WriteLine();

Write("New list of cities:");
foreach (string city in newList)
{
  Write($" {city}");
}
WriteLine();
```

2. Run the console application, view the result, and note that the immutable list of cities does not get modified when you call the Add method on it; instead, it returns a new list with the newly added city, as shown in the following output:

```
Immutable list of cities: Sydney Paris
New list of cities: Sydney Paris Rio
```

Good Practice: To improve performance, many applications store a shared copy of commonly accessed objects in a central cache. To safely allow multiple threads to work with those objects knowing they won't change, you should make them immutable or use a concurrent collection type that you can read about at the following link: https://docs.microsoft.com/en-us/dotnet/api/system.collections.concurrent

Working with spans, indexes, and ranges

One of Microsoft's goals with .NET Core 2.1 was to improve performance and resource usage. A key .NET feature that enables this is the Span<T> type.

More Information: You can read the official documentation for Span<T> at the following link: https://docs.microsoft.com/en-us/dotnet/api/system.span-1

Using memory efficiently using spans

When manipulating collections of objects, you will often create new collections from existing ones so that you can pass parts of a collection. This is not efficient because duplicate objects are created in memory.

If you need to work with a subset of a collection, instead of replicating the subset into a new collection, use a span because it is like a window into a subset of the original collection. This is more efficient in terms of memory usage and improves performance.

Before we look at spans in more detail, we need to understand some related objects: indexes and ranges.

Identifying positions with the Index type

C# 8.0 introduced two features for identifying an item's index within a collection and a range of items using two indexes.

You learned in the previous topic that objects in a list can be accessed by passing an integer into their indexer, as shown in the following code:

```
int index = 3;
Person p = people[index]; // fourth person in list or array
char letter = name[index]; // fourth letter in name
```

The Index value type is a more formal way of identifying a position, and supports counting from the end, as shown in the following code:

```
// two ways to define the same index, 3 in from the start
var i1 = new Index(value: 3); // counts from the start
Index i2 = 3; // using implicit int conversion operator

// two ways to define the same index, 5 in from the end
var i3 = new Index(value: 5, fromEnd: true);
var i4 = ^5; // using the caret operator
```

We had to explicitly define the Index type in the second statement because otherwise, the compiler would treat it as an int. In the fourth statement, the caret ^ was enough for the compiler to understand our meaning.

Identifying ranges with the Range type

The Range value type uses Index values to indicate the start and end of its range, using its constructor, C# syntax, or its static methods, as shown in the following code:

```
Range r1 = new Range(start: new Index(3), end: new Index(7));
Range r2 = new Range(start: 3, end: 7); // using implicit int conversion
Range r3 = 3..7; // using C# 8.0 syntax
Range r4 = Range.StartAt(3); // from index 3 to last index
Range r5 = 3..; // from index 3 to last index
Range r6 = Range.EndAt(3); // from index 0 to index 3
Range r7 = ..3; // from index 0 to index 3
```

Extension methods have been added to string values, int arrays, and spans to make ranges easier to work with. These extension methods accept a range as a parameter and return a Span<T>. This makes them very memory-efficient.

Using indexes and ranges

Let's explore using indexes and ranges to return spans:

1. Create a new console application named WorkingWithRanges, add it to the workspace, and select it as the active project for OmniSharp.

2. In the Main method, type statements to compare using the string type's Substring method with using ranges to extract parts of someone's name, as shown in the following code:

```
string name = "Samantha Jones";

int lengthOfFirst = name.IndexOf(' ');
int lengthOfLast = name.Length - lengthOfFirst - 1;

string firstName = name.Substring(
  startIndex: 0,
  length: lengthOfFirst);

string lastName = name.Substring(
  startIndex: name.Length - lengthOfLast,
  length: lengthOfLast);

WriteLine($"First name: {firstName}, Last name: {lastName}");

ReadOnlySpan<char> nameAsSpan = name.AsSpan();

var firstNameSpan = nameAsSpan[0..lengthOfFirst];

var lastNameSpan = nameAsSpan[^lengthOfLast..^0];

WriteLine("First name: {0}, Last name: {1}",
  arg0: firstNameSpan.ToString(),
  arg1: lastNameSpan.ToString());
```

3. Run the console application and view the result, as shown in the following output:

```
First name: Samantha, Last name: Jones
First name: Samantha, Last name: Jones
```

More Information: You can read more about how spans work internally at the following link: https://docs.microsoft.com/en-us/archive/msdn-magazine/2018/january/csharp-all-about-span-exploring-a-new-net-mainstay

Working with network resources

Sometimes you will need to work with network resources. The most common types in .NET for working with network resources are shown in the following table:

Namespace	Example type(s)	Description
`System.Net`	`Dns`, `Uri`, `Cookie`, `WebClient`, `IPAddress`	These are for working with DNS servers, URIs, IP addresses, and so on.
`System.Net`	`FtpStatusCode`, `FtpWebRequest`, `FtpWebResponse`	These are for working with FTP servers.
`System.Net`	`HttpStatusCode`, `HttpWebRequest`, `HttpWebResponse`	These are for working with HTTP servers; that is, websites and services. Types from `System.Net.Http` are easier to use.
`System.Net` `.Http`	`HttpClient`, `HttpMethod`, `HttpRequestMessage`, `HttpResponseMessage`	These are for working with HTTP servers; that is, websites and services. You will learn how to use these in *Chapter 18, Building and Consuming Web Services*.
`System.Net` `.Mail`	`Attachment`, `MailAddress`, `MailMessage`, `SmtpClient`	These are for working with SMTP servers; that is, sending email messages.
`System.Net` `.NetworkInformation`	`IPStatus`, `NetworkChange`, `Ping`, `TcpStatistics`	These are for working with low-level network protocols.

Working with URIs, DNS, and IP addresses

Let's explore some common types for working with network resources:

1. Create a new console application project named `WorkingWithNetworkResources`, add it to the workspace, and select it as the active project for OmniSharp.

2. At the top of the file, import the following namespace:

    ```
    using System.Net;
    ```

3. In the `Main` method, type statements to prompt the user to enter a website address, and then use the `Uri` type to break it down into its parts, including the scheme (HTTP, FTP, and so on), port number, and host, as shown in the following code:

    ```
    Write("Enter a valid web address: ");
    string url = ReadLine();

    if (string.IsNullOrWhiteSpace(url))
    {
    ```

```
    url = "https://world.episerver.com/cms/?q=pagetype";
  }

  var uri = new Uri(url);

  WriteLine($"URL: {url}");
  WriteLine($"Scheme: {uri.Scheme}");
  WriteLine($"Port: {uri.Port}");
  WriteLine($"Host: {uri.Host}");
  WriteLine($"Path: {uri.AbsolutePath}");
  WriteLine($"Query: {uri.Query}");
```

For convenience, I have also allowed the user to press *ENTER* to use an example URL.

4. Run the console application, enter a valid website address or press *ENTER*, and view the result, as shown in the following output:

```
Enter a valid web address:
URL: https://world.episerver.com/cms/?q=pagetype
Scheme: https
Port: 443
Host: world.episerver.com
Path: /cms/
Query: ?q=pagetype
```

5. Add statements to the Main method to get the IP address for the entered website, as shown in the following code:

```
IPHostEntry entry = Dns.GetHostEntry(uri.Host);
WriteLine($"{entry.HostName} has the following IP addresses:");
foreach (IPAddress address in entry.AddressList)
{
  WriteLine($"  {address}");
}
```

6. Run the console application, enter a valid website address or press *ENTER*, and view the result, as shown in the following output:

```
world.episerver.com.cdn.cloudflare.net has the following IP addresses:
  104.18.23.198
  104.18.22.198
```

Pinging a server

Now you will add code to ping a web server to check its health:

1. In Program.cs, add a statement to import System.Net.NetworkInformation, as shown in the following code:

```
using System.Net.NetworkInformation;
```

2. Add statements to `Main` to ping the entered website, as shown in the following code:

```
try
{
  var ping = new Ping();
  WriteLine("Pinging server. Please wait...");
  PingReply reply = ping.Send(uri.Host);

  WriteLine($"{uri.Host} was pinged and replied: {reply.Status}.");
  if (reply.Status == IPStatus.Success)
  {
    WriteLine("Reply from {0} took {1:N0}ms",
      reply.Address, reply.RoundtripTime);
  }
}
catch (Exception ex)
{
  WriteLine($"{ex.GetType().ToString()} says {ex.Message}");
}
```

3. Run the console application, press *ENTER*, and view the result, as shown in the following output on macOS:

```
Pinging server. Please wait...
world.episerver.com was pinged and replied: Success.
Reply from 104.18.23.198 took 4ms
```

4. Run the console application again and enter `http://google.com`, as shown in the following output:

```
Enter a valid web address: http://google.com
URL: http://google.com
Scheme: http
Port: 80
Host: google.com
Path: /
Query:
google.com has the following IP addresses:
 172.217.18.78
google.com was pinged and replied: Success.
Reply from 172.217.18.78 took 19ms
```

Working with types and attributes

Reflection is a programming feature that allows code to understand and manipulate itself. An assembly is made up of up to four parts:

- **Assembly metadata and manifest**: Name, assembly, and file version, referenced assemblies, and so on.
- **Type metadata**: Information about the types, their members, and so on.
- **IL code**: Implementation of methods, properties, constructors, and so on.
- **Embedded resources (optional)**: Images, strings, JavaScript, and so on.

The metadata comprises items of information about your code. The metadata is generated automatically from your code (for example, information about the types and members) or applied to your code using attributes.

Attributes can be applied at multiple levels: to assemblies, to types, and to their members, as shown in the following code:

```
// an assembly-level attribute
[assembly: AssemblyTitle("Working with Reflection")]

// a type-level attribute
[Serializable]
public class Person
{
  // a member-level attribute
  [Obsolete("Deprecated: use Run instead.")]
  public void Walk()
  {
    ...
```

Versioning of assemblies

Version numbers in .NET are a combination of three numbers, with two optional additions. If you follow the rules of semantic versioning:

- **Major**: Breaking changes.
- **Minor**: Non-breaking changes, including new features, and often bug fixes.
- **Patch**: Non-breaking bug fixes.

> **Good Practice**: When updating a NuGet package, you should specify an optional flag to make sure that you only upgrade to the highest minor to avoid breaking changes, or to the highest patch if you are extra cautious and only want to receive bug fixes, as shown in the following commands: `Update-Package Newtonsoft.Json -ToHighestMinor` or `Update-Package Newtonsoft.Json -ToHighestPatch`

Optionally, a version can include these:

- **Prerelease**: Unsupported preview releases.
- **Build number**: Nightly builds.

Good Practice: Follow the rules of semantic versioning, as described at the following link: `http://semver.org`

Reading assembly metadata

Let's explore working with attributes:

1. Create a new console application project named `WorkingWithReflection`, add it to the workspace, and select it as the active project for OmniSharp.

2. At the top of the file, import the following namespace:

    ```
    using System.Reflection;
    ```

3. In the `Main` method, enter statements to get the console app's assembly, output its name and location, and get all assembly-level attributes and output their types, as shown in the following code:

    ```
    WriteLine("Assembly metadata:");
    Assembly assembly = Assembly.GetEntryAssembly();

    WriteLine($" Full name: {assembly.FullName}");
    WriteLine($" Location: {assembly.Location}");

    var attributes = assembly.GetCustomAttributes();

    WriteLine($" Attributes:");
    foreach (Attribute a in attributes)
    {
      WriteLine($"  {a.GetType()}");
    }
    ```

4. Run the console application and view the result, as shown in the following output:

    ```
    Assembly metadata:
     Full name: WorkingWithReflection, Version=1.0.0.0, Culture=neutral,
    PublicKeyToken=null
     Location: /Users/markjprice/Code/Chapter08/WorkingWithReflection/bin/
    Debug/net5.0/WorkingWithReflection.dll
     Attributes:
      System.Runtime.CompilerServices.CompilationRelaxationsAttribute
      System.Runtime.CompilerServices.RuntimeCompatibilityAttribute
      System.Diagnostics.DebuggableAttribute
      System.Runtime.Versioning.TargetFrameworkAttribute
      System.Reflection.AssemblyCompanyAttribute
      System.Reflection.AssemblyConfigurationAttribute
    ```

```
System.Reflection.AssemblyFileVersionAttribute
System.Reflection.AssemblyInformationalVersionAttribute
System.Reflection.AssemblyProductAttribute
System.Reflection.AssemblyTitleAttribute
```

Now that we know some of the attributes decorating the assembly, we can ask for them specifically.

5. Add statements to the end of the Main method to get the AssemblyInformationalVersionAttribute and AssemblyCompanyAttribute classes, as shown in the following code:

```
var version = assembly.GetCustomAttribute
  <AssemblyInformationalVersionAttribute>();

WriteLine($" Version: {version.InformationalVersion}");

var company = assembly.GetCustomAttribute
  <AssemblyCompanyAttribute>();

WriteLine($" Company: {company.Company}");
```

6. Run the console application and view the result, as shown in the following output:

```
Version: 1.0.0
Company: WorkingWithReflection
```

Hmm, let's explicitly set this information. The legacy .NET Framework way to set these values was to add attributes in the C# source code file, as shown in the following code:

```
[assembly: AssemblyCompany("Packt Publishing")]
[assembly: AssemblyInformationalVersion("1.3.0")]
```

The Roslyn compiler used by .NET sets these attributes automatically, so we can't use the old way. Instead, they can be set in the project file.

7. Modify WorkingWithReflection.csproj, as shown in the following markup:

```
<Project Sdk="Microsoft.NET.Sdk">
  <PropertyGroup>
    <OutputType>Exe</OutputType>
    <TargetFramework>net5.0</TargetFramework>

    <Version>1.3.0</Version>
    <Company>Packt Publishing</Company>
  </PropertyGroup>
</Project>
```

8. Run the console application and view the result, as shown in the following output:

```
Version: 1.3.0
Company: Packt Publishing
```

Creating custom attributes

You can define your own attributes by inheriting from the `Attribute` class:

1. Add a class file to your project named `CoderAttribute.cs`.

2. Define an attribute class that can decorate either classes or methods with two properties to store the name of a coder and the date they last modified some code, as shown in the following code:

```
using System;

namespace Packt.Shared
{
  [AttributeUsage(AttributeTargets.Class | AttributeTargets.Method,
    AllowMultiple = true)]
  public class CoderAttribute : Attribute
  {
    public string Coder { get; set; }
    public DateTime LastModified { get; set; }

    public CoderAttribute(string coder, string lastModified)
    {
      Coder = coder;
      LastModified = DateTime.Parse(lastModified);
    }
  }
}
```

3. In `Program.cs`, import `System.Linq`, as shown in the following code:

```
using System.Linq; // to use OrderByDescending
using System.Runtime.CompilerServices; // to use CompilerGeneratedAttribute
using Packt.Shared; // CoderAttribute
```

You will learn more about LINQ in *Chapter 12, Querying and Manipulating Data Using LINQ*. We have imported it to use its `OrderByDescending` method.

4. In the `Program` class, add a method named `DoStuff`, and decorate it with the `Coder` attribute with data about two coders, as shown in the following code:

```
[Coder("Mark Price", "22 August 2019")]
[Coder("Johnni Rasmussen", "13 September 2019")]
public static void DoStuff()
{
}
```

5. In the `Main` method, add code to get the types, enumerate their members, read any `Coder` attributes on those members, and write the information to the console, as shown in the following code:

```
WriteLine();
WriteLine($"* Types:");
Type[] types = assembly.GetTypes();

foreach (Type type in types)
{
  WriteLine();
  WriteLine($"Type: {type.FullName}");
  MemberInfo[] members = type.GetMembers();

  foreach (MemberInfo member in members)
  {
    WriteLine("{0}: {1} ({2})",
      arg0: member.MemberType,
      arg1: member.Name,
      arg2: member.DeclaringType.Name);

    var coders = member.GetCustomAttributes<CoderAttribute>()
      .OrderByDescending(c => c.LastModified);

    foreach (CoderAttribute coder in coders)
    {
      WriteLine("-> Modified by {0} on {1}",
        coder.Coder, coder.LastModified.ToShortDateString());
    }
  }
}
```

6. Run the console application and view the result, as shown in the following output:

```
* Types:

Type: CoderAttribute
Method: get_Coder (CoderAttribute)
Method: set_Coder (CoderAttribute)
Method: get_LastModified (CoderAttribute)
Method: set_LastModified (CoderAttribute)
Method: Equals (Attribute)
Method: GetHashCode (Attribute)
Method: get_TypeId (Attribute)
Method: Match (Attribute)
Method: IsDefaultAttribute (Attribute)
Method: ToString (Object)
```

```
Method: GetType (Object)
Constructor: .ctor (CoderAttribute)
Property: Coder (CoderAttribute)
Property: LastModified (CoderAttribute)
Property: TypeId (Attribute)

Type: WorkingWithReflection.Program
Method: DoStuff (Program)
-> Modified by Johnni Rasmussen on 13/09/2019
-> Modified by Mark Price on 22/08/2019
Method: ToString (Object)
Method: Equals (Object)
Method: GetHashCode (Object)
Method: GetType (Object)
Constructor: .ctor (Program)

Type: WorkingWithReflection.Program+<>c
Method: ToString (Object)
Method: Equals (Object)
Method: GetHashCode (Object)
Method: GetType (Object)
Constructor: .ctor (<>c)
Field: <>9 (<>c)
Field: <>9__0_0 (<>c)
```

 More Information: What is the `WorkingWithReflection.Program+<>c` type? It is a compiler-generated display class. `<>` indicates compiler-generated and `c` indicates a display class. You can read more at the following link: http://stackoverflow.com/a/2509524/55847

As an optional challenge, add statements to your console application to filter compiler-generated types by skipping types decorated with `CompilerGeneratedAttribute`.

Doing more with reflection

This is just a taster of what can be achieved with reflection. We only used reflection to read metadata from our code. Reflection can also do the following:

- **Dynamically load assemblies that are not currently referenced**: https://docs.microsoft.com/en-us/dotnet/standard/assembly/unloadability-howto

- **Dynamically execute code**: https://docs.microsoft.com/en-us/dotnet/api/system.reflection.methodbase.invoke

- **Dynamically generate new code and assemblies**: https://docs.microsoft.com/en-us/dotnet/api/system.reflection.emit.assemblybuilder

Working with images

ImageSharp is a third-party cross-platform 2D graphics library. When .NET Core 1.0 was in development, there was negative feedback about the missing `System.Drawing` namespace for working with 2D images. The ImageSharp project was started to fill that gap for modern .NET applications.

In their official documentation for `System.Drawing`, Microsoft says, "The `System.Drawing` namespace is not recommended for new development, due to not being supported within a Windows or ASP.NET service and it is not cross-platform. ImageSharp and SkiaSharp are recommended as alternatives."

Let us see what can be achieved with ImageSharp:

1. Create a new console application project named `WorkingWithImages`, add it to the workspace, and select it as the active project for OmniSharp.

2. Create an `images` folder and download the nine images from the following link: `https://github.com/markjprice/cs9dotnet5/tree/master/Assets/Categories`

3. Open `WorkingWithImages.csproj` and add a package reference for `SixLabors.ImageSharp`, as shown highlighted in the following markup:

```xml
<Project Sdk="Microsoft.NET.Sdk">
  <PropertyGroup>
    <OutputType>Exe</OutputType>
    <TargetFramework>net5.0</TargetFramework>
  </PropertyGroup>
  <ItemGroup>
    <PackageReference Include="SixLabors.ImageSharp" Version="1.0.0" />
  </ItemGroup>
</Project>
```

4. At the top of the `Program.cs` file, import the following namespaces:

```csharp
using System.Collections.Generic;
using System.IO;
using SixLabors.ImageSharp;
using SixLabors.ImageSharp.Processing;
```

5. In the `Main` method, enter statements to convert all the files in the `images` folder into grayscale thumbnails at one-tenth size, as shown in the following code:

```csharp
string imagesFolder = Path.Combine(
  Environment.CurrentDirectory, "images");

IEnumerable<string> images =
  Directory.EnumerateFiles(imagesFolder);

foreach (string imagePath in images)
{
```

```
    string thumbnailPath = Path.Combine(
      Environment.CurrentDirectory, "images",
      Path.GetFileNameWithoutExtension(imagePath)
      + "-thumbnail" + Path.GetExtension(imagePath)
    );

    using (Image image = Image.Load(imagePath))
    {
      image.Mutate(x => x.Resize(image.Width / 10, image.Height / 10));
      image.Mutate(x => x.Grayscale());
      image.Save(thumbnailPath);
    }
}
```

6. Run the console application.

7. In the filesystem, open the images folder and note the much smaller in bytes grayscale thumbnails, as shown in the following screenshot:

Figure 8.2: Images after processing

 More Information: You can read about ImageSharp at the following link: https://github.com/SixLabors/ImageSharp

Internationalizing your code

Internationalization is the process of enabling your code to run correctly all over the world. It has two parts: **globalization** and **localization**.

Globalization is about writing your code to accommodate multiple languages and region combinations. The combination of a language and a region is known as a culture. It is important for your code to know both the language and region because the date and currency formats are different in Quebec and Paris, despite them both using the French language.

There are **International Organization for Standardization (ISO)** codes for all culture combinations. For example, in the code da-DK, da indicates the Danish language and DK indicates the Denmark region, and in the code fr-CA, fr indicates the French language and CA indicates the Canadian region.

ISO is not an acronym. ISO is a reference to the Greek word *isos* (which means equal).

Localization is about customizing the user interface to support a language, for example, changing the label of a button to be **Close** (en) or **Fermer** (fr). Since localization is more about the language, it doesn't always need to know about the region, although ironically enough, standardization (en-US) and standardisation (en-GB) suggest otherwise.

Detecting and changing the current culture

Internationalization is a huge topic on which several thousand-page books have been written. In this section, you will get a brief introduction to the basics using the CultureInfo type in the System.Globalization namespace:

1. Create a new console application project named Internationalization, add it to the workspace, and select it as the active project for OmniSharp.

2. At the top of the Program.cs file, import the following namespace:

    ```
    using System.Globalization;
    ```

3. In the Main method, enter statements to get the current globalization and localization cultures and write some information about them to the console, and then prompt the user to enter a new culture code and show how that affects the formatting of common values such as dates and currency, as shown in the following code:

    ```
    CultureInfo globalization = CultureInfo.CurrentCulture;
    CultureInfo localization = CultureInfo.CurrentUICulture;

    WriteLine("The current globalization culture is {0}: {1}",
      globalization.Name, globalization.DisplayName);
    WriteLine("The current localization culture is {0}: {1}",
      localization.Name, localization.DisplayName);
    WriteLine();

    WriteLine("en-US: English (United States)");
    WriteLine("da-DK: Danish (Denmark)");
    WriteLine("fr-CA: French (Canada)");
    Write("Enter an ISO culture code: ");
    string newCulture = ReadLine();

    if (!string.IsNullOrEmpty(newCulture))
    {
      var ci = new CultureInfo(newCulture);
      CultureInfo.CurrentCulture = ci;
    ```

```
        CultureInfo.CurrentUICulture = ci;
    }
    WriteLine();

    Write("Enter your name: ");
    string name = ReadLine();

    Write("Enter your date of birth: ");
    string dob = ReadLine();

    Write("Enter your salary: ");
    string salary = ReadLine();

    DateTime date = DateTime.Parse(dob);
    int minutes = (int)DateTime.Today.Subtract(date).TotalMinutes;
    decimal earns = decimal.Parse(salary);

    WriteLine(
        "{0} was born on a {1:dddd}, is {2:N0} minutes old, and earns {3:C}",
        name, date, minutes, earns);
```

When you run an application, it automatically sets its thread to use the culture of the operating system. I am running my code in London, UK, so the thread is set to English (United Kingdom).

The code prompts the user to enter an alternative ISO code. This allows your applications to replace the default culture at runtime.

The application then uses standard format codes to output the day of the week using format code dddd; the number of minutes with thousand separators using format code N0; and the salary with the currency symbol. These adapt automatically, based on the thread's culture.

4. Run the console application and enter en-GB for the ISO code and then enter some sample data including a date in a format valid for British English, as shown in the following output:

```
Enter an ISO culture code: en-GB
Enter your name: Alice
Enter your date of birth: 30/3/1967
Enter your salary: 23500
Alice was born on a Thursday, is 25,469,280 minutes old, and earns
£23,500.00
```

5. Rerun the application and try a different culture, such as Danish in Denmark, as shown in the following output:

```
Enter an ISO culture code: da-DK
Enter your name: Mikkel
```

```
Enter your date of birth: 12/3/1980
Enter your salary: 340000
Mikkel was born on a onsdag, is 18.656.640 minutes old, and earns
340.000,00 kr.
```

 Good Practice: Consider whether your application needs to be internationalized and plan for that before you start coding! Write down all the pieces of text in the user interface that will need to be localized. Think about all the data that will need to be globalized (date formats, number formats, and sorting text behavior).

Handling time zones

One of the trickiest areas of internationalization is handling time zones. It is too complex to cover in this book.

 More Information: You can read more about time zones at the following link: `https://devblogs.microsoft.com/dotnet/cross-platform-time-zones-with-net-core/`

Practicing and exploring

Test your knowledge and understanding by answering some questions, get some hands-on practice, and explore with deeper research into the topics in this chapter.

Exercise 8.1 – Test your knowledge

Use the web to answer the following questions:

1. What is the maximum number of characters that can be stored in a `string` variable?
2. When and why should you use a `SecureString` class?
3. When is it appropriate to use a `StringBuilder` type?
4. When should you use a `LinkedList<T>` class?
5. When should you use a `SortedDictionary<T>` class rather than a `SortedList<T>` class?
6. What is the ISO culture code for Welsh?
7. What is the difference between localization, globalization, and internationalization?
8. In a regular expression, what does $ mean?
9. In a regular expression, how could you represent digits?
10. Why should you *not* use the official standard for email addresses to create a regular expression to validate a user's email address?

Exercise 8.2 – Practice regular expressions

Create a console application named `Exercise02` that prompts the user to enter a regular expression, and then prompts the user to enter some input and compare the two for a match until the user presses *Esc*, as shown in the following output:

```
The default regular expression checks for at least one digit.
Enter a regular expression (or press ENTER to use the default): ^[a-z]+$
Enter some input: apples
apples matches ^[a-z]+$? True
Press ESC to end or any key to try again.
Enter a regular expression (or press ENTER to use the default): ^[a-z]+$
Enter some input: abc123xyz
abc123xyz matches ^[a-z]+$? False
Press ESC to end or any key to try again.
```

Exercise 8.3 – Practice writing extension methods

Create a class library named `Exercise03` that defines extension methods that extend number types such as `BigInteger` and `int` with a method named `Towards` that returns a `string` describing the number; for example, 18,000,000 would be eighteen million, and 18,456,002,032,011,000,007 would be eighteen quintillion, four hundred and fifty-six quadrillion, two trillion, thirty-two billion, eleven million, and seven.

 More Information: You can read more about names for large numbers at the following link: `https://en.wikipedia.org/wiki/Names_of_large_numbers`

Exercise 8.4 – Explore topics

Use the following links to read about the topics covered in this chapter in more detail:

- **.NET API Reference**: `https://docs.microsoft.com/en-us/dotnet/api/`
- **String Class**: `https://docs.microsoft.com/en-us/dotnet/api/system.string`
- **Regex Class**: `https://docs.microsoft.com/en-us/dotnet/api/system.text.regularexpressions.regex`
- **Regular expressions in .NET**: `https://docs.microsoft.com/en-us/dotnet/articles/standard/base-types/regular-expressions`
- **Regular Expression Language – Quick Reference**: `https://docs.microsoft.com/en-us/dotnet/standard/base-types/regular-expression-language-quick-reference`
- **Collections (C# and Visual Basic)**: `https://docs.microsoft.com/en-us/dotnet/api/system.collections`

- **Extending Metadata Using Attributes**: `https://docs.microsoft.com/en-us/dotnet/standard/attributes/`

- **Globalizing and localizing .NET applications**: `https://docs.microsoft.com/en-us/dotnet/standard/globalization-localization/`

Summary

In this chapter, you explored some choices for types to store and manipulate numbers and text, including regular expressions, which collections to use for storing multiple items; worked with indexes, ranges, and spans; used some network resources; reflected on code and attributes; manipulated images using a Microsoft-recommended third-party library; and learned how to internationalize your code.

In the next chapter, we will manage files and streams, encode and decode text, and perform serialization.

09

Working with Files, Streams, and Serialization

This chapter is about reading and writing to files and streams, text encoding, and serialization. We will be covering the following topics:

- Managing the filesystem
- Reading and writing with streams
- Encoding and decoding text
- Serializing object graphs

Managing the filesystem

Your applications will often need to perform input and output with files and directories in different environments. The System and System.IO namespaces contain classes for this purpose.

Handling cross-platform environments and filesystems

Let's explore how to handle cross-platform environments like the differences between Windows and Linux or macOS:

1. Create a new console application named WorkingWithFileSystems in a folder named Chapter09.
2. Save the workspace as Chapter09 and add WorkingWithFileSystems to it.

3. Import the `System.IO` namespace, and statically import the `System.Console`, `System.IO.Directory`, `System.Environment`, and `System.IO.Path` types, as shown in the following code:

```
using System.IO; // types for managing the filesystem
using static System.Console;
using static System.IO.Directory;
using static System.IO.Path;
using static System.Environment;
```

Paths are different for Windows, macOS, and Linux, so we will start by exploring how .NET handles this.

4. Create a static `OutputFileSystemInfo` method, and write statements to do the following:

   - Output the path and directory separation characters

   - Output the path of the current directory

   - Output some special paths for system files, temporary files, and documents

```
static void OutputFileSystemInfo()
{
  WriteLine("{0,-33} {1}", "Path.PathSeparator", PathSeparator);
  WriteLine("{0,-33} {1}", "Path.DirectorySeparatorChar",
    DirectorySeparatorChar);
  WriteLine("{0,-33} {1}", "Directory.GetCurrentDirectory()",
    GetCurrentDirectory());
  WriteLine("{0,-33} {1}", "Environment.CurrentDirectory",
    CurrentDirectory);
  WriteLine("{0,-33} {1}", "Environment.SystemDirectory",
    SystemDirectory);
  WriteLine("{0,-33} {1}", "Path.GetTempPath()", GetTempPath());
  WriteLine("GetFolderPath(SpecialFolder");
  WriteLine("{0,-33} {1}", " .System)",
    GetFolderPath(SpecialFolder.System));
  WriteLine("{0,-33} {1}", " .ApplicationData)",
    GetFolderPath(SpecialFolder.ApplicationData));
  WriteLine("{0,-33} {1}", " .MyDocuments)",
    GetFolderPath(SpecialFolder.MyDocuments));
  WriteLine("{0,-33} {1}", " .Personal)",
    GetFolderPath(SpecialFolder.Personal));
}
```

The `Environment` type has many other useful members, including the `GetEnvironmentVariables` method and the `OSVersion` and `ProcessorCount` properties.

5. In the `Main` method, call `OutputFileSystemInfo`, as shown in the following code:

```
static void Main(string[] args)
{
    OutputFileSystemInfo();
}
```

6. Run the console application and view the result, as shown in the following screenshot (when run on Windows):

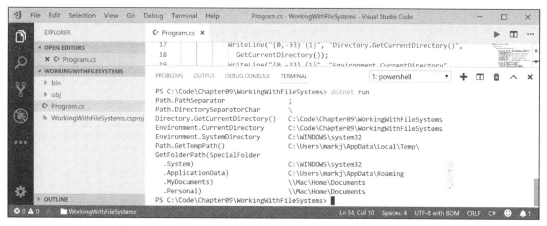

Figure 9.1: Running your application to show filesystem information

Windows uses a backslash for the directory separator character. macOS and Linux use a forward slash for the directory separator character.

Managing drives

To manage drives, use `DriveInfo`, which has a static method that returns information about all the drives connected to your computer. Each drive has a drive type. The steps are as follows:

1. Create a `WorkWithDrives` method, and write statements to get all the drives and output their name, type, size, available free space, and format, but only if the drive is ready, as shown in the following code:

```
static void WorkWithDrives()
{
    WriteLine("{0,-30} | {1,-10} | {2,-7} | {3,18} | {4,18}",
        "NAME", "TYPE", "FORMAT", "SIZE (BYTES)", "FREE SPACE");

    foreach (DriveInfo drive in DriveInfo.GetDrives())
    {
        if (drive.IsReady)
        {
            WriteLine(
                "{0,-30} | {1,-10} | {2,-7} | {3,18:N0} | {4,18:N0}",
                drive.Name, drive.DriveType, drive.DriveFormat,
                drive.TotalSize, drive.AvailableFreeSpace);
```

```
        }
        else
        {
            WriteLine("{0,-30} | {1,-10}", drive.Name, drive.DriveType);
        }
    }
}
```

 Good Practice: Check that a drive is ready before reading properties such as TotalSize or you will see an exception thrown with removable drives.

2. In Main, comment out the previous method call, and add a call to WorkWithDrives, as shown in the following code:

```
static void Main(string[] args)
{
    // OutputFileSystemInfo();
    WorkWithDrives();
}
```

3. Run the console application and view the result, as shown in the following screenshot:

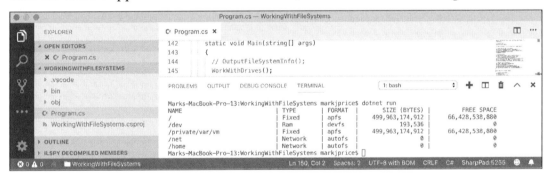

Figure 9.2: Showing drive information

Managing directories

To manage directories, use the Directory, Path, and Environment static classes.

These types include many properties and methods for working with the filesystem, as shown in the following diagram:

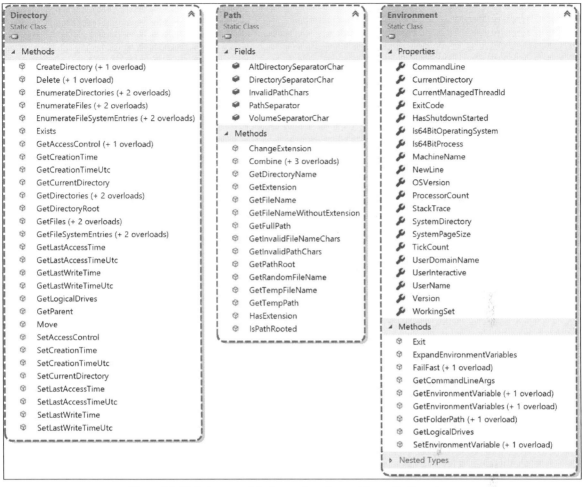

Figure 9.3: Static types and their members for working with filesystems

When constructing custom paths, you must be careful to write your code so that it makes no assumptions about the platform, for example, what to use for the directory separator character:

1. Create a WorkWithDirectories method, and write statements to do the following:

    a. Define a custom path under the user's home directory by creating an array of strings for the directory names, and then properly combining them with the Path type's static Combine method.

    b. Check for the existence of the custom directory path using the static Exists method of the Directory class.

c. Create and then delete the directory, including files and subdirectories within it, using the static `CreateDirectory` and `Delete` methods of the `Directory` class:

```
static void WorkWithDirectories()
{
  // define a directory path for a new folder
  // starting in the user's folder
  var newFolder = Combine(
    GetFolderPath(SpecialFolder.Personal),
    "Code", "Chapter09", "NewFolder");

  WriteLine($"Working with: {newFolder}");

  // check if it exists
  WriteLine($"Does it exist? {Exists(newFolder)}");

  // create directory
  WriteLine("Creating it...");
  CreateDirectory(newFolder);
  WriteLine($"Does it exist? {Exists(newFolder)}");
  Write("Confirm the directory exists, and then press ENTER: ");
  ReadLine();

  // delete directory
  WriteLine("Deleting it...");
  Delete(newFolder, recursive: true);
  WriteLine($"Does it exist? {Exists(newFolder)}");
}
```

2. In the `Main` method, comment out the previous method call, and add a call to `WorkWithDirectories`, as shown in the following code:

```
static void Main(string[] args)
{
  // OutputFileSystemInfo();
  // WorkWithDrives();
  WorkWithDirectories();
}
```

3. Run the console application and view the result, and use your favorite file management tool to confirm that the directory has been created before pressing *Enter* to delete it, as shown in the following output:

```
Working with: /Users/markjprice/Code/Chapter09/NewFolder
Does it exist? False
Creating it...
Does it exist? True
Confirm the directory exists, and then press ENTER:
```

```
Deleting it...
Does it exist? False
```

Managing files

When working with files, you could statically import the File type, just as we did for the Directory type, but, for the next example, we will not, because it has some of the same methods as the Directory type and they would conflict. The File type has a short enough name not to matter in this case. The steps are as follows:

1. Create a WorkWithFiles method, and write statements to do the following:

    a. Check for the existence of a file.

    b. Create a text file.

    c. Write a line of text to the file.

    d. Close the file to release system resources and file locks (this would normally be done inside a try-finally statement block to ensure that the file is closed even if an exception occurs when writing to it).

    e. Copy the file to a backup.

    f. Delete the original file.

    g. Read the backup file's contents and then close it.

```
static void WorkWithFiles()
{
  // define a directory path to output files
  // starting in the user's folder
  var dir = Combine(
    GetFolderPath(SpecialFolder.Personal),
    "Code", "Chapter09", "OutputFiles");

  CreateDirectory(dir);

  // define file paths
  string textFile = Combine(dir, "Dummy.txt");
  string backupFile = Combine(dir, "Dummy.bak");
  WriteLine($"Working with: {textFile}");

  // check if a file exists
  WriteLine($"Does it exist? {File.Exists(textFile)}");

  // create a new text file and write a line to it
  StreamWriter textWriter = File.CreateText(textFile);
  textWriter.WriteLine("Hello, C#!");
  textWriter.Close(); // close file and release resources
  WriteLine($"Does it exist? {File.Exists(textFile)}");
```

```
    // copy the file, and overwrite if it already exists
    File.Copy(sourceFileName: textFile,
      destFileName: backupFile, overwrite: true);
    WriteLine(
      $"Does {backupFile} exist? {File.Exists(backupFile)}");
    Write("Confirm the files exist, and then press ENTER: ");
    ReadLine();

    // delete file
    File.Delete(textFile);
    WriteLine($"Does it exist? {File.Exists(textFile)}");

    // read from the text file backup
    WriteLine($"Reading contents of {backupFile}:");
    StreamReader textReader = File.OpenText(backupFile);
    WriteLine(textReader.ReadToEnd());
    textReader.Close();
}
```

2. In `Main`, comment out the previous method call, and add a call to `WorkWithFiles`.

3. Run the application and view the result, as shown in the following output:

```
Working with: /Users/markjprice/Code/Chapter09/OutputFiles/Dummy.txt
Does it exist? False
Does it exist? True
Does /Users/markjprice/Code/Chapter09/OutputFiles/Dummy.bak exist? True
Confirm the files exist, and then press ENTER:
Does it exist? False
Reading contents of /Users/markjprice/Code/Chapter09/OutputFiles/Dummy.
bak:
Hello, C#!
```

Managing paths

Sometimes, you need to work with parts of a path; for example, you might want to extract just the folder name, the filename, or the extension. Sometimes, you need to generate temporary folders and filenames. You can do this with static methods of the `Path` class:

1. Add the following statements to the end of the WorkWithFiles method:

```
// Managing paths
WriteLine($"Folder Name: {GetDirectoryName(textFile)}");
WriteLine($"File Name: {GetFileName(textFile)}");
WriteLine("File Name without Extension: {0}",
  GetFileNameWithoutExtension(textFile));
WriteLine($"File Extension: {GetExtension(textFile)}");
WriteLine($"Random File Name: {GetRandomFileName()}");
WriteLine($"Temporary File Name: {GetTempFileName()}");
```

2. Run the application and view the result, as shown in the following output:

```
Folder Name: /Users/markjprice/Code/Chapter09/OutputFiles
File Name: Dummy.txt
File Name without Extension: Dummy
File Extension: .txt
Random File Name: u45w1zki.co3
Temporary File Name:
/var/folders/tz/xx0y_wld5sx0nv0fjtq4tnpc0000gn/T/tmpyqrepP.tmp
```

GetTempFileName creates a zero-byte file and returns its name, ready for you to use. GetRandomFileName just returns a filename; it doesn't create the file.

Getting file information

To get more information about a file or directory, for example, its size or when it was last accessed, you can create an instance of the FileInfo or DirectoryInfo class.

FileInfo and DirectoryInfo both inherit from FileSystemInfo, so they both have members such as LastAccessTime and Delete, as shown in the following diagram:

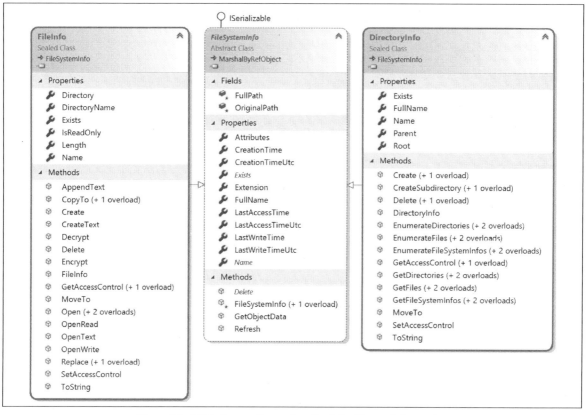

Figure 9.4: A list of properties and methods for files and directories

Let's write some code that uses a `FileInfo` instance for efficiently performing multiple actions on a file:

1. Add statements to the end of the `WorkWithFiles` method to create an instance of `FileInfo` for the backup file and write information about it to the console, as shown in the following code:

```
var info = new FileInfo(backupFile);
WriteLine($"{backupFile}:");
WriteLine($"Contains {info.Length} bytes");
WriteLine($"Last accessed {info.LastAccessTime}");
WriteLine($"Has readonly set to {info.IsReadOnly}");
```

2. Run the application and view the result, as shown in the following output:

```
/Users/markjprice/Code/Chapter09/OutputFiles/Dummy.bak:
Contains 11 bytes
Last accessed 26/11/2018 09:08:26
Has readonly set to False
```

The number of bytes might be different on your operating system because operating systems can use different line endings.

Controlling how you work with files

When working with files, you often need to control how they are opened. The `File.Open` method has overloads to specify additional options using enum values. The enum types are as follows:

- `FileMode`: This controls what you want to do with the file, like `CreateNew`, `OpenOrCreate`, or `Truncate`.
- `FileAccess`: This controls what level of access you need, like `ReadWrite`.
- `FileShare`: This controls locks on the file to allow other processes the specified level of access, like `Read`.

You might want to open a file and read from it, and allow other processes to read it too, as shown in the following code:

```
FileStream file = File.Open(pathToFile,
    FileMode.Open, FileAccess.Read, FileShare.Read);
```

There is also an enum for attributes of a file as follows:

- `FileAttributes`: This is to check a `FileSystemInfo`-derived types, `Attributes` property for values like `Archive` and `Encrypted`.

You could check a file or directory's attributes, as shown in the following code:

```
var info = new FileInfo(backupFile);
WriteLine("Is the backup file compressed? {0}",
    info.Attributes.HasFlag(FileAttributes.Compressed));
```

Reading and writing with streams

A **stream** is a sequence of bytes that can be read from and written to. Although files can be processed rather like arrays, with random access provided by knowing the position of a byte within the file, it can be useful to process files as a stream in which the bytes can be accessed in sequential order.

Streams can also be used to process terminal input and output and networking resources such as sockets and ports that do not provide random access and cannot seek (that is, move) to a position. You can write code to process some arbitrary bytes without knowing or caring where it comes from. Your code simply reads or writes to a stream, and another piece of code handles where the bytes are actually stored.

There is an abstract class named `Stream` that represents a stream. There are many classes that inherit from this base class, including `FileStream`, `MemoryStream`, `BufferedStream`, `GZipStream`, and `SslStream`, so they all work the same way.

All streams implement `IDisposable`, so they have a `Dispose` method to release unmanaged resources.

In the following table are some of the common members of the `Stream` class:

Member	Description
`CanRead, CanWrite`	This determines whether you can read from and write to the stream.
`Length, Position`	This determines the total number of bytes and the current position within the stream. These properties may throw an exception for some types of streams.
`Dispose()`	This closes the stream and releases its resources.
`Flush()`	If the stream has a buffer, then the bytes in the buffer are written to the stream and the buffer is cleared.
`Read(), ReadAsync()`	This reads a specified number of bytes from the stream into a byte array and advances the position.
`ReadByte()`	This reads the next byte from the stream and advances the position.
`Seek()`	This moves the position to the specified position (if CanSeek is true).
`Write(), WriteAsync()`	This writes the contents of a byte array into the stream.
`WriteByte()`	This writes a byte to the stream.

In the following table are some **storage streams** that represent a location where the bytes will be stored:

Namespace	Class	Description
`System.IO`	`FileStream`	Bytes stored in the filesystem.
`System.IO`	`MemoryStream`	Bytes stored in memory in the current process.
`System.Net.Sockets`	`NetworkStream`	Bytes stored at a network location.

In the following table are some **function streams** that cannot exist on their own. They can only be "plugged onto" other streams to add functionality:

Namespace	Class	Description
`System.Security.Cryptography`	`CryptoStream`	This encrypts and decrypts the stream.
`System.IO.Compression`	`GZipStream, DeflateStream`	This compresses and decompresses the stream.
`System.Net.Security`	`AuthenticatedStream`	This sends credentials across the stream.

Although there will be occasions where you need to work with streams at a low level, most often, you can plug helper classes into the chain to make things easier.

All the helper types for streams implement `IDisposable`, so they have a `Dispose` method to release unmanaged resources.

In the following table are some helper classes to handle common scenarios:

Namespace	Class	Description
System.IO	StreamReader	This reads from the underlying stream as text.
System.IO	StreamWriter	This writes to the underlying stream as text.
System.IO	BinaryReader	This reads from streams as .NET types. For example, the ReadDecimal method reads the next 16 bytes from the underlying stream as a decimal value and the ReadInt32 method reads the next 4 bytes as an int value.
System.IO	BinaryWriter	This writes to streams as .NET types. For example, the Write method with a decimal parameter writes 16 bytes to the underlying stream and the Write method with an int parameter writes 4 bytes.
System.Xml	XmlReader	This reads from the underlying stream as XML.
System.Xml	XmlWriter	This writes to the underlying stream as XML.

Writing to text streams

Let's type some code to write text to a stream:

1. Create a new console application project named WorkingWithStreams, add it to the Chapter09 workspace, and select the project as active for OmniSharp.

2. Import the System.IO and System.Xml namespaces, and statically import the System.Console, System.Environment and System.IO.Path types.

3. Define an array of string values, perhaps containing Viper pilot call signs, and create a WorkWithText method that enumerates the call signs, writing each one on its own line in a single text file, as shown in the following code:

```
// define an array of Viper pilot call signs
static string[] callsigns = new string[] {
  "Husker", "Starbuck", "Apollo", "Boomer",
  "Bulldog", "Athena", "Helo", "Racetrack" };

static void WorkWithText()
{
  // define a file to write to
  string textFile = Combine(CurrentDirectory, "streams.txt");

  // create a text file and return a helper writer
  StreamWriter text = File.CreateText(textFile);
```

```
    // enumerate the strings, writing each one
    // to the stream on a separate line
    foreach (string item in callsigns)
    {
      text.WriteLine(item);
    }
    text.Close(); // release resources

    // output the contents of the file
    WriteLine("{0} contains {1:N0} bytes.",
      arg0: textFile,
      arg1: new FileInfo(textFile).Length);
    WriteLine(File.ReadAllText(textFile));
}
```

4. In `Main`, call the `WorkWithText` method.

5. Run the application and view the result, as shown in the following output:

```
/Users/markjprice/Code/Chapter09/WorkingWithStreams/streams.txt contains
60 bytes.
Husker
Starbuck
Apollo
Boomer
Bulldog
Athena
Helo
Racetrack
```

6. Open the file that was created and check that it contains the list of call signs.

Writing to XML streams

There are two ways to write an XML element, as follows:

* `WriteStartElement` and `WriteEndElement`: use this pair when an element might have child elements.

* `WriteElementString`: use this when an element does not have children.

Now, let's try storing the same array of `string` values in an XML file:

1. Create a `WorkWithXml` method that enumerates the call signs, writing each one as an element in a single XML file, as shown in the following code:

```
static void WorkWithXml()
{
  // define a file to write to
```

```
    string xmlFile = Combine(CurrentDirectory, "streams.xml");

    // create a file stream
    FileStream xmlFileStream = File.Create(xmlFile);

    // wrap the file stream in an XML writer helper
    // and automatically indent nested elements
    XmlWriter xml = XmlWriter.Create(xmlFileStream,
      new XmlWriterSettings { Indent = true });

    // write the XML declaration
    xml.WriteStartDocument();

    // write a root element
    xml.WriteStartElement("callsigns");

    // enumerate the strings writing each one to the stream
    foreach (string item in callsigns)
    {
      xml.WriteElementString("callsign", item);
    }

    // write the close root element
    xml.WriteEndElement();

    // close helper and stream
    xml.Close();
    xmlFileStream.Close();

    // output all the contents of the file
    WriteLine("{0} contains {1:N0} bytes.",
      arg0: xmlFile,
      arg1: new FileInfo(xmlFile).Length);

    WriteLine(File.ReadAllText(xmlFile));
}
```

2. In `Main`, comment out the previous method call, and add a call to the `WorkWithXml` method.

3. Run the application and view the result, as shown in the following output:

```
/Users/markjprice/Code/Chapter09/WorkingWithStreams/streams.xml contains
310 bytes.
<?xml version="1.0" encoding="utf-8"?>
<callsigns>
  <callsign>Husker</callsign>
```

```
<callsign>Starbuck</callsign>
<callsign>Apollo</callsign>
<callsign>Boomer</callsign>
<callsign>Bulldog</callsign>
<callsign>Athena</callsign>
<callsign>Helo</callsign>
<callsign>Racetrack</callsign>
</callsigns>
```

Disposing of file resources

When you open a file to read or write to it, you are using resources outside of .NET. These are called unmanaged resources and must be disposed of when you are done working with them. To deterministically control when they are disposed of, we can call the `Dispose` method inside of a `finally` block.

Let's improve our previous code that works with XML to properly dispose of its unmanaged resources:

1. Modify the `WorkWithXml` method, as shown highlighted in the following code:

```
static void WorkWithXml()
{
  FileStream xmlFileStream = null;
  XmlWriter xml = null;

  try
  {
    // define a file to write to
    string xmlFile = Combine(CurrentDirectory, "streams.xml");

    // create a file stream
    xmlFileStream = File.Create(xmlFile);

    // wrap the file stream in an XML writer helper
    // and automatically indent nested elements
    xml = XmlWriter.Create(xmlFileStream,
      new XmlWriterSettings { Indent = true });

    // write the XML declaration
    xml.WriteStartDocument();

    // write a root element
    xml.WriteStartElement("callsigns");

    // enumerate the strings writing each one to the stream
    foreach (string item in callsigns)
```

```
      {
        xml.WriteElementString("callsign", item);
      }

      // write the close root element
      xml.WriteEndElement();

      // close helper and stream
      xml.Close();
      xmlFileStream.Close();

      // output all the contents of the file
      WriteLine($"{0} contains {1:N0} bytes.",
        arg0: xmlFile,
        arg1: new FileInfo(xmlFile).Length);
      WriteLine(File.ReadAllText(xmlFile));
    }
    catch(Exception ex)
    {
      // if the path doesn't exist the exception will be caught
      WriteLine($"{ex.GetType()} says {ex.Message}");
    }
    finally
    {
      if (xml != null)
      {
        xml.Dispose();
        WriteLine("The XML writer's unmanaged resources have been
disposed.");
      }
      if (xmlFileStream != null)
      {
        xmlFileStream.Dispose();
        WriteLine("The file stream's unmanaged resources have been
disposed.");
      }
    }
}
```

You could also go back and modify the other methods you previously created but I will leave that as an optional exercise for you.

2. Run the application and view the result, as shown in the following output:

```
The XML writer's unmanaged resources have been disposed.
The file stream's unmanaged resources have been disposed.
```

Good Practice: Before calling `Dispose`, check that the object is not null.

You can simplify the code that needs to check for a `null` object and then call its `Dispose` method by using the `using` statement. Generally, I would recommend using `using` rather than manually calling `Dispose` unless you need a greater level of control.

Confusingly, there are two uses for the `using` keyword: importing a namespace and generating a `finally` statement that calls `Dispose` on an object that implements `IDisposable`.

The compiler changes a `using` statement block into a `try-finally` statement without a `catch` statement. You can use nested `try` statements; so, if you do want to catch any exceptions, you can, as shown in the following code example:

```
using (FileStream file2 = File.OpenWrite(
  Path.Combine(path, "file2.txt")))
{
  using (StreamWriter writer2 = new StreamWriter(file2))
  {
    try
    {
      writer2.WriteLine("Welcome, .NET!");
    }
    catch(Exception ex)
    {
      WriteLine($"{ex.GetType()} says {ex.Message}");
    }
  } // automatically calls Dispose if the object is not null
} // automatically calls Dispose if the object is not null
```

Compressing streams

XML is relatively verbose, so it takes up more space in bytes than plain text. Let's see how we can squeeze the XML using a common compression algorithm known as **GZIP**:

1. Import the following namespace:

   ```
   using System.IO.Compression;
   ```

2. Add a `WorkWithCompression` method, which uses instances of `GZipSteam` to create a compressed file containing the same XML elements as before and then decompresses it while reading it and outputting to the console, as shown in the following code:

   ```
   static void WorkWithCompression()
   {
     // compress the XML output
   ```

```
    string gzipFilePath = Combine(
      CurrentDirectory, "streams.gzip");

    FileStream gzipFile = File.Create(gzipFilePath);

    using (GZipStream compressor = new GZipStream(
      gzipFile, CompressionMode.Compress))
    {
      using (XmlWriter xmlGzip = XmlWriter.Create(compressor))
      {
        xmlGzip.WriteStartDocument();
        xmlGzip.WriteStartElement("callsigns");
        foreach (string item in callsigns)
        {
          xmlGzip.WriteElementString("callsign", item);
        }

        // the normal call to WriteEndElement is not necessary
        // because when the XmlWriter disposes, it will
        // automatically end any elements of any depth
      }
    } // also closes the underlying stream

    // output all the contents of the compressed file
    WriteLine("{0} contains {1:N0} bytes.",
      gzipFilePath, new FileInfo(gzipFilePath).Length);
    WriteLine($"The compressed contents:");
    WriteLine(File.ReadAllText(gzipFilePath));

    // read a compressed file
    WriteLine("Reading the compressed XML file:");
      gzipFile = File.Open(gzipFilePath, FileMode.Open);

    using (GZipStream decompressor = new GZipStream(
      gzipFile, CompressionMode.Decompress))
    {
      using (XmlReader reader = XmlReader.Create(decompressor))
      {
        while (reader.Read()) // read the next XML node
        {
          // check if we are on an element node named callsign
          if ((reader.NodeType == XmlNodeType.Element)
            && (reader.Name == "callsign"))
          {
            reader.Read(); // move to the text inside element
            WriteLine($"{reader.Value}"); // read its value
```

```
        }
      }
    }
  }
}
```

3. In `Main`, leave the call to `WorkWithXml`, and add a call to `WorkWithCompression`, as shown in the following code:

```
static void Main(string[] args)
{
  // WorkWithText();
  WorkWithXml();
  WorkWithCompression();
}
```

4. Run the console application and compare the sizes of the XML file and the compressed XML file. It is less than half the size of the same XML without compression, as shown in the following edited output:

```
/Users/markjprice/Code/Chapter09/WorkingWithStreams/streams.xml contains
310 bytes.
/Users/markjprice/Code/Chapter09/WorkingWithStreams/streams.gzip contains
150 bytes.
```

Compressing with the Brotli algorithm

In .NET Core 2.1, Microsoft introduced an implementation of the Brotli compression algorithm. In performance, Brotli is similar to the algorithm used in **DEFLATE** and **GZIP**, but the output is about 20% denser. The steps are as follows:

1. Modify the `WorkWithCompression` method to have an optional parameter to indicate if Brotli should be used and to use Brotli by default, as shown highlighted in the following code:

```
static void WorkWithCompression(bool useBrotli = true)
{
  string fileExt = useBrotli ? "brotli" : "gzip";

  // compress the XML output
  string filePath = Combine(
    CurrentDirectory, $"streams.{fileExt}");

  FileStream file = File.Create(filePath);

  Stream compressor;
  if (useBrotli)
  {
    compressor = new BrotliStream(file, CompressionMode.Compress);
```

```
  }
  else
  {
    compressor = new GZipStream(file, CompressionMode.Compress);
  }

  using (compressor)
  {
    using (XmlWriter xml = XmlWriter.Create(compressor))
    {
      xml.WriteStartDocument();
      xml.WriteStartElement("callsigns");
      foreach (string item in callsigns)
      {
        xml.WriteElementString("callsign", item);
      }
    }
  } // also closes the underlying stream

  // output all the contents of the compressed file
  WriteLine("{0} contains {1:N0} bytes.",
    filePath, new FileInfo(filePath).Length);
  WriteLine(File.ReadAllText(filePath));

  // read a compressed file
  WriteLine("Reading the compressed XML file:");
  file = File.Open(filePath, FileMode.Open);

  Stream decompressor;
  if (useBrotli)
  {
    decompressor = new BrotliStream(
      file, CompressionMode.Decompress);
  }
  else
  {
    decompressor = new GZipStream(
      file, CompressionMode.Decompress);
  }

  using (decompressor)
  {
    using (XmlReader reader = XmlReader.Create(decompressor))
    {
      while (reader.Read())
      {
```

```
          // check if we are on an element node named callsign
          if ((reader.NodeType == XmlNodeType.Element)
            && (reader.Name == "callsign"))
          {
            reader.Read(); // move to the text inside element
            WriteLine($"{reader.Value}"); // read its value
          }
        }
      }
    }
  }
}
```

2. Modify the `Main` method to call `WorkWithCompression` twice, once with the default using Brotli and once with GZIP, as shown in the following code:

    ```
    WorkWithCompression();
    WorkWithCompression(useBrotli: false);
    ```

3. Run the console application and compare the sizes of the two compressed XML files. Brotli is more than 21% denser, as shown in the following edited output:

    ```
    /Users/markjprice/Code/Chapter09/WorkingWithStreams/streams.brotli
    contains 118 bytes.
    /Users/markjprice/Code/Chapter09/WorkingWithStreams/streams.gzip contains
    150 bytes.
    ```

High-performance streams using pipelines

In .NET Core 2.1, Microsoft introduced **pipelines**. Processing data from a stream correctly requires a lot of complex boilerplate code that is difficult to maintain. Testing on your local laptop often works with small example files, but it fails in the real world due to poor assumptions. Pipelines help with this.

Although pipelines are powerful for real-world use and eventually you will want to learn about them, a decent example gets complicated so I have no plans to cover them in this book.

 More Information: You can read a detailed description of the problem and how pipelines help at the following link: `https://devblogs.microsoft.com/dotnet/system-io-pipelines-high-performance-io-in-net/`

Asynchronous streams

With .NET Core 3.0, Microsoft introduced the asynchronous processing of streams. You will learn about this in *Chapter 13, Improving Performance and Scalability Using Multitasking*.

More Information: You can complete a tutorial about async streams at the following link: https://docs.microsoft.com/en-us/dotnet/csharp/tutorials/generate-consume-asynchronous-stream

Encoding and decoding text

Text characters can be represented in different ways. For example, the alphabet can be encoded using Morse code into a series of dots and dashes for transmission over a telegraph line.

In a similar way, text inside a computer is stored as bits (ones and zeros) representing a code point within a code space. Most code points represent a single character, but they can also have other meanings like formatting.

For example, ASCII has a code space with 128 code points. .NET uses a standard called **Unicode** to encode text internally. Unicode has more than one million code points.

Sometimes, you will need to move text outside .NET for use by systems that do not use Unicode or use a variation of Unicode so it is important to learn how to convert between encodings.

The following table lists some alternative text encodings commonly used by computers:

Encoding	Description
ASCII	This encodes a limited range of characters using the lower seven bits of a byte.
UTF-8	This represents each Unicode code point as a sequence of one to four bytes.
UTF-7	This is designed to be more efficient over 7-bit channels than UTF-8 but it has security and robustness issues so UTF-8 is recommended over UTF-7.
UTF-16	This represents each Unicode code point as a sequence of one or two 16-bit integers.
UTF-32	This represents each Unicode code point as a 32-bit integer and is therefore a fixed-length encoding unlike the other Unicode encodings, which are all variable-length encodings.
ANSI/ISO encodings	This provides support for a variety of code pages that are used to support a specific language or group of languages.

In most cases today, UTF-8 is a good default, which is why it is literally the default encoding, that is, `Encoding.Default`.

Encoding strings as byte arrays

Let's explore text encodings:

1. Create a new console application project named `WorkingWithEncodings`, add it to the `Chapter09` workspace, and select the project as active for OmniSharp.

2. Import the `System.Text` namespace and statically import the `Console` class.

3. Add statements to the `Main` method to encode a `string` using an encoding chosen by the user, loop through each byte, and then decode it back into a `string` and output it, as shown in the following code:

```
WriteLine("Encodings");
WriteLine("[1] ASCII");
WriteLine("[2] UTF-7");
WriteLine("[3] UTF-8");
WriteLine("[4] UTF-16 (Unicode)");
WriteLine("[5] UTF-32");
WriteLine("[any other key] Default");

// choose an encoding
Write("Press a number to choose an encoding: ");
ConsoleKey number = ReadKey(intercept: false).Key;
WriteLine();
WriteLine();

Encoding encoder = number switch
{
  ConsoleKey.D1 => Encoding.ASCII,
  ConsoleKey.D2 => Encoding.UTF7,
  ConsoleKey.D3 => Encoding.UTF8,
  ConsoleKey.D4 => Encoding.Unicode,
  ConsoleKey.D5 => Encoding.UTF32,
  _             => Encoding.Default
};

// define a string to encode
string message = "A pint of milk is £1.99";

// encode the string into a byte array
byte[] encoded = encoder.GetBytes(message);

// check how many bytes the encoding needed
WriteLine("{0} uses {1:N0} bytes.",
  encoder.GetType().Name, encoded.Length);

// enumerate each byte
WriteLine($"BYTE HEX CHAR");
foreach (byte b in encoded)
{
  WriteLine($"{b,4} {b.ToString("X"),4} {(char)b,5}");
}

// decode the byte array back into a string and display it
```

```
string decoded = encoder.GetString(encoded);
WriteLine(decoded);
```

4. Run the application and note the warning to avoid using UTF7 because it is insecure. Of course, if you need to generate text using that encoding for compatibility with another system, it needs to remain an option in .NET.

5. Press 1 to choose ASCII and note that when outputting the bytes, the pound sign (£) cannot be represented in ASCII, so it uses a question mark instead, as shown in the following output:

```
ASCIIEncodingSealed uses 23 bytes.
BYTE HEX CHAR
  65  41   A
  32  20
 112  70   p
 105  69   i
 110  6E   n
 116  74   t
  32  20
 111  6F   o
 102  66   f
  32  20
 109  6D   m
 105  69   i
 108  6C   l
 107  6B   k
  32  20
 105  69   i
 115  73   s
  32  20
  63  3F   ?
  49  31   1
  46  2E   .
  57  39   9
  57  39   9
A pint of milk is ?1.99
```

6. Rerun the application and press 3 to choose UTF-8 and note that UTF-8 requires one extra byte (24 bytes instead of 23 bytes) but it can store the £ sign.

7. Rerun the application and press 4 to choose Unicode (UTF-16) and note that UTF-16 requires two bytes for every character, taking 46 total bytes, and it can store the £ sign. This encoding is used internally by .NET to store char and string values.

Encoding and decoding text in files

When using stream helper classes, such as StreamReader and StreamWriter, you can specify the encoding you want to use. As you write to the helper, the text will automatically be encoded, and as you read from the helper, the bytes will be automatically decoded.

To specify an encoding, pass the encoding as a second parameter to the helper type's constructor, as shown in the following code:

```
var reader = new StreamReader(stream, Encoding.UTF7);
var writer = new StreamWriter(stream, Encoding.UTF7);
```

Good Practice: Often, you won't have the choice of which encoding to use, because you will be generating a file for use by another system. However, if you do, pick one that uses the least number of bytes, but can store every character you need.

Serializing object graphs

Serialization is the process of converting a live object into a sequence of bytes using a specified format. **Deserialization** is the reverse process.

There are dozens of formats you can specify, but the two most common ones are **eXtensible Markup Language (XML)** and **JavaScript Object Notation (JSON)**.

Good Practice: JSON is more compact and is best for web and mobile applications. XML is more verbose but is better supported in more legacy systems. Use JSON to minimize the size of serialized object graphs. JSON is also a good choice when sending object graphs to web applications and mobile applications because JSON is the native serialization format for JavaScript and mobile apps often make calls over limited bandwidth, so the number of bytes is important.

.NET has multiple classes that will serialize to and from XML and JSON. We will start by looking at XmlSerializer and JsonSerializer.

Serializing as XML

Let's start by looking at XML, probably the world's most used serialization format (for now). To show a typical example, we will define a custom class to store information about a person and then create an object graph using a list of Person instances with nesting:

1. Create a new console application project named WorkingWithSerialization, add it to the Chapter09 workspace, and select the project as active for OmniSharp.

2. Add a class named `Person` with a `Salary` property that is `protected`, meaning it is only accessible to itself and derived classes. To populate the salary, the class has a constructor with a single parameter to set the initial salary, as shown in the following code:

```
using System;
using System.Collections.Generic;

namespace Packt.Shared
{
  public class Person
  {
    public Person(decimal initialSalary)
    {
      Salary = initialSalary;
    }

    public string FirstName { get; set; }
    public string LastName { get; set; }
    public DateTime DateOfBirth { get; set; }
    public HashSet<Person> Children { get; set; }
    protected decimal Salary { get; set; }
  }
}
```

3. Back in `Program.cs`, import the following namespaces:

```
using System; // DateTime
using System.Collections.Generic; // List<T>, HashSet<T>
using System.Xml.Serialization; // XmlSerializer
using System.IO; // FileStream
using Packt.Shared; // Person
using static System.Console;
using static System.Environment;
using static System.IO.Path;
```

4. Add the following statements to the `Main` method:

```
// create an object graph
var people = new List<Person>
{
  new Person(30000M) { FirstName = "Alice",
    LastName = "Smith",
    DateOfBirth = new DateTime(1974, 3, 14) },
  new Person(40000M) { FirstName = "Bob",
    LastName = "Jones",
    DateOfBirth = new DateTime(1969, 11, 23) },
  new Person(20000M) { FirstName = "Charlie",
```

```
      LastName = "Cox",
      DateOfBirth = new DateTime(1984, 5, 4),
      Children = new HashSet<Person>
        { new Person(0M) { FirstName = "Sally",
          LastName = "Cox",
          DateOfBirth = new DateTime(2000, 7, 12) } } }
};

// create object that will format a List of Persons as XML
var xs = new XmlSerializer(typeof(List<Person>));

// create a file to write to
string path = Combine(CurrentDirectory, "people.xml");

using (FileStream stream = File.Create(path))
{
  // serialize the object graph to the stream
  xs.Serialize(stream, people);
}

WriteLine("Written {0:N0} bytes of XML to {1}",
   arg0: new FileInfo(path).Length,
   arg1: path);
WriteLine();

// Display the serialized object graph
WriteLine(File.ReadAllText(path));
```

5. Run the console application, view the result, and note that an exception is thrown, as shown in the following output:

```
Unhandled Exception: System.InvalidOperationException: Packt.Shared.Person
cannot be serialized because it does not have a parameterless constructor.
```

6. Back in the Person.cs file, add the following statement to define a parameterless constructor, as shown in the following code:

```
public Person() { }
```

The constructor does not need to do anything, but it must exist so that the XmlSerializer can call it to instantiate new Person instances during the deserialization process.

7. Rerun the console application and view the result, and note that the object graph is serialized as XML and the Salary property is not included, as shown in the following output:

```
Written 752 bytes of XML to
/Users/markjprice/Code/Chapter09/WorkingWithSerialization/people.xml
```

```xml
<?xml version="1.0"?>
<ArrayOfPerson xmlns:xsi="http://www.w3.org/2001/XMLSchema-instance"
xmlns:xsd="http://www.w3.org/2001/XMLSchema">
  <Person>
    <FirstName>Alice</FirstName>
    <LastName>Smith</LastName>
    <DateOfBirth>1974-03-14T00:00:00</DateOfBirth>
  </Person>
  <Person>
    <FirstName>Bob</FirstName>
    <LastName>Jones</LastName>
    <DateOfBirth>1969-11-23T00:00:00</DateOfBirth>
  </Person>
  <Person>
    <FirstName>Charlie</FirstName>
    <LastName>Cox</LastName>
    <DateOfBirth>1984-05-04T00:00:00</DateOfBirth>
    <Children>
      <Person>
        <FirstName>Sally</FirstName>
        <LastName>Cox</LastName>
        <DateOfBirth>2000-07-12T00:00:00</DateOfBirth>
      </Person>
    </Children>
  </Person>
</ArrayOfPerson>
```

Generating compact XML

We could make the XML more compact using attributes instead of elements for some fields:

1. In the Person.cs file, import the System.Xml.Serialization namespace.

2. Decorate all the properties, except Children, with the [XmlAttribute] attribute, and set a short name for each property, as shown in the following code:

```csharp
[XmlAttribute("fname")]
public string FirstName { get; set; }

[XmlAttribute("lname")]
public string LastName { get; set; }

[XmlAttribute("dob")]
public DateTime DateOfBirth { get; set; }
```

3. Rerun the application and note that the size of the file has been reduced from 752 to 462 bytes, a space-saving of more than a third, as shown in the following output:

```
Written 462 bytes of XML to /Users/markjprice/Code/Chapter09/
WorkingWithSerialization/people.xml
<?xml version="1.0"?>
<ArrayOfPerson xmlns:xsi="http://www.w3.org/2001/XMLSchema-instance"
xmlns:xsd="http://www.w3.org/2001/XMLSchema">
  <Person fname="Alice" lname="Smith" dob="1974-03-14T00:00:00" />
  <Person fname="Bob" lname="Jones" dob="1969-11-23T00:00:00" />
  <Person fname="Charlie" lname="Cox" dob="1984-05-04T00:00:00">
    <Children>
      <Person fname="Sally" lname="Cox" dob="2000-07-12T00:00:00" />
    </Children>
  </Person>
</ArrayOfPerson>
```

Deserializing XML files

Now let's try deserializing the XML file back into live objects in memory:

1. Add statements to the end of the Main method to open the XML file and then deserialize it, as shown in the following code:

```
using (FileStream xmlLoad = File.Open(path, FileMode.Open))
{
  // deserialize and cast the object graph into a List of Person
  var loadedPeople = (List<Person>)xs.Deserialize(xmlLoad);

  foreach (var item in loadedPeople)
  {
    WriteLine("{0} has {1} children.",
      item.LastName, item.Children.Count);
  }
}
```

2. Rerun the application and note that the people are loaded successfully from the XML file, as shown in the following output:

```
Smith has 0 children.
Jones has 0 children.
Cox has 1 children.
```

There are many other attributes that can be used to control the XML generated.

Good Practice: When using XmlSerializer, remember that only the public fields and properties are included, and the type must have a parameterless constructor. You can customize the output with attributes.

Serializing with JSON

One of the most popular .NET libraries for working with the JSON serialization format is Newtonsoft.Json, known as **Json.NET**. It is mature and powerful.

Let's see it in action:

1. Edit the WorkingWithSerialization.csproj file to add a package reference for the latest version of Newtonsoft.Json, as shown highlighted in the following markup:

```xml
<Project Sdk="Microsoft.NET.Sdk">
  <PropertyGroup>
    <OutputType>Exe</OutputType>
    <TargetFramework>net5.0</TargetFramework>
  </PropertyGroup>
  <ItemGroup>
    <PackageReference Include="Newtonsoft.Json"
      Version="12.0.3" />
  </ItemGroup>
</Project>
```

Good Practice: Search for NuGet packages on Microsoft's NuGet feed to discover the latest supported version, as shown at the following link: https://www.nuget.org/packages/Newtonsoft.Json/

2. Add statements to the end of the Main method to create a text file and then serialize the people into the file as JSON, as shown in the following code:

```csharp
// create a file to write to
string jsonPath = Combine(CurrentDirectory, "people.json");

using (StreamWriter jsonStream = File.CreateText(jsonPath))
{
  // create an object that will format as JSON
  var jss = new Newtonsoft.Json.JsonSerializer();

  // serialize the object graph into a string
  jss.Serialize(jsonStream, people);
}
WriteLine();
```

```
WriteLine("Written {0:N0} bytes of JSON to: {1}",
    arg0: new FileInfo(jsonPath).Length,
    arg1: jsonPath);

// Display the serialized object graph
WriteLine(File.ReadAllText(jsonPath));
```

3. Rerun the application and note that JSON requires less than half the number of bytes compared to XML with elements. It's even smaller than the XML file, which uses attributes, as shown in the following output:

```
Written 366 bytes of JSON to: /Users/markjprice/Code/Chapter09/
WorkingWithSerialization/people.json
[{"FirstName":"Alice","LastName":"Smith","DateOfBirth":"1974-03-
14T00:00:00","Children":null},{"FirstName":"Bob","LastName":"Jones","Date
OfBirth":"1969-11-23T00:00:00","Children":null},{"FirstName":"Charlie","L
astName":"Cox","DateOfBirth":"1984-05-04T00:00:00","Children":[{"FirstNam
e":"Sally","LastName":"Cox","DateOfBirth":"2000-07-12T00:00:00","Children
":null}]}]
```

High-performance JSON processing

.NET Core 3.0 introduced a new namespace for working with JSON: System.Text.Json, which is optimized for performance by leveraging APIs like Span<T>.

Also, Json.NET is implemented by reading UTF-16. It would be more performant to read and write JSON documents using UTF-8 because most network protocols, including HTTP, use UTF-8 and you can avoid transcoding UTF-8 to and from Json.NET's Unicode string values. With the new API, Microsoft achieved between 1.3x and 5x improvement, depending on the scenario.

 More Information: You can read more about the new System.Text.Json APIs at the following link: https://devblogs.microsoft.com/dotnet/try-the-new-system-text-json-apis/

The original author of Json.NET, James Newton-King, joined Microsoft and has been working with them to develop their new JSON types. As he says in a comment discussing the new JSON APIs, *"Json.NET isn't going away,"* as shown in the following screenshot:

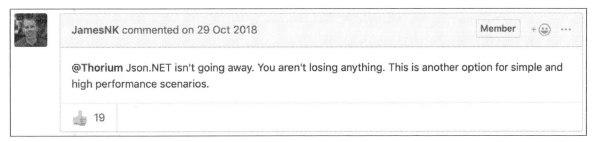

Figure 9.5: A comment by the original author of Json.NET

 More Information: You can read more about the issues solved by the new JSON APIs, including JamesNK's comments, at the following link: `https://github.com/dotnet/corefx/issues/33115`

Let's explore the new JSON APIs:

1. Import the `System.Threading.Tasks` namespace.

2. Modify the `Main` method to enable awaiting on tasks by changing void to `async Task`, as shown highlighted in the following code:

```
static async Task Main(string[] args)
```

3. Import the new JSON class for performing serialization using an alias to avoid conflicting names with the Json.NET one we used before, as shown in the following code:

```
using NuJson = System.Text.Json.JsonSerializer;
```

4. Add statements to open the JSON file, deserialize it, and output the names and counts of the children of the people, as shown in the following code:

```
using (FileStream jsonLoad = File.Open(
  jsonPath, FileMode.Open))
{
  // deserialize object graph into a List of Person
  var loadedPeople = (List<Person>)

  await NuJson.DeserializeAsync(
    utf8Json: jsonLoad,
    returnType: typeof(List<Person>));

  foreach (var item in loadedPeople)
  {
    WriteLine("{0} has {1} children.",
      item.LastName, item.Children?.Count ?? 0);
  }
}
```

5. Run the console application and view the result, as shown in the following output:

```
Smith has 0 children.
Jones has 0 children.
Cox has 1 children.
```

> **Good Practice**: Choose Json.NET for developer productivity and a large feature set or `System.Text.Json` for performance.

In .NET 5, Microsoft has added refinements to the types in the `System.Text.Json` namespace like extension methods for `HttpResponse`, which you will see in *Chapter 18, Building and Consuming Web Services*.

If you have existing code that uses the Newtonsoft Json.NET library and you want to migrate to the new `System.Text.Json` namespace, then Microsoft has specific documentation for that.

> **More Information**: You can read how to migrate from `Newtonsoft.Json` to `System.Text.Json` at the following link: `https://docs.microsoft.com/en-us/dotnet/standard/serialization/system-text-json-migrate-from-newtonsoft-how-to`

Practicing and exploring

Test your knowledge and understanding by answering some questions, get some hands-on practice, and explore this chapter's topics with more in-depth research.

Exercise 9.1 – Test your knowledge

Answer the following questions:

1. What is the difference between using the `File` class and the `FileInfo` class?
2. What is the difference between the `ReadByte` method and the `Read` method of a stream?
3. When would you use the `StringReader`, `TextReader`, and `StreamReader` classes?
4. What does the `DeflateStream` type do?
5. How many bytes per character does UTF-8 encoding use?
6. What is an object graph?
7. What is the best serialization format to choose for minimizing space requirements?
8. What is the best serialization format to choose for cross-platform compatibility?

9. Why is it bad to use a string value like \Code\Chapter01 to represent a path and what should you do instead?

10. Where can you find information about NuGet packages and their dependencies?

Exercise 9.2 – Practice serializing as XML

Create a console application named Exercise02 that creates a list of shapes, uses serialization to save it to the filesystem using XML, and then deserializes it back:

```
// create a list of Shapes to serialize
var listOfShapes = new List<Shape>
{
  new Circle { Colour = "Red", Radius = 2.5 },
  new Rectangle { Colour = "Blue", Height = 20.0, Width = 10.0 },
  new Circle { Colour = "Green", Radius = 8.0 },
  new Circle { Colour = "Purple", Radius = 12.3 },
  new Rectangle { Colour = "Blue", Height = 45.0, Width = 18.0 }
};
```

Shapes should have a read-only property named Area so that when you deserialize, you can output a list of shapes, including their areas, as shown here:

```
List<Shape> loadedShapesXml =
  serializerXml.Deserialize(fileXml) as List<Shape>;

foreach (Shape item in loadedShapesXml)
{
  WriteLine("{0} is {1} and has an area of {2:N2}",
    item.GetType().Name, item.Colour, item.Area);
}
```

This is what your output should look like when you run the application:

```
Loading shapes from XML:
Circle is Red and has an area of 19.63
Rectangle is Blue and has an area of 200.00
Circle is Green and has an area of 201.06
Circle is Purple and has an area of 475.29
Rectangle is Blue and has an area of 810.00
```

Exercise 9.3 – Explore topics

Use the following links to read more on this chapter's topics:

- **File System and the Registry (C# Programming Guide)**: `https://docs.microsoft.com/en-us/dotnet/csharp/programming-guide/file-system/`

- **Character encoding in .NET**: `https://docs.microsoft.com/en-us/dotnet/articles/standard/base-types/character-encoding`

- **Serialization (C#)**: `https://docs.microsoft.com/en-us/dotnet/articles/csharp/programming-guide/concepts/serialization/`

- **Serializing to Files, TextWriters, and XmlWriters**: `https://docs.microsoft.com/en-us/dotnet/standard/linq/serialize-files-textwriters-xmlwriters`

- **Newtonsoft Json.NET**: `https://www.newtonsoft.com/json`

Summary

In this chapter, you learned how to read from and write to text files and XML files, how to compress and decompress files, how to encode and decode text, and how to serialize an object into JSON and XML (and deserialize it back again).

In the next chapter, you will learn how to protect data and files using hashing, signing encryption, authentication, and authorization.

10

Protecting Your Data and Applications

This chapter is about protecting your data from being viewed by malicious users using encryption, and from being manipulated or corrupted using hashing and signing.

In .NET Core 2.1, Microsoft introduced new Span<T>-based cryptography APIs for hashing, random number generation, asymmetric signature generation and processing, and RSA encryption.

Cryptographic operations are performed by operating system implementations so that when an OS has a security vulnerability fixed, then .NET apps benefit immediately. But this means that those .NET apps can only use features that an OS supports.

 More Information: You can read about which features are supported by which OS at the following link: https://docs.microsoft.com/en-us/dotnet/standard/security/cross-platform-cryptography

This chapter covers the following topics:

- Understanding the vocabulary of protection
- Encrypting and decrypting data
- Hashing data
- Signing data
- Generating random numbers
- What's new in cryptography?
- Authenticating and authorizing users

Understanding the vocabulary of protection

There are many techniques to protect your data; below we'll briefly introduce six of the most popular ones and you will see more detailed explanations and practical implementations throughout this chapter:

- **Encryption and decryption**: These are a two-way process to convert your data from clear text into crypto-text and back again.
- **Hashes**: This is a one-way process to generate a hash value to securely store passwords, or can be used to detect malicious changes or corruption of your data.
- **Signatures**: This technique is used to ensure that data has come from someone you trust by validating a signature that has been applied to some data against someone's public key.
- **Authentication**: This technique is used to identify someone by checking their credentials.
- **Authorization**: This technique is used to ensure that someone has permission to perform an action or work with some data by checking the roles or groups they belong to.

Good Practice: If security is important to you (and it should be!), then hire an experienced security expert for guidance rather than relying on advice found online. It is very easy to make small mistakes and leave your applications and data vulnerable without realizing until it is too late!

Keys and key sizes

Protection algorithms often use a **key**. Keys are represented by byte arrays of varying size.

Good Practice: Choose a bigger key size for stronger protection.

Keys can be symmetric (also known as shared or secret because the same key is used to encrypt and decrypt) or asymmetric (a public-private key pair where the public key is used to encrypt and only the private key can be used to decrypt).

Good Practice: Symmetric key encryption algorithms are fast and can encrypt large amounts of data using a stream. Asymmetric key encryption algorithms are slow and can only encrypt small byte arrays.

In the real world, get the best of both worlds by using a symmetric key to encrypt your data, and an asymmetric key to share the symmetric key. This is how **Secure Sockets Layer (SSL)** encryption on the internet works.

Keys come in various byte array sizes.

IVs and block sizes

When encrypting large amounts of data, there are likely to be repeating sequences. For example, in an English document, in the sequence of characters, the would appear frequently, and each time it might get encrypted as hQ2. A good cracker would use this knowledge to make it easier to crack the encryption, as shown in the following output:

```
When the wind blew hard the umbrella broke.
5:s4&hQ2aj#D f9d1d£8fh"&hQ2s0)an DF8SFd#][1
```

We can avoid repeating sequences by dividing data into **blocks**. After encrypting a block, a byte array value is generated from that block, and this value is fed into the next block to adjust the algorithm so that the isn't encrypted in the same way. To encrypt the first block, we need a byte array to feed in. This is called the **initialization vector (IV)**.

 Good Practice: Choose a small block size for stronger encryption.

Salts

A **salt** is a random byte array that is used as an additional input to a one-way hash function. If you do not use a salt when generating hashes, then when many of your users register with 123456 as their password (about 8% of users still did this in 2016!), they will all have the same hashed value, and their accounts will be vulnerable to a dictionary attack.

 More Information: You can read a Dictionary Attacks 101 at the following link: https://blog.codinghorror.com/dictionary-attacks-101/

When a user registers, the salt should be randomly generated and concatenated with their chosen password before being hashed. The output (but not the original password) is stored with the salt in the database.

Then, when the user next logs in and enters their password, you look up their salt, concatenate it with the entered password, regenerate a hash, and then compare its value with the hash stored in the database. If they are the same, you know they entered the correct password.

Generating keys and IVs

Keys and IVs are byte arrays. Both of the two parties that want to exchange encrypted data need the key and IV values, but byte arrays can be difficult to exchange reliably.

You can reliably generate a key or IV using a **password-based key derivation function (PBKDF2)**. A good one is the Rfc2898DeriveBytes class, which takes a password, a salt, and an iteration count, and then generates keys and IVs by making calls to its GetBytes method.

 Good Practice: The salt size should be 8 bytes or larger, and the iteration count should be greater than zero. The minimum recommended number of iterations is 1,000.

Encrypting and decrypting data

In .NET, there are multiple encryption algorithms you can choose from.

In legacy .NET Framework, some algorithms are implemented by the operating system and their names are suffixed with CryptoServiceProvider. Some algorithms are implemented in the .NET BCL and their names are suffixed with Managed.

In modern .NET, all algorithms are implemented by the operating system. If the OS algorithms are certified by the **Federal Information Processing Standards (FIPS)**, then .NET uses FIPS-certified algorithms.

Generally, you will always use an abstract class like Aes and its Create factory method to get an instance of an algorithm so you will not need to know if you are using CryptoServiceProvider or Managed anyway.

Some algorithms use symmetric keys, and some use asymmetric keys. The main asymmetric encryption algorithm is RSA.

Symmetric encryption algorithms use CryptoStream to encrypt or decrypt large amounts of bytes efficiently. Asymmetric algorithms can only handle small amounts of bytes, stored in a byte array instead of a stream.

The most common symmetric encryption algorithms derive from the abstract class named SymmetricAlgorithm and are shown in the following list:

- AES
- DESCryptoServiceProvider
- TripleDESCryptoServiceProvider
- RC2CryptoServiceProvider
- RijndaelManaged

If you need to write code to decrypt some data sent by an external system, then you will have to use whatever algorithm the external system used to encrypt the data. Or if you need to send encrypted data to a system that can only decrypt using a specific algorithm, then again you will not have a choice of algorithm.

If your code will both encrypt and decrypt, then you can choose the algorithm that best suits your requirements for strength, performance, and so on.

> **Good Practice**: Choose the **Advanced Encryption Standard (AES)**, which is based on the Rijndael algorithm, for symmetric encryption. Choose RSA for asymmetric encryption. Do not confuse RSA with DSA. **Digital Signature Algorithm (DSA)** cannot encrypt data. It can only generate hashes and signatures.

Encrypting symmetrically with AES

To make it easier to reuse your protection code in the future, we will create a `static` class named `Protector` in its own class library:

1. In the `Code` folder, create a folder named `Chapter10`, with two subfolders named `CryptographyLib` and `EncryptionApp`.

2. In Visual Studio Code, save a workspace as `Chapter10` in the `Chapter10` folder.

3. Add the folder named `CryptographyLib` to the workspace.

4. Navigate to **Terminal | New Terminal**.

5. In **TERMINAL**, enter the following command:
   ```
   dotnet new classlib
   ```

6. Add the folder named `EncryptionApp` to the workspace.

7. Navigate to **Terminal | New Terminal** and select `EncryptionApp`.

8. In **TERMINAL**, enter the following command:
   ```
   dotnet new console
   ```

9. In **EXPLORER**, expand `CryptographyLib` and rename the `Class1.cs` file to `Protector.cs`.

10. In the `EncryptionApp` project folder, open the file named `EncryptionApp.csproj`, and add a package reference to the `CryptographyLib` library, as shown highlighted in the following markup:
    ```xml
    <Project Sdk="Microsoft.NET.Sdk">
      <PropertyGroup>
        <OutputType>Exe</OutputType>
        <TargetFramework>net5.0</TargetFramework>
      </PropertyGroup>
    ```

```xml
  <ItemGroup>
    <ProjectReference
      Include="..\CryptographyLib\CryptographyLib.csproj" />
  </ItemGroup>
</Project>
```

11. In **TERMINAL**, enter the following command:

```
dotnet build
```

12. Open the `Protector.cs` file and change its contents to define a static class named `Protector` with fields for storing a salt byte array and a number of iterations, and methods to `Encrypt` and `Decrypt`, as shown in the following code:

```csharp
using System;
using System.Collections.Generic;
using System.IO;
using System.Security.Cryptography;
using System.Security.Principal;
using System.Text;
using System.Xml.Linq;
using static System.Convert;

namespace Packt.Shared
{
  public static class Protector
  {
    // salt size must be at least 8 bytes, we will use 16 bytes
    private static readonly byte[] salt =
      Encoding.Unicode.GetBytes("7BANANAS");

    // iterations must be at least 1000, we will use 2000
    private static readonly int iterations = 2000;

    public static string Encrypt(
      string plainText, string password)
    {
      byte[] encryptedBytes;
      byte[] plainBytes = Encoding.Unicode
        .GetBytes(plainText);

      var aes = Aes.Create(); // abstract class factory method

      var pbkdf2 = new Rfc2898DeriveBytes(
        password, salt, iterations);

      aes.Key = pbkdf2.GetBytes(32); // set a 256-bit key
      aes.IV = pbkdf2.GetBytes(16); // set a 128-bit IV
```

```
    using (var ms = new MemoryStream())
    {
      using (var cs = new CryptoStream(
        ms, aes.CreateEncryptor(),
        CryptoStreamMode.Write))
      {
        cs.Write(plainBytes, 0, plainBytes.Length);
      }
      encryptedBytes = ms.ToArray();
    }
    return Convert.ToBase64String(encryptedBytes);
  }

  public static string Decrypt(
    string cryptoText, string password)
  {
    byte[] plainBytes;
    byte[] cryptoBytes = Convert
      .FromBase64String(cryptoText);

    var aes = Aes.Create();

    var pbkdf2 = new Rfc2898DeriveBytes(
      password, salt, iterations);

    aes.Key = pbkdf2.GetBytes(32);
    aes.IV = pbkdf2.GetBytes(16);

    using (var ms = new MemoryStream())
    {
      using (var cs = new CryptoStream(
        ms, aes.CreateDecryptor(),
        CryptoStreamMode.Write))
      {
        cs.Write(cryptoBytes, 0, cryptoBytes.Length);
      }
      plainBytes = ms.ToArray();
    }
    return Encoding.Unicode.GetString(plainBytes);
  }
}
}
```

Note the following points about the preceding code:

- We used double the recommended salt size and iteration count.
- Although the salt and iteration count can be hardcoded, the password must be passed at runtime when calling the `Encrypt` and `Decrypt` methods.
- We use a temporary `MemoryStream` type to store the results of encrypting and decrypting, and then call `ToArray` to turn the stream into a byte array.
- We convert the encrypted byte arrays to and from a Base64 encoding to make them easier to read.

 Good Practice: Never hardcode a password in your source code because, even after compilation, the password can be read in the assembly by using disassembler tools.

13. In the `EncryptionApp` project, open the `Program.cs` file and then import the namespace for the `Protector` class, the namespace for the `CryptographicException` class, and statically import the `Console` class, as shown in the following code:

```
using System.Security.Cryptography; // CryptographicException
using Packt.Shared;                 // Protector
using static System.Console;
```

14. In `Main`, add statements to prompt the user for a message and a password, and then encrypt and decrypt, as shown in the following code:

```
Write("Enter a message that you want to encrypt: ");
string message = ReadLine();

Write("Enter a password: ");
string password = ReadLine();

string cryptoText = Protector.Encrypt(message, password);

WriteLine($"Encrypted text: {cryptoText}");

Write("Enter the password: ");
string password2 = ReadLine();

try
{
  string clearText = Protector.Decrypt(cryptoText, password2);
  WriteLine($"Decrypted text: {clearText}");
}
catch (CryptographicException ex)
{
  WriteLine("{0}\nMore details: {1}",
```

```
      arg0: "You entered the wrong password!",
      arg1: ex.Message);
  }
  catch (Exception ex)
  {
    WriteLine("Non-cryptographic exception: {0}, {1}",
      arg0: ex.GetType().Name,
      arg1: ex.Message);
  }
```

15. Run the console application, try entering a message and password, and view the result, as shown in the following output:

```
Enter a message that you want to encrypt: Hello Bob
Enter a password: secret
Encrypted text: pV5qPDf1CCZmGzUMH2gapFSkn573lg7tMj5ajice3cQ=
Enter the password: secret
Decrypted text: Hello Bob
```

16. Rerun the application and try entering a message and password, but this time enter the password incorrectly after encrypting and view the output:

```
Enter a message that you want to encrypt: Hello Bob
Enter a password: secret
Encrypted text: pV5qPDf1CCZmGzUMH2gapFSkn573lg7tMj5ajice3cQ=
Enter the password: 123456
You entered the wrong password!
More details: Padding is invalid and cannot be removed.
```

Hashing data

In .NET, there are multiple hash algorithms you can choose from. Some do not use any key, some use symmetric keys, and some use asymmetric keys.

There are two important factors to consider when choosing a hash algorithm:

- **Collision resistance**: How rare is it to find two inputs that share the same hash?
- **Preimage resistance**: For a hash, how difficult would it be to find another input that shares the same hash?

Some common non-keyed hashing algorithms are shown in the following table:

Algorithm	Hash size	Description
MD5	16 bytes	This is commonly used because it is fast, but it is not collision-resistant.
SHA1	20 bytes	The use of SHA1 on the internet has been deprecated since 2011.
SHA256 SHA384 SHA512	32 bytes 48 bytes 64 bytes	These are the **Secure Hashing Algorithm 2nd generation (SHA2)** algorithms with different hash sizes.

Good Practice: Avoid MD5 and SHA1 because they have known weaknesses. Choose a larger hash size to reduce the possibility of repeated hashes. The first publicly known MD5 collision happened in 2010. The first publicly known SHA1 collision happened in 2017. You can read more at the following link: https://arstechnica.co.uk/information-technology/2017/02/at-deaths-door-for-years-widely-used-sha1-function-is-now-dead/

Hashing with the commonly used SHA256

We will now add a class to represent a user stored in memory, a file, or a database. We will use a dictionary to store multiple users in memory:

1. In the `CryptographyLib` class library project, add a new class file named `User.cs`, as shown in the following code:

    ```
    namespace Packt.Shared
    {
      public class User
      {
        public string Name { get; set; }
        public string Salt { get; set; }
        public string SaltedHashedPassword { get; set; }
      }
    }
    ```

2. Add statements to the `Protector` class to declare a dictionary to store users and define two methods, one to register a new user and one to validate their password when they subsequently log in, as shown in the following code:

    ```
    private static Dictionary<string, User> Users =
      new Dictionary<string, User>();

    public static User Register(
      string username, string password)
    {
      // generate a random salt
    ```

```
  var rng = RandomNumberGenerator.Create();
  var saltBytes = new byte[16];
  rng.GetBytes(saltBytes);
  var saltText = Convert.ToBase64String(saltBytes);

  // generate the salted and hashed password
  var saltedhashedPassword = SaltAndHashPassword(
    password, saltText);

  var user = new User
  {
    Name = username, Salt = saltText,
    SaltedHashedPassword = saltedhashedPassword
  };
  Users.Add(user.Name, user);
  return user;
}

public static bool CheckPassword(
  string username, string password)
{
  if (!Users.ContainsKey(username))
  {
    return false;
  }
  var user = Users[username];

  // re-generate the salted and hashed password
  var saltedhashedPassword = SaltAndHashPassword(
    password, user.Salt);

  return (saltedhashedPassword == user.SaltedHashedPassword);
}

private static string SaltAndHashPassword(
  string password, string salt)
{
  var sha = SHA256.Create();
  var saltedPassword = password + salt;
  return Convert.ToBase64String(
    sha.ComputeHash(Encoding.Unicode.GetBytes(saltedPassword)));
}
```

3. Create a new console application project named `HashingApp`, add it to the workspace, and select the project as active for OmniSharp.

4. Add a reference to the `CryptographyLib` assembly as you did before and import the `Packt.Shared` namespace.

5. In the `Main` method, add statements to register a user and prompt to register a second user, and then prompt to log in as one of those users and validate the password, as shown in the following code:

```
WriteLine("Registering Alice with Pa$$w0rd.");
var alice = Protector.Register("Alice", "Pa$$w0rd");

WriteLine($"Name: {alice.Name}");
WriteLine($"Salt: {alice.Salt}");
WriteLine("Password (salted and hashed): {0}",
  arg0: alice.SaltedHashedPassword);
WriteLine();

Write("Enter a new user to register: ");
string username = ReadLine();
Write($"Enter a password for {username}: ");
string password = ReadLine();

var user = Protector.Register(username, password);

WriteLine($"Name: {user.Name}");
WriteLine($"Salt: {user.Salt}");
WriteLine("Password (salted and hashed): {0}",
  arg0: user.SaltedHashedPassword);
WriteLine();

bool correctPassword = false;
while (!correctPassword)
{
  Write("Enter a username to log in: ");
  string loginUsername = ReadLine();
  Write("Enter a password to log in: ");
  string loginPassword = ReadLine();

  correctPassword = Protector.CheckPassword(
    loginUsername, loginPassword);

  if (correctPassword)
  {
    WriteLine($"Correct! {loginUsername} has been logged in.");
  }
  else
```

```
    {
        WriteLine("Invalid username or password. Try again.");
    }
}
```

When using multiple projects, remember to use a **TERMINAL** window for the correct console application before entering the `dotnet build` and `dotnet run` commands.

6. Run the console application, register a new user with the same password as Alice, and view the result, as shown in the following output:

```
Registering Alice with Pa$$w0rd.
Name: Alice
Salt: I1I1dzIjkd7EYDf/6jaf4w==
Password (salted and hashed): pIoadjE4W/XaRFkqS3br3UuAuPv/3LVQ8kzj6mvcz+s=
Enter a new user to register: Bob
Enter a password for Bob: Pa$$w0rd
Name: Bob
Salt: 1X7ym/UjxTiuEWBC/vIHpw==
Password (salted and hashed): DoBFtDhKeN0aaaLVdErtrZ3mpZSvpWDQ9TXDosTq0sQ=
Enter a username to log in: Alice
Enter a password to log in: secret
Invalid username or password. Try again.
Enter a username to log in: Bob
Enter a password to log in: secret
Invalid username or password. Try again.
Enter a username to log in: Bob
Enter a password to log in: Pa$$w0rd
Correct! Bob has been logged in.
```

Even if two users register with the same password, they have randomly generated salts so that their salted and hashed passwords are different.

Signing data

To prove that some data has come from someone we trust, it can be signed. Actually, you do not sign the data itself; instead, you sign a hash of the data.

We will be using the SHA256 algorithm for generating the hash, combined with the RSA algorithm for signing the hash.

We could use DSA for both hashing and signing. DSA is faster than RSA for generating a signature, but it is slower than RSA for validating a signature. Since a signature is generated once but validated many times, it is best to have faster validation than generation.

More Information: The RSA algorithm is based on the factorization of large integers, compared to the DSA algorithm, which is based on the discrete logarithm calculation. You can read more at the following link: `http://mathworld.wolfram.com/RSAEncryption.html`

Signing with SHA256 and RSA

Let's explore signing data and checking the signature with a public key:

1. In the `CryptographyLib` class library project, add statements to the `Protector` class to declare a field for the public key, two extension methods to convert an RSA instance to and from XML, and two methods to generate and validate a signature, as shown in the following code:

```
public static string PublicKey;

public static string ToXmlStringExt(
  this RSA rsa, bool includePrivateParameters)
{
  var p = rsa.ExportParameters(includePrivateParameters);

  XElement xml;

  if (includePrivateParameters)
  {
    xml = new XElement("RSAKeyValue",
      new XElement("Modulus", ToBase64String(p.Modulus)),
      new XElement("Exponent", ToBase64String(p.Exponent)),
      new XElement("P", ToBase64String(p.P)),
      new XElement("Q", ToBase64String(p.Q)),
      new XElement("DP", ToBase64String(p.DP)),
      new XElement("DQ", ToBase64String(p.DQ)),
      new XElement("InverseQ", ToBase64String(p.InverseQ))
    );
  }
  else
  {
    xml = new XElement("RSAKeyValue",
      new XElement("Modulus", ToBase64String(p.Modulus)),
      new XElement("Exponent", ToBase64String(p.Exponent)));
  }
  return xml?.ToString();
}

public static void FromXmlStringExt(
```

```
      this RSA rsa, string parametersAsXml)
  {
    var xml = XDocument.Parse(parametersAsXml);
    var root = xml.Element("RSAKeyValue");

    var p = new RSAParameters
    {
      Modulus = FromBase64String(root.Element("Modulus").Value),
      Exponent = FromBase64String(root.Element("Exponent").Value)
    };

    if (root.Element("P") != null)
    {
      p.P = FromBase64String(root.Element("P").Value);
      p.Q = FromBase64String(root.Element("Q").Value);
      p.DP = FromBase64String(root.Element("DP").Value);
      p.DQ = FromBase64String(root.Element("DQ").Value);
      p.InverseQ = FromBase64String(root.Element("InverseQ").Value);
    }
    rsa.ImportParameters(p);
  }


  public static string GenerateSignature(string data)
  {
    byte[] dataBytes = Encoding.Unicode.GetBytes(data);
    var sha = SHA256.Create();
    var hashedData = sha.ComputeHash(dataBytes);
    var rsa = RSA.Create();

    PublicKey = rsa.ToXmlStringExt(false); // exclude private key

    return ToBase64String(rsa.SignHash(hashedData,
      HashAlgorithmName.SHA256, RSASignaturePadding.Pkcs1));
  }

  public static bool ValidateSignature(
    string data, string signature)
  {
    byte[] dataBytes = Encoding.Unicode.GetBytes(data);
    var sha = SHA256.Create();
    var hashedData = sha.ComputeHash(dataBytes);
    byte[] signatureBytes = FromBase64String(signature);
    var rsa = RSA.Create();
    rsa.FromXmlStringExt(PublicKey);
    return rsa.VerifyHash(hashedData, signatureBytes,
      HashAlgorithmName.SHA256, RSASignaturePadding.Pkcs1);
  }
```

Note the following from the preceding code:

- The RSA type has two methods named ToXmlString and FromXmlString. These serialize and deserialize the RSAParameters structure, which contains the public and private keys. However, the implementation of these methods on macOS throws a PlatformNotSupportedException exception. I have had to re-implement them myself as extension methods named ToXmlStringExt and FromXmlStringExt using LINQ to XML types such as XDocument, which you will learn about in *Chapter 12, Querying and Manipulating Data Using LINQ*.

- Only the public part of the public-private key pair needs to be made available to the code that is checking the signature so that we can pass the false value when we call the ToXmlStringExt method. The private part is required to sign data and must be kept secret because anyone with the private part can sign data as if they are you!

- The hash algorithm used to generate the hash from the data by calling the SignHash method must match the hash algorithm set when calling the VerifyHash method. In the preceding code, we used SHA256.

Now we can test signing some data and checking its signature.

2. Create a new console application project named SigningApp, add it to the workspace, and select the project as active for OmniSharp.

3. Add a reference to the CryptographyLib assembly, in Program.cs import the appropriate namespaces, and then in Main, add statements to prompt the user to enter some text, sign it, check its signature, then modify the signature, and check the signature again to deliberately cause a mismatch, as shown in the following code:

```
Write("Enter some text to sign: ");
string data = ReadLine();

var signature = Protector.GenerateSignature(data);

WriteLine($"Signature: {signature}");
WriteLine("Public key used to check signature:");
WriteLine(Protector.PublicKey);

if (Protector.ValidateSignature(data, signature))
{
  WriteLine("Correct! Signature is valid.");
}
else
{
  WriteLine("Invalid signature.");
}

// simulate a fake signature by replacing the
// first character with an X
```

```
var fakeSignature = signature.Replace(signature[0], 'X');

if (Protector.ValidateSignature(data, fakeSignature))
{
  WriteLine("Correct! Signature is valid.");
}
else
{
  WriteLine($"Invalid signature: {fakeSignature}");
}
```

4. Run the console application and enter some text, as shown in the following output (edited for length):

```
Enter some text to sign: The cat sat on the mat.
Signature: BXSTdM...4Wrg==
Public key used to check signature:
<RSAKeyValue>
   <Modulus>nHtwl3...mw3w==</Modulus>
   <Exponent>AQAB</Exponent>
</RSAKeyValue>
Correct! Signature is valid.
Invalid signature: XXSTdM...4Wrg==
```

Generating random numbers

Sometimes you need to generate random numbers, perhaps in a game that simulates rolls of a die, or for use with cryptography in encryption or signing. There are a couple of classes that can generate random numbers in .NET.

Generating random numbers for games

In scenarios that don't need truly random numbers like games, you can create an instance of the Random class, as shown in the following code example:

```
var r = new Random();
```

Random has a constructor with a parameter for specifying a seed value used to initialize its pseudo-random number generator, as shown in the following code:

```
var r = new Random(Seed: 12345);
```

Good Practice: Shared seed values act as a secret key, so if you use the same random number generation algorithm with the same seed value in two applications, then they can generate the same "random" sequences of numbers. Sometimes this is necessary, for example, when synchronizing a GPS receiver with a satellite, or when a game needs to randomly generate the same level. But usually, you want to keep your seed secret.

As you learned in *Chapter 2, Speaking C#*, parameter names should use camel case. The developer who defined the constructor for the Random class broke this convention! The parameter name should be seed, not Seed.

Once you have a Random object, you can call its methods to generate random numbers, as shown in the following code examples:

```
int dieRoll = r.Next(minValue: 1, maxValue: 7); // returns 1 to 6

double randomReal = r.NextDouble(); // returns 0.0 to 1.0

var arrayOfBytes = new byte[256];
r.NextBytes(arrayOfBytes); // 256 random bytes in an array
```

The Next method takes two parameters: minValue and maxValue. Now, maxValue is not the maximum value that the method returns! It is an exclusive upper bound, meaning it is one more than the maximum value.

Generating random numbers for cryptography

Random generates pseudo-random numbers. This is not good enough for cryptography! If the random numbers are not truly random, then they are repeatable, and if they are repeatable, then a cracker can break your protection.

For truly random numbers, you must use a RandomNumberGenerator derived type, such as RNGCryptoServiceProvider.

We will now create a method to generate a truly random byte array that can be used in algorithms like encryption for key and IV values:

1. In the CryptographyLib class library project, add statements to the Protector class to define a method to get a random key or IV for use in encryption, as shown in the following code:

    ```
    public static byte[] GetRandomKeyOrIV(int size)
    {
      var r = RandomNumberGenerator.Create();
      var data = new byte[size];
      r.GetNonZeroBytes(data);
    ```

```
  // data is an array now filled with
  // cryptographically strong random bytes
  return data;
}
```

Now we can test the random bytes generated for a truly random encryption key or IV.

2. Create a new console application project named `RandomizingApp`, add it to the workspace, and select the project as active for OmniSharp.

3. Add a reference to the `CryptographyLib` assembly, import the appropriate namespaces, and in `Main`, add statements to prompt the user to enter a size of byte array and then generate random byte values and write them to the console, as shown in the following code:

```
Write("How big do you want the key (in bytes): ");
string size = ReadLine();

byte[] key = Protector.GetRandomKeyOrIV(int.Parse(size));

WriteLine($"Key as byte array:");
for (int b = 0; b < key.Length; b++)
{
  Write($"{key[b]:x2} ");
  if (((b + 1) % 16) == 0) WriteLine();
}
WriteLine();
```

4. Run the console application, enter a typical size for the key, such as 256, and view the randomly generated key, as shown in the following output:

```
How big do you want the key (in bytes): 256
Key as byte array:
f1 57 3f 44 80 e7 93 dc 8e 55 04 6c 76 6f 51 b9
e8 84 59 e5 8d eb 08 d5 e6 59 65 20 b1 56 fa 68
...
```

What's new in cryptography?

An automatic benefit of using .NET Core 3.0 or later is that algorithms for hashing, **hash-based message authentication code (HMAC)**, random number generation, asymmetric signature generation and processing, and RSA encryption have been rewritten to use `Span<T>` so they achieve better performance. For example, `Rfc2898DeriveBytes` is about 15% faster.

Some enhancements have been made to the cryptography APIs that are useful in advanced scenarios, including:

- Signing and verifying of CMS/PKCS #7 messages.
- Enable `X509Certificate.GetCertHash` and `X509Certificate.GetCertHashString` to get certificate thumbprint values using algorithms other than SHA-1.
- The `CryptographicOperations` class with useful methods like `ZeroMemory` to securely clear memory.
- `RandomNumberGenerator` has a `Fill` method that will fill a span with random values and doesn't require you to manage an `IDisposable` resource.
- APIs to read, validate, and create RFC 3161 `TimestampToken` values.
- Elliptic-Curve Diffie-Hellman support using the `ECDiffieHellman` classes.
- Support for RSA-OAEP-SHA2 and RSA-PSS on Linux platforms.

Authenticating and authorizing users

Authentication is the process of verifying the identity of a user by validating their credentials against some authority. Credentials include a username and password combination, or a fingerprint or face scan.

Once authenticated, the authority can make claims about the user, for example, what their email address is, and what groups or roles they belong to.

Authorization is the process of verifying membership of groups or roles before allowing access to resources such as application functions and data. Although authorization can be based on individual identity, it is good security practice to authorize based on group or role membership (that can be indicated via claims) even when there is only one user in the role or group. This is because that allows the user's membership to change in the future without reassigning the user's individual access rights.

For example, instead of assigning access rights to launch a nuclear strike to Donald Trump (a user), you would assign access rights to launch a nuclear strike to the President of the United States (a role) and then add Donald Trump as the sole member of that role. Then, in January 2021, you do not need to change any access rights for the POTUS role, you can just replace the Donald Trump user with the Joe Biden user. Or not. ;-)

There are multiple authentication and authorization mechanisms to choose from. They all implement a pair of interfaces in the `System.Security.Principal` namespace: `IIdentity` and `IPrincipal`.

`IIdentity` represents a user, so it has a `Name` property and an `IsAuthenticated` property to indicate if they are anonymous or if they have been successfully authenticated from their credentials.

The most common class that implements this interface is `GenericIdentity`, which inherits from `ClaimsIdentity`, as shown in the following diagram:

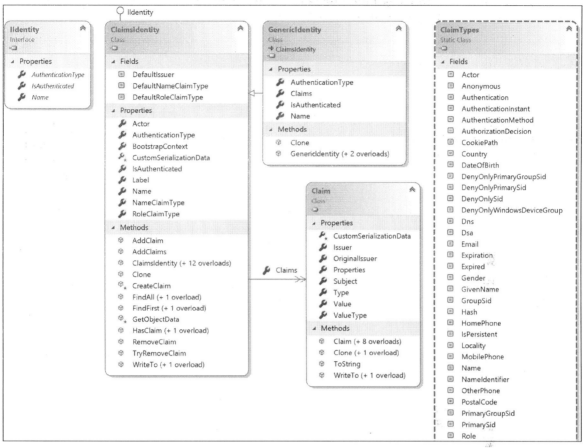

Figure 10.1: Types for working with authentication

Each `ClaimsIdentity` class has a `Claims` property that is shown in the preceding diagram as a double-arrowhead between the `ClaimsIdentity` and `Claim` classes.

The `Claim` objects have a `Type` property that indicates if the claim is for their name, their membership of a role or group, their date of birth, and so on.

`IPrincipal` is used to associate an identity with the roles and groups that they are members of, so it can be used for authorization purposes. The current thread executing your code has a `CurrentPrincipal` property that can be set to any object that implements `IPrincipal`, and it will be checked when permission is needed to perform a secure action.

The most common class that implements this interface is `GenericPrincipal`, which inherits from `ClaimsPrincipal`, as shown in the following diagram:

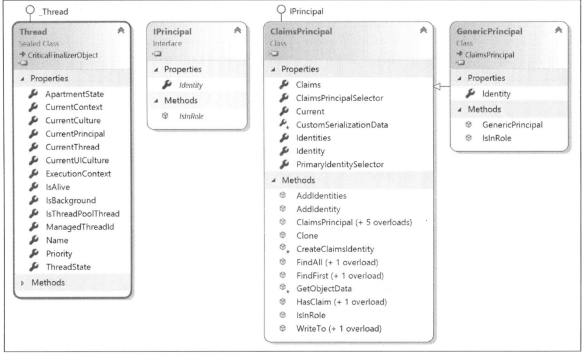

Figure 10.2: Types for working with authorization

Implementing authentication and authorization

Let's explore authentication and authorization:

1. In the `CryptographyLib` class library project, add a property to the `User` class to store an array of roles, as shown in the following code:

    ```
    public string[] Roles { get; set; }
    ```

2. Modify the `Register` method in the `Protector` class to allow an array of roles to be passed as an optional parameter, as shown highlighted in the following code:

    ```
    public static User Register(
        string username, string password,
        string[] roles = null)
    ```

3. Modify the `Register` method in the `Protector` class to set the array of roles in the `User` object, as shown in the following code:

    ```
    var user = new User
    {
        Name = username, Salt = saltText,
        SaltedHashedPassword = saltedhashedPassword,
        Roles = roles
    };
    ```

4. In the `CryptographyLib` class library project, add statements to the `Protector` class to define a `LogIn` method to log in a user, and use generic identity and principal to assign them to the current thread, as shown in the following code:

```
public static void LogIn(string username, string password)
{
  if (CheckPassword(username, password))
  {
    var identity = new GenericIdentity(
      username, "PacktAuth");
    var principal = new GenericPrincipal(
      identity, Users[username].Roles);
    System.Threading.Thread.CurrentPrincipal = principal;
  }
}
```

5. Create a new console application project named `SecureApp`, add it to the workspace, and select the project as active for OmniSharp.

6. Add a reference to the `CryptographyLib` assembly, and then in `Program.cs`, import the following namespaces:

```
using static System.Console;
using Packt.Shared;
using System.Threading;
using System.Security;
using System.Security.Permissions;
using System.Security.Principal;
using System.Security.Claims;
```

7. In the `Main` method, write statements to register three users, named Alice, Bob, and Eve, in various roles, prompt the user to log in, and then output information about them, as shown in the following code:

```
Protector.Register("Alice", "Pa$$w0rd",
  new[] { "Admins" });

Protector.Register("Bob", "Pa$$w0rd",
  new[] { "Sales", "TeamLeads" });

Protector.Register("Eve", "Pa$$w0rd");

Write($"Enter your user name: ");
string username = ReadLine();

Write($"Enter your password: ");
string password = ReadLine();

Protector.LogIn(username, password);
```

```
if (Thread.CurrentPrincipal == null)
{
  WriteLine("Log in failed.");
  return;
}

var p = Thread.CurrentPrincipal;

WriteLine(
  $"IsAuthenticated: {p.Identity.IsAuthenticated}");
WriteLine(
  $"AuthenticationType: {p.Identity.AuthenticationType}");
WriteLine($"Name: {p.Identity.Name}");
WriteLine($"IsInRole(\"Admins\"): {p.IsInRole("Admins")}");
WriteLine($"IsInRole(\"Sales\"): {p.IsInRole("Sales")}");

if (p is ClaimsPrincipal)
{
  WriteLine(
    $"{p.Identity.Name} has the following claims:");

  foreach (Claim claim in (p as ClaimsPrincipal).Claims)
  {
    WriteLine($"{claim.Type}: {claim.Value}");
  }
}
```

8. Run the console application, log in as Alice with Pa$$word, and view the results, as shown in the following output:

```
Enter your user name: Alice
Enter your password: Pa$$w0rd
IsAuthenticated: True
AuthenticationType: PacktAuth
Name: Alice
IsInRole("Admins"): True
IsInRole("Sales"): False
Alice has the following claims:
http://schemas.xmlsoap.org/ws/2005/05/identity/claims/name: Alice
http://schemas.microsoft.com/ws/2008/06/identity/claims/role: Admins
```

9. Run the console application, log in as Alice with secret, and view the results, as shown in the following output:

```
Enter your user name: Alice
Enter your password: secret
Log in failed.
```

10. Run the console application, log in as Bob with Pa$$word, and view the results, as shown in the following output:

```
Enter your user name: Bob
Enter your password: Pa$$w0rd
IsAuthenticated: True
AuthenticationType: PacktAuth
Name: Bob
IsInRole("Admins"): False
IsInRole("Sales"): True
Bob has the following claims:
http://schemas.xmlsoap.org/ws/2005/05/identity/claims/name: Bob
http://schemas.microsoft.com/ws/2008/06/identity/claims/role: Sales
http://schemas.microsoft.com/ws/2008/06/identity/claims/role: TeamLeads
```

Protecting application functionality

Now let's explore how we can use authorization to prevent some users from accessing some features of an application:

1. Add a method to the Program class, secured by checking for permission inside the method, and throw appropriate exceptions if the user is anonymous or not a member of the Admins role, as shown in the following code:

```
static void SecureFeature()
{
  if (Thread.CurrentPrincipal == null)
  {
    throw new SecurityException(
      "A user must be logged in to access this feature.");
  }

  if (!Thread.CurrentPrincipal.IsInRole("Admins"))
  {
    throw new SecurityException(
      "User must be a member of Admins to access this feature.");
  }
  WriteLine("You have access to this secure feature.");
}
```

2. Add statements to the end of the Main method to call the SecureFeature method in a try statement, as shown in the following code:

```
try
{
  SecureFeature();
}
catch (System.Exception ex)
```

```
{
    WriteLine($"{ex.GetType()}: {ex.Message}");
}
```

3. Run the console application, log in as `Alice` with `Pa$$word`, and view the results:

```
You have access to this secure feature.
```

4. Run the console application, log in as `Bob` with `Pa$$word`, and view the results:

```
System.Security.SecurityException: User must be a member of Admins to
access this feature.
```

Practicing and exploring

Test your knowledge and understanding by answering some questions, get some hands-on practice, and explore the topics covered in this chapter with deeper research.

Exercise 10.1 – Test your knowledge

Answer the following questions:

1. Of the encryption algorithms provided by .NET, which is the best choice for symmetric encryption?
2. Of the encryption algorithms provided by .NET, which is the best choice for asymmetric encryption?
3. What is a rainbow attack?
4. For encryption algorithms, is it better to have a larger or smaller block size?
5. What is a hash?
6. What is a signature?
7. What is the difference between symmetric and asymmetric encryption?
8. What does RSA stand for?
9. Why should passwords be salted before being stored?
10. SHA1 is a hashing algorithm designed by the United States National Security Agency. Why should you never use it?

Exercise 10.2 – Practice protecting data with encryption and hashing

Create a console application named `Exercise02` that protects an XML file, such as the following example:

```xml
<?xml version="1.0" encoding="utf-8" ?>
  <customers>
    <customer>
      <name>Bob Smith</name>
      <creditcard>1234-5678-9012-3456</creditcard>
      <password>Pa$$w0rd</password>
    </customer>
  ...
  </customers>
```

The customer's credit card number and password are currently stored in clear text. The credit card number must be encrypted so that it can be decrypted and used later, and the password must be salted and hashed.

Exercise 10.3 – Practice protecting data with decryption

Create a console application named Exercise03 that opens the XML file that you protected in the preceding code and decrypts the credit card number.

Exercise 10.4 – Explore topics

Use the following links to read more about the topics covered in this chapter:

- **Key Security Concepts**: https://docs.microsoft.com/en-us/dotnet/standard/security/key-security-concepts

- **Encrypting Data**: https://docs.microsoft.com/en-us/dotnet/standard/security/encrypting-data

- **Cryptographic Signatures**: https://docs.microsoft.com/en-us/dotnet/standard/security/cryptographic-signatures

Summary

In this chapter, you learned how to encrypt and decrypt using symmetric encryption, how to generate a salted hash, how to sign data and check the signature on the data, how to generate truly random numbers, and how to use authentication and authorization to protect features of your applications.

In the next chapter, you will learn how to work with databases using Entity Framework Core.

11

Working with Databases Using Entity Framework Core

This chapter is about reading and writing to data stores, such as Microsoft SQL Server, SQLite, and Azure Cosmos DB, by using the object-to-data store mapping technology named **Entity Framework Core (EF Core)**.

This chapter will cover the following topics:

- Understanding modern databases
- Setting up EF Core
- Defining EF Core models
- Querying EF Core models
- Loading patterns with EF Core
- Manipulating data with EF Core

Understanding modern databases

Two of the most common places to store data are in a **Relational Database Management System (RDBMS)** such as Microsoft SQL Server, PostgreSQL, MySQL, and SQLite, or in a NoSQL data store such as Microsoft Azure Cosmos DB, Redis, MongoDB, and Apache Cassandra.

This chapter will focus on RDBMSes such as SQL Server and SQLite. If you wish to learn more about NoSQL databases, such as Cosmos DB and MongoDB, and how to use them with EF Core, then I recommend the following links, which will go over them in detail:

- **Welcome to Azure Cosmos DB**: https://docs.microsoft.com/en-us/azure/cosmos-db/introduction

- **Use NoSQL databases as a persistence infrastructure**: https://docs.microsoft.com/en-us/dotnet/standard/microservices-architecture/microservice-ddd-cqrs-patterns/nosql-database-persistence-infrastructure

- **Document Database Providers for Entity Framework Core**: https://github.com/BlueshiftSoftware/EntityFrameworkCore

Understanding legacy Entity Framework

Entity Framework (EF) was first released as part of .NET Framework 3.5 with Service Pack 1 back in late 2008. Since then, Entity Framework has evolved, as Microsoft has observed how programmers use an **object-relational mapping (ORM)** tool in the real world.

ORMs use a mapping definition to associate columns in tables to properties in classes. Then, a programmer can interact with objects of different types in a way that they are familiar with, instead of having to deal with knowing how to store the values in a relational table or another structure provided by a NoSQL data store.

The version of EF included with .NET Framework is **Entity Framework 6 (EF6)**. It is mature, stable, and supports an old EDMX (XML file) way of defining the model as well as complex inheritance models, and a few other advanced features.

EF 6.3 and later have been extracted from .NET Framework as a separate package so it can be supported on .NET Core 3.0 and later, including .NET 5. This enables existing projects like web applications and services to be ported and run cross-platform. However, EF6 should be considered a legacy technology because it has some limitations when running cross-platform and no new features will be added to it.

> **More Information**: You can read more about Entity Framework 6.3 and its .NET Core 3.0 and later support at the following link: https://devblogs.microsoft.com/dotnet/announcing-ef-core-3-0-and-ef-6-3-general-availability/

To use the legacy Entity Framework in a .NET Core 3.0 or later project, you must add a package reference to it in your project file, as shown in the following markup:

```
<PackageReference Include="EntityFramework" Version="6.4.4" />
```

> **Good Practice**: Only use legacy EF6 if you have to. This book is about modern cross-platform development so, in the rest of this chapter, I will only cover the modern Entity Framework Core. You will not need to reference the legacy EF6 package as shown above in the projects for this chapter.

Understanding Entity Framework Core

The truly cross-platform version, EF Core, is different from the legacy Entity Framework. Although EF Core has a similar name, you should be aware of how it varies from EF6. For example, as well as traditional RDBMSes, EF Core also supports modern cloud-based, nonrelational, schema-less data stores, such as Microsoft Azure Cosmos DB and MongoDB, sometimes with third-party providers.

EF Core 5.0 runs on platforms that support .NET Standard 2.1, meaning .NET Core 3.0 and 3.1, as well as .NET 5. It will not run on .NET Standard 2.0 platforms like .NET Framework 4.8.

> **More Information**: You can read more about the EF Core team's plans at the following link: `https://docs.microsoft.com/en-us/ef/core/what-is-new/ef-core-5.0/plan`

EF Core 5.0 has so many improvements that this chapter cannot cover them all. I will focus on the fundamentals that all .NET developers should know and some of the cooler new features.

> **More Information**: You can read the complete list of new features in EF Core 5 at the following link: `https://docs.microsoft.com/en-us/ef/core/what-is-new/ef-core-5.0/whatsnew`

Using a sample relational database

To learn how to manage an RDBMS using .NET, it would be useful to have a sample one so that you can practice on one that has a medium complexity and a decent amount of sample records. Microsoft offers several sample databases, most of which are too complex for our needs, so instead, we will use a database that was first created in the early 1990s known as **Northwind**.

Let's take a minute to look at a diagram of the Northwind database. You can use the following diagram to refer to as we write code and queries throughout this book:

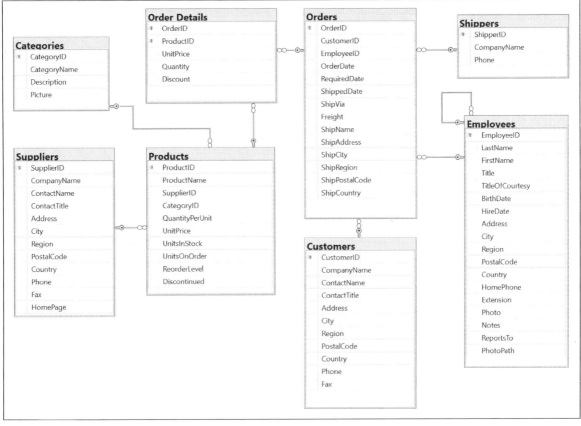

Figure 11.1: The Northwind database tables and relationships

You will write code to work with the `Categories` and `Products` tables later in this chapter and other tables in later chapters. But before we do, note that:

- Each category has a unique identifier, name, description, and picture.
- Each product has a unique identifier, name, unit price, units in stock, and other fields.
- Each product is associated with a category by storing the category's unique identifier.
- The relationship between `Categories` and `Products` is one-to-many, meaning each category can have zero or more products.

SQLite is a small, cross-platform, self-contained RDBMS that is available in the public domain. It's the most common RDBMS for mobile platforms such as iOS (iPhone and iPad) and Android.

Setting up SQLite for macOS

SQLite is included in macOS in the `/usr/bin/` directory as a command-line application named `sqlite3`.

Setting up SQLite for Windows

SQLite can be downloaded and installed for other OSes. On Windows, we also need to add the folder for SQLite to the system path so it will be found when we enter commands in Command Prompt:

1. Start your favorite browser and navigate to the following link: `https://www.sqlite.org/download.html`.

2. Scroll down the page to the **Precompiled Binaries for Windows** section.

3. Click `sqlite-tools-win32-x86-3330000.zip`. Note the file might have a higher version number after this book is published.

4. Extract the ZIP file into a folder named `C:\Sqlite\`.

5. Navigate to **Windows Settings**.

6. Search for `environment` and choose **Edit the system environment variables**.

7. Click the **Environment Variables** button.

8. In **System variables**, select **Path** in the list, and then click **Edit....**

9. Click **New**, enter `C:\Sqlite`, and press *Enter*.

10. Click **OK**.

11. Click **OK**.

12. Click **OK**.

13. Close **Windows Settings**.

Creating the Northwind sample database for SQLite

Now we can create the `Northwind` sample database using a SQL script:

1. Create a folder named `Chapter11` with a subfolder named `WorkingWithEFCore`.

2. If you have not previously cloned the GitHub repository for this book, then do so now using the following link: `https://github.com/markjprice/cs9dotnet5/`.

3. Copy the script to create the `Northwind` database for SQLite from the following path in your local Git repository: `/sql-scripts/Northwind.sql` into the `WorkingWithEFCore` folder.

4. In Visual Studio Code, open the `WorkingWithEFCore` folder.

5. Navigate to **TERMINAL** and execute the script using SQLite to create the `Northwind.db` database, as shown in the following command:

```
sqlite3 Northwind.db -init Northwind.sql
```

6. Be patient because this command might take a while to create the database structure, as shown in the following output:

```
-- Loading resources from Northwind.sql
SQLite version 3.28.0 2019-04-15 14:49:49
Enter ".help" for usage hints.
sqlite>
```

7. Press *Ctrl + C* on Windows or *Ctrl + D* on macOS to exit SQLite command mode.

 More Information: You can read about the SQL statements supported by SQLite at the following link: `https://sqlite.org/lang.html`

Managing the Northwind sample database with SQLiteStudio

You can use a cross-platform graphical database manager named **SQLiteStudio** to easily manage SQLite databases:

1. Navigate to the following link, `http://sqlitestudio.pl`, and download and unpack the application.
2. Launch **SQLiteStudio**.
3. On the **Database** menu, choose **Add a database**.
4. In the **Database** dialog, click on the folder button to browse for an existing database file on the local computer, and select the `Northwind.db` file in the `WorkingWithEFCore` folder, and then click **OK**.
5. Right-click on the `Northwind` database and choose **Connect to the database**. You will see the tables that were created by the script.
6. Right-click on the `Products` table and choose **Edit the table**.

   In the table editor window, you will see the structure of the `Products` table, including column names, data types, keys, and constraints, as shown in the following screenshot:

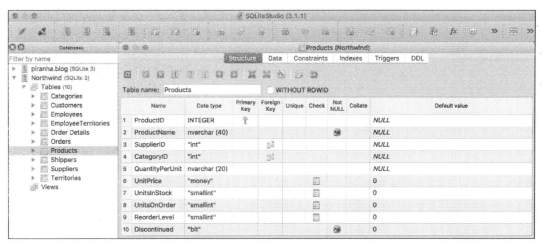

Figure 11.2: The table editor in SQLiteStudio showing the structure of the Products table

7. In the table editor window, click the **Data** tab. You will see 77 products, as shown in the following screenshot:

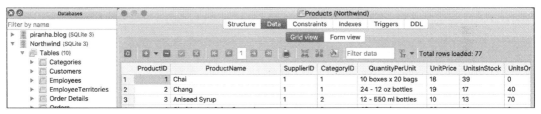

Figure 11.3: The Data tab showing the rows in the Products table

Setting up EF Core

Before we dive into the practicalities of managing data using EF Core, let's briefly talk about choosing between **EF Core data providers**.

Choosing an EF Core database provider

To manage data in a specific database, we need classes that know how to efficiently talk to that database.

EF Core database providers are sets of classes that are optimized for a specific data store. There is even a provider for storing the data in the memory of the current process, which is useful for high-performance unit testing since it avoids hitting an external system.

They are distributed as NuGet packages, as shown in the following table:

To manage this data store	Install this NuGet package
Microsoft SQL Server 2012 or later	`Microsoft.EntityFrameworkCore.SqlServer`
SQLite 3.7 or later	`Microsoft.EntityFrameworkCore.SQLite`
MySQL	`MySQL.Data.EntityFrameworkCore`
In-memory	`Microsoft.EntityFrameworkCore.InMemory`
Azure Cosmos DB SQL API	`Microsoft.EntityFrameworkCore.Cosmos`
Oracle DB 11.2	`Oracle.EntityFrameworkCore`

More Information: You can see the full list of EF Core database providers at the following link: `https://docs.microsoft.com/en-us/ef/core/providers/`

Devart is a third party that offers EF Core database providers for a wide range of data stores.

More Information: Read more about Devart database providers at the following link: `https://www.devart.com/dotconnect/entityframework.html`

Setting up the dotnet-ef tool

.NET has a command-line tool named `dotnet`. It can be extended with capabilities useful for working with EF Core. It can perform design-time tasks like create and apply migrations from an older model to a newer model and generate code for a model from an existing database.

Since .NET Core 3.0, the `dotnet ef` command-line tool is not automatically installed. You have to install this package as either a global or local tool. If you have already installed the tool, you should uninstall any existing version:

1. In **TERMINAL**, check if you have already installed `dotnet-ef` as a global tool, as shown in the following command:

   ```
   dotnet tool list --global
   ```

2. Check in the list if the tool has been installed, as shown in the following output:

   ```
   Package Id        Version                    Commands
   ------------------------------------------------------------
   dotnet-ef         3.1.0                      dotnet-ef
   ```

3. If an old version is already installed, then uninstall the tool, as shown in the following command:

   ```
   dotnet tool uninstall --global dotnet-ef
   ```

4. Install the latest version, as shown in the following command:

```
dotnet tool install --global dotnet-ef --version 5.0.0
```

Connecting to the database

To connect to SQLite, we just need to know the database filename. We specify this information in a connection string:

1. In Visual Studio Code, make sure that you have opened the WorkingWithEFCore folder, and then in **TERMINAL**, enter the dotnet new console command.

2. Edit WorkingWithEFCore.csproj to add a package reference to the EF Core data provider for SQLite, as shown highlighted in the following markup:

```xml
<Project Sdk="Microsoft.NET.Sdk">
  <PropertyGroup>
    <OutputType>Exe</OutputType>
    <TargetFramework>net5.0</TargetFramework>
  </PropertyGroup>
  <ItemGroup>
    <PackageReference
      Include="Microsoft.EntityFrameworkCore.Sqlite"
      Version="5.0.0" />
  </ItemGroup>
</Project>
```

3. In **TERMINAL**, build the project to restore packages, as shown in the following command:

```
dotnet build
```

 More Information: You can check the most recent version at the following link: https://www.nuget.org/packages/Microsoft.EntityFrameworkCore.Sqlite/

Defining EF Core models

EF Core uses a combination of **conventions**, **annotation attributes**, and **Fluent API** statements to build an entity model at runtime so that any actions performed on the classes can later be automatically translated into actions performed on the actual database. An entity class represents the structure of a table and an instance of the class represents a row in that table.

First, we will review the three ways to define a model, with code examples, and then we will create some classes that implement those techniques.

EF Core conventions

The code we will write will use the following conventions:

- The name of a table is assumed to match the name of a DbSet<T> property in the DbContext class, for example, Products.

- The names of the columns are assumed to match the names of properties in the class, for example, ProductID.

- The string .NET type is assumed to be a nvarchar type in the database.

- The int .NET type is assumed to be an int type in the database.

- A property that is named ID, or if the class is named Product, then the property can be named ProductID. That property is then assumed to be a primary key. If this property is an integer type or the Guid type, then it is also assumed to be IDENTITY (a column type that automatically assigns a value when inserting).

More Information: There are many other conventions, and you can even define your own, but that is beyond the scope of this book. You can read about them at the following link: https://docs.microsoft.com/en-us/ef/core/modeling/

EF Core annotation attributes

Conventions often aren't enough to completely map the classes to the database objects. A simple way of adding more smarts to your model is to apply annotation attributes.

For example, in the database, the maximum length of a product name is 40, and the value cannot be null, as shown highlighted in the following **Data Definition Language (DDL)** code:

```
CREATE TABLE Products (
  ProductID       INTEGER       PRIMARY KEY,
  ProductName     NVARCHAR (40) NOT NULL,
  SupplierID      "INT",
  CategoryID      "INT",
  QuantityPerUnit NVARCHAR (20),
  UnitPrice       "MONEY" CONSTRAINT DF_Products_UnitPrice DEFAULT (0),
  UnitsInStock    "SMALLINT" CONSTRAINT DF_Products_UnitsInStock DEFAULT (0),
  UnitsOnOrder    "SMALLINT" CONSTRAINT DF_Products_UnitsOnOrder DEFAULT (0),
  ReorderLevel    "SMALLINT" CONSTRAINT DF_Products_ReorderLevel DEFAULT (0),
  Discontinued    "BIT"     NOT NULL
                            CONSTRAINT DF_Products_Discontinued DEFAULT (0),
  CONSTRAINT FK_Products_Categories FOREIGN KEY (
    CategoryID
  )
  REFERENCES Categories (CategoryID),
```

```
  CONSTRAINT FK_Products_Suppliers FOREIGN KEY (
    SupplierID
  )
  REFERENCES Suppliers (SupplierID),
  CONSTRAINT CK_Products_UnitPrice CHECK (UnitPrice >= 0),
  CONSTRAINT CK_ReorderLevel CHECK (ReorderLevel >= 0),
  CONSTRAINT CK_UnitsInStock CHECK (UnitsInStock >= 0),
  CONSTRAINT CK_UnitsOnOrder CHECK (UnitsOnOrder >= 0)
);
```

In a Product class, we could apply attributes to specify this, as shown in the following code:

```
[Required]
[StringLength(40)]
public string ProductName { get; set; }
```

When there isn't an obvious map between .NET types and database types, an attribute can be used.

For example, in the database, the column type of UnitPrice for the Products table is money. .NET does not have a money type, so it should use decimal instead, as shown in the following code:

```
[Column(TypeName = "money")]
public decimal? UnitPrice { get; set; }
```

Another example is for the Categories table, as shown in the following DDL code:

```
CREATE TABLE Categories (
    CategoryID    INTEGER        PRIMARY KEY,
    CategoryName  NVARCHAR (15) NOT NULL,
    Description   "NTEXT",
    Picture       "IMAGE"
);
```

The Description column can be longer than the maximum 8,000 characters that can be stored in a nvarchar variable, so it needs to map to ntext instead, as shown in the following code:

```
[Column(TypeName = "ntext")]
public string Description { get; set; }
```

EF Core Fluent API

The last way that the model can be defined is by using the **Fluent API**. This API can be used instead of attributes, as well as being used in addition to them. For example, let's look at the following two attributes in a Product class, as shown in the following code:

```
[Required]
[StringLength(40)]
public string ProductName { get; set; }
```

The attributes could be removed from the class to keep it simpler, and replaced with an equivalent Fluent API statement in the OnModelCreating method of a database context class, as shown in the following code:

```
modelBuilder.Entity<Product>()
  .Property(product => product.ProductName)
  .IsRequired()
  .HasMaxLength(40);
```

Understanding data seeding

You can use the Fluent API to provide initial data to populate a database. EF Core automatically works out what insert, update, or delete operations must be executed. If we wanted to make sure that a new database has at least one row in the Product table, then we would call the HasData method, as shown in the following code:

```
modelBuilder.Entity<Product>()
  .HasData(new Product
  {
    ProductID = 1,
    ProductName = "Chai",
    UnitPrice = 8.99M
  });
```

Our model will map to an existing database that is already populated with data so we will not need to use this technique in our code.

 More Information: You can read more about data seeding at the following link: https://docs.microsoft.com/en-us/ef/core/modeling/data-seeding

Building an EF Core model

Now that you've learned about model conventions, let's build a model to represent two tables and the Northwind database. To make the classes more reusable, we will define them in the Packt.Shared namespace. These three classes will refer to each other, so to avoid compiler errors, we will create the three classes without any members first:

1. Add three class files to the WorkingWithEFCore project named Northwind.cs, Category.cs, and Product.cs.

2. In the file named `Northwind.cs`, define a class named `Northwind`, as shown in the following code:

```
namespace Packt.Shared
{
  public class Northwind
  {
  }
}
```

3. In the file named `Category.cs`, define a class named `Category`, as shown in the following code:

```
namespace Packt.Shared
{
  public class Category
  {
  }
}
```

4. In the file named `Product.cs`, define a class named `Product`, as shown in the following code:

```
namespace Packt.Shared
{
  public class Product
  {
  }
}
```

Defining the Category and Product entity classes

`Category` will be used to represent a row in the `Categories` table, which has four columns, as shown in the following screenshot:

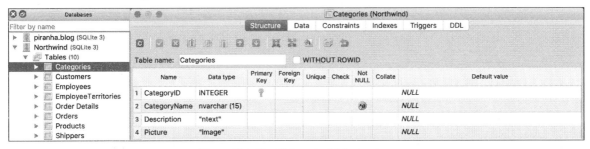

Figure 11.4: The Categories table structure

We will use conventions to define three of the four properties (we will not map the `Picture` column), the primary key, and the one-to-many relationship to the `Products` table. To map the `Description` column to the correct database type, we will need to decorate the `string` property with the `Column` attribute.

Later in this chapter, we will use the Fluent API to define that `CategoryName` cannot be `null` and is limited to a maximum of 15 characters:

1. Modify `Category.cs`, as shown in the following code:

```
using System.Collections.Generic;
using System.ComponentModel.DataAnnotations.Schema;

namespace Packt.Shared
{
  public class Category
  {
    // these properties map to columns in the database
    public int CategoryID { get; set; }
    public string CategoryName { get; set; }

    [Column(TypeName = "ntext")]
    public string Description { get; set; }

    // defines a navigation property for related rows
    public virtual ICollection<Product> Products { get; set; }

    public Category()
    {
      // to enable developers to add products to a Category we must
      // initialize the navigation property to an empty collection
      this.Products = new HashSet<Product>();
    }
  }
}
```

`Product` will be used to represent a row in the `Products` table, which has ten columns. You do not need to include all columns from a table as properties of a class. We will only map six properties: `ProductID`, `ProductName`, `UnitPrice`, `UnitsInStock`, `Discontinued`, and `CategoryID`.

Columns that are not mapped to properties cannot be read or set using the class instances. If you use the class to create a new object, then the new row in the table will have `NULL` or some other default value for the unmapped column values in that row. In this scenario, the rows already have data values and I have decided that I do not need to read those values in the console application.

We can rename a column by defining a property with a different name, like `Cost`, and then decorating the property with the `[Column]` attribute and specifying its column name, like `UnitPrice`.

The final property, `CategoryID`, is associated with a `Category` property that will be used to map each product to its parent category.

2. Modify `Product.cs`, as shown in the following code:

```
using System.ComponentModel.DataAnnotations;
using System.ComponentModel.DataAnnotations.Schema;

namespace Packt.Shared
{
  public class Product
  {
    public int ProductID { get; set; }

    [Required]
    [StringLength(40)]
    public string ProductName { get; set; }

    [Column("UnitPrice", TypeName = "money")]
    public decimal? Cost { get; set; } // property name != field name

    [Column("UnitsInStock")]
    public short? Stock { get; set; }

    public bool Discontinued { get; set; }

    // these two define the foreign key relationship
    // to the Categories table
    public int CategoryID { get; set; }
    public virtual Category Category { get; set; }
  }
}
```

The two properties that relate the two entities, `Category.Products` and `Product.Category`, are both marked as `virtual`. This allows EF Core to inherit and override the properties to provide extra features, such as lazy loading. Lazy loading is not available in EF Core 2.0 or earlier.

Defining the Northwind database context class

The `Northwind` class will be used to represent the database. To use EF Core, the class must inherit from `DbContext`. This class understands how to communicate with databases and dynamically generate SQL statements to query and manipulate data.

Inside your `DbContext`-derived class, you must define at least one property of the `DbSet<T>` type. These properties represent the tables. To tell EF Core what columns each table has, the `DbSet` properties use generics to specify a class that represents a row in the table, with properties that represent its columns.

Your `DbContext`-derived class should have an overridden method named `OnConfiguring`, which will set the database connection string.

Likewise, your `DbContext`-derived class can optionally have an overridden method named `OnModelCreating`. This is where you can write Fluent API statements as an alternative to decorating your entity classes with attributes:

1. Modify `Northwind.cs`, as shown in the following code:

```csharp
using Microsoft.EntityFrameworkCore;

namespace Packt.Shared
{
  // this manages the connection to the database
  public class Northwind : DbContext
  {
    // these properties map to tables in the database
    public DbSet<Category> Categories { get; set; }
    public DbSet<Product> Products { get; set; }

    protected override void OnConfiguring(
      DbContextOptionsBuilder optionsBuilder)
    {
      string path = System.IO.Path.Combine(
        System.Environment.CurrentDirectory, "Northwind.db");

      optionsBuilder.UseSqlite($"Filename={path}");
    }

    protected override void OnModelCreating(
      ModelBuilder modelBuilder)
    {
      // example of using Fluent API instead of attributes
      // to limit the length of a category name to 15
      modelBuilder.Entity<Category>()
        .Property(category => category.CategoryName)
        .IsRequired() // NOT NULL
        .HasMaxLength(15);

      // added to "fix" the lack of decimal support in SQLite
      modelBuilder.Entity<Product>()
        .Property(product => product.Cost)
        .HasConversion<double>();
    }
  }
}
```

In EF Core 3.0 and later, the `decimal` type is not supported for sorting and other operations. We can fix this by telling SQLite that `decimal` values can be converted to `double` values. This does not actually perform any conversion at runtime.

Now that you have seen some examples of defining an entity model manually, let's see a tool that can do some of the work for you.

Scaffolding models using an existing database

Scaffolding is the process of using a tool to create classes that represent the model of an existing database using reverse engineering. A good scaffolding tool allows you to extend the automatically generated classes and then regenerate those classes without losing your extended classes.

If you know that you will never regenerate the classes using the tool, then feel free to change the code for the automatically generated classes as much as you want. The code generated by the tool is just a best approximation. Do not be afraid to overrule the tool.

Let us see if the tool generates the same model as we did manually:

1. In **TERMINAL**, add the EF Core design package to the `WorkingWithEFCore` project, as shown in the following command:

   ```
   dotnet add package Microsoft.EntityFrameworkCore.Design
   ```

2. Generate a model for the `Categories` and `Products` tables in a new folder named `AutoGenModels`, as shown in the following command:

   ```
   dotnet ef dbcontext scaffold "Filename=Northwind.db" Microsoft.
   EntityFrameworkCore.Sqlite --table Categories --table Products --output-
   dir AutoGenModels --namespace Packt.Shared.AutoGen --data-annotations
   --context Northwind
   ```

   Note the following:

   - The command to perform: `dbcontext scaffold`
   - The connection string: `"Filename=Northwind.db"`
   - The database provider: `Microsoft.EntityFrameworkCore.Sqlite`
   - The tables to generate models for: `--table Categories --table Products`
   - The output folder: `--output-dir AutoGenModels`
   - The namespace: `--namespace Packt.Shared.AutoGen`
   - To use data annotations as well as Fluent API: `--data-annotations`
   - To rename the context from `[database_name]Context`: `--context Northwind`

3. Note the build messages and warnings, as shown in the following output:

   ```
   Build started...
   Build succeeded.
   To protect potentially sensitive information in your connection string,
   you should move it out of source code. You can avoid scaffolding the
   connection string by using the Name= syntax to read it from configuration
   - see https://go.microsoft.com/fwlink/?linkid=2131148. For more guidance
   on storing connection strings, see http://go.microsoft.com/
   ```

```
/?LinkId=723263.
Could not scaffold the foreign key '0'. The referenced table could not be
found. This most likely occurred because the referenced table was excluded
from scaffolding.
```

4. Open the `AutoGenModels` folder and note the three class files that were automatically generated: `Category.cs`, `Northwind.cs`, and `Product.cs`.

5. Open `Category.cs` and note the differences compared to the one you created manually, as shown in the following code:

```csharp
using System;
using System.Collections.Generic;
using System.ComponentModel.DataAnnotations;
using System.ComponentModel.DataAnnotations.Schema;
using Microsoft.EntityFrameworkCore;

#nullable disable

namespace Packt.Shared.AutoGen
{
    [Index(nameof(CategoryName), Name = "CategoryName")]
    public partial class Category
    {
        public Category()
        {
            Products = new HashSet<Product>();
        }

        [Key]
        [Column("CategoryID")]
        public long CategoryId { get; set; }
        [Required]
        [Column(TypeName = "nvarchar (15)")]
        public string CategoryName { get; set; }
        [Column(TypeName = "ntext")]
        public string Description { get; set; }
        [Column(TypeName = "image")]
        public byte[] Picture { get; set; }

        [InverseProperty(nameof(Product.Category))]
        public virtual ICollection<Product> Products { get; set; }
    }
}
```

Note the following:

- The `dotnet-ef` tool currently cannot use the nullable reference types language feature so it explicitly disables nullability.

- It decorates the entity class with the `[Index]` attribute introduced in EF Core 5.0 that indicates properties that match to fields that should have an index. In earlier versions, only the Fluent API was supported for defining indexes.

- The table name is `Categories` but the `dotnet-ef` tool uses the Humanizer third-party library to automatically singularize (or pluralize) the class name to `Category`, which is a more natural name when creating a single entity.

 More Information: You can learn about the Humanizer library and how you might use it in your own apps at the following link: `http://humanizr.net`

- The entity class is declared using the `partial` keyword so that you can create a matching `partial` class for adding additional code. This allows you to rerun the tool and regenerate the entity class without losing that extra code.

- The `CategoryId` property is decorated with the `[Key]` attribute to indicate that it is the primary key for this entity. It is also misnamed since Microsoft naming conventions say that two-letter abbreviations or acronyms should use all uppercase and not title case.

- The `Products` property uses the `[InverseProperty]` attribute to define the foreign key relationship to the `Category` property on the `Product` entity class.

6. Open `Product.cs` and note the differences compared to the one you created manually.

7. Open `Northwind.cs` and note the differences compared to the one you created manually, as shown in the following edited-for-space code:

```
using Microsoft.EntityFrameworkCore;

#nullable disable

namespace Packt.Shared.AutoGen
{
  public partial class Northwind : DbContext
  {
    public Northwind()
    {
    }

    public Northwind(DbContextOptions<Northwind> options)
        : base(options)
    {
    }
```

```
    public virtual DbSet<Category> Categories { get; set; }
    public virtual DbSet<Product> Products { get; set; }

    protected override void OnConfiguring(
      DbContextOptionsBuilder optionsBuilder)
    {
      if (!optionsBuilder.IsConfigured)
      {
#warning To protect potentially sensitive information in your connection
string, you should move it out of source code. You can avoid scaffolding
the connection string by using the Name= syntax to read it from
configuration - see https://go.microsoft.com/fwlink/?linkid=2131148. For
more guidance on storing connection strings, see http://go.microsoft.com/
fwlink/?LinkId=723263.
        optionsBuilder.UseSqlite("Filename=Northwind.db");
      }
    }

    protected override void OnModelCreating(ModelBuilder modelBuilder)
    {
      modelBuilder.Entity<Category>(entity =>
      {
        entity.Property(e => e.CategoryId)
          .ValueGeneratedNever()
          .HasColumnName("CategoryID");

        entity.Property(e => e.CategoryName)
          .HasAnnotation("Relational:ColumnType", "nvarchar (15)");

        entity.Property(e => e.Description)
          .HasAnnotation("Relational:ColumnType", "ntext");

        entity.Property(e => e.Picture)
          .HasAnnotation("Relational:ColumnType", "image");
      });

      modelBuilder.Entity<Product>(entity =>
      {
        ...
      });

      OnModelCreatingPartial(modelBuilder);
    }

    partial void OnModelCreatingPartial(ModelBuilder modelBuilder);
```

```
    }
  }
```

Note the following:

- The `Northwind` data context class is `partial` to allow you to extend it and regenerate it in the future.

- It has two constructors: a default parameter-less one and one that allows options to be passed in. This is useful in apps where you want to specify the connection string at runtime.

- In the `OnConfiguring` method, if options have not been specified in the constructor, then it defaults to using a connection string that looks for the database file in the current folder. It has a compiler warning to remind you that you should not hardcode security information in this connection string.

- In the `OnModelCreating` method, Fluent API is used to configure the two entity classes, and then a partial method named `OnModelCreatingPartial` is invoked. This allows you to implement that partial method in your own partial `Northwind` class to add your own Fluent API configuration that will not be lost if you regenerate the model classes.

8. Close the automatically generated class files.

 More Information: You can read more about scaffolding at the following link: `https://docs.microsoft.com/en-us/ef/core/managing-schemas/scaffolding?tabs=dotnet-core-cli`

In the rest of this chapter, we will use the classes that you manually created.

Querying EF Core models

Now that we have a model that maps to the `Northwind` database and two of its tables, we can write some simple LINQ queries to fetch data. You will learn much more about writing LINQ queries in *Chapter 12, Querying and Manipulating Data Using LINQ*. For now, just write the code and view the results:

1. Open `Program.cs` and import the following namespaces:

```
using static System.Console;
using Packt.Shared;
using Microsoft.EntityFrameworkCore;
using System.Linq;
```

2. In `Program`, define a `QueryingCategories` method, and add statements to do these tasks, as shown in the following code:

   - Create an instance of the `Northwind` class that will manage the database. Database context instances are designed for short lifetimes in a unit of work. They should be disposed as soon as possible so we will wrap it in a `using` statement.

   - Create a query for all categories that include their related products.

   - Enumerate through the categories, outputting the name and number of products for each one.

```
static void QueryingCategories()
{
  using (var db = new Northwind())
  {
    WriteLine("Categories and how many products they have:");

    // a query to get all categories and their related products
    IQueryable<Category> cats = db.Categories
      .Include(c => c.Products);

    foreach (Category c in cats)
    {
      WriteLine($"{c.CategoryName} has {c.Products.Count} products.");
    }
  }
}
```

3. In `Main`, call the `QueryingCategories` method, as shown in the following code:

```
static void Main(string[] args)
{
  QueryingCategories();
}
```

4. Run the application and view the result, as shown in the following output:

```
Categories and how many products they have:
Beverages has 12 products.
Condiments has 12 products.
Confections has 13 products.
Dairy Products has 10 products.
Grains/Cereals has 7 products.
Meat/Poultry has 6 products.
Produce has 5 products.
Seafood has 12 products.
```

Filtering included entities

EF Core 5.0 introduced filtered includes, which means you can specify a lambda expression in the `Include` method call to filter which entities are returned in the results:

1. In `Program`, define a `FilteredIncludes` method, and add statements to do these tasks, as shown in the following code:

   - Create an instance of the `Northwind` class that will manage the database.

   - Prompt the user to enter a minimum value for units in stock.

   - Create a query for categories that have products with that minimum number of units in stock.

   - Enumerate through the categories and products, outputting the name and units in stock for each one:

```
static void FilteredIncludes()
{
  using (var db = new Northwind())
  {
    Write("Enter a minimum for units in stock: ");
    string unitsInStock = ReadLine();
    int stock = int.Parse(unitsInStock);

    IQueryable<Category> cats = db.Categories
      .Include(c => c.Products.Where(p => p.Stock >= stock));

    foreach (Category c in cats)
    {
      WriteLine($"{c.CategoryName} has {c.Products.Count} products with a
minimum of {stock} units in stock.");

      foreach(Product p in c.Products)
      {
        WriteLine($"  {p.ProductName} has {p.Stock} units in stock.");
      }
    }
  }
}
```

2. In `Main`, comment out the `QueryingCategories` method and invoke the `FilteredIncludes` method, as shown in the following code:

```
static void Main(string[] args)
{
  // QueryingCategories();
  FilteredIncludes();
}
```

3. Run the application, enter a minimum for units in stock like 100, and view the result, as shown in the following output:

```
Enter a minimum for units in stock: 100
Beverages has 2 products with a minimum of 100 units in stock.
  Sasquatch Ale has 111 units in stock.
  Rhönbräu Klosterbier has 125 units in stock.
Condiments has 2 products with a minimum of 100 units in stock.
  Grandma's Boysenberry Spread has 120 units in stock.
  Sirop d'érable has 113 units in stock.
Confections has 0 products with a minimum of 100 units in stock.
Dairy Products has 1 products with a minimum of 100 units in stock.
  Geitost has 112 units in stock.
Grains/Cereals has 1 products with a minimum of 100 units in stock.
  Gustaf's Knäckebröd has 104 units in stock.
Meat/Poultry has 1 products with a minimum of 100 units in stock.
  Pâté chinois has 115 units in stock.
Produce has 0 products with a minimum of 100 units in stock.
Seafood has 3 products with a minimum of 100 units in stock.
  Inlagd Sill has 112 units in stock.
  Boston Crab Meat has 123 units in stock.
  Röd Kaviar has 101 units in stock.
```

More Information: You can read more about filtered include at the following link: https://docs.microsoft.com/en-us/ef/core/querying/related-data/eager#filtered-include

Filtering and sorting products

Let's explore a more complex query that filters and sorts data:

1. In `Program`, define a `QueryingProducts` method, and add statements to do the following, as shown in the following code:

    • Create an instance of the `Northwind` class that will manage the database.

    • Prompt the user for a price for products.

    • Create a query for products that cost more than the price using LINQ.

    • Loop through the results, outputting the ID, name, cost (formatted with US dollars), and the number of units in stock:

```
static void QueryingProducts()
{
  using (var db = new Northwind())
  {
```

```
    WriteLine("Products that cost more than a price, highest at top.");
    string input;
    decimal price;
    do
    {
      Write("Enter a product price: ");
      input = ReadLine();
    } while(!decimal.TryParse(input, out price));

    IQueryable<Product> prods = db.Products
      .Where(product => product.Cost > price)
      .OrderByDescending(product => product.Cost);

    foreach (Product item in prods)
    {
      WriteLine(
        "{0}: {1} costs {2:$#,##0.00} and has {3} in stock.",
        item.ProductID, item.ProductName, item.Cost, item.Stock);
    }
  }
}
```

2. In Main, comment the previous method, and call the method, as shown in the following code:

```
static void Main(string[] args)
{
  // QueryingCategories();
  // FilteredIncludes();
  QueryingProducts();
}
```

3. Run the application, enter 50 when prompted to enter a product price, and view the result, as shown in the following output:

```
Products that cost more than a price, highest at top.
Enter a product price: 50
38: Côte de Blaye costs $263.50 and has 17 in stock.
29: Thüringer Rostbratwurst costs $123.79 and has 0 in stock.
9: Mishi Kobe Niku costs $97.00 and has 29 in stock.
20: Sir Rodney's Marmalade costs $81.00 and has 40 in stock.
18: Carnarvon Tigers costs $62.50 and has 42 in stock.
59: Raclette Courdavault costs $55.00 and has 79 in stock.
51: Manjimup Dried Apples costs $53.00 and has 20 in stock.
```

There is a limitation with the console provided by Microsoft on versions of Windows before the Windows 10 Fall Creators Update. By default, the console cannot display Unicode characters. You can temporarily change the code page (also known as the character set) in a console to Unicode UTF-8 by entering the following command at the prompt before running the app:

```
chcp 65001
```

Getting the generated SQL

You might be wondering how well-written the SQL statements are that are generated from the C# queries we write. EF Core 5.0 introduces a quick and easy way to see the SQL generated:

1. In the `FilteredIncludes` method, after defining the query, add a statement to output the generated SQL, as shown highlighted in the following code:

    ```
    IQueryable<Category> cats = db.Categories
      .Include(c => c.Products.Where(p => p.Stock >= stock));

    WriteLine($"ToQueryString: {cats.ToQueryString()}");
    ```

2. Modify the `Main` method to comment out the call to the `QueryingProducts` method and uncomment the call to the `FilteredIncludes` method.

3. Run the application, enter a minimum for units in stock like 99, and view the result, as shown in the following output:

    ```
    Enter a minimum for units in stock: 99
    ToQueryString: .param set @__stock_0 99

    SELECT "c"."CategoryID", "c"."CategoryName", "c"."Description",
    "t"."ProductID", "t"."CategoryID", "t"."UnitPrice", "t"."Discontinued",
    "t"."ProductName", "t"."UnitsInStock"
    FROM "Categories" AS "c"
    LEFT JOIN (
        SELECT "p"."ProductID", "p"."CategoryID", "p"."UnitPrice",
    "p"."Discontinued", "p"."ProductName", "p"."UnitsInStock"
        FROM "Products" AS "p"
        WHERE ("p"."UnitsInStock" >= @__stock_0)
    ) AS "t" ON "c"."CategoryID" = "t"."CategoryID"
    ORDER BY "c"."CategoryID", "t"."ProductID"
    Beverages has 2 products with a minimum of 99 units in stock.
      Sasquatch Ale has 111 units in stock.
      Rhönbräu Klosterbier has 125 units in stock.
    ...
    ```

4. Note the SQL parameter named `@__stock_0` has been set to a minimum stock value of 99.

Logging EF Core

To monitor the interaction between EF Core and the database, we can enable logging. This requires the following two tasks:

- The registering of a **logging provider**.
- The implementation of a **logger**.

Let us see an example of this in action:

1. Add a file to your project named ConsoleLogger.cs.
2. Modify the file to define two classes, one to implement ILoggerProvider and one to implement ILogger, as shown in the following code, and note the following:

    - ConsoleLoggerProvider returns an instance of ConsoleLogger. It does not need any unmanaged resources, so the Dispose method does not do anything, but it must exist.

    - ConsoleLogger is disabled for log levels None, Trace, and Information. It is enabled for all other log levels.

    - ConsoleLogger implements its Log method by writing to Console:

```
using Microsoft.Extensions.Logging;
using System;
using static System.Console;

namespace Packt.Shared
{
  public class ConsoleLoggerProvider : ILoggerProvider
  {
    public ILogger CreateLogger(string categoryName)
    {
      return new ConsoleLogger();
    }

    // if your logger uses unmanaged resources,
    // you can release the memory here
    public void Dispose() { }
  }

  public class ConsoleLogger : ILogger
  {
    // if your logger uses unmanaged resources, you can
    // return the class that implements IDisposable here
    public IDisposable BeginScope<TState>(TState state)
    {
      return null;
```

```
        }

        public bool IsEnabled(LogLevel logLevel)
        {
          // to avoid overlogging, you can filter
          // on the Log Level
          switch(logLevel)
          {
            case LogLevel.Trace:
            case LogLevel.Information:
            case LogLevel.None:
              return false;
            case LogLevel.Debug:
            case LogLevel.Warning:
            case LogLevel.Error:
            case LogLevel.Critical:
            default:
              return true;
          };
        }

        public void Log<TState>(LogLevel logLevel,
          EventId eventId, TState state, Exception exception,
          Func<TState, Exception, string> formatter)
        {
          // log the level and event identifier
          Write($"Level: {logLevel}, Event ID: {eventId.Id}");

          // only output the state or exception if it exists
          if (state != null)
          {
            Write($", State: {state}");
          }

          if (exception != null)
          {
            Write($", Exception: {exception.Message}");
          }
          WriteLine();
        }
      }
    }
```

3. At the top of the `Program.cs` file, add statements to import the namespaces needed for logging, as shown in the following code:

```
using Microsoft.EntityFrameworkCore.Infrastructure;
```

```
using Microsoft.Extensions.DependencyInjection;
using Microsoft.Extensions.Logging;
```

4. To both the QueryingCategories and QueryingProducts methods, add statements immediately inside the using block for the Northwind database context to get the logging factory and register your custom console logger, as shown highlighted in the following code:

```
using (var db = new Northwind())
{
    var loggerFactory = db.GetService<ILoggerFactory>();
    loggerFactory.AddProvider(new ConsoleLoggerProvider());
```

5. Run the console application and view the logs, which are partially shown in the following output:

```
Level: Debug, Event ID: 20000, State: Opening connection to database
'main' on server '/Users/markjprice/Code/Chapter11/WorkingWithEFCore/
Northwind.db'.
Level: Debug, Event ID: 20001, State: Opened connection to database 'main'
on server '/Users/markjprice/Code/Chapter11/WorkingWithEFCore/Northwind.
db'.
Level: Debug, Event ID: 20100, State: Executing DbCommand [Parameters=[],
CommandType='Text', CommandTimeout='30']
PRAGMA foreign_keys=ON;
Level: Debug, Event ID: 20100, State: Executing DbCommand [Parameters=[],
CommandType='Text', CommandTimeout='30']
SELECT "product"."ProductID", "product"."CategoryID",
"product"."UnitPrice", "product"."Discontinued", "product"."ProductName",
"product"."UnitsInStock"
FROM "Products" AS "product"
ORDER BY "product"."UnitPrice" DESC
```

The event ID values and what they mean will be specific to the .NET data provider. If we want to know how the LINQ query has been translated into SQL statements and is executing, then the Event ID to output has an Id value of 20100.

6. Modify the Log method in ConsoleLogger to only output events with an Id of 20100, as highlighted in the following code:

```
public void Log<TState>(LogLevel logLevel, EventId eventId,
    TState state, Exception exception,
    Func<TState, Exception, string> formatter)
{
    if (eventId.Id == 20100)
    {
        // log the level and event identifier
        Write("Level: {0}, Event ID: {1}, Event: {2}"
            logLevel, eventId.Id, eventId.Name);
        // only output the state or exception if it exists
```

```
    if (state != null)
    {
      Write($", State: {state}");
    }

    if (exception != null)
    {
      Write($", Exception: {exception.Message}");
    }
    WriteLine();
  }
}
```

7. In `Main`, uncomment the `QueryingCategories` method and comment the `FilteredIncludes` method so that we can monitor the SQL statements that are generated when joining two tables.

8. Run the console application, and note the following SQL statements that were logged, as shown in the following output that has been edited for space:

```
Categories and how many products they have:
Level: Debug, Event ID: 20100, State: Executing DbCommand [Parameters=[],
CommandType='Text', CommandTimeout='30']
PRAGMA foreign_keys=ON;
Level: Debug, Event ID: 20100, State: Executing DbCommand [Parameters=[],
CommandType='Text', CommandTimeout='30']
SELECT "c"."CategoryID", "c"."CategoryName", "c"."Description"
FROM "Categories" AS "c"
ORDER BY "c"."CategoryID"
Level: Debug, Event ID: 20100, State: Executing DbCommand [Parameters=[],
CommandType='Text', CommandTimeout='30']
SELECT "c.Products"."ProductID", "c.Products"."CategoryID",
"c.Products"."UnitPrice", "c.Products"."Discontinued",
"c.Products"."ProductName", "c.Products"."UnitsInStock"
FROM "Products" AS "c.Products"
INNER JOIN (
SELECT "c0"."CategoryID"
FROM "Categories" AS "c0"
) AS "t" ON "c.Products"."CategoryID" = "t"."CategoryID"
ORDER BY "t"."CategoryID"
Beverages has 12 products.
Condiments has 12 products.
Confections has 13 products.
Dairy Products has 10 products.
Grains/Cereals has 7 products.
Meat/Poultry has 6 products.
Produce has 5 products.
Seafood has 12 products.
```

Logging with query tags

When logging LINQ queries, it can be tricky to correlate log messages in complex scenarios. EF Core 2.2 introduced the query tags feature to help by allowing you to add SQL comments to the log.

You can annotate a LINQ query using the `TagWith` method, as shown in the following code:

```
IQueryable<Product> prods = db.Products
  .TagWith("Products filtered by price and sorted.")
  .Where(product => product.Cost > price)
  .OrderByDescending(product => product.Cost);
```

This will add a SQL comment to the log, as shown in the following output:

```
-- Products filtered by price and sorted.
```

 More Information: You can read more about query tags at the following link: https://docs.microsoft.com/en-us/ef/core/querying/tags

Pattern matching with Like

EF Core supports common SQL statements including `Like` for pattern matching:

1. In `Program`, add a method named `QueryingWithLike`, as shown in the following code, and note:

   - We have enabled logging.
   - We prompt the user to enter part of a product name and then use the `EF.Functions.Like` method to search anywhere in the `ProductName` property.
   - For each matching product, we output its name, stock, and if it is discontinued:

```
static void QueryingWithLike()
{
  using (var db = new Northwind())
  {
    var loggerFactory = db.GetService<ILoggerFactory>();
    loggerFactory.AddProvider(new ConsoleLoggerProvider());

    Write("Enter part of a product name: ");
    string input = ReadLine();

    IQueryable<Product> prods = db.Products
      .Where(p => EF.Functions.Like(p.ProductName, $"%{input}%"));
```

```
      foreach (Product item in prods)
      {
        WriteLine("{0} has {1} units in stock. Discontinued? {2}",
          item.ProductName, item.Stock, item.Discontinued);
      }
    }
  }
```

2. In `Main`, comment the existing methods, and call `QueryingWithLike`.

3. Run the console application, enter a partial product name such as che, and view the result, as shown in the following output:

```
Enter part of a product name: che
Level: Debug, Event ID: 20100, State: Executing DbCommand [Parameters=[],
CommandType='Text', CommandTimeout='30']
PRAGMA foreign_keys=ON;
Level: Debug, Event ID: 20100, State: Executing DbCommand [Parameters=[@__
Format_1='?' (Size = 5)], CommandType='Text', CommandTimeout='30']
SELECT "p"."ProductID", "p"."CategoryID", "p"."UnitPrice",
"p"."Discontinued", "p"."ProductName", "p"."UnitsInStock"
FROM "Products" AS "p"
WHERE "p"."ProductName" LIKE @__Format_1
Chef Anton's Cajun Seasoning has 53 units in stock. Discontinued? False
Chef Anton's Gumbo Mix has 0 units in stock. Discontinued? True
Queso Manchego La Pastora has 86 units in stock. Discontinued? False
Gumbär Gummibärchen has 15 units in stock. Discontinued? False
```

Defining global filters

The `Northwind` products can be discontinued, so it might be useful to ensure that discontinued products are never returned in results, even if the programmer forgets to use `Where` to filter them out:

1. Modify the `OnModelCreating` method in the `Northwind` class to add a global filter to remove discontinued products, as shown highlighted in the following code:

```
protected override void OnModelCreating(ModelBuilder modelBuilder)
{
  // example of using Fluent API instead of attributes
  // to limit the length of a category name to under 15
  modelBuilder.Entity<Category>()
    .Property(category => category.CategoryName)
    .IsRequired() // NOT NULL
    .HasMaxLength(15);

  // added to "fix" the lack of decimal support in SQLite
```

```
modelBuilder.Entity<Product>()
  .Property(product => product.Cost)
  .HasConversion<double>();

// global filter to remove discontinued products
modelBuilder.Entity<Product>()
  .HasQueryFilter(p => !p.Discontinued);
}
```

2. Run the console application, enter the partial product name che, view the result, and note that **Chef Anton's Gumbo Mix** is now missing, because the SQL statement generated includes a filter for the Discontinued column, as shown in the following output:

```
SELECT "p"."ProductID", "p"."CategoryID", "p"."UnitPrice",
"p"."Discontinued", "p"."ProductName", "p"."UnitsInStock"
FROM "Products" AS "p"
WHERE ("p"."Discontinued" = 0) AND "p"."ProductName" LIKE @__Format_1
Chef Anton's Cajun Seasoning has 53 units in stock. Discontinued? False
Queso Manchego La Pastora has 86 units in stock. Discontinued? False
Gumbär Gummibärchen has 15 units in stock. Discontinued? False
```

Loading patterns with EF Core

There are three **loading patterns** that are commonly used with EF: **eager loading**, **lazy loading**, and **explicit loading**. In this section, we're going to introduce each of them.

Eager loading entities

In the QueryingCategories method, the code currently uses the Categories property to loop through each category, outputting the category name and the number of products in that category. This works because when we wrote the query, we used the Include method to use eager loading (also known as **early loading**) for the related products:

1. Modify the query to comment out the Include method call, as shown in the following code:

```
IQueryable<Category> cats =
  db.Categories; //.Include(c => c.Products);
```

2. In Main, comment all methods except QueryingCategories.

3. Run the console application and view the result, as shown in the following partial output:

```
Beverages has 0 products.
Condiments has 0 products.
Confections has 0 products.
```

```
Dairy Products has 0 products.
Grains/Cereals has 0 products.
Meat/Poultry has 0 products.
Produce has 0 products.
Seafood has 0 products.
```

Each item in foreach is an instance of the Category class, which has a property named Products, that is, the list of products in that category. Since the original query is only selected from the Categories table, this property is empty for each category.

Enabling lazy loading

Lazy loading was introduced in EF Core 2.1, and it can automatically load missing related data.

To enable lazy loading, developers must:

- Reference a NuGet package for proxies.
- Configure lazy loading to using a proxy.

Let us see this in action:

1. Open WorkingWithEFCore.csproj and add a package reference, as shown in the following markup:

   ```
   <PackageReference
     Include="Microsoft.EntityFrameworkCore.Proxies"
     Version="5.0.0" />
   ```

2. In **TERMINAL**, build the project to restore packages, as shown in the following command:

   ```
   dotnet build
   ```

3. Open Northwind.cs, import the Microsoft.EntityFrameworkCore.Proxies namespace, and call an extension method to use lazy loading proxies before using SQLite, as shown highlighted in the following code:

   ```
   optionsBuilder.UseLazyLoadingProxies()
     .UseSqlite($"Filename={path}");
   ```

   Now, every time the loop enumerates, and an attempt is made to read the Products property, the lazy loading proxy will check if they are loaded. If not, it will load them for us "lazily" by executing a SELECT statement to load just that set of products for the current category, and then the correct count would be returned to the output.

4. Run the console app and you will see that the problem with lazy loading is that multiple round trips to the database server are required to eventually fetch all the data, as shown in the following partial output:

```
Categories and how many products they have:
Level: Debug, Event ID: 20100, State: Executing DbCommand [Parameters=[],
CommandType='Text', CommandTimeout='30']
PRAGMA foreign_keys=ON;
Level: Debug, Event ID: 20100, State: Executing DbCommand [Parameters=[],
CommandType='Text', CommandTimeout='30']
SELECT "c"."CategoryID", "c"."CategoryName", "c"."Description"
FROM "Categories" AS "c"
Level: Debug, Event ID: 20100, State: Executing DbCommand
[Parameters=[@__p_0='?'], CommandType='Text', CommandTimeout='30']
SELECT "p"."ProductID", "p"."CategoryID", "p"."UnitPrice",
"p"."Discontinued", "p"."ProductName", "p"."UnitsInStock"
FROM "Products" AS "p"
WHERE ("p"."Discontinued" = 0) AND ("p"."CategoryID" = @__p_0)
Beverages has 11 products.
Level: Debug, Event ID: 20100, State: Executing DbCommand
[Parameters=[@__p_0='?'], CommandType='Text', CommandTimeout='30']
SELECT "p"."ProductID", "p"."CategoryID", "p"."UnitPrice",
"p"."Discontinued", "p"."ProductName", "p"."UnitsInStock"
FROM "Products" AS "p"
WHERE ("p"."Discontinued" = 0) AND ("p"."CategoryID" = @__p_0)
Condiments has 11 products.
```

Explicit loading entities

Another type of loading is explicit loading. It works in a similar way to lazy loading, with the difference being that you are in control of exactly what related data is loaded and when:

1. In the `QueryingCategories` method, modify the statements to disable lazy loading and then prompt the user if they want to enable eager loading and explicit loading, as shown in the following code:

```
IQueryable<Category> cats;
  // = db.Categories;
  // .Include(c => c.Products);

db.ChangeTracker.LazyLoadingEnabled = false;

Write("Enable eager loading? (Y/N): ");
bool eagerloading = (ReadKey().Key == ConsoleKey.Y);
bool explicitloading = false;
WriteLine();

if (eagerloading)
{
  cats = db.Categories.Include(c => c.Products);
}
```

```
else
{
  cats = db.Categories;

  Write("Enable explicit loading? (Y/N): ");
    explicitloading = (ReadKey().Key == ConsoleKey.Y);
  WriteLine();
}
```

2. Inside the `foreach` loop, before the `WriteLine` method call, add statements to check if explicit loading is enabled, and if so, prompt the user if they want to explicitly load each individual category, as shown in the following code:

```
if (explicitloading)
{
  Write($"Explicitly load products for {c.CategoryName}? (Y/N): ");
  ConsoleKeyInfo key = ReadKey();
  WriteLine();
  if (key.Key == ConsoleKey.Y)
  {
    var products = db.Entry(c).Collection(c2 => c2.Products);
    if (!products.IsLoaded) products.Load();
  }
}
WriteLine($"{c.CategoryName} has {c.Products.Count} products.");
```

3. Run the console application; press *N* to disable eager loading, and press *Y* to enable explicit loading. For each category, press *Y* or *N* to load its products as you wish. I chose to load products for only two of the eight categories, `Beverages` and `Seafood`, as shown in the following output that has been edited for space:

```
Categories and how many products they have:
Enable eager loading? (Y/N): n
Enable explicit loading? (Y/N): y
Level: Debug, Event ID: 20100, State: Executing DbCommand [Parameters=[],
CommandType='Text', CommandTimeout='30']
PRAGMA foreign_keys=ON;
Level: Debug, Event ID: 20100, State: Executing DbCommand [Parameters=[],
CommandType='Text', CommandTimeout='30']
SELECT "c"."CategoryID", "c"."CategoryName", "c"."Description"
FROM "Categories" AS "c"
Explicitly load products for Beverages? (Y/N): y
Level: Debug, Event ID: 20100, State: Executing DbCommand
[Parameters=[@__p_0='?'], CommandType='Text', CommandTimeout='30']
SELECT "p"."ProductID", "p"."CategoryID", "p"."UnitPrice",
"p"."Discontinued", "p"."ProductName", "p"."UnitsInStock"
FROM "Products" AS "p"
WHERE ("p"."Discontinued" = 0) AND ("p"."CategoryID" = @__p_0)
```

```
Beverages has 11 products.
Explicitly load products for Condiments? (Y/N): n
Condiments has 0 products.
Explicitly load products for Confections? (Y/N): n
Confections has 0 products.
Explicitly load products for Dairy Products? (Y/N): n
Dairy Products has 0 products.
Explicitly load products for Grains/Cereals? (Y/N): n
Grains/Cereals has 0 products.
Explicitly load products for Meat/Poultry? (Y/N): n
Meat/Poultry has 0 products.
Explicitly load products for Produce? (Y/N): n
Produce has 0 products.
Explicitly load products for Seafood? (Y/N): y
Level: Debug, Event ID: 20100, State: Executing DbCommand
[Parameters=[@__p_0='?'], CommandType='Text', CommandTimeout='30']
SELECT "p"."ProductID", "p"."CategoryID", "p"."UnitPrice",
"p"."Discontinued", "p"."ProductName", "p"."UnitsInStock"
FROM "Products" AS "p"
WHERE ("p"."Discontinued" = 0) AND ("p"."CategoryID" = @__p_0)
Seafood has 12 products.
```

> **Good Practice**: Carefully consider which loading pattern is best for your code. Lazy loading could literally make you a lazy database developer! Read more about loading patterns at the following link: https://docs.microsoft.com/en-us/ef/core/querying/related-data

Manipulating data with EF Core

Inserting, updating, and deleting entities using EF Core is an easy task to accomplish. DbContext maintains change tracking automatically, so the local entities can have multiple changes tracked, including adding new entities, modifying existing entities, and removing entities. When you are ready to send those changes to the underlying database, call the SaveChanges method. The number of entities successfully changed will be returned.

Inserting entities

Let's start by looking at how to add a new row to a table:

1. In Program, create a new method named AddProduct, as shown in the following code:

```
static bool AddProduct(
    int categoryID, string productName, decimal? price)
{
    using (var db = new Northwind())
    {
```

```
            var newProduct = new Product
            {
              CategoryID = categoryID,
              ProductName = productName,
              Cost = price
            };

            // mark product as added in change tracking
            db.Products.Add(newProduct);

            // save tracked change to database
            int affected = db.SaveChanges();
            return (affected == 1);
        }
    }
```

2. In `Program`, create a new method named `ListProducts` that outputs the ID, name, cost, stock, and discontinued properties of each product sorted with the costliest first, as shown in the following code:

```
    static void ListProducts()
    {
      using (var db = new Northwind())
      {
        WriteLine("{0,-3} {1,-35} {2,8} {3,5} {4}",
          "ID", "Product Name", "Cost", "Stock", "Disc.");

        foreach (var item in db.Products.OrderByDescending(p => p.Cost))
        {
          WriteLine("{0:000} {1,-35} {2,8:$#,##0.00} {3,5} {4}",
            item.ProductID, item.ProductName, item.Cost,
            item.Stock, item.Discontinued);
        }
      }
    }
```

Remember that `1,-35` means left-align argument number 1 within a 35 character-wide column and `3,5` means right-align argument number 3 within a 5 character-wide column.

3. In `Main`, comment previous method calls, and then call `AddProduct` and `ListProducts`, as shown in the following code:

```
    static void Main(string[] args)
    {
      // QueryingCategories();
      // FilteredIncludes();
      // QueryingProducts();
```

```
// QueryingWithLike();

if (AddProduct(6, "Bob's Burgers", 500M))
{
  WriteLine("Add product successful.");
}
ListProducts();
}
```

4. Run the application, view the result, and note the new product has been added, as shown in the following partial output:

```
Add product successful.
ID  Product Name              Cost Stock Disc.
078 Bob's Burgers          $500.00       False
038 Côte de Blaye          $263.50    17 False
020 Sir Rodney's Marmalade $81.00     40 False
...
```

Updating entities

Now, let's modify an existing row in a table:

1. In `Program`, add a method to increase the price of the first product with a name that begins with a specified value (we'll use `Bob` in our example) by a specified amount like $20, as shown in the following code:

```
static bool IncreaseProductPrice(string name, decimal amount)
{
  using (var db = new Northwind())
  {
    // get first product whose name starts with name
    Product updateProduct = db.Products.First(
      p => p.ProductName.StartsWith(name));

    updateProduct.Cost += amount;
    int affected = db.SaveChanges();
    return (affected == 1);
  }
}
```

2. In `Main`, comment the whole `if` statement block that calls `AddProduct`, and add a call to `IncreaseProductPrice` before the call to list products, as shown highlighted in the following code:

```
if (IncreaseProductPrice("Bob", 20M))
{
  WriteLine("Update product price successful.");
```

```
    }
    ListProducts();
```

3. Run the console application, view the result, and note that the existing entity for Bob's Burgers has increased in price by $20, as shown in the following partial output:

```
Update product price successful.
ID  Product Name         Cost Stock Disc.
078 Bob's Burgers       $520.00       False
038 Côte de Blaye       $263.50    17 False
...
```

Deleting entities

Now let's see how to delete a row from a table:

1. In `Program`, import `System.Collections.Generic`.

2. Add a method to delete all products with a name that begins with a specified value (`Bob` in our example), as shown in the following code:

```
static int DeleteProducts(string name)
{
  using (var db = new Northwind())
  {
    IEnumerable<Product> products = db.Products.Where(
      p => p.ProductName.StartsWith(name));

    db.Products.RemoveRange(products);
    int affected = db.SaveChanges();
    return affected;
  }
}
```

You can remove individual entities with the `Remove` method. `RemoveRange` is more efficient when you want to delete multiple entities.

3. In `Main`, comment the whole `if` statement block that calls `IncreaseProductPrice`, and add a call to `DeleteProducts`, as shown highlighted in the following code:

```
int deleted = DeleteProducts("Bob");
WriteLine($"{deleted} product(s) were deleted.");
ListProducts();
```

4. Run the console application and view the result, as shown in the following output:

```
1 product(s) were deleted.
ID Product Name Cost Stock Disc.
038 Côte de Blaye $263.50 17 False
020 Sir Rodney's Marmalade $81.00 40 False
```

If multiple product names started with Bob, then they are all deleted. As an optional challenge, uncomment the statements to add three new products that start with Bob and then delete them.

Pooling database contexts

The DbContext class is disposable and is designed following the single-unit-of-work principle. In the previous code examples, we created all the DbContext-derived Northwind instances in a using block.

A feature of ASP.NET Core that is related to EF Core is that it makes your code more efficient by pooling database contexts when building web applications and web services.

This allows you to create and dispose of as many DbContext-derived objects as you want, knowing your code is still very efficient.

 More Information: You can read more about pooling database contexts at the following link: https://docs.microsoft.com/en-us/ef/core/what-is-new/ef-core-2.0#dbcontext-pooling

Transactions

Every time you call the SaveChanges method, an **implicit transaction** is started so that if something goes wrong, it would automatically roll back all the changes. If the multiple changes within the transaction succeed, then the transaction and all changes are committed.

Transactions maintain the integrity of your database by applying locks to prevent reads and writes while a sequence of changes is occurring.

Transactions are **ACID**, which is an acronym explained in the following list:

- **A** is for atomic. Either all the operations in the transaction commit, or none of them do.
- **C** is for consistent. The state of the database before and after a transaction is consistent. This is dependent on your code logic; for example, when transferring money between bank accounts, it is up to your business logic to ensure that if you debit $100 in one account, you credit $100 in the other account.
- **I** is for isolated. During a transaction, changes are hidden from other processes. There are multiple isolation levels that you can pick from (refer to the following table). The stronger the level, the better the integrity of the data. However, more locks must be applied, which will negatively affect other processes. Snapshot is a special case because it creates multiple copies of rows to avoid locks, but this will increase the size of your database while transactions occur.
- **D** is for durable. If a failure occurs during a transaction, it can be recovered. This is often implemented as a two-phase commit and transaction logs. The opposite of durable is volatile:

Isolation level	Lock(s)	Integrity problems allowed
ReadUncommitted	None	Dirty reads, nonrepeatable reads, and phantom data
ReadCommitted	When editing, it applies read lock(s) to block other users from reading the record(s) until the transaction ends	Nonrepeatable reads and phantom data
RepeatableRead	When reading, it applies edit lock(s) to block other users from editing the record(s) until the transaction ends	Phantom data
Serializable	Applies key-range locks to prevent any action that would affect the results, including inserts and deletes	None
Snapshot	None	None

Defining an explicit transaction

You can control explicit transactions using the Database property of the database context:

1. Import the following namespace in Program.cs to use the IDbContextTransaction interface:

    ```
    using Microsoft.EntityFrameworkCore.Storage;
    ```

2. In the DeleteProducts method, after the instantiation of the db variable, add the following highlighted statements to start an explicit transaction and output its isolation level. At the bottom of the method, commit the transaction, and close the brace, as shown in the following code:

    ```
    static int DeleteProducts(string name)
    {
      using (var db = new Northwind())
      {
        using (IDbContextTransaction t = db.Database.BeginTransaction())
        {
          WriteLine("Transaction isolation level: {0}",
            t.GetDbTransaction().IsolationLevel);

          var products = db.Products.Where(
            p => p.ProductName.StartsWith(name));

          db.Products.RemoveRange(products);

          int affected = db.SaveChanges();
          t.Commit();
          return affected;
        }
    ```

```
    }
  }
```

3. Run the console application and view the result, as shown in the following output:

```
Transaction isolation level: Serializable
```

Practicing and exploring

Test your knowledge and understanding by answering some questions, get some hands-on practice, and explore this chapter's topics with deeper research.

Exercise 11.1 – Test your knowledge

Answer the following questions:

1. What type would you use for the property that represents a table, for example, the Products property of a database context?
2. What type would you use for the property that represents a one-to-many relationship, for example, the Products property of a Category entity?
3. What is the EF Core convention for primary keys?
4. When would you use an annotation attribute in an entity class?
5. Why might you choose the Fluent API in preference to annotation attributes?
6. What does a transaction isolation level of Serializable mean?
7. What does the DbContext.SaveChanges() method return?
8. What is the difference between eager loading and explicit loading?
9. How should you define an EF Core entity class to match the following table?

```
CREATE TABLE Employees(
  EmpID INT IDENTITY,
  FirstName NVARCHAR(40) NOT NULL,
  Salary MONEY
)
```

10. What benefit do you get from declaring entity navigation properties as virtual?

Exercise 11.2 – Practice exporting data using different serialization formats

Create a console application named Exercise02 that queries the Northwind database for all the categories and products, and then serializes the data using at least three formats of serialization available to .NET.

Which format of serialization uses the least number of bytes?

Exercise 11.3 – Explore the EF Core documentation

Use the following link to read more about the topics covered in this chapter:

```
https://docs.microsoft.com/en-us/ef/core/
```

Summary

In this chapter, you learned how to connect to a database, how to execute a simple LINQ query and process the results, how to use filtered includes, how to add, modify, and delete data, and how to build entity data models for an existing database, such as Northwind.

In the next chapter, you will learn how to write more advanced LINQ queries to select, filter, sort, join, and group.

12

Querying and Manipulating Data Using LINQ

This chapter is about **Language Integrated Query (LINQ)**, a set of language extensions that add the ability to work with sequences of items and then filter, sort, and project them into different outputs.

This chapter will cover the following topics:

- Writing LINQ queries
- Working with sets using LINQ
- Using LINQ with EF Core
- Sweetening LINQ syntax with syntactic sugar
- Using multiple threads with parallel LINQ
- Creating your own LINQ extension methods
- Working with LINQ to XML

Writing LINQ queries

Although we wrote a few LINQ queries in *Chapter 11, Working with Databases Using Entity Framework Core*, they weren't the focus, and so I didn't properly explain how LINQ works, but let's now take time to properly understand them.

LINQ has several parts; some are required, and some are optional:

- **Extension methods (required)**: These include examples such as Where, OrderBy, and Select. These are what provide the functionality of LINQ.

- **LINQ providers (required)**: These include LINQ to Objects, LINQ to Entities, LINQ to XML, LINQ to OData, and LINQ to Amazon. These are what convert standard LINQ operations into specific commands for different types of data.
- **Lambda expressions (optional)**: These can be used instead of named methods to simplify LINQ extension method calls.
- **LINQ query comprehension syntax (optional)**: These include `from`, `in`, `where`, `orderby`, `descending`, and `select`. These are C# keywords that are aliases for some of the LINQ extension methods, and their use can simplify the queries you write, especially if you already have experience with other query languages, such as **Structured Query Language (SQL)**.

When programmers are first introduced to LINQ, they often believe that LINQ query comprehension syntax is LINQ, but ironically, that is one of the parts of LINQ that is optional!

Extending sequences with the Enumerable class

The LINQ extension methods, such as `Where` and `Select`, are appended by the `Enumerable` static class to any type, known as a **sequence**, that implements `IEnumerable<T>`.

For example, an array of any type implements the `IEnumerable<T>` class, where `T` is the type of item in the array, so all arrays support LINQ to query and manipulate them.

All generic collections, such as `List<T>`, `Dictionary<TKey, TValue>`, `Stack<T>`, and `Queue<T>`, implement `IEnumerable<T>`, so they can be queried and manipulated with LINQ.

`Enumerable` defines more than 45 extension methods, as summarized in the following table:

Method(s)	Description
`First, FirstOrDefault, Last, LastOrDefault`	Gets the first or last item in the sequence or throws an exception, or returns the default value for the type, for example, 0 for an `int` and `null` for a reference type, if there is no first or last item.
`Where`	Returns a sequence of items that match a specified filter.
`Single, SingleOrDefault`	Returns an item that matches a specific filter or throws an exception, or returns the default value for the type, if there is not exactly one match.
`ElementAt, ElementAtOrDefault`	Returns an item at a specified index position or throws an exception, or returns the default value for the type, if there is not an item at that position.
`Select, SelectMany`	Projects items into a different shape, that is, type, and flattens a nested hierarchy of items.
`OrderBy, OrderByDescending, ThenBy, ThenByDescending`	Sorts items by a specified property.
`Reverse`	Reverses the order of items.
`GroupBy, GroupJoin, Join`	Group and join sequences.

Skip, SkipWhile	Skips a number of items or skips while an expression is true.
Take, TakeWhile	Take a number of items or take while an expression is true.
Aggregate, Average, Count, LongCount, Max, Min, Sum	Calculates aggregate values.
All, Any, Contains	Returns true if all or any of the items match the filter, or if the sequence contains a specified item.
Cast	Converts items into a specified type.
OfType	Removes items that do not match a specified type.
Except, Intersect, Union	Performs operations that return sets. Sets cannot have duplicate items. Although the inputs of these methods can be any sequence and so can have duplicates, the result is always a set.
Append, Concat, Prepend	Performs sequence-combining operations.
Zip	Performs a match operation on two sequences based on the position of items, for example, the item at position 1 in the first sequence matches the item at position 1 in the second sequence.
Distinct	Removes duplicate items from the sequence.
ToArray, ToList, ToDictionary, ToLookup	Converts the sequence into an array or collection.

Filtering entities with Where

The most common reason for using LINQ is to filter items in a sequence using the Where extension method. Let's explore filtering by defining a sequence of names and then applying LINQ operations to it:

1. In the Code folder, create a folder named Chapter12, with a subfolder named LinqWithObjects.

2. In Visual Studio Code, save a workspace as Chapter12.code-workspace in the Chapter12 folder.

3. Add the folder named LinqWithObjects to the workspace.

4. Navigate to **Terminal | New Terminal**.

5. In **TERMINAL**, enter the following command:

```
dotnet new console
```

6. In Program.cs, add a LinqWithArrayOfStrings method, which defines an array of string values and then attempts to call the Where extension method on it, as shown in the following code:

```
static void LinqWithArrayOfStrings()
{
  var names = new string[] { "Michael", "Pam", "Jim", "Dwight",
    "Angela", "Kevin", "Toby", "Creed" };
  var query = names.
}
```

7. As you type the `Where` method, note that it is missing from the IntelliSense list of members of a `string` array, as shown in the following screenshot:

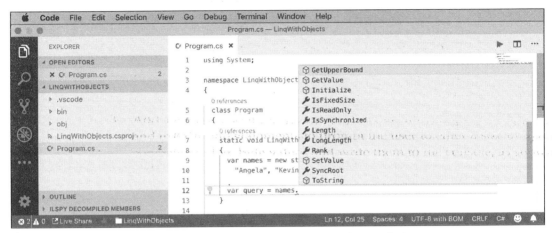

Figure 12.1: IntelliSense not showing the Where method

This is because `Where` is an **extension method**. It does not exist on the array type. To make the `Where` extension method available, we must import the `System.Linq` namespace.

8. Add the following statement to the top of the `Program.cs` file:

```
using System.Linq;
```

9. Retype the `Where` method and note that the IntelliSense list shows many more methods, including the extension methods added by the `Enumerable` class, as shown in the following screenshot:

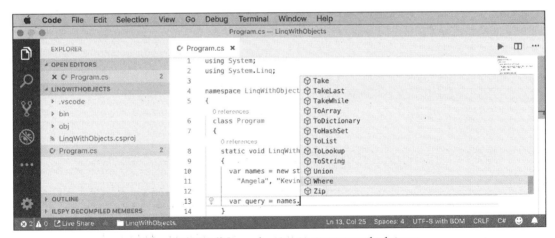

Figure 12.2: IntelliSense showing many more methods now

10. As you type the parentheses for the `Where` method, IntelliSense tells us that to call `Where`, we must pass in an instance of a `Func<string, bool>` delegate, as shown in the following screenshot:

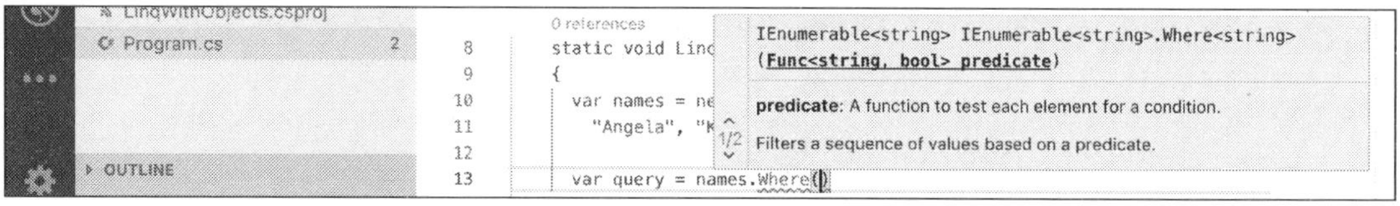

Figure 12.3: Method signature showing you must pass in a Func<string, bool> delegate

11. Enter an expression to create a new instance of a `Func<string, bool>` delegate, and for now note that we have not yet supplied a method name because we will define it in the next step, as shown in the following code:

```
var query = names.Where(new Func<string, bool>())
```

The `Func<string, bool>` delegate tells us that for each `string` variable passed to the method, the method must return a `bool` value. If the method returns `true`, it indicates that we should include the `string` in the results, and if the method returns `false`, it indicates that we should exclude it.

Targeting a named method

Let's define a method that only includes names that are longer than four characters:

1. Add a method to `Program`, as shown in the following code:
   ```
   static bool NameLongerThanFour(string name)
   {
       return name.Length > 4;
   }
   ```

2. Back in the `LinqWithArrayOfStrings` method, pass the method's name into the `Func<string, bool>` delegate, and then loop through the query items, as shown in the following code:
   ```
   var query = names.Where(
       new Func<string, bool>(NameLongerThanFour));

   foreach (string item in query)
   {
       WriteLine(item);
   }
   ```

3. In `Main`, call the `LinqWithArrayOfStrings` method, run the console application, and view the results, noting that only names longer than four letters are listed, as shown in the following output:

```
Michael
Dwight
Angela
Kevin
Creed
```

Simplifying the code by removing the explicit delegate instantiation

We can simplify the code by deleting the explicit instantiation of the `Func<string, bool>` delegate because the C# compiler can instantiate the delegate for us.

1. To help you learn by seeing progressively improved code, copy and paste the query.
2. Comment out the first example, as shown in the following code:

    ```
    // var query = names.Where(
    // new Func<string, bool>(NameLongerThanFour));
    ```

3. Modify the copy to remove the explicit instantiation of the delegate, as shown in the following code:

    ```
    var query = names.Where(NameLongerThanFour);
    ```

4. Rerun the application and note that it has the same behavior.

Targeting a lambda expression

We can simplify our code even further using a **lambda expression** in place of a named method.

Although it can look complicated at first, a lambda expression is simply a **nameless function**. It uses the => (read as "goes to") symbol to indicate the return value.

1. Copy and paste the query, comment the second example, and modify the query, as shown in the following code:

    ```
    var query = names.Where(name => name.Length > 4);
    ```

    Note that the syntax for a lambda expression includes all the important parts of the `NameLongerThanFour` method, but nothing more. A lambda expression only needs to define the following:

    *   The names of input parameters
    *   A return value expression

    The type of the name input parameter is inferred from the fact that the sequence contains `string` values, and the return type must be a `bool` value for `Where` to work, so the expression after the => symbol must return a `bool` value.

    The compiler does most of the work for us, so our code can be as concise as possible.

2. Rerun the application and note that it has the same behavior.

Sorting entities

Other commonly used extension methods are `OrderBy` and `ThenBy`, used for sorting a sequence.

Extension methods can be chained if the previous method returns another sequence, that is, a type that implements the `IEnumerable<T>` interface.

Sorting by a single property using OrderBy

Let's continue working with the current project to explore sorting.

1. Append a call to OrderBy to the end of the existing query, as shown in the following code:

```
var query = names
  .Where(name => name.Length > 4)
  .OrderBy(name => name.Length);
```

 Good Practice: Format the LINQ statement so that each extension method call happens on its own line to make them easier to read.

2. Rerun the application and note that the names are now sorted by shortest first, as shown in the following output:

```
Kevin
Creed
Dwight
Angela
Michael
```

To put the longest name first, you would use OrderByDescending.

Sorting by a subsequent property using ThenBy

We might want to sort by more than one property, for example, to sort names of the same length in alphabetical order.

1. Add a call to the ThenBy method at the end of the existing query, as shown highlighted in the following code:

```
var query = names
  .Where(name => name.Length > 4)
  .OrderBy(name => name.Length)
  .ThenBy(name => name);
```

2. Rerun the application and note the slight difference in the following sort order. Within a group of names of the same length, the names are sorted alphabetically by the full value of the string, so Creed comes before Kevin, and Angela comes before Dwight, as shown in the following output:

```
Creed
Kevin
Angela
Dwight
Michael
```

Filtering by type

Where is great for filtering by values, such as text and numbers. But what if the sequence contains multiple types, and you want to filter by a specific type and respect any inheritance hierarchy?

Imagine that you have a sequence of exceptions. Exceptions have a complex hierarchy, as shown in the following diagram:

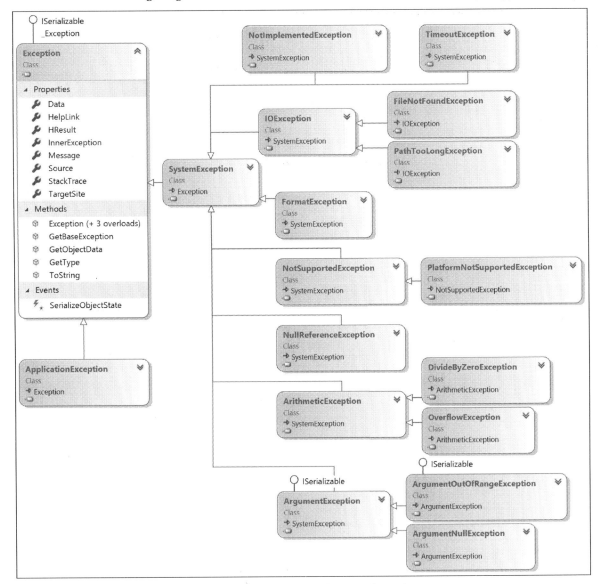

Figure 12.4: An exception's inheritance hierarchy

Let's explore filtering by type:

1. In `Program`, add a `LinqWithArrayOfExceptions` method, which defines an array of `Exception`-derived objects, as shown in the following code:

```
static void LinqWithArrayOfExceptions()
{
  var errors = new Exception[]
  {
    new ArgumentException(),
    new SystemException(),
    new IndexOutOfRangeException(),
    new InvalidOperationException(),
    new NullReferenceException(),
    new InvalidCastException(),
    new OverflowException(),
    new DivideByZeroException(),
    new ApplicationException()
  };
}
```

2. Write statements using the `OfType<T>` extension method to filter exceptions that are not arithmetic exceptions and write them to the console, as shown in the following code:

```
var numberErrors = errors.OfType<ArithmeticException>();

foreach (var error in numberErrors)
{
  WriteLine(error);
}
```

3. In the `Main` method, comment out the call to the `LinqWithArrayOfStrings` method and add a call to the `LinqWithArrayOfExceptions` method.

4. Run the console application and note that the results only include exceptions of the `ArithmeticException` type, or the `ArithmeticException`-derived types, as shown in the following output:

```
System.OverflowException: Arithmetic operation resulted in an overflow.
System.DivideByZeroException: Attempted to divide by zero.
```

Working with sets and bags using LINQ

Sets are one of the most fundamental concepts in mathematics. A **set** is a collection of one or more unique objects. A **multiset** or **bag** is a collection of one or more objects that can have duplicates. You might remember being taught about Venn diagrams in school. Common set operations include the **intersect** or **union** between sets.

Let's create a console application that will define three arrays of `string` values for cohorts of apprentices and then perform some common set and multiset operations on them.

1. Create a new console application project named `LinqWithSets`, add it to the workspace for this chapter, and select the project as active for `OmniSharp`.

2. Import the following additional namespaces:

```
using System.Collections.Generic; // for IEnumerable<T>
using System.Linq; // for LINQ extension methods
```

3. In `Program`, before the `Main` method, add the following method that outputs any sequence of `string` variables as a comma-separated single `string` to the console output, along with an optional description:

```
static void Output(IEnumerable<string> cohort,
  string description = "")
{
  if (!string.IsNullOrEmpty(description))
  {
    WriteLine(description);
  }
  Write(" ");
  WriteLine(string.Join(", ", cohort.ToArray()));
}
```

4. In `Main`, add statements to define three arrays of names, output them, and then perform various set operations on them, as shown in the following code:

```
var cohort1 = new string[]
  { "Rachel", "Gareth", "Jonathan", "George" };
var cohort2 = new string[]
  { "Jack", "Stephen", "Daniel", "Jack", "Jared" };
var cohort3 = new string[]
  { "Declan", "Jack", "Jack", "Jasmine", "Conor" };
Output(cohort1, "Cohort 1");
Output(cohort2, "Cohort 2");
Output(cohort3, "Cohort 3");
WriteLine();

Output(cohort2.Distinct(), "cohort2.Distinct():");
WriteLine();
Output(cohort2.Union(cohort3), "cohort2.Union(cohort3):");
WriteLine();
Output(cohort2.Concat(cohort3), "cohort2.Concat(cohort3):");
WriteLine();
Output(cohort2.Intersect(cohort3), "cohort2.Intersect(cohort3):");
WriteLine();
Output(cohort2.Except(cohort3), "cohort2.Except(cohort3):");
WriteLine();
Output(cohort1.Zip(cohort2,(c1, c2) => $"{c1} matched with {c2}"),
  "cohort1.Zip(cohort2):");
```

5. Run the console application and view the results, as shown in the following output:

```
Cohort 1
 Rachel, Gareth, Jonathan, George
Cohort 2
 Jack, Stephen, Daniel, Jack, Jared
Cohort 3
 Declan, Jack, Jack, Jasmine, Conor
cohort2.Distinct():
 Jack, Stephen, Daniel, Jared
cohort2.Union(cohort3):
 Jack, Stephen, Daniel, Jared, Declan, Jasmine, Conor
cohort2.Concat(cohort3):
 Jack, Stephen, Daniel, Jack, Jared, Declan, Jack, Jack, Jasmine, Conor
cohort2.Intersect(cohort3):
 Jack
cohort2.Except(cohort3):
 Stephen, Daniel, Jared
cohort1.Zip(cohort2):
 Rachel matched with Jack, Gareth matched with Stephen, Jonathan matched
with Daniel, George matched with Jack
```

With Zip, if there are unequal numbers of items in the two sequences, then some items will not have a matching partner. Those without a partner will not be included in the result.

Using LINQ with EF Core

To learn about **projection**, it is best to have some more complex sequences to work with, so in the next project, we will use the Northwind sample database.

Building an EF Core model

Let's define an **Entity Framework (EF)** Core model to represent the database and tables that we will work with. We will define the entity classes manually to take complete control and to prevent a relationship from being automatically defined. Later, you will use LINQ to join the two entity sets.

1. Create a new console application project named LinqWithEFCore, add it to the workspace for this chapter, and select the project as active for OmniSharp.

2. Modify the LinqWithEFCore.csproj file, as shown highlighted in the following markup:

```
<Project Sdk="Microsoft.NET.Sdk">
  <PropertyGroup>
    <OutputType>Exe</OutputType>
    <TargetFramework>net5.0</TargetFramework>
  </PropertyGroup>
```

```xml
  <ItemGroup>
    <PackageReference
      Include="Microsoft.EntityFrameworkCore.Sqlite"
      Version="5.0.0" />
  </ItemGroup>
</Project>
```

3. In **TERMINAL**, download the referenced package and compile the current project, as shown in the following command:

```
dotnet build
```

4. Copy the Northwind.sql file into the LinqWithEFCore folder, and then use **TERMINAL** to create the Northwind database by executing the following command:

```
sqlite3 Northwind.db -init Northwind.sql
```

5. Be patient because this command might take a while to create the database structure, as shown in the following output:

```
-- Loading resources from Northwind.sql
SQLite version 3.28.0 2019-04-15 14:49:49
Enter ".help" for usage hints.
sqlite>
```

6. Press *Ctrl* + *D* on macOS or *Ctrl* + *C* on Windows to exit SQLite command mode.

7. Add three class files to the project, named Northwind.cs, Category.cs, and Product.cs.

8. Modify the class file named Northwind.cs, as shown in the following code:

```csharp
using Microsoft.EntityFrameworkCore;

namespace Packt.Shared
{
  // this manages the connection to the database
  public class Northwind : DbContext
  {
    // these properties map to tables in the database
    public DbSet<Category> Categories { get; set; }
    public DbSet<Product> Products { get; set; }

    protected override void OnConfiguring(
      DbContextOptionsBuilder optionsBuilder)
    {
      string path = System.IO.Path.Combine(
        System.Environment.CurrentDirectory, "Northwind.db");
      optionsBuilder.UseSqlite($"Filename={path}");
    }

    protected override void OnModelCreating(
```

```
    ModelBuilder modelBuilder)
  {
    modelBuilder.Entity<Product>()
      .Property(product => product.UnitPrice)
      .HasConversion<double>();
  }
 }
}
```

9. Modify the class file named `Category.cs`, as shown in the following code:

```
using System.ComponentModel.DataAnnotations;

namespace Packt.Shared
{
  public class Category
  {
    public int CategoryID { get; set; }
    [Required]
    [StringLength(15)]
    public string CategoryName { get; set; }
    public string Description { get; set; }
  }
}
```

10. Modify the class file named `Product.cs`, as shown in the following code:

```
using System.ComponentModel.DataAnnotations;
namespace Packt.Shared
{
  public class Product
  {
    public int ProductID { get; set; }
    [Required]
    [StringLength(40)]
    public string ProductName { get; set; }
    public int? SupplierID { get; set; }
    public int? CategoryID { get; set; }
    [StringLength(20)]
    public string QuantityPerUnit { get; set; }
    public decimal? UnitPrice { get; set; }
    public short? UnitsInStock { get; set; }
    public short? UnitsOnOrder { get; set; }
    public short? ReorderLevel { get; set; }
    public bool Discontinued { get; set; }
  }
}
```

Filtering and sorting sequences

Now let's write statements to filter and sort sequences of rows from the tables.

1. Open the `Program.cs` file and import the following type and namespaces:

```
using static System.Console;
using Packt.Shared;
using Microsoft.EntityFrameworkCore;
using System.Linq;
```

2. Create a method to filter and sort products, as shown in the following code:

```
static void FilterAndSort()
{
  using (var db = new Northwind())
  {
    var query = db.Products
      // query is a DbSet<Product>
      .Where(product => product.UnitPrice < 10M)
      // query is now an IQueryable<Product>
      .OrderByDescending(product => product.UnitPrice);

    WriteLine("Products that cost less than $10:");
    foreach (var item in query)
    {
      WriteLine("{0}: {1} costs {2:$#,##0.00}",
        item.ProductID, item.ProductName, item.UnitPrice);
    }
    WriteLine();
  }
}
```

`DbSet<T>` implements `IQueryable<T>`, which implements `IEnumerable<T>`, so LINQ can be used to query and manipulate collections of entities in models built for EF Core.

You might have also noticed that the sequences implement `IQueryable<T>` (or `IOrderedQueryable<T>` after a call to an ordering LINQ method) instead of `IEnumerable<T>` or `IOrderedEnumerable<T>`.

This is an indication that we are using a LINQ provider that builds the query in memory using expression trees. They represent code in a tree-like data structure and enable the creation of dynamic queries, which is useful for building LINQ queries for external data providers like SQLite.

More Information: You can read more about expression trees at the following link: https://docs.microsoft.com/en-us/dotnet/csharp/programming-guide/concepts/expression-trees/

The LINQ query will be converted into another query language, such as SQL. Enumerating the query with `foreach` or calling a method such as `ToArray` will force the execution of the query.

3. In `Main`, call the `FilterAndSort` method.

4. Run the console application and view the result, as shown in the following output:

```
Products that cost less than $10:
41: Jack's New England Clam Chowder costs $9.65
45: Rogede sild costs $9.50
47: Zaanse koeken costs $9.50
19: Teatime Chocolate Biscuits costs $9.20
23: Tunnbröd costs $9.00
75: Rhönbräu Klosterbier costs $7.75
54: Tourtière costs $7.45
52: Filo Mix costs $7.00
13: Konbu costs $6.00
24: Guaraná Fantástica costs $4.50
33: Geitost costs $2.50
```

Although this query outputs the information we want, it does so inefficiently because it gets all columns from the `Products` table instead of just the three columns we need, which is the equivalent of the following SQL statement:

```
SELECT * FROM Products;
```

In *Chapter 11*, *Working with Databases Using Entity Framework Core*, you learned how to log the SQL commands executed against SQLite to see this for yourself.

Projecting sequences into new types

Before we look at projection, we need to review object initialization syntax. If you have a class defined, then you can instantiate an object using `new`, the class name, and curly braces to set initial values for fields and properties, as shown in the following code:

```
var alice = new Person
{
  Name = "Alice Jones",
  DateOfBirth = new DateTime(1998, 3, 7)
};
```

C# 3.0 and later allow instances of **anonymous types** to be instantiated, as shown in the following code:

```
var anonymouslyTypedObject = new
{
  Name = "Alice Jones",
  DateOfBirth = new DateTime(1998, 3, 7)
};
```

Although we did not specify a type name, the compiler could infer an anonymous type from the setting of two properties named Name and DateOfBirth. This capability is especially useful when writing LINQ queries to project an existing type into a new type without having to explicitly define the new type. Since the type is anonymous, this can only work with var-declared local variables.

Let's add a call to the Select method to make the SQL command executed against the database table more efficient by projecting instances of the Product class into instances of a new anonymous type with only three properties.

1. In Main, modify the LINQ query to use the Select method to return only the three properties (that is, table columns) that we need, as shown highlighted in the following code:

```
var query = db.Products
  // query is a DbSet<Product>
  .Where(product => product.UnitPrice < 10M)
  // query is now an IQueryable<Product>
  .OrderByDescending(product => product.UnitPrice)
  // query is now an IOrderedQueryable<Product>
  .Select(product => new // anonymous type
  {
    product.ProductID,
    product.ProductName,
    product.UnitPrice
  });
```

2. Run the console application and confirm that the output is the same as before.

Joining and grouping sequences

There are two extension methods for joining and grouping:

-   Join: This method has four parameters: the sequence that you want to join with, the property or properties on the *left* sequence to match on, the property or properties on the *right* sequence to match on, and a projection.

- **GroupJoin**: This method has the same parameters, but it combines the matches into a group object with a Key property for the matching value and an IEnumerable<T> type for the multiple matches.

Let's explore these methods when working with two tables: categories and products.

1. Create a method to select categories and products, join them, and output them, as shown in the following code:

```
static void JoinCategoriesAndProducts()
{
  using (var db = new Northwind())
  {
    // join every product to its category to return 77 matches
    var queryJoin = db.Categories.Join(
      inner: db.Products,
      outerKeySelector: category => category.CategoryID,
      innerKeySelector: product => product.CategoryID,
      resultSelector: (c, p) =>
        new { c.CategoryName, p.ProductName, p.ProductID });

    foreach (var item in queryJoin)
    {
      WriteLine("{0}: {1} is in {2}.",
        arg0: item.ProductID,
        arg1: item.ProductName,
        arg2: item.CategoryName);
    }
  }
}
```

In a join, there are two sequences, outer and inner. In the previous example, categories is the outer sequence and products is the inner sequence.

2. In Main, comment out the call to FilterAndSort and call JoinCategoriesAndProducts.

3. Run the console application and view the results. Note that there is a single line of output for each of the 77 products, as shown in the following output (edited to only include the first 10 items):

```
1: Chai is in Beverages.
2: Chang is in Beverages.
3: Aniseed Syrup is in Condiments.
4: Chef Anton's Cajun Seasoning is in Condiments.
5: Chef Anton's Gumbo Mix is in Condiments.
6: Grandma's Boysenberry Spread is in Condiments.
7: Uncle Bob's Organic Dried Pears is in Produce.
8: Northwoods Cranberry Sauce is in Condiments.
```

```
9: Mishi Kobe Niku is in Meat/Poultry.
10: Ikura is in Seafood.
```

4. At the end of the existing query, call the OrderBy method to sort by CategoryName, as shown in the following code:

```
.OrderBy(cp => cp.CategoryName);
```

5. Rerun the console application and view the results. Note that there is a single line of output for each of the 77 products, and the results show all products in the Beverages category first, then the Condiments category, and so on, as shown in the following partial output:

```
1: Chai is in Beverages.
2: Chang is in Beverages.
24: Guaraná Fantástica is in Beverages.
34: Sasquatch Ale is in Beverages.
35: Steeleye Stout is in Beverages.
38: Côte de Blaye is in Beverages.
39: Chartreuse verte is in Beverages.
43: Ipoh Coffee is in Beverages.
67: Laughing Lumberjack Lager is in Beverages.
70: Outback Lager is in Beverages.
75: Rhönbräu Klosterbier is in Beverages.
76: Lakkalikööri is in Beverages.
3: Aniseed Syrup is in Condiments.
4: Chef Anton's Cajun Seasoning is in Condiments.
```

6. Create a method to group and join, show the group name, and then show all the items within each group, as shown in the following code:

```csharp
static void GroupJoinCategoriesAndProducts()
{
  using (var db = new Northwind())
  {
    // group all products by their category to return 8 matches
    var queryGroup = db.Categories.AsEnumerable().GroupJoin(
      inner: db.Products,
      outerKeySelector: category => category.CategoryID,
      innerKeySelector: product => product.CategoryID,
      resultSelector: (c, matchingProducts) => new {
        c.CategoryName,
        Products = matchingProducts.OrderBy(p => p.ProductName)
      });

    foreach (var item in queryGroup)
    {
      WriteLine("{0} has {1} products.",
        arg0: item.CategoryName,
```

```
      arg1: item.Products.Count());

    foreach (var product in item.Products)
    {
      WriteLine($"  {product.ProductName}");
    }
    }
  }
}
```

If we had not called the `AsEnumerable` method, then a runtime exception is thrown, as shown in the following output:

```
Unhandled exception. System.NotImplementedException: The method or
operation is not implemented.
  at Microsoft.EntityFrameworkCore.Relational.Query.Pipeline.
RelationalQueryableMethodTranslatingExpressionVisitor.TranslateGroupJoin(S
hapedQueryExpression outer, ShapedQueryExpression inner, LambdaExpression
outerKeySelector, LambdaExpression innerKeySelector, LambdaExpression
resultSelector)
```

This is because not all LINQ extension methods can be converted from expression trees into other query syntax like SQL. In these cases, we can convert from `IQueryable<T>` to `IEnumerable<T>` by calling the `AsEnumerable` method, which forces query processing to use LINQ to EF Core only to bring the data into the application and then use LINQ to Objects to execute more complex processing in-memory. But, often, this is less efficient.

7. In `Main`, comment the previous method call and call `GroupJoinCategoriesAndProducts`.

8. Rerun the console application, view the results, and note that the products inside each category have been sorted by their name, as defined in the query and as shown in the following partial output:

```
Beverages has 12 products.
  Chai
  Chang
  Chartreuse verte
  Côte de Blaye
  Guaraná Fantástica
  Ipoh Coffee
  Lakkalikööri
  Laughing Lumberjack Lager
  Outback Lager
  Rhönbräu Klosterbier
  Sasquatch Ale
  Steeleye Stout
Condiments has 12 products.
  Aniseed Syrup
  Chef Anton's Cajun Seasoning
```

```
  Chef Anton's Gumbo Mix
  ...
```

Aggregating sequences

There are LINQ extension methods to perform aggregation functions, such as `Average` and `Sum`. Let's write some code to see some of these methods in action aggregating information from the `Products` table.

1. Create a method to show the use of the aggregation extension methods, as shown in the following code:

```
static void AggregateProducts()
{
  using (var db = new Northwind())
  {
    WriteLine("{0,-25} {1,10}",
      arg0: "Product count:",
      arg1: db.Products.Count());
    WriteLine("{0,-25} {1,10:$#,##0.00}",
      arg0: "Highest product price:",
      arg1: db.Products.Max(p => p.UnitPrice));
    WriteLine("{0,-25} {1,10:N0}",
      arg0: "Sum of units in stock:",
      arg1: db.Products.Sum(p => p.UnitsInStock));
    WriteLine("{0,-25} {1,10:N0}",
      arg0: "Sum of units on order:",
      arg1: db.Products.Sum(p => p.UnitsOnOrder));
    WriteLine("{0,-25} {1,10:$#,##0.00}",
      arg0: "Average unit price:",
      arg1: db.Products.Average(p => p.UnitPrice));
    WriteLine("{0,-25} {1,10:$#,##0.00}",
      arg0: "Value of units in stock:",
      arg1: db.Products.AsEnumerable()
        .Sum(p => p.UnitPrice * p.UnitsInStock));
  }
}
```

2. In `Main`, comment the previous method and call `AggregateProducts`.

3. Run the console application and view the result, as shown in the following output:

```
Product count:                    77
Highest product price:        $263.50
Sum of units in stock:          3,119
Sum of units on order:            780
Average unit price:            $28.87
Value of units in stock:  $74,050.85
```

In EF Core 3.0 and later, LINQ operations that cannot be translated to SQL are no longer automatically evaluated on the client side, so you must explicitly call AsEnumerable to force further processing of the query on the client.

> **More Information**: You can learn more about this breaking change at the following link: https://docs.microsoft.com/en-us/ef/core/what-is-new/ef-core-3.x/breaking-changes#linq-queries-are-no-longer-evaluated-on-the-client

Sweetening LINQ syntax with syntactic sugar

C# 3.0 introduced some new language keywords in 2008 in order to make it easier for programmers with experience with SQL to write LINQ queries. This **syntactic sugar** is sometimes called the **LINQ query comprehension syntax**.

> **More Information**: The LINQ query comprehension syntax is limited in functionality. It only provides C# keywords for the most commonly used LINQ features. You must use extension methods to access all the features of LINQ. You can read more about why it is called comprehension syntax at the following link: https://stackoverflow.com/questions/6229187/linq-why-is-it-called-comprehension-syntax

Consider the following array of string values:

```
var names = new string[] { "Michael", "Pam", "Jim", "Dwight",
  "Angela", "Kevin", "Toby", "Creed" };
```

To filter and sort the names, you could use **extension methods** and **lambda expressions**, as shown in the following code:

```
var query = names
  .Where(name => name.Length > 4)
  .OrderBy(name => name.Length)
  .ThenBy(name => name);
```

Or, you could achieve the same results by using **query comprehension syntax**, as shown in the following code:

```
var query = from name in names
  where name.Length > 4
  orderby name.Length, name
  select name;
```

The compiler changes the query comprehension syntax to the equivalent extension methods and lambda expressions for you.

The select keyword is always required for LINQ query comprehension syntax. The Select extension method is optional when using extension methods and lambda expressions because the whole item is implicitly selected.

Not all extension methods have a C# keyword equivalent, for example, the Skip and Take extension methods, which are commonly used to implement paging for lots of data.

A query that skips and takes cannot be written using only the query comprehension syntax, so we could write the query using all extension methods, as shown in the following code:

```
var query = names
  .Where(name => name.Length > 4)
  .Skip(80)
  .Take(10);
```

Or, you can wrap query comprehension syntax in parentheses and then switch to using extension methods, as shown in the following code:

```
var query = (from name in names
  where name.Length > 4
  select name)
  .Skip(80)
  .Take(10);
```

Good Practice: Learn both extension methods with lambda expressions and the query comprehension syntax ways of writing LINQ queries, because you are likely to have to maintain code that uses both.

Using multiple threads with parallel LINQ

By default, only one thread is used to execute a LINQ query. **Parallel LINQ (PLINQ)** is an easy way to enable multiple threads to execute a LINQ query.

Good Practice: Do not assume that using parallel threads will improve the performance of your applications. Always measure real-world timings and resource usage.

Creating an app that benefits from multiple threads

To see it in action, we will start with some code that only uses a single thread to square 2 billion integers. We will use the StopWatch type to measure the change in performance.

We will use operating system tools to monitor CPU and CPU core usage. If you do not have multiple CPUs or at least multiple cores, then this exercise won't show much!

1. Create a new console application project named `LinqInParallel`, add it to the workspace for this chapter, and select the project as active for OmniSharp.

2. Import the `System.Diagnostics` namespace so that we can use the `StopWatch` type, `System.Collections.Generic` so that we can use the `IEnumerable<T>` type, and `System.Linq` so that we can use LINQ; and statically import the `System.Console` type.

3. Add statements to `Main` to create a stopwatch to record timings, wait for a keypress before starting the timer, create 2 billion integers, square each of them, stop the timer, and display the elapsed milliseconds, as shown in the following code:

```
var watch = new Stopwatch();
Write("Press ENTER to start: ");
ReadLine();
watch.Start();

IEnumerable<int> numbers = Enumerable.Range(1, 2_000_000_000);

var squares = numbers.Select(number => number * number).ToArray();

watch.Stop();
WriteLine("{0:#,##0} elapsed milliseconds.",
    arg0: watch.ElapsedMilliseconds);
```

4. Run the console application, but do not press *Enter* to start yet.

Using Windows 10

1. If you are using Windows 10, then right-click on the Windows **Start** button or press *Ctrl + Alt + Delete*, and then click on **Task Manager**.

2. At the bottom of the **Task Manager** window, click on the **More details** button. At the top of the **Task Manager** window, click on the **Performance** tab.

3. Right-click on the **CPU Utilization** graph, choose **Change graph to**, and then select **Logical processors**.

Using macOS

1. If you are using macOS, then launch **Activity Monitor**.

2. Navigate to **View | Update Frequency Very often (1 sec)**.

3. To see the CPU graphs, navigate to **Window | CPU History**.

For all operating systems

1. Rearrange **Task Manager** or **CPU History** or your Linux tool and Visual Studio Code so that they are side by side.

2. Wait for the CPUs to settle and then press *Enter* to start the stopwatch and run the query. The result should be an amount of elapsed milliseconds, as shown in the following output and screenshot:

```
Press ENTER to start.
173,689 elapsed milliseconds.
```

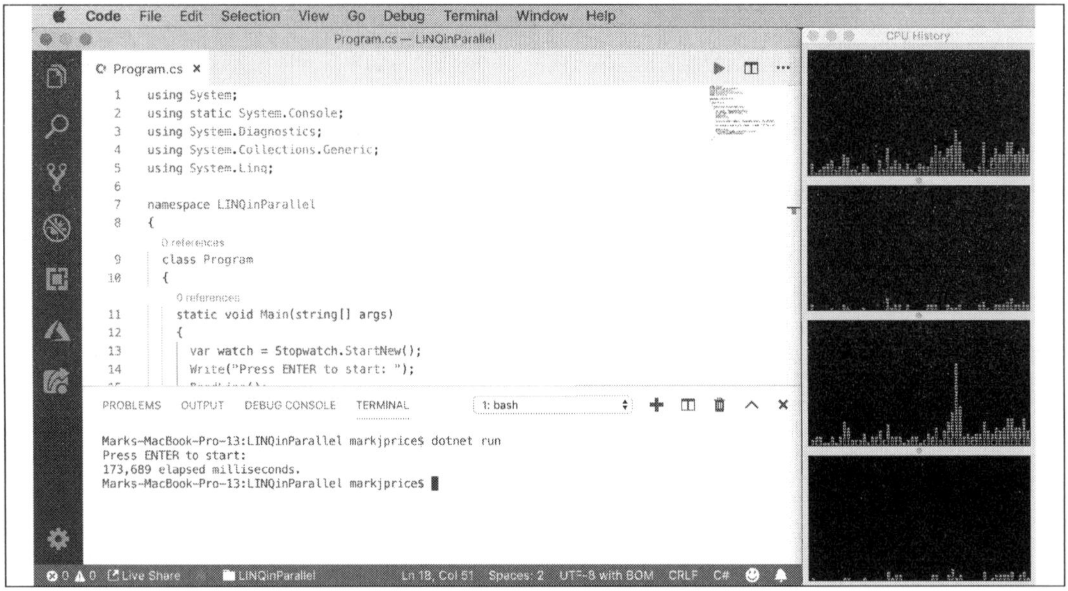

Figure 12.5: The app using a single thread

The **Task Manager** or **CPU History** windows should show that one or two CPUs were used the most. Others may execute background tasks at the same time, such as the garbage collector, so the other CPUs or cores won't be completely flat, but the work is certainly not being evenly spread among all the possible CPUs or cores.

3. In `Main`, modify the query to make a call to the `AsParallel` extension method, as shown in the following code:

```
var squares = numbers.AsParallel()
  .Select(number => number * number).ToArray();
```

4. Run the application again.

5. Wait for the **Task Manager** or **CPU History** windows to settle and then press *Enter* to start the stopwatch and run the query. This time, the application should complete in less time (although it might not be as less as you might hope for — managing those multiple threads takes extra effort!):

```
Press ENTER to start.
145,904 elapsed milliseconds.
```

6. The **Task Manager** or **CPU History** windows should show that all CPUs were used equally to execute the LINQ query, as shown in the following screenshot:

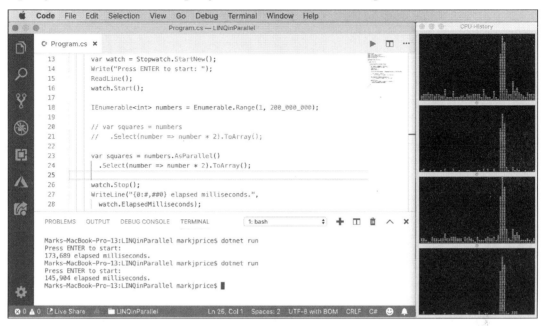

Figure 12.6: The app using multiple threads

You will learn more about managing multiple threads in *Chapter 13, Improving Performance and Scalability Using Multitasking*.

Creating your own LINQ extension methods

In *Chapter 6, Implementing Interfaces and Inheriting Classes*, you learned how to create your own extension methods. To create LINQ extension methods, all you must do is extend the `IEnumerable<T>` type.

> **Good Practice**: Put your own extension methods in a separate class library so that they can be easily deployed as their own assembly or NuGet package.

We will look at the `Average` extension method as an example. A well-educated school child will tell you that average can mean one of three things:

- **Mean**: Sum the numbers and divide by the count.
- **Mode**: The most common number.
- **Median**: The number in the middle of the numbers when ordered.

Microsoft's implementation of the `Average` extension method calculates the mean. We might want to define our own extension methods for `Mode` and `Median`.

1. In the `LinqWithEFCore` project, add a new class file named `MyLinqExtensions.cs`.

2. Modify the class, as shown in the following code:

```csharp
using System.Collections.Generic;

namespace System.Linq // extend Microsoft's namespace
{
  public static class MyLinqExtensions
  {
    // this is a chainable LINQ extension method
    public static IEnumerable<T> ProcessSequence<T>(
      this IEnumerable<T> sequence)
    {
      // you could do some processing here
      return sequence;
    }

    // these are scalar LINQ extension methods
    public static int? Median(this IEnumerable<int?> sequence)
    {
      var ordered = sequence.OrderBy(item => item);
      int middlePosition = ordered.Count() / 2;
      return ordered.ElementAt(middlePosition);
    }

    public static int? Median<T>(
      this IEnumerable<T> sequence, Func<T, int?> selector)
    {
      return sequence.Select(selector).Median();
    }

    public static decimal? Median(
      this IEnumerable<decimal?> sequence)
    {
      var ordered = sequence.OrderBy(item => item);
      int middlePosition = ordered.Count() / 2;
      return ordered.ElementAt(middlePosition);
    }

    public static decimal? Median<T>(
      this IEnumerable<T> sequence, Func<T, decimal?> selector)
    {
      return sequence.Select(selector).Median();
    }

    public static int? Mode(this IEnumerable<int?> sequence)
```

```
  {
    var grouped = sequence.GroupBy(item => item);
    var orderedGroups = grouped.OrderByDescending(
      group => group.Count());
    return orderedGroups.FirstOrDefault().Key;
  }

  public static int? Mode<T>(
    this IEnumerable<T> sequence, Func<T, int?> selector)
  {
    return sequence.Select(selector).Mode();
  }

  public static decimal? Mode(
    this IEnumerable<decimal?> sequence)
  {
    var grouped = sequence.GroupBy(item => item);
    var orderedGroups = grouped.OrderByDescending(
      group => group.Count());
    return orderedGroups.FirstOrDefault().Key;
  }

  public static decimal? Mode<T>(
    this IEnumerable<T> sequence, Func<T, decimal?> selector)
  {
    return sequence.Select(selector).Mode();
  }
  }
}
```

If this class was in a separate class library, to use your LINQ extension methods, you simply need to reference the class library assembly because the `System.Linq` namespace is often already imported.

3. In `Program.cs`, in the `FilterAndSort` method, modify the LINQ query for `Products` to call your custom chainable extension method, as shown highlighted in the following code:

```
var query = db.Products
  // query is a DbSet<Product>
  .ProcessSequence()
  .Where(product => product.UnitPrice < 10M)
  // query is now an IQueryable<Product>
  .OrderByDescending(product => product.UnitPrice)
  // query is now an IOrderedQueryable<Product>
  .Select(product => new // anonymous type
  {
```

```
      product.ProductID,
      product.ProductName,
      product.UnitPrice
  });
```

4. In the `Main` method, uncomment the `FilterAndSort` method and comment out any calls to other methods.

5. Run the console application and note that you see the same output as before because your method doesn't modify the sequence. But you now know how to extend LINQ with your own functionality.

6. Create a method to output the mean, median, and mode, for `UnitsInStock` and `UnitPrice` for products, using your custom extension methods and the built-in `Average` extension method, as shown in the following code:

```
static void CustomExtensionMethods()
{
  using (var db = new Northwind())
  {
    WriteLine("Mean units in stock: {0:N0}",
      db.Products.Average(p => p.UnitsInStock));
    WriteLine("Mean unit price: {0:$#,##0.00}",
      db.Products.Average(p => p.UnitPrice));
    WriteLine("Median units in stock: {0:N0}",
      db.Products.Median(p => p.UnitsInStock));
    WriteLine("Median unit price: {0:$#,##0.00}",
      db.Products.Median(p => p.UnitPrice));
    WriteLine("Mode units in stock: {0:N0}",
      db.Products.Mode(p => p.UnitsInStock));
    WriteLine("Mode unit price: {0:$#,##0.00}",
      db.Products.Mode(p => p.UnitPrice));
  }
}
```

7. In `Main`, comment any previous method calls and call `CustomExtensionMethods`.

8. Run the console application and view the result, as shown in the following output:

```
Mean units in stock: 41
Mean unit price: $28.87
Median units in stock: 26
Median unit price: $19.50
Mode units in stock: 0
Mode unit price: $18.00
```

There are four products with a unit price of $18.00. There are five products with 0 units in stock.

Working with LINQ to XML

LINQ to XML is a LINQ provider that allows you to query and manipulate XML.

Generating XML using LINQ to XML

Let's create a method to convert the Products table into XML.

1. In `Program.cs`, import the `System.Xml.Linq` namespace.
2. Create a method to output the products in XML format, as shown in the following code:

```
static void OutputProductsAsXml()
{
  using (var db = new Northwind())
  {
    var productsForXml = db.Products.ToArray();
    var xml = new XElement("products",
      from p in productsForXml
      select new XElement("product",
        new XAttribute("id", p.ProductID),
        new XAttribute("price", p.UnitPrice),
        new XElement("name", p.ProductName)));
    WriteLine(xml.ToString());
  }
}
```

3. In `Main`, comment the previous method call and call `OutputProductsAsXml`.
4. Run the console application, view the result, and note that the structure of the XML generated matches the elements and attributes that the LINQ to XML statement declaratively described in the preceding code, as shown in the following partial output:

```
<products>
  <product id="1" price="18">
    <name>Chai</name>
  </product>
  <product id="2" price="19">
    <name>Chang</name>
  </product>
...
```

Reading XML using LINQ to XML

You might want to use LINQ to XML to easily query or process XML files.

1. In the `LinqWithEFCore` project, add a file named `settings.xml`.

2. Modify its contents, as shown in the following markup:

```xml
<?xml version="1.0" encoding="utf-8" ?>
<appSettings>
  <add key="color" value="red" />
  <add key="size" value="large" />
  <add key="price" value="23.99" />
</appSettings>
```

3. Create a method to complete these tasks:

   - Load the XML file.

   - Use LINQ to XML to search for an element named appSettings and its descendants named add.

   - Project the XML into an array of an anonymous type with Key and Value properties.

   - Enumerate through the array to show the results:

```csharp
static void ProcessSettings()
{
  XDocument doc = XDocument.Load("settings.xml");
  var appSettings = doc.Descendants("appSettings")
    .Descendants("add")
    .Select(node => new
    {
      Key = node.Attribute("key").Value,
      Value = node.Attribute("value").Value
    }).ToArray();

  foreach (var item in appSettings)
  {
    WriteLine($"{item.Key}: {item.Value}");
  }
}
```

4. In Main, comment the previous method call and call ProcessSettings.

5. Run the console application and view the result, as shown in the following output:

```
color: red
size: large
price: 23.99
```

Practicing and exploring

Test your knowledge and understanding by answering some questions, get some hands-on practice, and explore with deeper research into the topics covered in this chapter.

Exercise 12.1 – Test your knowledge

Answer the following questions:

1. What are the two required parts of LINQ?
2. Which LINQ extension method would you use to return a subset of properties from a type?
3. Which LINQ extension method would you use to filter a sequence?
4. List five LINQ extension methods that perform aggregation.
5. What is the difference between the `Select` and `SelectMany` extension methods?
6. What is the difference between `IEnumerable<T>` and `IQueryable<T>`? And how do you switch between them?
7. What does the last type parameter in the generic `Func` delegates represent?
8. What is the benefit of a LINQ extension method that ends with `OrDefault`?
9. Why is query comprehension syntax optional?
10. How can you create your own LINQ extension methods?

Exercise 12.2 – Practice querying with LINQ

Create a console application, named `Exercise02`, that prompts the user for a city and then lists the company names for Northwind customers in that city, as shown in the following output:

```
Enter the name of a city: London
There are 6 customers in London:
Around the Horn
B's Beverages
Consolidated Holdings
Eastern Connection
North/South
Seven Seas Imports
```

Then, enhance the application by displaying a list of all unique cities that customers already reside in as a prompt to the user before they enter their preferred city, as shown in the following output:

```
Aachen, Albuquerque, Anchorage, Århus, Barcelona, Barquisimeto, Bergamo, Berlin,
Bern, Boise, Bräcke, Brandenburg, Bruxelles, Buenos Aires, Butte, Campinas,
Caracas, Charleroi, Cork, Cowes, Cunewalde, Elgin, Eugene, Frankfurt a.M.,
Genève, Graz, Helsinki, I. de Margarita, Kirkland, Kobenhavn, Köln, Lander,
Leipzig, Lille, Lisboa, London, Luleå, Lyon, Madrid, Mannheim, Marseille,
México D.F., Montréal, München, Münster, Nantes, Oulu, Paris, Portland, Reggio
Emilia, Reims, Resende, Rio de Janeiro, Salzburg, San Cristóbal, San Francisco,
Sao Paulo, Seattle, Sevilla, Stavern, Strasbourg, Stuttgart, Torino, Toulouse,
Tsawassen, Vancouver, Versailles, Walla Walla, Warszawa
```

Exercise 12.3 – Explore topics

Use the following links to read more details about the topics covered in this chapter:

- **LINQ in C#**: https://docs.microsoft.com/en-us/dotnet/csharp/linq/linq-in-csharp
- **101 LINQ Samples**: https://docs.microsoft.com/en-us/samples/dotnet/try-samples/101-linq-samples/
- **Parallel LINQ (PLINQ)**: https://docs.microsoft.com/en-us/dotnet/standard/parallel-programming/introduction-to-plinq
- **LINQ to XML Overview (C#)**: https://docs.microsoft.com/en-gb/dotnet/csharp/programming-guide/concepts/linq/linq-to-xml-overview
- **LINQPad**: https://www.linqpad.net/

Summary

In this chapter, you learned how to write LINQ queries to select, project, filter, sort, join, and group data in many different formats, including XML, which are tasks you will perform every day.

In the next chapter, you will use the Task type to improve the performance of your applications.

13

Improving Performance and Scalability Using Multitasking

This chapter is about allowing multiple actions to occur at the same time to improve performance, scalability, and user productivity for the applications that you build.

In this chapter, we will cover the following topics:

- Understanding processes, threads, and tasks
- Monitoring performance and resource usage
- Running tasks asynchronously
- Synchronizing access to shared resources
- Understanding `async` and `await`

Understanding processes, threads, and tasks

A **process**, with one example being each of the console applications we have created, has resources like memory and threads allocated to it. A **thread** executes your code, statement by statement. By default, each process only has one thread, and this can cause problems when we need to do more than one **task** at the same time. Threads are also responsible for keeping track of things like the currently authenticated user and any internationalization rules that should be followed for the current language and region.

Windows and most other modern operating systems use **preemptive multitasking**, which simulates the parallel execution of tasks. It divides the processor time among the threads, allocating a **time slice** to each thread one after another. The current thread is suspended when its time slice finishes. The processor then allows another thread to run for a time slice.

When Windows switches from one thread to another, it saves the context of the thread and reloads the previously saved context of the next thread in the thread queue. This takes both time and resources to complete.

Threads have a `Priority` property and a `ThreadState` property. In addition, there is a `ThreadPool` class, which is for managing a pool of background worker threads, as shown in the following diagram:

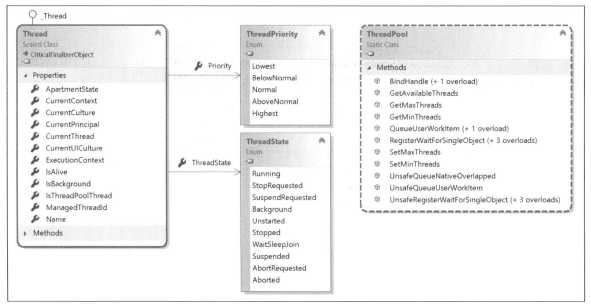

Figure 13.1: The Thread class and related types

As a developer, if you have a small number of complex pieces of work and you want complete control over them, then you can create and manage individual `Thread` instances. If you have one main thread and multiple small pieces of work that can be executed in the background, then you can add delegate instances that point to those pieces of work implemented as methods to a queue, and they will be automatically allocated to threads in the thread pool.

More Information: You can read more about the thread pool at the following link: `https://docs.microsoft.com/en-us/dotnet/standard/threading/the-managed-thread-pool`

Threads may have to compete for and also wait for access to shared resources, such as variables, files, and database objects.

Depending on the task, doubling the number of threads (workers) to perform a task does not halve the number of seconds that it will take to complete that task. In fact, it can *increase* the duration of the task, as pointed out in the following tweet:

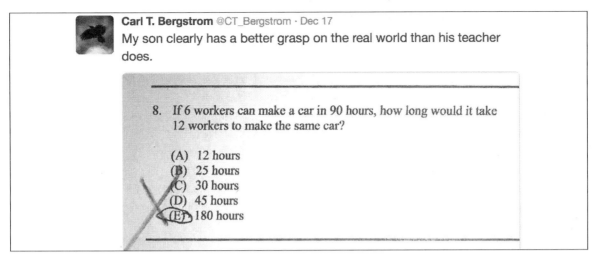

Figure 13.2: Doubling the number of workers doesn't necessarily half the time to complete a task

Good Practice: Never assume that more threads will improve performance! Run performance tests on a baseline code implementation without multiple threads, and then again on a code implementation with multiple threads. You should also perform performance tests in a staging environment that is as close as possible to the production environment.

Monitoring performance and resource usage

Before we can improve the performance of any code, we need to be able to monitor its speed and efficiency in order to record a baseline that we can then measure improvements from.

Evaluating the efficiency of types

What is the best type to use for a scenario? To answer this question, we need to carefully consider what we mean by *best*, and through this, we should consider the following factors:

- **Functionality**: This can be decided by checking whether the type provides the features you need.
- **Memory size**: This can be decided by the number of bytes of memory the type takes up.
- **Performance**: This can be decided by how fast the type is.
- **Future needs**: This depends on the changes in requirements and maintainability.

There will be scenarios, such as when storing numbers, where multiple types have the same functionality, so we will need to consider memory and performance to make a choice.

If we need to store millions of numbers, then the best type to use would be the one that requires the least bytes of memory. But if we only need to store a few numbers, yet we need to perform lots of calculations on them, then the best type to use would be the one that runs fastest on a specific CPU.

You have seen the use of the `sizeof()` function, which shows the number of bytes a single instance of a type uses in memory. When we are storing a large number of values in more complex data structures, such as arrays and lists, then we need a better way of measuring memory usage.

You can read lots of advice online and in books, but the only way to know for sure what the best type would be for your code is to compare the types yourself.

In the next section, you will learn how to write code to monitor the actual memory requirements and performance when using different types.

Today a `short` variable might be the best choice, but it might be an even better choice to use an `int` variable, even though it takes twice as much space in the memory. This is because we might need a wider range of values to be stored in the future.

There is another metric we should consider: **maintenance**. This is a measure of how much effort another programmer would have to put in to understand and modify your code. If you use a nonobvious type choice without explaining that choice with a helpful comment, then it might confuse the programmer who comes along later and needs to fix a bug or add a feature.

Monitoring performance and memory use

The `System.Diagnostics` namespace has lots of useful types for monitoring your code. The first one we will look at is the `Stopwatch` type:

1. In the `Code` folder, create a folder named `Chapter13` with two subfolders named `MonitoringLib` and `MonitoringApp`.
2. In Visual Studio Code, save a workspace as `Chapter13.code-workspace`.
3. Add the folder named `MonitoringLib` to the workspace, open a new **TERMINAL** window for it, and create a new class library project, as shown in the following command:

```
dotnet new classlib
```

4. Add the folder named `MonitoringApp` to the workspace, open a new **TERMINAL** window for it, and create a new console app project, as shown in the following command:

```
dotnet new console
```

5. In the `MonitoringLib` project, rename the `Class1.cs` file to `Recorder.cs`.
6. In the `MonitoringApp` project, open `MonitoringApp.csproj` and add a project reference to the `MonitoringLib` class library, as shown highlighted in the following markup:

```
<Project Sdk="Microsoft.NET.Sdk">
  <PropertyGroup>
    <OutputType>Exe</OutputType>
    <TargetFramework>net5.0</TargetFramework>
  </PropertyGroup>
  <ItemGroup>
```

```
    <ProjectReference
      Include="..\MonitoringLib\MonitoringLib.csproj" />
  </ItemGroup>
</Project>
```

7. In **TERMINAL**, compile the projects, as shown in the following command:

```
dotnet build
```

Implementing the Recorder class

We will create a `Recorder` class that makes it easy to monitor time and memory resource usage.

The `Stopwatch` type has some useful members, as shown in the following table:

Member	Description
`Restart` method	This resets the elapsed time to zero and then starts the timer.
`Stop` method	This stops the timer.
`Elapsed` property	This is the elapsed time stored as a TimeSpan format (for example, hours:minutes:seconds)
`ElapsedMilliseconds` property	This is the elapsed time in milliseconds stored as a long.

The `Process` type has some useful members, as shown in the following table:

Member	Description
`VirtualMemorySize64`	This displays the amount of virtual memory, in bytes, allocated for the process.
`WorkingSet64`	This displays the amount of physical memory, in bytes, allocated for the process.

To implement our `Recorder` class, we will use the `Stopwatch` and `Process` classes:

1. Open `Recorder.cs`, and change its contents to use a `Stopwatch` instance to record timings and the current `Process` instance to record memory usage, as shown in the following code:

```
using System;
using System.Diagnostics;
using static System.Console;
using static System.Diagnostics.Process;

namespace Packt.Shared
{
  public static class Recorder
  {
    static Stopwatch timer = new Stopwatch();

    static long bytesPhysicalBefore = 0;
```

```
    static long bytesVirtualBefore = 0;

    public static void Start()
    {
      // force two garbage collections to release memory that is
      // no longer referenced but has not been released yet
      GC.Collect();
      GC.WaitForPendingFinalizers();
      GC.Collect();

      // store the current physical and virtual memory use
      bytesPhysicalBefore = GetCurrentProcess().WorkingSet64;
      bytesVirtualBefore = GetCurrentProcess().VirtualMemorySize64;
      timer.Restart();
    }

    public static void Stop()
    {
      timer.Stop();
      long bytesPhysicalAfter = GetCurrentProcess().WorkingSet64;
      long bytesVirtualAfter =
        GetCurrentProcess().VirtualMemorySize64;
      WriteLine("{0:N0} physical bytes used.",
        bytesPhysicalAfter - bytesPhysicalBefore);
      WriteLine("{0:N0} virtual bytes used.",
        bytesVirtualAfter - bytesVirtualBefore);
      WriteLine("{0} time span ellapsed.", timer.Elapsed);
      WriteLine("{0:N0} total milliseconds ellapsed.",
        timer.ElapsedMilliseconds);
    }
  }
}
```

The `Start` method of the `Recorder` class uses the garbage collector (the `GC` class) type to ensure that any currently allocated but not referenced memory is collected before recording the amount of used memory. This is an advanced technique that you should almost never use in application code.

2. In the `Program` class, in `Main`, write statements to start and stop the `Recorder` while generating an array of 10,000 integers, as shown in the following code:

```
using System;
using System.Linq;
using Packt.Shared;
using static System.Console;

namespace MonitoringApp
```

```
{
  class Program
  {
    static void Main(string[] args)
    {
      WriteLine("Processing. Please wait...");
      Recorder.Start();

      // simulate a process that requires some memory resources...
      int[] largeArrayOfInts =
        Enumerable.Range(1, 10_000).ToArray();

      // ...and takes some time to complete
      System.Threading.Thread.Sleep(
        new Random().Next(5, 10) * 1000);

      Recorder.Stop();
    }
  }
}
```

3. Run the console application and view the result, as shown in the following output:

```
Processing. Please wait...
655,360 physical bytes used.
536,576 virtual bytes used.
00:00:09.0038702 time span ellapsed.
9,003 total milliseconds ellapsed.
```

Measuring the efficiency of processing strings

Now that you've seen how the Stopwatch and Process types can be used to monitor your code, we will use them to evaluate the best way to process string variables.

1. Comment out the previous statements in the Main method by wrapping them in /* */.

2. Add statements to the Main method to create an array of 50,000 int variables and then concatenate them with commas as separators using a string and StringBuilder class, as shown in the following code:

```
int[] numbers = Enumerable.Range(1, 50_000).ToArray();

WriteLine("Using string with +");
Recorder.Start();
string s = "";
for (int i = 0; i < numbers.Length; i++)
{
  s += numbers[i] + ", ";
```

```
    }
    Recorder.Stop();

    WriteLine("Using StringBuilder");
    Recorder.Start();
    var builder = new System.Text.StringBuilder();
    for (int i = 0; i < numbers.Length; i++)
    {
        builder.Append(numbers[i]); builder.Append(", ");
    }
    Recorder.Stop();
```

3. Run the console application and view the result, as shown in the following output:

```
Using string with +
10,883,072 physical bytes used.
1,609,728 virtual bytes used.
00:00:02.6220879 time span ellapsed.
2,622 total milliseconds ellapsed.
Using StringBuilder
4,096 physical bytes used.
0 virtual bytes used.
00:00:00.0014265 time span ellapsed.
1 total milliseconds ellapsed.
```

We can summarize the results as follows:

- The `string` class with the + operator used about 11 MB of physical memory, 1.5 MB of virtual memory, and took 2.6 seconds.

- The `StringBuilder` class used 4 KB of physical memory, 0 virtual memory, and took only 1 millisecond.

In this scenario, `StringBuilder` is more than 1,000 times faster and about 10,000 times more memory efficient when concatenating text!

 Good Practice: Avoid using the `String.Concat` method or the + operator inside loops. Use `StringBuilder` instead.

Now that you've learned how to measure the performance and resource efficiency of your code, let's learn about processes, threads, and tasks.

Running tasks asynchronously

To understand how multiple tasks can be run simultaneously (at the same time), we will create a console application that needs to execute three methods.

There will be three methods that need to be executed: the first takes 3 seconds, the second takes 2 seconds, and the third takes 1 second. To simulate that work, we can use the Thread class to tell the current thread to go to sleep for a specified number of milliseconds.

Running multiple actions synchronously

Before we make the tasks run simultaneously, we will run them synchronously, that is, one after the other.

1. Create a new console application named WorkingWithTasks, add its folder to your Chapter13 workspace, and select the project as active for OmniSharp.

2. In Program.cs, import namespaces to work with threading and tasks, as shown in the following code:

```
using System;
using System.Threading;
using System.Threading.Tasks;
using System.Diagnostics;
using static System.Console;
```

3. In the Program class, add the three methods, as shown in the following code:

```
static void MethodA()
{
  WriteLine("Starting Method A...");
  Thread.Sleep(3000); // simulate three seconds of work
  WriteLine("Finished Method A.");
}

static void MethodB()
{
  WriteLine("Starting Method B...");
  Thread.Sleep(2000); // simulate two seconds of work
  WriteLine("Finished Method B.");
}

static void MethodC()
{
  WriteLine("Starting Method C...");
  Thread.Sleep(1000); // simulate one second of work
  WriteLine("Finished Method C.");
}
```

4. In `Main`, add statements to define a stopwatch and output the milliseconds elapsed, as shown in the following code:

```
static void Main(string[] args)
{
    var timer = Stopwatch.StartNew();
    WriteLine("Running methods synchronously on one thread.");
    MethodA();
    MethodB();
    MethodC();
    WriteLine($"{timer.ElapsedMilliseconds:#,##0}ms elapsed.");
}
```

5. Run the console application, view the result, and note that when there is only one thread doing the work, the total time required is just over 6 seconds, as shown in the following output:

```
Running methods synchronously on one thread.
Starting Method A...
Finished Method A.
Starting Method B...
Finished Method B.
Starting Method C...
Finished Method C.
6,015ms elapsed.
```

Running multiple actions asynchronously using tasks

The `Thread` class has been available since the first version of .NET and can be used to create new threads and manage them, but it can be tricky to work with directly.

.NET Framework 4.0 introduced the `Task` class in 2010, which is a wrapper around a thread that enables easier creation and management. Managing multiple threads wrapped in tasks will allow our code to execute at the same time, aka asynchronously.

Each `Task` has a `Status` property, and a `CreationOptions` property has a `ContinueWith` method that can be customized with the `TaskContinuationOptions` enum, and can be managed with the `TaskFactory` class, as shown in the following diagram:

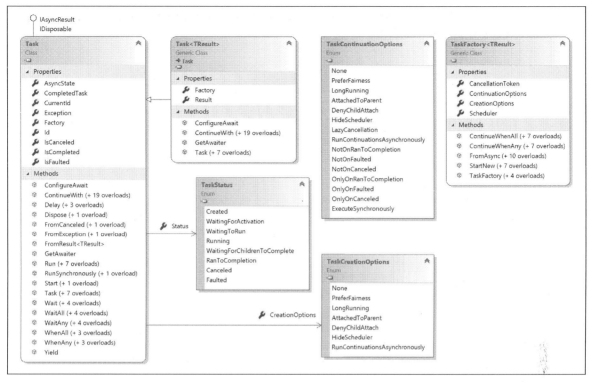

Figure 13.3: The Task class and related types

We will look at three ways to start the methods using `Task` instances. Each has a slightly different syntax, but they all define a `Task` and start it:

1. Comment out the calls to the three methods and the associated console message.

2. Add statements to create and start three tasks, one for each method, as shown in the following code:

```
static void Main(string[] args)
{
  var timer = Stopwatch.StartNew();
  // WriteLine("Running methods synchronously on one thread.");
  // MethodA();
  // MethodB();
  // MethodC();

  WriteLine("Running methods asynchronously on multiple threads.");
  Task taskA = new Task(MethodA);
  taskA.Start();
  Task taskB = Task.Factory.StartNew(MethodB);
  Task taskC = Task.Run(new Action(MethodC));
  WriteLine($"{timer.ElapsedMilliseconds:#,##0}ms elapsed.");
}
```

3. Run the console application, view the result, and note that the elapsed milliseconds appear almost immediately. This is because each of the three methods is now being executed by three *new* threads and the original thread can, therefore, write the elapsed time before they finish, as shown in the following output:

```
Running methods asynchronously on multiple threads.
Starting Method A...
Starting Method B...
Starting Method C...
3ms elapsed.
```

It is even possible that the console app will end before one or more of the tasks have a chance to start and write to the console!

 More Information: You can read more about the pros and cons of different ways to start tasks at the following link: https://devblogs.microsoft.com/pfxteam/task-factory-startnew-vs-new-task-start/

Waiting for tasks

Sometimes, you need to wait for a task to complete before continuing. To do this, you can use the Wait method on a Task instance, or the WaitAll or WaitAny static methods on an array of tasks, as described in the following table:

Method	Description
t.Wait()	This waits for the task instance named t to complete execution.
Task.WaitAny(Task[])	This waits for any of the tasks in the array to complete execution.
Task.WaitAll(Task[])	This waits for all the tasks in the array to complete execution.

Let's see how we can use these wait methods to fix the problem with our console app.

1. Add statements to the Main method (after creating the three tasks and before outputting the elapsed time) to combine references to the three tasks into an array and pass them to the WaitAll method, as shown in the following code:

```
Task[] tasks = { taskA, taskB, taskC };
Task.WaitAll(tasks);
```

Now, the original thread will pause on that statement, waiting for all three tasks to finish before outputting the elapsed time.

2. Run the console application and view the result, as shown in the following output:

```
Running methods asynchronously on multiple threads.
Starting Method C...
Starting Method A...
Starting Method B...
```

```
Finished Method C.
Finished Method B.
Finished Method A.
3,006ms elapsed.
```

The three new threads execute their code simultaneously, and they start in any order. `MethodC` should finish first because it takes only 1 second, then `MethodB`, which takes 2 seconds, and finally `MethodA`, because it takes 3 seconds.

However, the actual CPU used has a big effect on the results. It is the CPU that allocates time slices to each process to allow them to execute their threads. You have no control over when the methods run.

Continuing with another task

If all three tasks can be performed at the same time, then waiting for all tasks to finish will be all we need to do. However, often a task is dependent on the output from another task. To handle this scenario, we need to define **continuation tasks**.

We will create some methods to simulate a call to a web service that returns a monetary amount that then needs to be used to retrieve how many products cost more than that amount in a database. The result returned from the first method needs to be fed into the input of the second method. We will use the `Random` class to wait for a random interval between 2 and 4 seconds for each method call to simulate the work.

1. Add two methods to the `Program` class that simulate calling a web service and a database-stored procedure, as shown in the following code:

    ```
    static decimal CallWebService()
    {
      WriteLine("Starting call to web service...");
      Thread.Sleep((new Random()).Next(2000, 4000));
      WriteLine("Finished call to web service.");
      return 89.99M;
    }

    static string CallStoredProcedure(decimal amount)
    {
      WriteLine("Starting call to stored procedure...");
      Thread.Sleep((new Random()).Next(2000, 4000));
      WriteLine("Finished call to stored procedure.");
      return $"12 products cost more than {amount:C}.";
    }
    ```

2. In the `Main` method, comment out the previous three tasks by wrapping them in multiline comment characters, `/* */`. Leave the statement that outputs the elapsed milliseconds.

3. Add statements before the existing statement to output the total time elapsed and then call `ReadLine` to wait for the user to press `Enter`, as shown in the following code:

```
WriteLine("Passing the result of one task as an input into another.");
var taskCallWebServiceAndThenStoredProcedure =
  Task.Factory.StartNew(CallWebService)
    .ContinueWith(previousTask =>
      CallStoredProcedure(previousTask.Result));
WriteLine($"Result: {taskCallWebServiceAndThenStoredProcedure.Result}");
```

4. Run the console application and view the result, as shown in the following output:

```
Passing the result of one task as an input into another.
Starting call to web service...
Finished call to web service.
Starting call to stored procedure...
Finished call to stored procedure.
Result: 12 products cost more than £89.99.
5,971ms elapsed.
```

Nested and child tasks

As well as defining dependencies between tasks, you can define nested and child tasks. A **nested task** is a task that is created inside another task. A **child task** is a nested task that must finish before its parent task is allowed to finish.

Let's explore how these types of task work:

1. Create a new console application named `NestedAndChildTasks`, add it to the `Chapter13` workspace, and select the project as active for OmniSharp.

2. In `Program.cs`, import namespaces to work with threads and tasks, as shown in the following code:

```
using System;
using System.Threading;
using System.Threading.Tasks;
using System.Diagnostics;
using static System.Console;
```

3. Add two methods, one of which starts a task to run the other, as shown in the following code:

```
static void OuterMethod()
{
  WriteLine("Outer method starting...");
```

```
    var inner = Task.Factory.StartNew(InnerMethod);
    WriteLine("Outer method finished.");
}
static void InnerMethod()
{
    WriteLine("Inner method starting...");
    Thread.Sleep(2000);
    WriteLine("Inner method finished.");
}
```

4. In `Main`, add statements to start a task to run the outer method and wait for it to finish before stopping, as shown in the following code:

```
var outer = Task.Factory.StartNew(OuterMethod);
outer.Wait();
WriteLine("Console app is stopping.");
```

5. Run the console application and view the result, as shown in the following output:

```
Outer method starting...
Outer method finished.
Console app is stopping.
Inner method starting...
```

Note that, although we wait for the outer task to finish, its inner task does not have to finish as well. In fact, the outer task might finish, and the console app could end, before the inner task even starts! To link these nested tasks, we must use a special option.

6. Modify the existing code that defines the inner task to add a `TaskCreationOption` value of `AttachedToParent`, as shown highlighted in the following code:

```
var inner = Task.Factory.StartNew(InnerMethod,
    TaskCreationOptions.AttachedToParent);
```

7. Run the console application, view the result, and note that the inner task must finish before the outer task can, as shown in the following output:

```
Outer method starting...
Outer method finished.
Inner method starting...
Inner method finished.
Console app is stopping.
```

The `OuterMethod` can finish before the `InnerMethod`, as shown by its writing to the console, but its task must wait, as shown by the console not stopping until both the outer and inner tasks finish.

Synchronizing access to shared resources

When you have multiple threads executing at the same time, there is a possibility that two or more of the threads may access the same variable or another resource at the same time, and as a result, may cause a problem. For this reason, you should carefully consider how to make your code *thread-safe*.

The simplest mechanism for implementing thread safety is to use an object variable as a *flag* or *traffic light* to indicate when a shared resource has an exclusive lock applied.

In William Golding's *Lord of the Flies*, Piggy and Ralph spot a conch shell and use it to call a meeting. The boys impose a "rule of the conch" on themselves, deciding that no one can speak unless they're holding the conch.

I like to name the object variable I use for implementing thread-safe code the "conch." When a thread has the conch, no other thread can access the shared resource(s) represented by that conch.

We will explore a couple of types that can be used to synchronize access to resources:

- `Monitor`: A flag to prevent multiple threads from accessing a resource simultaneously within the same process.
- `Interlocked`: An object for manipulating simple numeric types at the CPU level.

Accessing a resource from multiple threads

1. Create a console application named `SynchronizingResourceAccess`, add it to the `Chapter13` workspace, and select the project as active for OmniSharp.

2. Import namespaces for working with threads and tasks, as shown in the following code:

```
using System;
using System.Threading;
using System.Threading.Tasks;
using System.Diagnostics;
using static System.Console;
```

3. In `Program`, add statements to do the following:

   - Declare and instantiate an object to generate random wait times.
   - Declare a `string` variable to store a message (this is the shared resource).
   - Declare two methods that add a letter, `A` or `B`, to the shared `string` five times in a loop, and wait for a random interval of up to 2 seconds for each iteration:

```
static Random r = new Random();
static string Message; // a shared resource

static void MethodA()
{
  for (int i = 0; i < 5; i++)
  {
    Thread.Sleep(r.Next(2000));
    Message += "A";
    Write(".");
  }
}

static void MethodB()
{
  for (int i = 0; i < 5; i++)
  {
    Thread.Sleep(r.Next(2000));
    Message += "B";
    Write(".");
  }
}
```

4. In `Main`, execute both methods on separate threads using a pair of tasks and wait for them to complete before outputting the elapsed milliseconds, as shown in the following code:

```
WriteLine("Please wait for the tasks to complete.");
Stopwatch watch = Stopwatch.StartNew();
Task a = Task.Factory.StartNew(MethodA);
Task b = Task.Factory.StartNew(MethodB);
Task.WaitAll(new Task[] { a, b });
WriteLine();
WriteLine($"Results: {Message}.");
WriteLine($"{watch.ElapsedMilliseconds:#,##0} elapsed milliseconds.");
```

5. Run the console application and view the result, as shown in the following output:

```
Please wait for the tasks to complete.
..........
Results: BABABAABBA.
5,753 elapsed milliseconds.
```

This shows that both threads were modifying the message concurrently. In an actual application, this could be a problem. But we can prevent concurrent access by applying a mutually exclusive lock to the resource, which we will do in the following section.

Applying a mutually exclusive lock to a resource

Now, let's use a conch to ensure that only one thread has access to the shared resource at a time.

1. In `Program`, declare and instantiate an object variable to act as a *conch*, as shown in the following code:

   ```
   static object conch = new object();
   ```

2. In both `MethodA` and `MethodB`, add a `lock` statement around the `for` statement, as shown in the following code:

   ```
   lock (conch)
   {
     for (int i = 0; i < 5; i++)
     {
       Thread.Sleep(r.Next(2000));
       Message += "A";
       Write(".");
     }
   }
   ```

3. Run the console application and view the result, as shown in the following output:

   ```
   Please wait for the tasks to complete.
   ..........
   Results: BBBBBAAAAA.
   10,345 elapsed milliseconds.
   ```

Although the time elapsed was longer, only one method at a time could access the shared resource. Either `MethodA` or `MethodB` can start first. Once a method has finished its work on the shared resource, then the conch gets released, and the other method has the chance to do its work.

Understanding the lock statement and avoiding deadlocks

You might wonder how the `lock` statement works when it *locks* an object variable, as shown in the following code:

```
lock (conch)
{
  // work with shared resource
}
```

The C# compiler changes the `lock` statement into a `try-finally` statement that uses the `Monitor` class to enter and exit the conch object variable, as shown in the following code:

```
try
{
  Monitor.Enter(conch);
  // work with shared resource
}
finally
{
  Monitor.Exit(conch);
}
```

Knowing how the lock statement works internally is important because using the lock statement can cause a deadlock.

Deadlocks occur when there are two or more shared resources (and therefore conches), and the following sequence of events happens:

- Thread X locks conch A.
- Thread Y locks conch B.
- Thread X attempts to lock conch B but is blocked because thread Y already has it.
- Thread Y attempts to lock conch A but is blocked because thread X already has it.

A proven way to prevent deadlocks is to specify a timeout when attempting to get a lock. To do this, you must manually use the Monitor class instead of using the lock statement.

1. Modify your code to replace the lock statements with code that tries to enter the conch with a timeout, as shown in the following code:

    ```
    try
    {
      if (Monitor.TryEnter(conch, TimeSpan.FromSeconds(15)))
      {
        for (int i = 0; i < 5; i++)
        {
          Thread.Sleep(r.Next(2000));
          Message += "A";
          Write(".");
        }
      }
      else
      {
        WriteLine("Method A failed to enter a monitor lock.");
      }
    }
    finally
    {
      Monitor.Exit(conch);
    }
    ```

2. Run the console application and view the result, which should return the same results as before (although either A or B could grab the conch first) but is better code because it will avoid potential deadlocks.

Good Practice: Only use the `lock` keyword if you can write your code such that it avoids potential deadlocks. If you cannot avoid potential deadlocks, then always use the `Monitor.TryEnter` method instead of `lock`, in combination with a `try-finally` statement, so that you can supply a timeout and one of the threads will back out of a deadlock if it occurs.

Synchronizing events

In *Chapter 6, Implementing Interfaces and Inheriting Classes*, you learned how to raise and handle events. But .NET events are not thread-safe, so you should avoid using them in multithreaded scenarios and follow the standard event raising code I showed you earlier.

Many developers attempt to use exclusive locks when adding and removing event handlers or when raising an event, which is a bad idea, as shown in the following code:

```csharp
// event delegate field
public EventHandler Shout;

// conch
private readonly object eventLock = new object();

// method
public void Poke()
{
  lock (eventLock)
  {
    // if something is listening...
    if (Shout != null)
    {
      // ...then call the delegate to raise the event
      Shout(this, EventArgs.Empty);
    }
  }
}
```

More Information: You can read more about events and thread-safety at the following link: `https://docs.microsoft.com/en-us/archive/blogs/cburrows/field-like-events-considered-harmful`

Good Practice: It is complicated, as explained by Stephen Cleary in the following blog post: `https://blog.stephencleary.com/2009/06/threadsafe-events.html`

Making CPU operations atomic

Atomic is from the Greek word **atomos**, which means *undividable*. It is important to understand which operations are atomic in multithreading because if they are not atomic, then they could be interrupted by another thread partway through their operation. Is the C# increment operator atomic, as shown in the following code?

```
int x = 3;
x++; // is this an atomic CPU operation?
```

It is not atomic! Incrementing an integer requires the following three CPU operations:

1. Load a value from an instance variable into a register.
2. Increment the value.
3. Store the value in the instance variable.

A thread could be interrupted after executing the first two steps. A second thread could then execute all three steps. When the first thread resumes execution, it will overwrite the value in the variable, and the effect of the increment or decrement performed by the second thread will be lost!

There is a type named `Interlocked` that can perform atomic actions on value types, such as integers and floats. Let's see it in action:

1. Declare another shared resource that will count how many operations have occurred, as shown in the following code:
   ```
   static int Counter; // another shared resource
   ```
2. In both methods, inside the `for` statement and after modifying the `string` value, add a statement to safely increment the counter, as shown in the following code:
   ```
   Interlocked.Increment(ref Counter);
   ```
3. After outputting the elapsed time, write the current value of the counter to the console, as shown in the following code:
   ```
   WriteLine($"{Counter} string modifications.");
   ```
4. Run the console application and view the result, as shown in the following partial output:
   ```
   10 string modifications.
   ```

Observant readers will realize that the existing conch object variable protects *all* shared resources accessed within a block of code locked by the conch, and therefore it is actually unnecessary to use Interlocked in this specific example. But if we had not already been protecting another shared resource like Message then using Interlocked would be necessary.

Applying other types of synchronization

Monitor and Interlocked are mutually exclusive locks that are simple and effective, but sometimes, you need more advanced options to synchronize access to shared resources, as shown in the following table:

Type	Description
ReaderWriterLock and ReaderWriterLockSlim (recommended)	These allow multiple threads to be in the **read mode**, one thread to be in the **write mode** with exclusive ownership of the lock, and one thread that has read access to be in the **upgradeable read mode**, from which the thread can upgrade to the write mode without having to relinquish its read access to the resource.
Mutex	Like Monitor, this provides exclusive access to a shared resource, except it is used for inter-process synchronization.
Semaphore and SemaphoreSlim	These limit the number of threads that can access a resource or pool of resources concurrently by defining slots.
AutoResetEvent and ManualResetEvent	Event wait handles allow threads to synchronize activities by signaling each other and by waiting for each other's signals.

Understanding async and await

C# 5 introduced two keywords to simplify working with the Task type. They are especially useful for the following:

- Implementing multitasking for a **graphical user interface (GUI)**.
- Improving the scalability of web applications and web services.

In *Chapter 16, Building Websites Using the Model-View-Controller Pattern*, we will see how the async and await keywords can improve scalability in websites.

In *Chapter 21, Building Cross-Platform Mobile Apps*, we will see how the async and await keywords can implement multitasking with a GUI.

But for now, let's learn the theory of why these two C# keywords were introduced, and then later you will see them used in practice.

Improving responsiveness for console apps

One of the limitations with console applications is that you can only use the await keyword inside methods that are marked as async but C# 7 and earlier do not allow the Main method to be marked as async! Luckily, a new feature introduced in C# 7.1 was support for async in Main:

1. Create a console app named AsyncConsole, add it to the Chapter13 workspace, and select the project as active for OmniSharp.

2. Import namespaces for making HTTP requests and working with tasks, and statically import Console, as shown in the following code:

```
using System.Net.Http;
using System.Threading.Tasks;
using static System.Console;
```

3. In the Main method, add statements to create an HttpClient instance, make a request for Apple's home page, and output how many bytes it has, as shown in the following code:

```
var client = new HttpClient();

HttpResponseMessage response =
  await client.GetAsync("http://www.apple.com/");

WriteLine("Apple's home page has {0:N0} bytes.",
  response.Content.Headers.ContentLength);
```

4. Build the project and note the error message, as shown in the following output:

```
Program.cs(14,9): error CS4033: The 'await' operator can only be used
within an async method. Consider marking this method with the 'async'
modifier and changing its return type to 'Task'. [/Users/markjprice/Code/
Chapter13/AsyncConsole/AsyncConsole.csproj]
```

5. Add the async keyword to the Main method and change its return type to Task.

6. Build the project and note that it now builds successfully.

7. Run the console application and view the result, which is likely to have a different number of bytes since Apple changes its home page frequently, as shown in the following output:

```
Apple's home page has 40,252 bytes.
```

Improving responsiveness for GUI apps

So far in this book, we have only built console applications. Life for a programmer gets more complicated when building web applications, web services, and apps with GUIs such as Windows desktop and mobile apps.

One reason for this is that for a GUI app, there is a special thread: the **user interface (UI)** thread.

There are two rules for working in GUIs:

- Do not perform long-running tasks on the UI thread.
- Do not access UI elements on any thread except the UI thread.

To handle these rules, programmers used to have to write complex code to ensure that long-running tasks were executed by a non-UI thread, but once complete, the results of the task were safely passed to the UI thread to present to the user. It could quickly get messy!

Luckily, with C# 5 and later, you have the use of async and await. They allow you to continue to write your code as if it is synchronous, which keeps your code clean and easy to understand, but underneath, the C# compiler creates a complex state machine and keeps track of running threads. It's kind of magical!

Improving scalability for web applications and web services

The async and await keywords can also be applied on the server side when building websites, applications, and services. From the client application's point of view, nothing changes (or they might even notice a small increase in the time taken for a request to return). So, from a single client's point of view, the use of async and await to implement multitasking on the server side makes their experience worse!

On the server side, additional, cheaper worker threads are created to wait for long-running tasks to finish so that expensive I/O threads can handle other client requests instead of being blocked. This improves the overall scalability of a web application or service. More clients can be supported simultaneously.

Common types that support multitasking

There are many common types that have asynchronous methods that you can await, as shown in the following table:

Type	Methods
DbContext\<T>	AddAsync, AddRangeAsync, FindAsync, and SaveChangesAsync
DbSet\<T>	AddAsync, AddRangeAsync, ForEachAsync, SumAsync, ToListAsync, ToDictionaryAsync, AverageAsync, and CountAsync
HttpClient	GetAsync, PostAsync, PutAsync, DeleteAsync, and SendAsync
StreamReader	ReadAsync, ReadLineAsync, and ReadToEndAsync
StreamWriter	WriteAsync, WriteLineAsync, and FlushAsync

 Good Practice: Any time you see a method that ends in the suffix Async, check to see whether it returns Task or Task\<T>. If it does, then you should use it instead of the synchronous non-Async suffixed method. Remember to call it using await and decorate your method with async.

Using await in catch blocks

In C# 5, it was only possible to use the await keyword in a try block, but not in a catch block. In C# 6 and later, it is now possible to use await in both the try and catch blocks.

Working with async streams

Before C# 8.0 and .NET Core 3.0, the await keyword only worked with tasks that return scalar values. Async stream support in .NET Standard 2.1 allows an async method to return a sequence of values.

Let's see a simulated example.

1. Create a console app named AsyncEnumerable, add it to the Chapter13 workspace, and select the project as active for OmniSharp.

2. Import extra namespaces for working with tasks, and statically import Console, as shown in the following code:

```
using System.Collections.Generic;
using System.Threading.Tasks;
using static System.Console;
```

3. Create a method that yield returns a random sequence of three numbers asynchronously, as shown in the following code:

```csharp
async static IAsyncEnumerable<int> GetNumbers()
{
    var r = new Random();

    // simulate work
    await Task.Run(() => Task.Delay(r.Next(1500, 3000)));
    yield return r.Next(0, 1001);

    await Task.Run(() => Task.Delay(r.Next(1500, 3000)));
    yield return r.Next(0, 1001);

    await Task.Run(() => Task.Delay(r.Next(1500, 3000)));
    yield return r.Next(0, 1001);
}
```

4. In the Main method, add statements to enumerate the sequence of numbers, as shown in the following code:

```csharp
static async Task Main(string[] args)
{
    await foreach (int number in GetNumbers())
    {
        WriteLine($"Number: {number}");
    }
}
```

5. Run the console application and view the result, as shown in the following output:

```
Number: 509
Number: 813
Number: 307
```

Practicing and exploring

Test your knowledge and understanding by answering some questions, get some hands-on practice, and explore this chapter's topics with deeper research.

Exercise 13.1 – Test your knowledge

Answer the following questions:

1. What information can you find out about a process?
2. How accurate is the Stopwatch class?

3. By convention, what suffix should be applied to a method that returns `Task` or `Task<T>`?

4. To use the `await` keyword inside a method, what keyword must be applied to the method declaration?

5. How do you create a `child` task?

6. Why should you avoid the `lock` keyword?

7. When should you use the `Interlocked` class?

8. When should you use the `Mutex` class instead of the `Monitor` class?

9. What is the benefit of using `async` and `await` in a website or web service?

10. Can you cancel a task? How?

Exercise 13.2 – Explore topics

Use the following links to read more about this chapter's topics:

- **Threads and threading**: `https://docs.microsoft.com/en-us/dotnet/standard/threading/threads-and-threading`

- **Async in depth**: `https://docs.microsoft.com/en-us/dotnet/standard/async-in-depth`

- **await (C# reference)**: `https://docs.microsoft.com/en-us/dotnet/csharp/language-reference/keywords/await`

- **Parallel Programming in .NET**: `https://docs.microsoft.com/en-us/dotnet/standard/parallel-programming/`

- **Overview of synchronization primitives**: `https://docs.microsoft.com/en-us/dotnet/standard/threading/overview-of-synchronization-primitives`

Summary

In this chapter, you have learned not only how to define and start a task, but also how to wait for one or more tasks to finish, and how to control task completion order. You've also learned how to synchronize access to shared resources, and the theory behind `async` and `await`.

In the remaining chapters, you will learn how to create applications for the **App Models** supported by .NET, such as websites, web applications, and web services. As a bonus, you will also learn how you can build Windows desktop apps using .NET 5 and cross-platform mobile apps.

14

Introducing Practical Applications of C# and .NET

The third part of this book is about practical applications of C# and .NET. You will learn how to build cross-platform projects such as websites, web services, Windows desktop apps, and cross-platform mobile apps, as well as how to add intelligence to them with machine learning.

Microsoft calls platforms for building applications **App Models**.

I recommend that you work through this and subsequent chapters sequentially because later chapters will reference projects in earlier chapters, and you will build up sufficient knowledge and skills to tackle the trickier problems in later chapters.

In this chapter, we will cover the following topics:

- Understanding app models for C# and .NET
- New features in ASP.NET Core
- Understanding SignalR
- Understanding Blazor
- Understanding the bonus chapters
- Building an entity data model for Northwind

Understanding app models for C# and .NET

Since this book is about C# 9 and .NET 5, we will learn about app models that use them to build the practical applications that we will encounter in the remaining chapters of this book.

> **More Information**: Microsoft has extensive guidance for implementing App
> Models such as ASP.NET web applications, Xamarin mobile apps, and UWP
> apps in its .NET Application Architecture Guidance documentation, which
> you can read at the following link: `https://www.microsoft.com/net/`
> `learn/architecture`

Building websites using ASP.NET Core

Websites are made up of multiple web pages loaded statically from the filesystem or generated
dynamically by a server-side technology such as ASP.NET Core. A web browser makes GET
requests using URLs that identify each page and can manipulate data stored on the server
using POST, PUT, and DELETE requests.

With many websites, the web browser is treated as a presentation layer, with almost all of the
processing performed on the server side. A small amount of JavaScript might be used on the
client side to implement some presentation features, such as carousels.

ASP.NET Core provides multiple technologies for building websites:

- **ASP.NET Core Razor Pages** and **Razor class libraries** are ways to dynamically
  generate HTML for simple websites. You will learn about them in detail in *Chapter 15,
  Building Websites Using ASP.NET Core Razor Pages*.

- **ASP.NET Core MVC** is an implementation of the Model-View-Controller design
  pattern that is popular for developing complex websites. You will learn about it in
  detail in *Chapter 16, Building Websites Using the Model-View-Controller Pattern*.

- **Blazor** lets you build server-side or client-side components and user interfaces using C#
  instead of JavaScript. You will learn about it in detail in *Chapter 20, Building Web User
  Interfaces Using Blazor*.

Building websites using a web content management system

Most websites have a lot of content, and if developers had to be involved every time some
content needed to be changed, that would not scale well. A web **Content Management System
(CMS)** enables developers to define content structure and templates to provide consistency
and good design while making it easy for a non-technical content owner to manage the actual
content. They can create new pages or blocks of content, and update existing content, knowing
it will look great for visitors with minimal effort.

There is a multitude of CMSs available for all web platforms, like WordPress for PHP or django
CMS for Python. Enterprise-level CMSs for .NET Framework include Episerver and Sitecore,
but neither is available yet for .NET Core or .NET 5 and later. CMSs that support .NET Core
include Piranha CMS, Squidex, and Orchard Core.

The key benefit of using a CMS is that it provides a friendly content management user interface. Content owners log in to the website and manage the content themselves. The content is then rendered and returned to visitors using ASP.NET Core MVC controllers and views.

In summary, C# and .NET can be used on both the server side and the client side to build websites, as shown in the following diagram:

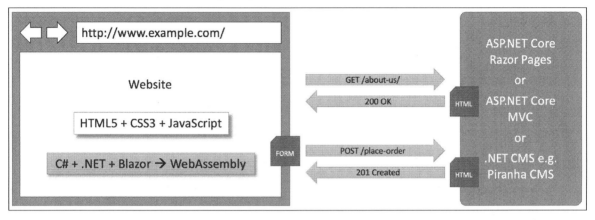

Figure 14.1: The use of C# and .NET to build websites

Understanding web applications

Web applications, also known as **Single-Page Applications (SPAs)**, are made up of a single web page built with a frontend technology such as Angular, React, Vue, or a proprietary JavaScript library that can make requests to a backend web service for getting more data when needed and posting updated data, using common serialization formats, such as XML and JSON. The canonical examples are Google web apps like Gmail, Maps, and Docs.

With a web application, the client side uses JavaScript libraries to implement sophisticated user interactions, but most of the important processing and data access still happens on the server side, because the web browser has limited access to local system resources.

 More Information: JavaScript is loosely typed and is not designed for complex projects so most JavaScript libraries these days use Microsoft TypeScript, which adds strong typing to JavaScript and is designed with many modern language features for handling complex implementations. TypeScript 4.0 was released in August 2020. You can read more about TypeScript at the following link: https://www.typescriptlang.org

.NET has project templates for JavaScript and TypeScript-based SPAs, but we will not spend any time learning how to build JavaScript and TypeScript-based SPAs in this book, even though these are commonly used with ASP.NET Core as the backend.

More Information: To learn more about building frontends to .NET using JavaScript and TypeScript-based SPAs, Packt has a few books of interest, which you can read about at the following links:

- ASP.NET Core 2 and Vue.js: `https://www.packtpub.com/product/asp-net-core-2-and-vue-js/9781788839464`

- ASP.NET Core 3 and React: `https://www.packtpub.com/product/asp-net-core-3-and-react/9781789950229`

- ASP.NET Core 3 and Angular 9: `https://www.packtpub.com/product/asp-net-core-3-and-angular-9-third-edition/9781789612165`

Building and consuming web services

Although we will not learn about JavaScript and TypeScript-based SPAs, we will learn how to build a web service using the **ASP.NET Core Web API**, and then call that web service from the server-side code in our ASP.NET Core websites, and then later, we will call that web service from Blazor web components, Windows desktop, and cross-platform mobile apps.

Building intelligent apps

In a traditional app, the algorithms it uses to process its data are designed and implemented by a human. Humans are good at many things, but writing complex algorithms is not one of them, especially algorithms for spotting meaningful patterns in vast quantities of data.

Machine learning algorithms that work with custom trained models like those provided by Microsoft's **ML.NET** can add intelligence to your apps. We will use ML.NET algorithms with custom trained models to process the tracked behavior of visitors to a product website and then make recommendations for other product pages that they might be interested in. It will work rather like how Netflix recommends films and TV shows you might like based on your previous behavior and the behavior of people who have expressed similar interests to you.

New features in ASP.NET Core

Over the past few years, Microsoft has rapidly expanded the capabilities of ASP.NET Core. You should note which .NET platforms are supported, as shown in the following list:

- ASP.NET 1.0 to 2.2 runs on either .NET Core or .NET Framework.
- ASP.NET Core 3.0 or later only runs on .NET Core 3.0 or later.

ASP.NET Core 1.0

ASP.NET Core 1.0 was released in June 2016 and focused on implementing a minimum API suitable for building modern cross-platform web apps and services for Windows, macOS, and Linux.

More Information: You can read the ASP.NET Core 1.0 announcement at the following link: `https://devblogs.microsoft.com/aspnet/announcing-asp-net-core-1-0/`

ASP.NET Core 1.1

ASP.NET Core 1.1 was released in November 2016 and focused on bug fixes and general improvements to features and performance.

More Information: You can read the ASP.NET Core 1.1 announcement at the following link: `https://devblogs.microsoft.com/aspnet/announcing-asp-net-core-1-1/`

ASP.NET Core 2.0

ASP.NET Core 2.0 was released in August 2017 and focused on adding new features such as Razor Pages, bundling assemblies into a `Microsoft.AspNetCore.All` metapackage, targeting .NET Standard 2.0, providing a new authentication model, and performance improvements. The biggest new feature is covered in *Chapter 15, Building Websites Using ASP.NET Core Razor Pages*.

More Information: You can read the ASP.NET Core 2.0 announcement at the following link: `https://devblogs.microsoft.com/aspnet/announcing-asp-net-core-2-0/`

ASP.NET Core 2.1

ASP.NET Core 2.1 was released in May 2018 and is a **Long-Term Support (LTS)** release, meaning it will be supported until August 21, 2021.

It focused on adding new features such as SignalR for real-time communication, Razor class libraries for reusing code, ASP.NET Core Identity for authentication, and better support for HTTPS and the European Union's **General Data Protection Regulation (GDPR)**, including the topics listed in the following table:

Feature	Chapter	Topic
SignalR	14	Understanding SignalR
Razor class libraries	15	Using Razor class libraries
GDPR support	16	Creating and exploring an ASP.NET Core MVC website

Identity UI library and scaffolding	16	Exploring an ASP.NET Core MVC website
Integration tests	16	Testing an ASP.NET Core MVC website
`[ApiController]`, `ActionResult<T>`	18	Creating an ASP.NET Core Web API project
Problem details	18	Implementing a Web API controller
`IHttpClientFactory`	18	Configuring HTTP clients using `HttpClientFactory`

 More Information: You can read the ASP.NET Core 2.1 announcement at the following link: `https://devblogs.microsoft.com/aspnet/asp-net-core-2-1-0-now-available/`

ASP.NET Core 2.2

ASP.NET Core 2.2 was released in December 2018 and focused on improving the building of RESTful HTTP APIs, updating the project templates to Bootstrap 4 and Angular 6, an optimized configuration for hosting in Azure, and performance improvements, including the topics listed in the following table:

Feature	Chapter	Topic
HTTP/2 in Kestrel	15	Classic ASP.NET versus modern ASP.NET Core
In-process hosting model	15	Creating an ASP.NET Core project
Health Check API	18	Implementing Health Check API
Open API Analyzers	18	Implementing Open API analyzers and conventions
Endpoint Routing	18	Understanding endpoint routing

 More Information: You can read the ASP.NET Core 2.2 announcement at the following link: `https://devblogs.microsoft.com/aspnet/asp-net-core-2-2-available-today/`

ASP.NET Core 3.0

ASP.NET Core 3.0 was released in September 2019 and focused on fully leveraging .NET Core 3.0, which means it can no longer support .NET Framework, and added useful refinements, including the topics listed in the following table:

Feature	Chapter	Topic
Blazor; server- and client-side	14	Understanding Blazor
Static assets in Razor class libraries	15	Using Razor class libraries
New options for MVC service registration	16	Understanding ASP.NET Core MVC startup

More Information: You can read the ASP.NET Core 3.0 announcement at the following link: `https://devblogs.microsoft.com/aspnet/a-first-look-at-changes-coming-in-asp-net-core-3-0/`

ASP.NET Core 3.1

ASP.NET Core 3.1 was released in December 2019 and is an LTS release, meaning it will be supported until December 3, 2022. It focused on refinements like partial class support for Razor components and a new component tag helper.

 More Information: You can read the ASP.NET Core 3.1 announcement at the following link: `https://devblogs.microsoft.com/aspnet/asp-net-core-updates-in-net-core-3-1/`

Blazor WebAssembly 3.2

Blazor WebAssembly 3.2 was released in May 2020 and is a Current release meaning that projects must be upgraded to the .NET 5 version within three months of the .NET 5 release, i.e. by February 10, 2021.

Microsoft has finally delivered on the promise of full stack web development with .NET, and both Blazor Server and Blazor WebAssembly are covered in *Chapter 20, Building Web User Interfaces Using Blazor*.

 More Information: You can read the Blazor WebAssembly announcement at the following link: `https://devblogs.microsoft.com/aspnet/blazor-webassembly-3-2-0-now-available/`

ASP.NET Core 5.0

ASP.NET Core 5.0 was released in November 2020 and focused on bug fixes, performance improvements using caching for certificate authentication, HPack dynamic compression of HTTP/2 response headers in Kestrel, nullable annotations for ASP.NET Core assemblies, and a reduction in container image sizes, including the topics listed in the following table:

Feature	Chapter	Topic
Extension method to allow anonymous access to an endpoint	18	Securing web services
JSON extension methods for HttpRequest and HttpResponse	18	Getting customers as JSON in the controller

> **More Information**: You can read the ASP.NET Core 5.0 announcement by finding the link on the book's GitHub repository at the following link:
> https://github.com/markjprice/cs9dotnet5/

Understanding SignalR

In the early days of the Web in the 1990s, browsers had to make a full-page HTTP GET request to the web server to get fresh information to show to the visitor.

In late 1999, Microsoft released Internet Explorer 5.0 with a component named **XMLHttpRequest** that could make asynchronous HTTP calls in the background. This alongside **dynamic HTML (DHTML)** allowed parts of the web page to be updated with fresh data smoothly.

The benefits of this technique were obvious and soon all browsers added the same component. Google took maximum advantage of this capability to build clever web applications such as Google Maps and Gmail. A few years later, the technique became popularly known as **Asynchronous JavaScript and XML (AJAX)**.

AJAX still uses HTTP to communicate, however, and that has limitations. First, HTTP is a request-response communication protocol, meaning that the server cannot push data to the client. It must wait for the client to make a request. Second, HTTP request and response messages have headers with lots of potentially unnecessary overhead. Third, HTTP typically requires a new underlying TCP connection to be created on each request.

WebSocket is full-duplex, meaning that either the client or server can initiate communicating new data. WebSocket uses the same TCP connection for the lifecycle of the connection. It is also more efficient in the message sizes that it sends because they are minimally framed with 2 bytes.

WebSocket works over HTTP ports 80 and 443 so it is compatible with the HTTP protocol and the WebSocket handshake uses the HTTP Upgrade header to switch from the HTTP protocol to the WebSocket protocol.

> **More Information**: You can read more about WebSocket at the following link:
> https://en.wikipedia.org/wiki/WebSocket

Modern web apps are expected to deliver up-to-date information. Live chat is the canonical example, but there are lots of potential applications, from stock prices to games.

Whenever you need the server to push updates to the web page, you need a web-compatible, real-time communication technology. WebSocket could be used but it is not supported by all clients.

ASP.NET Core SignalR is an open source library that simplifies adding real-time web functionality to apps by being an abstraction over multiple underlying communication technologies, which allows you to add real-time communication capabilities using C# code.

The developer does not need to understand or implement the underlying technology used, and SignalR will automatically switch between underlying technologies depending on what the visitor's web browser supports. For example, SignalR will use WebSocket when it's available, and gracefully falls back on other technologies such as AJAX long polling when it isn't, while your application code stays the same.

SignalR is an API for server-to-client **remote procedure calls** (**RPCs**). The RPCs call JavaScript functions on clients from server-side .NET Core code. SignalR has hubs to define the pipeline and handles the message dispatching automatically using two built-in hub protocols: JSON and a binary one based on MessagePack.

More Information: You can read more about MessagePack at the following link: https://msgpack.org

On the server side, SignalR runs everywhere that ASP.NET Core runs: Windows, macOS, or Linux servers. SignalR supports the following client platforms:

- JavaScript clients for current browsers including Chrome, Firefox, Safari, Edge, and Internet Explorer 11.
- .NET clients including Blazor and Xamarin for Android and iOS mobile apps.
- Java 8 and later.

More Information: You can read more about SignalR at the following link: https://docs.microsoft.com/en-us/aspnet/core/signalr/introduction

Understanding Blazor

Blazor lets you build shared components and interactive web user interfaces using C# instead of JavaScript. In April 2019, Microsoft announced that Blazor "is no longer experimental and we are committing to ship it as a supported web UI framework including support for running client-side in the browser on WebAssembly."

JavaScript and friends

Traditionally, any code that needs to execute in a web browser is written using the JavaScript programming language or a higher-level technology that **transpiles** (transforms or compiles) into JavaScript. This is because all browsers have supported JavaScript for about two decades, so it has become the lowest common denominator for implementing business logic on the client side.

JavaScript does have some issues, however. First, although it has superficial similarities to C-style languages like C# and Java, it is actually very different once you dig beneath the surface. Second, it is a dynamically typed pseudo-functional language that uses prototypes instead of class inheritance for object reuse. It might look human, but you will get a surprise when it's revealed to actually be a Skrull.

Wouldn't it be great if we could use the same language and libraries in a web browser as we do on the server side?

Silverlight – C# and .NET using a plugin

Microsoft made a previous attempt at achieving this goal with a technology named **Silverlight**. When Silverlight 2.0 was released in 2008, a C# and .NET developer could use their skills to build libraries and visual components that were executed in the web browser by the Silverlight plugin.

By 2011 and Silverlight 5.0, Apple's success with the iPhone and Steve Jobs' hatred of browser plugins like Flash eventually led to Microsoft abandoning Silverlight since, like Flash, Silverlight is banned from iPhones and iPads.

WebAssembly – a target for Blazor

A recent development in browsers has given Microsoft the opportunity to make another attempt. In 2017, the WebAssembly Consensus was completed and all major browsers now support it: Chromium (Chrome, Edge, Opera, Brave), Firefox, and WebKit (Safari). It is not supported by Microsoft's Internet Explorer because it is a legacy web browser.

WebAssembly (Wasm) is a binary instruction format for a virtual machine that provides a way to run code written in multiple languages on the web at near-native speed. Wasm is designed as a portable target for the compilation of high-level languages like C#.

More Information: You can learn more about WebAssembly at the following link: https://webassembly.org

Blazor on the server side or client side

Blazor is a single programming or **app** model with two **hosting** models:

- Server-side Blazor runs on the server side using SignalR to communicate with the client side, and it shipped as part of .NET Core 3.0.
- Client-side Blazor runs on the client side using WebAssembly, and it shipped as an extension to .NET Core 3.1, although it is only a Current release, which is why it was versioned as 3.2.

This means that a web developer can write Blazor components once, and then run them either on the server side or client side (with careful planning).

More Information: You can read the official documentation for Blazor at the following link: https://dotnet.microsoft.com/apps/aspnet/web-apps/blazor

Understanding the bonus chapters

The bonus chapters in this book are the last chapter and appendix B:

- *Chapter 21, Building Cross-Platform Mobile Apps*
- *Appendix B, Building Windows Desktop Apps*

Since this book is about modern cross-platform development using C# 9 and .NET 5, technically, it should not include coverage of Windows desktop apps because they are Windows-only. Nor should it include coverage of cross-platform mobile apps because they use Xamarin instead of .NET 5.

In *Chapters 1* to *20*, we are using cross-platform Visual Studio Code to build all the apps. Cross-platform mobile apps are built using Visual Studio 2019 for Mac and require macOS to compile. Windows desktop apps are built using Visual Studio 2019 on Windows 10.

But Windows and mobile are important platforms for current and future client app development using C# and .NET, so I did not want to take away the opportunity to introduce you to them.

Appendix B, Building Windows Desktop Apps can be found online at: https://static.packt-cdn.com/downloads/9781800568105_Appendices.pdf

Building cross-platform mobile and desktop apps

There are two major mobile platforms: Apple's iOS and Google's Android, each with their own different programming languages and platform APIs. There are also two major desktop platforms: Apple's macOS and Microsoft's Windows, each with their own different programming languages and platform APIs.

Cross-platform mobile and desktop apps can be built once for the Xamarin platform using C#, and then can run on mobile and desktop platforms. Xamarin.Forms makes it even easier to develop those apps by sharing user interface components as well as business logic. Much of the XAML for defining the user interface can even be shared between Xamarin.Forms, WPF, and UWP apps.

The apps can exist on their own, but they usually call web services to provide an experience that spans across all of your computing devices, from servers and laptops to phones and gaming systems.

Once .NET 6 is released in November 2021, you will be able to create cross-platform mobile and desktop apps that target the same .NET 6 APIs as used by console apps, websites, web services, and Windows desktop apps, and it will be executed by the Xamarin runtime on mobile devices. This will use an evolution of Xamarin.Forms known as .NET MAUI or Multi-platform App UI (User Interface).

The current version of Xamarin.Forms requires Visual Studio for Mac or Visual Studio 2019 (for Windows). MAUI will support these tools as well as Visual Studio Code through an extension. The sixth edition of this book will finally be able to use only Visual Studio Code for 100% of its code examples.

.NET MAUI will support existing MVVM and XAML patterns as well as ones like **Model-View-Update (MVU)** with C#, which is similar to Apple's Swift UI, and of course Blazor.

> **More Information**: You can read an introduction to .NET MAUI at the following link: https://devblogs.microsoft.com/dotnet/introducing-net-multi-platform-app-ui/

The last chapter in the sixth edition of this book will be retitled to *Chapter 21, Building Cross-Platform Mobile and Desktop Apps*, and will cover using .NET **Multi-platform App User Interfaces (MAUI)** to build cross-platform mobile and desktop apps.

> **More Information**: You can review the GitHub repository for .NET MAUI at the following link: https://github.com/dotnet/maui

Building Windows desktop apps using legacy technologies

With the first version of C# and .NET Framework released in 2002, Microsoft provided technology for building Windows desktop applications named **Windows Forms**. The equivalent at the time for web development was named **Web Forms**, hence the complimentary names.

In 2007, Microsoft released a more powerful technology for building Windows desktop applications, named **Windows Presentation Foundation (WPF)**. WPF can use **eXtensible Application Markup Language (XAML)** to specify its user interface, which is easy for both humans and code to understand. Visual Studio 2019 is built with WPF.

There are many enterprise applications built using Windows Forms and WPF that need to be maintained or enhanced with new features, but until recently they were stuck on .NET Framework, which is now a legacy platform. With .NET 5 and Windows Desktop Pack, these apps can now use the full modern capabilities of .NET.

In 2015 Microsoft released Windows 10, and with it a new technology named **Universal Windows Platform (UWP)**. UWP apps can be built using C++ and DirectX UI, or JavaScript and HTML, or C# using a custom fork of .NET Core that is not cross-platform but provides full access to the underlying WinRT APIs.

UWP apps can only execute on the Windows 10 platform, not earlier versions of Windows. UWP apps can also run on Xbox and Windows Mixed Reality headsets with motion controllers.

The Windows Forms and WPF technologies for building Windows desktop apps are legacy, and very few developers want to build UWP apps, so the chapter about them has been moved to an online-only appendix.

> **More Information**: You can download *Appendix B, Building Windows Desktop Apps* at the following link: https://static.packt-cdn.com/downloads/9781800568105_Appendices.pdf

This appendix will be removed in the sixth edition of the book when .NET 6 and .NET MAUI are available to create cross-platform apps that can run on Windows desktop as well as many other platforms.

> **More Information**: If you are interested in building WPF apps, you might be interested in the following Packt book: https://www.packtpub.com/product/mastering-windows-presentation-foundation/9781785883002

Building an entity data model for Northwind

Practical applications usually need to work with data in a relational database or another data store. In this chapter, we will define an entity data model for the Northwind database stored in SQLite. It will be used in most of the apps that we create in subsequent chapters.

Although macOS includes an installation of SQLite by default, if you are using Windows or a variety of Linux then you might need to download, install, and configure SQLite for your operating system. Instructions to do so can be found in *Chapter 11, Working with Databases Using Entity Framework Core*. In that chapter, you will also find instructions for installing the dotnet-ef tool, which you will use to scaffold an entity model from an existing database.

 Good Practice: You should create a separate class library project for your entity data models. This allows easier sharing between backend web servers and frontend desktop, mobile, and Blazor clients.

Creating a class library for Northwind entity models

You will now define entity data models in a .NET 5 class library so that they can be reused in other types of projects including client-side app models.

Generating entity models using dotnet-ef

First, we will automatically generate some entity models using the EF Core command-line tool:

1. In your existing Code folder, create a folder named PracticalApps.

2. In Visual Studio Code, open the PracticalApps folder.

3. Create the Northwind.db file by copying the Northwind.sql file into the PracticalApps folder, and then enter the following command in **TERMINAL**:

    ```
    sqlite3 Northwind.db -init Northwind.sql
    ```

4. Be patient because this command might take a while to create the database structure, as shown in the following output:

    ```
    -- Loading resources from Northwind.sql
    SQLite version 3.28.0 2019-04-15 14:49:49
    Enter ".help" for usage hints.
    sqlite>
    ```

5. Press *Ctrl* + *D* on macOS or *Ctrl* + *C* on Windows to exit SQLite command mode.

6. In the **File** menu, close the PracticalApps folder.

7. In Visual Studio Code, navigate to **File | Save Workspace As…**, enter the name `PracticalApps`, change to the `PracticalApps` folder, and click **Save**.

8. In the `PracticalApps` folder, create a folder named `NorthwindEntitiesLib`.

9. Add the `NorthwindEntitiesLib` folder to the workspace.

10. Navigate to **Terminal | New Terminal** and select **NorthwindEntitiesLib**.

11. In **TERMINAL**, enter the command `dotnet new classlib`.

12. Open the `NorthwindEntitiesLib.csproj` file, and add two package references for EF Core for SQLite and design-time support, as shown highlighted in the following markup:

```
<Project Sdk="Microsoft.NET.Sdk">
  <PropertyGroup>
    <TargetFramework>net5.0</TargetFramework>
  </PropertyGroup>
  <ItemGroup>
    <PackageReference
      Include="Microsoft.EntityFrameworkCore.Sqlite"
      Version="5.0.0" />
    <PackageReference
      Include="Microsoft.EntityFrameworkCore.Design"
      Version="5.0.0" />
  </ItemGroup>
</Project>
```

13. In **TERMINAL**, download the referenced package and compile the current project, as shown in the following command:

```
dotnet build
```

14. Delete the `Class1.cs` file.

15. In **TERMINAL**, generate entity class models for all tables, as shown in the following command:

```
dotnet ef dbcontext scaffold "Filename=../Northwind.db" Microsoft.
EntityFrameworkCore.Sqlite --namespace Packt.Shared --data-annotations
--context Northwind
```

Note the following:

- The command to perform: `dbcontext scaffold`
- The connection string: `"Filename=../Northwind.db"`
- The database provider: `Microsoft.EntityFrameworkCore.Sqlite`
- The namespace: `--namespace Packt.Shared`
- To use data annotations as well as the Fluent API: `--data-annotations`
- To rename the context from [database_name]Context: `--context Northwind`

16. Note the build messages and warnings, as shown in the following output:

```
Build started...
Build succeeded.
To protect potentially sensitive information in your connection string,
you should move it out of source code. You can avoid scaffolding the
connection string by using the Name= syntax to read it from configuration
- see https://go.microsoft.com/fwlink/?linkid=2131148. For more
guidance on storing connection strings, see http://go.microsoft.com/
fwlink/?LinkId=723263.
```

Manually improving the class-to-table mapping

Second, we will make some small changes to improve the model mapping.

We will make the changes to these entity classes: Category.cs, Customer.cs, Employee.cs, Order.cs, OrderDetail.cs, Product.cs, Shipper.cs, Supplier.cs, and Territory.cs.

The changes we will make to each entity class are the following:

1. Change all primary or foreign key properties to use standard naming, for example, change CategoryId to CategoryID. This will allow you to also remove the attribute [Column] attribute that maps the property to the column in the table, as shown in the following code:

    ```
    // before
    [Key]
    [Column("CategoryID")]
    public long CategoryId { get; set; }

    // after
    [Key]
    public long CategoryID { get; set; }
    ```

2. Decorate all string properties with the [StringLength] attribute to limit the maximum number of characters allowed for the matching field using the information in the [Column] attribute, as shown in the following code:

    ```
    // before
    [Required]
    [Column(TypeName = "nvarchar (15)")]
    public string CategoryName { get; set; }

    // after
    [Required]
    [Column(TypeName = "nvarchar (15)")]
    [StringLength(15)]
    public string CategoryName { get; set; }
    ```

3. Open the `Customer.cs` file and add a regular expression to validate its primary key value to only allow uppercase Western characters, as shown in the following code:

```
[Key]
[Column(TypeName = "nchar (5)")]
[StringLength(5)]
[RegularExpression("[A-Z]{5}")]
public string CustomerID { get; set; }
```

4. Change any date/time properties, for example, in `Employee.cs`, to use a nullable `DateTime` instead of an array of bytes, as shown in the following code:

```
// before
[Column(TypeName = "datetime")]
public byte[] BirthDate { get; set; }

// after
[Column(TypeName = "datetime")]
public DateTime? BirthDate { get; set; }
```

5. Change any money properties, for example, in `Order.cs`, to use a nullable `decimal` instead of an array of bytes, as shown in the following code:

```
// before
[Column(TypeName = "money")]
public byte[] Freight { get; set; }

// after
[Column(TypeName = "money")]
public decimal? Freight { get; set; }
```

6. Change any bit properties, for example, in `Product.cs`, to use a `bool` instead of an array of bytes, as shown in the following code:

```
// before
[Required]
[Column(TypeName = "bit")]
public byte[] Discontinued { get; set; }

// after
[Required]
[Column(TypeName = "bit")]
public bool Discontinued { get; set; }
```

Now that we have a class library for the entity classes, we can create a class library for the database context.

Creating a class library for a Northwind database context

You will now define a database context class library:

1. In the `PracticalApps` folder, create a folder named `NorthwindContextLib`.

2. Add the `NorthwindContextLib` folder to the workspace.

3. Navigate to **Terminal | New Terminal** and select `NorthwindContextLib`.

4. In **TERMINAL**, enter the command `dotnet new classlib`.

5. Navigate to **View | Command Palette**, enter and select **OmniSharp: Select Project**, and select the `NorthwindContextLib` project.

6. Modify `NorthwindContextLib.csproj` to add a reference to the `NorthwindEntitiesLib` project and the Entity Framework Core package for SQLite, as shown highlighted in the following markup:

```xml
<Project Sdk="Microsoft.NET.Sdk">
  <PropertyGroup>
    <TargetFramework>net5.0</TargetFramework>
  </PropertyGroup>
  <ItemGroup>
    <ProjectReference Include=
      "..\NorthwindEntitiesLib\NorthwindEntitiesLib.csproj" />
    <PackageReference
      Include="Microsoft.EntityFrameworkCore.SQLite"
      Version="5.0.0" />
  </ItemGroup>
</Project>
```

7. In the `NorthwindContextLib` project, delete the `Class1.cs` class file.

8. Drag and drop the `Northwind.cs` file from the `NorthwindEntitiesLib` folder to the `NorthwindContextLib` folder.

9. In `Northwind.cs`, modify the statements to remove the compiler warning about the connection string. Then remove the Fluent API statements for validation and defining keys and relationships except for `OrderDetail` because multi-field primary keys can only be defined using the Fluent API. This is because they are duplicating work done by the attributes in the entity model classes, as shown in the following code:

```csharp
using Microsoft.EntityFrameworkCore;

#nullable disable

namespace Packt.Shared
{
  public partial class Northwind : DbContext
  {
```

```csharp
    public Northwind()
    {
    }

    public Northwind(DbContextOptions<Northwind> options)
      : base(options)
    {
    }
    public virtual DbSet<Category> Categories { get; set; }
    public virtual DbSet<Customer> Customers { get; set; }
    public virtual DbSet<Employee> Employees { get; set; }
    public virtual DbSet<EmployeeTerritory> EmployeeTerritories
      { get; set; }
    public virtual DbSet<Order> Orders { get; set; }
    public virtual DbSet<OrderDetail> OrderDetails { get; set; }
    public virtual DbSet<Product> Products { get; set; }
    public virtual DbSet<Shipper> Shippers { get; set; }
    public virtual DbSet<Supplier> Suppliers { get; set; }
    public virtual DbSet<Territory> Territories { get; set; }

    protected override void OnConfiguring(
      DbContextOptionsBuilder optionsBuilder)
    {
      if (!optionsBuilder.IsConfigured)
      {
        optionsBuilder.UseSqlite("Filename=../Northwind.db");
      }
    }

    protected override void OnModelCreating(
      ModelBuilder modelBuilder)
    {
      modelBuilder.Entity<OrderDetail>(entity =>
      {
        entity.HasKey(x => new { x.OrderID, x.ProductID });

        entity.HasOne(d => d.Order)
          .WithMany(p => p.OrderDetails)
          .HasForeignKey(x => x.OrderID)
          .OnDelete(DeleteBehavior.ClientSetNull);

        entity.HasOne(d => d.Product)
                     .WithMany(p => p.OrderDetails)
                     .HasForeignKey(x => x.ProductID)
                     .OnDelete(DeleteBehavior.ClientSetNull);
      });
```

```
        modelBuilder.Entity<Product>()
          .Property(product => product.UnitPrice)
          .HasConversion<double>();

        OnModelCreatingPartial(modelBuilder);
    }
    partial void OnModelCreatingPartial(ModelBuilder modelBuilder);
  }
}
```

10. In **TERMINAL**, restore packages and compile the class libraries to check for errors by entering the command dotnet build.

We will override the default database connection string in any projects such as websites that need to work with the Northwind database, so the class derived from DbContext must have a constructor with a DbContextOptions parameter for this to work.

Summary

In this chapter, you have been introduced to some of the app models that you can use to build practical applications using C# and .NET, and you have created two class libraries to define an entity data model for working with the Northwind database.

In the following chapters, you will learn the details about how to build the following:

- Simple websites with static HTML pages and dynamic Razor Pages.
- Complex websites with the **Model-View-Controller** (**MVC**) design pattern.
- Complex websites with content that can be managed by end users with a web **Content Management System** (**CMS**).
- Web services that can be called by any platform that can make an HTTP request and client websites and apps that call those services.
- Intelligent apps that use machine learning to implement features like product recommendations.
- Blazor web user interface components that can be hosted either on the server or in the browser.
- Cross-platform mobile apps using Xamarin.Forms.

15
Building Websites Using ASP.NET Core Razor Pages

This chapter is about building websites with a modern HTTP architecture on the server side using Microsoft ASP.NET Core. You will learn about building simple websites using the ASP.NET Core Razor Pages feature introduced with .NET Core 2.0 and the Razor class library feature introduced with .NET Core 2.1.

This chapter will cover the following topics:

- Understanding web development
- Understanding ASP.NET Core
- Exploring Razor Pages
- Using Entity Framework Core with ASP.NET Core
- Using Razor class libraries
- Configuring services and the HTTP request pipeline

Understanding web development

Developing for the web is developing with **Hypertext Transfer Protocol** (HTTP).

Understanding HTTP

To communicate with a web server, the client, also known as the **user agent**, makes calls over the network using HTTP. As such, HTTP is the technical underpinning of the **web**. So, when we talk about web applications or web services, we mean that they use HTTP to communicate between a client (often a web browser) and a server.

A client makes an HTTP request for a resource, such as a page, uniquely identified by a **Uniform Resource Locator (URL)**, and the server sends back an HTTP response, as shown in the following diagram:

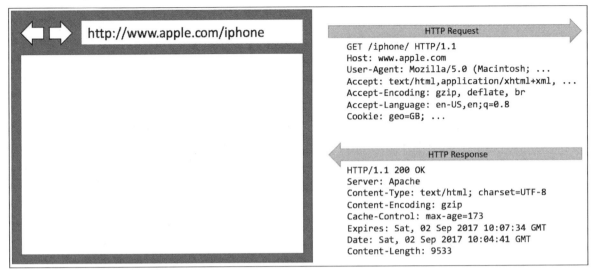

Figure 15.1: An HTTP request and response

You can use Google Chrome and other browsers to record requests and responses.

Good Practice: Google Chrome is available on more operating systems than any other browser, and it has powerful, built-in developer tools, so it is a good first choice of browser for testing your websites. Always test your web application with Chrome and at least two other browsers, for example, Firefox and Safari for macOS and iPhone. Microsoft Edge switched from using Microsoft's own rendering engine to using Chromium in 2019 so it is less important to test with it. If Microsoft's Internet Explorer is used at all, it tends to mostly be inside organizations for intranets.

Let's explore how to use Google Chrome to make HTTP requests:

1. Start **Google Chrome**.
2. To show developer tools in Chrome, do the following:
   - On macOS, press *Alt + Cmd + I*
   - On Windows, press *F12* or *Ctrl + Shift + I*

3. Click on the **Network** tab, and Chrome should immediately start recording the network traffic between your browser and any web servers, as shown in the following screenshot:

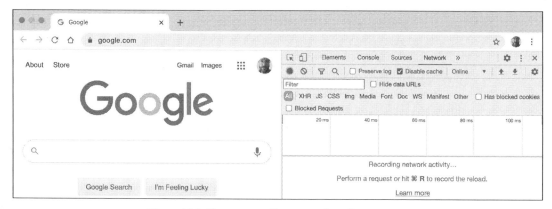

Figure 15.2: Chrome recording network traffic

4. In Chrome's address box, enter the following URL: `https://dotnet.microsoft.com/learn/aspnet`.

5. In the **Developer tools** window, in the list of recorded requests, scroll to the top and click on the first entry, the **document**, as shown in the following screenshot:

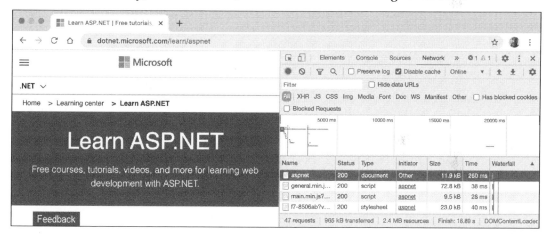

Figure 15.3: Recorded requests

6. On the right-hand side, click on the **Headers** tab, and you will see details about the request and the response, as shown in the following screenshot:

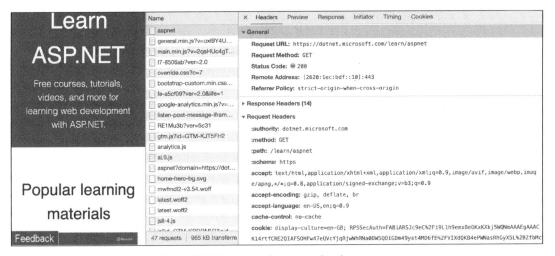

Figure 15.4: Request and response details

Note the following aspects:

- **Request Method** is GET. Other methods that HTTP defines include POST, PUT, DELETE, HEAD, and PATCH.

- **Status Code** is 200 OK. This means that the server found the resource that the browser requested and has returned it in the body of the response. Other status codes that you might see in response to a GET request include 301 Moved Permanently, 400 Bad Request, 401 Unauthorized, and 404 Not Found.

- **Request Headers** sent by the browser to the web server include:

  - **accept**, which lists what formats the browser accepts. In this case, the browser is saying it understands HTML, XHTML, XML, and some image formats, but it will accept all other files */*. Default weightings, also known as quality values, are 1.0. XML is specified with a quality value of 0.9 so it is preferred less than HTML or XHTML. All other file types are given a quality value of 0.8 so are least preferred.

  - **accept-encoding**, which lists what compression algorithms the browser understands. In this case, GZIP, DEFLATE, and Brotli.

  - **accept-language**, which lists the human languages it would prefer the content to use. In this case, US English, which has a default quality value of 1.0, and then any dialect of English that has an explicitly specified quality value of 0.9.

- **Response Headers, content-encoding** tells me the server has sent back the HTML web page response compressed using the GZIP algorithm because it knows that the client can decompress that format.

7. Close Chrome.

Client-side web development

When building websites, a developer needs to know more than just C# and .NET Core. On the client (that is, in the web browser), you will use a combination of the following technologies:

- **HTML5**: This is used for the content and structure of a web page.
- **CSS3**: This is used for the styles applied to elements on the web page.
- **JavaScript**: This is used to code any business logic needed on the web page, for example, validating form input or making calls to a web service to fetch more data needed by the web page.

Although HTML5, CSS3, and JavaScript are the fundamental components of frontend web development, there are many additional technologies that can make frontend web development more productive, including Bootstrap, the world's most popular frontend open source toolkit, and CSS preprocessors like SASS and LESS for styling, Microsoft's TypeScript language for writing more robust code, and JavaScript libraries like jQuery, Angular, React, and Vue. All these higher-level technologies ultimately translate or compile to the underlying three core technologies, so they work across all modern browsers.

As part of the build and deploy process, you will likely use technologies like Node.js; **Node Package Manager** (**NPM**) and Yarn, which are both client-side package managers; and Webpack, which is a popular module bundler, a tool for compiling, transforming, and bundling website source files.

 More Information: This book is about C# and .NET Core, so we will cover some of the basics of frontend web development, but for more detail, try *HTML5 and CSS3: Building Responsive Websites*, at: `https://www.packtpub.com/product/html5-and-css3-building-responsive-websites/9781787124813h`

Understanding ASP.NET Core

Microsoft ASP.NET Core is part of a history of Microsoft technologies used to build websites and web services that have evolved over the years:

- **Active Server Pages** (**ASP**) was released in 1996 and was Microsoft's first attempt at a platform for dynamic server-side execution of website code. ASP files contain a mix of HTML and code that executes on the server written in the VBScript language.
- **ASP.NET Web Forms** was released in 2002 with the .NET Framework, and is designed to enable non-web developers, such as those familiar with Visual Basic, to quickly create websites by dragging and dropping visual components and writing event-driven code in Visual Basic or C#. Web Forms can only be hosted on Windows, but it is still used today in products such as Microsoft SharePoint. It should be avoided for new web projects in favor of ASP.NET Core.

- **Windows Communication Foundation (WCF)** was released in 2006 and enables developers to build SOAP and REST services. SOAP is powerful but complex, so it should be avoided unless you need advanced features, such as distributed transactions and complex messaging topologies.

- **ASP.NET MVC** was released in 2009 and is designed to cleanly separate the concerns of web developers between the *models*, which temporarily store the data; the *views* that present the data using various formats in the UI; and the *controllers*, which fetch the model and pass it to a view. This separation enables improved reuse and unit testing.

- **ASP.NET Web API** was released in 2012 and enables developers to create HTTP services, also known as REST services that are simpler and more scalable than SOAP services.

- **ASP.NET SignalR** was released in 2013 and enables real-time communication in websites by abstracting underlying technologies and techniques, such as WebSockets and Long Polling. This enables website features like live chat or updates to time-sensitive data like stock prices across a wide variety of web browsers even when they do not support an underlying technology like Web Sockets.

- **ASP.NET Core** was released in 2016 and combines MVC, Web API, and SignalR, running on .NET Core. Therefore, it can execute cross-platform. ASP.NET Core has many project templates to get you started with its supported technologies.

 Good Practice: Choose ASP.NET Core to develop websites and web services because it includes web-related technologies that are modern and cross-platform.

ASP.NET Core 2.0 to 2.2 can run on .NET Framework 4.6.1 or later (Windows only) as well as .NET Core 2.0 or later (cross-platform). ASP.NET Core 3.0 only supports .NET Core 3.0. ASP.NET Core 5 only supports .NET 5.

Classic ASP.NET versus modern ASP.NET Core

Until now, ASP.NET has been built on top of a large assembly in the .NET Framework named System.Web.dll and it is tightly coupled to Microsoft's Windows-only web server named **Internet Information Services (IIS)**. Over the years, this assembly has accumulated a lot of features, many of which are not suitable for modern cross-platform development.

ASP.NET Core is a major redesign of ASP.NET. It removes the dependency on the System.Web. dll assembly and IIS and is composed of modular lightweight packages, just like the rest of .NET Core.

You can develop and run ASP.NET Core applications cross-platform on Windows, macOS, and Linux. Microsoft has even created a cross-platform, super-performant web server named **Kestrel**, and the entire stack is open source.

More Information: You can read more about Kestrel, including its HTTP/2 support, at the following link: `https://docs.microsoft.com/en-us/aspnet/core/fundamentals/servers/kestrel`

ASP.NET Core 2.2 or later projects default to the new in-process hosting model. This gives a 400% performance improvement when hosting in Microsoft IIS, but Microsoft still recommends using Kestrel for even better performance.

Creating an ASP.NET Core project

We will create an ASP.NET Core project that will show a list of suppliers from the Northwind database.

The **dotnet** tool has many project templates that do a lot of work for you, but it can be difficult to discern which work best in a given situation, so we will start with the simplest web template and slowly add features step by step so that you can understand all the pieces:

1. In your existing `PracticalApps` folder, create a subfolder named `NorthwindWeb`, and add it to the `PracticalApps` workspace.
2. Navigate to **Terminal | New Terminal** and select `NorthwindWeb`.
3. In **TERMINAL**, enter the following command to create an **ASP.NET Core Empty** website: `dotnet new web`
4. In **TERMINAL**, enter the following command to restore packages and compile the website: `dotnet build`
5. Edit `NorthwindWeb.csproj`, and note the SDK is `Microsoft.NET.Sdk.Web`, as shown in the following markup:

    ```
    <Project Sdk="Microsoft.NET.Sdk.Web">
      <PropertyGroup>
        <TargetFramework>net5.0</TargetFramework>
      </PropertyGroup>
    </Project>
    ```

    In ASP.NET Core 1.0, you would need to include lots of package references. With ASP.NET Core 2.0, you would need a package reference named `Microsoft.AspNetCore.All`. With ASP.NET Core 3.0 and later, simply using this Web SDK is enough.
6. Open `Program.cs`, and note the following:
    *   A website is like a console application, with a `Main` method as its entry point.
    *   A website has a `CreateHostBuilder` method that creates a host for the website using defaults for a web host which is then built and run and specifies a `Startup` class that is used to further configure the website, as shown in the following code:

```
public class Program
{
  public static void Main(string[] args)
  {
    CreateHostBuilder(args).Build().Run();
  }

  public static IHostBuilder CreateHostBuilder(string[] args) =>
    Host.CreateDefaultBuilder(args)
      .ConfigureWebHostDefaults(webBuilder =>
      {
        webBuilder.UseStartup<Startup>();
      });
}
```

7. Open `Startup.cs`, and note its two methods:

   - The `ConfigureServices` method is currently empty. We will use it later to add services like Razor Pages and a database context for working with the `Northwind` database.

   - The `Configure` method sets up the HTTP request pipeline and currently does three things: first, it configures that when developing, any unhandled exceptions will be shown in the browser window for the developer to see its details; second, it uses routing; and third, it uses endpoints to wait for requests, and then for each HTTP GET request it asynchronously responds by returning the plain text "Hello World!", as shown in the following code:

```
public class Startup
{
  // This method gets called by the runtime.
  // Use this method to add services to the container.
  public void ConfigureServices(IServiceCollection services)
  {
  }

  // This method gets called by the runtime.
  // Use this method to configure the HTTP request pipeline.
  public void Configure(
    IApplicationBuilder app, IWebHostEnvironment env)
  {
    if (env.IsDevelopment())
    {
      app.UseDeveloperExceptionPage();
```

```
        }

        app.UseRouting();
        app.UseEndpoints(endpoints =>
        {
          endpoints.MapGet("/", async context =>
          {
            await context.Response.WriteAsync("Hello World!");
          });
        });
      }
    }
```

8. Close the `Startup.cs` class file.

How does ASP.NET Core know when we are running in development mode so that the `IsDevelopment` method returns `true`? Let's find out.

Testing and securing the website

We will now test the functionality of the ASP.NET Core Empty website project. We will also enable encryption of all traffic between the browser and web server for privacy by switching from HTTP to HTTPS. HTTPS is the secure encrypted version of HTTP.

1. In **TERMINAL**, enter the `dotnet run` command, and note the web server has started listening on ports `5000` and `5001` and the hosting environment is `Development`, as shown in the following output:

```
info: Microsoft.Hosting.Lifetime[0]
  Now listening on: https://localhost:5001
info: Microsoft.Hosting.Lifetime[0]
  Now listening on: http://localhost:5000
info: Microsoft.Hosting.Lifetime[0]
  Application started. Press Ctrl+C to shut down.
info: Microsoft.Hosting.Lifetime[0]
  Hosting environment: Development
info: Microsoft.Hosting.Lifetime[0]
  Content root path: /Users/markjprice/Code/PracticalApps/NorthwindWeb
```

2. Start Chrome.

3. Enter the address `http://localhost:5000/`, and note the response is `Hello World!` in plain text, from the cross-platform Kestrel web server, as shown in the following screenshot:

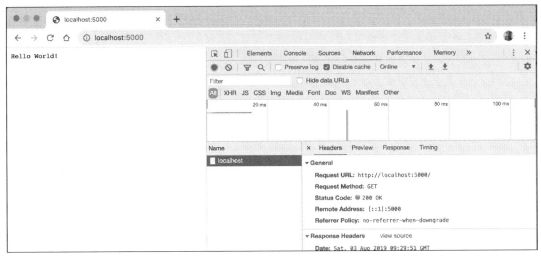

Figure 15.5: Plain text response from http://localhost:5000/

4. Enter the address `https://localhost:5001/`, and note the response is a privacy error, as shown in the following screenshot:

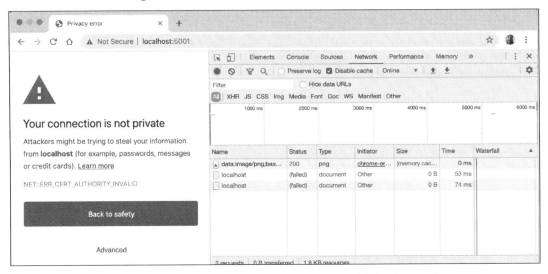

Figure 15.6: Privacy error showing SSL encryption has not been enabled with a certificate

This is because we have not configured a certificate that the browser can trust to encrypt and decrypt HTTPS traffic (so if you do not see this error, it is because you have already configured a certificate). In a production environment, you would want to pay a company like Verisign for one because they provide liability protection and technical support.

More Information: If you use a Linux variant that cannot create self-signed certificates or you do not mind reapplying for a new certificate every 90 days, then you can get a free certificate from the following link: https://letsencrypt.org

During development, you can tell your OS to trust a temporary development certificate provided by ASP.NET Core.

5. In **TERMINAL**, press *Ctrl + C* to stop the web server.

6. In **TERMINAL**, enter the `dotnet dev-certs https --trust` command, and note the message, **Trusting the HTTPS development certificate was requested**. You might be prompted to enter your password and a valid HTTPS certificate may already be present.

7. If Chrome is still running, close and restart it to ensure it has read the new certificate.

8. In `Startup.cs`, in the `Configure` method, add an `else` statement to enable HSTS when not in development, as shown highlighted in the following code:

```
if (env.IsDevelopment())
{
    app.UseDeveloperExceptionPage();
}
else
{
    app.UseHsts();
}
```

HTTP Strict Transport Security (HSTS) is an opt-in security enhancement. If a website specifies it and a browser supports it, then it forces all communication over HTTPS and prevents the visitor from using untrusted or invalid certificates.

9. Add a statement after the call to `app.UseRouting` to redirect HTTP requests to HTTPS, as shown in the following code:

```
app.UseHttpsRedirection();
```

10. In **TERMINAL**, enter the `dotnet run` command to start the web server.

11. In Chrome, request the address `http://localhost:5000/`, and note how the server responds with a `307 Temporary Redirect` to port `5001`, and that the certificate is now valid and trusted, as shown in the following screenshot:

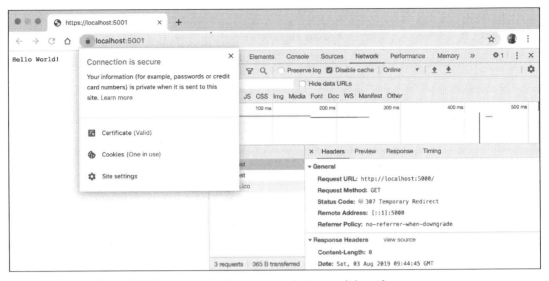

Figure 15.7: The connection is now secured using a valid certificate

12. Close Chrome.

13. In **TERMINAL**, press *Ctrl + C* to stop the web server.

Remember to stop the Kestrel web server whenever you have finished testing a website.

Controlling the hosting environment

ASP.NET Core can read from environment variables to determine what hosting environment to use, for example, DOTNET_ENVIRONMENT or ASPNETCORE_ENVIRONMENT when the ConfigureWebHostDefaults method is called, as it is in Program.cs in this project.

You can override these settings during local development:

1. In the NorthwindWeb folder, expand the folder named Properties, open the file named launchSettings.json, and note the profile named NorthwindWeb that sets the hosting environment to Development, as shown highlighted in the following configuration:

```json
{
  "iisSettings": {
    "windowsAuthentication": false,
    "anonymousAuthentication": true,
    "iisExpress": {
      "applicationUrl": "http://localhost:56111",
      "sslPort": 44329
    }
  },
  "profiles": {
    "IIS Express": {
      "commandName": "IISExpress",
```

```
      "launchBrowser": true,
      "environmentVariables": {
        "ASPNETCORE_ENVIRONMENT": "Development"
      }
    },
    "NorthwindWeb": {
      "commandName": "Project",
      "launchBrowser": true,
      "applicationUrl": "https://localhost:5001;http://localhost:5000",
      "environmentVariables": {
        "ASPNETCORE_ENVIRONMENT": "Development"
      }
    }
  }
}
```

2. Change the environment to Production.

3. In **TERMINAL**, start the website using the dotnet run command and note the hosting environment is Production, as shown in the following output:

```
info: Microsoft.Hosting.Lifetime[0]
   Hosting environment: Production
```

4. In **TERMINAL**, press *Ctrl* + *C* to stop the website.

5. In launchSettings.json, change the environment back to Development.

 More Information: You can learn more about working with ASP.NET Core hosting environments at the following link: https://docs.microsoft.com/en-us/aspnet/core/fundamentals/environments

Enabling static and default files

A website that only ever returns a single plain text message isn't very useful!

At a minimum, it ought to return static HTML pages, CSS that the web pages will use for styling, and any other static resources such as images and videos.

You will now create a folder for your static website resources and a basic index page that uses Bootstrap for styling:

 More Information: Web technologies like Bootstrap commonly use a **Content Delivery Network (CDN)** to efficiently deliver their source files globally. You can read more about CDNs at the following link: https://en.wikipedia.org/wiki/Content_delivery_network

1. In the NorthwindWeb folder, create a folder named wwwroot.

2. Add a new file to the wwwroot folder named index.html.

3. Modify its content to link to CDN-hosted Bootstrap for styling, and use modern good practices such as setting the viewport, as shown in the following markup:

```html
<!DOCTYPE html>
<html lang="en">

<head>
  <!-- Required meta tags -->
  <meta charset="utf-8" />
  <meta name="viewport" content=
    "width=device-width, initial-scale=1, shrink-to-fit=no" />

  <!-- Bootstrap CSS -->
  <link rel="stylesheet" href="https://stackpath.bootstrapcdn.com/
bootstrap/4.5.2/css/bootstrap.min.css" integrity="sha384-JcKb8q3iqJ61gNV9K
Gb8thSsNjpSL0n8PARn9HuZOnIxN0hoP+VmmDGMN5t9UJ0Z" crossorigin="anonymous">

  <title>Welcome ASP.NET Core!</title>
</head>

<body>
  <div class="container">
    <div class="jumbotron">
      <h1 class="display-3">Welcome to Northwind!</h1>
      <p class="lead">We supply products to our customers.</p>
      <hr />
      <h2>This is a static HTML page.</h2>
      <p>Our customers include restaurants, hotels, and cruise lines.</p>
      <p>
        <a class="btn btn-primary"
          href="https://www.asp.net/">Learn more</a>
      </p>
    </div>
  </div>
</body>

</html>
```

More Information: To get the latest <link> element for Bootstrap, copy and paste it from the *Getting Started - Introduction* page in the documentation at the following link: https://getbootstrap.com/

If you were to start the website now, and enter `http://localhost:5000/index.html` in the address box, the website would return a `404 Not Found` error saying no web page was found. To enable the website to return static files such as `index.html`, we must explicitly configure that feature.

Even if we enable static files, if you were to start the website and enter `http://localhost:5000/` in the address box, the website would return a `404 Not Found` error because the web server doesn't know what to return by default if no named file is requested.

You will now enable static files, explicitly configure default files, and change the URL path registered that returns `Hello World`:

1. In `Startup.cs`, in the `Configure` method, modify the statement that maps a `GET` request to returning the `Hello World!` plain text response to only respond to the URL path `/hello`, and add statements to enable static files and default files, as shown highlighted in the following code:

```
public void Configure(
    IApplicationBuilder app, IWebHostEnvironment env)
{
    if (env.IsDevelopment())
    {
        app.UseDeveloperExceptionPage();
    }
    else
    {
        app.UseHsts();
    }

    app.UseRouting();

    app.UseHttpsRedirection();
    app.UseDefaultFiles(); // index.html, default.html, and so on
    app.UseStaticFiles();

    app.UseEndpoints(endpoints =>
    {
        endpoints.MapGet("/hello", async context =>
        {
            await context.Response.WriteAsync("Hello World!");
        });
    });
}
```

The call to `UseDefaultFiles` must be before the call to `UseStaticFiles`, or it won't work!

2. Start the website by entering `dotnet run` in **TERMINAL**.

3. In Chrome, enter `http://localhost:5000/`, and note that you are redirected to the HTTPS address on port 5001, and the `index.html` file is now returned because it is one of the possible default files for this website.

4. In Chrome, enter `http://localhost:5000/hello`, and note that it returns the plain text `Hello World!` as before.

If all web pages are static, that is, they only get changed manually by a web editor, then our website programming work is complete. But almost all websites need dynamic content, which means a web page that is generated at runtime by executing code.

The easiest way to do that is to use a feature of ASP.NET Core named **Razor Pages**.

Exploring Razor Pages

Razor Pages allow a developer to easily mix HTML markup with C# code statements. That is why they use the `.cshtml` file extension.

By default, ASP.NET Core looks for Razor Pages in a folder named `Pages`.

Enabling Razor Pages

You will now change the static HTML page into a dynamic Razor Page, and then add and enable the Razor Pages service:

1. In the `NorthwindWeb` project, create a folder named `Pages`.

2. Copy the `index.html` file into the `Pages` folder.

3. Rename the file extension from `.html` to `.cshtml`.

4. Remove the `<h2>` element that says that this is a static HTML page.

5. In `Startup.cs`, in the `ConfigureServices` method, add statements to add Razor Pages and its related services like model binding, authorization, anti-forgery, views, and tag helpers, as shown highlighted in the following code:

```
public void ConfigureServices(IServiceCollection services)
{
    services.AddRazorPages();
}
```

6. In `Startup.cs`, in the `Configure` method, in the configuration to use endpoints, add a statement to use `MapRazorPages`, as shown highlighted in the following code:

```
app.UseEndpoints(endpoints =>
{
    endpoints.MapRazorPages();

    endpoints.MapGet("/hello", async context =>
    {
```

```
        await context.Response.WriteAsync("Hello World!");
    });
});
```

Defining a Razor Page

In the HTML markup of a web page, Razor syntax is indicated by the @ symbol.

Razor Pages can be described as follows:

- They require the @page directive at the top of the file.
- They can have an @functions section that defines any of the following:

    - Properties for storing data values, like in a class definition. An instance of that class is automatically instantiated named Model that can have its properties set in special methods and you can get the property values in the markup.
    - Methods named OnGet, OnPost, OnDelete, and so on, that execute when HTTP requests are made, such as GET, POST, and DELETE.

Let's now convert the static HTML page into a Razor page:

1. In Visual Studio Code, open index.cshtml.
2. Add the @page statement to the top of the file.
3. After the @page statement, add an @functions statement block.
4. Define a property to store the name of the current day as a string value.
5. Define a method to set DayName that executes when an HTTP GET request is made for the page, as shown in the following code:

```
@page
@functions
{
    public string DayName { get; set; }

    public void OnGet()
    {
        Model.DayName = DateTime.Now.ToString("dddd");
    }
}
```

6. Output the day name inside one of the paragraphs, as shown in the following markup:

```
<p>It's @Model.DayName! Our customers include restaurants, hotels, and
cruise lines.</p>
```

7. Start the website, visit it with Chrome as you did before by navigating to the URL http://localhost:5000/, and note the current day name is output on the page, as shown in the following screenshot:

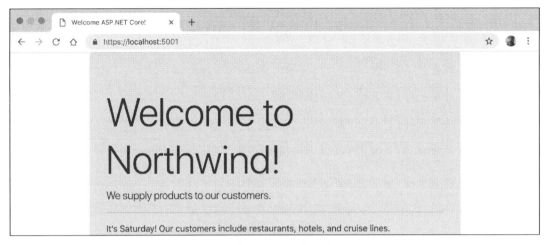

Figure 15.8: Welcome to Northwind!

8. In Chrome, enter `http://localhost:5000/index.html`, which exactly matches the static filename, and note that it returns the static HTML page as before.

9. Close Chrome and stop the web server by pressing *Ctrl + C* in **TERMINAL**.

Using shared layouts with Razor Pages

Most websites have more than one page. If every page had to contain all of the boilerplate markup that is currently in `index.cshtml`, that would become a pain to manage. So, ASP.NET Core has **layouts**.

To use layouts, we must create a Razor file to define the default layout for all Razor Pages (and all MVC views) and store it in a `Shared` folder so that it can be easily found by convention. The name of this file can be anything, but `_Layout.cshtml` is good practice. We must also create a specially named file to set the default layout for all Razor Pages (and all MVC views). This file must be named `_ViewStart.cshtml`:

1. In the `Pages` folder, create a file named `_ViewStart.cshtml`.

2. Modify its content, as shown in the following markup:

```
@{
    Layout = "_Layout";
}
```

3. In the `Pages` folder, create a folder named `Shared`.

4. In the `Shared` folder, create a file named `_Layout.cshtml`.

5. Modify the content of `_Layout.cshtml` (it is similar to `index.cshtml` so you can copy and paste the HTML markup from there), as shown in the following markup:

```
<!DOCTYPE html>
<html lang="en">

<head>
  <!-- Required meta tags -->
  <meta charset="utf-8" />
  <meta name="viewport" content=
    "width=device-width, initial-scale=1, shrink-to-fit=no" />

  <!-- Bootstrap CSS -->
  <link rel="stylesheet" href="https://stackpath.bootstrapcdn.com/
bootstrap/4.5.2/css/bootstrap.min.css" integrity="sha384-JcKb8q3iqJ61gNV9K
Gb8thSsNjpSL0n8PARn9HuZOnIxN0hoP+VmmDGMN5t9UJ0Z " crossorigin="anonymous">

  <title>@ViewData["Title"]</title>
</head>

<body>
  <div class="container">
  @RenderBody()
  <hr />
  <footer>
    <p>Copyright &copy; 2020 - @ViewData["Title"]</p>
  </footer>
  </div>

  <!-- JavaScript to enable features like carousel -->
  <!-- jQuery first, then Popper.js, then Bootstrap JS -->
  <script src="https://code.jquery.com/jquery-3.5.1.slim.min.js"
integrity="sha384-DfXdz2htPH0lsSSs5nCTpuj/zy4C+OGpamoFVy38MVBnE+IbbVYUew+O
rCXaRkfj" crossorigin="anonymous"></script>

  <script src="https://cdnjs.cloudflare.com/ajax/libs/popper.js/1.14.7/
umd/popper.min.js" integrity="sha384-UO2eT0CpHqdSJQ6hJty5KVphtPhzWj9WO1clH
TMGa3JDZwrnQq4sF86dIHNDz0W1" crossorigin="anonymous"></script>

  <script src="https://stackpath.bootstrapcdn.com/bootstrap/4.3.1/js/
bootstrap.min.js" integrity="sha384-JjSmVgyd0p3pXB1rRibZUAYoIIy6OrQ6VrjIEa
Ff/nJGzIxFDsf4x0xIM+B07jRM" crossorigin="anonymous"></script>

  @RenderSection("Scripts", required: false)

</body>
</html>
```

While reviewing the preceding markup, note the following:

- `<title>` is set dynamically using server-side code from a dictionary named `ViewData`. This is a simple way to pass data between different parts of an ASP. NET Core website. In this case, the data will be set in a Razor Page class file and then output in the shared layout.

- `@RenderBody()` marks the insertion point for the page being requested.

- A horizontal rule and footer will appear at the bottom of each page.

- At the bottom of the layout are some scripts to implement some cool features of Bootstrap that we can use later like a carousel of images.

- After the `<script>` elements for Bootstrap, we have defined a section named `Scripts` so that a Razor Page can optionally inject additional scripts that it needs.

6. Modify `index.cshtml` to remove all HTML markup except `<div class="jumbotron">` and its contents, and leave the C# code in the `@functions` block that you added earlier.

7. Add a statement to the `OnGet` method to store a page title in the `ViewData` dictionary, and modify the button to navigate to a suppliers page (which we will create in the next section), as shown highlighted in the following markup:

```
@page
@functions
{
    public string DayName { get; set; }

    public void OnGet()
    {
        ViewData["Title"] = "Northwind Website";

        Model.DayName = DateTime.Now.ToString("dddd");
    }
}
<div class="jumbotron">
    <h1 class="display-3">Welcome to Northwind!</h1>
    <p class="lead">We supply products to our customers.</p>
    <hr />
    <p>It's @Model.DayName! Our customers include restaurants, hotels, and
cruise lines.</p>
    <p>
        <a class="btn btn-primary" href="suppliers">
        Learn more about our suppliers</a>
    </p>
</div>
```

8. Start the website, visit it with Chrome, and note that it has similar behavior as before, although clicking the button for suppliers will give a 404 Not Found error because we have not created that page yet.

Using code-behind files with Razor Pages

Sometimes, it is better to separate the HTML markup from the data and executable code, so Razor Pages allows **code-behind** class files.

You will now create a page that shows a list of suppliers. In this example, we are focusing on learning about code-behind files. In the next topic, we will load the list of suppliers from a database, but for now, we will simulate that with a hardcoded array of string values:

1. In the Pages folder, add two new files named suppliers.cshtml and suppliers.cshtml. cs.

2. Add statements to suppliers.cshtml.cs, as shown in the following code:

```
using Microsoft.AspNetCore.Mvc.RazorPages;
using System.Collections.Generic;

namespace NorthwindWeb.Pages
{
  public class SuppliersModel : PageModel
  {
    public IEnumerable<string> Suppliers { get; set; }

    public void OnGet()
    {
      ViewData["Title"] = "Northwind Web Site - Suppliers";


      Suppliers = new[] {
        "Alpha Co", "Beta Limited", "Gamma Corp"
      };
    }
  }
}
```

While reviewing the preceding markup, note the following:

- SuppliersModel inherits from PageModel, so it has members such as the ViewData dictionary for sharing data. You can click on PageModel and press F12 to see that it has lots more useful features, like the entire HttpContext of the current request.

- SuppliersModel defines a property for storing a collection of string values named Suppliers.

- When an HTTP GET request is made for this Razor Page, the Suppliers property is populated with some example supplier names.

3. Modify the contents of suppliers.cshtml, as shown in the following markup:

```
@page
@model NorthwindWeb.Pages.SuppliersModel
<div class="row">
  <h1 class="display-2">Suppliers</h1>
  <table class="table">
    <thead class="thead-inverse">
      <tr><th>Company Name</th></tr>
    </thead>
    <tbody>
    @foreach(string name in Model.Suppliers)
    {
      <tr><td>@name</td></tr>
    }
    </tbody>
  </table>
</div>
```

While reviewing the preceding markup, note the following:

- The model type for this Razor Page is set to SuppliersModel.
- The page outputs an HTML table with Bootstrap styles.
- The data rows in the table are generated by looping through the Suppliers property of Model.

4. Start the website, visit it using Chrome, click on the button to learn more about suppliers, and note the table of suppliers, as shown in the following screenshot:

Figure 15.9: The temporary list of suppliers

Using Entity Framework Core with ASP.NET Core

Entity Framework Core is a natural way to get real data into a website. In *Chapter 14*, *Introducing Practical Applications of C# and .NET*, you created two class libraries: one for the entity models and one for the Northwind database context.

Configure Entity Framework Core as a service

Functionality like Entity Framework Core database contexts that are needed by ASP.NET Core must be registered as a service during website startup:

1. In the NorthwindWeb project, modify NorthwindWeb.csproj to add a reference to the NorthwindContextLib project, as shown highlighted in the following markup:

```
<Project Sdk="Microsoft.NET.Sdk.Web">
  <PropertyGroup>
    <TargetFramework>net5.0</TargetFramework>
  </PropertyGroup>
  <ItemGroup>
    <ProjectReference Include=
      "..\NorthwindContextLib\NorthwindContextLib.csproj" />
  </ItemGroup>
</Project>
```

2. In **TERMINAL**, restore packages and compile the project by entering the following command: dotnet build

3. Open Startup.cs and import the System.IO, Microsoft.EntityFrameworkCore, and Packt.Shared namespaces, as shown in the following code:

```
using System.IO;
using Microsoft.EntityFrameworkCore;
using Packt.Shared;
```

4. Add statements to the ConfigureServices method to register the Northwind database context class to use SQLite as its database provider and specify its database connection string, as shown in the following code:

```
string databasePath = Path.Combine("..", "Northwind.db");

services.AddDbContext<Northwind>(options =>
  options.UseSqlite($"Data Source={databasePath}"));
```

5. In the NorthwindWeb project, in the Pages folder, open suppliers.cshtml.cs, and import the Packt.Shared and System.Linq namespaces, as shown in the following code:

```
using System.Linq;
using Packt.Shared;
```

6. In the `SuppliersModel` class, add a private field and a constructor to get the `Northwind` database context, as shown in the following code:

```
private Northwind db;

public SuppliersModel(Northwind injectedContext)
{
  db = injectedContext;
}
```

7. In the `OnGet` method, modify the statements to get the names of suppliers by selecting the company names from the `Suppliers` property of the database context, as shown highlighted in the following code:

```
public void OnGet()
{
  ViewData["Title"] = "Northwind Web Site - Suppliers";

  Suppliers = db.Suppliers.Select(s => s.CompanyName);
}
```

8. In **TERMINAL**, enter the command `dotnet run` to start the website, in Chrome, enter `http://localhost:5000/`, click the button to go to the `Suppliers` page, and note that the supplier table now loads from the database, as shown in the following screenshot:

Figure 15.10: The suppliers table loading from the database

Manipulating data using Razor Pages

You will now add functionality to insert a new supplier.

Enabling a model to insert entities

First, you will modify the supplier model so that it responds to HTTP POST requests when a visitor submits a form to insert a new supplier:

1. In the `NorthwindWeb` project, in the `Pages` folder, open `suppliers.cshtml.cs` and import the following namespace:

```
using Microsoft.AspNetCore.Mvc;
```

2. In the `SuppliersModel` class, add a property to store a supplier, and a method named `OnPost` that adds the supplier if its model is valid, as shown in the following code:

```
[BindProperty]
public Supplier Supplier { get; set; }

public IActionResult OnPost()
{
  if (ModelState.IsValid)
  {
    db.Suppliers.Add(Supplier);
    db.SaveChanges();
    return RedirectToPage("/suppliers");
  }
  return Page();
}
```

While reviewing the preceding code, note the following:

- We added a property named `Supplier` that is decorated with the `[BindProperty]` attribute so that we can easily connect HTML elements on the web page to properties in the `Supplier` class.

- We added a method that responds to HTTP POST requests. It checks that all property values conform to validation rules and then adds the supplier to the existing table and saves changes to the database context. This will generate a SQL statement to perform the insert into the database. Then it redirects to the **Suppliers** page so that the visitor sees the newly added supplier.

Defining a form to insert new suppliers

Second, you will modify the Razor page to define a form that a visitor can fill in and submit to insert a new supplier:

1. Open `suppliers.cshtml`, and add tag helpers after the `@model` declaration so that we can use tag helpers like `asp-for` on this Razor page, as shown in the following markup:

```
@addTagHelper *, Microsoft.AspNetCore.Mvc.TagHelpers
```

2. At the bottom of the file, add a form to insert a new supplier, and use the `asp-for` tag helper to connect the `CompanyName` property of the `Supplier` class to the input box, as shown in the following markup:

```
<div class="row">
  <p>Enter a name for a new supplier:</p>
  <form method="POST">
    <div><input asp-for="Supplier.CompanyName" /></div>
    <input type="submit" />
  </form>
</div>
```

While reviewing the preceding markup, note the following:

- The `<form>` element with a POST method is normal HTML, so an `<input type="submit" />` element inside it will make an HTTP POST request back to the current page with values of any other elements inside that form.

- An `<input>` element with a tag helper named `asp-for` enables data binding to the model behind the Razor page.

3. Start the website, click **Learn more about our suppliers**, scroll down the table of suppliers to the bottom of the form to add a new supplier, enter Bob's Burgers, and click on **Submit**, as shown in the following screenshot:

Figure 15.11: Entering a new supplier

4. Note that you see a refreshed *Suppliers* list with the new supplier added.

5. Close the browser.

As an optional exercise, add the other fields for a Supplier like **Country** and **Phone**.

Using Razor class libraries

Everything related to a Razor page can be compiled into a class library for easier reuse. With .NET Core 3.0 and later, this can include static files. A website can either use the Razor page's view as defined in the class library or override it.

Creating a Razor class library

Let us create a new Razor class library:

1. Create a subfolder in PracticalApps named NorthwindEmployees.

2. In Visual Studio Code, add the NorthwindEmployees folder to the PracticalApps workspace.

3. Navigate to **Terminal** | **New Terminal** and select NorthwindEmployees.

4. In **TERMINAL**, enter the following command to create a **Razor Class Library** project:

```
dotnet new razorclasslib -s
```

 More Information: The -s option is short for --support-pages-and-views that enables the class library to use Razor Pages and .cshtml file views

Disabling compact folders

Before we implement our Razor class library, I want to explain a recent Visual Studio Code feature that confused some readers of the previous edition because the feature was added after publishing.

The **compact folders** feature means that nested folders like /Areas/MyFeature/Pages/ are shown in a compact form if the intermediate folders in the hierarchy do not contain files, as shown in the following screenshot:

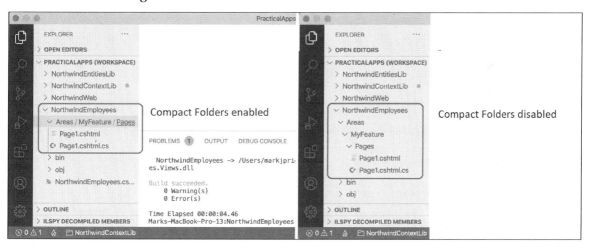

Figure 15.12: Compact folders enabled or disabled

If you would like to disable the Visual Studio Code compact folders feature, complete the following steps:

1. On macOS, navigate to **Code** | **Preferences** | **Settings**, or press *Cmd* + ,. On Windows, navigate to **File** | **Preferences** | **Settings**, or press *Ctrl* + ,.

2. In the **Search** settings box, enter compact.

3. Clear the **Explorer: Compact Folders** checkbox, as shown in the following screenshot:

Figure 15.13: Disabling compact folders

4. Close the **Settings** tab.

 More Information: You can read about the Compact Folders feature introduced with Visual Studio Code 1.41 in November 2019 at the following link: https://github.com/microsoft/vscode-docs/blob/vnext/release-notes/v1_41.md#compact-folders-in-explorer

Implementing the employees feature using EF Core

Now we can add a reference to our entity models to get the employees to show in the Razor class library:

1. Edit NorthwindEmployees.csproj, note the SDK is Microsoft.NET.Sdk.Razor, and add a reference to the NorthwindContextLib project, as shown highlighted in the following markup:

```
<Project Sdk="Microsoft.NET.Sdk.Razor">
  <PropertyGroup>
    <TargetFramework>net5.0</TargetFramework>
    <AddRazorSupportForMvc>true</AddRazorSupportForMvc>
  </PropertyGroup>
  <ItemGroup>
    <FrameworkReference Include="Microsoft.AspNetCore.App" />
  </ItemGroup>
  <ItemGroup>
```

```
    <ProjectReference Include=
        "..\NorthwindContextLib\NorthwindContextLib.csproj" />
    </ItemGroup>
</Project>
```

2. In **TERMINAL**, enter the following command to restore packages and compile the project: `dotnet build`

3. In **EXPLORER**, under the `Areas` folder, right-click the `MyFeature` folder, select **Rename**, enter the new name `PacktFeatures`, and press *Enter*.

4. In **EXPLORER**, under the `PacktFeatures` folder, and in the `Pages` subfolder, add a new file named `_ViewStart.cshtml`.

5. Modify its content, as shown in the following markup:

```
@{
    Layout = "_Layout";
}
```

6. In the `Pages` subfolder, rename `Page1.cshtml` to `employees.cshtml`, and rename `Page1.cshtml.cs` to `employees.cshtml.cs`.

7. Modify `employees.cshtml.cs`, to define a page model with an array of `Employee` entity instances loaded from the `Northwind` database, as shown in the following code:

```
using Microsoft.AspNetCore.Mvc.RazorPages; // PageModel
using Packt.Shared;                        // Employee
using System.Linq;                         // ToArray()
using System.Collections.Generic;          // IEnumerable<T>

namespace PacktFeatures.Pages
{
  public class EmployeesPageModel : PageModel
  {
    private Northwind db;

    public EmployeesPageModel(Northwind injectedContext)
    {
      db = injectedContext;
    }

    public IEnumerable<Employee> Employees { get; set; }

    public void OnGet()
    {
      Employees = db.Employees.ToArray();
    }
  }
}
```

8. Modify `employees.cshtml`, as shown in the following markup:

```
@page
@using Packt.Shared
@addTagHelper *, Microsoft.AspNetCore.Mvc.TagHelpers
@model PacktFeatures.Pages.EmployeesPageModel
<div class="row">
  <h1 class="display-2">Employees</h2>
</div>
<div class="row">
@foreach(Employee employee in Model.Employees)
{
  <div class="col-sm-3">
    <partial name="_Employee" model="employee" />
  </div>
}
</div>
```

While reviewing the preceding markup, note the following:

- We import the `Packt.Shared` namespace so that we can use classes in it like `Employee`.

- We add support for tag helpers so that we can use the `<partial>` element.

- We declare the model type for this Razor page to use the class that you just defined.

- We enumerate through the `Employees` in the model, outputting each one using a partial view. Partial views are like small pieces of a Razor page and you will create one in the next few steps.

 More Information: The `<partial>` tag helper was introduced in ASP.NET Core 2.1. You can read more about it at the following link: https://docs. microsoft.com/en-us/aspnet/core/mvc/views/tag-helpers/built-in/ partial-tag-helper

Implementing a partial view to show a single employee

Now we will define a partial view to render a single employee:

1. In the `Pages` folder, create a `Shared` folder.

2. In the `Shared` folder, create a file named `_Employee.cshtml`.

3. Modify `_Employee.cshtml`, as shown in the following markup:

```
@model Packt.Shared.Employee
<div class="card border-dark mb-3" style="max-width: 18rem;">
  <div class="card-header">@Model.FirstName
    @Model.LastName</div>
  <div class="card-body text-dark">
    <h5 class="card-title">@Model.Country</h5>
    <p class="card-text">@Model.Notes</p>
  </div>
</div>
```

While reviewing the preceding markup, note the following:

- By convention, the names of partial views start with an underscore.
- If you put a partial view in the Shared folder, then it can be found automatically.
- The model type for this partial view is an Employee entity.
- We use Bootstrap card styles to output information about each employee.

Using and testing a Razor class library

You will now reference and use the Razor class library in the website project:

1. Modify the NorthwindWeb.csproj file to add a reference to the NorthwindEmployees project, as shown highlighted in the following markup:

```
<Project Sdk="Microsoft.NET.Sdk.Web">
  <PropertyGroup>
    <TargetFramework>net5.0</TargetFramework>
  </PropertyGroup>
  <ItemGroup>
    <ProjectReference Include=
      "..\NorthwindContextLib\NorthwindContextLib.csproj" />
    <ProjectReference Include=
      "..\NorthwindEmployees\NorthwindEmployees.csproj" />
  </ItemGroup>
</Project>
```

2. Modify Pages\index.cshtml to add a link to the Packt feature employees page after the link to the suppliers page, as shown in the following markup:

```
<p>
  <a class="btn btn-primary" href="packtfeatures/employees">
    Contact our employees
  </a>
</p>
```

3. Start the website, visit the website using Chrome, and click the button to see the cards of employees, as shown in the following screenshot:

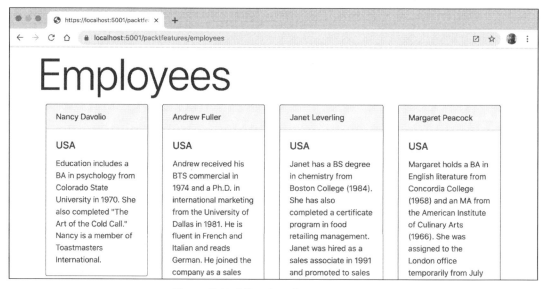

Figure 15.14: A list of employees

Configuring services and the HTTP request pipeline

Now that we have built a website we can return to the configuration and review how services and the HTTP request pipeline work in more detail.

Review the `Startup.cs` class file, as shown in the following code:

```
using Microsoft.AspNetCore.Builder;
using Microsoft.AspNetCore.Hosting;
using Microsoft.AspNetCore.Http;
using Microsoft.Extensions.DependencyInjection;
using Microsoft.Extensions.Hosting;
using Microsoft.EntityFrameworkCore;
using Packt.Shared;
using System;
using System.IO;
using System.Threading.Tasks;

namespace NorthwindWeb
{
  public class Startup
  {
    // This method gets called by the runtime.
```

```csharp
    // Use this method to add services to the container.
    // For more information on how to configure your application,
    // visit https://go.microsoft.com/fwlink/?LinkID=398940
    public void ConfigureServices(IServiceCollection services)
    {
      services.AddRazorPages();

      string databasePath = Path.Combine("..", "Northwind.db");

      services.AddDbContext<Northwind>(options =>
        options.UseSqlite($"Data Source={databasePath}"));
    }

    // This method gets called by the runtime.
    // Use this method to configure the HTTP request pipeline.
    public void Configure(
      IApplicationBuilder app, IWebHostEnvironment env)
    {
      if (env.IsDevelopment())
      {
        app.UseDeveloperExceptionPage();
      }
      else
      {
        app.UseHsts();
      }

      app.UseRouting();

      app.UseHttpsRedirection();

      app.UseDefaultFiles(); // index.html, default.html, and so on
      app.UseStaticFiles();

      app.UseEndpoints(endpoints =>
      {
        endpoints.MapRazorPages();

        endpoints.MapGet("/hello", async context =>
        {
         await context.Response.WriteAsync("Hello World!");
        });
      });
    }
  }
}
```

The Startup class has two methods that are called automatically by the host to configure the website. The ConfigureServices method registers services that can then be retrieved when the functionality they provide is needed using dependency injection. Our code registers two services: Razor Pages and an EF Core database context.

Registering services

Common methods that register dependency services, including services that combine other method calls that register services, are shown in the following table:

Method	Services that it registers
AddMvcCore	Minimum set of services necessary to route requests and invoke controllers. Most websites will need more configuration than this.
AddAuthorization	Authentication and authorization services.
AddDataAnnotations	MVC data annotations service.
AddCacheTagHelper	MVC cache tag helper service.
AddRazorPages	Razor Pages service including the Razor view engine. Commonly used in simple website projects. Calls the following additional methods: • AddMvcCore • AddAuthorization • AddDataAnnotations • AddCacheTagHelper
AddApiExplorer	Web API explorer service.
AddCors	**Cross-Origin Resource Sharing** (**CORS**) support for enhanced security.
AddFormatterMappings	Mappings between a URL Format and its corresponding media type.
AddControllers	Controller services but not services for views or pages. Commonly used in ASP.NET Core Web API projects. Calls the following additional methods: • AddMvcCore • AddAuthorization • AddDataAnnotations • AddCacheTagHelper • AddApiExplorer • AddCors • AddFormatterMappings
AddViews	Support for .cshtml views including default conventions.
AddRazorViewEngine	Support for Razor view engine including processing the @ symbol.

AddControllersWithViews	Controller, views, and pages services. Commonly used in ASP.NET Core MVC website projects.
	Calls the following additional methods:
	• AddMvcCore
	• AddAuthorization
	• AddDataAnnotations
	• AddCacheTagHelper
	• AddApiExplorer
	• AddCors
	• AddFormatterMappings
	• AddViews
	• AddRazorViewEngine
AddMvc	Similar to above, but you should only use it for backward compatibility.
AddDbContext<T>	Your DbContext type and its optional DbContextOptions<TContext>.

More Information: You can read more about registering a database context for use as a dependency service at the following link: https://docs.microsoft.com/en-us/ef/core/miscellaneous/configuring-dbcontext#using-dbcontext-with-dependency-injection

You will see more examples of using these extension methods for registering services in the next few chapters when working with MVC and Web API services.

Configuring the HTTP request pipeline

The Configure method configures the HTTP request pipeline, which is made up of a connected sequence of delegates that can perform processing and then decide to either return a response themselves or pass processing on to the next delegate in the pipeline. Responses that come back can also be manipulated.

Remember that delegates define a method signature that a delegate implementation can plug into. The delegate for the HTTP request pipeline looks like the following code:

```
public delegate Task RequestDelegate(HttpContext context);
```

You can see that the input parameter is an HttpContext. This provides access to everything you might need to process the incoming HTTP request, including the URL path, query string parameters, cookies, user agent, and so on.

More Information: You can read more about HttpContext at the following link: https://docs.microsoft.com/en-us/dotnet/api/system.web.httpcontext

These delegates are often called middleware because they sit in between the browser client and the website or service.

Middleware delegates are configured using one of the following methods or a custom method that calls them itself:

- Run: Adds a middleware delegate that terminates the pipeline by immediately returning a response instead of calling the next middleware delegate.
- Map: Adds a middleware delegate that creates a branch in the pipeline when there is a matching request usually based on a URL path like /hello.
- Use: Adds a middleware delegate that forms part of the pipeline so it can decide if it wants to pass the request to the next delegate in the pipeline and it can modify the request and response before and after the next delegate.

 More Information: You can review simple examples of each of these methods at the following link: https://www.vaughanreid.com/2020/05/using-in-line-middleware-in-asp-net-core/

For convenience, there are many extension methods that make it easier to build the pipeline, for example, UseMiddleware<T> where T is a class that has (1) a constructor with a RequestDelegate parameter that will be passed the next pipeline component, and (2) an Invoke method with a HttpContext parameter and returns a Task.

Key middleware extension methods used in our code include the following:

- UseDeveloperExceptionPage: Captures synchronous and asynchronous System. Exception instances from the pipeline and generates HTML error responses.
- UseHsts: Adds middleware for using HSTS, which adds the Strict-Transport-Security header.
- UseRouting: Adds middleware that defines a point in the pipeline where routing decisions are made and must be combined with a call to UseEndpoints where the processing is then executed. This means that for our code, any URL paths that match / or /index or /suppliers will be mapped to Razor Pages and a match on /hello will be mapped to the anonymous delegate. Any other URL paths will be passed on to the next delegate for matching, for example, static files. This is why, although it looks like the mapping for Razor Pages and /hello happen after static files in the pipeline, they actually take priority because the call to UseRouting happens before UseStaticFiles.
- UseHttpsRedirection: Adds middleware for redirecting HTTP Requests to HTTPS, so in our code a request for http://localhost:5000 would be modified to https://localhost:5001.
- UseDefaultFiles: Adds middleware that enables default file mapping on the current path, so in our code it would identify files like index.html.

- **UseStaticFiles**: Adds middleware that looks in `wwwroot` for static files to return in the HTTP response.
- **UseEndpoints**: Adds middleware to execute to generate responses from decisions made earlier in the pipeline. Two endpoints are added, as shown in the following sub-list:
  - **MapRazorPages**: Adds middleware that will map URL paths like `/suppliers` to a Razor Page file in the `/Pages` folder named `suppliers.cshtml` and return the results as the HTTP response.
  - **MapGet**: Adds middleware that will map URL paths like `/hello` to an inline delegate that writes plain text directly to the HTTP response.

The HTTP request and response pipeline can be visualized as a sequence of request delegates, called one after the other, as shown in the following simplified diagram that excludes some middleware delegates like `UseHsts`:

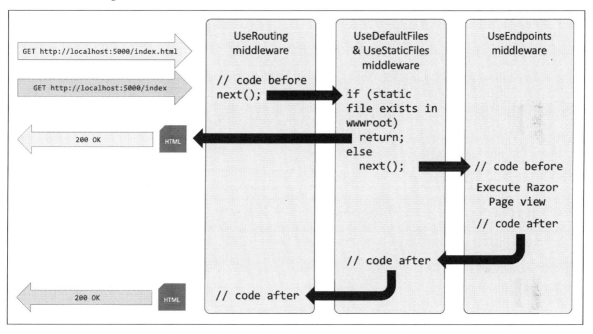

Figure 15.15: The HTTP request and response pipeline

 More Information: You can learn how to automatically visualize your endpoints by reading the article at the following link: `https://andrewlock.net/visualizing-asp-net-core-endpoints-using-graphvizonline-and-the-dot-language/`

As mentioned before, the `UseRouting` and `UseEndpoints` methods must be used together. Although the code to define the mapped routes like `/hello` are written in `UseEndpoints`, the decision if an incoming HTTP request URL path matches and therefore which endpoint to execute is made at the `UseRouting` point in the pipeline.

A delegate can be specified as an inline anonymous method. We will register one that plugs into the pipeline after routing decisions for endpoints have been made. It will output which endpoint was chosen, as well as handling one specific route: /bonjour. If that route is matched, it will respond with plain text, without calling any further into the pipeline:

1. Open the Startup.cs class file and import the Microsoft.AspNetCore.Routing namespace and statically import Console.

2. Add statements before the call to UseHttpsRedirection to use an anonymous method as a middleware delegate, as shown in the following code:

```csharp
app.Use(async (HttpContext context, Func<Task> next) =>
{
  var rep = context.GetEndpoint() as RouteEndpoint;
  if (rep != null)
  {
    WriteLine($"Endpoint name: {rep.DisplayName}");
    WriteLine($"Endpoint route pattern: {rep.RoutePattern.RawText}");
  }

  if (context.Request.Path == "/bonjour")
  {
    // in the case of a match on URL path, this becomes a terminating
    // delegate that returns so does not call the next delegate
    await context.Response.WriteAsync("Bonjour Monde!");
    return;
  }
  // we could modify the request before calling the next delegate
  await next();
  // we could modify the response after calling the next delegate
});
```

3. Start the website.

4. In Chrome, navigate to https://localhost:5001/ and note in **TERMINAL** that there was a match on an endpoint route /, it was processed as /index, and the Index.cshtml Razor Page was executed to return the response, as shown in the following output:

```
Endpoint name: /index
Endpoint route pattern:
```

5. Navigate to https://localhost:5001/suppliers and note in **TERMINAL** that you can see that there was a match on an endpoint route /supplier and the supplier.cshtml Razor Page was executed to return the response, as shown in the following output:

```
Endpoint name: /suppliers
Endpoint route pattern: suppliers
```

6. Navigate to `https://localhost:5001/index` and note in **TERMINAL** that there was a match on an endpoint route /index and the `Index.cshtml` Razor Page was executed to return the response, as shown in the following output:

```
Endpoint name: /index
Endpoint route pattern: index
```

7. Navigate to `https://localhost:5001/index.html` and note in **TERMINAL** that there was no match on an endpoint route but there was a match for a static file, so it was returned as the response.

8. Navigate to `https://localhost:5001/hello` and note in **TERMINAL** that there was a match on an endpoint route /hello and the anonymous method was executed to return the plain text response, as shown in the following output:

```
Endpoint name: /hello HTTP: GET
Endpoint route pattern: /hello
```

9. Close Chrome and stop the website.

 More Information: You can read more about configuring the HTTP pipeline with middleware at the following link: `https://docs.microsoft.com/en-us/aspnet/core/fundamentals/middleware`

Simplest possible ASP.NET Core website project

We will end by creating the simplest possible ASP.NET Core website in 15 lines of code using the C# 9 top-level program feature and a request pipeline implementation that always returns the same HTTP response:

1. In your existing `PracticalApps` folder, create a subfolder named `SimpleWeb`, and add it to the `PracticalApps` workspace.

2. Navigate to **Terminal | New Terminal** and select `SimpleWeb`.

3. In **TERMINAL**, enter the following command to create a console app: `dotnet new console`

4. Select `SimpleWeb` as the active project.

5. Edit `SimpleWeb.csproj`, and modify the SDK to `Microsoft.NET.Sdk.Web`, as shown highlighted in the following markup:

```
<Project Sdk="Microsoft.NET.Sdk.Web">
  <PropertyGroup>
    <TargetFramework>net5.0</TargetFramework>
  </PropertyGroup>
</Project>
```

6. Edit the `Program.cs` file, as shown in the following code:

```
using Microsoft.AspNetCore.Hosting; // IWebHostBuilder.Configure
using Microsoft.AspNetCore.Builder; // IApplicationBuilder.Run
using Microsoft.AspNetCore.Http;    // HttpResponse.WriteAsync
using Microsoft.Extensions.Hosting; // Host

Host.CreateDefaultBuilder(args)
  .ConfigureWebHostDefaults(webBuilder =>
  {
    webBuilder.Configure(app =>
    {
      app.Run(context =>
        context.Response.WriteAsync("Hello World Wide Web!"));
    });
  })
  .Build().Run();
```

7. Start the website.

8. In Chrome, navigate to `http://localhost:5000/`, and note the response is always the same plain text whatever URL path is used.

9. Close Chrome and stop the web server.

Practicing and exploring

Test your knowledge and understanding by answering some questions, get some hands-on practice, and explore this chapter's topics with deeper research.

Exercise 15.1 – Test your knowledge

Answer the following questions:

1. List six method names that can be specific in an HTTP request.
2. List six status codes and their descriptions that can be returned in an HTTP response.
3. In ASP.NET Core, what is the `Startup` class used for?
4. What does the acronym HSTS stand for and what does it do?
5. How do you enable static HTML pages for a website?
6. How do you mix C# code into the middle of HTML to create a dynamic page?
7. How can you define shared layouts for Razor Pages?
8. How can you separate the markup from the code behind in a Razor Page?

9. How do you configure an Entity Framework Core data context for use with an ASP. NET Core website?

10. How can you reuse Razor Pages with ASP.NET Core 2.2 or later?

Exercise 15.2 – Practice building a data-driven web page

Add a Razor Page to the **NorthwindWeb** website that enables the user to see a list of customers grouped by country. When the user clicks on a customer record, they then see a page showing the full contact details of that customer, and a list of their orders.

Exercise 15.3 – Practice building web pages for console apps

Re-implement some of the console apps from earlier chapters as Razor Pages, for example, from *Chapter 4, Writing, Debugging, and Testing Functions*, provide a web user interface to output times tables, calculate tax, and generate factorials and the Fibonacci sequence.

Exercise 15.4 – Explore topics

Use the following links to read more details about this chapter's topics:

- **ASP.NET Core fundamentals**: `https://docs.microsoft.com/en-us/aspnet/core/fundamentals/`

- **Static files in ASP.NET Core**: `https://docs.microsoft.com/en-us/aspnet/core/fundamentals/static-files`

- **Introduction to Razor Pages in ASP.NET Core**: `https://docs.microsoft.com/en-us/aspnet/core/razor-pages/`

- **Razor syntax reference for ASP.NET Core**: `https://docs.microsoft.com/en-us/aspnet/core/mvc/views/razor`

- **Layout in ASP.NET Core**: `https://docs.microsoft.com/en-us/aspnet/core/mvc/views/layout`

- **Tag Helpers in ASP.NET Core**: `https://docs.microsoft.com/en-us/aspnet/core/mvc/views/tag-helpers/intro`

- **ASP.NET Core Razor Pages with EF Core**: `https://docs.microsoft.com/en-us/aspnet/core/data/ef-rp/intro`

- **DEEP DIVE: HOW IS THE ASP.NET CORE MIDDLEWARE PIPELINE BUILT?** `https://www.stevejgordon.co.uk/how-is-the-asp-net-core-middleware-pipeline-built`

Summary

In this chapter, you learned about the foundations of web development using HTTP, how to build a simple website that returns static files, and you used ASP.NET Core Razor Pages with Entity Framework Core to create web pages that were dynamically generated from information in a database.

We reviewed the HTTP request and response pipeline, what the helper extension methods do, and how you can add your own middleware that affects processing.

In the next chapter, you will learn how to build more complex websites using ASP.NET Core MVC, which separates the technical concerns of building a website into models, views, and controllers to make them easier to manage.

16

Building Websites Using the Model-View-Controller Pattern

This chapter is about building websites with a modern HTTP architecture on the server side using Microsoft ASP.NET Core MVC, including the startup configuration, authentication, authorization, routes, request and response pipeline, models, views, and controllers that make up an ASP.NET Core MVC project.

This chapter will cover the following topics:

- Setting up an ASP.NET Core MVC website
- Exploring an ASP.NET Core MVC website
- Customizing an ASP.NET Core MVC website
- Using other project templates

Setting up an ASP.NET Core MVC website

ASP.NET Core Razor Pages are great for simple websites. For more complex websites, it would be better to have a more formal structure to manage that complexity.

This is where the **Model-View-Controller** (**MVC**) design pattern is useful. It uses technologies similar to Razor Pages, but allows a cleaner separation between technical concerns, as shown in the following list:

- **Models**: Classes that represent the data entities and view models used in the website.
- **Views**: Razor files, that is, .cshtml files, that render data in view models into HTML web pages. Blazor uses the .razor file extension, but do not confuse them with Razor files!
- **Controllers**: Classes that execute code when an HTTP request arrives at the web server.

- The code usually creates a view model that may contain entity models and passes it to a view to generate an HTTP response to send back to the web browser or other client.

The best way to understand using the MVC design pattern for web development is to see a working example.

Creating and exploring an ASP.NET Core MVC website

You will use the mvc project template to create an ASP.NET Core MVC application with a database for authenticating and authorizing users:

1. In the folder named PracticalApps, create a folder named NorthwindMvc.
2. In Visual Studio Code, open the PracticalApps workspace and then add the NorthwindMvc folder to the workspace.
3. Navigate to **Terminal | New Terminal** and select NorthwindMvc.
4. In **TERMINAL**, create a new MVC website project with authentication stored in a SQLite database, as shown in the following command:

```
dotnet new mvc --auth Individual
```

You can enter the following command to see other options for this template:

```
dotnet new mvc --help
```

5. In **TERMINAL**, enter the command dotnet run to start the website.
6. Start Chrome and open **Developer tools**.
7. Navigate to http://localhost:5000/ and note the following, as shown in the following screenshot:
   - Requests for HTTP are automatically redirected to HTTPS on port 5001.
   - The navigation menu at the top with links to **Home**, **Privacy**, **Register**, and **Login**. If the viewport width is 575 pixels or less, then the navigation collapses into a hamburger menu.
   - The title of the website, **NorthwindMvc**, shown in the header and footer.

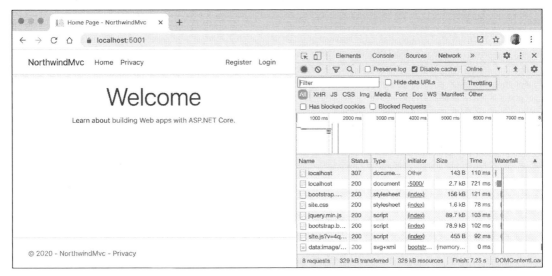

Figure 16.1: The Northwind MVC website homepage

8. Click **Register**, enter an email and password, and click the **Register** button.

   By default, passwords must have at least one non-alphanumeric character, they must have at least one digit (0-9), and they must have at least one uppercase letter (A-Z). I use Pa$$w0rd in scenarios like this when I am just exploring.

   The MVC project template follows best practice for **double-opt-in (DOI)**, meaning that after filling in an email and password to register, an email is sent to the email address, and the visitor must click a link in that email to confirm that they want to register.

   We have not yet configured an email provider to send that email, so we must simulate that step.

9. Click the link with the text **Click here to confirm your account** and note that you are redirected to a **Confirm email** web page that you can customize.

10. In the top navigation menu, click **Login**, enter your email and password (note that there is an optional checkbox to remember you, and there are links if the visitor has forgotten their password or they want to register as a new visitor), and then click the **Log in** button.

11. Click your email in the top navigation menu to navigate to an account management page, and note that you can set a phone number, change your email address, change your password, enable two-factor authentication (if you add an authenticator app), and download and delete your personal data, as shown in the following screenshot:

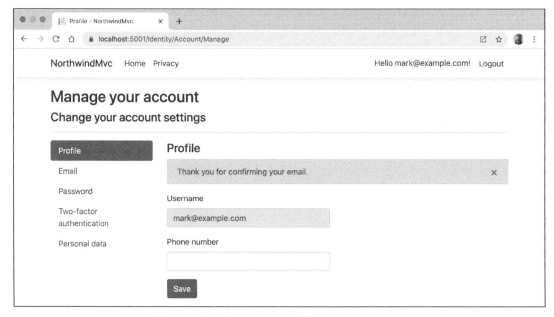

Figure 16.2: Website visitor Profile settings

 More Information: Some of these built-in features of the basic MVC project template make it easier for your website to be compliant with modern privacy requirements, like the European Union's **General Data Protection Regulation (GDPR)** that became active in May 2018. You can read more at the following link: https://docs.microsoft.com/en-us/aspnet/core/security/gdpr

12. Close the browser.

13. In **TERMINAL**, press *Ctrl + C* to stop the console application and shut down the Kestrel web server that is hosting your ASP.NET Core website.

 More Information: You can read more about ASP.NET Core's support for authenticator apps at the following link: https://docs.microsoft.com/en-us/aspnet/core/security/authentication/identity-enable-qrcodes

Reviewing the ASP.NET Core MVC website

In Visual Studio Code, look at the **EXPLORER** pane, as shown in the following screenshot:

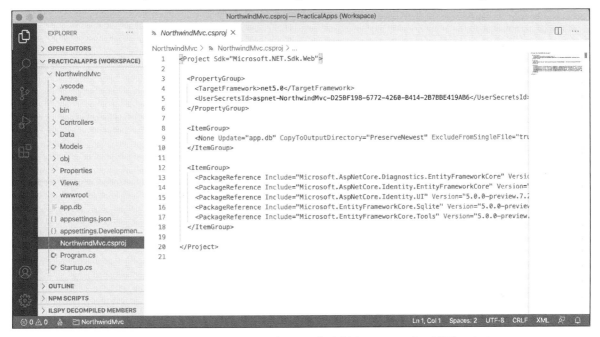

Figure 16.3: The EXPLORER pane showing the initial structure of an MVC project

We will look in more detail at some of these parts later, but for now, note the following:

- `Areas`: This folder contains nested folders and a file needed to integrate your website project with **ASP.NET Core Identity**, which is used for authentication.

- `bin`, `obj`: These folders contain the compiled assemblies for the project.

- `Controllers`: This folder contains C# classes that have methods (known as actions) that fetch a *model* and pass it to a *view*, for example, `HomeController.cs`.

- `Data`: This folder contains Entity Framework Core migration classes used by the **ASP.NET Core Identity** system to provide data storage for authentication and authorization, for example, `ApplicationDbContext.cs`.

- `Models`: This folder contains C# classes that represent all of the data gathered together by a controller and passed to a view, for example, `ErrorViewModel.cs`.

- `Properties`: This folder contains a configuration file for IIS or IIS Express on Windows and for launching the website during development named `launchSettings.json`. This file is only used on the local development machine and is not deployed to your production website.

- Views: This folder contains the .cshtml Razor files that combine HTML and C# code to dynamically generate HTML responses. The _ViewStart file sets the default layout and _ViewImports imports common namespaces used in all views like tag helpers:
    - Home: This subfolder contains Razor files for the home and privacy pages.
    - Shared: This subfolder contains Razor files for the shared layout, an error page, and two partial views for logging in and validation scripts.
- wwwroot: This folder contains static content used by the website, such as CSS for styling, libraries of JavaScript, JavaScript for this website project, and a favicon.ico file. You would also put images and other static file resources like documents in here.
- app.db: This is the SQLite database that stores registered visitors.
- appsettings.json and appsettings.Development.json: These files contain settings that your website can load at runtime, for example, the database connection string for the ASP.NET Identity system and logging levels.
- NorthwindMvc.csproj: This file contains project settings like use of the Web .NET SDK, an entry to ensure that the app.db file is copied to the website's output folder, and a list of NuGet packages that your project requires, including:
    - Microsoft.AspNetCore.Diagnostics.EntityFrameworkCore
    - Microsoft.AspNetCore.Identity.EntityFrameworkCore
    - Microsoft.AspNetCore.Identity.UI
    - Microsoft.EntityFrameworkCore.Sqlite
    - Microsoft.EntityFrameworkCore.Tools
- Program.cs: This file defines a class that contains the Main entry point that builds a pipeline for processing incoming HTTP requests and hosts the website using default options like configuring the Kestrel web server and loading appsettings. While building the host, it calls the UseStartup<T>() method to specify another class that performs additional configuration.
- Startup.cs: This file adds and configures services that your website needs, for example, ASP.NET Core Identity for authentication, SQLite for data storage, and so on, and routes for your application.

 More Information: You can read more about default configuration of web hosts at the following link: https://docs.microsoft.com/en-us/aspnet/core/fundamentals/host/web-host

---

Reviewing the ASP.NET Core Identity database

If you installed an SQLite tool such as **SQLiteStudio**, then you can open the database and see the tables that the ASP.NET Core Identity system uses to register users and roles, including the AspNetUsers table used to store the registered visitor, as shown in the following screenshot:

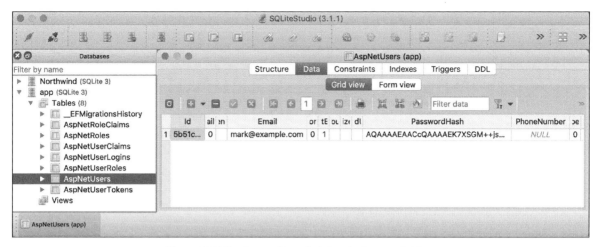

Figure 16.4: Viewing registered visitors in the app database

 Good Practice: The ASP.NET Core MVC project template follows good practice by storing a hash of the password instead of the password itself, as you learned how to do in *Chapter 10, Protecting Your Data and Applications*.

Exploring an ASP.NET Core MVC website

Let's walk through the parts that make up a modern ASP.NET Core MVC website.

Understanding ASP.NET Core MVC startup

Appropriately enough, we will start by exploring the MVC website's default startup configuration:

1. Open the `Startup.cs` file.

2. Note the read-only `Configuration` property that can be passed in and set in the class constructor, as shown in the following code:

```
public Startup(IConfiguration configuration)
{
  Configuration = configuration;
}

public IConfiguration Configuration { get; }
```

3. Note that the `ConfigureServices` method adds an application database context using SQLite with its database connection string loaded from the `appsettings.json` file for its data storage, adds ASP.NET Core Identity for authentication and configures it to use the application database, and adds support for MVC controllers with views, as shown in the following code:

```
public void ConfigureServices(IServiceCollection services)
{
  services.AddDbContext<ApplicationDbContext>(options =>
    options.UseSqlite(
      Configuration.GetConnectionString("DefaultConnection")));

  services.AddDatabaseDeveloperPageExceptionFilter();

  services.AddDefaultIdentity<IdentityUser>(options =>
    options.SignIn.RequireConfirmedAccount = true)
    .AddEntityFrameworkStores<ApplicationDbContext>();

  services.AddControllersWithViews();
}
```

> **More Information**: You can learn more about the Identity UI library that is distributed as a Razor class library and can be overridden by a website at the following link: https://docs.microsoft.com/en-us/aspnet/core/security/authentication/scaffold-identity?tabs=netcore-cli

The call to AddDbContext is an example of registering a dependency service. ASP.NET Core implements the **dependency injection (DI)** design pattern so that controllers can request needed services through their constructors. Developers register those services in the ConfigureServices method.

> **More Information**: You can read more about dependency injection at the following link: https://docs.microsoft.com/en-us/aspnet/core/fundamentals/dependency-injection

4. Next, we have the Configure method, which configures a detailed exception and database error page if the website runs in development, or a friendlier error page and HSTS for production. HTTPS redirection, static files, routing, and ASP.NET Identity are enabled, and an MVC default route and Razor Pages are configured, as shown in the following code:

```
public void Configure(IApplicationBuilder app,
    IWebHostEnvironment env)
{
  if (env.IsDevelopment())
  {
    app.UseDeveloperExceptionPage();
  }
  else
  {
    app.UseExceptionHandler("/Home/Error");
    // The default HSTS value is 30 days.
```

```
      app.UseHsts();
    }
    app.UseHttpsRedirection();
    app.UseStaticFiles();

    app.UseRouting();

    app.UseAuthentication();
    app.UseAuthorization();

    app.UseEndpoints(endpoints =>
    {
      endpoints.MapControllerRoute(
        name: "default",
        pattern: "{controller=Home}/{action=Index}/{id?}");

      endpoints.MapRazorPages();
    });
}
```

We learned about most of these methods in *Chapter 15, Building Websites Using ASP.NET Core Razor Pages.* Apart from the UseAuthentication and UseAuthorization methods, the most important new method in the Configure method is MapControllerRoute, which maps a default route for use by MVC. This route is very flexible because it will map to almost any incoming URL, as you will see in the next section.

Although we will not create any Razor Pages in this chapter, we need to leave the method call that maps Razor Page support because our MVC website uses ASP.NET Core Identity for authentication and authorization, and it uses a Razor Class Library for its user interface components, like visitor registration and login.

 More Information: You can read more about configuring middleware at the following link: https://docs.microsoft.com/en-us/aspnet/core/fundamentals/middleware/

Understanding the default MVC route

The responsibility of a route is to discover the name of a controller class to instantiate an action method to execute with an optional id parameter to pass into the method that will generate an HTTP response.

A default route is configured for MVC, as shown in the following code:

```
endpoints.MapControllerRoute(
  name: "default",
  pattern: "{controller=Home}/{action=Index}/{id?}");
```

The route pattern has parts in curly brackets {} called **segments**, and they are like named parameters of a method. The value of these segments can be any `string`. Segments in URLs are not case-sensitive.

The route pattern looks at any URL path requested by the browser and matches it to extract the name of a `controller`, the name of an `action`, and an optional `id` value (the `?` symbol makes it optional).

If the user hasn't entered these names, it uses defaults of `Home` for the controller and `Index` for the action (the `=` assignment sets a default for a named segment).

The following table contains example URLs and how the default route would work out the names of a controller and action:

URL	Controller	Action	ID
/	Home	Index	
/Muppet	Muppet	Index	
/Muppet/Kermit	Muppet	Kermit	
/Muppet/Kermit/Green	Muppet	Kermit	Green
/Products	Products	Index	
/Products/Detail	Products	Detail	
/Products/Detail/3	Products	Detail	3

Understanding controllers and actions

In ASP.NET Core MVC, the *C* stands for *controller*. From the route and an incoming URL, ASP.NET Core MVC knows the name of the controller, so it will then look for a class that is decorated with the [Controller] attribute or derives from a class decorated with that attribute, for example, the Microsoft provided class named `ControllerBase`, as shown in the following code:

```
namespace Microsoft.AspNetCore.Mvc
{
    //
    // Summary:
    // A base class for an MVC controller without view support.
    [Controller]
    public abstract class ControllerBase
    ...
```

As you can see in the XML comment, `ControllerBase` does not support views. It is used for creating web services, as you will see in *Chapter 18, Building and Consuming Web Services*.

Microsoft provides a class named `Controller` that your classes can inherit from if they do need view support.

The responsibilities of a controller are as follows:

- Identify the services that the controller needs in order to be in a valid state and to function properly in their class constructor(s).
- Use the action name to identify a method to execute.
- Extract parameters from the HTTP request.
- Use the parameters to fetch any additional data needed to construct a view model and pass it to the appropriate view for the client. For example, if the client is a web browser, then a view that renders HTML would be most appropriate. Other clients might prefer alternative renderings, like document formats such as a PDF file or an Excel file, or data formats, like JSON or XML.
- Return the results from the view to the client as an HTTP response with an appropriate status code.

Let's review the controller used to generate the home, privacy, and error pages:

1. Expand the Controllers folder.
2. Open the file named HomeController.cs.
3. Note, as shown in the following code, that:
    - A private field is declared to store a reference to a logger for the HomeController that is set in a constructor.
    - All three action methods call a method named View() and return the results as an IActionResult interface to the client.
    - The Error action method passes a view model into its view with a request ID used for tracing. The error response will not be cached:

```
public class HomeController : Controller
{
  private readonly ILogger<HomeController> _logger;

  public HomeController(ILogger<HomeController> logger)
  {
    _logger = logger;
  }

  public IActionResult Index()
  {
    return View();
  }

  public IActionResult Privacy()
  {
    return View();
  }
```

```
[ResponseCache(Duration = 0,
  Location = ResponseCacheLocation.None, NoStore = true)]
public IActionResult Error()
{
  return View(new ErrorViewModel { RequestId =
    Activity.Current?.Id ?? HttpContext.TraceIdentifier });
}
}
```

If the visitor enters / or /Home, then it is the equivalent of /Home/Index because those were the defaults.

Understanding the view search path convention

Both the Index and Privacy methods have identical implementation, yet they return different web pages. This is because of conventions. The call to the View method looks in different paths for the Razor file to generate the web page:

1. In the NorthwindMvc project, expand the Views and then Home folders.
2. Rename the Privacy.cshtml file to Privacy2.cshtml.
3. In **TERMINAL**, enter the command dotnet run to start the website.
4. Start Chrome, navigate to http://localhost:5000/, click **Privacy**, and note the paths that are searched for a view to render the web page including in Shared folders, as shown in the following output:

```
InvalidOperationException: The view 'Privacy' was not found. The following
locations were searched:
/Views/Home/Privacy.cshtml
/Views/Shared/Privacy.cshtml
/Pages/Shared/Privacy.cshtml
```

5. Close Chrome.
6. Rename the Privacy2.cshtml file back to Privacy.cshtml.

The view search path convention is shown in the following list:

- Specific Razor view: /Views/{controller}/{action}.cshtml
- Shared Razor view: /Views/Shared/{action}.cshtml
- Shared Razor page: /Pages/Shared/{action}.cshtml

Unit testing MVC

Controllers are where the business logic of your website runs, so it is important to test the correctness of that logic using unit tests, as you learned in *Chapter 4, Writing, Debugging, and Testing Functions*.

More Information: You can read more about how to unit test controllers at the following link: https://docs.microsoft.com/en-us/aspnet/core/mvc/controllers/testing

Understanding filters

When you need to add some functionality to multiple controllers and actions, then you can use or define your own filters that are implemented as an attribute class.

Filters can be applied at the following levels:

- At the action-level by decorating the method with the attribute. This will only affect the one method.

- At the controller-level by decorating the class with the attribute. This will affect all methods of this controller.

- At the global level by adding an instance of the attribute to the `Filters` collection of the `IServiceCollection` in the `ConfigureServices` method of the `Startup` class. This will affect all methods of all controllers in the project.

More Information: You can read more about filters at the following link: https://docs.microsoft.com/en-us/aspnet/core/mvc/controllers/filters

Using a filter to secure an action method

For example, you might want to ensure that one particular method of a controller can only be called by members of certain security roles. You do this by decorating the method with the `[Authorize]` attribute, as shown in the following code:

```
[Authorize(Roles = "Sales,Marketing")]
public IActionResult SalesAndMarketingEmployeesOnly()
{
  return View();
}
```

More Information: You can read more about authorization at the following link: https://docs.microsoft.com/en-us/aspnet/core/security/authorization/introduction

Using a filter to cache a response

You might want to cache the HTTP response that is generated by an action method by decorating the method with the [ResponseCache] attribute, as shown in the following code:

```
[ResponseCache(Duration = 3600, // in seconds therefore 1 hour
  Location = ResponseCacheLocation.Any)]
public IActionResult AboutUs()
{
  return View();
}
```

You control where the response is cached and for how long by setting parameters, as shown in the following list:

- Duration: In seconds. This sets the max-age HTTP response header.
- Location: One of the ResponseCacheLocation values, Any, Client, or None. This sets the cache-control HTTP response header.
- NoStore: If true, this ignores Duration and Location and sets the cache-control HTTP response header to no-store.

More Information: You can read more about response caching at the following link: https://docs.microsoft.com/en-us/aspnet/core/performance/caching/response

Using a filter to define a custom route

You might want to define a simplified route for an action method instead of using the default route.

For example, to show the privacy page currently requires the following URL path, which specifies both the controller and action:

```
https://localhost:5001/home/privacy
```

We could decorate the action method to make the route simpler, as shown in the following code:

```
[Route("private")]
public IActionResult Privacy()
```

```
{
  return View();
}
```

Now, we can use the following URL path, which uses the attribute-defined route:

```
https://localhost:5001/private
```

Understanding entity and view models

In ASP.NET Core MVC, the *M* stands for *model*. Models represent the data required to respond to a request. **Entity models** represent entities in a data store like SQLite. Based on the request, one or more entities might need to be retrieved from data storage. All of the data that we want to show in response to a request is the MVC model, sometimes called a **view model**, because it is a *model* that is passed into a *view* for rendering into a response format like HTML or JSON.

For example, the following HTTP GET request might mean that the browser is asking for the product details page for product number 3:

```
http://www.example.com/products/details/3
```

The controller would need to use the ID value 3 to retrieve the entity for that product and pass it to a view that can then turn the model into HTML for display in the browser.

Imagine that when a user comes to our website, we want to show them a carousel of categories, a list of products, and a count of the number of visitors we have had this month.

We will reference the Entity Framework Core entity data model for the Northwind database that you created in *Chapter 14, Introducing Practical Applications of C# and .NET*:

1. In the NorthwindMvc project, open NorthwindMvc.csproj.
2. Add a project reference to NorthwindContextLib, as shown in the following markup:
   ```
   <ItemGroup>
     <ProjectReference Include=
       "..\NorthwindContextLib\NorthwindContextLib.csproj" />
   </ItemGroup>
   ```
3. In **TERMINAL**, enter the following command to rebuild the project:
   ```
   dotnet build
   ```
4. Modify Startup.cs to import the System.IO and Packt.Shared namespaces and add a statement to the ConfigureServices method to configure the Northwind database context, as shown in the following code:
   ```
   string databasePath = Path.Combine("..", "Northwind.db");
   services.AddDbContext<Northwind>(options =>
     options.UseSqlite($"Data Source={databasePath}"));
   ```
5. Add a class file to the Models folder and name it HomeIndexViewModel.cs.

Good Practice: Although the `ErrorViewModel` class created by the MVC project template does not follow this convention, I recommend that you use the naming convention `{Controller}{Action}ViewModel` for your view model classes.

6. Modify the class definition to have three properties for a count of the number of visitors, and lists of categories and products, as shown in the following code:

```
using System.Collections.Generic;
using Packt.Shared;

namespace NorthwindMvc.Models
{
  public class HomeIndexViewModel
  {
    public int VisitorCount;
    public IList<Category> Categories { get; set; }
    public IList<Product> Products { get; set; }
  }
}
```

7. Open the `HomeController` class.

8. Import the `Packt.Shared` namespace.

9. Add a field to store a reference to a `Northwind` instance, and initialize it in the constructor, as shown highlighted in the following code:

```
public class HomeController : Controller
{
  private readonly ILogger<HomeController> _logger;
  private Northwind db;

  public HomeController(ILogger<HomeController> logger,
    Northwind injectedContext)
  {
    _logger = logger;
    db = injectedContext;
  }
```

ASP.NET Core will use constructor parameter injection to pass an instance of the `Northwind` database context using the database path you specified in the `Startup` class.

10. Modify the contents of the `Index` action method to create an instance of the view model for this method, simulating a visitor count using the `Random` class to generate a number between 1 and 1000, and using the `Northwind` database to get lists of categories and products, and then pass the model to the view, as shown in the following code:

```
var model = new HomeIndexViewModel
{
  VisitorCount = (new Random()).Next(1, 1001),
  Categories = db.Categories.ToList(),
  Products = db.Products.ToList()
};
return View(model); // pass model to view
```

When the `View()` method is called in a controller's action method, ASP.NET Core MVC looks in the `Views` folder for a subfolder with the same name as the current controller, that is, `Home`. It then looks for a file with the same name as the current action, that is, `Index.cshtml`. It will also search for shared views.

Understanding views

In ASP.NET Core MVC, the *V* stands for *view*. The responsibility of a view is to transform a model into HTML or other formats.

There are multiple **view engines** that could be used to do this. The default view engine is called **Razor**, and it uses the @ symbol to indicate server-side code execution.

The Razor Pages feature introduced with ASP.NET Core 2.0 uses the same view engine and so can use the same Razor syntax.

Let's modify the home page view to render the lists of categories and products:

1. Expand the `Views` folder, and then expand the `Home` folder.

2. Open the `Index.cshtml` file and note the block of C# code wrapped in `@{ }`. This will execute first and can be used to store data that needs to be passed into a shared layout file like the title of the web page, as shown in the following code:

   ```
   @{
       ViewData["Title"] = "Home Page";
   }
   ```

3. Note the static HTML content in the `<div>` element that uses Bootstrap for styling.

 Good Practice: As well as defining your own styles, base your styles on a common library, such as Bootstrap, that implements responsive design.

Just as with Razor Pages, there is a file named `_ViewStart.cshtml` that gets executed by the `View()` method. It is used to set defaults that apply to all views.

For example, it sets the `Layout` property of all views to a shared layout file, as shown in the following markup:

```
@{
   Layout = "_Layout";
}
```

4. In the `Views` folder, open the `_ViewImports.cshtml` file and note that it imports some namespaces and then adds the ASP.NET Core tag helpers, as shown in the following code:

```
@using NorthwindMvc
@using NorthwindMvc.Models
@addTagHelper *, Microsoft.AspNetCore.Mvc.TagHelpers
```

5. In the `Shared` folder, open the `_Layout.cshtml` file.

6. Note that the title is being read from the `ViewData` dictionary that was set earlier in the `Index.cshtml` view, as shown in the following markup:

```
<title>@ViewData["Title"] - NorthwindMvc</title>
```

7. Note the rendering of links to support Bootstrap and a site stylesheet, where ~ means the `wwwroot` folder, as shown in the following markup:

```
<link rel="stylesheet"
  href="~/lib/bootstrap/dist/css/bootstrap.css" />
<link rel="stylesheet" href="~/css/site.css" />
```

8. Note the rendering of a navigation bar in the header, as shown in the following markup:

```
<body>
  <header>
    <nav class="navbar ...">
```

9. Note the rendering of a collapsible `<div>` containing a partial view for logging in and hyperlinks to allow users to navigate between pages using ASP.NET Core tag helpers with attributes like `asp-controller` and `asp-action`, as shown in the following markup:

```
<div class=
  "navbar-collapse collapse d-sm-inline-flex flex-sm-row-reverse">
  <partial name="_LoginPartial" />
  <ul class="navbar-nav flex-grow-1">
    <li class="nav-item">
      <a class="nav-link text-dark" asp-area=""
        asp-controller="Home" asp-action="Index">Home</a>
    </li>
    <li class="nav-item">
      <a class="nav-link text-dark"
        asp-area="" asp-controller="Home"
        asp-action="Privacy">Privacy</a>
    </li>
  </ul>
</div>
```

The <a> elements use tag helper attributes named `asp-controller` and `asp-action` to specify the controller name and action name that will execute when the link is clicked on. If you want to navigate to a feature in a Razor Class Library, then you use `asp-area` to specify the feature name.

10. Note the rendering of the body inside the `<main>` element, as shown in the following markup:

```
<div class="container">
  <main role="main" class="pb-3">
    @RenderBody()
  </main>
</div>
```

The `@RenderBody()` method call injects the contents of a specific Razor view for a page like the `Index.cshtml` file at that point in the shared layout.

More Information: You can read about why it is good to put `<script>` elements at the bottom of the `<body>` at the following link: `https://stackoverflow.com/questions/436411/where-should-i-put-script-tags-in-html-markup`

11. Note the rendering of `<script>` elements at the bottom of the page so that it doesn't slow down the display of the page and that you can add your own script blocks into an optional defined section named `scripts`, as shown in the following markup:

```
<script src="~/lib/jquery/dist/jquery.js"></script>
<script src="~/lib/bootstrap/dist/js/bootstrap.bundle.js">
</script>
<script src="~/js/site.js" asp-append-version="true"></script>
@await RenderSectionAsync("scripts", required: false)
```

When `asp-append-version` is specified with a `true` value in any element along with an `src` attribute, the Image Tag Helper is invoked (it does not only affect images!).

It works by automatically appending a query string value named v that is generated from a hash of the referenced source file, as shown in the following example generated output:

```
<script src="~/js/site.js?
v=Kl_dqr9NVtnMdsM2MUg4qthUnWZm5T1fCEimBPWDNgM"></script>
```

If even a single byte within the `site.js` file changes, then its hash value will be different, and therefore if a browser or CDN is caching the script file, then it will bust the cached copy and replace it with the new version.

More Information: You can read how cache busting using query strings works at the following link: `https://stackoverflow.com/questions/9692665/cache-busting-via-params`

Customizing an ASP.NET Core MVC website

Now that you've reviewed the structure of a basic MVC website, you will customize it. You have already added code to retrieve entities from the Northwind database, so the next task is to output that information on the home page.

 More Information: To find suitable images for the eight categories, I searched on a site that has free stock photos for commercial use with no attribution at the following link: https://www.pexels.com/

Defining a custom style

The home page will show a list of the 77 products in the Northwind database. To make efficient use of space, we want to show the list in three columns. To do this, we need to customize the stylesheet for the website:

1. In the wwwroot\css folder, open the site.css file.

2. At the bottom of the file, add a new style that will apply to an element with the newspaper ID, as shown in the following code:

```
#newspaper
{
  column-count: 3;
}
```

Setting up the category images

The Northwind database includes a table of categories, but they do not have images, and websites look better with some colorful pictures:

1. In the wwwroot folder, create a folder named images.

2. In the images folder, add eight image files named category1.jpeg, category2.jpeg, and so on, up to category8.jpeg.

 More Information: You can download images from the GitHub repository for this book at the following link: https://github.com/markjprice/cs9dotnet5/tree/master/Assets/Categories

Understanding Razor syntax

Before we customize the home page view, let's review an example Razor file that has an initial Razor code block that instantiates an order with price and quantity and then outputs information about the order on the web page, as shown in the following markup:

```
@{
  var order = new Order
  {
    OrderID = 123,
    Product = "Sushi",
    Price = 8.49M,
    Quantity = 3
  };
}
<div>Your order for @order.Quantity of @order.Product has a total cost of $@
order.Price * @order.Quantity</div>
```

The preceding Razor file would result in the following incorrect output:

```
Your order for 3 of Sushi has a total cost of $8.49 * 3
```

Although Razor markup can include the value of any single property using the @object.property syntax, you should wrap expressions in parentheses, as shown in the following markup:

```
<div>Your order for @order.Quantity of @order.Product has a total cost of $@
(order.Price * @order.Quantity)</div>
```

The preceding Razor expression results in the following correct output:

```
Your order for 3 of Sushi has a total cost of $25.47
```

Defining a typed view

To improve the IntelliSense when writing a view, you can define what type the view can expect using an @model directive at the top:

1. In the Views\Home folder, open Index.cshtml.
2. At the top of the file, add a statement to set the model type to use the HomeIndexViewModel, as shown in the following code:

    ```
    @model NorthwindMvc.Models.HomeIndexViewModel
    ```

Now, whenever we type Model in this view, the Visual Studio Code C# extension will know the correct type for the model and will provide IntelliSense for it.

While entering code in a view, remember the following:

- To declare the type for the model, use @model (with lowercase m).
- To interact with the model instance, use @Model (with uppercase M).

Let's continue customizing the view for the home page.

3. In the initial Razor code block, add a statement to declare a string variable for the current item and replace the existing <div> element with the new markup to output categories in a carousel and products as an unordered list, as shown in the following markup:

```
@model NorthwindMvc.Models.HomeIndexViewModel
@{
    ViewData["Title"] = "Home Page";
    string currentItem = "";
}
<div id="categories" class="carousel slide" data-ride="carousel"
    data-interval="3000" data-keyboard="true">
    <ol class="carousel-indicators">
    @for (int c = 0; c < Model.Categories.Count; c++)
    {
        if (c == 0)
        {
            currentItem = "active";
        }
        else
        {
            currentItem = "";
        }
        <li data-target="#categories" data-slide-to="@c"
            class="@currentItem"></li>
    }
    </ol>
    <div class="carousel-inner">
    @for (int c = 0; c < Model.Categories.Count; c++)
    {
        if (c == 0)
        {
            currentItem = "active";
        }
        else
        {
            currentItem = "";
        }
        <div class="carousel-item @currentItem">
```

```
          <img class="d-block w-100" src=
            "~/images/category@(Model.Categories[c].CategoryID).jpeg"
            alt="@Model.Categories[c].CategoryName" />
          <div class="carousel-caption d-none d-md-block">
            <h2>@Model.Categories[c].CategoryName</h2>
            <h3>@Model.Categories[c].Description</h3>
            <p>
              <a class="btn btn-primary"
                href="/category/@Model.Categories[c].CategoryID">View</a>
            </p>
          </div>
        </div>
      }
    </div>
    <a class="carousel-control-prev" href="#categories"
      role="button" data-slide="prev">
      <span class="carousel-control-prev-icon"
        aria-hidden="true"></span>
      <span class="sr-only">Previous</span>
    </a>
    <a class="carousel-control-next" href="#categories"
      role="button" data-slide="next">
      <span class="carousel-control-next-icon"
        aria-hidden="true"></span>
      <span class="sr-only">Next</span>
    </a>
  </div>
  <div class="row">
    <div class="col-md-12">
      <h1>Northwind</h1>
      <p class="lead">
        We have had @Model.VisitorCount visitors this month.
      </p>
      <h2>Products</h2>
      <div id="newspaper">
        <ul>
        @foreach (var item in @Model.Products)
        {
          <li>
            <a asp-controller="Home"
              asp-action="ProductDetail"
              asp-route-id="@item.ProductID">
              @item.ProductName costs
              @item.UnitPrice.ToString("C")
            </a>
          </li>
```

```
        }
      </ul>
    </div>
  </div>
</div>
```

While reviewing the preceding Razor markup, note the following:

- It is easy to mix static HTML elements such as `<ul>` and `<li>` with C# code to output the carousel of categories and the list of product names.

- The `<div>` element with the `id` attribute of `newspaper` will use the custom style that we defined earlier, so all of the content in that element will display in three columns.

- The `<img>` element for each category uses parentheses around a Razor expression to ensure that the compiler does not include the `.jpeg` as part of the expression, as shown in the following markup: `"~/images/category@(Model. Categories[c].CategoryID).jpeg"`

- The `<a>` elements for the product links use tag helpers to generate URL paths. Clicks on these hyperlinks will be handled by the `Home` controller and its `ProductDetail` action method. This action method does not exist yet, but you will add it later in this chapter. The ID of the product is passed as a route segment named `id`, as shown in the following URL path for Ipoh Coffee:

  `https://localhost:5001/Home/ProductDetail/43`

Reviewing the customized home page

Let's see the result of our customized home page:

1. Start the website by entering the following command: `dotnet run`.

2. Start Chrome and navigate to `http://localhost:5000`.

3. Note the home page has a rotating carousel showing categories, a random number of visitors, and a list of products in three columns, as shown in the following screenshot:

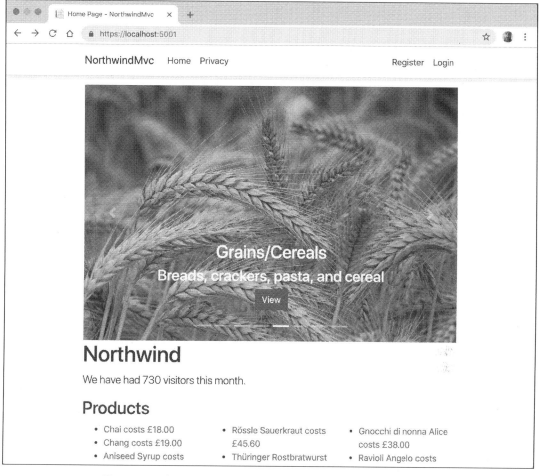

Figure 16.5: The updated Northwind MVC website homepage

At the moment, clicking on any of the categories or product links gives 404 Not Found errors, so let's see how we can pass parameters so that we can see the details of a product or category.

4. Close Chrome.

5. Stop the website by pressing *Ctrl + C* in **TERMINAL**.

Passing parameters using a route value

One way to pass a simple parameter is to use the id segment defined in the default route:

1. In the HomeController class, add an action method named ProductDetail, as shown in the following code:

```
public IActionResult ProductDetail(int? id)
{
  if (!id.HasValue)
```

```
{
    return NotFound("You must pass a product ID in the route, for example,
/Home/ProductDetail/21");
  }

  var model = db.Products
    .SingleOrDefault(p => p.ProductID == id);

  if (model == null)
  {
    return NotFound($"Product with ID of {id} not found.");
  }
  return View(model); // pass model to view and then return result
}
```

Note the following:

- This method uses a feature of ASP.NET Core called **model binding** to automatically match the id passed in the route to the parameter named id in the method.

- Inside the method, we check to see whether id does not have a value, and if so, we call the NotFound method to return a 404 status code with a custom message explaining the correct URL path format.

- Otherwise, we can connect to the database and try to retrieve a product using the id variable.

- If we find a product, we pass it to a view; otherwise, we call the NotFound method to return a 404 status code and a custom message explaining that a product with that ID was not found in the database.

Remember that if the view is named to match the action method and is placed in a folder that matches the controller name or a shared folder, then ASP.NET Core MVC's conventions will find it automatically.

2. Inside the Views/Home folder, add a new file named ProductDetail.cshtml.

3. Modify the contents, as shown in the following markup:

```
@model Packt.Shared.Product
@{
    ViewData["Title"] = "Product Detail - " + Model.ProductName;
}
<h2>Product Detail</h2>
```

```
<hr />
<div>
  <dl class="dl-horizontal">
    <dt>Product ID</dt>
    <dd>@Model.ProductID</dd>
    <dt>Product Name</dt>
    <dd>@Model.ProductName</dd>
    <dt>Category ID</dt>
    <dd>@Model.CategoryID</dd>
    <dt>Unit Price</dt>
    <dd>@Model.UnitPrice.ToString("C")</dd>
    <dt>Units In Stock</dt>
    <dd>@Model.UnitsInStock</dd>
  </dl>
</div>
```

4. Start the website by entering the following command: `dotnet run`.

5. Start Chrome and navigate to `http://localhost:5000`.

6. When the home page appears with the list of products, click on one of them, for example, the second product, **Chang**.

7. Note the URL path in the browser's address bar, the page title shown in the browser tab, and the product details page, as shown in the following screenshot:

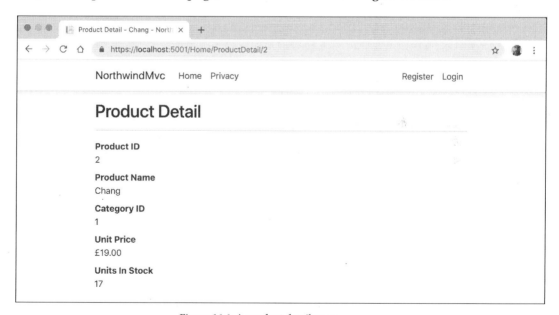

Figure 16.6: A product detail page

8. Toggle on the developer tools pane.

9. Edit the URL in the address box of Chrome to request a product ID that does not exist, like 99, and note the 404 Not Found status code and custom error response, as shown in the following screenshot:

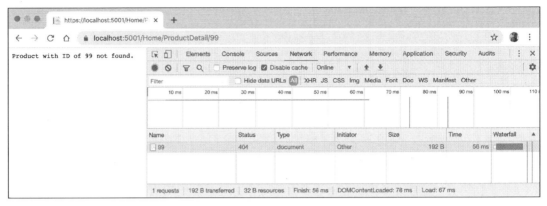

Figure 16.7: Requesting a product ID that doesn't exist

Understanding model binders

Model binders are very powerful, and the default one does a lot for you. After the default route identifies a controller class to instantiate and an action method to call, if that method has parameters, then those parameters need to have values set.

Model binders do this by looking for parameter values passed in the HTTP request as any of the following types of parameters:

- **Route parameter**, like id as we did in the previous section, as shown in the following URL path: /Home/ProductDetail/2
- **Query string parameter**, as shown in the following URL path: /Home/ProductDetail?id=2
- **Form parameter**, as shown in the following markup:
  ```html
  <form action="post" action="/Home/ProductDetail">
    <input type="text" name="id" />
    <input type="submit" />
  </form>
  ```

Model binders can populate almost any type:

- Simple types, like int, string, DateTime, and bool.
- Complex types defined by class or struct.
- Collections types, like arrays and lists.

Let's create a somewhat artificial example to illustrate what can be achieved using the default model binder:

1. In the Models folder, add a new file named Thing.cs.

2. Modify the contents to define a class with two properties for a nullable number named
ID and a string named color, as shown in the following code:

```
namespace NorthwindMvc.Models
{
  public class Thing
  {
    public int? ID { get; set; }
    public string Color { get; set; }
  }
}
```

3. Open HomeController.cs and add two new action methods, one to show a page with a
form and one to display it with a parameter using your new model type, as shown in
the following code:

```
public IActionResult ModelBinding()
{
  return View(); // the page with a form to submit
}

public IActionResult ModelBinding(Thing thing)
{
  return View(thing); // show the model bound thing
}
```

4. In the Views\Home folder, add a new file named ModelBinding.cshtml.

5. Modify its contents, as shown in the following markup:

```
@model NorthwindMvc.Models.Thing
@{
  ViewData["Title"] = "Model Binding Demo";
}
<h1>@ViewData["Title"]</h1>
<div>
  Enter values for your thing in the following form:
</div>
<form method="POST" action="/home/modelbinding?id=3">
  <input name="color" value="Red" />
  <input type="submit" />
</form>
@if (Model != null)
{
<h2>Submitted Thing</h2>
<hr />
<div>
  <dl class="dl-horizontal">
    <dt>Model.ID</dt>
```

```
        <dd>@Model.ID</dd>
        <dt>Model.Color</dt>
        <dd>@Model.Color</dd>
      </dl>
    </div>
    }
```

6. Start the website, start Chrome, and navigate to `https://localhost:5001/home/modelbinding`.

7. Note the unhandled exception about an ambiguous match, as shown in the following screenshot:

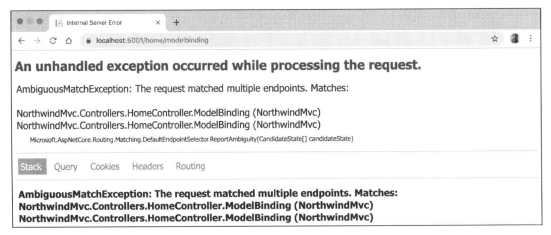

Figure 16.8: An unhandled exception error

Although the C# compiler can differentiate between the two methods by noting that the signatures are different, from HTTP's point of view, both methods are potential matches. We need an HTTP-specific way to disambiguate the action methods. We could do this by creating different names for the actions, or by specifying that one method should be used for a specific HTTP verb, like GET, POST, or DELETE.

8. Stop the website by pressing *Ctrl + C* in **TERMINAL**.

9. In `HomeController.cs`, decorate the second `ModelBinding` action method to indicate that it should be used for processing HTTP POST requests, that is, when a form is submitted, as shown highlighted in the following code:

```
[HttpPost]
public IActionResult ModelBinding(Thing thing)
```

10. Start the website, start Chrome, and navigate to `https://localhost:5001/home/modelbinding`.

11. Click the **Submit** button and note the value for the ID property is set from the query string parameter and the value for the color property is set from the form parameter, as shown in the following screenshot:

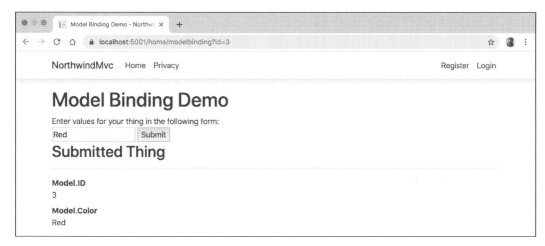

Figure 16.9: The Model Binding Demo page

12. Stop the website.

13. Modify the action for the form to pass the value 2 as a route parameter, as shown highlighted in the following markup:

```
<form method="POST" action="/home/modelbinding/2?id=3">
```

14. Start the website, start Chrome, and navigate to https://localhost:5001/home/modelbinding.

15. Click the **Submit** button and note the value for the ID property is set from the route parameter and the value for the color property is set from the form parameter.

16. Stop the website.

17. Modify the action for the form to pass the value 1 as a form parameter, as shown highlighted in the following markup:

```
<form method="POST" action="/home/modelbinding/2?id=3">
    <input name="id" value="1" />
    <input name="color" value="Red" />
    <input type="submit" />
</form>
```

18. Start the website, start Chrome, and navigate to https://localhost:5001/home/modelbinding.

19. Click the Submit button and note the values for the ID and color properties are both set from the form parameters.

20. If you have multiple parameters with the same name, then form parameters have the highest priority and query string parameters have the lowest priority for automatic model binding.

> **More Information**: For advanced scenarios, you can create your own model binders by implementing the IModelBinder interface: https://docs.microsoft.com/en-us/aspnet/core/mvc/advanced/custom-model-binding

Validating the model

The process of model binding can cause errors, for example, data type conversions or validation errors if the model has been decorated with validation rules. What data has been bound and any binding or validation errors are stored in `ControllerBase.ModelState`.

Let's explore what we can do with model state by applying some validation rules to the bound model and then showing invalid data messages in the view:

1. In the `Models` folder, open `Thing.cs`.

2. Import the `System.ComponentModel.DataAnnotations` namespace.

3. Decorate the `ID` property with a validation attribute to limit the range of allowed numbers to 1 to 10, and one to ensure that the visitor supplies a color, as shown in the following highlighted code:

    ```
    public class Thing
    {
      [Range(1, 10)]
      public int? ID { get; set; }

      [Required]
      public string Color { get; set; }
    }
    ```

4. In the `Models` folder, add a new file named `HomeModelBindingViewModel.cs`.

5. Modify its contents to define a class with two properties for the bound model and for any errors, as shown in the following code:

    ```
    using System.Collections.Generic;

    namespace NorthwindMvc.Models
    {
      public class HomeModelBindingViewModel
      {
        public Thing Thing { get; set; }
        public bool HasErrors { get; set; }
        public IEnumerable<string> ValidationErrors { get; set; }
      }
    }
    ```

6. In the `Controllers` folder, open `HomeController.cs`.

7. In the second `ModelBinding` method, comment out the previous statement that passed the thing to the view, and instead add statements to create an instance of the view model. Validate the model and store an array of error messages, and then pass the view model to the view, as shown in the following code:

    ```
    public IActionResult ModelBinding(Thing thing)
    {
    ```

```
// return View(thing); // show the model bound thing

var model = new HomeModelBindingViewModel
{
  Thing = thing,
  HasErrors = !ModelState.IsValid,
  ValidationErrors = ModelState.Values
    .SelectMany(state => state.Errors)
    .Select(error => error.ErrorMessage)
};
return View(model);
}
```

8. In Views\Home, open ModelBinding.cshtml.

9. Modify the model type declaration to use the view model class, add a <div> to show any model validation errors, and change the output of the thing's properties because the view model has changed, as shown highlighted in the following markup:

```
@model NorthwindMvc.Models.HomeModelBindingViewModel
@{
  ViewData["Title"] = "Model Binding Demo";
}
<h1>@ViewData["Title"]</h1>
<div>
  Enter values for your thing in the following form:
</div>
<form method="POST" action="/home/modelbinding/2?id=3">
  <input name="id" value="1" />
  <input name="color" value="Red" />
  <input type="submit" />
</form>
@if (Model != null)
{
  <h2>Submitted Thing</h2>
  <hr />
  <div>
    <dl class="dl-horizontal">
      <dt>Model.Thing.ID</dt>
      <dd>@Model.Thing.ID</dd>
      <dt>Model.Thing.Color</dt>
      <dd>@Model.Thing.Color</dd>
    </dl>
  </div>
  @if (Model.HasErrors)
  {
    <div>
```

```
    @foreach(string errorMessage in Model.ValidationErrors)
    {
        <div class="alert alert-danger" role="alert">@errorMessage</div>
    }
    </div>
}
}
```

10. Start the website, start Chrome, and navigate to https://localhost:5001/home/
    modelbinding.

11. Click the **Submit** button and note that 1 and Red are valid values.

12. Enter an ID of 99, clear the color textbox, click the **Submit** button, and note the error
    messages, as shown in the following screenshot:

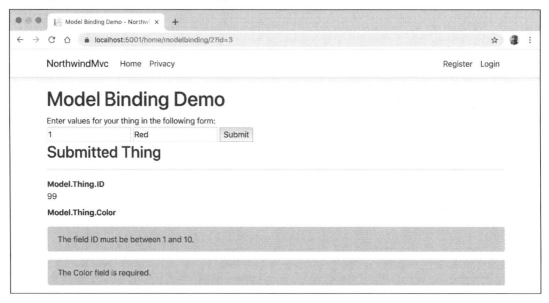

Figure 16.10: The Model Binding Demo page with field validations

13. Close the browser and stop the website.

More Information: You can read more about model validation at the following
link: https://docs.microsoft.com/en-us/aspnet/core/mvc/models/
validation

Understanding view helper methods

While creating a view for ASP.NET Core MVC, you can use the Html object and its methods to
generate markup.

Some useful methods include the following:

- `ActionLink`: Use this to generate an anchor `<a>` element that contains a URL path to the specified controller and action.

- `AntiForgeryToken`: Use this inside a `<form>` to insert a `<hidden>` element containing an anti-forgery token that will be validated when the form is submitted.

> **More Information**: You can read more about anti-forgery tokens at the following link: https://docs.microsoft.com/en-us/aspnet/core/security/anti-request-forgery

- `Display` and `DisplayFor`: Use this to generate HTML markup for the expression relative to the current model using a display template. There are built-in display templates for .NET types and custom templates can be created in the `DisplayTemplates` folder. The folder name is case-sensitive on case-sensitive filesystems.

- `DisplayForModel`: Use this to generate HTML markup for an entire model instead of a single expression.

- `Editor` and `EditorFor`: Use this to generate HTML markup for the expression relative to the current model using an editor template. There are built-in editor templates for .NET types that use `<label>` and `<input>` elements, and custom templates can be created in the `EditorTemplates` folder. The folder name is case-sensitive on case-sensitive filesystems.

- `EditorForModel`: Use this to generate HTML markup for an entire model instead of a single expression.

- `Encode`: Use this to safely encode an object or string into HTML. For example, the string value "`<script>`" would be encoded as "`&lt;script&gt;`". This is not normally necessary since the Razor @ symbol encodes `string` values by default.

- `Raw`: Use this to render a `string` value *without* encoding as HTML.

- `PartialAsync` and `RenderPartialAsync`: Use these to generate HTML markup for a partial view. You can optionally pass a model and view data.

> **More Information**: You can read more about the `HtmlHelper` class at the following link: https://docs.microsoft.com/en-us/dotnet/api/microsoft.aspnetcore.mvc.viewfeatures.htmlhelper

Querying a database and using display templates

Let's create a new action method that can have a query string parameter passed to it and use that to query the `Northwind` database for products that cost more than a specified price:

1. In the `HomeController` class, import the `Microsoft.EntityFrameworkCore` namespace. We need this to add the `Include` extension method so that we can include related entities, as you learned in *Chapter 11, Working with Databases Using Entity Framework Core*.

2. Add a new action method, as shown in the following code:

```
public IActionResult ProductsThatCostMoreThan(decimal? price)
{
  if (!price.HasValue)
  {
    return NotFound("You must pass a product price in the query string,
for example, /Home/ProductsThatCostMoreThan?price=50");
  }

  IEnumerable<Product> model = db.Products
    .Include(p => p.Category)
    .Include(p => p.Supplier)
    .Where(p => p.UnitPrice > price);

  if (model.Count() == 0)
  {
    return NotFound(
      $"No products cost more than {price:C}.");
  }

  ViewData["MaxPrice"] = price.Value.ToString("C");
  return View(model); // pass model to view
}
```

3. Inside the `Views/Home` folder, add a new file named `ProductsThatCostMoreThan.cshtml`.

4. Modify the contents, as shown in the following code:

```
@model IEnumerable<Packt.Shared.Product>
@{
  string title =
    "Products That Cost More Than " + ViewData["MaxPrice"];
  ViewData["Title"] = title;
}
<h2>@title</h2>
<table class="table">
  <thead>
    <tr>
      <th>Category Name</th>
      <th>Supplier's Company Name</th>
      <th>Product Name</th>
      <th>Unit Price</th>
      <th>Units In Stock</th>
```

```
        </tr>
      </thead>
      <tbody>
      @foreach (var item in Model)
      {
        <tr>
          <td>
            @Html.DisplayFor(modelItem => item.Category.CategoryName)
          </td>
          <td>
            @Html.DisplayFor(modelItem => item.Supplier.CompanyName)
          </td>
          <td>
            @Html.DisplayFor(modelItem => item.ProductName)
          </td>
          <td>
            @Html.DisplayFor(modelItem => item.UnitPrice)
          </td>
          <td>
            @Html.DisplayFor(modelItem => item.UnitsInStock)
          </td>
        </tr>
      }
      <tbody>
    </table>
```

5. In the `Views/Home` folder, open `Index.cshtml`.

6. Add the following `form` element below the visitor count and above the `Products` heading and its listing of products. This will provide a form for the user to enter a price. The user can then click on the **Submit** button to call the action method that shows only products that cost more than the entered price:

```
<h3>Query products by price</h3>
<form asp-action="ProductsThatCostMoreThan" method="get">
  <input name="price" placeholder="Enter a product price" />
  <input type="submit" />
</form>
```

7. Start the website, use Chrome to navigate to the website, and on the home page, enter a price in the form, for example, 50, and then click on **Submit**. You will see a table of the products that cost more than the price that you entered, as shown in the following screenshot:

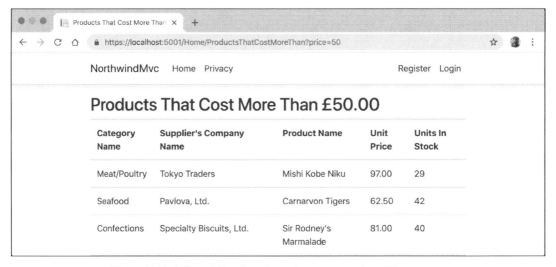

Figure 16.11: A filtered list of products that cost more than £50

8. Close the browser and stop the website.

Improving scalability using asynchronous tasks

When building a desktop or mobile app, multiple tasks (and their underlying threads) can be used to improve responsiveness, because while one thread is busy with the task, another can handle interactions with the user.

Tasks and their threads can be useful on the server side too, especially with websites that work with files, or request data from a store or a web service that could take a while to respond. But they are detrimental to complex calculations that are CPU-bound, so leave these to be processed synchronously as normal.

When an HTTP request arrives at the web server, a thread from its pool is allocated to handle the request. But if that thread must wait for a resource, then it is blocked from handling any more incoming requests. If a website receives more simultaneous requests than it has threads in its pool, then some of those requests will respond with a server timeout error, 503 Service Unavailable.

The threads that are locked are not doing useful work. They *could* handle one of those other requests but only if we implement asynchronous code in our websites.

Whenever a thread is waiting for a resource it needs, it can return to the thread pool and handle a different incoming request, improving the scalability of the website, that is, increasing the number of simultaneous requests it can handle.

Why not just have a larger thread pool? In modern operating systems, every thread pool thread has a 1 MB stack. An asynchronous method uses a smaller amount of memory. It also removes the need to create new threads in the pool, which takes time. The rate at which new threads are added to the pool is typically one every two seconds, which is a looooong time compared to switching between asynchronous threads.

Making controller action methods asynchronous

It is easy to make an existing action method asynchronous:

1. In the `HomeController` class, make sure that the `System.Threading.Tasks` namespace has been imported.

2. Modify the `Index` action method to be asynchronous, to return a `Task<T>`, and to await the calls to asynchronous methods to get the categories and products, as shown highlighted in the following code:

```
public async Task<IActionResult> Index()
{
  var model = new HomeIndexViewModel
  {
    VisitorCount = (new Random()).Next(1, 1001),
    Categories = await db.Categories.ToListAsync(),
    Products = await db.Products.ToListAsync()
  };
  return View(model); // pass model to view
}
```

3. Modify the `ProductDetail` action method in a similar way, as shown highlighted in the following code:

```
public async Task<IActionResult> ProductDetail(int? id)
{
  if (!id.HasValue)
  {
    return NotFound("You must pass a product ID in the route, for example,
/Home/ProductDetail/21");
  }

  var model = await db.Products
    .SingleOrDefaultAsync(p => p.ProductID == id);

  if (model == null)
  {
    return NotFound($"Product with ID of {id} not found.");
  }
  return View(model); // pass model to view and then return result
}
```

4. Start the website, use Chrome to navigate to the website, and note that the functionality of the website is the same, but trust that it will now scale better.

5. Close the browser and stop the website.

Using other project templates

When you install the .NET Core SDK, there are many project templates included:

1. In **TERMINAL**, enter the following command:

    ```
    dotnet new --help
    ```

2. You will see a list of currently installed templates, including templates for Windows desktop development if you are running on Windows, as shown in the following screenshot:

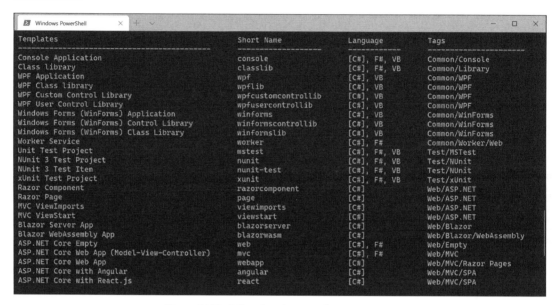

Figure 16.12: A list of project templates

3. Note the web-related project templates, including ones for creating SPAs using Blazor.

Installing additional template packs

Developers can install lots of additional template packs:

1. Start a browser and navigate to http://dotnetnew.azurewebsites.net/.

2. Enter vue in the textbox, click the **Search templates** button, and note the list of available templates for Vue.js, including one published by Microsoft, as shown in the following screenshot:

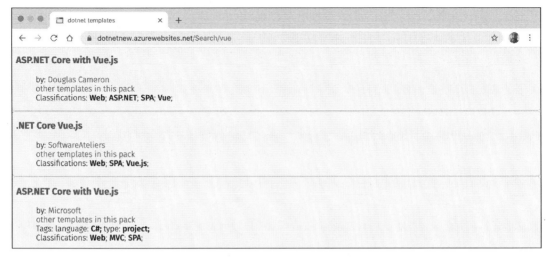

Figure 16.13: A list of Vue.js templates

3. Click on **ASP.NET Core with Vue.js** by Microsoft, and note the instructions for installing and using this template, as shown in the following command:

```
dotnet new --install "Microsoft.AspNetCore.SpaTemplates"
```

More Information: You can see more templates at the following link: https://github.com/dotnet/templating/wiki/Available-templates-for-dotnet-new

Practicing and exploring

Test your knowledge and understanding by answering some questions, get some hands-on practice, and explore this chapter's topics with deeper research.

Exercise 16.1 – Test your knowledge

Answer the following questions:

1. What do the files with the special names _ViewStart and _ViewImports do when created in the Views folder?

2. What are the names of the three segments defined in the default ASP.NET Core MVC route, what do they represent, and which are optional?

3. What does the default model binder do, and what data types can it handle?

4. In a shared layout file like _Layout.cshtml, how do you output the content of the current view?

5. In a shared layout file like _Layout.cshtml, how do you output a section that the current view can supply content for, and how does the view supply the contents for that section?

6. When calling the View method inside a controller's action method, what paths are searched for the view by convention?

7. How can you instruct the visitor's browser to cache the response for 24 hours?

8. Why might you enable Razor Pages even if you are not creating any yourself?

9. How does ASP.NET Core MVC identify classes that can act as controllers?

10. In what ways does ASP.NET Core MVC make it easier to test a website?

Exercise 16.2 – Practice implementing MVC by implementing a category detail page

The NorthwindMvc project has a home page that shows categories, but when the **View** button is clicked, the website returns a 404 Not Found error, for example, for the following URL: https://localhost:5001/category/1

Extend the NorthwindMvc project by adding the ability to show a detail page for a category.

Exercise 16.3 – Practice improving scalability by understanding and implementing async action methods

A few years ago, Stephen Cleary wrote an excellent article for MSDN Magazine explaining the scalability benefits of implementing async action methods for ASP.NET. The same principles apply to ASP.NET Core, but even more so, because unlike old ASP.NET as described in the article, ASP.NET Core supports asynchronous filters and other components.

Read the article at the following link and change all the remaining non-async action methods in the controller: https://docs.microsoft.com/en-us/archive/msdn-magazine/2014/october/async-programming-introduction-to-async-await-on-asp-net.

Exercise 16.4 – Explore topics

Use the following links to read more details about this chapter's topics:

- **Overview of ASP.NET Core MVC**: https://docs.microsoft.com/en-us/aspnet/core/mvc/overview

- **Tutorial: Get started with EF Core in an ASP.NET MVC web app**: https://docs.microsoft.com/en-us/aspnet/core/data/ef-mvc/intro

- **Handle requests with controllers in ASP.NET Core MVC**: https://docs.microsoft.com/en-us/aspnet/core/mvc/controllers/actions

- **Model Binding in ASP.NET Core**: `https://docs.microsoft.com/en-us/aspnet/core/mvc/models/model-binding`
- **Views in ASP.NET Core MVC**: `https://docs.microsoft.com/en-us/aspnet/core/mvc/views/overview`

Summary

In this chapter, you learned how to build large, complex websites in a way that is easy to unit test and manage with teams of programmers using ASP.NET Core. You learned about startup configuration, authentication, routes, models, views, and controllers in ASP.NET Core MVC.

In the next chapter, you will learn how to build websites using a cross-platform **Content Management System (CMS)**. This allows developers to put responsibility for the content where it belongs: into the hands of users.

17
Building Websites Using a Content Management System

This chapter is about building websites using a modern cross-platform **Content Management System (CMS)**.

There are many choices of CMS for most web development platforms. For cross-platform C# and .NET web developers, the best for learning the important principles is currently Piranha CMS. It was the first CMS to support .NET Core, with Piranha CMS 4.0 released on December 1, 2017.

This chapter will cover the following topics:

- Understanding the benefits of a CMS
- Understanding Piranha CMS
- Defining components, content types, and templates
- Testing the Northwind CMS website

Understanding the benefits of a CMS

In previous chapters, you learned how to create static HTML web pages and configure ASP.NET Core to serve them when requested by a visitor's browser.

You also learned how ASP.NET Core Razor Pages can add C# code that executes on the server side to generate HTML dynamically, including from information loaded live from a database. Additionally, you learned how ASP.NET Core MVC provides the separation of technical concerns to make building more complex websites more manageable.

On its own, ASP.NET Core does not solve the problem of managing content. In those previous websites, the person creating and managing the content would have to have programming and HTML editing skills, or the ability to edit the data in the Northwind database, to change what visitors see on the website.

This is where a CMS becomes useful. A CMS separates the content (data values) from templates (layout, format, and style). Most CMSs generate web responses like HTML for humans viewing the website with a browser.

Some CMSs generate open data formats like JSON and XML to be processed by a web service or rendered in a browser using client-side technologies like Angular, React, or Vue. This is often called a **headless CMS**.

Developers define the structure of data stored in the CMS using content type classes for different purposes, like a product page, with content templates that render the content data into HTML, JSON, or other formats.

Non-technical content owners can log in to the CMS and use a simple user interface to create, edit, delete, and publish content that will fit the structure defined by the content type classes, without needing the involvement of developers or tools like Visual Studio Code.

Understanding basic CMS features

Any decent basic CMS will include the following core features:

- A user interface that allows non-technical content owners to log in and manage their content.
- Media asset management of images, videos, documents, and other files.
- Sharing and reuse of pieces of content, often named *blocks*.
- Saved drafts of content that are hidden from website visitors until they are published.
- **Search Engine Optimized (SEO)** URLs, page titles and related metadata, sitemaps, and so on.
- Authentication and authorization, including management of users, groups, and their access rights to content.
- A content delivery system that converts the content from simple data into one or more formats, like HTML and JSON.

Understanding enterprise CMS features

Any decent commercial enterprise-level CMS would add the following additional features:

- Forms designer for gathering input from visitors.
- Marketing tools like tracking visitor behavior and A/B testing of content.
- Personalization of content based on rules like geographic location or machine learning processing of tracked visitor behavior.

- Retaining multiple versions of content and enabling the republishing of old versions.
- Translation of content into multiple human languages, like English and German.

Understanding CMS platforms

CMSs exist for most development platforms and languages, as shown in the following table:

Development platform	Content Management Systems
PHP	WordPress, Drupal, Joomla!, Magento
Python	django CMS
Java	Adobe Experience Manager, Bloomreach Experience Manager (formerly Hippo CMS)
.NET Framework	Episerver CMS, Sitecore, Umbraco, Kentico CMS
.NET Core and .NET 5	Piranha CMS, Orchard Core CMS

More Information: Orchard Core CMS version 1.0 was planned to be released in September 2020 but at the time of publishing it is still a release candidate and is more complicated than Piranha CMS, so I decided to use Piranha CMS as it is simpler and more mature. It has supported .NET Core since its version 4.0 and it is now up to version 8.4. After learning about Piranha CMS, if you want another option to compare it to, then you can read about Orchard Core CMS at the following link: `https://orchardcore.readthedocs.io/en/dev/`

Understanding Piranha CMS

Piranha CMS is a good choice for learning how to develop for a CMS because it is open source, simple, and flexible.

As described by its lead developer and creator, Håkan Edling, "Piranha CMS is a lightweight, unobtrusive and cross-platform CMS library for .NET Standard 2.0. It can be used to add CMS functionality to an already existing application, build a new website from scratch, or even be used as a backend for a mobile application."

Piranha CMS has three design principles:

- An open and extendible platform.
- Easy and intuitive for the content administrators.
- Fast, efficient, and fun for the developers.

Instead of adding more and more complex functions for commercial enterprise customers, Piranha CMS focuses on providing a platform for small- to medium-sized websites that need non-technical users to edit content on their current websites.

Piranha is not WordPress, meaning it will never have thousands of predefined themes and plugins to install. In the words of Piranha themselves, *"The heart and soul of Piranha is about structuring content and editing it in the most intuitive way possible – the rest we leave up to you."*

 More Information: You can read the official documentation for Piranha CMS at the following link: `https://piranhacms.org/`

Open source libraries and licensing

Piranha CMS is built using some open source libraries, including the following:

- **Font Awesome**, the web's most popular icon set and toolkit: `https://fontawesome.com`
- **AutoMapper**, a convention-based object-object mapper: `https://automapper.org`
- **Markdig**, a fast, powerful, CommonMark-compliant, extensible Markdown processor for .NET: `https://github.com/lunet-io/markdig`
- **Newtonsoft Json.NET**, a popular high-performance JSON framework for .NET: `https://www.newtonsoft.com/json`

Piranha CMS is released under the MIT license, meaning that it permits reuse within proprietary software provided all copies of the licensed software include a copy of the MIT License terms and the copyright notice.

Creating a Piranha CMS website

Piranha CMS has four project templates: **Empty**, **MVC**, **Razor Pages**, and **Module**. **MVC** and **Razor Pages** include models, controllers, and views for basic pages and a blog archive with blog posts. It is up to you if you prefer MVC or Razor Pages to implement your website.

We will need to install these templates before we can create a Piranha CMS website project.

You will use the `piranha.mvc` project template to create a Piranha CMS website based on MVC with a SQLite database for storing content including pages, blog posts, and usernames and passwords for authentication:

1. In the folder named `PracticalApps`, create a folder named `NorthwindCms`.
2. In **Visual Studio Code**, open the `PracticalApps` workspace.
3. Add the `NorthwindCms` folder to the workspace.
4. Navigate to **Terminal | New Terminal** and select `NorthwindCms`.
5. In **TERMINAL**, install Piranha project templates, as shown in the following command:

```
dotnet new -i Piranha.Templates
```

6. In **TERMINAL**, enter a command to list the Piranha CMS templates, as shown in the following command:

```
dotnet new "piranha cms" --list
```

7. Note the templates, as shown in the following output:

```
Templates                                        Short Name      Language
------------------------------------------------------------------------
ASP.NET Core Empty with Piranha CMS              piranha.empty   [C#]
ASP.NET Core MVC Web with Piranha CMS            piranha.mvc     [C#]
ASP.NET Core Razor Pages Web with Piranha CMS    piranha.razor   [C#]
ASP.NET Core Razor pages Piranha CMS Module      piranha.module  [C#]
```

8. In **TERMINAL**, enter the command to create a Piranha CMS website using MVC, as shown in the following command:

```
dotnet new piranha.mvc
```

9. In **EXPLORER**, open the NorthwindCms.csproj file, and note that at the time of writing, Piranha CMS is version 8.4 and that it targets ASP.NET Core 3.1, the Long-Term Support version that will retain support until December 3, 2022, as shown in the following markup:

```
<Project Sdk="Microsoft.NET.Sdk.Web">
  <PropertyGroup>
    <TargetFramework>netcoreapp3.1</TargetFramework>
  </PropertyGroup>

  <ItemGroup>
    <PackageReference Include="Piranha" Version="8.4.2" />
    <PackageReference Include="Piranha.AspNetCore" Version="8.4.1" />
    <PackageReference Include="Piranha.AspNetCore.Identity.SQLite"
      Version="8.4.0" />
    <PackageReference Include="Piranha.AttributeBuilder"
      Version="8.4.0" />
    <PackageReference
      Include="Piranha.Data.EF.SQLite" Version="8.4.0" />
    <PackageReference Include="Piranha.ImageSharp" Version="8.4.0" />
    <PackageReference Include="Piranha.Local.FileStorage"
      Version="8.4.0" />
    <PackageReference Include="Piranha.Manager" Version="8.4.0" />
    <PackageReference Include="Piranha.Manager.TinyMCE"
      Version="8.4.0" />
  </ItemGroup>
</Project>
```

I expect Piranha CMS and its project templates to be updated to support .NET 5 by the end of 2020, so by the time you read this book the target framework will be net5.0 and the version numbers of the Piranha packages in your .csproj file are likely to be 9.0 or higher.

Exploring a Piranha CMS website

Let's explore a Piranha CMS website:

1. In **TERMINAL**, build and start the website, as shown in the following command:

    ```
    dotnet run
    ```

2. Start Chrome and navigate to the following URL: `https://localhost:5001/`.

3. Note the default home page for a Piranha CMS website that welcomes you and explains, "You can log into the admin panel at ~/manager with the default credentials `admin`/`password`. If you want, we can seed some data for you which will give you an example of how to create and structure with Piranha CMS. After you're done with the setup, you can delete the `SetupController` and the ~/seed directory from your project."

4. At the bottom of the page, click **Seed some data**, and note the following:

    *   The home page for the website has blocks of content arranged in pleasing ways that leads a visitor deeper into the website using page links that can show some of the page content, like a primary image and description.

    *   The website has a blog archive that shows the latest posts. Each blog post has an image, title, category, some hashtags, comments, and a publish date, as well as summary text with a button to **Read more**, as shown in the following screenshot:

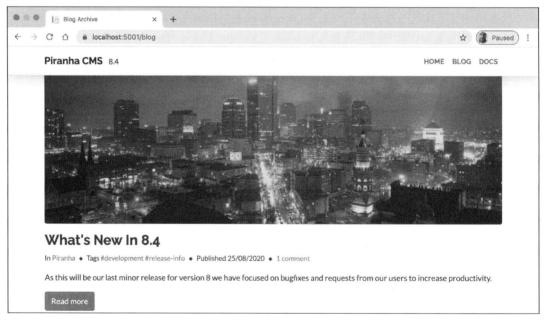

Figure 17.1: A Piranha CMS website

Editing site and page content

Let's log in as if we are the content owner for the website and manage some of the content:

1. In your browser's address box, enter the following URL: `https://localhost:5001/manager`.

2. Enter a username of `admin` and a password of `password`.

3. In the manager, note the existing pages named **Home** (which is an example of the **Standard page** type), **Blog** (which is an example of the **Standard archive** type), and **Docs** (which is another example of the **Standard page** type), and then at the root of the page structure, click **Default Site**, as shown in the following screenshot:

Figure 17.2: The Default Site and its pages

4. In the **Edit site** dialog box, on the **Settings** tab, change the **Title** to `Northwind CMS` and **Description** to `Providing fresh tasty food to restaurants for three generations`, and then click the **Save** button, as shown in the following screenshot:

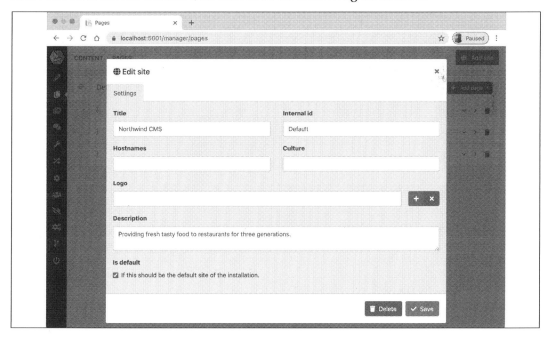

Figure 17.3: Editing site settings

5. If you are not already in the **CONTENT : PAGES** section, then in the menu navigation bar on the left, click **Pages**, and then click **Home** to edit that page.

6. Change the page title to `Welcome To Northwind CMS`, and note that beneath it the content owner can set a primary image and some text, and then beneath that they can add any number of blocks to the page, as shown in the following screenshot, including:

   - Horizontal dividers between each block with a circular button to insert a new block.

   - When a block has the focus, it has buttons to collapse, expand, and delete the block, and a menu of additional actions.

   - A **CONTENT** block with rich text, images, and links, easily styled with a toolbar when it has the focus.

   - A **COLUMNS** block that can have multiple columns of rich text, with a + button to add columns and trash can icon buttons to remove columns or the whole block.

   - A **GALLERY** block that can have multiple images and rotate them in a carousel-style animation:

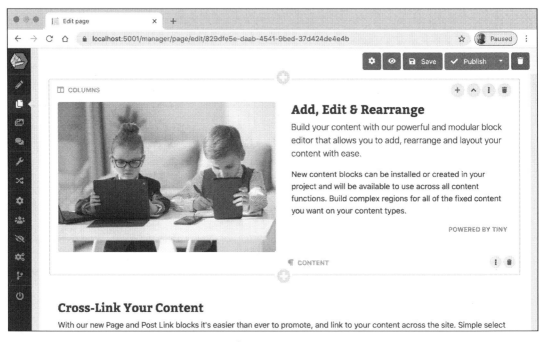

Figure 17.4: Changing your page

7. At the top of **CONTENT : PAGES / EDIT**, click the gear icon to show the **Settings** dialog box, where the content owner can set the slug used in the URL path, publish date, navigation title, if the page should be hidden in the sitemap, redirections, and enabling comments for a specified number of days, as shown in the following screenshot:

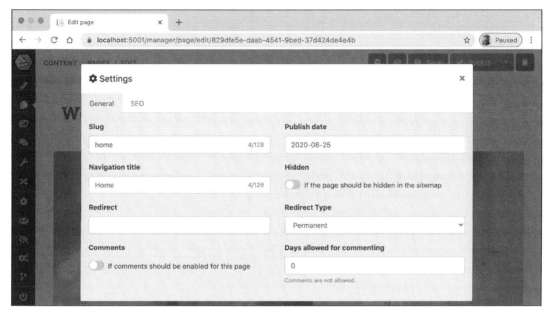

Figure 17.5: The page General Settings dialog box

8. Click the **SEO** tab, where the content owner can set the meta title, meta keywords, the meta description, and **OpenGraph (OG)** metadata.

> **More Information**: You can read more about why you would want to set OpenGraph metadata for your web pages at the following link: `https://ogp.me/`

9. Change **Meta title** to Northwind CMS.

10. Change **Meta keywords** to beverages, condiments, meat, seafood.

11. Change **Meta description** to Providing fresh tasty food to restaurants for three generations.

12. Note the OpenGraph title and description metadata is set for you but you need to select an image yourself. Select the cute children image, as shown in the following screenshot:

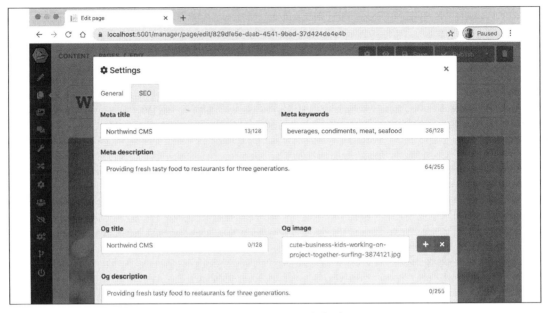

Figure 17.6: The page SEO Settings dialog box

13. Close the dialog box.

14. At the top of **CONTENT : PAGES / EDIT**, click the **Save** button, and note that the changes have been saved as a draft, as shown in the following screenshot:

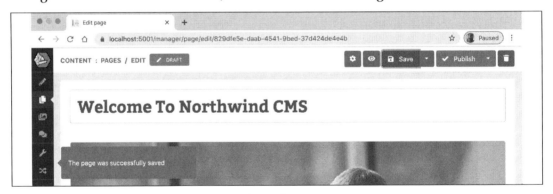

Figure 17.7: Saving the page

15. Click the **Publish** button to make those changes visible to website visitors.

Creating a new top-level page

Let's create a new page with some blocks for its content:

1. In the menu navigation bar on the left, click **Pages**, click the **+ Add page** button, and then click **Standard page**.

2. In the **Your page title** box, enter Contact Us.

3. For the page image, select the cheerful diverse colleagues.

4. For the page text, type We welcome your contact.

5. In the blocks section, click the circular **+** button and choose **Columns**, as shown in the following screenshot:

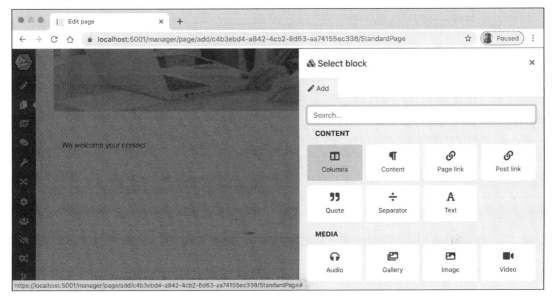

Figure 17.8: Adding a block of content to a page

6. At the top of the **COLUMNS** block, click the **+** button, click **Content**, and then enter a fake postal address, like 123 Main Street, New York City, United States, and a fake email address and phone number, like admin@northwind.com and (123) 555-1234.

7. At the top of the **COLUMNS** block, click the **+** button, click **Quote**, and then enter We love our customers by the Customer Success Team, as shown in the following screenshot:

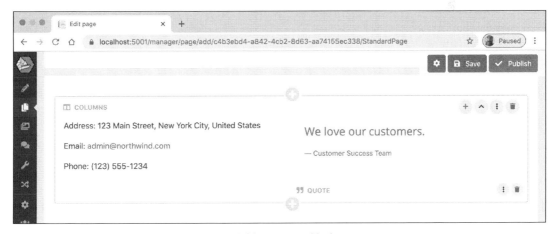

Figure 17.9: Adding a quote block

8. At the top of **CONTENT : PAGES / EDIT**, click **Publish**.

If you just click the **Save** button, then the new page is saved to the CMS database, but it will not yet be visible to website visitors.

Creating a new child page

To create new pages in Piranha CMS, you must consider the page hierarchy.

To create the **Contact Us** page, we clicked the **+ Add page** button at the top of the **Pages** structure. But to insert a new page within the existing page hierarchy, you must click either the down or right arrow icons for an existing page:

*   **Down arrow**: Creates a new page *after* the current page, that is, at the same level.
*   **Right arrow**: Creates a new page *under* the current page, that is, a child page.

If you ever create a page in the wrong place, it is easy to drag and drop it into the correct position within the page hierarchy. Some content owners might even prefer this technique, that is, always create new pages at the bottom of the list and then drag and drop them to the desired position within the page tree.

Let's try creating a new child page for the **Contact Us** page:

1. In the menu navigation bar on the left, click **Pages**; in the **Contact Us** row, click the right arrow icon, and then click **Standard page**. Note that there is also an option to copy the content of an existing page, but we will start with a blank standard page.
2. Enter Our Location for the page title and then click **Publish**.
3. In the menu navigation bar on the left, click **Pages**, and note the **Our Location** page is a child of **Contact Us**, as shown in the following screenshot:

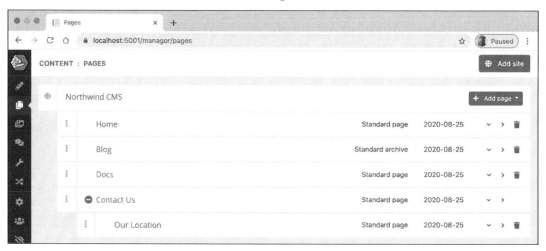

Figure 17.10: The page structure of the Northwind CMS website

4. Click the **Our Location** page to edit it.

5. Click the gear button to open the **Settings** dialog box, and note the **Slug** has been set automatically based on where the page was initially created and uses characters that are better for URL paths like hyphens for spaces and lowercase, as shown in the following screenshot:

Figure 17.11: The Our Location page's slug

The slug for a page will not automatically change if the page is later dragged and dropped to a different position within the page hierarchy. You would have to change the slug manually.

Reviewing the blog archive

Let's review the blog archive:

1. In the menu navigation bar on the left, click **Pages**, click **Blog**, and note the **Standard archive** type of page has a tab for **Main content** with image, text, and blocks just like a **Standard page**.

2. Click the **Archive** tab and note that it has a table of blog post items, each row with the item's title, published date, item type (**Standard post**), category (**Piranha**, **Tristique**, and **Magna**), and the ability to delete individual posts, as shown in the following screenshot:

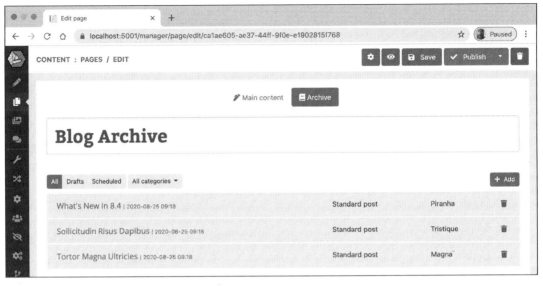

Figure 17.12: The Blog Archive with list of published posts

3. Click the **+ Add** button at the top of the table of blog posts.

4. Enter a post title like `Northwind has some cool new fish to sell you!`, enter `Fish` for the category, add some tags like `seafood` and `cool`, and then add at least one block like a quote saying `"This fish is the tastiest ever!"`.

5. Click **Publish**.

6. Click the **Preview** button (with the "eye" icon) to the left of the **Save** button.

7. In the **Live Preview** browser tab, click **MOBILE** to see how the blog post will look on mobile devices, as shown in the following screenshot:

Figure 17.13: The Live Preview tab

Commenting on posts and pages

One of the recent new features in Piranha CMS is built-in support for comments on posts and pages:

1. Click **TABLET**, scroll down to the bottom of the post, and note that a visitor can post a comment, as shown in the following screenshot:

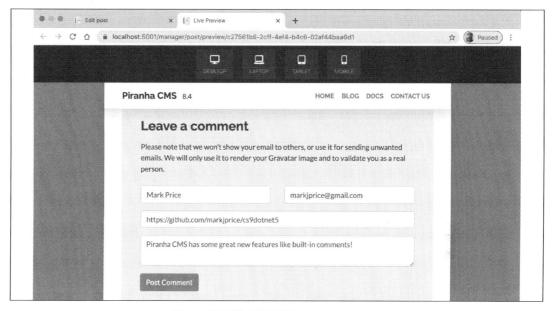

Figure 17.14: The TABLET preview

2. Post your own comment.

3. Close the **Live Preview** browser tab.

4. In the menu navigation bar on the left, click **Comments**, and note the table of comments for all pages, as shown in the following screenshot:

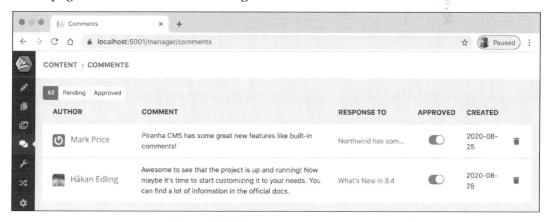

Figure 17.15: The comments page

5. Click the toggle button in the **APPROVED** column to unapprove the comment you made.

6. Click the post title in the **RESPONSE TO** column to quickly navigate back to the post.

7. Note the warning notification showing the number of pending comments, as shown in the following screenshot:

Figure 17.16: There is one comment notification

8. Click the **Comments** tab.

9. Click **Pending**.

10. Click the toggle button to approve your comment.

11. Close the **Comments** browser tab.

Exploring authentication and authorization

Let's see what system settings are available to secure content:

1. In the menu navigation bar on the left, click **Users**, and note the **admin** user is a member of the **SysAdmin** role, as shown in the following screenshot:

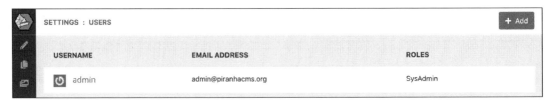

Figure 17.17: A roles of the admin user

2. In the menu navigation bar on the left, click **Roles**, click the **SysAdmin** role, and note that you can assign dozens of permissions to a role, as shown in the following screenshot:

Figure 17.18: Managing permissions

3. In the menu navigation bar on the left, click **Roles**, and then click the **+ Add** button.

4. In the **GENERAL** section, enter the name Editors.

5. In the **CORE PERMISSIONS** section, select both **Page Preview** and **Post Preview** permissions.

6. In the **MANAGER PERMISSIONS** section, select the following permissions:

   - **Comments**: **List Comments**.
   - **Media**: **Add Media**, **Add Media Folders**, **Edit Media**, **List Media**.
   - **Pages**: **Add Pages**, **Edit Pages**, **List Pages**, **Pages - Save**.
   - **Posts**: **Add Posts**, **Edit Posts**, **List Posts**, **Save Posts**.

7. Click **Save**.

8. In the menu navigation bar on the left, click **Users**, and then click the **+ Add** button.

9. Enter a name of Eve, an email address of eve@northwind.com, assign her to the Editors role, and set her password to Pa$$w0rd, as shown in the following screenshot:

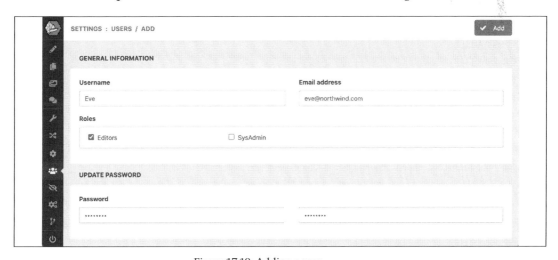

Figure 17.19: Adding a user

10. Click **Add**.

> **Good Practice**: You should carefully consider what permissions different roles will need. The SysAdmin role should have all permissions. An Editor role might be allowed to add, delete, edit, and save pages, posts, and media, but perhaps only a Publisher role would be allowed to publish content because only they should control when to allow website visitors to see the content.

Exploring configuration

Let's see how you can control the URL paths, the number of versions of each page and posts that are retained in the CMS database, and caching to improve scalability and performance:

1. In the menu navigation bar on the left, click **Config**, and note some of the common configuration settings, including the ones shown in the following list:

    - **Hierarchical page slugs**: By default, if the content owner creates a hierarchical tree of pages, then the URL path will use hierarchical slugs, as shown in the following example URL path: /about-us/news-and-events/northwind-wins-award.

    - **Close comments after**: By default, the value is 0 days, so comments are open forever.

    - **Enable post/page comments**: By default, posts allow comments, but pages do not.

    - **Approve comments**: By default, comments are automatically approved. It would be safer to disable this setting so toggle it off now, but then you will need to moderate the comments for individual pages and posts.

    - **HISTORY**: By default, 10 revisions of each post and page are stored.

    - **CACHING**: By default, pages and posts are not cached so every visitor request is served by loading the content from the database. Common values are 120 minutes (two hours), 720 minutes (12 hours), and 1440 minutes (24 hours).

> **Good Practice**: While developing, keep caching switched off because it is likely to cause you confusion when you make a change to your code, but it is not reflected in the website! After you deploy to production, then log in and set these values to sensible values depending on how frequently content owners update pages and how quickly they expect a website visitor to then see those changes. Caching is a balance.

2. Click **Save**.

Testing the new content

Let's see if the **Contact Us** and **Our Location** pages are published and therefore visible to website visitors:

1. In the menu navigation bar on the left, click **Logout**.
2. Navigate to the website at `https://localhost:5001/` and note that the **Contact Us** page and the blog post are now shown to visitors, as shown in the following screenshot:

Figure 17.20: The updated Piranha CMS site with Contact Us page in the top menu

3. Only top-level pages are shown in the navigation menu, so click **CONTACT US** to navigate to that page and then, in the browser's address bar, append the rest of the slug and press *Enter*, as shown in the following URL:

```
https://localhost:5001/contact-us/our-location
```

In a real website, you would want to provide navigation to child pages like **Our Location** using something like a Bootstrap navbar with drop-down menus.

 More Information: You can read about Bootstrap's navbar at the following link: `https://getbootstrap.com/docs/4.5/components/navbar/`

4. Close the browser.
5. Stop the website running by pressing *Ctrl + C* in **TERMINAL**.

Understanding routing

Piranha CMS uses the normal ASP.NET Core routing system underneath.

In the current website, we have five pages that are the responses to HTTP requests for relative paths, also known as slugs, as shown in the following list:

- **Home**: / or /home
- **Blog**: /blog
- **Docs**: /docs
- **Contact Us**: /contact-us
- **Our Location**: /contact-us/our-location

When a request arrives for a slug, Piranha CMS looks in the content database for a content item with a matching slug. When found, it looks up the type of content, so for /contact-us it would then know that it is a **Standard page**. If a slug match is not found, it returns a 404 Missing resource HTTP response.

The **Standard page** and **Standard archive** do not need custom routes defined in order to work because the following routes are configured by default:

- /page for all page types except archives
- /archive for archives
- /post for post items in an archive
- /post/comment for comments on a post

So, incoming HTTP request URLs are translated into a route that can be processed by ASP.NET Core in the normal way. For example, the following request:

```
https://localhost:5001/contact-us
```

Is translated by Piranha CMS middleware into:

```
https://localhost:5001/page?id=154b519d-b5ed-4f75-8aa4-d092559363b0
```

This is then processed by a normal ASP.NET Core MVC controller. The page id is a GUID that can be used to look up the page content data in the Piranha CMS database. Let's see how:

1. In the Controllers folder, open CmsController.cs.
2. Note that CmsController derives from Microsoft's Controller class.
3. Scroll down to find the Page action method, and note that it uses Microsoft's [Route] attribute to indicate that this action method responds to HTTP requests for the relative URL path, /page, and will extract the Guid using Microsoft's model binder and use it to look up the page's model from the database using Piranha's API, as shown in the following code:

```
/// <summary>
/// Gets the page with the given id.
/// </summary>
/// <param name="id">The unique page id</param>
```

```
/// <param name="draft">If a draft is requested</param>
[Route("page")]
public async Task<IActionResult> Page(
  Guid id, bool draft = false)
{
  try
  {
    var model = await _loader.GetPageAsync<StandardPage>(
      id, HttpContext.User, draft);

    return View(model);
  }
  catch (UnauthorizedAccessException)
  {
    return Unauthorized();
  }
}
```

Note that this controller also has similar action methods with custom simplified routes for archives and posts, as well as an action method for handling posting comments and saving them to the database.

So that a request is not processed repeatedly by Piranha, a query string parameter, `piranha_handled=true`, is added to the rewritten URL.

As well as the built-in custom routes, you can define additional ones. For example, if you are building an e-commerce website, then you might want special routes for product catalogs and categories:

- **Product catalog**: `/catalog`
- **Product category**: `/catalog/beverages`

> **More Information**: You can read about advanced routing for Piranha CMS at the following link: `http://piranhacms.org/docs/application/advanced-routing`

Understanding media

Media files can be uploaded through the manager user interface or programmatically using an API provided by Piranha CMS with streams and byte arrays.

> **More Information**: You can read more about programmatically uploading media using the Piranha CMS APIs at the following link: `http://piranhacms.org/docs/content/media`

To make it more likely that uploaded media is compatible with common devices, Piranha CMS limits the types of media that can be uploaded to the following file types by default:

- `.jpg`, `.jpeg`, and `.png` images
- `.mp4` videos
- `.pdf` documents

If you need to upload other types of file, like GIF images, then you can register additional media file types in the `Startup` class:

1. Open the `Startup.cs` file.
2. In the `Configure` method, after Piranha is initialized, register the GIF file extension as a recognized file type, as shown highlighted in the following code:

```
// Initialize Piranha
App.Init(api);


// register GIFs as a media type
App.MediaTypes.Images.Add(".gif", "image/gif");
```

Understanding the application service

`ApplicationService` simplifies programmatic access to common objects for the current request. It is usually injected into all Razor files using `_ViewImports.cshtml` with the name `WebApp`, as shown in the following code:

```
@inject Piranha.AspNetCore.Services.IApplicationService WebApp
```

Common uses of the application service are shown in the following table:

Code	Description
`@WebApp.PageId`	GUID of the requested page.
`@WebApp.Url`	Browser requested original URL before it was rewritten by the middleware.
`@WebApp.Api`	Access to the complete Piranha API.
`@WebApp.Media.ResizeImage(ImageField image, int width, int? height = null)`	Resizes the given `ImageField` to the specified dimensions and returns the generated URL path to the resized file. `ImageField` is a Piranha type that can reference an uploaded image.

Understanding content types

Piranha allows a developer to define three categories of **content type**, as shown in the following list:

- **Sites**: For properties shared across all other content. If you don't need to share properties, then you don't need a site content type. Even if you do need one, each site usually only needs one site content type. The class must be decorated with [SiteType]. The piranha.mvc project template does not include an example of a custom site.

 More Information: You can read about sites at the following link: https://piranhacms.org/docs/content/sites

- **Pages**: For informational pages like **Contact Us** and landing pages like a home or category page that can have other pages as their children. Pages form a hierarchical tree that provides the URL path structure of the site, like /contact-us/our-location and /about-us/job-vacancies. Each site usually has multiple page content types, like **Standard page**, **Standard archive**, **Category page**, and **Product page**. The class must be decorated with [PageType].

- **Posts**: For "pages" that do not have children and can only be listed in a page with an archive property. Posts can be filtered and grouped by date, category, and tags. The PostArchive<T> type provides the user interaction with the posts through a page property named **Archive** by convention. Each site usually has only one or two post content types, like NewsPost or EventPost. The class must be decorated with [PostType].

Understanding component types

Registered content types are given built-in support for creating, editing, and deleting in the Piranha manager. The structure of a content type is provided by dividing it into three categories of **component type**, as shown in the following list:

- **Fields**: The smallest component of content. They can be as simple as a number, date, or string value. Fields are like properties in a C# class. The property must be decorated with [Field].

- **Regions**: Small pieces of content that appear in a fixed location on the page or post rendered to the visitor under the control of the developer. Regions are composed of one or more fields, or a sortable collection of fields. Regions are like titled complex properties in a C# class. The property must be decorated with [Region].

- **Blocks**: Small pieces of content that can be added, reordered, and deleted. Blocks provide complete flexibility to the content editor. By default, all pages and posts can contain any number of blocks, although this can be disabled for a specific page or post content type with the [PageType] attribute that sets UseBlocks to false. Standard block types include multi-column rich text, quote, and image. Developers can define custom block types with a custom editing experience in the Piranha manager.

Understanding standard fields

Standard fields each have a built-in editing experience and include the following:

- `CheckBoxField`, `DateField`, `NumberField`, `StringField`, `TextField`: Simple field values.

- `PageField` and `PostField`: Reference a page or post using its GUID.

- `DocumentField`, `ImageField`, `VideoField`, `MediaField`: Reference a document, image, video, or any media file using its `Guid`. By default, `DocumentField` can be `.pdf`, `ImageField` can be `.jpg`, `.jpeg`, or `.png`, `VideoField` can be `.mp4`, and `MediaField` can be any file type.

- `HtmlField`, `MarkdownField`: Formatted text values with a customizable `TinyMCE` editor with a toolbar and a Markdown editor.

Customizing the rich text editor

By default, Piranha CMS includes the open source TinyMCE rich text editor.

 More Information: You can read the documentation for TinyMCE at the following link: `https://www.tiny.cloud/docs/`

TinyMCE is configured using the file named `editorconfig.json`, as shown in the following markup:

```
{
  "plugins": "autoresize autolink code hr paste lists piranhalink piranhaimage",
  "toolbar": "bold italic | bullist numlist hr | alignleft aligncenter alignright
| formatselect styleselect | piranhalink piranhaimage",
  "blockformats": "Paragraph=p;Header 1=h1;Header 2=h2;Header 3=h3;Header 4=h4;C
ode=pre;Quote=blockquote",
  "styleformats": [
    { "title": "Small", "tag": "small", "type": "inline" },
    { "title": "Code", "tag": "code", "type": "format" },
    { "title": "Lead", "tag": "p", "type": "block", "classes": "lead" },
    { "title": "Button Primary", "tag": "a", "type": "inline", "classes": "btn
btn-primary" },
    { "title": "Button Light", "tag": "a", "type": "inline", "classes": "btn
btn-light" }
  ]
}
```

Piranha CMS provides two custom TinyMCE plugins to enable integrated embedded links and images.

Reviewing the Standard page type

Let's review some of the content types defined by the Piranha Blog project template:

1. Open `Models/StandardPage.cs`, and note that a page type must inherit from `Page<T>`, where `T` is the derived class, and be decorated with the `[PageType]` attribute, as shown in the following code:

```
using Piranha.AttributeBuilder; // [PageType]
using Piranha.Models;           // Page<T>

namespace NorthwindCms.Models
{
  [PageType(Title = "Standard page")]
  public class StandardPage : Page<StandardPage>
  {
  }
}
```

2. Click in `Page<StandardPage>` and press *F12* to view the source.

3. Click in `GenericPage<T>` and press *F12* to view the source.

4. Click in `PageBase` and press *F12* to view the source.

5. Review the `PageBase` class, as shown in the following code, and note that every page has the following properties:

   • `SiteId` and `ParentId`, which are `Guid` values.

   • `Blocks`, which is a list of `Block` instances:

```
#region Assembly Piranha, Version=8.4.2.0, Culture=neutral,
PublicKeyToken=null
// Piranha.dll
#endregion
using System;
using System.Collections.Generic;
using System.ComponentModel.DataAnnotations;
using Piranha.Extend;

namespace Piranha.Models
{
  public abstract class PageBase :
    RoutedContentBase, IBlockContent, IMeta, ICommentModel
  {
    protected PageBase();

    public Guid SiteId { get; set; }
    [StringLength(256)]
    public Guid? ParentId { get; set; }
```

```
      public int SortOrder { get; set; }
      [StringLength(128)]
      public string NavigationTitle { get; set; }
      public bool IsHidden { get; set; }
      [StringLength(256)]
      public string RedirectUrl { get; set; }
      public RedirectType RedirectType { get; set; }
      public Guid? OriginalPageId { get; set; }
      public IList<Block> Blocks { get; set; }
      public bool EnableComments { get; set; }
      public int CloseCommentsAfterDays { get; set; }
      public int CommentCount { get; set; }
      public bool IsCommentsOpen { get; }
      public bool IsStartPage { get; }
    }
  }
```

6. Click in `RoutedContentBase`, press *F12* to view the source, and note that this is the class that defines properties like `Slug` for the segment name used in URL paths, SEO and OpenGraph metadata like a description and keywords, a primary image and excerpt, and the published date.

7. Click in `ContentBase` and press *F12* to view the source, as shown in the following code, and note that all content has:

    *   `Id` as a `Guid`

    *   `TypeId` as a string

    *   `Title` as a string

    *   `DateTime` values for when it was created and last modified:

```
using System;
using System.ComponentModel.DataAnnotations;

namespace Piranha.Models
{
  public abstract class ContentBase
  {
    protected ContentBase();

    public Guid Id { get; set; }
    [StringLength(64)]
    public string TypeId { get; set; }
    [StringLength(128)]
    public string Title { get; set; }
    public IList<string> Permissions { get; set; }
    public DateTime Created { get; set; }
    public DateTime LastModified { get; set; }
```

```
      }
   }
```

8. Open `Views/Cms/Page.cshtml`, and note this view:

    *   Is strongly typed to be passed an instance of the `StandardPage` class as its `Model` property.

    *   Stores the `Title` in the `ViewData` dictionary so it can be rendered into a shared layout.

    *   Renders additional meta tags from the model.

    *   Renders the `Title`, background primary image and excerpt (if set), and `Blocks` in Bootstrap-styled `<div>` elements, as shown in the following code:

```
@model StandardPage
@{
  ViewData["Title"] = !string.IsNullOrEmpty(Model.MetaTitle)
    ? Model.MetaTitle : Model.Title;
  var hasImage = Model.PrimaryImage.HasValue;
}
@section head {
  @WebApp.MetaTags(Model)
}

<header @(hasImage ? "class=has-image" : "") @(hasImage ?
$"style=background-image:url({ @Url.Content(WebApp.Media.
ResizeImage(Model.PrimaryImage, 1920, 400)) })" : "")>
  <div class="dimmer"></div>
  <div class="container text-center">
    <h1>@Model.Title</h1>
    @if (!string.IsNullOrWhiteSpace(Model.Excerpt))
    {
      <div class="row justify-content-center">
        <div class="col-lg-8 lead">
          @Html.Raw(Model.Excerpt)
        </div>
      </div>
    }
  </div>
</header>

<main>
  @foreach (var block in Model.Blocks)
  {
    <div class="block @block.CssName()">
      <div class="container">
        @Html.DisplayFor(m => block, block.GetType().Name)
```

```
        </div>
      </div>
    }
  </main>
```

Reviewing the Standard archive and post types

Blog archives on a website require a minimum of two types: a page type and a post type. The page type acts as a container for listing, filtering, and grouping the blog posts that use the post type:

1. Open `Models/StandardArchive.cs` and note this is a page type so is decorated with the `[PageType]` attribute, but it also has the `IsArchive` property set to `true`, and it has a property named `Archive` of type `PostArchive<PostInfo>`, as shown in the following code:

    ```
    using Piranha.AttributeBuilder;
    using Piranha.Models;

    namespace NorthwindCms.Models
    {
      [PageType(Title = "Standard archive", IsArchive = true)]
      public class StandardArchive : Page<StandardArchive>
      {
        public PostArchive<PostInfo> Archive { get; set; }
      }
    }
    ```

2. Open `Models/StandardPost.cs` and note that a post type must inherit from `Post<T>`, where `T` is the derived class, and be decorated with the `[PostType]` attribute, and that this post has a single property to store any comments, as shown in the following code:

    ```
    using System.Collections.Generic;
    using Piranha.AttributeBuilder;
    using Piranha.Models;
    namespace NorthwindCms.Models
    {
      [PostType(Title = "Standard post")]
      public class StandardPost : Post<StandardPost>
      {
        public IEnumerable<Comment> Comments
          { get; set; } = new List<Comment>();
      }
    }
    ```

Understanding standard blocks

Standard blocks include the following:

- **Columns**: Has an `Items` property with one or more items that are `Block` instances.
- **Image**: Has a `Body` property that is an `ImageField` with a view that outputs it as the `src` for an `<img>` element.
- **Quote**: Has a `Body` property that is a `TextField` with a view that outputs it wrapped in a `<blockquote>` element.
- **Text**: Has a `Body` property that is a `TextField`.

Reviewing component types and standard blocks

Let's review some of the component types defined by the project template:

1. In the `Models` folder, add a new temporary class without a namespace, named `ExploreBlocks.cs`, and enter statements to define properties, one for each of the most common block types, as shown in the following code:

    ```
    using Piranha.Extend.Blocks;

    class ExploreBlocks
    {
      AudioBlock ab;
      HtmlBlock hb;
      ColumnBlock cb;
      ImageBlock ib;
      ImageGalleryBlock igb;
      PageBlock pb;
      QuoteBlock qb;
      SeparatorBlock sb;
      TextBlock tb;
      VideoBlock vb;
    }
    ```

2. Click inside each block type, press *F12*, review its definition, and note that to define a block, the class must inherit from `Block` and be decorated with the `[BlockType]` attribute. For example, the `HtmlBlock` class, as shown in the following code:

    ```
    #region Assembly Piranha, Version=8.4.2.0, Culture=neutral,
    PublicKeyToken=null
    // Piranha.dll
    #endregion

    using Piranha.Extend.Fields;

    namespace Piranha.Extend.Blocks
    ```

```
{
  [BlockType(Name = "Content", Category = "Content",
    Icon = "fas fa-paragraph", Component = "html-block")]
  public class HtmlBlock : Block, ISearchable
  {
    public HtmlBlock();
    public HtmlField Body { get; set; }
    public string GetIndexedContent();
    public override string GetTitle();
  }
}
```

3. Open `Views/Cms/DisplayTemplates/HtmlBlock.cshtml` and note that it renders the block by simply rendering the raw HTML stored in the `Body` property, as shown in the following code:

```
@model Piranha.Extend.Blocks.HtmlBlock


@Html.Raw(Model.Body)
```

4. Open `Views/Cms/DisplayTemplates/ColumnBlock.cshtml` and note that it renders the collection of block items by calling the Microsoft `DisplayFor` method that will pass the block model into the appropriate view inside `<div>` elements styled with Bootstrap, as shown in the following markup:

```
@model Piranha.Extend.Blocks.ColumnBlock

<div class="row">
  @for (var n = 0; n < Model.Items.Count; n++)
  {
    <div class="col-md">
      @Html.DisplayFor(m => Model.Items[n],
        Model.Items[n].GetType().Name)
    </div>
  }
</div>
```

5. Review the models and views for the other built-in block types.

6. Comment out the whole class or delete the file from your project. We only created it to review how the built-in block types are implemented.

 More Information: If you are not familiar with the Bootstrap grid system, then you can read about it at the following link: `https://getbootstrap.com/docs/4.1/layout/grid/`

Defining components, content types, and templates

Now that you have seen the functionality of the content and component types provided with the project template, we will define custom pages and regions for storing categories and products imported from the Northwind database to show a catalog of Northwind products.

First, we will create an MVC controller that responds to an HTTP GET request for the /import relative path by querying the Northwind database for categories and their products.

Then, using the Piranha CMS API to find a special page that represents the root of the product catalog, and as children of that page, we will programmatically create instances of a custom CategoryPage type with a custom region to store details like the name, description, and image of each category, and a list of instances of a custom region to store details of each product, including name, price, and units in stock, as shown in the following diagram:

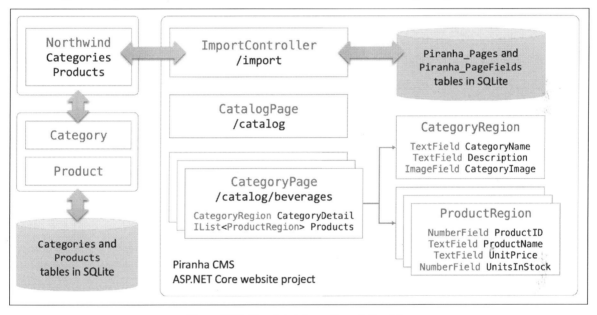

Figure 17.21: The site's information relationships

Creating custom regions

Let's start by creating custom regions for a category and product so that data can be stored in the Piranha CMS database and edited by a content owner through the manager user interface:

1. In the Models folder, add a new class named CategoryRegion.cs, and add statements to define a region for storing information about a category from the Northwind database using suitable field types, as shown in the following code:

```
using Piranha.Extend;
using Piranha.Extend.Fields;

namespace NorthwindCms.Models
{
  public class CategoryRegion
  {
    [Field(Title = "Category ID")]
    public NumberField CategoryID { get; set; }

    [Field(Title = "Category name")]
    public TextField CategoryName { get; set; }

    [Field]
    public HtmlField Description { get; set; }

    [Field(Title = "Category image")]
    public ImageField CategoryImage { get; set; }
  }
}
```

2. In the `Models` folder, add a new class named `ProductRegion.cs` and add statements to define a region for storing information about a product from the `Northwind` database using suitable field types, as shown in the following code:

```
using Piranha.Extend;
using Piranha.Extend.Fields;
using Piranha.Models;

namespace NorthwindCms.Models
{
  public class ProductRegion
  {
    [Field(Title = "Product ID")]
    public NumberField ProductID { get; set; }

    [Field(Title = "Product name")]
    public TextField ProductName { get; set; }

    [Field(Title = "Unit price", Options = FieldOption.HalfWidth)]
    public StringField UnitPrice { get; set; }

    [Field(Title = "Units in stock", Options = FieldOption.HalfWidth)]
    public NumberField UnitsInStock { get; set; }
  }
}
```

Creating an entity data model

At the time of writing, Piranha CMS 8.4 does not support .NET 5, so we cannot use the EF Core database context and entity model class projects. But since we only need basic functionality to import categories and products, we will create a new simplified `Northwind` database context and entity model classes in the current Piranha CMS project:

1. In the `Models` folder, add a class named `Northwind.cs`.

2. Add statements to define three classes: `Northwind`, `Category`, and `Product`, as shown in the following code:

```csharp
using Microsoft.EntityFrameworkCore;
using System.Collections.Generic;

namespace Packt.Shared
{
  public class Category
  {
    public int CategoryID { get; set; }
    public string CategoryName { get; set; }
    public string Description { get; set; }

    public virtual ICollection<Product> Products { get; set; }

    public Category()
    {
      this.Products = new HashSet<Product>();
    }
  }

  public class Product
  {
    public int ProductID { get; set; }
    public string ProductName { get; set; }
    public decimal? UnitPrice { get; set; }
    public short? UnitsInStock { get; set; }
    public bool Discontinued { get; set; }
    public int CategoryID { get; set; }

    public virtual Category Category { get; set; }
  }
  public class Northwind : DbContext
  {
    public DbSet<Category> Categories { get; set; }
    public DbSet<Product> Products { get; set; }
```

```
    public Northwind(DbContextOptions options)
      : base(options) { }

    protected override void OnModelCreating(ModelBuilder modelBuilder)
    {
      modelBuilder.Entity<Category>()
        .HasMany(c => c.Products)
        .WithOne(p => p.Category);

      modelBuilder.Entity<Product>()
        .HasOne(p => p.Category)
        .WithMany(c => c.Products);
    }
  }
}
```

Creating custom page types

Now we need to define custom page types for the catalog and a product category:

1. In the Models folder, add a class named CatalogPage.cs that does not allow blocks,
    has no content regions because it will just act as an entry point and container for
    enumerated category pages, and has a custom route path /catalog, as shown in the
    following code:

    ```
    using Piranha.AttributeBuilder;
    using Piranha.Models;

    namespace NorthwindCms.Models
    {
      [PageType(Title = "Catalog page", UseBlocks = false)]
      [PageTypeRoute(Title = "Default", Route = "/catalog")]
      public class CatalogPage : Page<CatalogPage>
      {
      }
    }
    ```

2. In the Models folder, add a class named CategoryPage.cs that does not allow blocks,
    has a custom route path /catalog-category, and has a property to store details of the
    category using a region and a property to store a list of products using a region, as
    shown in the following code:

    ```
    using Piranha.AttributeBuilder;
    using Piranha.Extend;
    using Piranha.Models;
    using System.Collections.Generic;
    ```

```
namespace NorthwindCms.Models
{
  [PageType(Title = "Category Page", UseBlocks = false)]
  [PageTypeRoute(Title = "Default", Route = "/catalog-category")]
  public class CategoryPage : Page<CategoryPage>
  {
    [Region(Title = "Category detail")]
    [RegionDescription("The details for this category.")]
    public CategoryRegion CategoryDetail { get; set; }

    [Region(Title = "Category products")]
    [RegionDescription("The products for this category.")]
    public IList<ProductRegion> Products
      { get; set; } = new List<ProductRegion>();
  }
}
```

Creating custom view models

Next, we need to define some types for populating the catalog page because it will use the page hierarchy structure to determine product categories to show in the catalog page:

1. In the Models folder, add a class named CategoryItem.cs that has properties to store a summary of a category, including links to its image and the full category page, as shown in the following code:

    ```
    namespace NorthwindCms.Models
    {
      public class CategoryItem
      {
        public string Title { get; set; }
        public string Description { get; set; }
        public string PageUrl { get; set; }
        public string ImageUrl { get; set; }
      }
    }
    ```

2. In the Models folder, add a class named CatalogViewModel.cs that has a property to reference the catalog page and a property to store a list of category summary items, as shown in the following code:

    ```
    using System.Collections.Generic;

    namespace NorthwindCms.Models
    {
      public class CatalogViewModel
      {
    ```

```
    public CatalogPage CatalogPage { get; set; }
    public IEnumerable<CategoryItem> Categories { get; set; }
  }
}
```

Defining custom content templates for content types

Now we must define the controllers and views to render the content types. We will use the sitemap to fetch the children of the catalog page to find out which categories should be shown in the catalog:

1. Open `Controllers/CmsController.cs`, import the `System.Linq` namespace, and add statements to define two new action methods named `Catalog` and `Category` configured for the routes for the catalog and each catalog category, as shown highlighted in the following partial code:

```csharp
using System;
using System.Threading.Tasks;
using Microsoft.AspNetCore.Mvc;
using Piranha;
using Piranha.AspNetCore.Services;
using Piranha.Models;
using NorthwindCms.Models;
using System.Linq;

namespace NorthwindCms.Controllers
{
  [ApiExplorerSettings(IgnoreApi = true)]
  public class CmsController : Controller
  {
    ...

    [Route("catalog")]
    public async Task<IActionResult> Catalog(Guid id)
    {
      var catalog = await _api.Pages.GetByIdAsync<CatalogPage>(id);

      var model = new CatalogViewModel
      {
        CatalogPage = catalog,
        Categories = (await _api.Sites.GetSitemapAsync())
          // get the catalog page
          .Where(item => item.Id == catalog.Id)
          // get its children
          .SelectMany(item => item.Items)
```

```
            // for each child sitemap item, get the page
            // and return a simplified model for the view
            .Select(item =>
            {
                var page = _api.Pages.GetByIdAsync<CategoryPage>
                    (item.Id).Result;

                var ci = new CategoryItem
                {
                    Title = page.Title,
                    Description = page.CategoryDetail.Description,
                    PageUrl = page.Permalink,
                    ImageUrl = page.CategoryDetail.CategoryImage
                        .Resize(_api, 200)
                };
                return ci;
            })
        };
        return View(model);
    }


    [Route("catalog-category")]
    public async Task<IActionResult> Category(Guid id)
    {
        var model = await _api.Pages
            .GetByIdAsync<Models.CategoryPage>(id);
        return View(model);
    }
  }
}
```

We used catalog-category for the name of the route because there is already a route named category that is used for grouping blog posts into categories.

In Views/Cms, add a Razor file named Catalog.cshtml, as shown in the following markup:

```
@using NorthwindCms.Models
@model CatalogViewModel
@{
  ViewBag.Title = Model.CatalogPage.Title;
}
<div class="container">
  <div class="row justify-content-center">
    <div class="col-sm-10">
      <h1 class="display-3">@Model.CatalogPage.Title</h1>
    </div>
```

```
    </div>
    <div class="row">
    @foreach(CategoryItem c in Model.Categories)
    {
      <div class="col-sm-4">
        <a class="card-link" href="@c.PageUrl">
          <div class="card border-dark" style="width: 18rem;">
            <img class="card-img-top" src="@c.ImageUrl"
              alt="Image of @c.Title" asp-append-version="true" />
            <div class="card-body">
              <h5 class="card-title text-info">@c.Title</h5>
              <p class="card-text text-info">@c.Description</p>
            </div>
          </div>
        </a>
      </div>
    }
    </div>
</div>
```

2. In Views/Cms, add a Razor file named Category.cshtml, as shown in the following markup:

```
@using NorthwindCms.Models
@model CategoryPage
@{
  ViewBag.Title = Model.Title;
}
<div class="container">
  <div class="row justify-content-center">
    <div class="col-sm-10">
      <h1 class="display-4">
        @Model.CategoryDetail.CategoryName
      </h1>
      <p class="lead">@Model.CategoryDetail.Description</p>
    </div>
  </div>
  <div class="row">
  @if (Model.Products.Count == 0)
  {
    <div class="col-sm-10">
      There are no products in this category!
    </div>
  }
  else
  {
```

```
@foreach(ProductRegion p in Model.Products)
{
<div class="col-sm-4">
  <div class="card border-dark" style="width: 18rem;">
    <div class="card-header">
      In Stock: @p.UnitsInStock.Value
    </div>
    <div class="card-body">
      <h5 class="card-title text-info">
        <small class="text-muted">@p.ProductID.Value</small>
        @p.ProductName.Value
      </h5>
      <p class="card-text text-info">
        Price: @p.UnitPrice.Value
      </p>
    </div>
  </div>
</div>
}
}
</div>
</div>
```

Configuring startup and importing from a database

Finally, we must configure the content types and Northwind database connection string:

1. Open Startup.cs and import the System.IO namespace.

2. At the bottom of the ConfigureServices method, add a statement to register the Northwind database context, as shown in the following partial code:

```
public void ConfigureServices(IServiceCollection services)
{
  ...
  string databasePath = Path.Combine("..", "Northwind.db");
  services.AddDbContext<Packt.Shared.Northwind>(options =>
    options.UseSqlite($"Data Source={databasePath}"));
}
```

3. In the Controllers folder, add a new class named ImportController.cs to define a controller to import categories and products from Northwind into instances of the new custom content types, as shown in the following code:

```
using Microsoft.AspNetCore.Mvc;
using Piranha;
using Piranha.Models;
using System;
```

```csharp
using System.Linq;
using System.Threading.Tasks;
using Packt.Shared;
using NorthwindCms.Models;
using Microsoft.EntityFrameworkCore; // Include() extension method

namespace NorthwindCms.Controllers
{
  public class ImportController : Controller
  {
    private readonly IApi api;
    private readonly Northwind db;

    public ImportController(IApi api, Northwind injectedContext)
    {
      this.api = api;
      db = injectedContext;
    }

    [Route("/import")]
    public async Task<IActionResult> Import()
    {
      int importCount = 0;
      int existCount = 0;

      var site = await api.Sites.GetDefaultAsync();

      var catalog = await api.Pages
        .GetBySlugAsync<CatalogPage>("catalog");

      foreach (Category c in
        db.Categories.Include(c => c.Products))
      {
        // if the category page already exists,
        // then skip to the next iteration of the loop
        CategoryPage cp = await api.Pages.GetBySlugAsync<CategoryPage>(
          $"catalog/{c.CategoryName.ToLower().Replace(' ', '-') }");

        if (cp == null)
        {
          importCount++;

          cp = await CategoryPage.CreateAsync(api);

          cp.Id = Guid.NewGuid();
          cp.SiteId = site.Id;
```

```
    cp.ParentId = catalog.Id;
    cp.CategoryDetail.CategoryID = c.CategoryID;
    cp.CategoryDetail.CategoryName = c.CategoryName;
    cp.CategoryDetail.Description = c.Description;

    // find the media folder named Categories
    Guid categoriesFolderID =
      (await api.Media.GetAllFoldersAsync())
      .First(folder => folder.Name == "Categories").Id;

    // find image with correct filename for category id
    var image = (await api.Media
      .GetAllByFolderIdAsync(categoriesFolderID))
      .First(media => media.Type == MediaType.Image
      && media.Filename == $"category{c.CategoryID}.jpeg");

    cp.CategoryDetail.CategoryImage = image;

    if (cp.Products.Count == 0)
    {
      // convert the products for this category into
      // a list of instances of ProductRegion
      cp.Products = c.Products
        .Select(p => new ProductRegion
        {
          ProductID = p.ProductID,
          ProductName = p.ProductName,
          UnitPrice = p.UnitPrice.HasValue
            ? p.UnitPrice.Value.ToString("c") : "n/a",
          UnitsInStock = p.UnitsInStock ?? 0
        }).ToList();
    }

    cp.Title = c.CategoryName;
    cp.MetaDescription = c.Description;
    cp.NavigationTitle = c.CategoryName;
    cp.Published = DateTime.Now;

    await api.Pages.SaveAsync(cp);
  }
  else
  {
    existCount++;
  }
}
```

```
        TempData["import_message"] = $"{existCount} categories already
    existed. {importCount} new categories imported.";


        return Redirect("~/");
      }
    }
  }
```

4. In the `Views\Cms` folder, open `Page.cshtml` and add statements to the top of the `<main>` element that output an import message if it has been set, as shown highlighted in the following code:

```
<main>
  @if(TempData["import_message"] != null)
  {
  <div class="container">
    <div class="row">
      <div class="col">
        <div class="alert alert-info" role="alert">
          <h4 class="alert-heading">Import</h4>
          <p>@TempData["import_message"]</p>
        </div>
      </div>
    </div>
  </div>
  }
```

Learning how to create content using the project template

You can get more inspiration for how to programmatically work with content by reviewing the `SetupController.cs` class file that creates the initial pages in the example Piranha CMS website. For example, how to create a page like **Docs** that redirects to another page, as shown in the following clipped code:

```
// Add docs page
var docsPage = await StandardPage.CreateAsync(_api);
docsPage.Id = Guid.NewGuid();
docsPage.SiteId = site.Id;
docsPage.SortOrder = 1;
docsPage.Title = "Read The Docs";
docsPage.NavigationTitle = "Docs"; // used to generate the slug
...
docsPage.RedirectUrl = "https://piranhacms.org/docs";
docsPage.RedirectType = RedirectType.Temporary;
...
```

```
docsPage.Published = DateTime.Now;
await _api.Pages.SaveAsync(docsPage);
```

Or how to programmatically add blocks to a page like the **Home** page, as shown in the following clipped code:

```
// Add start page
var startPage = await StandardPage.CreateAsync(_api);
...


startPage.Blocks.Add(new HtmlBlock
{
  Body = "<h2>Because First Impressions Last</h2>" +
    "<p class=\"lead\">All pages and posts you create have a primary image and
excerpt available that you can use both to create nice looking headers for your
content, but also when listing or linking to it on your site. These fields are
totally optional and can be disabled for each content type.</p>"
});


startPage.Blocks.Add(new ColumnBlock
{
  Items = new List<Block>()
  {
    new ImageBlock
    {
      Aspect = new SelectField<ImageAspect>
        { Value = ImageAspect.Widescreen },
      Body = images["concentrated-little-kids-...jpg"]
    },
    new HtmlBlock
    {
      Body = "<h3>Add, Edit & Rearrange</h3>" + ...
    }
  }
});
```

Testing the Northwind CMS website

We are now ready to run the website.

Uploading images and creating the catalog root

First, we will upload some images to use for the eight categories of products and then we will create a catalog page to act as a root in the page hierarchy that we will later import content from the Northwind database into:

> **More Information**: You can download images from `https://github.com/markjprice/cs9dotnet5/tree/master/Assets/Categories`

1. In **TERMINAL**, enter the command `dotnet run` to build and start the website.

2. Start Chrome, navigate to `https://localhost:5001/manager/`, and log in as `admin` with `password`.

3. In the menu navigation bar on the left, click **Media**, and click the **+** button to add a folder named `Categories`.

4. Select the `Categories` folder and import the eight category images, as shown in the following screenshot:

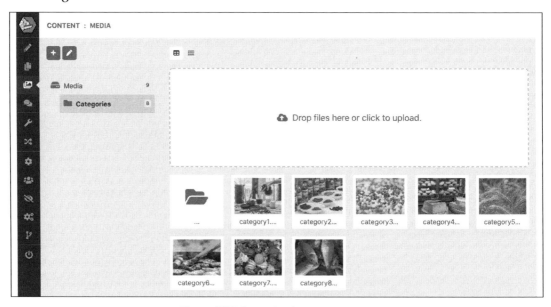

Figure 17.22: Importing images

5. In the menu navigation bar on the left, click **Pages**, add a new **Catalog page**, set its title to `Catalog`, and then click **Publish**.

Importing category and product content

In the **CONTENT : PAGES** section, a content owner could manually add a new **Category page** under the **Catalog**, but we will use the import controller to create all the categories and products automatically:

1. In the Chrome address box, change the URL to `https://localhost:5001/` and press *Enter*.

2. On the home page, in the top navigation menu, click **Catalog**, and note the new page is currently empty.

3. In the Chrome address box, change the URL to `https://localhost:5001/import/`, press *Enter*, and note that after importing the Northwind categories and products, you are redirected to the home page where you will see an import message informing you that eight categories were imported. If you were to go to the `/import` path again, it should inform you that eight categories already exist and none were imported.

4. Click **Catalog**, and note the categories have been successfully imported, as shown in the following screenshot:

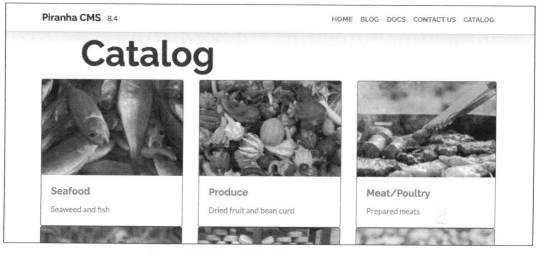

Figure 17.23: The published Catalog page

5. Click **Meat/Poultry**. Note that the URL is `https://localhost:5001/catalog/meat/poultry` and that it has some products, as shown in the following screenshot:

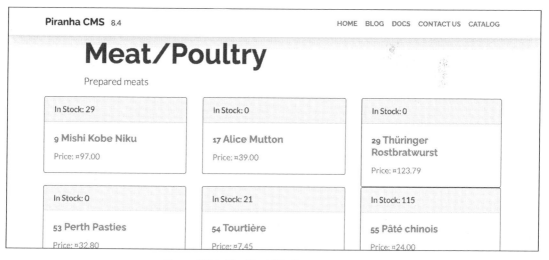

Figure 17.24: The Meat/Poultry page

Managing catalog content

Now that we have imported the catalog content, a content owner can use the Piranha manager interface to make changes instead of editing the original data in the Northwind database:

1. In the Chrome address box, change the URL to `https://localhost:5001/manager/` and, if necessary, log in as admin with password.

2. In **CONTENT : PAGES**, under the **Catalog** page, click the **Meat/Poultry** page, as shown in the following screenshot:

Figure 17.25: The Catalog structure in the Pages hierarchy

3. In **Meat/Poultry**, note the category details, including a link to the uploaded image media, and then click the **Category products** tab.

4. In **Category products**, note that although there are six rows representing the six products, the rows do not show the product details. You can write manager extensions to improve the view of a product in a row, but that is an advanced topic.

5. Click the three dots icons in any row to expand or collapse that row, and note the admin could edit the data, or click the delete icon to completely remove that product, as shown in the following screenshot:

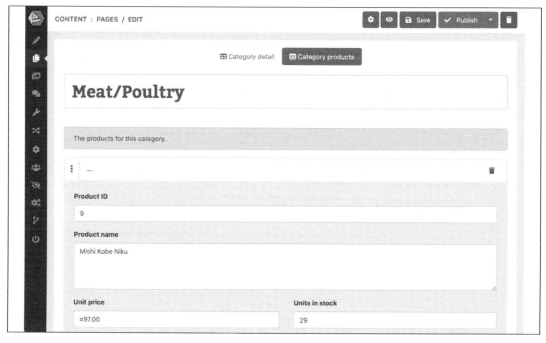

Figure 17.26: Editing the Meat/Poultry page

6. Close the browser.

Reviewing how Piranha stores content

Let's see how content is stored in the Piranha CMS database:

1. Start **SQLiteStudio**.
2. Navigate to **Database | Add a database.**
3. Click the yellow folder to browse for existing database files on the local computer.
4. Navigate to the `Code/PracticalApps/NorthwindCms` folder, select `piranha.db`, and click **Open**.
5. In the **Database** dialog box, click **OK**.
6. In the **Databases** pane, double-click the `piranha` database to connect to it.
7. Expand **Tables**, right-click the `Piranha_Pages` table, and select **Edit the table**.

8. Click the **Data** tab and note the column values stored for each page, including **LastModified**, **MetaDescription**, **NavigationTitle**, and **PageTypeId**, as shown in the following screenshot:

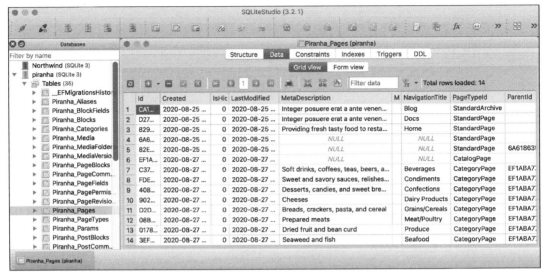

Figure 17.27: The Piranha_Pages Data tab

9. Right-click the `Piranha_PageFields` table and select **Edit the table**.

10. Click the **Data** tab, and note the column values stored for each page, including **CLRType**, **FieldId**, **RegionId**, and **Value**, as shown in the following screenshot:

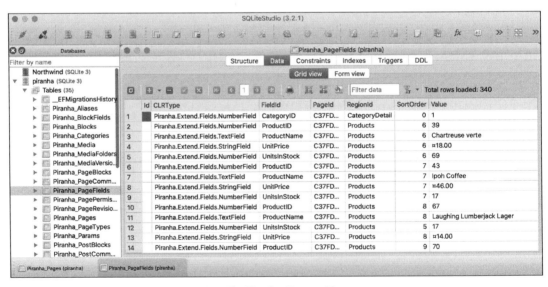

Figure 17.28: The Piranha_Pages table

11. Right-click the `piranha` database and select **Disconnect from the database**.

12. Close **SQLiteStudio**.

Practicing and exploring

Test your knowledge and understanding by answering some questions, get some hands-on practice, and explore this chapter's topics with deeper research.

Exercise 17.1 – Test your knowledge

Answer the following questions:

1. What are some of the benefits of using a CMS to build a website compared to using ASP.NET Core alone?
2. What is the special relative URL path to access the Piranha CMS management user interface and what is the username and password configured by default?
3. What is a slug?
4. What is the difference between saving content and publishing content?
5. What are the three Piranha CMS content types and what are they used for?
6. What are the three Piranha CMS component types and what are they used for?
7. List three properties that a Page type inherits from its base classes and explain what they are used for.
8. How do you define a custom region for a content type?
9. How do you define routes for Piranha CMS?
10. How do you retrieve a page from the Piranha CMS database?

Exercise 17.2 – Practice defining a block type for rendering YouTube videos

Read the following support article and then define a block type with properties to control options like auto play with a display template that uses the correct HTML markup:

https://support.google.com/youtube/answer/171780

You should also refer to the official documentation for defining custom blocks. Note that for Piranha CMS 7.0 and later, to define a manager view to enable block editing, you must use Vue.js: http://piranhacms.org/docs/extensions/blocks

Exercise 17.3 – Explore topics

Use the following links to read more details about this chapter's topics:

- **Piranha CMS**: `https://piranhacms.org/`
- **Piranha CMS repository**: `https://github.com/PiranhaCMS/piranha.core`
- **Piranha questions on Stack Overflow**: `https://stackoverflow.com/questions/tagged/piranha-cms`

Summary

In this chapter, you learned how a web CMS can enable developers to rapidly build websites that non-technical users can use to create and manage their own content.

As an example, you learned about a simple open source .NET Core-based one named Piranha CMS, you reviewed some content types provided by its blog project template, and you defined custom regions and page types for working with content imported from the `Northwind` sample database.

In the next chapter, you will learn how to build and consume web services.

18

Building and Consuming Web Services

This chapter is about learning how to build web services using the ASP.NET Core Web API, and then consuming web services using HTTP clients that could be any other type of .NET app, including a website, a Windows desktop app, or a mobile app.

This chapter assumes knowledge and skills that you learned in *Chapter 11, Working with Databases Using Entity Framework Core*, and Chapters 14 to 16, about building websites using ASP.NET Core.

In this chapter, we will cover the following topics:

- Building web services using the ASP.NET Core Web API
- Documenting and testing web services
- Consuming services using HTTP clients
- Implementing advanced features
- Understanding other communication technologies

Building web services using the ASP.NET Core Web API

Before we build a modern web service, we need to cover some background to set the context for this chapter.

Understanding web service acronyms

Although HTTP was originally designed to request and respond with HTML and other resources for humans to look at, it is also good for building services.

Roy Fielding stated in his doctoral dissertation, describing the **Representational State Transfer (REST)** architectural style, that the HTTP standard would be great for building services because it defines the following:

- URIs to uniquely identify resources, like `https://localhost:5001/api/products/23`.
- Methods to perform common tasks on those resources, like `GET`, `POST`, `PUT`, and `DELETE`.
- The ability to negotiate the media type of content exchanged in requests and responses, such as XML and JSON. Content negotiation happens when the client specifies a request header like `Accept: application/xml,*/*;q=0.8`. The default response format used by the ASP.NET Core Web API is JSON, which means one of the response headers would be `Content-Type: application/json; charset=utf-8`.

 More Information: You can read more about media types at the following link: `http://en.wikipedia.org/wiki/Media_type`

Web services are services that use the HTTP communication standard, so they are sometimes called HTTP or RESTful services. HTTP or RESTful services are what this chapter is about.

Web services can also mean **Simple Object Access Protocol (SOAP)** services that implement some of the WS-* standards.

 More Information: You can read more about WS-* standards at the following link: `https://en.wikipedia.org/wiki/List_of_web_service_specifications`

Microsoft .NET Framework 3.0 and later includes a **remote procedure call (RPC)** technology named **Windows Communication Foundation (WCF)**, which makes it easy for developers to create services including SOAP services that implement WS-* standards, but Microsoft decided it is legacy and has not ported it to modern .NET platforms.

gRPC is a modern cross-platform open source RPC framework created by Google (the "g" in gRPC).

 More Information: You can read about using gRPC as an alternative to WCF at the following link: `https://devblogs.microsoft.com/premier-developer/grpc-asp-net-core-as-a-migration-path-for-wcfs-in-net-core/`

Creating an ASP.NET Core Web API project

We will build a web service that provides a way to work with data in the Northwind database using ASP.NET Core so that the data can be used by any client application on any platform that can make HTTP requests and receive HTTP responses:

1. In the folder named PracticalApps, create a folder named NorthwindService.

2. In Visual Studio Code, open the PracticalApps workspace and add the NorthwindService folder.

3. Navigate to **Terminal | New Terminal** and select NorthwindService.

4. In **TERMINAL**, use the webapi template to create a new ASP.NET Core Web API project, as shown in the following command:

```
dotnet new webapi
```

5. Set NorthwindService as the active project and add required assets when prompted.

6. In the Controllers folder, open WeatherForecastController.cs, as shown in the following code:

```
using System;
using System.Collections.Generic;
using System.Linq;
using System.Threading.Tasks;
using Microsoft.AspNetCore.Mvc;
using Microsoft.Extensions.Logging;

namespace NorthwindService.Controllers
{
  [ApiController]
  [Route("[controller]")]
  public class WeatherForecastController : ControllerBase
  {
    private static readonly string[] Summaries = new[]
    {
      "Freezing", "Bracing", "Chilly", "Cool", "Mild",
      "Warm", "Balmy", "Hot", "Sweltering", "Scorching"
    };

    private readonly ILogger<WeatherForecastController> _logger;

    // The Web API will only accept tokens 1) for users, and
    // 2) having the access_as_user scope for this API
    static readonly string[] scopeRequiredByApi =
      new string[] { "access_as_user" };

    public WeatherForecastController(
```

```
    ILogger<WeatherForecastController> logger)
{
  _logger = logger;
}

[HttpGet]
public IEnumerable<WeatherForecast> Get()
{
  var rng = new Random();
  return Enumerable.Range(1, 5).Select(index =>
    new WeatherForecast
    {
      Date = DateTime.Now.AddDays(index),
      TemperatureC = rng.Next(-20, 55),
      Summary = Summaries[rng.Next(Summaries.Length)]
    })
    .ToArray();
}
  }
}
```

While reviewing the preceding code, note the following:

- The `Controller` class inherits from `ControllerBase`. This is simpler than the `Controller` class used in MVC because it does not have methods like `View` to generate HTML responses using a Razor file.

- The `[Route]` attribute registers the `weatherforecast` relative URL for clients to use to make HTTP requests that will be handled by this controller. For example, an HTTP request for `http://localhost:5001/weatherforecast/` would be handled by this controller. Some developers like to prefix the controller name with `api/`, which is a convention to differentiate between MVC and Web API in mixed projects. If you use `[controller]` as shown, it uses the characters before `Controller` in the class name, in this case, `WeatherForecast`, or you can simply enter a different name without the square brackets, for example, `[Route("api/forecast")]`.

- The `[ApiController]` attribute was introduced with ASP.NET Core 2.1 and it enables REST-specific behavior for controllers, like automatic HTTP 400 responses for invalid models, as you will see later in this chapter.

- The `scopeRequiredByApi` field can be used to add authorization to ensure that your web API is only called by client apps and websites on behalf of users who have the right scopes.

 More Information: You can read more about verifying that the tokens used to call your web APIs are requested with the expected claims at the following link: `https://docs.microsoft.com/en-us/azure/active-directory/develop/scenario-protected-web-api-verification-scope-app-roles`

- The [HttpGet] attribute registers the Get method in the Controller class to respond to HTTP GET requests, and its implementation uses a Random object to return an array of WeatherForecast values with random temperatures and summaries like Bracing or Balmy for the next five days of weather.

7. Add a second Get method that allows the call to specify how many days ahead the forecast should be by implementing the following:

   - Add a comment above the original method to show the GET and URL path it responds to.

   - Add a new method with an integer parameter named days.

   - Cut and paste the original Get method implementation code statements into the new Get method.

   - Modify the new method to create an IEnumerable of int values up to the number of days requested, and modify the original Get method to call the new Get method and pass the value 5.

Your methods should be as shown highlighted in the following code:

```
// GET /weatherforecast
[HttpGet]
public IEnumerable<WeatherForecast> Get() // original method
{
  return Get(5); // five day forecast
}


// GET /weatherforecast/7
[HttpGet("{days:int}")]
public IEnumerable<WeatherForecast> Get(int days) // new method
{
  var rng = new Random();

  return Enumerable.Range(1, days).Select(index =>
    new WeatherForecast
    {
      Date = DateTime.Now.AddDays(index),
      TemperatureC = rng.Next(-20, 55),
      Summary = Summaries[rng.Next(Summaries.Length)]
    })
    .ToArray();
}
```

In the [HttpGet] attribute, note the route format pattern that constrains the days parameter to int values.

> **More Information**: You can read more about route constraints at the following link: https://docs.microsoft.com/en-us/aspnet/core/fundamentals/routing#route-constraint-reference

Reviewing the web service's functionality

Now, we will test the web service's functionality:

1. In **TERMINAL**, start the website by entering dotnet run.

2. Start Chrome, navigate to https://localhost:5001/, and note you will get a 404 status code response because we have not enabled static files and there is not an index.html, nor is there an MVC controller with a route configured, either. Remember that this project is not designed for a human to view and interact with.

3. In Chrome, show the **Developer tools**, navigate to https://localhost:5001/weatherforecast, and note the Web API service should return a JSON document with five random weather forecast objects in an array, as shown in the following screenshot:

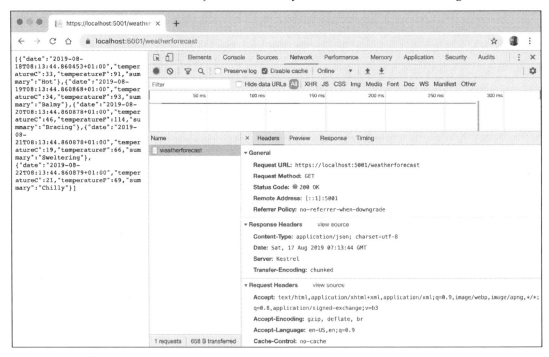

Figure 18.1: A request and response from a weather forecast web service

4. Close **Developer Tools**.

5. Navigate to `https://localhost:5001/weatherforecast/14`, and note the response when requesting a two-week weather forecast, as shown in the following screenshot:

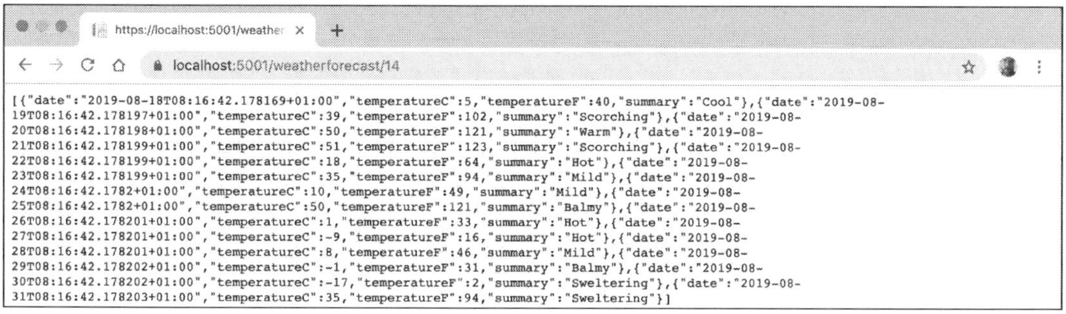

Figure 18.2: A two-week weather forecast as JSON

6. Close Chrome.

7. In **TERMINAL**, press *Ctrl + C* to stop the console application and shut down the Kestrel web server that is hosting your ASP.NET Core Web API service.

Creating a web service for the Northwind database

Unlike MVC controllers, Web API controllers do not call Razor views to return HTML responses for humans to see in browsers. Instead, they use **content negotiation** with the client application that made the HTTP request to return data in formats such as XML, JSON, or X-WWW-FORM-URLENCODED in their HTTP response.

The client application must then deserialize the data from the negotiated format. The most commonly used format for modern web services is **JavaScript Object Notation (JSON)** because it is compact and works natively with JavaScript in a browser when building **Single-Page Applications (SPAs)** with client-side technologies like Angular, React, and Vue.

We will reference the Entity Framework Core entity data model for the Northwind database that you created in *Chapter 14, Introducing Practical Applications of C# and .NET*:

1. In the `NorthwindService` project, open `NorthwindService.csproj`.

2. Add a project reference to `NorthwindContextLib`, as shown in the following markup:

```
<ItemGroup>
  <ProjectReference Include=
    "..\NorthwindContextLib\NorthwindContextLib.csproj" />
</ItemGroup>
```

3. In **TERMINAL**, enter the following command and ensure that the project builds:

```
dotnet build
```

4. Open `Startup.cs` and modify it to import the `System.IO`, `Microsoft.EntityFrameworkCore`, `Microsoft.AspNetCore.Mvc.Formatters`, and `Packt.Shared` namespaces, and statically import the `System.Console` class.

5. Add statements to the `ConfigureServices` method, before the call to `AddControllers`, to configure the Northwind data context, as shown in the following code:

```
string databasePath = Path.Combine("..", "Northwind.db");
services.AddDbContext<Northwind>(options =>
  options.UseSqlite($"Data Source={databasePath}"));
```

6. In the call to `AddControllers`, add statements to write the names and supported media types of the default output formatters to the console, and then add XML serializer formatters and set the compatibility to ASP.NET Core 3.0 after the method call to add controller support, as shown in the following code:

```
services.AddControllers(options =>
  {
    WriteLine("Default output formatters:");
    foreach(IOutputFormatter formatter in options.OutputFormatters)
    {
      var mediaFormatter = formatter as OutputFormatter;
      if (mediaFormatter == null)
      {
        WriteLine($" {formatter.GetType().Name}");
      }
      else // OutputFormatter class has SupportedMediaTypes
      {
        WriteLine(" {0}, Media types: {1}",
          arg0: mediaFormatter.GetType().Name,
          arg1: string.Join(", ",
            mediaFormatter.SupportedMediaTypes));
      }
    }
  })
  .AddXmlDataContractSerializerFormatters()
  .AddXmlSerializerFormatters()
  .SetCompatibilityVersion(CompatibilityVersion.Version_3_0);
```

> **More Information**: You can read more about the benefits of setting version compatibility at the following link: https://docs. microsoft.com/en-us/aspnet/core/mvc/compatibility-version

7. Start the web service and note that there are four default output formatters, including ones that convert `null` values into `204 No Content` and ones to support responses that are plain text and JSON, as shown in the following output:

```
Default output formatters:
  HttpNoContentOutputFormatter
  StringOutputFormatter, Media types: text/plain
  StreamOutputFormatter
```

```
    SystemTextJsonOutputFormatter, Media types: application/json, text/json,
    application/*+json
```

8. Stop the web service.

Creating data repositories for entities

Defining and implementing a data repository to provide CRUD operations is good practice. The CRUD acronym includes the following operations:

- C for Create
- R for Retrieve (or Read)
- U for Update
- D for Delete

We will create a data repository for the `Customers` table in `Northwind`. There are only 91 customers in this table, so we will store a copy of the whole table in memory to improve scalability and performance when reading customer records. In a real web service, you should use a distributed cache like **Redis**, an open source data structure store that can be used as a high-performance, high-availability database, cache, or message broker.

 More Information: You can read more about Redis at the following link: `https://redis.io`

We will follow modern good practice and make the repository API asynchronous. It will be instantiated by a `Controller` class using constructor parameter injection, so a new instance is created to handle every HTTP request:

1. In the `NorthwindService` project, create a `Repositories` folder.
2. Add two class files to the `Repositories` folder named `ICustomerRepository.cs` and `CustomerRepository.cs`.
3. The `ICustomerRepository` interface will define five methods, as shown in the following code:

```
using Packt.Shared;
using System.Collections.Generic;
using System.Threading.Tasks;

namespace NorthwindService.Repositories
{
  public interface ICustomerRepository
  {
    Task<Customer> CreateAsync(Customer c);
    Task<IEnumerable<Customer>> RetrieveAllAsync();
```

```
      Task<Customer> RetrieveAsync(string id);
      Task<Customer> UpdateAsync(string id, Customer c);
      Task<bool?> DeleteAsync(string id);
    }
  }
```

4. The `CustomerRepository` class will implement the five methods, as shown in the following code:

```
using Microsoft.EntityFrameworkCore.ChangeTracking;
using Packt.Shared;
using System.Collections.Generic;
using System.Collections.Concurrent;
using System.Linq;
using System.Threading.Tasks;

namespace NorthwindService.Repositories
{
  public class CustomerRepository : ICustomerRepository
  {
    // use a static thread-safe dictionary field to cache the customers
    private static ConcurrentDictionary
      <string, Customer> customersCache;

    // use an instance data context field because it should not be
    // cached due to their internal caching
    private Northwind db;

    public CustomerRepository(Northwind db)
    {
      this.db = db;

      // pre-load customers from database as a normal
      // Dictionary with CustomerID as the key,
      // then convert to a thread-safe ConcurrentDictionary
      if (customersCache == null)
      {
        customersCache = new ConcurrentDictionary<string, Customer>(
          db.Customers.ToDictionary(c => c.CustomerID));
      }
    }

    public async Task<Customer> CreateAsync(Customer c)
    {
      // normalize CustomerID into uppercase
      c.CustomerID = c.CustomerID.ToUpper();
```

```csharp
// add to database using EF Core
EntityEntry<Customer> added = await db.Customers.AddAsync(c);
int affected = await db.SaveChangesAsync();
if (affected == 1)
{
  // if the customer is new, add it to cache, else
  // call UpdateCache method
  return customersCache.AddOrUpdate(c.CustomerID, c, UpdateCache);
}
else
{
  return null;
}
}

public Task<IEnumerable<Customer>> RetrieveAllAsync()
{
  // for performance, get from cache
  return Task.Run<IEnumerable<Customer>>(
    () => customersCache.Values);
}

public Task<Customer> RetrieveAsync(string id)
{
  return Task.Run(() =>
  {
    // for performance, get from cache
    id = id.ToUpper();
    customersCache.TryGetValue(id, out Customer c);
    return c;
  });
}

private Customer UpdateCache(string id, Customer c)
{
  Customer old;
  if (customersCache.TryGetValue(id, out old))
  {
    if (customersCache.TryUpdate(id, c, old))
    {
      return c;
    }
  }
  return null;
}
```

```csharp
    public async Task<Customer> UpdateAsync(string id, Customer c)
    {
      // normalize customer ID
      id = id.ToUpper();
      c.CustomerID = c.CustomerID.ToUpper();

      // update in database
      db.Customers.Update(c);
      int affected = await db.SaveChangesAsync();
      if (affected == 1)
      {
        // update in cache
        return UpdateCache(id, c);
      }
      return null;
    }

    public async Task<bool?> DeleteAsync(string id)
    {
      id = id.ToUpper();

      // remove from database
      Customer c = db.Customers.Find(id);
      db.Customers.Remove(c);
      int affected = await db.SaveChangesAsync();
      if (affected == 1)
      {
        // remove from cache
        return customersCache.TryRemove(id, out c);
      }
      else
      {
        return null;
      }
    }
  }
}
```

Implementing a Web API controller

There are some useful attributes and methods for implementing a controller that returns data instead of HTML.

With MVC controllers, a route like /home/index/ tells us the Controller class name and the action method name, for example, the HomeController class and the Index action method.

With Web API controllers, a route like /weatherforecast/ only tells us the Controller class name, for example, WeatherForecastController. To determine the action method name to execute, we must map HTTP methods like GET and POST to methods in the Controller class.

You should decorate Controller methods with the following attributes to indicate the HTTP method to respond to:

- [HttpGet], [HttpHead]: These action methods respond to HTTP GET or HEAD requests to retrieve a resource and return either the resource and its response headers or just the headers.
- [HttpPost]: This action method responds to HTTP POST requests to create a new resource.
- [HttpPut], [HttpPatch]: These action methods respond to HTTP PUT or PATCH requests to update an existing resource either by replacing it or updating some of its properties.
- [HttpDelete]: This action method responds to HTTP DELETE requests to remove a resource.
- [HttpOptions]: This action method responds to HTTP OPTIONS requests.

> **More Information**: You can read more about the HTTP OPTIONS method and other HTTP methods at the following link: https://developer.mozilla.org/en-US/docs/Web/HTTP/Methods/OPTIONS

An action method can return .NET types like a single string value, complex objects defined by a class, record, or struct, or collections of complex objects, and the ASP.NET Core Web API will automatically serialize them into the requested data format set in the HTTP request Accept header, for example, JSON, if a suitable serializer has been registered.

For more control over the response, there are helper methods that return an ActionResult wrapper around the .NET type.

Declare the action method's return type to be IActionResult if it could return different return types based on inputs or other variables. Declare the action method's return type to be ActionResult<T> if it will only return a single type but with different status codes.

> **Good Practice**: Decorate action methods with the [ProducesResponseType] attribute to indicate all the known types and HTTP status codes that the client should expect in a response. This information can then be publicly exposed to document how a client should interact with your web service. Think of it as part of your formal documentation. Later in this chapter, you will learn how you can install a code analyzer to give you warnings when you do not decorate your action methods like this.

For example, an action method that gets a product based on an `id` parameter would be decorated with three attributes – one to indicate that it responds to GET requests and has an `id` parameter, and two to indicate what happens when it succeeds and when the client has supplied an invalid product ID, as shown in the following code:

```
[HttpGet("{id}")]
[ProducesResponseType(200, Type = typeof(Product))]
[ProducesResponseType(404)]
public IActionResult Get(string id)
```

The `ControllerBase` class has methods to make it easy to return different responses:

- `Ok`: Returns an HTTP 200 status code with a resource converted to the client's preferred format, like JSON or XML. Commonly used in response to an HTTP GET request.

- `CreatedAtRoute`: Returns an HTTP 201 status code with the path to the new resource. Commonly used in response to a POST request to create a resource that can be performed quickly.

- `Accepted`: Returns an HTTP 202 status code to indicate the request is being processed but has not completed. Commonly used in response to a request that triggers a background process that takes a long time to complete.

- `NoContentResult`: Returns an HTTP 204 status code. Commonly used in response to a DELETE request or a PUT request to update an existing resource when the response does not need to contain the updated resource.

- `BadRequest`: Returns an HTTP 400 status code with the optional message `string`.

- `NotFound`: Returns an HTTP 404 status code with an automatically populated `ProblemDetails` body (requires a compatibility version of 2.2 or later).

Configuring the customers repository and Web API controller

Now you will configure the repository so that it can be called from within a Web API controller.

You will register a scoped dependency service implementation for the repository when the web service starts up and then use constructor parameter injection to get it in a new Web API controller for working with customers.

 More Information: You can read more about dependency injection at the following link: https://docs.microsoft.com/en-us/aspnet/core/fundamentals/dependency-injection

To show an example of differentiating between MVC and Web API controllers using routes, we will use the common /api URL prefix convention for the customers controller:

1. Open `Startup.cs` and import the `NorthwindService.Repositories` namespace.

2. Add the following statement to the bottom of the `ConfigureServices` method, which will register the `CustomerRepository` for use at runtime, as shown in the following code:

   ```
   services.AddScoped<ICustomerRepository, CustomerRepository>();
   ```

3. In the `Controllers` folder, add a new class named `CustomersController.cs`.

4. In the `CustomersController` class file, add statements to define a Web API `Controller` class to work with customers, as shown in the following code:

   ```csharp
   using Microsoft.AspNetCore.Mvc;
   using Packt.Shared;
   using NorthwindService.Repositories;
   using System.Collections.Generic;
   using System.Linq;
   using System.Threading.Tasks;

   namespace NorthwindService.Controllers
   {
     // base address: api/customers
     [Route("api/[controller]")]
     [ApiController]
     public class CustomersController : ControllerBase
     {
       private ICustomerRepository repo;

       // constructor injects repository registered in Startup
       public CustomersController(ICustomerRepository repo)
       {
         this.repo = repo;
       }

       // GET: api/customers
       // GET: api/customers/?country=[country]
       // this will always return a list of customers even if its empty
       [HttpGet]
       [ProducesResponseType(200,
         Type = typeof(IEnumerable<Customer>))]
       public async Task<IEnumerable<Customer>> GetCustomers(
         string country)
       {
         if (string.IsNullOrWhiteSpace(country))
         {
           return await repo.RetrieveAllAsync();
   ```

```
    }
    else
    {
      return (await repo.RetrieveAllAsync())
        .Where(customer => customer.Country == country);
    }
  }

  // GET: api/customers/[id]
  [HttpGet("{id}", Name = nameof(GetCustomer))] // named route
  [ProducesResponseType(200, Type = typeof(Customer))]
  [ProducesResponseType(404)]
  public async Task<IActionResult> GetCustomer(string id)
  {
    Customer c = await repo.RetrieveAsync(id);
    if (c == null)
    {
      return NotFound(); // 404 Resource not found
    }
    return Ok(c); // 200 OK with customer in body
  }

  // POST: api/customers
  // BODY: Customer (JSON, XML)
  [HttpPost]
  [ProducesResponseType(201, Type = typeof(Customer))]
  [ProducesResponseType(400)]
  public async Task<IActionResult> Create([FromBody] Customer c)
  {
    if (c == null)
    {
      return BadRequest(); // 400 Bad request
    }
    if (!ModelState.IsValid)
    {
      return BadRequest(ModelState); // 400 Bad request
    }
    Customer added = await repo.CreateAsync(c);
    return CreatedAtRoute( // 201 Created
      routeName: nameof(GetCustomer),
      routeValues: new { id = added.CustomerID.ToLower() },
      value: added);
  }

  // PUT: api/customers/[id]
  // BODY: Customer (JSON, XML)
```

```
[HttpPut("{id}")]
[ProducesResponseType(204)]
[ProducesResponseType(400)]
[ProducesResponseType(404)]
public async Task<IActionResult> Update(
  string id, [FromBody] Customer c)
{
  id = id.ToUpper();
  c.CustomerID = c.CustomerID.ToUpper();

  if (c == null || c.CustomerID != id)
  {
    return BadRequest(); // 400 Bad request
  }
  if (!ModelState.IsValid)
  {
    return BadRequest(ModelState); // 400 Bad request
  }

  var existing = await repo.RetrieveAsync(id);
  if (existing == null)
  {
    return NotFound(); // 404 Resource not found
  }
  await repo.UpdateAsync(id, c);
  return new NoContentResult(); // 204 No content
}

// DELETE: api/customers/[id]
[HttpDelete("{id}")]
[ProducesResponseType(204)]
[ProducesResponseType(400)]
[ProducesResponseType(404)]
public async Task<IActionResult> Delete(string id)
{
  var existing = await repo.RetrieveAsync(id);
  if (existing == null)
  {
    return NotFound(); // 404 Resource not found
  }

  bool? deleted = await repo.DeleteAsync(id);
  if (deleted.HasValue && deleted.Value) // short circuit AND
  {
    return new NoContentResult(); // 204 No content
  }
```

```
        else
        {
          return BadRequest( // 400 Bad request
            $"Customer {id} was found but failed to delete.");
        }
      }
    }
  }
```

While reviewing this Web API controller class, note the following:

- The `Controller` class registers a route that starts with `api/` and includes the name of the controller, that is, `api/customers`.

- The constructor uses dependency injection to get the registered repository for working with customers.

- There are five methods to perform CRUD operations on customers — two `GET` methods (all customers or one customer), `POST` (create), `PUT` (update), and `DELETE`.

- `GetCustomers` can have a `string` parameter passed with a country name. If it is missing, all customers are returned. If it is present, it is used to filter customers by country.

- `GetCustomer` has a route explicitly named `GetCustomer` so that it can be used to generate a URL after inserting a new customer.

- `Create` decorates the `customer` parameter with `[FromBody]` to tell the model binder to populate it with values from the body of the HTTP `POST` request.

- `Create` returns a response that uses the `GetCustomer` route so that the client knows how to get the newly created resource in the future. We are matching up two methods to create and then get a customer.

- `Create` and `Update` both check the model state of the customer passed in the body of the HTTP request and return a `400 Bad Request` containing details of the model validation errors if it is not valid.

When an HTTP request is received by the service, then it will create an instance of the `Controller` class, call the appropriate action method, return the response in the format preferred by the client, and release the resources used by the controller, including the repository and its data context.

Specifying problem details

A feature added in ASP.NET Core 2.1 and later is an implementation of a web standard for specifying problem details.

 More Information: You can read more about the proposed standard for Problem Details for HTTP APIs at the following link: `https://tools.ietf.org/html/rfc7807`

In Web API controllers decorated with [ApiController] in a project with ASP.NET Core 2.2 or later compatibility enabled, action methods that return IActionResult and return a client error status code, that is, 4xx, will automatically include a serialized instance of the ProblemDetails class in the response body.

> **More Information**: You can read more about implementing problem details at the following link: https://docs.microsoft.com/en-us/dotnet/api/ microsoft.aspnetcore.mvc.problemdetails

If you want to take control, then you can create a ProblemDetails instance yourself and include additional information.

Let's simulate a bad request that needs custom data returned to the client:

1. At the top of the CustomersController class, import the Microsoft.AspNetCore.Http namespace.

2. At the top of the Delete method, add statements to check if the id matches the string value "bad", and if so, then return a custom problem details object, as shown in the following example code:

```
// take control of problem details
if (id == "bad")
{
  var problemDetails = new ProblemDetails
  {
    Status = StatusCodes.Status400BadRequest,
    Type = "https://localhost:5001/customers/failed-to-delete",
    Title = $"Customer ID {id} found but failed to delete.",
    Detail = "More details like Company Name, Country and so on.",
    Instance = HttpContext.Request.Path
  };
  return BadRequest(problemDetails); // 400 Bad request
}
```

Controlling XML serialization

In the Startup.cs file, we added the XmlSerializer so that our Web API service can return XML as well as JSON if the client requests that.

However, the XmlSerializer cannot serialize interfaces, and our entity classes use ICollection<T> to define related child entities. This causes a warning at runtime, for example, for the Customer class and its Orders property, as shown in the following output:

```
warn: Microsoft.AspNetCore.Mvc.Formatters.XmlSerializerOutputFormatter[1]
      An error occurred while trying to create an XmlSerializer for the type
'Packt.Shared.Customer'.
```

```
      System.InvalidOperationException: There was an error reflecting type
'Packt.Shared.Customer'.
      ---> System.InvalidOperationException: Cannot serialize member 'Packt.
Shared.Customer.Orders' of type 'System.Collections.Generic.ICollection`1[[Packt.
Shared.Order, NorthwindEntitiesLib, Version=1.0.0.0, Culture=neutral,
PublicKeyToken=null]]', see inner exception for more details.
```

We can prevent this warning by excluding the Orders property when serializing a Customer to XML:

1. In the NorthwindEntitiesLib project, open Customers.cs.

2. Import the System.Xml.Serialization namespace.

3. Decorate the Orders property with an attribute to ignore it when serializing, as shown highlighted in the following code:

```
[InverseProperty(nameof(Order.Customer))]
[XmlIgnore]
public virtual ICollection<Order> Orders { get; set; }
```

Documenting and testing web services

You can easily test a web service by making HTTP GET requests using a browser. To test other HTTP methods, we need a more advanced tool.

Testing GET requests using a browser

You will use Chrome to test the three implementations of a GET request – for all customers, for customers in a specified country, and for a single customer using their unique customer ID:

1. In **TERMINAL**, start the NorthwindService Web API web service by entering the command dotnet run.

2. In Chrome, navigate to https://localhost:5001/api/customers and note the JSON document returned, containing all 91 customers in the Northwind database (unsorted), as shown in the following screenshot:

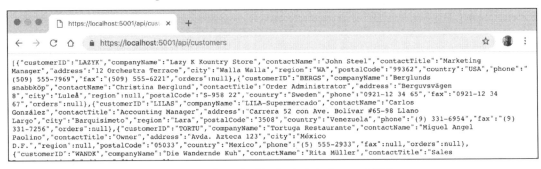

Figure 18.3: Customers from the Northwind database as JSON

3. Navigate to `https://localhost:5001/api/customers/?country=Germany` and note the JSON document returned, containing only the customers in Germany, as shown in the following screenshot:

Figure 18.4: A list of customers from Germany as JSON

If you get an empty array returned, then make sure you have entered the country name using the correct casing because the database query is case-sensitive.

4. Navigate to `https://localhost:5001/api/customers/alfki` and note the JSON document returned containing only the customer named **Alfreds Futterkiste**, as shown in the following screenshot:

Figure 18.5: Specific customer information as JSON

We do not need to worry about casing for the customer `id` value because inside the `Controller` class, we normalized the `string` value to uppercase in code.

But how can we test the other HTTP methods, such as `POST`, `PUT`, and `DELETE`? And how can we document our web service so it's easy for anyone to understand how to interact with it?

To solve the first problem, we can install a Visual Studio Code extension named **REST Client**. To solve the second, we can enable **Swagger**, the world's most popular technology for documenting and testing HTTP APIs. But first, let's see what is possible with the Visual Studio Code extension.

Testing HTTP requests with the REST Client extension

REST Client is an extension that allows you to send any type of HTTP request and view the response in Visual Studio Code:

> **More Information**: You can read more about how you can use REST Client at the following link: `https://github.com/Huachao/vscode-restclient/blob/master/README.md`

1. If you have not already installed REST Client by Huachao Mao (`humao.rest-client`), then install it now.

2. In Visual Studio Code, open the `NorthwindService` project.

3. If the web service is not already running, then start it by entering the following command in **TERMINAL**: `dotnet run`.

4. In the `NorthwindService` folder, create a `RestClientTests` folder.

5. In the `RestClientTests` folder, create a file named `get-customers.http`, and modify its contents to contain an HTTP `GET` request to retrieve all customers, as shown in the following code:

```
GET https://localhost:5001/api/customers/ HTTP/1.1
```

6. Navigate to **View | Command Palette**, enter `rest client`, select the command **Rest Client: Send Request**, and press *Enter*, as shown in the following screenshot:

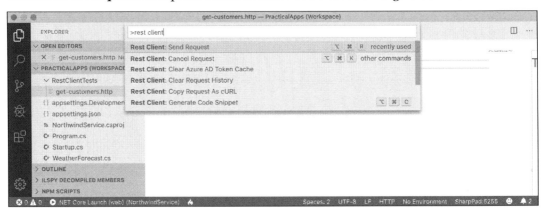

Figure 18.6: Testing HTTP requests with Rest Client

7. Note the **Response** is shown in a new tabbed window pane vertically and that you can rearrange the open tabs to a horizontal layout by dragging and dropping tabs.

8. Enter more HTTP GET requests, each separated by three hash symbols, to test getting customers in various countries and getting a single customer using their ID, as shown in the following code:

```
###
GET https://localhost:5001/api/customers/?country=Germany HTTP/1.1
###
GET https://localhost:5001/api/customers/?country=USA HTTP/1.1
Accept: application/xml
###
GET https://localhost:5001/api/customers/ALFKI HTTP/1.1
###
GET https://localhost:5001/api/customers/abcxy HTTP/1.1
```

9. Click inside each statement and press *Ctrl* or *Cmd* + *Alt* + *R* or click the **Send Request** link above each request to send it, as shown in the following screenshot:

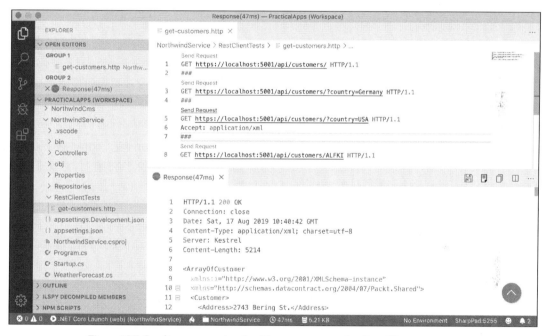

Figure 18.7: Sending a request and getting a response using Rest Client

10. In the `RestClientTests` folder, create a file named `create-customer.http` and modify its contents to define a `POST` request to create a new customer, as shown in the following code:

```
POST https://localhost:5001/api/customers/ HTTP/1.1
Content-Type: application/json
Content-Length: 287


{
    "customerID": "ABCXY",
    "companyName": "ABC Corp",
    "contactName": "John Smith",
    "contactTitle": "Sir",
    "address": "Main Street",
    "city": "New York",
    "region": "NY",
    "postalCode": "90210",
    "country": "USA",
    "phone": "(123) 555-1234",
    "fax": null,
    "orders": null
}
```

Note that REST Client will provide IntelliSense while you type common HTTP requests.

Due to different line endings in different operating systems, the value for the `Content-Length` header will be different on Windows and macOS or Linux. If the value is wrong, then the request will fail.

11. To discover the correct content length, select the body of the request and then look in the status bar for the number of characters, as shown in the following screenshot:

Figure 18.8: Checking the correct content length

12. Send the request and note the response is `201 Created`. Also note the location (that is, URL) of the newly created customer is `https://localhost:5001/api/Customers/abcxy`, and includes the newly created customer in the response body, as shown in the following screenshot:

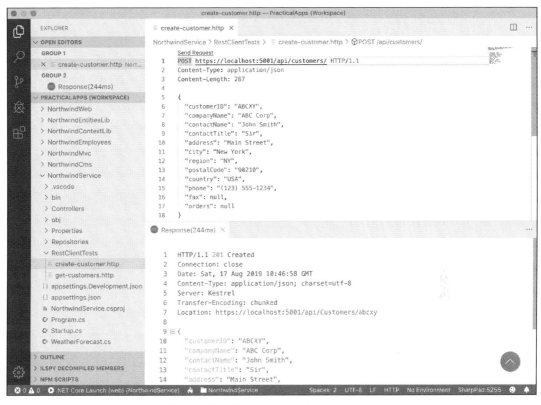

Figure 18.9: Adding a new customer

> **More Information**: Learn more details about HTTP POST requests at the following link: `https://developer.mozilla.org/en-US/docs/Web/HTTP/Methods/POST`

I will leave as an optional challenge to the reader the task of creating REST Client files to test updating a customer (using `PUT`) and deleting a customer (using `DELETE`). Test them on customers that do exist as well as customers that do not. Solutions are in the GitHub repository for this book.

Now that we've seen a quick and easy way to test our service, which also happens to be a great way to learn HTTP, what about external developers? We want it to be as easy as possible for them to learn and then call our service. For that purpose, we will use Swagger.

Understanding Swagger

The most important part of Swagger is the **OpenAPI Specification**, which defines a REST-style contract for your API, detailing all of its resources and operations in a human- and machine-readable format for easy development, discovery, and integration.

For us, another useful feature is **Swagger UI**, because it automatically generates documentation for your API with built-in visual testing capabilities.

 More Information: You can read more about Swagger at the following link: `https://swagger.io/`

Let's review how Swagger is enabled for our web service using the `Swashbuckle` package:

1. If the web service is running, stop it by pressing *Ctrl + C* in **TERMINAL**.

2. Open `NorthwindService.csproj` and note the package reference for `Swashbuckle.AspNetCore`, as shown in the following markup:

```
<ItemGroup>
    <PackageReference Include="Swashbuckle.AspNetCore" Version="5.5.1" />
</ItemGroup>
```

3. Open `Startup.cs` and note the import for Microsoft's OpenAPI models namespace, and add statements to import Swashbuckle's `Swagger` and `SwaggerUI` namespaces, as shown in the following code:

```
using Swashbuckle.AspNetCore.Swagger;
using Swashbuckle.AspNetCore.SwaggerUI;
using Microsoft.OpenApi.Models;
```

4. At the bottom of the `ConfigureServices` method, note the statement to add Swagger support including documentation for the Northwind service, indicating that this is the first version of your service, and change the title, as shown in the following code:

```
// Register the Swagger generator and define a Swagger document
// for Northwind service
services.AddSwaggerGen(options =>
  {
    options.SwaggerDoc(name: "v1", info: new OpenApiInfo
      { Title = "Northwind Service API", Version = "v1" });
  });
```

 More Information: You can read about how Swagger can support multiple versions of an API at the following link: `https://stackoverflow.com/questions/30789045/leverage-multipleapiversions-in-swagger-with-attribute-versioning/30789944`

5. In the `Configure` method, note the statements to use Swagger and Swagger UI, define an endpoint for the OpenAPI specification JSON document, and add code to list the HTTP methods supported by our web service, as shown highlighted in the following code:

```
app.UseSwagger();
app.UseSwaggerUI(c =>
{
    c.SwaggerEndpoint("/swagger/v1/swagger.json",
        "Northwind Service API Version 1");

    c.SupportedSubmitMethods(new[] {
        SubmitMethod.Get, SubmitMethod.Post,
        SubmitMethod.Put, SubmitMethod.Delete });
});
```

Testing requests with Swagger UI

You are now ready to test an HTTP request using Swagger:

1. Start the `NorthwindService` ASP.NET Web API service.

2. In Chrome, navigate to `https://localhost:5001/swagger/` and note that both the **Customers** and **WeatherForecast** Web API controllers have been discovered and documented, as well as **Schemas** used by the API.

3. Click `GET /api/Customers/{id}` to expand that endpoint and note the required parameter for the `id` of a customer, as shown in the following screenshot:

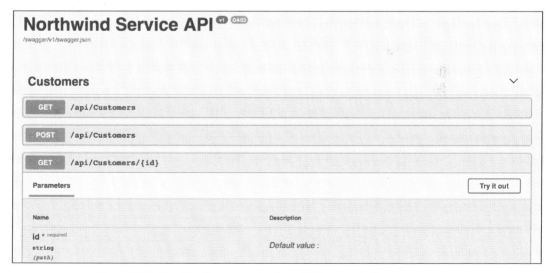

Figure 18.10: Checking the parameters for a GET request in Swagger

4. Click **Try it out**, enter an ID of ALFKI, and then click the wide blue **Execute** button, as shown in the following screenshot:

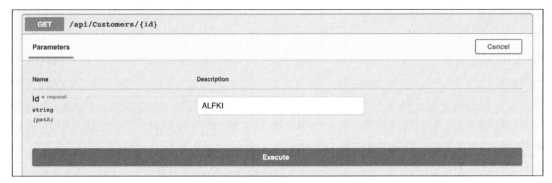

Figure 18.11: Inputting an id before execution

5. Scroll down and note the **Request URL**, **Server response** with **Code**, and **Details** including **Response body** and **Response headers**, as shown in the following screenshot:

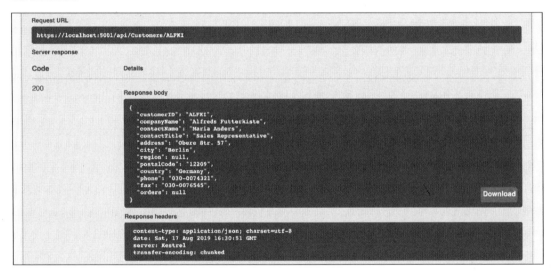

Figure 18.12: Information on ALFKI in a successful Swagger request

6. Scroll back up to the top of the page, click POST /api/Customers to expand that section, and then click **Try it out**.

7. Click inside the **Request body** box, and modify the JSON to define a new customer, as shown in the following JSON:

```
{
    "customerID": "SUPER",
    "companyName": "Super Company",
    "contactName": "Rasmus Ibensen",
    "contactTitle": "Sales Leader",
    "address": "Rotterslef 23",
    "city": "Billund",
    "region": null,
    "postalCode": "4371",
    "country": "Denmark",
    "phone": "31 21 43 21",
    "fax": "31 21 43 22",
    "orders": null
}
```

8. Click **Execute**, and note the **Request URL**, **Server response** with **Code**, and **Details** including **Response body** and **Response headers**, as shown in the following screenshot:

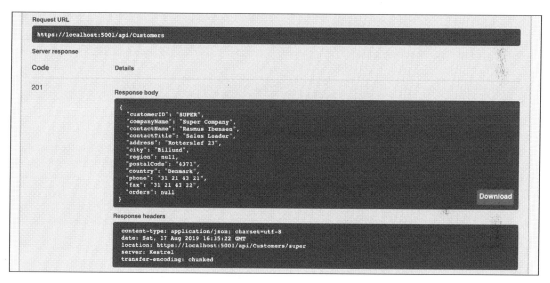

Figure 18.13: Successfully adding a new customer

A response code of 201 means the customer was successfully created.

9. Scroll back up to the top of the page, click `GET` `/api/Customers`, click **Try it out**, enter `Denmark` for the country parameter, and click **Execute**, to confirm that the new customer was added to the database, as shown in the following screenshot:

Figure 18.14: Successfully getting customers in Denmark

10. Click `DELETE` `/api/Customers/{id}`, click **Try it out**, enter super for the id, click **Execute**, and note that the **Server response Code** is 204, indicating that it was successfully deleted, as shown in the following screenshot:

Figure 18.15: Successfully deleting a customer

11. Click **Execute** again, and note that the **Server response Code** is 404, indicating that the customer does not exist anymore, and the **Response body** contains a problem details JSON document, as shown in the following screenshot:

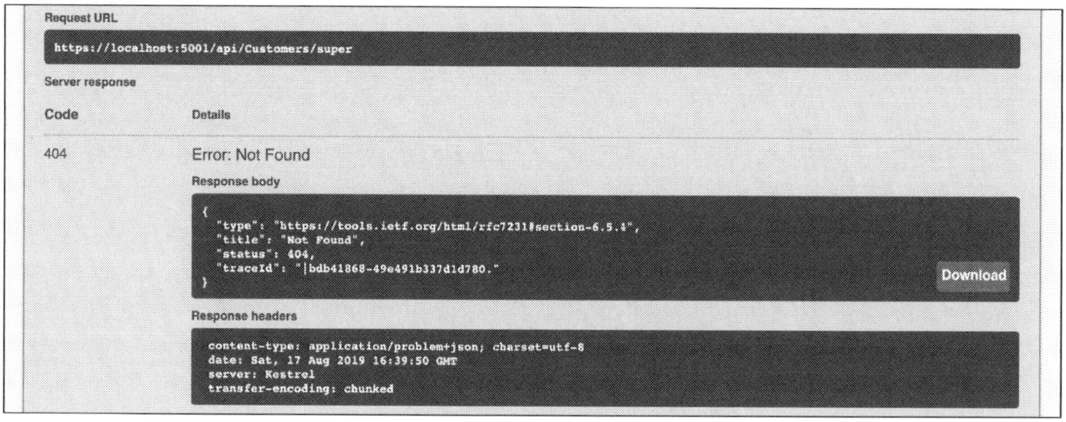

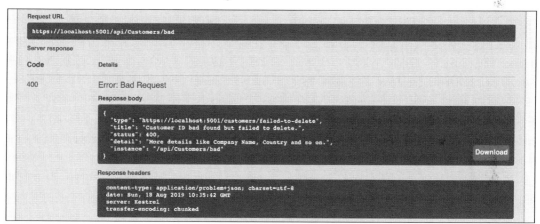

Figure 18.16: The deleted customer does not exist anymore

12. Enter bad, click **Execute** again, and note that the **Server response Code** is 400, indicating that the customer did exist but failed to delete (in this case, because the web service is simulating this error), and the **Response body** contains a custom problem details JSON document, as shown in the following screenshot:

Figure 18.17: The customer did exist but failed to delete

13. Use the GET methods to confirm that the new customer has been deleted from the database (there were originally only two customers in Denmark).

    I will leave testing updates to an existing customer by using PUT to the reader.

14. Close Chrome.

15. In **TERMINAL**, press *Ctrl* + *C* to stop the console application and shut down the Kestrel web server that is hosting your service.

> **More Information**: You can read more about the importance of documenting services at the following link: `https://idratherbewriting.com/learnapidoc/`

You are now ready to build applications that consume your web service.

Consuming services using HTTP clients

Now that we have built and tested our Northwind service, we will learn how to call it from any .NET app using the HttpClient class and its new factory.

Understanding HttpClient

The easiest way to consume a web service is to use the HttpClient class. However, many people use it wrongly because it implements IDisposable and Microsoft's own documentation shows poor usage of it.

Usually, when a type implements IDisposable, you should create it inside a using statement to ensure that it is disposed of as soon as possible. HttpClient is different because it is shared, reentrant, and partially thread-safe.

> **More Information**: It is the BaseAddress and DefaultRequestHeaders properties that you should treat with caution with multiple threads. You can read more details and recommendations at the following link: `https://medium.com/@nuno.caneco/c-httpclient-should-not-be-disposed-or-should-it-45d2a8f568bc`

The problem has to do with how the underlying network sockets have to be managed. The bottom line is that you should use a single instance of it for each HTTP endpoint that you consume during the life of your application.

This will allow each HttpClient instance to have defaults set that are appropriate for the endpoint it works with, while managing the underlying network sockets efficiently.

> **More Information**: You're using HttpClient wrong and it is destabilizing your software: `https://aspnetmonsters.com/2016/08/2016-08-27-httpclientwrong/`

Configuring HTTP clients using HttpClientFactory

Microsoft is aware of the issue, and in .NET Core 2.1 they introduced HttpClientFactory to encourage best practice; that is the technique we will use.

 More Information: You can read more about how to initiate HTTP requests at the following link: https://docs.microsoft.com/en-us/aspnet/core/fundamentals/http-requests

In the following example, we will use the Northwind MVC website as a client to the Northwind Web API service. Since both need to be hosted on a web server simultaneously, we first need to configure them to use different port numbers, as shown in the following list:

- The Northwind Web API service will continue to listen on port 5001 using HTTPS.
- Northwind MVC will listen on ports 5000 using HTTP and 5002 using HTTPS.

Let's configure those ports:

1. In the NorthwindMvc project, open Program.cs.

2. In the CreateHostBuilder method, add an extension method call to UseUrls to specify port number 5000 for HTTP and port number 5002 for HTTPS, as shown highlighted in the following code:

```
public static IHostBuilder CreateHostBuilder(string[] args) =>
  Host.CreateDefaultBuilder(args)
    .ConfigureWebHostDefaults(webBuilder =>
    {
      webBuilder.UseStartup<Startup>();
      webBuilder.UseUrls(
        "http://localhost:5000",
        "https://localhost:5002"
      );
    });
```

3. Open Startup.cs and import the System.Net.Http.Headers namespace.

4. In the ConfigureServices method, add a statement to enable HttpClientFactory with a named client to make calls to the Northwind Web API service using HTTPS on port 5001 and request JSON as the default response format, as shown in the following code:

```
services.AddHttpClient(name: "NorthwindService",
  configureClient: options =>
  {
    options.BaseAddress = new Uri("https://localhost:5001/");
```

```
    options.DefaultRequestHeaders.Accept.Add(
      new MediaTypeWithQualityHeaderValue(
      "application/json", 1.0));
});
```

Getting customers as JSON in the controller

We can now create an MVC controller action method that uses the factory to create an HTTP client, makes a GET request for customers, and deserializes the JSON response using convenience extension methods introduced with .NET 5 in the System.Net.Http.Json assembly and namespace.

> **More Information**: You can read more about the HttpClient extension methods for easily working with JSON at the following link: https:// github.com/dotnet/designs/blob/main/accepted/2020/json-http-extensions/json-http-extensions.md

1. Open Controllers/HomeController.cs and import the System.Net.Http and System. Net.Http.Json namespaces.

2. Declare a field to store the HTTP client factory, as shown in the following code:

    ```
    private readonly IHttpClientFactory clientFactory;
    ```

3. Set the field in the constructor, as shown in the following code:

    ```
    public HomeController(
      ILogger<HomeController> logger,
      Northwind injectedContext,
      IHttpClientFactory httpClientFactory)
    {
      _logger = logger;
      db = injectedContext;
      clientFactory = httpClientFactory;
    }
    ```

4. Create a new action method for calling the Northwind service, fetching all customers, and passing them to a view, as shown in the following code:

    ```
    public async Task<IActionResult> Customers(string country)
    {
      string uri;
      if (string.IsNullOrEmpty(country))
      {
        ViewData["Title"] = "All Customers Worldwide";
        uri = "api/customers/";
      }
      else
      {
    ```

```
      ViewData["Title"] = $"Customers in {country}";
      uri = $"api/customers/?country={country}";
    }

    var client = clientFactory.CreateClient(
      name: "NorthwindService");

    var request = new HttpRequestMessage(
      method: HttpMethod.Get, requestUri: uri);

    HttpResponseMessage response = await client.SendAsync(request);

    var model = await response.Content
      .ReadFromJsonAsync<IEnumerable<Customer>>();

    return View(model);
}
```

5. In the `Views/Home` folder, create a Razor file named `Customers.cshtml`.

6. Modify the Razor file to render the customers, as shown in the following markup:

```
@model IEnumerable<Packt.Shared.Customer>
<h2>@ViewData["Title"]</h2>
<table class="table">
  <thead>
    <tr>
      <th>Company Name</th>
      <th>Contact Name</th>
      <th>Address</th>
      <th>Phone</th>
    </tr>
  </thead>
  <tbody>
@foreach (var item in Model)
{
    <tr>
      <td>
        @Html.DisplayFor(modelItem => item.CompanyName)
      </td>
      <td>
        @Html.DisplayFor(modelItem => item.ContactName)
      </td>
      <td>
        @Html.DisplayFor(modelItem => item.Address)
        @Html.DisplayFor(modelItem => item.City)
        @Html.DisplayFor(modelItem => item.Region)
```

```
      @Html.DisplayFor(modelItem => item.Country)
      @Html.DisplayFor(modelItem => item.PostalCode)
    </td>
    <td>
      @Html.DisplayFor(modelItem => item.Phone)
    </td>
  </tr>
}
  </tbody>
</table>
```

7. Open `Views/Home/Index.cshtml` and add a form after rendering the visitor count to allow visitors to enter a country and see the customers, as shown in the following markup:

```
<h3>Query customers from a service</h3>
<form asp-action="Customers" method="get">
  <input name="country" placeholder="Enter a country" />
  <input type="submit" />
</form>
```

Enabling Cross-Origin Resource Sharing

It would be useful to explicitly specify the port number for the NorthwindService so that it does not conflict with the defaults of 5000 for HTTP and 5002 for HTTPS used by websites like NorthwindMvc, and to enable **Cross-Origin Resource Sharing (CORS)**:

More Information: The default browser same-origin policy prevents code downloaded from one origin from accessing resources downloaded from a different origin to improve security. CORS can be enabled to allow requests in ASP.NET Core at the following link: https://docs.microsoft.com/en-us/aspnet/core/security/cors

1. In the NorthwindService project, open Program.cs.

2. In the CreateHostBuilder method, add an extension method call to UseUrls and to specify port number 5001 for HTTPS, as shown highlighted in the following code:

```
public static IHostBuilder CreateHostBuilder(string[] args) =>
  Host.CreateDefaultBuilder(args)
    .ConfigureWebHostDefaults(webBuilder =>
    {
      webBuilder.UseStartup<Startup>();
      webBuilder.UseUrls("https://localhost:5001");
    });
```

3. Open `Startup.cs`, and add a statement to the top of the `ConfigureServices` method, to add support for CORS, as shown highlighted in the following code:

```
public void ConfigureServices(IServiceCollection services)
{
    services.AddCors();
```

4. Add a statement to the `Configure` method, before calling `UseEndpoints`, to use CORS and allow `HTTP GET`, `POST`, `PUT`, and `DELETE` requests from any website like Northwind MVC that has an origin of `https://localhost:5002`, as shown in the following code:

```
// must be after UseRouting and before UseEndpoints
app.UseCors(configurePolicy: options =>
{
    options.WithMethods("GET", "POST", "PUT", "DELETE");
    options.WithOrigins(
        "https://localhost:5002" // for MVC client
    );
});
```

5. Navigate to **Terminal | New Terminal** and select `NorthwindService`.

6. In **TERMINAL**, start the `NorthwindService` project by entering the command `dotnet run`. Confirm that the web service is listening only on port `5001`, as shown in the following output:

```
info: Microsoft.Hosting.Lifetime[0]
      Now listening on: https://localhost:5001
```

7. Navigate to **Terminal | New Terminal** and select `NorthwindMvc`.

8. In **TERMINAL**, start the `NorthwindMvc` project by entering the command `dotnet run`. Confirm that the website is listening on ports `5000` and `5002`, as shown in the following output:

```
info: Microsoft.Hosting.Lifetime[0]
      Now listening on: http://localhost:5000
info: Microsoft.Hosting.Lifetime[0]
      Now listening on: https://localhost:5002
```

9. Start Chrome, navigate to `http://localhost:5000/`, and note that it redirects to HTTPS on port `5002` and shows the home page of the Northwind MVC website.

10. In the customer form, enter a country like Germany, UK, or USA, click **Submit**, and note the list of customers, as shown in the following screenshot:

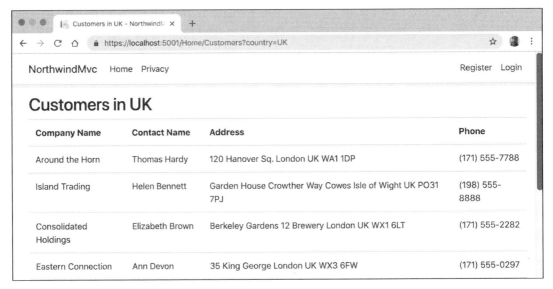

Figure 18.18: Customers in the UK

11. Click back into your browser, clear the country textbox, click **Submit**, and note the worldwide list of customers.

Implementing advanced features

Now that you have seen the fundamentals of building a web service and then calling it from a client, let us look at some more advanced features.

Implementing a Health Check API

There are many paid services that perform site availability tests that are basic pings, some with more advanced analysis of the HTTP response.

ASP.NET Core 2.2 and later makes it easy to implement more detailed website health checks. For example, your website might be live, but is it ready? Can it retrieve data from its database?

1. Open NorthwindService.csproj.

2. In the <ItemGroup> for the Swashbuckle package, add a project reference to enable Entity Framework Core database health checks, as shown in the following markup:

```
<PackageReference Include=
  "Microsoft.Extensions.Diagnostics.HealthChecks.EntityFrameworkCore"
  Version="5.0.0" />
```

3. In **TERMINAL**, restore packages and compile the website project, as shown in the following command:

```
dotnet build
```

4. Open `Startup.cs`.

5. At the bottom of the `ConfigureServices` method, add a statement to add health checks, including to the `Northwind` database context, as shown in the following code:

```
services.AddHealthChecks().AddDbContextCheck<Northwind>();
```

By default, the database context check calls EF Core's `CanConnectAsync` method. You can customize what operation is run using the `AddDbContextCheck` method.

6. In the `Configure` method, before the call to `UseEndpoints`, add a statement to use basic health checks, as shown in the following code:

```
app.UseHealthChecks(path: "/howdoyoufeel");
```

7. Start the web service and navigate to `https://localhost:5001/howdoyoufeel`.

8. Note the website responds with plain text: `Healthy`.

 More Information: You can extend the health check response as much as you want. Read more at the following link: `https://blogs.msdn.microsoft.com/webdev/2018/08/22/asp-net-core-2-2-0-preview1-healthcheck/`

Implementing Open API analyzers and conventions

In this chapter, you learned how to enable Swagger to document a web service by manually decorating a `Controller` class with attributes.

In ASP.NET Core 2.2 or later, there are API analyzers that reflect over `Controller` classes that have been annotated with the `[ApiController]` attribute to document it automatically. The analyzer assumes some API conventions.

To use it, your project must reference the NuGet package, as shown in the following markup:

```
<PackageReference Include="Microsoft.AspNetCore.Mvc.Api.Analyzers"
  Version="3.0.0" PrivateAssets="All" />
```

 More Information: At the time of writing, the preceding package was version 3.0.0-preview3-19153-02, but after publishing, it should be a full version 3.0.0 release. You can check the latest version to use at the following link: `http://www.nuget.org/packages/Microsoft.AspNetCore.Mvc.Api.Analyzers/`

After installing, controllers that have not been properly decorated should have warnings (green squiggles) and warnings when you compile the source code using the `dotnet build` command. For example, the `WeatherForecastController` class.

Automatic code fixes can then add the appropriate [Produces] and [ProducesResponseType] attributes, although this only currently works in Visual Studio 2019. In Visual Studio Code, you will see warnings about where the analyzer thinks you should add attributes, but you must add them yourself.

Implementing transient fault handling

When a client app or website calls a web service, it could be from across the other side of the world. Network problems between the client and the server could cause issues that are nothing to do with your implementation code. If a client makes a call and it fails, the app should not just give up. If it tries again, the issue may now have resolved. We need a way to handle these temporary faults.

To handle these transient faults, Microsoft recommends that you use the third-party library Polly to implement automatic retries with exponential backoff. You define a policy and the library handles everything else.

More Information: You can read more about how Polly can make your web services more reliable at the following link: https://docs.microsoft.com/en-us/dotnet/architecture/microservices/implement-resilient-applications/implement-http-call-retries-exponential-backoff-polly

Understanding endpoint routing

In earlier versions of ASP.NET Core, the routing system and the extendable middleware system did not always work easily together, for example, if you wanted to implement a policy like CORS in both middleware and MVC, so Microsoft has invested in improving routing with a system named **Endpoint Routing** introduced with ASP.NET Core 2.2.

Good Practice: Microsoft recommends every older ASP.NET Core project migrates to endpoint routing if possible.

Endpoint routing is designed to enable better interoperability between frameworks that need routing, like Razor Pages, MVC, or Web APIs, and middleware that need to understand how routing affects them, like localization, authorization, CORS, and so on.

More Information: You can read more about the design decisions around endpoint routing at the following link: https://devblogs.microsoft.com/aspnet/asp-net-core-2-2-0-preview1-endpoint-routing/

It gets its name because it represents the route table as a compiled tree of endpoints that can be walked efficiently by the routing system. One of the biggest improvements is the performance of routing and action method selection.

It is on by default with ASP.NET Core 2.2 or later if compatibility is set to 2.2 or later. Traditional routes registered using the MapRoute method or with attributes are mapped to the new system.

The new routing system includes a link generation service registered as a dependency service that does not need an HttpContext.

Configuring endpoint routing

Endpoint routing requires a pair of calls to app.UseRouting() and app.UseEndpoints().

- app.UseRouting() marks the pipeline position where a routing decision is made.
- app.UseEndpoints() marks the pipeline position where the selected endpoint is executed.

Middleware like localization that runs in between these can see the selected endpoint and can switch to a different endpoint if necessary.

Endpoint routing uses the same route template syntax that has been used in ASP.NET MVC since 2010 and the [Route] attribute introduced with ASP.NET MVC 5 in 2013. Migration often only requires changes to the Startup configuration.

MVC controllers, Razor Pages, and frameworks like SignalR used to be enabled by a call to UseMvc() or similar methods, but they are now added inside UseEndpoints() because they are all integrated into the same routing system along with middleware.

Let's define some middleware that can output information about endpoints:

1. Open Startup.cs and import namespaces for working with endpoint routing, as shown in the following code:

```
using Microsoft.AspNetCore.Http;    // GetEndpoint() extension method
using Microsoft.AspNetCore.Routing; // RouteEndpoint
```

2. In the Configure method, add a statement before UseEndpoints to define a lambda statement to output information about the selected endpoint during every request, as shown in the following code:

```
app.Use(next => (context) =>
{
  var endpoint = context.GetEndpoint();
  if (endpoint != null)
  {
    WriteLine("*** Name: {0}; Route: {1}; Metadata: {2}",
      arg0: endpoint.DisplayName,
      arg1: (endpoint as RouteEndpoint)?.RoutePattern,
```

```
        arg2: string.Join(", ", endpoint.Metadata));
    }

    // pass context to next middleware in pipeline
    return next(context);
});
```

While reviewing the preceding code, note the following:

- The `Use` method requires an instance of `RequestDelegate` or a lambda statement equivalent.

- `RequestDelegate` has a single `HttpContext` parameter that wraps all information about the current HTTP request (and its matching response).

- Importing the `Microsoft.AspNetCore.Http` namespace adds the `GetEndpoint` extension method to the `HttpContext` instance.

3. Start the web service.

4. In Chrome, navigate to `https://localhost:5001/weatherforecast`.

5. In **TERMINAL**, note the result, as shown in the following output:

```
Request starting HTTP/1.1 GET https://localhost:5001/weatherforecast
*** Name: NorthwindService.Controllers.WeatherForecastController.
Get (NorthwindService); Route: Microsoft.AspNetCore.Routing.Patterns.
RoutePattern; Metadata: Microsoft.AspNetCore.Mvc.ApiControllerAttribute,
Microsoft.AspNetCore.Mvc.ControllerAttribute, Microsoft.AspNetCore.
Mvc.RouteAttribute, Microsoft.AspNetCore.Mvc.HttpGetAttribute,
Microsoft.AspNetCore.Routing.HttpMethodMetadata, Microsoft.
AspNetCore.Mvc.Controllers.ControllerActionDescriptor, Microsoft.
AspNetCore.Routing.RouteNameMetadata, Microsoft.AspNetCore.Mvc.
ModelBinding.UnsupportedContentTypeFilter, Microsoft.AspNetCore.Mvc.
Infrastructure.ClientErrorResultFilterFactory, Microsoft.AspNetCore.Mvc.
Infrastructure.ModelStateInvalidFilterFactory, Microsoft.AspNetCore.
Mvc.ApiControllerAttribute, Microsoft.AspNetCore.Mvc.ActionConstraints.
HttpMethodActionConstraint
```

6. Close Chrome and stop the web service.

More Information: You can read more about endpoint routing at the following link: `https://docs.microsoft.com/en-us/aspnet/core/fundamentals/routing`

Endpoint routing replaces the `IRouter`-based routing used in ASP.NET Core 2.1 and earlier.

More Information: If you need to work with ASP.NET Core 2.1 or earlier, then you can read about the old routing system at the following link: `https://docs.microsoft.com/en-us/aspnet/core/fundamentals/routing?view=aspnetcore-2.1`

Adding security HTTP headers

ASP.NET Core has built-in support for common security HTTP headers like HSTS. But there are many more HTTP headers that you should consider implementing.

The easiest way to add these headers is using a middleware class:

1. In the `NorthwindService` folder, create a file named `SecurityHeadersMiddleware.cs` and modify its statements, as shown in the following code:

```
using System.Threading.Tasks;
using Microsoft.AspNetCore.Http;
using Microsoft.Extensions.Primitives;

namespace Packt.Shared
{
  public class SecurityHeaders
  {
    private readonly RequestDelegate next;

    public SecurityHeaders(RequestDelegate next)
    {
      this.next = next;
    }

    public Task Invoke(HttpContext context)
    {
      // add any HTTP response headers you want here
      context.Response.Headers.Add(
        "super-secure", new StringValues("enable"));

      return next(context);
    }
  }
}
```

2. Open the `Startup.cs` file and add a statement to register the middleware before the call to `UseEndpoints`, as shown in the following code:

```
app.UseMiddleware<SecurityHeaders>();
```

3. Start the web service.

4. Start Chrome and show **Developer Tools** and its **Network** tab to record requests and responses.

5. Navigate to `https://localhost:5001/weatherforecast`.

6. Note the custom HTTP response header that we added named super-secure, as shown in the following screenshot:

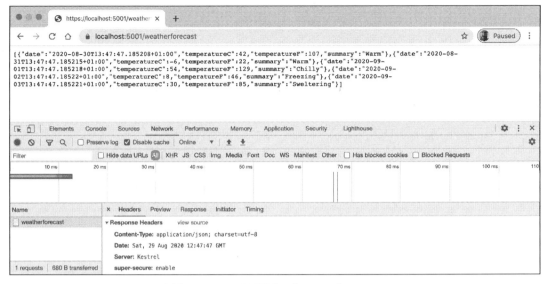

Figure 18.19: Adding a custom HTTP header named super-secure

More Information: You can read more about common HTTP security headers that you might want to add at the following link: `https://www.meziantou.net/security-headers-in-asp-net-core.htm`

Securing web services

An improvement for web services in .NET 5 includes a simple extension method for enabling anonymous HTTP calls when using endpoint routing, as shown highlighted in the following code:

```
app.UseEndpoints(endpoints =>
{
  endpoints.MapControllers()
  .AllowAnonymous();
});
```

Understanding other communication technologies

The ASP.NET Core Web API is not the only Microsoft technology for implementing services or communicating between components of a distributed application. Although we will not cover these technologies in detail, you should be aware of what they can do and when they should be used.

Understanding Windows Communication Foundation (WCF)

In 2006, Microsoft released .NET Framework 3.0 with some major frameworks, one of which was **Windows Communication Foundation (WCF)**. It abstracted the business logic implementation of a service from the technology used to communicate with it. It heavily used XML configuration to declaratively define endpoints, including their address, binding, and contract (known as the ABCs of endpoints). Once you have understood how to do this, it is a powerful yet flexible technology.

Microsoft has decided not to officially port WCF to .NET Core, but there is a community-owned OSS project named **Core WCF** managed by the .NET Foundation. If you need to migrate an existing service from .NET Framework to .NET Core, or build a client to a WCF service, then you could use Core WCF. Be aware that it can never be a full port since parts of WCF are Windows-specific.

 More Information: You can read more and download the Core WCF repository from the following link: https://github.com/CoreWCF/CoreWCF

Technologies like WCF allow for the building of distributed applications. A client application can make **remote procedure calls (RPC)** to a server application. Instead of using a port of WCF to do this, we could use an alternative RPC technology.

Understanding gRPC

gRPC is a modern open source high-performance RPC framework that can run in any environment.

 More Information: You can read about gRPC at the following link: https://grpc.io

Like WCF, gRPC uses contract-first API development that supports language-agnostic implementations. You write the contracts using .proto files with their own language syntax and tools to convert them into various languages like C#. It minimizes network usage by using Protobuf binary serialization.

 More Information: Microsoft officially supports gRPC with ASP.NET Core. You can learn how to use gRPC with ASP.NET Core at the following link: https://docs.microsoft.com/en-us/aspnet/core/grpc/aspnetcore

Practicing and exploring

Test your knowledge and understanding by answering some questions, get some hands-on practice, and explore this chapter's topics with deeper research.

Exercise 18.1 – Test your knowledge

Answer the following questions:

1. Which base class should you inherit from to create a controller class for an ASP.NET Core Web API service?

2. If you decorate your Controller class with the [ApiController] attribute to get default behavior like automatic 400 responses for invalid models, what else must you do?

3. What must you do to specify which controller action method will be executed in response to an HTTP request?

4. What must you do to specify what responses should be expected when calling an action method?

5. List three methods that can be called to return responses with different status codes.

6. List four ways that you can test a web service.

7. Why should you not wrap your use of HttpClient in a using statement to dispose of it when you are finished even though it implements the IDisposable interface, and what should you use instead?

8. What does the acronym CORS stand for and why is it important to enable it in a web service?

9. How can you enable clients to detect if your web service is healthy with ASP.NET Core 2.2 and later?

10. What benefits does endpoint routing provide?

Exercise 18.2 – Practice creating and deleting customers with HttpClient

Extend the NorthwindMvc website project to have pages where a visitor can fill in a form to create a new customer, or search for a customer and then delete them. The MVC controller should make calls to the Northwind service to create and delete customers.

Exercise 18.3 – Explore topics

Use the following links to read more about this chapter's topics:

- **Create web APIs with ASP.NET Core**: `https://docs.microsoft.com/en-us/aspnet/core/web-api/`

- **Swagger Tools**: `https://swagger.io/tools/`

- **Swashbuckle for ASP.NET Core**: `https://github.com/domaindrivendev/Swashbuckle.AspNetCore`

- **Health checks in ASP.NET Core**: `https://docs.microsoft.com/en-us/aspnet/core/host-and-deploy/health-checks`

- **Use HttpClientFactory to implement resilient HTTP requests**: `https://docs.microsoft.com/en-us/dotnet/architecture/microservices/implement-resilient-applications/use-httpclientfactory-to-implement-resilient-http-requests`

Summary

In this chapter, you learned how to build an ASP.NET Core Web API service that can be called by any app on any platform that can make an HTTP request and process an HTTP response. You also learned how to test and document web service APIs with Swagger, as well as how to consume services efficiently.

In the next chapter, you will learn how to add intelligence to any type of application using machine learning.

19
Building Intelligent Apps Using Machine Learning

This chapter is about embedding intelligence into your apps using machine learning algorithms. Microsoft has created a cross-platform machine learning library named ML.NET designed specifically for C# and .NET developers.

This chapter will cover the following topics:

- Understanding machine learning
- Understanding ML.NET
- Making product recommendations

Understanding machine learning

Marketing folk love to use terms like **artificial intelligence** or **data science** in their promotional materials. **Machine learning** is a subset of data science. It is one practical way to add intelligence to software.

 More Information: You can learn the science behind one of the most popular and successful data science techniques by enrolling in Harvard University's free *Data Science: Machine Learning* 8-week course at the following link: https://www.edx.org/course/data-science-machine-learning-2

This book cannot teach machine learning in one chapter. If you want to know how machine learning algorithms work internally, then you would need to understand data science topics including calculus, statistics, probability theory, and linear algebra. Then you would need to learn about machine learning in depth.

More Information: To learn about machine learning in depth, read *Python Machine Learning, Third Edition* by Sebastian Raschka and Vahid Mirjalili: https://www.packtpub.com/product/python-machine-learning-third-edition/9781789955750

My goal with this chapter is to give you the minimum conceptual knowledge needed to implement a valuable and practical application of machine learning: making product recommendations in an e-commerce website to increase the value of each order. By seeing all the tasks required, you can then decide for yourself if the effort required to properly learn it all is worth it for you, or if you'd rather put your efforts into other topics like building websites or mobile apps.

Understanding the machine learning lifecycle

The machine learning lifecycle has four steps:

- **Problem analysis**: What is the problem you are trying to solve?
- **Data gathering and processing**: The raw data needed to solve the problem often needs transforming into formats suitable for a machine learning algorithm to process.
- **Modeling** is divided into three sub-steps:
    - **Identifying features**: Features are the values that influence predictions, for example, the distance traveled and time of day, which influence the cost of a taxi journey.
    - **Training the model**: Select and apply algorithms and set hyperparameters to generate one or more models. Hyperparameters are parameters that are set before the learning process begins in contrast to other parameters derived during training.
    - **Evaluating the model**: Choose which model best solves the original problem. Evaluating models is a manual task that can take months.
- **Deploying the model**: Embed the model in an app where it is used to make predictions on real data inputs.

But even then, your work is not done!

After deploying the model, you should regularly reassess the model to maintain its efficiency. Over time, the predictions it makes could drift and become poorer because data can change over time.

You should not assume a static relationship between inputs and outputs, especially when predicting human behavior, since fashions change. Just because superhero movies are currently popular does not mean they always will be. This problem is named **concept drift** or model decay. If you suspect this problem, then you should retrain the model, or even switch to a better algorithm or hyperparameter values.

Deciding which algorithm to use and the values for its hyperparameters is tricky because the combination of potential algorithms and hyperparameter values is infinite. This is why machine learning and its wider data science field is a full-time specialized career.

 More Information: You can read more about roles like the types of data scientist who are involved with machine learning at the following link: https://www.datasciencecentral.com/profiles/blogs/difference-between-machine-learning-data-science-ai-deep-learning

Understanding datasets for training and testing

You must not use your entire dataset to train your model. You need to split your dataset into a **training dataset** and a **testing dataset**. The training dataset is used to train the model, unsurprisingly. Then, the testing dataset is used to evaluate that the model makes good enough predictions before it is deployed. If you were to use the whole dataset for training, then you would have no data left over to test your model.

The splitting between training and testing can be random for some scenarios, but be careful! You must consider if the dataset could have regular variations. For example, taxi usage varies based on time of day, and even varies based on season and city. For example, New York City will typically be busy for taxis all year, at all hours, but Munich might get extra busy for taxis during Oktoberfest.

When your dataset is affected by seasonality and other factors, you must split the dataset strategically. You also need to ensure that the model is not **overfitted** with the training data. Let's talk about an example of overfitting.

When I was studying Computer Science at the University of Bristol between 1990 and 1993, we were told a story during our neural networks class (possibly apocryphal, but it illustrates an important point). The British Army employed data scientists to build a machine learning model to detect Russian tanks camouflaged in the woods of Eastern Europe. The model was fed with thousands of images, yet when it came time to show off its abilities in the real world, it failed dismally.

During the project autopsy, the scientists realized that all the images they used to train the model were from spring when the foliage was lively shades of green, but the live test happened in autumn when the foliage was reds, yellows, and browns.

The model was *overfitted* to the spring foliage. If the model was more generalized, then it might have performed better in other seasons. Underfitting is the opposite; it describes a model that is too generalized and doesn't provide satisfactory outputs when applied to specific contexts.

 More Information: You can read more about overfitting and underfitting and how to compensate for it at the following link: https://elitedatascience.com/overfitting-in-machine-learning

Understanding machine learning tasks

There are many tasks or scenarios that machine learning can help developers with:

- **Binary classification** is classifying the items in an input dataset between two groups, predicting which group each item belongs to. For example, deciding if an Amazon book review is *positive* or *negative*, also known as sentiment analysis. Other examples include spam email message and credit card purchase fraud detection.

- **Multi-class classification** is classifying instances into one of three or more classes, predicting which group each one belongs to. For example, deciding if a news article should be categorized as *celebrity gossip, sports, politics,* or *science and technology*. Binary and multi-class are examples of **supervised** classification because the labels must be predefined.

- **Clustering** is for grouping input data items so that items in the same cluster are more similar to each other than to those in other clusters. It is not the same as classification because it does not give each cluster a label and therefore the labels do not have to be predefined as with classification. Clustering is therefore an example of **unsupervised** classification. After clustering, a group can be processed to spot patterns and then assign a label.

- **Ranking** is for ordering input data items based on properties like star reviews, context, likes, and so on.

- **Recommendations** are for suggesting other items like products or content that a user might like based on their past behavior compared to other users.

- **Regression** is for predicting a numeric value from input data. It can be used for forecasting and suggesting how much a product should sell for or how much it will cost to get a taxi from Heathrow Airport to a central London hotel, or how many bikes will be needed in a particular area of Amsterdam for a bike sharing scheme.

- **Anomaly detection** is for identifying "black swans," or unusual data that could indicate a problem that needs to be fixed, in fields like medical, financial, and mechanical maintenance.

- **Deep learning** is for handling large and complex binary input data instead of input data in a more structured format, for example, computer vision tasks like detecting objects and classifying images, or audio tasks like speech recognition and **natural language processing (NLP)**.

Understanding Microsoft Azure Machine Learning

The rest of this chapter will cover using an open source .NET package to implement machine learning, but before we dive into that, let's take a quick diversion to understand an important alternative.

Implementing machine learning well requires people with strong skills in mathematics or related areas. Data scientists are in high demand and the difficulty and cost of hiring them prevents some organizations from adopting machine learning in their own apps.

An organization might have access to warehouses of data accumulated over many years, but they might struggle to use machine learning to improve the decisions they make.

Microsoft Azure Machine Learning overcomes these obstacles by providing pre-built machine learning models for common tasks like face recognition and language processing. This enables organizations without their own data scientists to get some benefit from their data. As an organization hires their own data scientists, or their developers gain data science skills, they can then develop their own models to work within Azure ML.

But as organizations become more sophisticated and recognize the value of owning their machine learning models and being able to run them anywhere, more and more will need a platform that their existing developers can get started on that has as shallow a learning curve as possible.

Understanding ML.NET

ML.NET is Microsoft's open source and cross-platform machine learning framework for .NET. C# developers can use their existing skills and familiarity with .NET Standard APIs to integrate custom machine learning inside their apps without knowing details about how to build and maintain machine learning models.

More Information: You can read the official announcement for ML.NET at the following link: `https://devblogs.microsoft.com/dotnet/introducing-ml-net-cross-platform-proven-and-open-source-machine-learning-framework/`

Today, ML.NET contains machine learning libraries created by Microsoft Research and used by Microsoft products like PowerPoint for intelligently recommending style templates based on the content of a presentation. Soon, ML.NET will also support other popular libraries like Accord.NET, CNTK, Light GBM, and TensorFlow, but we will not cover those in this book.

More Information: The Accord.NET Framework is a .NET machine learning framework combined with audio and image processing libraries completely written in C#. You can read more at the following link: `http://accord-framework.net`

Understanding Infer.NET

Infer.NET was created by Microsoft Research in Cambridge in 2004. It was made available to academics in 2008. Since then, hundreds of academic papers have been written about Infer.NET.

More Information: You can read more about Microsoft Infer.NET at the following link: https://www.microsoft.com/en-us/research/blog/the-microsoft-infer-net-machine-learning-framework-goes-open-source/

Developers can incorporate domain knowledge into a model to create custom algorithms instead of mapping your problem to existing algorithms as you would do with ML.NET.

Infer.NET is used by Microsoft for products including Microsoft Azure, Xbox, and Bing search and translator.

Infer.NET can be used for classification, recommendations, and clustering.

We will not be looking at Infer.NET in this book.

More Information: You can read how to create a game match up list app with Infer.NET and probabilistic programming at the following link: https://docs.microsoft.com/en-us/dotnet/machine-learning/how-to-guides/matchup-app-infer-net

Understanding ML.NET learning pipelines

A typical learning pipeline comprises six steps:

- **Data loading** – ML.NET supports loading data from the following formats: text (CSV, TSV), Parquet, binary, `IEnumerable<T>`, and file sets.

- **Transformations** – ML.NET supports the following transformations: text manipulation, schema (that is, structure) modification, handling missing values, categorical value encoding, normalization, and feature selection.

- **Algorithms** – ML.NET supports the following algorithms: linear, boosted trees, k-means, **Support Vector Machine (SVM)**, and averaged perceptron.

- **Model training** – Call the ML.NET `Train` method to create a `PredictionModel` that you can use to make predictions.

- **Model evaluation** – ML.NET supports multiple evaluators to assess the accuracy of your model against various metrics.

- **Model deployment** – ML.NET allows you to export your model as a binary file for deployment with any type of .NET app.

More Information: The traditional "Hello World" app for machine learning is one that can predict the type of iris flower based on four features: petal length, petal width, sepal length, and sepal width. You can follow a 10-minute tutorial for it at the following link: `https://dotnet.microsoft.com/learn/machinelearning-ai/ml-dotnet-get-started-tutorial/intro`

Understanding model training concepts

The .NET type system was not designed for machine learning and data analysis, so it needs some specialized types to make it better suited for these tasks.

ML.NET uses the following .NET types when working with models:

- The `IDataView` interface represents a dataset that is:
  - **Immutable**, meaning it cannot change.
  - **Cursorable**, meaning cursors can iterate over the data.
  - **Lazily evaluated**, meaning that work like transformations is only done when a cursor iterates over the data.
  - **Heterogenous**, meaning data can have mixed types.
  - **Schematized**, meaning it has a strongly defined structure.

More Information: You can read more about the design of the `IDataView` interface at the following link: `https://github.com/dotnet/machinelearning/blob/master/docs/code/IDataViewDesignPrinciples.md`

- `DataViewType`: All `IDataView` column types derive from the abstract class `DataViewType`. Vector types require dimensionality information to indicate the length of the vector type.

- The `ITransformer` interface represents a component that accepts input data, changes it in some way, and returns output data. For example, a tokenizer transformer takes a text column containing phrases as input and outputs a vector column with individual words extracted out of the phrases and arranged vertically in a column. Most transformers work on one column at a time. New transformers can be constructed by combining other transformers in a chain.

- The `IDataReader<T>` interface represents a component to create data. It takes an instance of `T` and returns data out of it.

- The `IEstimator<T>` interface represents an object that learns from data. The result of the learning is a transformer. Estimators are eager, meaning every call to their `Fit` method causes learning to occur, which can take a lot of time!

- The `PredictionEngine<TSrc, TDst>` class represents a function that can be seen as a machine that applies a transformer to one row at prediction time. If you have a lot of input data that you want to make predictions for, you would create a data view, call `Transform` on the model to generate prediction rows, and then use a cursor to read the results. In the real world, a common scenario is to have one data row as input that you want to make a prediction for, so to simplify the process you can use a prediction engine.

Understanding missing values and key types

The R language is popular for machine learning and it uses the special value NA to indicate a missing value. ML.NET follows that convention.

Key types are used for data that is represented as number values within a cardinality set, as shown in the following code:

```
[KeyType(10)]
public uint NumberInRange1To10 { get; set; }
```

The representational, also known as underlying, type must be one of the four .NET unsigned integer types: byte, ushort, uint, and ulong. The value 0 always means NA, indicating its value is missing. The representational value 1 is always the first valid value of the key type.

The count should be set to one more than the maximum value to account for counting starting at 1, because 0 is reserved for missing values. For example, the cardinality of the 0-9 range should be 10. Any values outside of the specified cardinality will be mapped to the missing value representation: 0.

Understanding features and labels

The inputs of a machine learning model are called **features**. For example, if there was a linear regression model where one continuous quantity, like the price of a bottle of wine, is proportional to another, like the rating given by vintners, then price is the only feature.

The values used to train a machine learning model are called **labels**. In the wine example, the rating values in the training dataset are the labels.

In some models, the label value is not important since the existence of a row represents a match. This is especially common in recommendations.

Making product recommendations

The practical application of machine learning we will implement is making product recommendations on an e-commerce website, with the goal being to increase the value of a customer order.

The problem is how to decide what products to recommend to the visitor.

Problem analysis

On October 2, 2006, Netflix started an open prize challenge for the best algorithm for predicting customer ratings for films based only on previous ratings. The dataset that Netflix provided had 17,000 movies, 500,000 users, and 100 million ratings. For example, user 437822 gives movie 12934 a rating of 4 out of 5.

Singular Value Decomposition (SVD) is a decomposition method for reducing a matrix to make later calculations simpler, and Simon Funk shared with the community how he and his team used it to get near the top of the rankings during the competition.

 More Information: You can read more about Simon Funk's use of SVD at the following link: `https://sifter.org/~simon/journal/20061027.2.html`

Since Funk's initial work, similar approaches have been proposed for recommender systems. Matrix factorization is a class of collaborative filtering algorithms used in recommender systems that use SVD.

 More Information: You can read more about the use of matrix factorization in recommender systems at the following link: `https://en.wikipedia.org/wiki/Matrix_factorization_(recommender_systems)`

We will use the One-Class Matrix Factorization algorithm because we only have information on purchase order history. The products have not been given ratings or other factors that could be used in other multi-class factorization approaches.

The score produced by matrix factorization tells us the likelihood of being a positive case. The larger the score value, the higher the probability. The score is not a probability, so when making predictions, we have to predict multiple product co-purchase scores and sort with the highest score at the top.

Matrix factorization uses a supervised collaborative filtering approach, which assumes that if Alice has the same opinion as Bob about a product, Alice is more likely to have Bob's opinion on a different product than that of a random other person. Hence, they are more likely to add that product Bob liked to their shopping cart.

Data gathering and processing

The Northwind sample database has the following tables:

- **Products** has 77 rows, each with an integer product ID.

- **Orders** has 830 rows, each order having one or more related detail rows.

- **Order Details** has 2,155 rows, each with an integer product ID indicating the product that was ordered.

We can use this data to create datasets for training and testing models that can then make predictions of other products a customer might want to add to their cart based on what they have already added to it.

For example, order **10248** was made by customer **VINET** for three products with IDs of **11**, **42**, and **72**, as shown in the following screenshot:

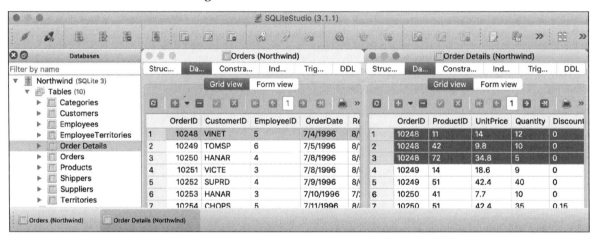

Figure 19.1: Order details for order 10248

We will write a LINQ query to cross-join this data to generate a simple text file with two columns showing products that are co-bought, as shown in the following output:

```
ProductID CoboughtProductID
11        42
11        72
42        11
42        72
72        11
72        42
```

Unfortunately, the Northwind database matches almost every product with every other product. To produce more realistic datasets, we will filter by country. We will generate one dataset for Germany, one for the UK, and one for the USA. The USA dataset will be used for testing.

Creating the NorthwindML website project

We will build an ASP.NET Core MVC website that shows a list of all products, grouped by category, and allows a visitor to add products to a shopping cart. Their shopping cart will be stored in a temporary cookie as a dash-separated list of product IDs:

1. In the folder named `PracticalApps`, create a folder named `NorthwindML`.

2. In Visual Studio Code, open the `PracticalApps` workspace and add the `NorthwindML` folder to the workspace.

3. Navigate to **Terminal** | **New Terminal** and select `NorthwindML`.

4. In **TERMINAL**, enter the following command to create a new ASP.NET Core MVC project, as shown in the following command:

```
dotnet new mvc
```

5. Select `NorthwindML` as the active project.

6. Open the `NorthwindML.csproj` project file, add references to the SQLite, ML.NET, and ML.NET Recommender packages, and to the Northwind context and entity class library projects that you created in *Chapter 14, Introducing Practical Applications of C# and .NET*, as shown highlighted in the following markup:

```xml
<Project Sdk="Microsoft.NET.Sdk.Web">
  <PropertyGroup>
    <TargetFramework>net5.0</TargetFramework>
  </PropertyGroup>

  <ItemGroup>
    <PackageReference
      Include="Microsoft.AspNetCore.Mvc.NewtonsoftJson"
      Version="5.0.0" />
    <PackageReference
      Include="Microsoft.EntityFrameworkCore.Sqlite"
      Version="5.0.0" />
    <PackageReference Include="Microsoft.ML" Version="1.5.1" />
    <PackageReference Include="Microsoft.ML.Recommender"
      Version="0.17.1" />
  </ItemGroup>

  <ItemGroup>
    <ProjectReference Include=
      "..\NorthwindContextLib\NorthwindContextLib.csproj" />
    <ProjectReference Include=
      "..\NorthwindEmployees\NorthwindEmployees.csproj" />
  </ItemGroup>
</Project>
```

7. In **TERMINAL**, restore packages and compile the project, as shown in the following command:

```
dotnet build
```

8. Open the `Startup.cs` class file and import the `Packt.Shared`, `System.IO`, and `Microsoft.EntityFrameworkCore` namespaces.

9. Add statements to the `ConfigureServices` method to register the Northwind data context, as shown in the following code:

```
string databasePath = Path.Combine("..", "Northwind.db");
services.AddDbContext<Northwind>(options =>
  options.UseSqlite($"Data Source={databasePath}"));
```

Creating the data and view models

The `NorthwindML` project will simulate an e-commerce website that allows visitors to add products that they want to order to their shopping cart. We will start by defining some models to represent this:

1. In the `Models` folder, create a class file named `CartItem.cs`, and add statements to define a class with properties for the ID and name of a product, as shown in the following code:

```
namespace NorthwindML.Models
{
  public class CartItem
  {
    public long ProductID { get; set; }
    public string ProductName { get; set; }
  }
}
```

2. In the `Models` folder, create a class file named `Cart.cs`, and add statements to define a class with properties for the items in a cart, as shown in the following code:

```
using System.Collections.Generic;

namespace NorthwindML.Models
{
  public class Cart
  {
    public IEnumerable<CartItem> Items { get; set; }
  }
}
```

3. In the Models folder, create a class file named `ProductCobought.cs`, and add statements to define a class with properties used to record when a product is purchased with another product, and the cardinality (aka maximum possible value) of the `ProductID` property, as shown in the following code:

```
using Microsoft.ML.Data;

namespace NorthwindML.Models
{
  public class ProductCobought
  {
    [KeyType(77)] // maximum possible value of a ProductID
    public uint ProductID { get; set; }

    [KeyType(77)]
    public uint CoboughtProductID { get; set; }
  }
}
```

4. In the Models folder, create a class file named `Recommendation.cs` that will be used as the output of the machine learning algorithm, and add statements to define a class with properties used to show a recommended product ID with its score that will be used as the result of the machine learning algorithm, as shown in the following code:

```
namespace NorthwindML.Models
{
  public class Recommendation
  {
    public uint CoboughtProductID { get; set; }
    public float Score { get; set; }
  }
}
```

5. In the Models folder, create a class file named `EnrichedRecommendation.cs`, and add statements to inherit from the `Recommendation` class with an extra property to show the product name for display, as shown in the following code:

```
namespace NorthwindML.Models
{
  public class EnrichedRecommendation : Recommendation
  {
    public string ProductName { get; set; }
  }
}
```

6. In the Models folder, create a class file named `HomeCartViewModel.cs`, and add statements to define a class with properties to store the visitor's shopping cart and a list of recommendations, as shown in the following code:

```
using System.Collections.Generic;

namespace NorthwindML.Models
{
  public class HomeCartViewModel
  {
    public Cart Cart { get; set; }
    public List<EnrichedRecommendation> Recommendations { get; set; }
  }
}
```

7. In the Models folder, create a class file named `HomeIndexViewModel.cs`, and add statements to define a class with properties to show if the training datasets have been created, as shown in the following code:

```
using System.Collections.Generic;
using Packt.Shared;

namespace NorthwindML.Models
{
  public class HomeIndexViewModel
  {
    public IEnumerable<Category> Categories { get; set; }
    public bool GermanyDatasetExists { get; set; }
    public bool UKDatasetExists { get; set; }
    public bool USADatasetExists { get; set; }
    public long Milliseconds { get; set; }
  }
}
```

8. In **TERMINAL**, compile the project, as shown in the following command:

```
dotnet build
```

Implementing the controller

Now we can modify the existing home controller to perform the operations we need:

1. In the wwwroot folder, create a folder named Data. This is where datasets for training models will be stored.

2. In the Controllers folder, open `HomeController.cs`, and import some namespaces, as shown in the following code:

```
using Packt.Shared;
using Microsoft.EntityFrameworkCore;
using Microsoft.AspNetCore.Hosting;
using System.IO;
using Microsoft.ML;
using Microsoft.ML.Data;
using Microsoft.Data;
using Microsoft.ML.Trainers;
```

3. In the `HomeController` class, declare some fields for the filename and countries that we
    will generate datasets for, as shown in the following code:

```
private readonly static string datasetName = "dataset.txt";
private readonly static string[] countries =
  new[] { "Germany", "UK", "USA" };
```

4. Declare some fields for the Northwind data context and web host environment
    dependency services and set them in the constructor, as shown in the following code:

```
// dependency services
private readonly ILogger<HomeController> _logger;
private readonly Northwind db;
private readonly IWebHostEnvironment webHostEnvironment;

public HomeController(ILogger<HomeController> logger,
  Northwind db, IWebHostEnvironment webHostEnvironment)
{
  _logger = logger;
  this.db = db;
  this.webHostEnvironment = webHostEnvironment;
}
```

5. Add a private method to return the path to a file stored in the `Data` folder of the
    website, as shown in the following code:

```
private string GetDataPath(string file)
{
  return Path.Combine(webHostEnvironment.ContentRootPath,
    "wwwroot", "Data", file);
}
```

6. Add a private method to create an instance of the `HomeIndexViewModel` class loaded with
    all the products from the `Northwind` database and indicating if the datasets have been
    created, as shown in the following code:

```
private HomeIndexViewModel CreateHomeIndexViewModel()
{
  return new HomeIndexViewModel
  {
    Categories = db.Categories
```

```
      .Include(category => category.Products),
    GermanyDatasetExists = System.IO.File.Exists(
      GetDataPath("germany-dataset.txt")),
    UKDatasetExists = System.IO.File.Exists(
      GetDataPath("uk-dataset.txt")),
    USADatasetExists = System.IO.File.Exists(
      GetDataPath("usa-dataset.txt"))
  };
}
```

We had to prefix the `File` class with `System.IO` because the `ControllerBase` class has a `File` method that would cause a naming conflict.

7. In the `Index` action method, add statements to create its view model and pass it to its Razor view, as shown highlighted in the following code:

```
public IActionResult Index()
{
  var model = CreateHomeIndexViewModel();
  return View(model);
}
```

8. Add an action method to generate the datasets for each country and then return to the default `Index` view, as shown in the following code:

```
public IActionResult GenerateDatasets()
{
  foreach (string country in countries)
  {
    IEnumerable<Order> ordersInCountry = db.Orders
      // filter by country to create different datasets
      .Where(order => order.Customer.Country == country)
      .Include(order => order.OrderDetails)
      .AsEnumerable(); // switch to client-side

    IEnumerable<ProductCobought> coboughtProducts =
      ordersInCountry.SelectMany(order =>
        from lineItem1 in order.OrderDetails // cross-join
        from lineItem2 in order.OrderDetails
        select new ProductCobought
        {
          ProductID = (uint)lineItem1.ProductID,
          CoboughtProductID = (uint)lineItem2.ProductID
        })
        // exclude matches between a product and itself
        .Where(p => p.ProductID != p.CoboughtProductID)
        // remove duplicates by grouping by both values
        .GroupBy(p => new { p.ProductID, p.CoboughtProductID })
```

```
      .Select(p => p.FirstOrDefault())
      // make it easier for humans to read results by sorting
      .OrderBy(p => p.ProductID)
      .ThenBy(p => p.CoboughtProductID);

    StreamWriter datasetFile = System.IO.File.CreateText(
      path: GetDataPath($"{country.ToLower()}-{datasetName}"));

    // tab-separated header
    datasetFile.WriteLine("ProductID\tCoboughtProductID");

    foreach (var item in coboughtProducts)
    {
      datasetFile.WriteLine("{0}\t{1}",
        item.ProductID, item.CoboughtProductID);
    }
    datasetFile.Close();
  }
  var model = CreateHomeIndexViewModel();
  return View("Index", model);
}
```

Training the recommendation models

In the dataset, we already provide a `KeyType` to set the maximum value for a product ID. The product IDs are already encoded as integers, which is what's needed for the algorithm we will use, so to train the models, all we need to do is call the `MatrixFactorizationTrainer` with a few extra parameters:

1. In the `HomeController.cs` file, add an action method to train the models, as shown in the following code:

```
public IActionResult TrainModels()
{
  var stopWatch = Stopwatch.StartNew();

  foreach (string country in countries)
  {
    var mlContext = new MLContext();

    IDataView dataView = mlContext.Data.LoadFromTextFile(
      path: GetDataPath($"{country}-{datasetName}"),
      columns: new[]
      {
        new TextLoader.Column(name: "Label",
          dataKind: DataKind.Double, index: 0),
        // The key count is the cardinality i.e. maximum
```

```
        // valid value. This column is used internally when
        // training the model. When results are shown, the
        // columns are mapped to instances of our model
        // which could have a different cardinality but
        // happen to have the same.
        new TextLoader.Column(
          name: nameof(ProductCobought.ProductID),
          dataKind: DataKind.UInt32,
          source: new [] { new TextLoader.Range(0) },
          keyCount: new KeyCount(77)),
        new TextLoader.Column(
          name: nameof(ProductCobought.CoboughtProductID),
          dataKind: DataKind.UInt32,
          source: new [] { new TextLoader.Range(1) },
          keyCount: new KeyCount(77))
      },
      hasHeader: true,
      separatorChar: '\t');

   var options = new MatrixFactorizationTrainer.Options
   {
      MatrixColumnIndexColumnName =
        nameof(ProductCobought.ProductID),
      MatrixRowIndexColumnName =
        nameof(ProductCobought.CoboughtProductID),
      LabelColumnName = "Label",
      LossFunction = MatrixFactorizationTrainer
        .LossFunctionType.SquareLossOneClass,
      Alpha = 0.01,
      Lambda = 0.025,
      C = 0.00001
   };

   MatrixFactorizationTrainer mft = mlContext.Recommendation()
      .Trainers.MatrixFactorization(options);

   ITransformer trainedModel = mft.Fit(dataView);

   mlContext.Model.Save(trainedModel,
      inputSchema: dataView.Schema,
      filePath: GetDataPath($"{country}-model.zip"));
}

stopWatch.Stop();

var model = CreateHomeIndexViewModel();
```

```
        model.Milliseconds = stopWatch.ElapsedMilliseconds;
        return View("Index", model);
}
```

Implementing a shopping cart with recommendations

We will now build a shopping cart feature and allow visitors to add products to their cart. In the cart, they will see recommendations of other products they can quickly add to their cart.

This type of recommendation is known as **co-purchase** or "products frequently bought together," which means it will recommend customers a set of products based upon their and other customers' purchase histories.

In this example, we will always use the Germany model to make predictions. In a real website, you might choose to select the model based on the current location of the visitor so that they get recommendations similar to other visitors from their country:

1. In the HomeController.cs file, add an action method to add a product to the shopping cart and then show the cart with the best three recommendations of other products the visitor might like to add, as shown in the following code:

```
// GET /Home/Cart
// To show the cart and recommendations
// GET /Home/Cart/5
// To add a product to the cart
public IActionResult Cart(int? id)
{
  // the current cart is stored as a cookie
  string cartCookie = Request.Cookies["nw_cart"] ?? string.Empty;

  // if visitor clicked Add to Cart button
  if (id.HasValue)
  {
    if (string.IsNullOrWhiteSpace(cartCookie))
    {
      cartCookie = id.ToString();
    }
    else
    {
      string[] ids = cartCookie.Split('-');

      if (!ids.Contains(id.ToString()))
      {
        cartCookie = string.Join('-', cartCookie, id.ToString());
      }
    }
    Response.Cookies.Append("nw_cart", cartCookie);
```

```
    }

    var model = new HomeCartViewModel
    {
      Cart = new Cart
      {
        Items = Enumerable.Empty<CartItem>()
      },
      Recommendations = new List<EnrichedRecommendation>()
    };

    if (cartCookie.Length > 0)
    {
      model.Cart.Items = cartCookie.Split('-').Select(item =>
        new CartItem
        {
          ProductID = long.Parse(item),
          ProductName = db.Products.Find(long.Parse(item)).ProductName
        });
    }

    if (System.IO.File.Exists(GetDataPath("germany-model.zip")))
    {
      var mlContext = new MLContext();
      ITransformer modelGermany;

      using (var stream = new FileStream(
        path: GetDataPath("germany-model.zip"),
        mode: FileMode.Open,
        access: FileAccess.Read,
        share: FileShare.Read))
      {
        modelGermany = mlContext.Model.Load(stream,
          out DataViewSchema schema);
      }

      var predictionEngine = mlContext.Model.CreatePredictionEngine
        <ProductCobought, Recommendation>(modelGermany);

      var products = db.Products.ToArray();

      foreach (var item in model.Cart.Items)
      {
        var topThree = products.Select(product =>
          predictionEngine.Predict(
            new ProductCobought
```

```
          {
            ProductID = (uint)item.ProductID,
            CoboughtProductID = (uint)product.ProductID
          })
        ) // returns IEnumerable<Recommendation>
        .OrderByDescending(x => x.Score)
        .Take(3)
        .ToArray();

      model.Recommendations.AddRange(topThree
        .Select(rec => new EnrichedRecommendation
        {
          CoboughtProductID = rec.CoboughtProductID,
          Score = rec.Score,
          ProductName = db.Products.Find(
            (long)rec.CoboughtProductID).ProductName
        }));
    }

    // show the best three product recommendations
    model.Recommendations = model.Recommendations
      .OrderByDescending(rec => rec.Score)
      .Take(3)
      .ToList();
  }
  return View(model);
}
```

2. In the Views folder, in its Home subfolder, open Index.cshtml and modify it to output its view model and include links to generate the datasets and train the models, as shown in the following markup:

```
@using Packt.Shared
@model HomeIndexViewModel
@{
  ViewData["Title"] = "Products - Northwind ML";
}
<h1 class="display-3">@ViewData["Title"]</h1>
<p class="lead">
<div>See product recommendations in your shopping cart.</div>
<ol>
  <li>First,
    <a asp-controller="Home"
      asp-action="GenerateDatasets">
      generate some datasets</a>.</li>
  <li>Second,
    <a asp-controller="Home" asp-action="TrainModels">
```

```
      train the models</a>.</li>
  <li>Third, add some products to your
    <a asp-controller="Home" asp-action="Cart">cart</a>.</li>
</ol>
<div>
@if (Model.GermanyDatasetExists || Model.UKDatasetExists)
{
  <text>Datasets for training:</text>
}
@if (Model.GermanyDatasetExists)
{
  <a href="/Data/germany-dataset.txt"
    class="btn btn-outline-primary">Germany</a>
}
@if (Model.UKDatasetExists)
{
  <a href="/Data/uk-dataset.txt"
    class="btn btn-outline-primary">UK</a>
}
@if (Model.USADatasetExists)
{
  <text>Dataset for testing:</text>
  <a href="/Data/usa-dataset.txt"
    class="btn btn-outline-primary">USA</a>
}
</div>
@if (Model.Milliseconds > 0)
{
<hr />
<div class="alert alert-success">
  It took @Model.Milliseconds milliseconds to train the models.
</div>
}
</p>
<h2>Products</h2>
@foreach (Category category in Model.Categories)
{
<h3>@category.CategoryName <small>@category.Description</small></h3>
<table>
<tbody>
@foreach (Product product in category.Products)
{
  <tr>
    <td>
      <a asp-controller="Home" asp-action="Cart"
        asp-route-id="@product.ProductID"
```

```
          class="btn btn-outline-success">Add to Cart</a>
      </td>
      <td>
        @product.ProductName
      </td>
    </tr>
  }
  </tbody>
  </table>
}
```

3. In the Views folder, in its Home subfolder, create a new Razor file named Cart.cshtml and modify it to output its view model, as shown in the following markup:

```
@model HomeCartViewModel
@{
  ViewData["Title"] = "Shopping Cart - Northwind ML";
}
<h1>@ViewData["Title"]</h1>
<table class="table table-bordered">
  <thead>
    <tr>
      <th>Product ID</th>
      <th>Product Name</th>
    </tr>
  </thead>
  <tbody>
  @foreach (CartItem item in Model.Cart.Items)
  {
    <tr>
      <td>@item.ProductID</td>
      <td>@item.ProductName</td>
    </tr>
  }
  </tbody>
</table>
<h2>Customers who bought items in your cart also bought the following
products</h2>
@if (Model.Recommendations.Count() == 0)
{
<div>No recommendations.</div>
}
else
{
<table class="table table-bordered">
  <thead>
```

```
    <tr>
      <th></th>
      <th>Co-bought Product</th>
      <th>Score</th>
    </tr>
  </thead>
  <tbody>
  @foreach (EnrichedRecommendation rec in Model.Recommendations)
  {
    <tr>
      <td>
        <a asp-controller="Home" asp-action="Cart"
           asp-route-id="@rec.CoboughtProductID"
           class="btn btn-outline-success">Add to Cart</a>
      </td>
      <td>
        @rec.ProductName
      </td>
      <td>
        @rec.Score
      </td>
    </tr>
  }
  </tbody>
</table>
}
```

Testing the product recommendations website

Now we are ready to test the website product recommendations feature:

1. Start the website using the following command:

```
dotnet run
```

2. Start Chrome and navigate to `https://localhost:5001/`.

3. On the home page, click **generate some datasets**, and note that buttons for the three datasets are created, as shown in the following screenshot:

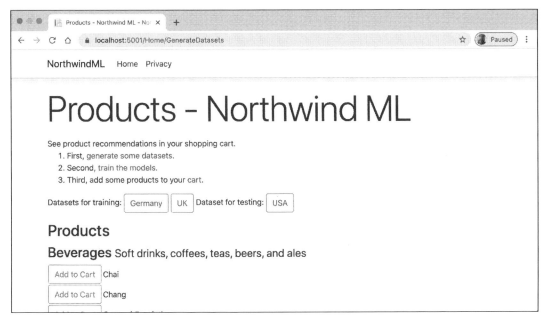

Figure 19.2: The Generating Datasets page

4. Click the **UK** dataset, and note that five products were co-bought with **Product ID 1**: **5**, **11**, **23**, **68**, and **69**, as shown in the following screenshot:

Figure 19.3: The UK dataset

5. Navigate back in your browser.

6. Click **train the models** and note how long it took to train the models.

7. In Visual Studio Code, in the NorthwindML project, expand the wwwroot folder, expand the Data folder, and note the models in the filesystem saved as binary ZIP files.

8. In Chrome, on the **Products - Northwind ML** home page, scroll down the list of products, click **Add to Cart** next to any product, like **Outback Lager**, and note the **Shopping Cart** page appears with the product as a cart item and recommended products with scores, as shown in the following screenshot:

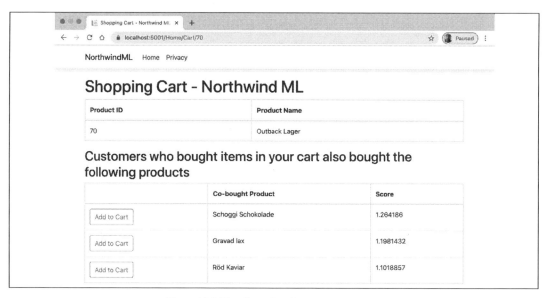

Figure 19.4: The Shopping Cart page

9. Navigate back in your browser, add another product to your cart, like **Ipoh Coffee**, and note the changes in the top three product recommendations due to **NuNuCa Nuß-Nougat-Creme** being even more likely to be co-bought than the previous top recommendation, **Schoggi Schokolade**, as shown in the following screenshot:

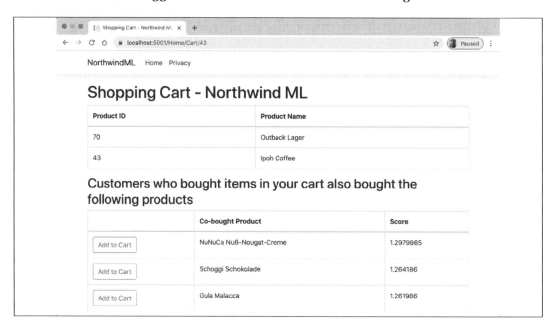

Figure 19.5: Two of the top three products have changed

10. Close the browser and stop the website.

Practicing and exploring

Test your knowledge and understanding by answering some questions, get some hands-on practice, and explore this chapter's topics with deeper research.

Exercise 19.1 – Test your knowledge

Answer the following questions:

1. What are the four main steps of the machine learning lifecycle?
2. What are the three sub-steps of the modeling step?
3. Why do models need to be retrained after deployment?
4. Why must you split your dataset into a training dataset and a testing dataset?
5. What are some of the differences between clustering and classification machine learning tasks?
6. What class must you instantiate to perform any machine learning task?
7. What is the difference between a label and a feature?
8. What does `IDataView` represent?
9. What does the `count` parameter in the `[KeyType(count: 10)]` attribute represent?
10. What does the score represent with matrix factorization?

Exercise 19.2 – Practice with samples

Microsoft has many sample projects for learning ML.NET, as shown in the following list:

- **Sentiment Analysis for User Reviews**: `https://github.com/dotnet/machinelearning-samples/tree/master/samples/csharp/getting-started/BinaryClassification_SentimentAnalysis`

- **Customer Segmentation - Clustering sample**: `https://github.com/dotnet/machinelearning-samples/tree/master/samples/csharp/getting-started/Clustering_CustomerSegmentation`

- **Spam Detection for Text Messages**: `https://github.com/dotnet/machinelearning-samples/tree/master/samples/csharp/getting-started/BinaryClassification_SpamDetection`

- **GitHub Issues Labeler**: `https://github.com/dotnet/machinelearning-samples/tree/master/samples/csharp/end-to-end-apps/MulticlassClassification-GitHubLabeler`

- **Movie Recommendation - Matrix Factorization problem sample**: `https://github.com/dotnet/machinelearning-samples/tree/master/samples/csharp/getting-started/MatrixFactorization_MovieRecommendation`

- **Taxi Fare Prediction**: `https://github.com/dotnet/machinelearning-samples/tree/master/samples/csharp/getting-started/Regression_TaxiFarePrediction`

- **Bike Sharing Demand - Regression problem sample**: `https://github.com/dotnet/ machinelearning-samples/tree/master/samples/csharp/getting-started/Regression_ BikeSharingDemand`

- **eShopDashboardML - Sales forecasting**: `https://github.com/dotnet/ machinelearning-samples/tree/master/samples/csharp/end-to-end-apps/ Forecasting-Sales`

Exercise 19.3 – Explore topics

Use the following links to read more details about this chapter's topics:

- **August 2020 ML.NET API and Tooling Updates**: `https://devblogs.microsoft.com/ dotnet/august-ml-net-api-and-tooling-updates/`

- **What is ML.Net and how does it work?**: `https://docs.microsoft.com/en-us/dotnet/ machine-learning/how-does-mldotnet-work`

- **Machine learning glossary of important terms**: `https://docs.microsoft.com/en-us/ dotnet/machine-learning/resources/glossary`

- **Channel 9 ML.NET videos**: `https://aka.ms/dotnet3-mlnet`

- **YouTube ML.NET videos**: `https://aka.ms/mlnetyoutube`

- **Machine Learning Explainability vs Interpretability: Two concepts that could help restore trust in AI**: `https://www.kdnuggets.com/2018/12/machine-learning-explainability-interpretability-ai.html`

- **Machine learning tasks in ML.NET**: `https://docs.microsoft.com/en-us/dotnet/ machine-learning/resources/tasks`

- **Machine learning data transforms - ML.NET**: `https://docs.microsoft.com/en-us/ dotnet/machine-learning/resources/transforms`

- **ML.NET Samples**: `https://github.com/dotnet/machinelearning-samples/blob/ master/README.md`

- **Community Samples**: `https://github.com/dotnet/machinelearning-samples/blob/ master/docs/COMMUNITY-SAMPLES.md`

- **ML.NET API reference**: `https://docs.microsoft.com/en-gb/dotnet/api/?view=ml-dotnet`

- **ML.NET: The Machine Learning Framework for .NET Developers**: `https://msdn. microsoft.com/en-us/magazine/mt848634`

- **Building recommendation engine for .NET applications using Azure Machine Learning**: `https://devblogs.microsoft.com/dotnet/dot-net-recommendation-system-for-net-applications-using-azure-machine-learning/`

Summary

In this chapter, you were introduced to some of the theoretical background to machine learning, the key classes in the ML.NET library, and one practical example of how to add intelligence to a website using ML.NET.

The current solution would not scale well since it currently loads the entire product list into memory. Building intelligence like this into apps is more than a full-time profession. I hope that this chapter has either sparked an interest in diving deeper into machine learning and data science or has shown you enough that you can make an informed decision about whether to pursue other areas of C# and .NET development.

In the next chapter, you will learn how to build web user interfaces using Blazor, Microsoft's cool new web component technology that enables web developers to build client-side, **single-page applications (SPAs)** using C# instead of JavaScript.

20

Building Web User Interfaces Using Blazor

This chapter is about using Microsoft Blazor to build user interfaces for the web.

I will describe the different flavors of Blazor and their pros and cons. You will learn how to build Blazor components that can execute their code on the web server or in the web browser. When hosted with Blazor Server, it uses SignalR to communicate updates needed to the user interface in the browser. When hosted with Blazor WebAssembly, the components execute their code in the client and must make HTTP calls to interact with the server.

In this chapter, we will cover the following topics:

- Understanding Blazor
- Building components using Blazor Server
- Building components using Blazor WebAssembly

Understanding Blazor

In *Chapter 14, Introducing Practical Applications of C# and .NET*, I introduced you to Blazor (and SignalR that is used by Blazor Server). Blazor is supported on all modern browsers.

 More Information: You can read the official list of supported platforms at the following link: `https://docs.microsoft.com/en-us/aspnet/core/blazor/supported-platforms`

Understanding Blazor hosting models

As a reminder, Blazor is a single app model with two main hosting models:

- **Blazor Server** runs on the server side, so the C# code that you write has full access to all resources that your business logic might need without needing to authenticate. It then uses SignalR to communicate user interface updates to the client side. The server must keep a live SignalR connection to each client and track the current state of every client, so Blazor Server does not scale well if you need to support lots of clients. It first shipped as part of .NET Core 3.0 in September 2019 and is included with .NET 5.0 and later.

- **Blazor WebAssembly** runs on the client side, so the C# code that you write only has access to resources in the browser and it must make HTTP calls (that might require authentication) before it can access resources on the server. It first shipped as an extension to .NET Core 3.1 in May 2020 and was versioned 3.2 because it is a Current release and therefore not covered by .NET Core 3.1's Long Term Support. The .NET Core 3.2 version used the Mono runtime and Mono libraries; the .NET 5 version uses the Mono runtime and the .NET 5 libraries. *"Blazor WebAssembly runs on a .NET IL interpreter without any JIT so it's not going to win any speed competitions. We have made some significant speed improvements though in .NET 5, and we expect to improve things further for .NET 6."* — Daniel Roth

Although Blazor Server is supported on Internet Explorer 11, Blazor WebAssembly is not.

Blazor WebAssembly has optional support for **Progressive Web Apps (PWAs)**, meaning a website visitor can use a browser menu to add the app to their desktop and run the app offline.

 More Information: You can read more about hosting models in the official documentation: `https://docs.microsoft.com/en-us/aspnet/core/blazor/hosting-models`

Understanding Blazor components

It is important to understand that Blazor is used to create **user interface components**. Components define how to render the user interface, react to user events, and can be composed and nested, and compiled into a NuGet Razor class library for packaging and distribution.

In the future, Blazor might not be limited to only creating user interface components using web technologies. Microsoft has an experimental technology known as **Blazor Mobile Bindings** that allows developers to use Blazor to build mobile user interface components. Instead of using HTML and CSS to build a web user interface, it uses XAML and Xamarin.Forms to build a cross-platform mobile user interface.

More Information: You can read more about Blazor Mobile Bindings at the following link: `https://devblogs.microsoft.com/aspnet/mobile-blazor-bindings-experiment/`

Microsoft is also experimenting with a hybrid model that enables building apps with a mixture of web and mobile.

 More Information: You can read more about Blazor Hybrid apps at the following link: `https://devblogs.microsoft.com/aspnet/hybrid-blazor-apps-in-mobile-blazor-bindings-july-update/`

What is the deal with Blazor and Razor?

You might wonder why Blazor components use `.razor` as their file extension. Razor is a template markup syntax that allows the mixing of HTML and C#. Older technologies that support Razor use the `.cshtml` file extension to indicate the mix of C# and HTML.

Razor is used for:

- ASP.NET Core MVC **views** and **partial views** that use the `.cshtml` file extension. The business logic is separated into a controller class that treats the view as a template to push the view model to, that then outputs it to a web page.
- **Razor Pages** that use the `.cshtml` file extension. The business logic can be embedded or separated into a file that uses the `.cshtml.cs` file extension. The output is a web page.
- **Blazor components** that use the `.razor` file extension. The output is not a web page although layouts can be used to wrap a component so it outputs as a web page and the @page directive can be used to assign a route that defines the URL path to retrieve the component as a page.

Comparing Blazor project templates

One way to understand the choice between the Blazor Server and Blazor WebAssembly hosting models is to review the differences in their default project templates.

Reviewing the Blazor Server project template

Let us look at the default template for a Blazor Server project. Mostly you will see that it is the same as an ASP.NET Core Razor Pages template, with a few key additions:

1. In the folder named `PracticalApps`, create a folder named `NorthwindBlazorServer`.
2. In **Visual Studio Code**, open the `PracticalApps` workspace and add the `NorthwindBlazorServer` folder.

3. Navigate to **Terminal | New Terminal** and select `NorthwindBlazorServer`.

4. In **TERMINAL**, use the `blazorserver` template to create a new Blazor Server project, as shown in the following command:

```
dotnet new blazorserver
```

5. Select `NorthwindBlazorServer` as the active OmniSharp project.

6. In the `NorthwindBlazorServer` folder, open `NorthwindBlazorServer.csproj`, and note it is identical to an ASP.NET Core project that uses the Web SDK and targets .NET 5.0.

7. Open `Program.cs`, and note it is identical to an ASP.NET Core project.

8. Open `Startup.cs`, and note the `ConfigureServices` method, with its call to the `AddServerSideBlazor` method, as shown highlighted in the following code:

```csharp
public void ConfigureServices(IServiceCollection services)
{
    services.AddRazorPages();
    services.AddServerSideBlazor();
    services.AddSingleton<WeatherForecastService>();
}
```

9. Note the `Configure` method, which is similar to an ASP.NET Core Razor Pages project except for the calls to the `MapBlazorHub` and `MapFallbackToPage` methods when configuring endpoints that configure an ASP.NET Core app to accept incoming SignalR connections for Blazor components, and other requests fall back to a Razor Page named `_Host.cshtml`, as shown in the following code:

```csharp
app.UseEndpoints(endpoints =>
{
    endpoints.MapBlazorHub();
    endpoints.MapFallbackToPage("/_Host");
});
```

10. In the `Pages` folder, open `_Host.cshtml`, as shown in the following markup:

```
@page "/"
@namespace NorthwindBlazorServer.Pages
@addTagHelper *, Microsoft.AspNetCore.Mvc.TagHelpers
@{
    Layout = null;
}

<!DOCTYPE html>
<html lang="en">
<head>
    <meta charset="utf-8" />
    <meta name="viewport"
          content="width=device-width, initial-scale=1.0" />
    <title>NorthwindBlazorServer</title>
```

```
    <base href="~/" />
    <link rel="stylesheet"
          href="css/bootstrap/bootstrap.min.css" />
    <link href="css/site.css" rel="stylesheet" />
    <link href="_content/NorthwindBlazorServer/_framework/scoped.styles.css"
rel="stylesheet" />
</head>
<body>
    <component type="typeof(App)"
               render-mode="ServerPrerendered" />

    <div id="blazor-error-ui">
      <environment include="Staging,Production">
        An error has occurred. This application may no longer respond until
reloaded.
      </environment>
      <environment include="Development">
        An unhandled exception has occurred. See browser dev tools for
details.
      </environment>
      <a href="" class="reload">Reload</a>
      <a class="dismiss">✕</a>
    </div>

    <script src="_framework/blazor.server.js"></script>
</body>
</html>
```

While reviewing the preceding markup, note the following:

- In the <body>, the Blazor component of type App that is prerendered on the server.

- The <div id="blazor-error-ui"> for showing Blazor errors that will appear as a yellow bar at the bottom of the web page when an error occurs.

- The script block for blazor.server.js manages the SignalR connection back to the server.

11. In the NorthwindBlazorServer folder, open App.razor, and note it defines a Router for all components found in the current assembly, as shown in the following code:

```
<Router AppAssembly="@typeof(Program).Assembly">
  <Found Context="routeData">
    <RouteView RouteData="@routeData"
               DefaultLayout="@typeof(MainLayout)" />
  </Found>
  <NotFound>
    <LayoutView Layout="@typeof(MainLayout)">
```

```
        <p>Sorry, there's nothing at this address.</p>
      </LayoutView>
    </NotFound>
  </Router>
```

While reviewing the preceding markup, note the following:

- If a matching route is found, then a RouteView is executed that sets the default layout for the component to MainLayout and passes any route data parameters to the component.

- If a matching route is not found, then a LayoutView is executed that outputs the internal markup (in this case a simple paragraph element with a message telling the visitor there is nothing at this address) inside the MainLayout.

12. In the Shared folder, open MainLayout.razor, and note it defines a <div> for a sidebar containing a navigation menu and a <div> for the main content, as shown in the following code:

```
@inherits LayoutComponentBase

<div class="page">
  <div class="sidebar">
    <NavMenu />
  </div>

  <div class="main">
    <div class="top-row px-4">
      <a href="https://docs.microsoft.com/aspnet/"
         target="_blank">About</a>
    </div>
    <div class="content px-4">
      @Body
    </div>
  </div>
</div>
```

13. In the Shared folder, open MainLayout.razor.css, and note it contains isolated CSS styles for the component.

14. In the Shared folder, open NavMenu.razor, and note it has three menu items for Home, Counter, and Fetch data. We will return to this later when we add our own component.

15. In the Pages folder, open FetchData.razor, and note it defines a component that fetches weather forecasts from an injected dependency weather service and then renders them in a table, as shown in the following code:

```
@page "/fetchdata"

@using NorthwindBlazorServer.Data
@inject WeatherForecastService ForecastService
```

```
<h1>Weather forecast</h1>

<p>This component demonstrates fetching data from a service.</p>

@if (forecasts == null)
{
  <p><em>Loading...</em></p>
}
else
{
  <table class="table">
    <thead>
      <tr>
        <th>Date</th>
        <th>Temp. (C)</th>
        <th>Temp. (F)</th>
        <th>Summary</th>
      </tr>
    </thead>
    <tbody>
      @foreach (var forecast in forecasts)
      {
        <tr>
          <td>@forecast.Date.ToShortDateString()</td>
          <td>@forecast.TemperatureC</td>
          <td>@forecast.TemperatureF</td>
          <td>@forecast.Summary</td>
        </tr>
      }
    </tbody>
  </table>
}

@code {
  private WeatherForecast[] forecasts;

  protected override async Task OnInitializedAsync()
  {
    forecasts = await ForecastService
      .GetForecastAsync(DateTime.Now);
  }
}
```

16. In the `Data` folder, open `WeatherForecastService.cs`, and note it is *not* a Web API controller class, it is just an ordinary class that returns random weather data, as shown in the following code:

```
using System;
using System.Linq;
using System.Threading.Tasks;

namespace NorthwindBlazorServer.Data
{
  public class WeatherForecastService
  {
    private static readonly string[] Summaries = new[]
    {
      "Freezing", "Bracing", "Chilly", "Cool", "Mild", "Warm", "Balmy",
"Hot", "Sweltering", "Scorching"
    };

    public Task<WeatherForecast[]> GetForecastAsync(
      DateTime startDate)
    {
      var rng = new Random();
      return Task.FromResult(
        Enumerable.Range(1, 5)
        .Select(index => new WeatherForecast
      {
        Date = startDate.AddDays(index),
        TemperatureC = rng.Next(-20, 55),
        Summary = Summaries[rng.Next(Summaries.Length)]
      }).ToArray());
    }
  }
}
```

Understanding CSS isolation

Blazor components often need to provide their own CSS to apply styling. To ensure this does not conflict with site-level CSS, Blazor supports CSS isolation. If you have a component named `Index.razor`, simply create a CSS file named `Index.razor.css`.

More Information: You can read more about the reason for needing CSS isolation for Blazor components at the following link: https://github.com/dotnet/aspnetcore/issues/10170

Running the Blazor Server project template

Now that we have reviewed the project template and the important parts that are specific to Blazor Server, we can start the website and review its behavior:

1. In **TERMINAL**, enter a command to run the website, as shown in the following command line:

   ```
   dotnet run
   ```

2. Start your browser and navigate to https://localhost:5001/, and click **Fetch data**, as shown in the following screenshot:

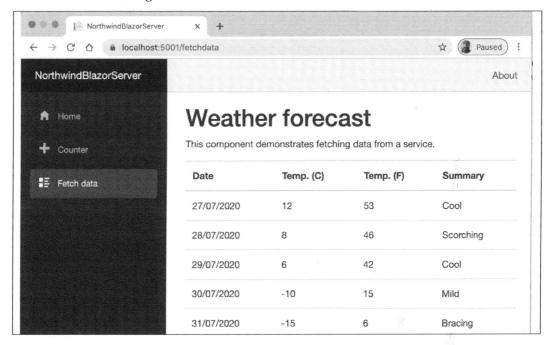

Figure 20.1: Fetching weather data

3. Change the route to /apples, and note the missing message, as shown in the following screenshot:

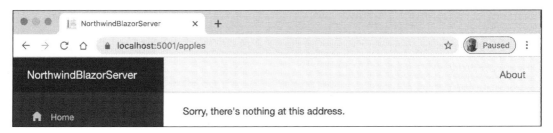

Figure 20.2: The missing component message

4. Close Chrome.

5. In **Visual Studio Code**, press *Ctrl* + *C* in **TERMINAL** to stop the web server.

Reviewing the Blazor WebAssembly project template

Now we will create a Blazor WebAssembly project. I will not show code in the book if the code is the same as in a Blazor Server project:

1. In the folder named `PracticalApps`, create a folder named `NorthwindBlazorWasm`.

2. In **Visual Studio Code**, open the `PracticalApps` workspace and add the `NorthwindBlazorWasm` folder.

3. Navigate to **Terminal | New Terminal** and select `NorthwindBlazorWasm`.

4. In **TERMINAL**, use the `blazorwasm` template with the `--pwa` and `--hosted` flags to create a new Blazor WebAssembly project hosted in ASP.NET Core that supports the PWA feature of your operating system, as shown in the following command:

    ```
    dotnet new blazorwasm --pwa --hosted
    ```

    While reviewing the generated project, note the following:

    *   A solution and three project folders are generated: **Client**, **Server**, and **Shared**.

    *   **Shared** is a class library that contains models for the weather service.

    *   **Server** is an ASP.NET Core website for hosting the weather service that has the same implementation for returning random weather forecasts as before but is implemented as a proper Web API controller class. The project file has project references to **Shared** and **Client**, and a package reference to support WebAssembly on the server side.

    *   **Client** is the Blazor WebAssembly project.

5. In the `Client` folder, open `NorthwindBlazorWasm.Client.csproj`, and note it uses the Blazor WebAssembly SDK and has three package references, as well as the service worker required for PWA support, as shown in the following markup:

    ```xml
    <Project Sdk="Microsoft.NET.Sdk.BlazorWebAssembly">

      <PropertyGroup>
        <TargetFramework>net5.0</TargetFramework>
        <ServiceWorkerAssetsManifest>service-worker-assets.js</
    ServiceWorkerAssetsManifest>
      </PropertyGroup>

      <ItemGroup>
        <PackageReference
          Include="Microsoft.AspNetCore.Components.WebAssembly"
          Version="5.0.0" />
        <PackageReference
          Include="Microsoft.AspNetCore.Components
            .WebAssembly.DevServer"
          Version="5.0.0" PrivateAssets="all" />
        <PackageReference
          Include="System.Net.Http.Json"
    ```

```
      Version="5.0.0" />
  </ItemGroup>

  <ItemGroup>
    <ProjectReference Include=
      "..\Shared\NorthwindBlazorWasm.Shared.csproj" />
  </ItemGroup>

  <ItemGroup>
    <ServiceWorker Include=
      "wwwroot\service-worker.js" PublishedContent=
      "wwwroot\service-worker.published.js" />
  </ItemGroup>

</Project>
```

6. In the `Client` folder, open `Program.cs`, and note the host builder is for `WebAssembly` instead of server-side ASP.NET Core, and it registers a dependency service for making HTTP requests, which is an extremely common requirement for Blazor WebAssembly apps, as shown in the following code:

```
var builder = WebAssemblyHostBuilder.CreateDefault(args);
builder.RootComponents.Add<App>("#app");

builder.Services.AddScoped(sp => new HttpClient
  { BaseAddress = new Uri(
    builder.HostEnvironment.BaseAddress) });

await builder.Build().RunAsync();
```

7. In the `wwwroot` folder, open `index.html`, and note the `manifest.json` and `service-worker.js` files to support offline work, and the `blazor.webassembly.js` script that downloads all the NuGet packages for Blazor WebAssembly, as shown highlighted in the following markup:

```
<!DOCTYPE html>
<html>

<head>
  <meta charset="utf-8" />
  <meta name="viewport" content="width=device-width, initial-scale=1.0,
maximum-scale=1.0, user-scalable=no" />
  <title>NorthwindBlazorWasm</title>
  <base href="/" />
  <link href="css/bootstrap/bootstrap.min.css"
        rel="stylesheet" />
  <link href="css/app.css" rel="stylesheet" />
  <link href="_framework/scoped.styles.css"
```

```
        rel="stylesheet" />
<link href="manifest.json" rel="manifest" />
  <link rel="apple-touch-icon" sizes="512x512"
        href="icon-512.png" />
</head>

<body>
  <div id="app">Loading...</div>

  <div id="blazor-error-ui">
    An unhandled error has occurred.
    <a href="" class="reload">Reload</a>
    <a class="dismiss">✕</a>
  </div>
  <script src="_framework/blazor.webassembly.js"></script>
  <script>navigator.serviceWorker
    .register('service-worker.js');</script>
</body>

</html>
```

8. In the `Client` folder, note the following files are identical to Blazor Server: `App.razor`, `Shared\MainLayout.razor`, `Shared\NavMenu.razor`, `SurveyPrompt.razor`, `Pages\Counter.razor`, and `Pages\Index.razor`.

9. In the `Pages` folder, open `FetchData.razor`, and note the markup is similar to Blazor Server except for the injected dependency service for making HTTP requests, as shown highlighted in the following partial markup:

```
@page "/fetchdata"
@using NorthwindBlazorWasm.Shared
@inject HttpClient Http

<h1>Weather forecast</h1>

...

@code {
  private WeatherForecast[] forecasts;

  protected override async Task OnInitializedAsync()
  {
    forecasts = await
      Http.GetFromJsonAsync<WeatherForecast[]>(
        "WeatherForecast");
  }
}
```

10. Start the Server project, as shown in the following commands:

```
cd Server
dotnet run
```

11. Note the app has the same functionality as before, but the code is executing inside the browser instead of on the server.

12. Close Chrome.

13. In **Visual Studio Code**, press *Ctrl + C* in **TERMINAL** to stop the web server.

Building components using Blazor Server

In this section we will build a component to list, create, and edit customers in the Northwind database.

Defining and testing a simple component

We will add the new component to the existing Blazor Server project:

1. In the NorthwindBlazorServer project, add a new file to the Pages folder named Customers.razor.

>
>
> **Good Practice**: Component filenames must start with an uppercase letter or you will see compile errors!

2. Add statements to register /customers as its route, output a heading for the customers component, and define a code block, as shown in the following markup:

```
@page "/customers"

<h1>Customers</h1>

@code {

}
```

3. In the Shared folder, open NavMenu.razor and add a list item element for our new component labeled Customers that uses an icon of people, as shown in the following markup:

```
<li class="nav-item px-3">
  <NavLink class="nav-link" href="customers">
    <span class="oi oi-people"
      aria-hidden="true"></span> Customers
  </NavLink>
</li>
```

More Information: You can see the available icons at the following link: https://iconify.design/icon-sets/oi/

4. Start the website project and navigate to it, and click **Customers**, as shown in the following screenshot:

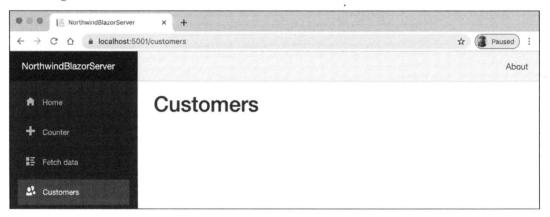

Figure 20.3: The Customers component shown as a page

5. Close Chrome.

6. In **Visual Studio Code**, press *Ctrl + C* in **TERMINAL** to stop the web server.

Getting entities into a component

Now that you have seen the minimum implementation of a component, we can add some useful functionality to it. In this case, we will use the Northwind database context to fetch customers from the database:

1. Open NorthwindBlazorServer.csproj, and add statements to reference the Northwind database context project, as shown highlighted in the following markup:

```
<Project Sdk="Microsoft.NET.Sdk.Web">

  <PropertyGroup>
    <TargetFramework>net5.0</TargetFramework>
  </PropertyGroup>

  <ItemGroup>
    <ProjectReference Include=
      "..\NorthwindContextLib\NorthwindContextLib.csproj" />
  </ItemGroup>

</Project>
```

2. In **TERMINAL**, restore packages and compile the project by entering the following command: dotnet build

3. Open Startup.cs and add the System.IO, Microsoft.EntityFrameworkCore, and Packt.Shared namespaces, as shown in the following code:

```
using Microsoft.EntityFrameworkCore;
using Packt.Shared;
using System.IO;
```

4. Add a statement to the ConfigureServices method to register the Northwind database context class to use SQLite as its database provider and specify its database connection string, as shown in the following code:

```
string databasePath = Path.Combine("..", "Northwind.db");
services.AddDbContext<Northwind>(options =>
    options.UseSqlite($"Data Source={databasePath}"));
```

5. Open _Imports.razor and import the NorthwindBlazorServer.Data, Microsoft. EntityFrameworkCore, and Packt.Shared namespaces, so that Blazor components that we build do not need to import the namespaces individually, as shown highlighted in the following markup:

```
@using System.Net.Http
@using Microsoft.AspNetCore.Authorization
@using Microsoft.AspNetCore.Components.Authorization
@using Microsoft.AspNetCore.Components.Forms
@using Microsoft.AspNetCore.Components.Routing
@using Microsoft.AspNetCore.Components.Web
@using Microsoft.JSInterop
@using NorthwindBlazorServer
@using NorthwindBlazorServer.Shared
@using NorthwindBlazorServer.Data
@using Microsoft.EntityFrameworkCore
@using Packt.Shared
```

6. In the Pages folder, open Customers.razor, inject the Northwind database context, and use it to output a table of all customers, as shown in the following code:

```
@page "/customers"
@inject Northwind db

<h1>Customers</h1>
@if (customers == null)
{
    <p><em>Loading...</em></p>
}
else
{
    <table class="table">
```

```
    <thead>
      <tr>
        <th>ID</th>
        <th>Company Name</th>
        <th>Address</th>
        <th>Phone</th>
        <th></th>
      </tr>
    </thead>
    <tbody>
      @foreach (var customer in customers)
      {
      <tr>
        <td>@customer.CustomerID</td>
        <td>@customer.CompanyName</td>
        <td>@customer.Address<br/>
        @customer.City<br/>
        @customer.PostalCode<br/>
        @customer.Country</td>
        <td>@customer.Phone</td>
        <td>
          <a class="btn btn-info"
             href="editcustomer/@customer.CustomerID">
               <i class="oi oi-pencil"></i></a>
          <a class="btn btn-danger"
             href="deletecustomer/@customer.CustomerID">
               <i class="oi oi-trash"></i></a>
        </td>
      </tr>
      }
    </tbody>
  </table>
}

@code {
  private IEnumerable<Customer> customers;

  protected override async Task OnInitializedAsync()
  {
    customers = await db.Customers.ToListAsync();
  }
}
```

7. In **TERMINAL**, enter the command `dotnet run` to start the website.

8. In Chrome, enter `https://localhost:5001/`, click **Customers**, and note the table of customers loads from the database and renders in the web page, as shown in the following screenshot:

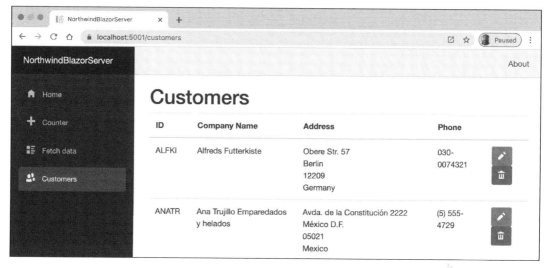

Figure 20.4: The list of customers

9. Close the browser.

10. In **Visual Studio Code**, press *Ctrl + C* in **TERMINAL** to stop the web server.

There are many built-in Blazor components, including ones to set elements like `<title>` in the `<head>` section of a web page, and plenty of third parties who will sell you components for common purposes.

 More Information: You can read more about setting `<head>` elements at the following link: `https://docs.microsoft.com/en-us/aspnet/core/blazor/fundamentals/additional-scenarios-influence-html-head-tag-elements`

Abstracting a service for a Blazor component

Currently, the Blazor component directly calls the `Northwind` database context to fetch the customers. This works fine in Blazor Server since the component executes on the server. But this component would not work when hosted in Blazor WebAssembly.

We will now create a local dependency service to enable better reuse of the components:

1. In the `Data` folder, add a new file named `INorthwindService.cs` and modify its contents to define a contract for a local service that abstracts CRUD operations, as shown in the following code:

```
using System.Collections.Generic;
using System.Threading.Tasks;

namespace Packt.Shared
{
  public interface INorthwindService
  {
    Task<List<Customer>> GetCustomersAsync();
    Task<Customer> GetCustomerAsync(string id);
    Task<Customer> CreateCustomerAsync(Customer c);
    Task<Customer> UpdateCustomerAsync(Customer c);
    Task DeleteCustomerAsync(string id);
  }
}
```

2. In the Data folder, add a new file named NorthwindService.cs, and modify its contents
   to implement the INorthwindService interface by using the Northwind database context,
   as shown in the following code:

```
using System.Collections.Generic;
using System.Threading.Tasks;
using Microsoft.EntityFrameworkCore;
using Packt.Shared;

namespace NorthwindBlazorServer.Data
{
  public class NorthwindService : INorthwindService
  {
    private readonly Northwind db;

    public NorthwindService(Northwind db)
    {
      this.db = db;
    }

    public Task<List<Customer>> GetCustomersAsync()
    {
      return db.Customers.ToListAsync();
    }

    public Task<Customer> GetCustomerAsync(string id)
    {
      return db.Customers.FirstOrDefaultAsync
        (c => c.CustomerID == id);
    }

    public Task<Customer> CreateCustomerAsync(Customer c)
```

```
    {
      db.Customers.Add(c);
      db.SaveChangesAsync();
      return Task.FromResult<Customer>(c);
    }

    public Task<Customer> UpdateCustomerAsync(Customer c)
    {
      db.Entry(c).State = EntityState.Modified;
      db.SaveChangesAsync();
      return Task.FromResult<Customer>(c);
    }

    public Task DeleteCustomerAsync(string id)
    {
      Customer customer = db.Customers.FirstOrDefaultAsync
        (c => c.CustomerID == id).Result;
      db.Customers.Remove(customer);
      return db.SaveChangesAsync();
    }
  }
}
```

3. Open `Startup.cs` and in the `ConfigureServices` method add a statement to register the `NorthwindService` as a transient service that implements the `INorthwindService` interface, as shown in the following code:

    ```
    services.AddTransient
      <INorthwindService, NorthwindService>();
    ```

4. In the `Pages` folder, open `Customers.razor`, remove the directive to inject the `Northwind` database context, and add a directive to inject the registered Northwind service, as shown in the following code:

    ```
    @inject INorthwindService service
    ```

5. Modify the `OnInitializedAsync` method to call the service, as shown in the following code:

    ```
    customers = await service.GetCustomersAsync();
    ```

6. If you would like, run the `NorthwindBlazorServer` website project to test that it retains the same functionality as before.

Using Blazor forms

Microsoft provides ready-made components for building forms. We will use them to provide, create, and edit functionality for customers.

Defining forms using the EditForm component

Microsoft provides the **EditForm** component and several form elements like InputText to make it easier to use forms with Blazor.

EditForm can have a model set to bind it to an object with properties and event handlers for custom validation, as well as recognizing standard Microsoft validation attributes on the model class, as shown in the following code:

```
<EditForm Model="@customer" OnSubmit="ExtraValidation">
  <DataAnnotationsValidator />
  <ValidationSummary />
  <InputText id="name" @bind-Value="customer.CompanyName" />
  <button type="submit">Submit</button>
</EditForm>

@code {
  private Customer customer = new Customer();

  private void ExtraValidation()
  {
    // perform validation
  }
}
```

As an alternative to a ValidationSummary component, you can use the ValidationMessage component to show a message next to an individual form element.

More Information: You can read more about forms and validation at the following link: https://docs.microsoft.com/en-us/aspnet/core/blazor/forms-validation

Navigating Blazor routes

Microsoft provides a dependency service named NavigationManager that understands Blazor routing and the NavLink component.

The NavigateTo method is used to go to the specified URL.

More Information: You can read more about using NavigationManager with Blazor routes at the following link: https://docs.microsoft.com/en-us/aspnet/core/blazor/fundamentals/routing#uri-and-navigation-state-helpers

Building and using a customer form component

Now we can create a custom component to create or edit a customer:

1. In the Pages folder, create a new file named CustomerDetail.razor and modify its contents to define a form to edit the properties of a customer, as shown in the following code:

```
<EditForm Model="@Customer" OnValidSubmit="@OnValidSubmit">
  <DataAnnotationsValidator />
  <div class="form-group">
    <div>
      <label>Customer ID</label>
      <div>
        <InputText @bind-Value="@Customer.CustomerID" />
        <ValidationMessage
          For="@(() => Customer.CustomerID)" />
      </div>
    </div>
  </div>
  <div class="form-group ">
    <div>
      <label>Company Name</label>
      <div>
        <InputText @bind-Value="@Customer.CompanyName" />
        <ValidationMessage
          For="@(() => Customer.CompanyName)" />
      </div>
    </div>
  </div>
  <div class="form-group ">
    <div>
      <label>Address</label>
      <div>
        <InputText @bind-Value="@Customer.Address" />
        <ValidationMessage
          For="@(() => Customer.Address)" />
      </div>
    </div>
  </div>
  <div class="form-group ">
    <div>
      <label>Country</label>
      <div>
        <InputText @bind-Value="@Customer.Country" />
        <ValidationMessage
          For="@(() => Customer.Country)" />
```

```
          </div>
        </div>
      </div>
      <button type="submit" class="btn btn-@ButtonStyle">
        @ButtonText
      </button>
  </EditForm>

  @code {
    [Parameter]
    public Customer Customer { get; set; }

    [Parameter]
    public string ButtonText { get; set; } = "Save Changes";

    [Parameter]
    public string ButtonStyle { get; set; } = "info";

    [Parameter]
    public EventCallback OnValidSubmit { get; set; }
  }
```

2. In the Pages folder, create a new file named CreateCustomer.razor and modify its contents to use the customer detail component to create a new customer, as shown in the following code:

```
@page "/createcustomer"
@inject INorthwindService service
@inject NavigationManager navigation

<h3>Create Customer</h3>
<CustomerDetail ButtonText="Create Customer"
                Customer="@customer"
                OnValidSubmit="@Create" />

@code {
  private Customer customer = new Customer();

  private async Task Create()
  {
    await service.CreateCustomerAsync(customer);
    navigation.NavigateTo("customers");
  }
}
```

3. In the Pages folder, open the file named `Customers.razor` and after the `<h1>` element, add a `<div>` element with a button to navigate to the create customer component, as shown in the following markup:

```
<div class="form-group">
  <a class="btn btn-info" href="createcustomer">
    <i class="oi oi-plus"></i> Create New</a>
</div>
```

4. In the Pages folder, create a new file named `EditCustomer.razor` and modify its contents to use the customer detail component to edit and save changes to an existing customer, as shown in the following code:

```
@page "/editcustomer/{customerid}"
@inject INorthwindService service
@inject NavigationManager navigation
<h3>Edit Customer</h3>
<CustomerDetail ButtonText="Update"
                Customer="@customer"
                OnValidSubmit="@Update" />
@code {
  [Parameter]
  public string CustomerID { get; set; }

  private Customer customer = new Customer();

  protected async override Task OnParametersSetAsync()
  {
    customer = await service.GetCustomerAsync(CustomerID);
  }

  private async Task Update()
  {
    await service.UpdateCustomerAsync(customer);
    navigation.NavigateTo("customers");
  }
}
```

5. In the Pages folder, create a new file named `DeleteCustomer.razor` and modify its contents to use the customer detail component to show the customer that is about to be deleted, as shown in the following code:

```
@page "/deletecustomer/{customerid}"
@inject INorthwindService service
@inject NavigationManager navigation
<h3>Delete Customer</h3>
<div class="alert alert-danger">
  Warning! This action cannot be undone!
</div>
<CustomerDetail ButtonText="Delete Customer"
```

```
                        ButtonStyle="danger"
                        Customer="@customer"
                        OnValidSubmit="@Delete" />
    @code {
      [Parameter]
      public string CustomerID { get; set; }

      private Customer customer = new Customer();

      protected async override Task OnParametersSetAsync()
      {
        customer = await service.GetCustomerAsync(CustomerID);
      }

      private async Task Delete()
      {
        await service.DeleteCustomerAsync(CustomerID);
        navigation.NavigateTo("customers");
      }
    }
  }
```

6. Start the website project and navigate to `https://localhost:5001/`.

7. Navigate to **Customers** and click the **+ Create New** button.

8. Enter an invalid **Customer ID** like ABCDEF, leave the text box, and note the validation message, as shown in the following screenshot:

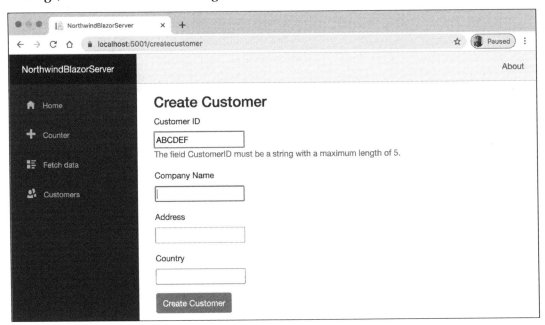

Figure 20.5: Creating a new customer and entering an invalid Customer ID

9. Change the **Customer ID** to ABCDE, enter values for the other textboxes, and click the **Create Customer** button, as shown in the following screenshot:

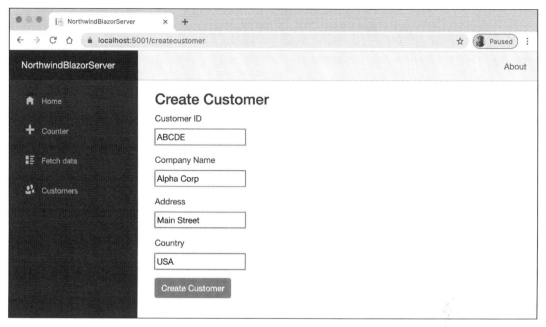

Figure 20.6: New customer information that validates successfully

10. When the list of customers appears, scroll down to the bottom of the page to see the new customer, as shown in the following screenshot:

Figure 20.7: Viewing the new customer

11. On the **ABCDE** customer row, click the **Edit** icon button, change the address, click **Update**, and note that the customer record has been updated.

12. On the **ABCDE** customer row, click the **Delete** icon button, note the warning, click the **Delete Customer** button, and note that the customer record has been deleted, as shown in the following screenshot:

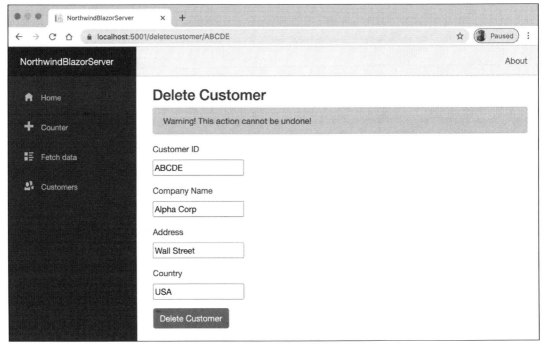

Figure 20.8: Deleting a customer

13. Close Chrome.
14. In **Visual Studio Code**, press *Ctrl + C* in **TERMINAL** to stop the web server.

Building components using Blazor WebAssembly

Now we will build the same functionality using Blazor WebAssembly so that you can clearly see the key differences.

Since we abstracted the local dependency service in the INorthwindService interface, we will be able to reuse all the components and that interface, as well as the entity model classes, and just rewrite the implementation of the NorthwindService class and create a customer controller for its implementation to call for Blazor WebAssembly, as shown in the following diagram:

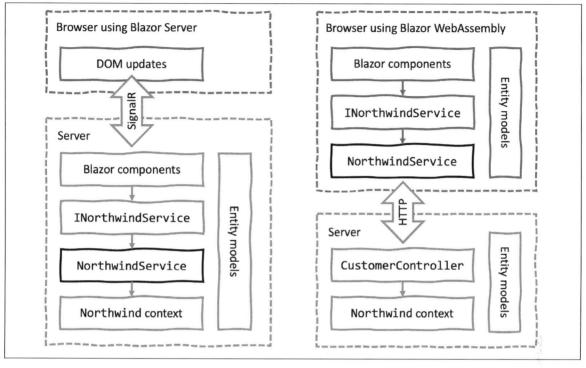

Figure 20.9: Comparing Blazor implementations using Server and WebAssembly

Configuring the server for Blazor WebAssembly

First, we need to build a service that the client app can call using HTTP:

> **Warning!** All relative path references for projects and the database are two levels up, for example, `"..\..\"`.

1. In the **Server** project, open `NorthwindBlazorWasm.Server.csproj`, and add statements to reference the `Northwind` database context project, as shown in the following markup:

```
<ItemGroup>
  <ProjectReference Include=
    "..\..\NorthwindContextLib\NorthwindContextLib.csproj" />
</ItemGroup>
```

2. In **TERMINAL**, in the `Server` folder, restore packages and compile the project, as shown in the following command:

```
dotnet build
```

3. In the **Server** project, open `Startup.cs`, and add statements to import some namespaces, as shown in the following code:

```
using Packt.Shared;
using Microsoft.EntityFrameworkCore;
using System.IO;
```

4. In the `ConfigureServices` method, add statements to register the `Northwind` database context, as shown in the following code:

```
string databasePath = Path.Combine(
  "..", "..", "Northwind.db");


services.AddDbContext<Northwind>(options =>
  options.UseSqlite($"Data Source={databasePath}"));
```

5. In the **Server** project, in the `Controllers` folder, create a file named `CustomersController.cs`, and add statements to define a Web API controller class with similar CRUD methods as before, as shown in the following code:

```
using System.Collections.Generic;
using System.Threading.Tasks;
using Microsoft.AspNetCore.Mvc;
using Microsoft.EntityFrameworkCore;
using Packt.Shared;

namespace NorthwindBlazorWasm.Server.Controllers
{
  [ApiController]
  [Route("api/[controller]")]
  public class CustomersController : ControllerBase
  {
    private readonly Northwind db;

    public CustomersController(Northwind db)
    {
      this.db = db;
    }


    [HttpGet]
    public async Task<List<Customer>> GetCustomersAsync()
    {
      return await db.Customers.ToListAsync();
    }
```

```csharp
[HttpGet("{id}")]
public async Task<Customer> GetCustomerAsync(string id)
{
  return await db.Customers.FirstOrDefaultAsync
    (c => c.CustomerID == id);
}

[HttpPost]
public async Task<Customer>CreateCustomerAsync
  (Customer customerToAdd)
{
  Customer existing = await db.Customers
    .FirstOrDefaultAsync
    (c => c.CustomerID == customerToAdd.CustomerID);

  if (existing == null)
  {
    db.Customers.Add(customerToAdd);
    int affected = await db.SaveChangesAsync();
    if (affected == 1)
    {
      return customerToAdd;
    }
  }
  return existing;
}

[HttpPut]
public async Task<Customer> UpdateCustomerAsync
  (Customer c)
{
  db.Entry(c).State = EntityState.Modified;
  int affected = await db.SaveChangesAsync();
  if (affected == 1)
  {
    return c;
  }
  return null;
}

[HttpDelete("{id}")]
public async Task<int> DeleteCustomerAsync(string id)
{
  Customer c = await db.Customers.FirstOrDefaultAsync
    (c => c.CustomerID == id);
```

```
        if (c != null)
        {
          db.Customers.Remove(c);
          int affected = await db.SaveChangesAsync();
          return affected;
        }
        return 0;
    }
  }
}
```

Configuring the client for Blazor WebAssembly

Second, we can reuse the components from the Blazor Server project. Since the components will be identical, we can copy them and only need to make changes to the local implementation of the abstracted Northwind service:

1. In the **Client** project, open `NorthwindBlazorWasm.Client.csproj`, and add statements to reference the Northwind entities library project, as shown in the following markup:

    ```
    <ItemGroup>
      <ProjectReference Include=
    "..\..\NorthwindEntitiesLib\NorthwindEntitiesLib.csproj" />
    </ItemGroup>
    ```

2. In **TERMINAL**, in the `Client` folder, restore packages and compile the project, as shown in the following commands:

    ```
    cd ..
    cd Client
    dotnet build
    ```

3. In the **Client** project, open `_Imports.razor` and import the `Packt.Shared` namespace to make the Northwind entity model types available in all Blazor components, as shown in the following code:

    ```
    @using Packt.Shared
    ```

4. In the **Client** project, in the `Shared` folder, open `NavMenu.razor` and add a `NavLink` element for customers, as shown in the following markup:

    ```
    <li class="nav-item px-3">
      <NavLink class="nav-link" href="customers">
        <span class="oi oi-people" aria-hidden="true">
          </span> Customers
      </NavLink>
    </li>
    ```

5. Copy the following five components from the `NorthwindBlazorServer` project `Pages` folder to the `NorthwindBlazorWasm` `Client` project `Pages` folder:

   - `CreateCustomer.razor`

   - `CustomerDetail.razor`

   - `Customers.razor`

   - `DeleteCustomer.razor`

   - `EditCustomer.razor`

6. In the **Client** project, create a `Data` folder.

7. Copy the `INorthwindService.cs` file from the `NorthwindBlazorServer` project `Data` folder into the `Client` project `Data` folder.

8. In the `Data` folder, add a new file named `NorthwindService.cs`, and modify its contents to implement the `INorthwindService` interface by using an `HttpClient` to call the customers Web API service, as shown in the following code:

```
using System.Collections.Generic;
using System.Net.Http;
using System.Net.Http.Json;
using System.Threading.Tasks;
using Packt.Shared;

namespace NorthwindBlazorWasm.Client.Data
{
  public class NorthwindService : INorthwindService
  {
    private readonly HttpClient http;

    public NorthwindService(HttpClient http)
    {
      this.http = http;
    }

    public Task<List<Customer>> GetCustomersAsync()
    {
      return http.GetFromJsonAsync
        <List<Customer>>("api/customers");
    }

    public Task<Customer> GetCustomerAsync(string id)
    {
      return http.GetFromJsonAsync
        <Customer>($"api/customers/{id}");
    }
```

```
    public async Task<Customer> CreateCustomerAsync
      (Customer c)
    {
      HttpResponseMessage response = await
        http.PostAsJsonAsync<Customer>
        ("api/customers", c);

      return await response.Content
        .ReadFromJsonAsync<Customer>();
    }

    public async Task<Customer> UpdateCustomerAsync
      (Customer c)
    {
      HttpResponseMessage response = await
        http.PutAsJsonAsync<Customer>
        ("api/customers", c);

      return await response.Content
        .ReadFromJsonAsync<Customer>();
    }

    public async Task DeleteCustomerAsync(string id)
    {
      HttpResponseMessage response = await
        http.DeleteAsync($"api/customers/{id}");
    }
  }
}
```

9. Open `Program.cs` and import the `Packt.Shared` and `NorthwindBlazorWasm.Client.Data` namespaces.

10. In the `ConfigureServices` method, add a statement to register the Northwind dependency service, as shown in the following code:

```
builder.Services.AddTransient
  <INorthwindService, NorthwindService>();
```

11. In **TERMINAL**, in the `Server` folder, compile the project, as shown in the following commands:

```
cd ..
cd Server
dotnet run
```

12. Start Chrome, show **Developer Tools**, and select the **Network** tab.

13. In the address bar, enter the following: `https://localhost:5001/`.

14. Select the **Console** tab and note that Blazor WebAssembly has loaded .NET 5 assemblies into the browser cache, as shown in the following screenshot:

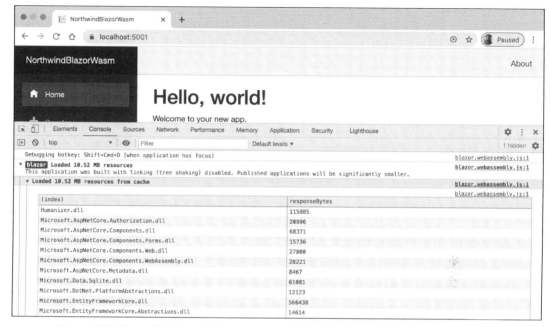

Figure 20.10: Blazor WebAssembly loading .NET 5 assemblies into the browser cache

15. Select the **Network** tab.

16. Click **Customers** and note the HTTP GET request with the JSON response containing all the customers, as shown in the following screenshot:

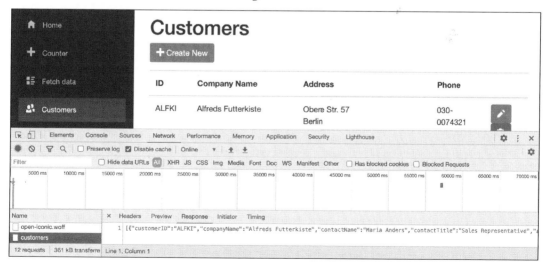

Figure 20.11: The HTTP GET request with JSON response for customers

17. Click the **+ Create New** button, complete the form to add a new customer as before, and note the HTTP POST request made, as shown in the following screenshot:

Figure 20.12: The HTTP POST request for creating a new customer

Exploring Progressive Web App support

Progressive Web App (PWA) support in Blazor WebAssembly projects means that the web app gains the following benefits:

- It acts as a normal web page until the visitor explicitly decides to progress to a full app experience.

- After the app is installed, launch it from the OS's start menu or desktop.

- It visually appears in its own app window instead of a browser tab.

- It works offline (if the developer has put in the effort to make this work well).

- It automatically updates.

Let us see PWA support in action:

1. In Chrome, in the address bar on the right, click the circled plus button with the tooltip **Install NorthwindBlazorWasm** and then click the **Install** button, as shown in the following screenshot:

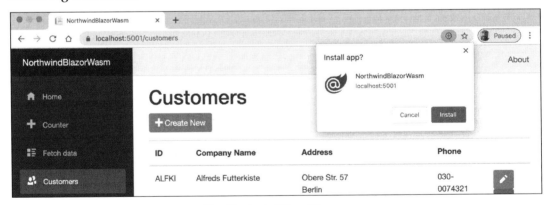

Figure 20.13: Installing NorthwindBlazorWasm as an app

2. Close Chrome.

3. Launch the **NorthwindBlazorWasm** app from your macOS Launchpad or Windows Start menu, and note it has a full app experience.

4. On the right of the title bar, click the three dots menu, and note that you can uninstall the app, but do not do so yet, as shown in the following screenshot:

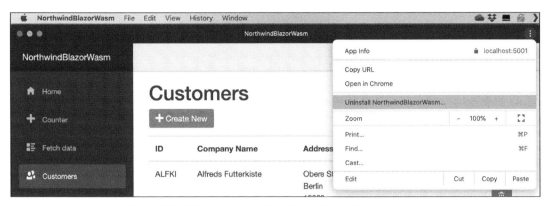

Figure 20.14: How to uninstall NorthwindBlazorWasm

5. Navigate to **View** | **Developer** | **Developer Tools** or, on Windows, press *F12*.

6. Select the **Network** tab, in the **Throttling** dropdown, select **Offline**, then in the app navigate to **Customers**, and note the failure to load any customers and the error message at the bottom of the app window, as shown in the following screenshot:

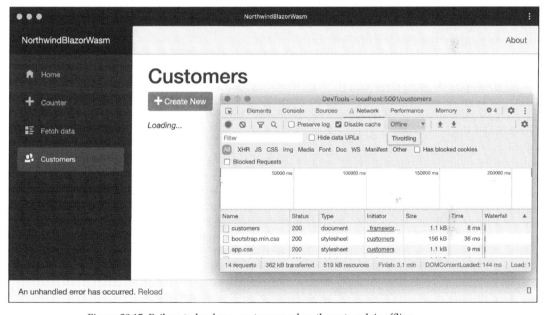

Figure 20.15: Failure to load any customers when the network is offline

7. In **Developer Tools**, set **Throttling** back to **Online**.

8. Click the **Reload** link in the yellow error bar at the bottom of the app and note that functionality returns.

9. Close the app.

We could improve the experience by caching HTTP GET responses from the Web API service locally, and storing new customers and modified or deleted customers locally, and then synchronizing with the server later by making the HTTP requests once network connectivity is restored, but that takes a lot of effort to implement well.

More Information: You can read more about implementing offline support for Blazor WebAssembly projects at the following link: `https://docs.microsoft.com/en-us/aspnet/core/blazor/progressive-web-app#offline-support`

Another way to improve Blazor WebAssembly projects is to use lazy loading of assemblies.

More Information: You can read about lazy loading assemblies at the following link: `https://docs.microsoft.com/en-us/aspnet/core/blazor/webassembly-lazy-load-assemblies?view=aspnetcore-5.0`

Practicing and exploring

Test your knowledge and understanding by answering some questions, get some hands-on practice, and explore this chapter's topics with deeper research.

Exercise 20.1 – Test your knowledge

Answer the following questions:

1. What are the two primary hosting models for Blazor and how are they different?
2. In a Blazor Server website project, compared to an ASP.NET Core MVC website project, what extra configuration is required in the `Startup` class?
3. One of the benefits of Blazor is being able to implement user interface components using C# and .NET instead of JavaScript. Does Blazor need any JavaScript?
4. In a Blazor project, what does the `App.razor` file do?
5. What is a benefit of using the `<NavLink>` component?
6. How can you pass a value into a component?
7. What is a benefit of using the `<EditForm>` component?
8. How can you execute some statements when parameters are set?
9. How can you execute some statements when a component appears?
10. What are two key differences in the `Program` class between a Blazor Server and Blazor WebAssembly project?

Exercise 20.2 – Practice creating a component

Create a component that renders a times table based on a parameter named `Number` and then test your component in two ways.

First, by adding an instance of your component to the `Index.razor` file, as shown in the following markup:

```
<timestable Number="6" />
```

Second, by entering a path in the browser address bar, as shown in the following link:

```
https://localhost:5001/timestable/6
```

Exercise 20.3 – Explore topics

Use the following links to read more about this chapter's topics:

- **Awesome Blazor**: A collection of awesome Blazor resources: `https://github.com/AdrienTorris/awesome-blazor`

- **Blazor University**: Learn the new .NET SPA framework from Microsoft: `https://blazor-university.com`

- **Blazor - app building workshop**: In this workshop, we will build a complete Blazor app and learn about the various Blazor framework features along the way: `https://github.com/dotnet-presentations/blazor-workshop/`

- **Carl Franklin's Blazor Train**: `https://www.youtube.com/playlist?list=PL8h4jt35t1wjvwFnvcB2LlYL4jLRzRmoz`

- **Routing in Blazor Apps**: Comparing the routing of popular web frameworks like React and Angular with Blazor: `https://devblogs.microsoft.com/premier-developer/routing-in-blazor-apps/`

- **Welcome to PACMAN written in C# and running on Blazor WebAssembly**: `https://github.com/SteveDunn/PacManBlazor`

Summary

In this chapter, you learned how to build Blazor components for both Server and WebAssembly. You saw some of the key differences between the two hosting models, like how data should be managed using dependency services.

In the next chapter, you will learn how to build mobile apps using Xamarin.Forms.

21

Building Cross-Platform Mobile Apps

This chapter is about learning how to take C# mobile by building a cross-platform mobile app for iOS and Android. The mobile app will allow the listing and management of customers in the Northwind database.

You will see how **eXtensible Application Markup Language (XAML)** makes it easy to define the user interface for a graphical app.

Apart from **Universal Windows Platform (UWP)** apps covered in *Appendix B, Building Windows Desktop Apps*, this is the only chapter that does not use .NET 5. But by 2021, with the release of .NET 6, all app models, including mobile, will share the same unified .NET platform.

Mobile development cannot be learned in a single chapter, but like web development, mobile development is so important that I want to introduce you to some of what is possible. Think of this chapter as a bonus. This chapter will give you a taste to inspire you, and then you can learn more from a book dedicated to mobile development.

> **More Information**: Packt has two books about Xamarin.Forms with 4.5 stars on Amazon – *Xamarin.Forms Projects*, available at the following link: https://www.packtpub.com/product/xamarin-forms-projects-second-edition/9781839210051, and *Mastering Xamarin.Forms*, available at the following link: https://www.packtpub.com/product/mastering-xamarin-forms-third-edition/9781839213380

The mobile app that you create will call the Northwind service that you built using ASP.NET Core Web API in *Chapter 18, Building and Consuming Web Services*. If you have not built the Northwind service, please go back and build it now or download it from the GitHub repository for this book at the following link: https://github.com/markjprice/cs9dotnet5.

You will need a computer with macOS, Xcode, and Visual Studio for Mac to complete this chapter.

In this chapter, we will cover the following topics:

- Understanding XAML
- Understanding Xamarin and Xamarin.Forms
- Building mobile apps using Xamarin.Forms
- Consuming a web service from a mobile app

Understanding XAML

In 2006, Microsoft released **Windows Presentation Foundation (WPF)**, which was the first technology to use XAML. Silverlight, for web and mobile apps, quickly followed, but it is no longer supported by Microsoft. WPF is still used today to create Windows desktop applications; for example, Microsoft Visual Studio 2019 is partially built using WPF.

XAML can be used to build parts of the following apps:

- **UWP apps** for Windows 10 devices, Xbox One, and Mixed Reality headsets.
- **WPF apps** for Windows desktop, including Windows 7 and later.
- **Xamarin.Forms apps** for mobile and desktop devices, including Android, iOS, Windows, and macOS. In 2021, with the release of .NET 6, this will evolve into .NET MAUI (**Multi-platform App User Interface**).

Simplifying code using XAML

XAML simplifies C# code, especially when building a user interface.

Imagine that you need two or more buttons laid out horizontally to create a toolbar.

In C#, you might write this code:

```
var toolbar = new StackPanel();
toolbar.Orientation = Orientation.Horizontal;
var newButton = new Button();
newButton.Content = "New";
newButton.Background = new SolidColorBrush(Colors.Pink);
toolbar.Children.Add(newButton);
var openButton = new Button();
openButton.Content = "Open";
openButton.Background = new SolidColorBrush(Colors.Pink);
toolbar.Children.Add(openButton);
```

In XAML, this could be simplified to the following lines of code. When this XAML is processed, the equivalent properties are set, and methods are called to achieve the same goal as the preceding C# code:

```
<StackPanel Name="toolbar" Orientation="Horizontal">
  <Button Name="newButton" Background="Pink">New</Button>
  <Button Name="openButton" Background="Pink">Open</Button>
</StackPanel>
```

XAML is an alternative and better way of declaring and instantiating .NET types for use in a user interface.

Choosing common controls

There are lots of predefined controls that you can choose from for common user interface scenarios. Almost all dialects of XAML support these controls:

Controls	Description
Button, Menu, Toolbar	Executing actions
CheckBox, RadioButton	Choosing options
Calendar, DatePicker	Choosing dates
ComboBox, ListBox, ListView, TreeView	Choosing items from lists and hierarchical trees
Canvas, DockPanel, Grid, StackPanel, WrapPanel	Layout containers that affect their children in different ways
Label, TextBlock	Displaying read-only text
RichTextBox, TextBox	Editing text
Image, MediaElement	Embedding images, videos, and audio files
DataGrid	Viewing and editing data as quickly and easily as possible
Scrollbar, Slider, StatusBar	Miscellaneous user interface elements

Understanding markup extensions

To support some advanced features, XAML uses markup extensions. Some of the most important enable element and data binding and the reuse of resources, as shown in the following list:

- {Binding} links an element to a value from another element or a data source.
- {StaticResource} links an element to a shared resource.
- {ThemeResource} links an element to a shared resource defined in a theme.

You will see some practical examples of markup extensions throughout this chapter.

Understanding Xamarin and Xamarin.Forms

To create a mobile app that only needs to run on iPhones, you might choose to build it with either the Objective-C or Swift language and the UIKit libraries using the Xcode development tool.

To create a mobile app that only needs to run on Android phones, you might choose to build it with either the Java or Kotlin language and the Android SDK libraries using the Android Studio development tool.

 More Information: In 2020, iPhone and Android have a combined global smartphone market share of 99.6%. What about the other 0.4%? Xamarin supports creating Tizen mobile apps for Samsung devices. You can read about Tizen .NET at the following link: `https://docs.microsoft.com/en-us/xamarin/xamarin-forms/platform/other/tizen`

But what if you need to create a mobile app that can run on iPhones and Android phones? And what if you only want to create that mobile app once using a programming language and development platform that you are already familiar with?

Xamarin enables developers to build cross-platform mobile apps for Apple iOS (iPhone), iPadOS, macOS, and Google Android using C# and .NET, which are then compiled to native APIs and run on native phone and desktop platforms. It is based on the open source implementation of .NET known as **Mono**.

Business logic layer code can be written once and shared between all platforms. User interface interactions and APIs are different on various mobile platforms, so the user interface layer is often custom for each platform. But even here, there is a technology that can ease development.

How Xamarin.Forms extends Xamarin

Xamarin.Forms extends Xamarin to make cross-platform mobile development even easier by sharing most of the user interface layer, as well as the business logic layer.

Like WPF and UWP apps, Xamarin.Forms uses XAML to define the user interface once for all platforms using abstractions of platform-specific user interface components. Applications built with Xamarin.Forms draw the user interface using native platform widgets, so the app's look-and-feel fits naturally with the target mobile platform.

A user experience built using Xamarin.Forms will never perfectly fit a specific platform like one custom built with Xamarin, but for mobile apps that will not have millions of users, it is good enough.

Development tools for mobile first, cloud first

Mobile apps are often supported by services in the cloud.

Satya Nadella, CEO of Microsoft, famously said this:

> *To me, when we say mobile first, it's not the mobility of the device, it's actually the mobility of the individual experience. [...] The only way you are going to be able to orchestrate the mobility of these applications and data is through the cloud.*

As you have seen earlier in this book, to create an ASP.NET Core Web API service to support a mobile app, we can use Visual Studio Code. To create Xamarin.Forms apps, developers can use either Visual Studio 2019 or Visual Studio for Mac. To compile iOS apps, you will require a Mac and Xcode.

 More Information: If you want to use Visual Studio 2019 to create a mobile app, then you can read how to connect to a Mac build host at the following link: `https://docs.microsoft.com/en-us/xamarin/ios/get-started/installation/windows/connecting-to-mac/`

A summary of which coding tool can be used on its own to build which type of app is shown in the following table:

	iOS	Android	ASP.NET Core Web API
Visual Studio Code	No	No	Yes
Visual Studio for Mac	Yes	Yes	Yes
Visual Studio 2019	No	Yes	Yes

Mobile platform market share

Market share numbers should be taken in the context that iOS users engage far more with their devices, which is important for monetizing mobile apps, either through up-front sales, in-app purchases, or advertising. Recent analyst reports show that iPhone apps tend to generate at least 60% more revenue than Android apps but do your own research here as the mobile world moves fast.

 More Information: You can read about the pros and cons of the two major mobile platforms based on aspects such as revenue generation and user engagement at the following link: `https://fueled.com/blog/app-store-vs-google-play/`

Understanding additional functionality

We will build a mobile app that uses a lot of the skills and knowledge that you learned in previous chapters. We will also use some functionality that you have not seen before.

Understanding the INotificationPropertyChanged interface

The `INotifyPropertyChanged` interface enables a model class to support two-way data binding. It works by forcing the class to have an event named `PropertyChanged`, as shown in the following code:

```
using System.ComponentModel;

public interface INotifyPropertyChanged
{
  event PropertyChangedEventHandler PropertyChanged;
}
```

Inside each property in the class, when setting a new value, you must raise the event (if it is not `null`) with an instance of `PropertyChangedEventArgs` containing the name of the property as a `string` value, as shown in the following code:

```
private string companyName;

public string CompanyName
{
  get => companyName;

  set
  {
    companyName = value; // store the new value being set

    PropertyChanged?.Invoke(this,
      new PropertyChangedEventArgs(nameof(CompanyName)));
  }
}
```

When a user interface control is data-bound to the property, it will automatically update to show the new value when it changes.

This interface is not just for mobile apps. It can also be used in other graphical user interfaces such as Windows desktop apps.

Understanding dependency services

Mobile platforms such as iOS and Android implement common features in different ways, so we need a way to get a platform-native implementation of common features. We can do that using dependency services. It works like this:

- Define an interface for the common feature, for example, `IDialer` for a phone number dialer.

- Implement the interface for all the mobile platforms that you need to support, for example, iOS and Android, and register the implementations with an attribute, as shown in the following code:

```
[assembly: Dependency(typeof(PhoneDialer))]
namespace NorthwindMobile.iOS
{
    public class PhoneDialer : IDialer
```

- In the common mobile project, get the platform-native implementation of an interface by using the dependency service, as shown in the following code:

```
var dialer = DependencyService.Get<IDialer>();
```

 More Information: You can read more about Xamarin dependency services at the following link: https://docs.microsoft.com/en-us/xamarin/ xamarin-forms/app-fundamentals/dependency-service/introduction

Understanding Xamarin.Forms user interface components

Xamarin.Forms includes some specialized controls for building mobile user interfaces. They are divided into four categories:

- **Pages**: represent cross-platform mobile application screens, for example, ContentPage, NavigationPage, and CarouselPage.

- **Layouts**: represent the structure of a combination of other user interface components, for example, StackLayout, RelativeLayout, and FlexLayout.

- **Views**: represent a single user interface component, for example, Label, Entry, Editor, and Button.

- **Cells**: represent a single item in a list or table view, for example, TextCell, ImageCell, SwitchCell, and EntryCell.

Understanding the ContentPage view

The ContentPage view is for simple user interfaces.

It has a ToolbarItems property that shows actions the user can perform in a platform-native way. Each ToolbarItem can have an icon and text:

```
<ContentPage.ToolbarItems>
  <ToolbarItem Text="Add" Activated="Add_Activated"
    Order="Primary" Priority="0" />
</ContentPage.ToolbarItems>
```

More Information: You can read more about Xamarin.Forms Pages at the following link: https://docs.microsoft.com/en-us/xamarin/xamarin-forms/user-interface/controls/pages

Understanding the Entry and Editor controls

The `Entry` and `Editor` controls are used for editing text values and are often data-bound to an entity model property, as shown in the following markup:

```
<Editor Text="{Binding CompanyName, Mode=TwoWay}" />
```

Use `Entry` for a single line of text.

More Information: You can read about the `Entry` control at the following link: https://docs.microsoft.com/en-us/xamarin/xamarin-forms/user-interface/text/entry

Use `Editor` for multiple lines of text.

More Information: You can read about the `Editor` control at the following link: https://docs.microsoft.com/en-us/xamarin/xamarin-forms/user-interface/text/editor

Understanding the ListView control

The `ListView` control is used for long lists of data-bound values of the same type. It can have headers and footers and its list items can be grouped.

It has cells to contain each list item. There are two built-in cell types: text and image. Developers can define custom cell types.

Cells can have context actions that appear when the cell is swiped on iPhone or long pressed on Android. A context action that is destructive can be shown in red, as shown in the following markup:

```
<TextCell Text="{Binding CompanyName}" Detail="{Binding Location}">
  <TextCell.ContextActions>
    <MenuItem Clicked="Customer_Phoned" Text="Phone" />
    <MenuItem Clicked="Customer_Deleted" Text="Delete" IsDestructive="True" />
  </TextCell.ContextActions>
</TextCell>
```

More Information: You can read more about the ListView control at the following link: `https://docs.microsoft.com/en-us/xamarin/xamarin-forms/user-interface/listview/`

Building mobile apps using Xamarin.Forms

We will build a mobile app that runs on either iOS or Android for managing customers in Northwind.

Good Practice: If you have never run Xcode, run it now until you see the Start window to ensure that all its required components are installed and registered. If you do not run Xcode, then you might get errors with your projects later in Visual Studio for Mac.

Adding Android SDKs

To target Android, you must install at least one Android SDK. A default installation of Visual Studio for Mac already includes one Android SDK, but it is often an older version to support as many Android devices as possible.

To use the latest features of Xamarin.Forms, you must install a more recent Android SDK. You might also have to set the paths on the **Locations** tab:

1. In macOS, start **Visual Studio for Mac** and navigate to **Visual Studio | Preferences**.

2. In **Preferences**, navigate to **Projects | SDK Locations | Android**, and select the **Android Platform SDK** and **System Image** that you want, for example, **Android 11.0 - R**. When installing an Android SDK, you must select at least one **System Image** to use as a virtual machine emulator for testing, for example, **Google APIs Intel x86 Atom System Image**.

3. Select or clear checkboxes to decide what to install or remove, or click the **Updates Available** button to update existing selections and then click **Install Updates**.

Creating a Xamarin.Forms solution

We will now create a solution with projects for a cross-platform mobile app:

1. Either click **New** in the Start window, navigate to **File | New Solution...** or press *Shift + Command + N*.

2. In the **New Project** dialog, select **Multiplatform | App** in the left-hand column, and select **Xamarin.Forms | Blank Forms App** using C# in the middle column, and then click on **Next**.

3. Enter **App Name** as NorthwindMobile, **Organization Identifier** as com.packt, and select **Target Platforms** checkboxes for both **Android** and **iOS**.

4. Click on **Next**.

5. Leave the **Project Name** and **Solution Name** unchanged. Change **Location** to /Users/ [user_folder]/Code/PracticalApps, and then click **Create**. After a few moments, the NorthwindMobile solution and three projects will be created, as shown in the following list:

    1. NorthwindMobile: Components shared cross-device, including XAML files defining the user interface.

    2. NorthwindMobile.Android: Components specific to Android.

    3. NorthwindMobile.iOS: Components specific to iOS.

6. NuGet packages should be automatically restored, but if not, then right-click on the NorthwindMobile solution, choose **Update NuGet Packages**, and accept any license agreements.

7. Navigate to **Build | Build All** and wait for the solution to successfully build the projects.

8. To the right of the **Run** button in the toolbar, select the **NorthwindMobile.iOS** project, select **Debug,** and select **iPhone 11 iOS 13.6** (or later).

9. Click the **Run** button in the toolbar and wait for the **Simulator** to start the iOS operating system and launch your mobile app.

10. In the **Simulator** toolbar, click the orientation rotation button to rotate the iPhone to be horizontal, as shown in the following screenshot:

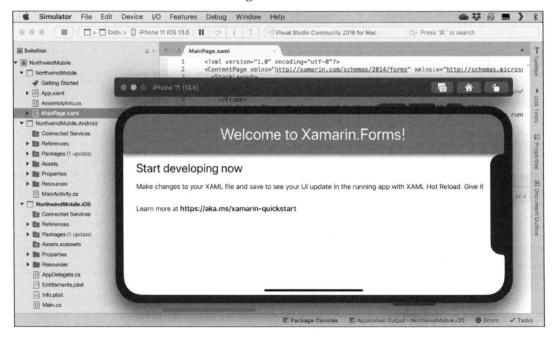

Figure 21.1: Rotating the iPhone layout

11. Quit the **Simulator**.

12. To the right of the **Run** button in the toolbar, select the `NorthwindMobile.Android` project, select **Debug**, and select `pixel_3a_xl_pie_9.0_-_api_28` (or whatever you named your device).

13. Click the **Run** button in the toolbar and wait for the device emulator to start the Android operating system and launch your mobile app, as shown in the following screenshot:

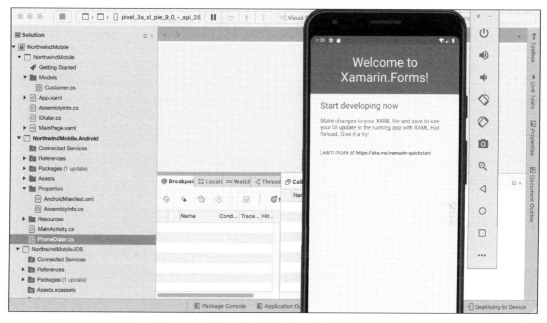

Figure 21.2: Launching the Android mobile app

14. Close the Android device emulator.

Creating an entity model with two-way data binding

After November 2021, with the release of .NET 6, we will be able to reuse the .NET entity data model library that you created in *Chapter 14, Introducing Practical Applications of C# and .NET* in mobile apps like this one.

But we need the entities to implement two-way data binding anyway, so we will create a new `Customer` entity class and it can be put in the project shared by both iOS and Android:

1. Right-click on the project named `NorthwindMobile`, go to **Add** | **New Folder**, and name the folder `Models`.

2. Right-click on the `Models` folder and go to **Add** | **New File...**.

3. In the **New File** dialog, go to **General** | **Empty Class**, enter the name `Customer`, and click **New**.

4. Modify the statements to define a `Customer` class that implements the `INotifyPropertyChanged` interface and has six properties, as shown in the following code:

```
using System.Collections.Generic;
using System.Collections.ObjectModel;
using System.ComponentModel;
using System.Runtime.CompilerServices;

namespace NorthwindMobile.Models
{
  public class Customer : INotifyPropertyChanged
  {
    public static IList<Customer> Customers;

    static Customer()
    {
      Customers = new ObservableCollection<Customer>();
    }

    public event PropertyChangedEventHandler PropertyChanged;

    private string customerID;
    private string companyName;
    private string contactName;
    private string city;
    private string country;
    private string phone;

    // this attribute sets the propertyName parameter
    // using the context in which this method is called
    private void NotifyPropertyChanged(
      [CallerMemberName] string propertyName = "")
    {
      // if an event handler has been set then invoke
      // the delegate and pass the name of the property
      PropertyChanged?.Invoke(this,
        new PropertyChangedEventArgs(propertyName));
    }

    public string CustomerID
    {
      get => customerID;
      set
      {
        customerID = value;
```

```
        NotifyPropertyChanged();
    }
}

public string CompanyName
{
  get => companyName;
  set
  {
    companyName = value;
    NotifyPropertyChanged();
  }
}

public string ContactName
{
  get => contactName;
  set
  {
    contactName = value;
    NotifyPropertyChanged();
  }
}

public string City
{
  get => city;
  set
  {
    city = value;
    NotifyPropertyChanged();
  }
}

public string Country
{
  get => country;
  set
  {
    country = value;
    NotifyPropertyChanged();
  }
}

public string Phone
{
```

```
    get => phone;
    set
    {
      phone = value;
      NotifyPropertyChanged();
    }
  }

  public string Location
  {
    get => $"{City}, {Country}";
  }

  // for testing before calling web service
  public static void AddSampleData()
  {
    Customers.Add(new Customer
    {
      CustomerID = "ALFKI",
      CompanyName = "Alfreds Futterkiste",
      ContactName = "Maria Anders",
      City = "Berlin",
      Country = "Germany",
      Phone = "030-0074321"
    });

    Customers.Add(new Customer
    {
      CustomerID = "FRANK",
      CompanyName = "Frankenversand",
      ContactName = "Peter Franken",
      City = "München",
      Country = "Germany",
      Phone = "089-0877310"
    });

    Customers.Add(new Customer
    {
      CustomerID = "SEVES",
      CompanyName = "Seven Seas Imports",
      ContactName = "Hari Kumar",
      City = "London",
      Country = "UK",
      Phone = "(171) 555-1717"
    });
```

```
            }
        }
    }
```

Note the following:

- The class implements INotifyPropertyChanged, so a two-way bound user interface component such as Editor will update the property and vice versa. There is a PropertyChanged event that is raised whenever one of the properties is modified using a NotifyPropertyChanged private method to simplify the implementation.

- After loading from the service, which will be implemented later in this chapter, the customers are cached locally using ObservableCollection. This supports notifications to any bound user interface components, such as ListView so that the user interface can redraw itself when the underlying data adds or removes items from the collection.

- In addition to properties for storing values retrieved from the HTTP service, the class defines a read-only Location property. This will be bound to a summary list of customers to show the location of each one.

- For testing purposes, when the HTTP service is not available, there is a method to populate three sample customers.

Creating a component for dialing phone numbers

To show an example of a component that is specific to Android and iOS, you will define and then implement a phone dialer component:

1. Right-click on the NorthwindMobile folder and choose **Add | New File...**.
2. Go to **General | Empty Interface**, name the file IDialer, and click **New**.
3. Modify the IDialer contents, as shown in the following code:
    ```
    namespace NorthwindMobile
    {
        public interface IDialer
        {
            bool Dial(string number);
        }
    }
    ```
4. Right-click on the NorthwindMobile.iOS folder and choose **Add | New File...**.
5. Go to **General | Empty Class**, name the file PhoneDialer, and click **New**.
6. Modify its contents, as shown in the following code:
    ```
    using Foundation;
    using NorthwindMobile.iOS;
    using UIKit;
    using Xamarin.Forms;
    ```

```
[assembly: Dependency(typeof(PhoneDialer))]

namespace NorthwindMobile.iOS
{
  public class PhoneDialer : IDialer
  {
    public bool Dial(string number)
    {
      return UIApplication.SharedApplication.OpenUrl(
        new NSUrl("tel:" + number));
    }
  }
}
```

7. Right-click the `Packages` folder in the `NorthwindMobile.Android` project and choose **Manage NuGet Packages...**.

8. Search for `Plugin.CurrentActivity` and click **Add Package**.

9. Open `MainActivity.cs` and import the `Plugin.CurrentActivity` namespace, as shown in the following code:

```
using Plugin.CurrentActivity;
```

10. At the top of the `OnCreate` method, add a statement to initialize the current activity, as shown in the following code:

```
CrossCurrentActivity.Current.Init(this, savedInstanceState);
```

11. Right-click the `NorthwindMobile.Android` folder and choose **Add | New File...**.

12. Choose **General | Empty Class**, name the file `PhoneDialer`, and click **New**.

13. Modify its contents, as shown in the following code:

```
using Android.Content;
using Android.Telephony;
using NorthwindMobile.Droid;
using Plugin.CurrentActivity;
using System.Linq;
using Xamarin.Forms;
using Uri = Android.Net.Uri;

[assembly: Dependency(typeof(PhoneDialer))]

namespace NorthwindMobile.Droid
{
  public class PhoneDialer : IDialer
  {
    public bool Dial(string number)
```

```
  {
    var context = CrossCurrentActivity.Current.Activity;

    if (context == null) return false;

    var intent = new Intent(Intent.ActionCall);
    intent.SetData(Uri.Parse("tel:" + number));

    if (IsIntentAvailable(context, intent))
    {
      context.StartActivity(intent); return true;
    }
    return false;
  }

  public static bool IsIntentAvailable(Context context, Intent intent)
  {
    var packageManager = context.PackageManager;

    var list = packageManager
      .QueryIntentServices(intent, 0)
      .Union(packageManager
      .QueryIntentActivities(intent, 0));

    if (list.Any()) return true;

    var manager = TelephonyManager.FromContext(context);
    return manager.PhoneType != PhoneType.None;
  }
 }
}
```

14. In the `NorthwindMobile.Android` project, expand **Properties**, and open `AndroidManifest.xml`.

15. In **Required permissions**, check the **CallPhone** permission, as shown in the following screenshot:

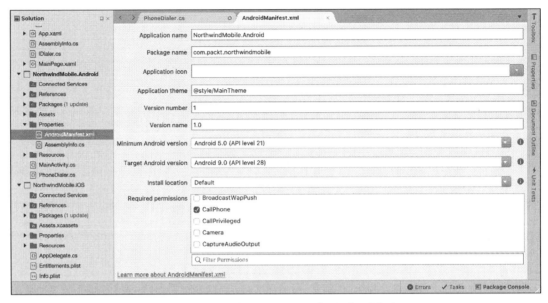

Figure 21.3: Checking the CallPhone permission for Android devices

Creating views for the customers list and customer details

You will now replace the existing MainPage with a view to show a list of customers and a view to show the details for a customer:

1. In the NorthwindMobile project, right-click MainPage.xaml, select **Delete**, and then in the confirmation dialog click **Delete**.

2. Right-click the NorthwindMobile project, select **Add** | **New Folder**, and name the new folder Views.

3. Right-click the Views folder, choose **Add** | **New File...**, and then select **Forms** | **Forms ContentPage XAML**.

4. Name the file CustomersList and click **New**.

5. Right-click the Views folder, choose **Add** | **New File...**, and then select **Forms** | **Forms ContentPage XAML**.

6. Name the file CustomerDetails and click **New**.

Implementing the customer list view

First, we will implement the list of customers:

1. Open `CustomersList.xaml` and modify its contents, as shown in the following markup:

```xml
<?xml version="1.0" encoding="UTF-8"?>
<ContentPage
    xmlns="http://xamarin.com/schemas/2014/forms"
    xmlns:x="http://schemas.microsoft.com/winfx/2009/xaml"
    x:Class="NorthwindMobile.Views.CustomersList"
    Title="List">

  <ContentPage.Content>
    <ListView ItemsSource="{Binding .}"
              VerticalOptions="Center"
              HorizontalOptions="Center"
              IsPullToRefreshEnabled="True"
              ItemTapped="Customer_Tapped"
              Refreshing="Customers_Refreshing">
      <ListView.Header>
        <Label Text="Northwind Customers" BackgroundColor="Silver" />
      </ListView.Header>
      <ListView.ItemTemplate>
        <DataTemplate>
          <TextCell Text="{Binding CompanyName}"
                    Detail="{Binding Location}">
            <TextCell.ContextActions>
              <MenuItem Clicked="Customer_Phoned" Text="Phone" />
              <MenuItem Clicked="Customer_Deleted" Text="Delete"
                        IsDestructive="True" />
            </TextCell.ContextActions>
          </TextCell>
        </DataTemplate>
      </ListView.ItemTemplate>
    </ListView>
  </ContentPage.Content>
  <ContentPage.ToolbarItems>
    <ToolbarItem Text="Add" Activated="Add_Activated"
                 Order="Primary" Priority="0" />
  </ContentPage.ToolbarItems>
</ContentPage>
```

Note the following:

- ContentPage has had its Title attribute set to List.
- ListView has its IsPullToRefreshEnabled set to true.
- Handlers have been written for the following events:

  Customer_Tapped: A customer being tapped to show their details.

  Customers_Refreshing: The list being pulled down to refresh its items.

  Customer_Phoned: A cell being swiped left on iPhone or long pressed on Android and then tapping **Phone**.

  Customer_Deleted: A cell being swiped left on iPhone or long pressed on Android and then tapping **Delete**.

  Add_Activated: The **Add** button being tapped.

- A data template defines how to display each customer: large text for the company name and smaller text for the location underneath.
- An **Add** button is displayed so that users can navigate to a detail view to add a new customer.

2. Open CustomersList.xaml.cs and modify the contents, as shown in the following code:

```
using System;
using System.Threading.Tasks;
using NorthwindMobile.Models;
using Xamarin.Forms;

namespace NorthwindMobile.Views
{
  public partial class CustomersList : ContentPage
  {
    public CustomersList()
    {
      InitializeComponent();

      Customer.Customers.Clear();
      Customer.AddSampleData();
      BindingContext = Customer.Customers;
    }

    async void Customer_Tapped(
      object sender, ItemTappedEventArgs e)
    {
      var c = e.Item as Customer;

      if (c == null) return;
```

```
            // navigate to the detail view and show the tapped customer
            await Navigation.PushAsync(new CustomerDetails(c));
        }

    async void Customers_Refreshing(object sender, EventArgs e)
    {
        var listView = sender as ListView;
        listView.IsRefreshing = true;
        // simulate a refresh
        await Task.Delay(1500);
        listView.IsRefreshing = false;
    }

    void Customer_Deleted(object sender, EventArgs e)
    {
        var menuItem = sender as MenuItem;
        Customer c = menuItem.BindingContext as Customer;
        Customer.Customers.Remove(c);
    }

    async void Customer_Phoned(object sender, EventArgs e)
    {
        var menuItem = sender as MenuItem;
        var c = menuItem.BindingContext as Customer;

        if (await this.DisplayAlert("Dial a Number",
            "Would you like to call " + c.Phone + "?",
            "Yes", "No"))
        {
            var dialer = DependencyService.Get<IDialer>();

            if (dialer != null) dialer.Dial(c.Phone);
        }
    }

    async void Add_Activated(object sender, EventArgs e)
    {
        await Navigation.PushAsync(new CustomerDetails());
    }
  }
}
```

Note the following:

- `BindingContext` is set to the sample list of `Customers` in the constructor of the page.
- When a customer in the list view is tapped, the user is taken to a details view (which you will create in the next step).
- When the list view is pulled down, it triggers a simulated refresh that takes 1.5 seconds.
- When a customer is deleted in the list view, they are removed from the bound collection of customers.
- When a customer in the list view is swiped, and the **Phone** button is tapped, a dialog prompts the user as to whether they want to dial the number, and if so, the platform-native implementation will be retrieved using the dependency resolver and then used to dial the number.
- When the **Add** button is tapped, the user is taken to the customer detail page to enter details for a new customer.

Implementing the customer detail view

Next, we will implement the customer detail view:

1. Open `CustomerDetails.xaml` and modify its contents, as shown in the following markup, and note the following:
   - `Title` of `ContentPage` has been set to `Edit`.
   - A customer `Grid` with two columns and six rows is used for the layout.
   - `Entry` views are two-way data bound to properties of the `Customer` class.
   - `InsertButton` has an event handler to execute code to add a new customer.

```xml
<?xml version="1.0" encoding="UTF-8"?>
<ContentPage
  xmlns="http://xamarin.com/schemas/2014/forms"
  xmlns:x="http://schemas.microsoft.com/winfx/2009/xaml"
  x:Class="NorthwindMobile.Views.CustomerDetails"
  Title="Edit">

  <ContentPage.Content>
    <StackLayout VerticalOptions="Fill" HorizontalOptions="Fill">
      <Grid BackgroundColor="Silver">
        <Grid.ColumnDefinitions>
          <ColumnDefinition/>
          <ColumnDefinition/>
        </Grid.ColumnDefinitions>
        <Grid.RowDefinitions>
          <RowDefinition/>
          <RowDefinition/>
```

```xml
                <RowDefinition/>
                <RowDefinition/>
                <RowDefinition/>
                <RowDefinition/>
            </Grid.RowDefinitions>
            <Label Text="Customer ID" VerticalOptions="Center" Margin="6" />
            <Entry Text="{Binding CustomerID, Mode=TwoWay}"
                    Grid.Column="1" />
            <Label Text="Company Name" Grid.Row="1"
                    VerticalOptions="Center" Margin="6" />
            <Entry Text="{Binding CompanyName, Mode=TwoWay}"
                    Grid.Column="1" Grid.Row="1" />
            <Label Text="Contact Name" Grid.Row="2"
                    VerticalOptions="Center" Margin="6" />
            <Entry Text="{Binding ContactName, Mode=TwoWay}"
                    Grid.Column="1" Grid.Row="2" />
            <Label Text="City" Grid.Row="3"
                    VerticalOptions="Center" Margin="6" />
            <Entry Text="{Binding City, Mode=TwoWay}"
                    Grid.Column="1" Grid.Row="3" />
            <Label Text="Country" Grid.Row="4"
                    VerticalOptions="Center" Margin="6" />
            <Entry Text="{Binding Country, Mode=TwoWay}"
                    Grid.Column="1" Grid.Row="4" />
            <Label Text="Phone" Grid.Row="5"
                    VerticalOptions="Center" Margin="6" />
            <Entry Text="{Binding Phone, Mode=TwoWay}"
                    Grid.Column="1" Grid.Row="5" />
        </Grid>
        <Button x:Name="InsertButton" Text="Insert Customer"
                Clicked="InsertButton_Clicked" />
    </StackLayout>
  </ContentPage.Content>
</ContentPage>
```

2. Open `CustomerDetails.xaml.cs` and modify its contents, as shown in the following code:

```csharp
using System;
using NorthwindMobile.Models;
using Xamarin.Forms;

namespace NorthwindMobile.Views
{
  public partial class CustomerDetails : ContentPage
  {
```

```
    public CustomerDetails()
    {
      InitializeComponent();

      BindingContext = new Customer();
      Title = "Add Customer";
    }

    public CustomerDetails(Customer customer)
    {
      InitializeComponent();

      BindingContext = customer;
      InsertButton.IsVisible = false;
    }

    async void InsertButton_Clicked(object sender, EventArgs e)
    {
      Customer.Customers.Add((Customer)BindingContext);
      await Navigation.PopAsync(animated: true);
    }
  }
}
```

Note the following:

- The default constructor sets the binding context to a new customer instance and the view title is changed to Add Customer.

- The constructor with a customer parameter sets the binding context to that instance and hides the **Insert** button because it is not needed when editing an existing customer due to two-way data binding.

- When **Insert** is tapped, the new customer is added to the collection and the navigation is moved back to the previous view asynchronously.

Setting the main page for the mobile app

Finally, we need to modify the mobile app to use our customer list wrapped in a navigation page as the main page instead of the old one that we deleted, which was created by the project template:

1. Open App.xaml.cs.

2. Import the NorthwindMobile.Views namespace.

3. Modify the statement that sets MainPage to create an instance of CustomersList wrapped in an instance of NavigationPage, as shown in the following code:

   ```
   MainPage = new NavigationPage(new CustomersList());
   ```

Testing the mobile app

We will now test the mobile app using an iPhone Simulator:

1. In Visual Studio for Mac, to the right of the **Run** button in the toolbar, select the **NorthwindMobile.iOS** project, select **Debug**, and select **iPhone 11 iOS 13.6** (or later).

2. Click on the **Run** button in the toolbar or navigate to **Run | Start Debugging**. The project will build, and then after a few moments, **Simulator** will appear with your running mobile app, as shown in the following screenshot:

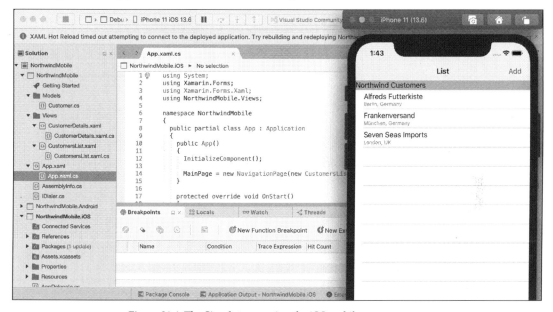

Figure 21.4: The Simulator running the iOS mobile app

3. Click **Seven Seas Imports** and modify **Company Name** to Seven Oceans Imports, as shown in the following screenshot of the customer details page:

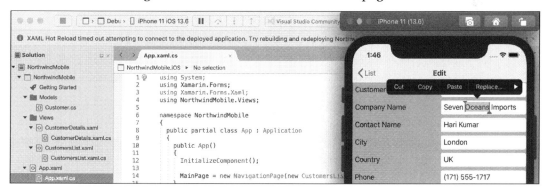

Figure 21.5: The customer details page

4. Click **List** to return to the list of customers and note that the company name has been updated due to the two-way data binding.

5. Click **Add**, and then fill in the fields for a new customer, as shown in the following screenshot:

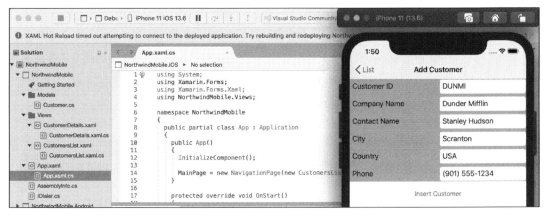

Figure 21.6: Adding a new customer

6. Click **Insert Customer** and note that the new customer has been added to the bottom of the list.

7. Slide one of the customers to the left to reveal two action buttons, **Phone** and **Delete**, as shown in the following screenshot:

Figure 21.7: Deleting a customer

8. Click **Phone** and note the pop-up prompt to the user to dial the number of that customer with **Yes** and **No** buttons.

9. Click **No**.

10. Slide one of the customers to the left to reveal two action buttons, **Phone** and **Delete**, and then click on **Delete**, and note that the customer is removed.

11. Click, hold, and drag the list down and then release, and note the animation effect for refreshing the list, but remember that we did not implement this feature, so the list does not change.

12. Navigate to **Simulator | Quit Simulator** or press *Cmd + Q*.

13. Change to the Android device emulator and repeat the same steps to test its functionality, as shown in the following screenshot:

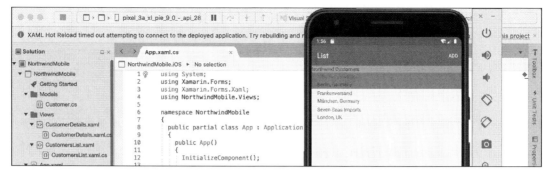

Figure 21.8: Testing the app on the Android device emulator

Note that instead of swiping left, you must press and hold to show the **Phone** and **Delete** buttons, which then appear at the top of the user interface.

We will now make the mobile app call `NorthwindService` to get the list of customers.

Consuming a web service from a mobile app

Apple's **App Transport Security** (**ATS**) forces developers to use good practice, including secure connections between an app and a web service. ATS is enabled by default and your mobile apps will throw an exception if they do not connect securely.

 More Information: You can read more about ATS at the following link: https://docs.microsoft.com/en-us/xamarin/ios/app-fundamentals/ats

If you need to call a web service that is secured with a self-signed certificate like our `NorthwindService` is, it is possible but complicated.

 More Information: You can read more about handling self-signed certificates at the following link: https://docs.remotingsdk.com/Clients/Tasks/HandlingSelfSignedCertificates/NET/

For simplicity, we will allow insecure connections to the web service and disable the security checks in the mobile app.

Configuring the web service to allow insecure requests

First, we will enable the web service to handle insecure connections at a new URL:

1. Start **Visual Studio Code** and open the `NorthwindService` project.

2. Open `Startup.cs`, and in the `Configure` method, comment out the HTTPS redirection, as shown highlighted in the following code:

```
public void Configure(IApplicationBuilder app,
  IWebHostEnvironment env)
{
  if (env.IsDevelopment())
  {
    app.UseDeveloperExceptionPage();
  }
  // commented out for mobile app in Chapter 21
  // app.UseHttpsRedirection();

  app.UseRouting();
```

3. Open `Program.cs`, and in the `CreateHostBuilder` method, add the insecure URL, as shown highlighted in the following code:

```
public static IHostBuilder CreateHostBuilder(string[] args) =>
  Host.CreateDefaultBuilder(args)
    .ConfigureWebHostDefaults(webBuilder =>
    {
      webBuilder.UseStartup<Startup>();
      webBuilder.UseUrls(
        "https://localhost:5001", // for MVC client
        "http://localhost:5003" // for mobile client
      );
    });
```

4. Navigate to **Terminal | New Terminal** and select `NorthwindService`.

5. In **TERMINAL**, start the web service by entering the following command: `dotnet run`.

6. Start Chrome and test that the web service is returning customers as JSON by navigating to the following URL: `http://localhost:5003/api/customers/`.

7. Close Chrome but leave the web service running.

Configuring the iOS app to allow insecure connections

Now you will configure the `NorthwindMobile.iOS` project to disable ATS to allow insecure HTTP requests to the web service:

1. In the `NorthwindMobile.iOS` project, open `Info.plist`.

2. On the **Source** tab, add a new entry named `NSAppTransportSecurity`, and set its **Type** to **Dictionary**.

3. In the dictionary, add a new entry named NSAllowsArbitraryLoads and set its **Type** to **Boolean** with a value of **Yes**, as shown in the following screenshot:

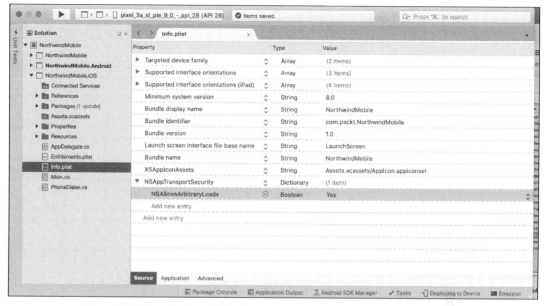

Figure 21.9: The info.plist tab disabling the SSL encryption requirement

Configuring the Android app to allow insecure connections

In a similar way to Apple and ATS, with Android 9 (API level 28) cleartext (that is, non-HTTPS) support is disabled by default.

 More Information: You can read more about Android and cleartext support at the following link: https://devblogs.microsoft.com/xamarin/cleartext-http-android-network-security/

Now you will configure the NorthwindMobile.Android project to enable cleartext to allow insecure HTTP requests to the web service:

1. In the NorthwindMobile.Android project, in the Properties folder, open AssemblyInfo.cs.

2. At the bottom of the file, add an attribute to enable cleartext, as shown in the following code:

```
[assembly: Application(UsesCleartextTraffic = true)]
```

Adding NuGet packages for consuming a web service

Next, we must add some NuGet packages to each of the platform-specific projects to enable HTTP requests and process the JSON responses:

1. In the `NorthwindMobile.iOS` project, right-click on the folder named `Packages` and choose **Manage NuGet Packages...**.

2. In the **Manage NuGet Packages** dialog, in the **Search** box, enter `System.Net.Http`.

3. Select the package named **System.Net.Http** and then click **Add Package**.

4. In the **License Acceptance** dialog, click **Accept**.

5. In `NorthwindMobile.iOS`, right-click on the folder named `Packages` and choose **Manage NuGet Packages...**.

6. In the **Manage Packages** dialog, in the **Search** box, enter `Newtonsoft.Json`.

7. Select the package named **Newtonsoft.Json** and then click **Add Package**.

8. Repeat the previous steps, 1 to 7, to add the same two NuGet packages to the project named `NorthwindMobile.Android`.

Getting customers from the web service

Now, we can modify the customers list page to get its list of customers from the web service instead of using sample data:

1. In the `NorthwindMobile` project, open `Views\CustomersList.xaml.cs`.

2. Import the following namespaces:
   ```
   using System;
   using System.Collections.Generic;
   using System.Linq;
   using System.Net.Http;
   using System.Net.Http.Headers;
   using System.Threading.Tasks;
   using Newtonsoft.Json;
   using NorthwindMobile.Models;
   using Xamarin.Forms;
   ```

3. Modify the `CustomersList` constructor to load the list of customers using the service proxy and only call the `AddSampleData` method if an exception occurs, as shown in the following code:
   ```
   public CustomersList()
   {
       InitializeComponent();
   ```

```
      Customer.Customers.Clear();

      try
      {
        var client = new HttpClient
        {
          BaseAddress = new Uri("http://localhost:5003/")
        };

        client.DefaultRequestHeaders.Accept.Add(
          new MediaTypeWithQualityHeaderValue(
            "application/json"));

        HttpResponseMessage response = client
          .GetAsync("api/customers").Result;

        response.EnsureSuccessStatusCode();

        string content = response.Content
          .ReadAsStringAsync().Result;

        var customersFromService = JsonConvert
          .DeserializeObject<IEnumerable<Customer>>(content);

        foreach (Customer c in customersFromService
          .OrderBy(customer => customer.CompanyName))
        {
          Customer.Customers.Add(c);
        }
      }
      catch (Exception ex)
      {
        DisplayAlert(title: "Exception",
          message: $"App will use sample data due to: {ex.Message}",
          cancel: "OK");

        Customer.AddSampleData();
      }

      BindingContext = Customer.Customers;
    }
```

4. Navigate to **Build | Clean All**. Changes to Info.plist like allowing insecure connections sometimes require a clean build.

5. Navigate to **Build | Build All**.

6.   Run the `NorthwindMobile` project in the iPhone Simulator and note that 91 customers are loaded from the web service, as shown in the following screenshot:

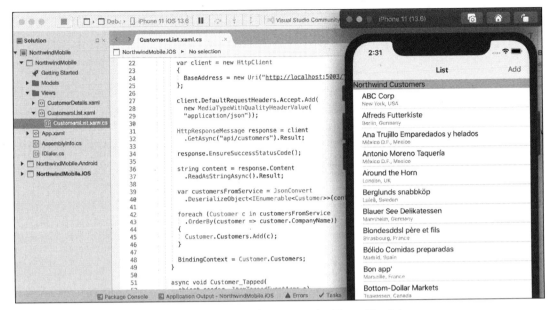

Figure 21.10: The NorthwindMobile project in the iPhone Simulator

7.   Navigate to **Simulator | Quit Simulator** or press *Cmd* + *Q*.

Practicing and exploring

Test your knowledge and understanding by answering some questions, get some hands-on practice, and explore this chapter's topics with more in-depth research.

Exercise 21.1 – Test your knowledge

Answer the following questions:

1.   What is the difference between Xamarin and Xamarin.Forms?

2.   What are the four categories of Xamarin.Forms user interface components, and what do they represent?

3.   List four types of cell.

4.   How can you enable a user to perform an action on a cell in a list view?

5.   How do you define a dependency service to implement platform-specific functionality?

6.   When would you use an `Entry` instead of an `Editor`?

7.   What is the effect of setting `IsDestructive` to `true` for a menu item in a cell's context actions?

8. When would you call the methods `PushAsync` and `PopAsync` in a Xamarin.Forms mobile app?

9. How do you show a pop-up modal message with simple button choices like Yes or No?

10. What is Apple's ATS and why is it important?

Exercise 21.2 – Explore topics

Use the following links to read more about this chapter's topics:

- **Xamarin.Forms documentation**: `https://docs.microsoft.com/en-us/xamarin/ xamarin-forms/`

- **Xamarin.Essentials provides developers with cross-platform APIs for their mobile applications**: `https://docs.microsoft.com/en-us/xamarin/essentials/`

- **Self Signed iOS Certifcates and Certificate Pinning in a Xamarin.Forms application**: `https://nicksnettravels.builttoroam.com/ios-certificate/`

- **Protecting your users with certificate pinning**: `https://www.basdecort.com/ protecting-your-users-with-certificate-pinning/`

- **HttpClient and SSL/TLS implementation selector for iOS/macOS**: `https://docs. microsoft.com/en-us/xamarin/cross-platform/macios/http-stack`

Summary

In this chapter, you learned how to build a mobile app using Xamarin.Forms, which is cross-platform for iOS and Android (and potentially other platforms) and consumes data from a web service using the `System.Net.Http` and `Newtonsoft.Json` NuGet packages.

In *Appendix B, Building Windows Desktop Apps*, you will learn how to build desktop apps for Windows using **Windows Presentation Foundation (WPF)** and **Universal Windows Platform (UWP)**, and how to migrate **Windows Forms** apps to .NET 5. *Appendix B, Building Windows Desktop Apps* can be found at `https://static.packt-cdn.com/downloads/9781800568105_ Appendices.pdf`.

Epilogue

I wanted this book to be different from the others on the market. I hope that you found it to be a brisk, fun read, packed with practical hands-on walk-throughs of each subject.

For subjects that you wanted to learn more about, I hope that the More Information notes and links that I provided pointed you in the right direction.

I have already started work on the sixth edition, which we plan to publish soon after the release of .NET 6.0 in November 2021. If you have suggestions for subjects that you would like to see covered, or you spot mistakes that need fixing in the book or code, please let me know via my GitHub account at the following link:

https://github.com/markjprice/cs9dotnet5

I wish you the best of luck with all your C# and .NET projects!

Index

reference link 147
URL 3
used, for building console apps 17
used, for code writing 18, 19
using, for cross-platform development 2, 3
Visual Studio Code debugger
URL 128
Visual Studio Code workspaces
using 51
Visual Studio for Mac 9
using, for mobile development 4

W

Web API controller
configuring 634, 638
implementing 632, 634
web applications 467
scalability, improving for 460
WebAssembly (Wasm) 474
reference link 475
web content management system
used, for building websites 466, 467
web development 485
client-side web development 489
with HTTP 485-488
Web Forms 477
web hosts, default configuration
reference link 532
web programming information
finding 22
web services 622
acronyms 622
advanced features 658
building 468
building, with ASP.NET Core Web API 621
consuming 468
creating, for Northwind database 627, 628
documenting 640
functionality, reviewing 626, 627
scalability, improving for 460
securing 664
testing 640
websites
building, with ASP.NET Core 466
building, with web content management system
466, 467
WebSocket 472
reference link 472
Where extension method
used, for filtering entities 407-409
while statement

looping with 88
whole numbers 46
storing 46, 47
Windows
used, for setting up SQLite 365
**Windows Communication Foundation
(WCF) 14, 490**
Windows desktop apps
building, with legacy technologies 477
Windows Desktop Pack 14
Windows Forms 14, 477
Windows Presentation Foundation (WPF) 14, 477
write mode 458

X

Xamarin project 9
Xamarin.Forms
user interface 743-744
used, for building mobile apps 745-760
Xamarin Studio development tool 9
XML 433
generating, with LINQ 433
object graphs, serializing 322-324
reading, with LINQ 433, 434
XML element
writing, to stream 310, 311
XML files
deserializing 326
XMLHttpRequest 472
XML serialization
controlling 639
xUnit.net 135

Printed in Great Britain
by Amazon